Street by Street

LONDON

3rd edition July 2003

© Automobile Association
Developments Limited 2004

Original edition printed May
2001

Ordnance Survey® This product
includes map
data licensed from Ordnance
Survey® with the permission of
the Controller of Her Majesty's
Stationery Office.
© Crown copyright 2004.
All rights reserved.
Licence No: 399221.

Published by AA Publishing
(a trading name of
Automobile Association
Developments Limited,
whose registered office is
Millstream, Maidenhead Road,
Windsor, Berkshire SL4 5GD.
Registered number 1878835).

Mapping produced by the
Cartography Department of The
Automobile Association. A02343

A CIP Catalogue record for this book is available from the British Library.

Printed by GRAFIASA S.A., Porto, Portugal

The contents of this atlas are believed to be correct at the time of the latest revision. However,
the publishers cannot be held responsible for loss occasioned to any person acting or refraining
from action as a result of any material in this atlas, nor for any errors, omissions or changes in
such material. This does not affect your statutory rights. The publishers would welcome
information to correct any errors or omissions and to keep this atlas up to date. Please write to
Publishing, The Automobile Association, Fanum House (FH17), Basing View, Basingstoke,
Hampshire, RG21 4EA.

Ref: MN037y

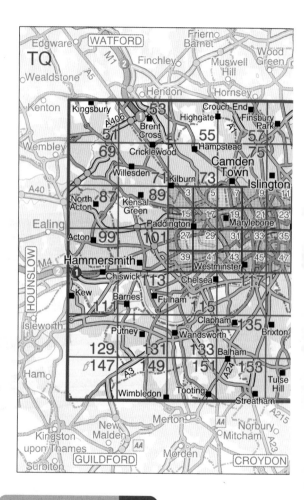

ii

Enlarged scale pages 1:10,000 6.3 inches to 1 mile

| 0 | miles | 1/4 |
| 0 | 1/4 kilometres | 1/2 |

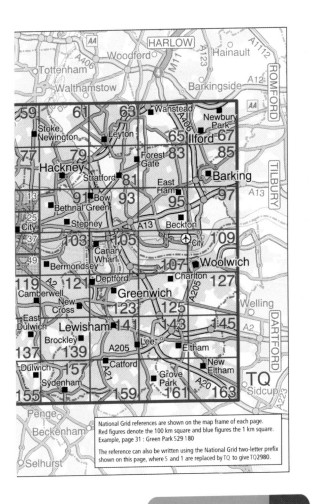

National Grid references are shown on the map frame of each page.
Red figures denote the 100 km square and blue figures the 1 km square.
Example, page 31 : Green Park 529 180

The reference can also be written using the National Grid two-letter prefix
shown on this page, where 5 and 1 are replaced by TQ to give TQ2980.

3.2 inches to 1 mile   **Scale of main map pages 1:20,000**

Junction 9 ▬▬	Motorway & junction
Services	Motorway service area
▬▬	Primary road single/dual carriageway
Services	Primary road service area
▬▬	A road single/dual carriageway
▬▬	B road single/dual carriageway
▬▬	Other road single/dual carriageway
▬▬	Minor/private road, access may be restricted
← ←	One-way street
▦▦▦	Pedestrian area
=======	Track or footpath
▮▮▮▮	Road under construction
⌐ = = ⌐	Road tunnel
AA	AA Service Centre
P	Parking
P+🚌	Park & Ride
🚌	Bus/coach station
▬▬ ⇄	Railway & main railway station
⇄ ▬	Railway & minor railway station

⊖	Underground station
⊖ ▬▬	Light railway & station
┿┿┿┿┿	Preserved private railway
_LC_ ╱	Level crossing
●—●—●—●	Tramway
– – – – –	Ferry route
··············	Airport runway
▬ · ▬ · ▬	County, administrative Boundary
▨	Congestion Charging Zone *
ᴠᴠᴠᴠᴠᴠᴠ	Mounds
93	Page continuation 1:20,000
7	Page continuation to enlarged scale 1:10,000
~	River/canal, lake, pier
~	Aqueduct, lock, weir
465 ▲ Winter Hill	Peak (with height in metres)
	Beach
▨	Woodland
	Park
✝ ✝ ✝✝ ✝ ✝	Cemetery

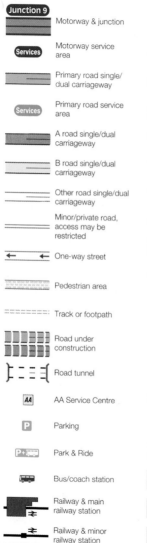
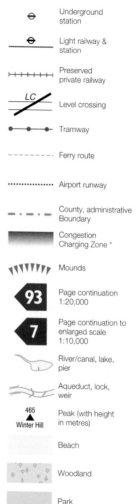

* The AA Central London Congestion Charging map is also available

	Built-up area			Abbey, cathedral or priory
	Featured building		♜	Castle
⊓⊔⊓⊔⊓⊔	City wall		🏛	Historic house or building
A&E	Hospital with 24-hour A&E department		Wakehurst Place NT	National Trust property
PO	Post Office		Ⓜ	Museum or art gallery
📖	Public library		🦅	Roman antiquity
𝒊	Tourist Information Centre		⬇	Ancient site, battlefield or monument
⛽⛽	Petrol station, 24 hour Major suppliers only			Industrial interest
✝	Church/chapel		✳	Garden
🚻	Public toilets		🌳	Arboretum
♿	Toilet with disabled facilities			Farm or animal centre
PH	Public house AA recommended		🦌	Zoological or wildlife collection
🍴	Restaurant AA inspected		🦜	Bird collection
🎭	Theatre or performing arts centre		🐋	Nature reserve
🎥	Cinema		🐟	Aquarium
⚑	Golf course		V	Visitor or heritage centre
▲	Camping AA inspected		¥	Country park
🚐	Caravan site AA inspected		⊙	Cave
▲🚐	Camping & caravan site AA inspected		✖	Windmill
	Theme park		🛢	Distillery, brewery or vineyard

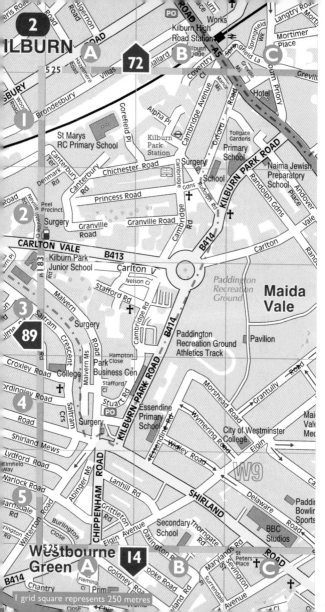

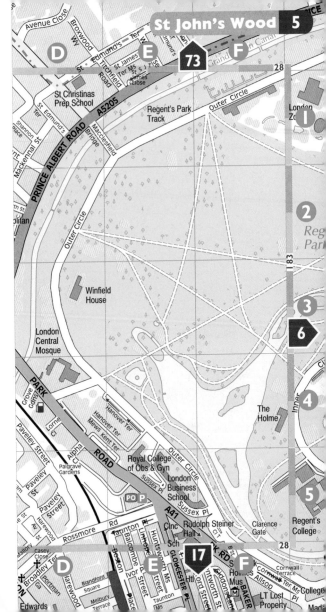

Avenue Close

Broxwood W.

St Edmund's Ter

Titchfield

St James
St James Ms
James
Close

Grand Union Canal

73

St Christinas
Prep School

PRINCE ALBERT ROAD A5205

Macclesfield
Bridge

Regent's Park
Track

Outer Circle

28

London
Zo

1

St Edmund's Ter

St Edmund's

Shannon St

Mackennal St

olitan

Outer Circle

2

Reg
Par

l 83

Winfield
House

London
Central
Mosque

3

6

PARK

Grove Gdns

Lorne
Cl

Paveley Street

Alpha
Cl

ROAD

Palgrave
Gardens

Hanover Ter

Hanover Ter
Mews Kent Ter

Outer Circle

Royal College
of Obs & Gyn

London
Business
School

Sussex Pl

Sussex Pl

The
Holme

Inner

4

Cl

5

Regent's
College

Paveley
St

Paveley
Street

Rossmore   Rd

Harewood

Av St

Taunton

Balcombe St

Linhope

Huntsworth Ms

Beston

Ivor Pl

PO P

A41

Clnc

Sch

Rudolph Steiner
Hall

Sussex Pl

Clarence
Gate

28

17

PK RD

F

Cornwall
Terrace

College

Holmes
Mus

Cornwall Ter Ms

Allsop

Mallory St

Casey
Close

Broadley Ter

Portman

Harewood

D

ON

Edwards

Blandford
Square

Melbury
Terrace

Portman

Square

E

Taunton

Place

GLOUCESTER PL

Itl

dsworth St

BAKER

Maryl

LT Lost
Property

F

M

Mada

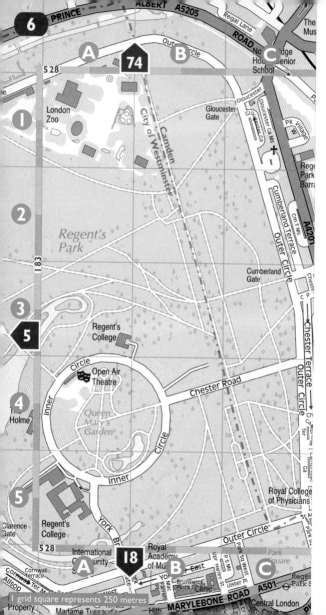

PRINCE ALBERT A5205 ROAD

Regal Lane

The
Mus

A

74

B

Outer Circle

No
Ho dge
Hou Senior
School

C

5 28

London
Zoo

Gloucester
Gate

City of Westminster

Camden

Gloucester
Ga

Gloucester Ga Ms

Pk Village
VI

Rege
Park
Barra

1

Regent's
Park

Cumberland Terrace

Cm t Ms

A4201

2

1 83

Outer Circle

Cumberland
Gate

Cheste

Chester Terrace

3

5

Regent's
College

Inner Circle

Open Air
Theatre

Chester Road

Outer Circle

Ter

Ch

Ga

4

The
Holme

Queen
Mary's
Garden

Inner Circle

5

Clarence
Gate

Regent's
College

York Br

Inner Circle

Royal College
of Physicians

St

Park Ro

5 28

International
Co unity
S l

A

18

Royal
Academy
of Mu

B

East

Upr Harley St

P S Ms

Ulster Pl

Park
Square

C

Rege
Park Sq

York Br

Pk Sq West

Cornwall
Terrace

Allsop

Cornwa Ter

Brunswick
Place

MARYLEBONE ROAD A501

Central London

Property

Madame Tussaud's

Hlth

Co d

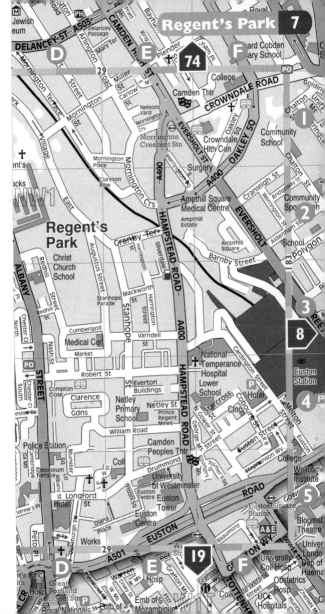

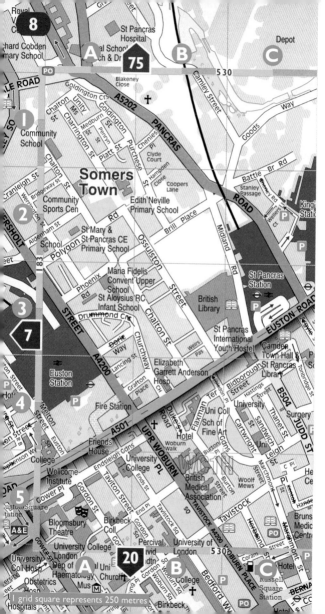

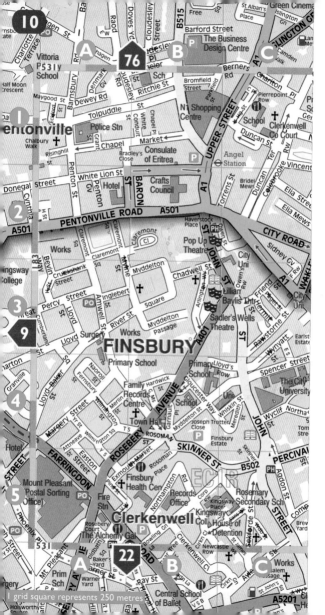

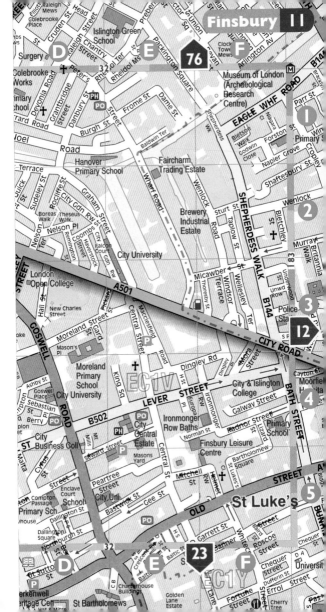

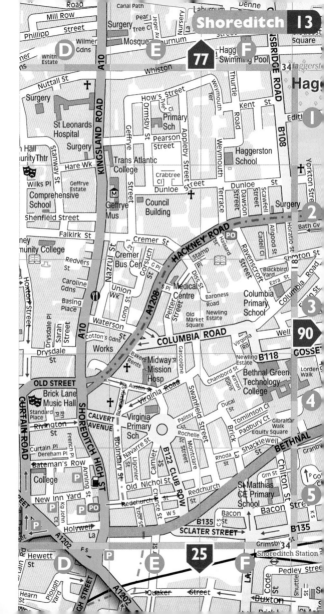

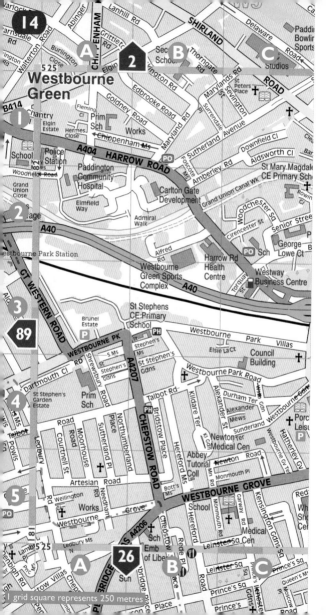

1 grid square represents 250 metres

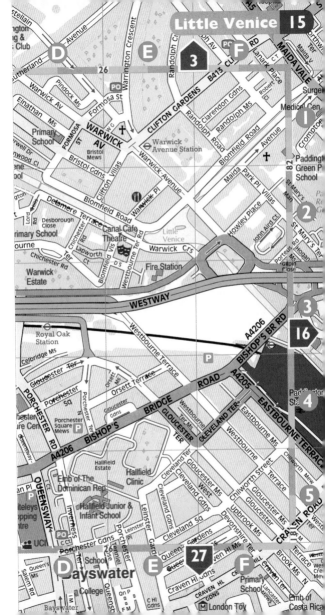

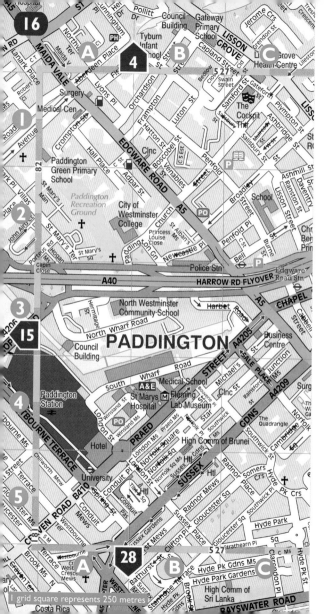

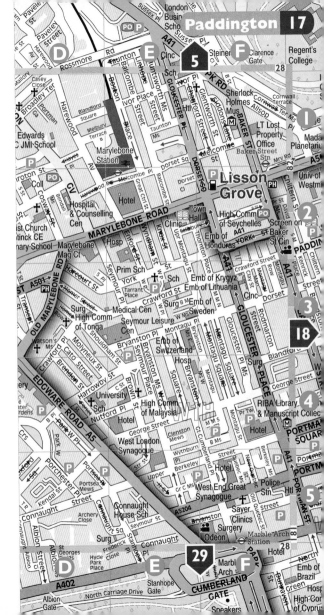

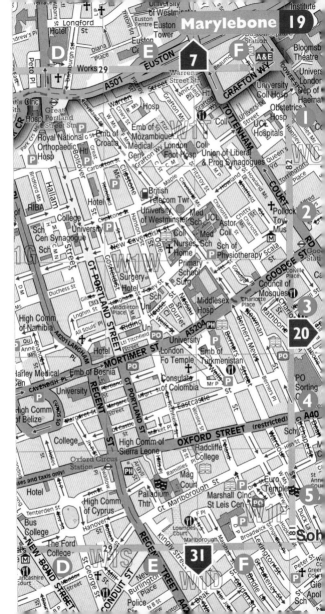

I grid square represents 250 metres

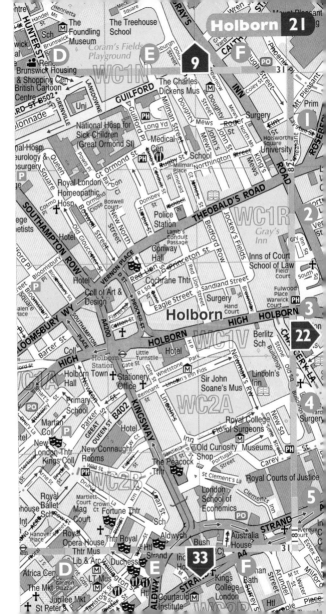

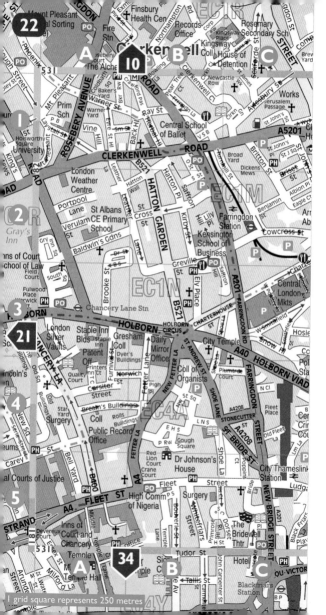

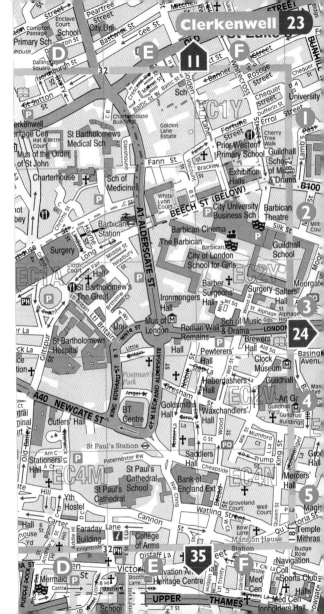

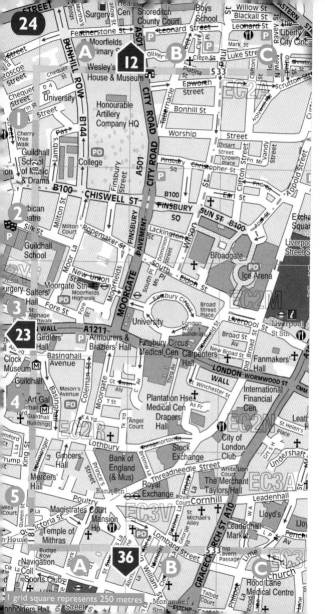

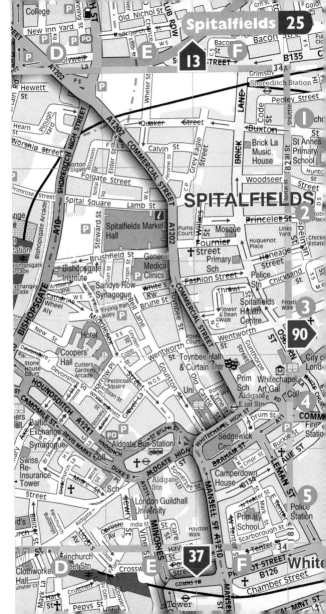

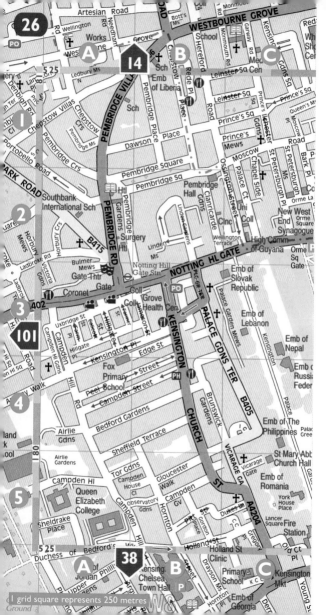

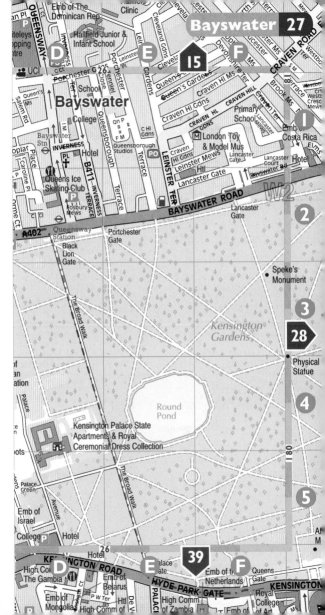

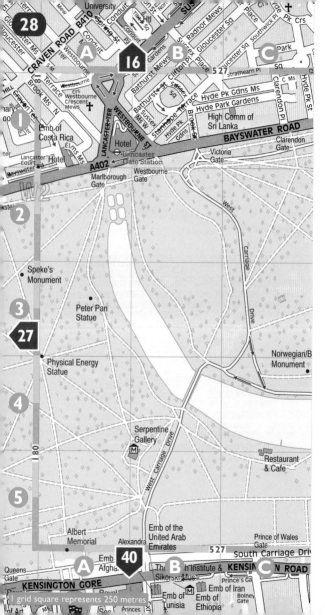

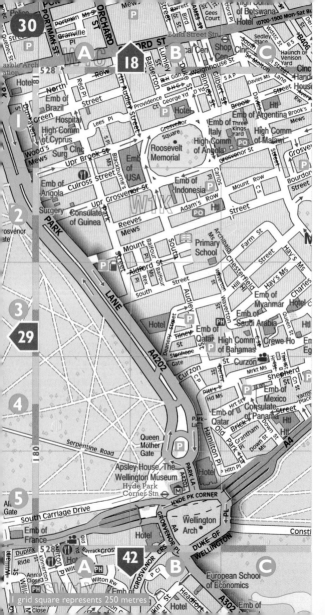

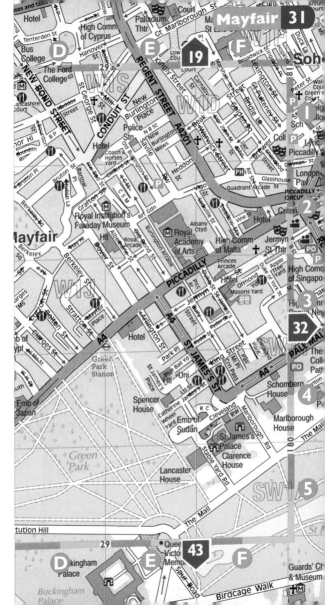

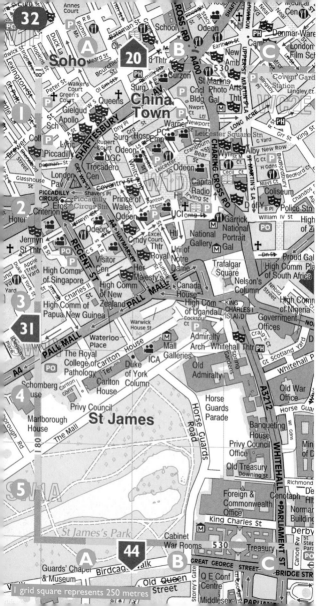

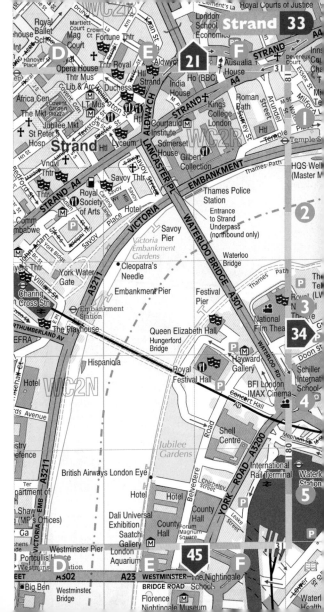

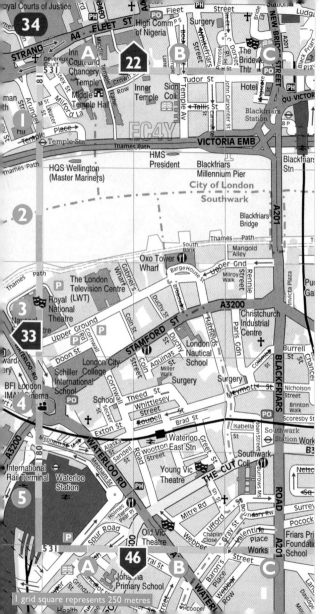

I grid square represents 250 metres

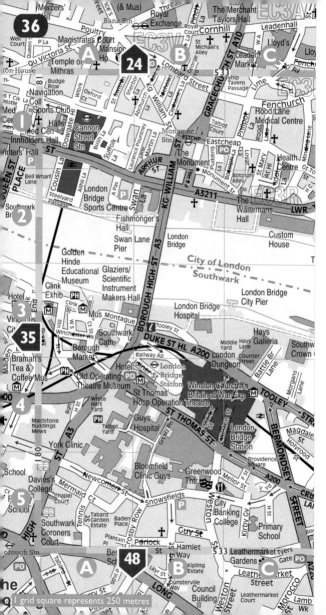

36

24

35

2

3

4

5

48

Mercers'

(& Mus)

Threadneedle

The Merchant Taylors' Hall

EC3A

Royal Exchange

Royal Court

Cornhill

Leadenhall

EC3V

St Michael's Alley

A10

WA

Lloyd's

Lloy

Well Court

Queen St Pla

Poultry

Bank Stn

Magistrates Court

Mansion Ho

St Michael's Alley

Leadenhall Market

C

Pench

QU Victoria St

Temple of Mithras

Lombard Street

Ship Tavern Passage

Lime

Fenchurch

EC3

Budge Row

Navigation

Work

Oxford Ct

Sherbor

William La

Clements La

Talbot

Rood Lane

Fenchurch Medical Centre

Lime St

St Coll

Sports Club

Halls

Cannon Street Stn

Bush La

Abchurch La

Laurence Pountney

Martin La

Monument Stn

ESTCHP

Eastcheap

Pudding

Botolph Alley

St Mary At Hl

Health Centre

Innholders' Hall

Winters' Hall

ST

Dowgate Hi

Suffolk La

KG-WILLIAM ST

The Monument

Monument St

St Mary At Hl

PO

P

Bell Wharf Lane

QUEEN ST

PLACE

Cousin La

Allhil La

London Bridge Sports Centre

P

Swan La

ARTHUR

A3211

The Watermans Hall

LWR

Steelyard Passage

Fishmonger's Hall

Swan Lane Pier

London Bridge

Custom House

Golden Hinde Educational Museum

Clink Exhib

Glaziers/ Scientific Instrument Makers Hall

City of London

Southwark

London Bridge City Pier

Hotel

PH

Mus

Montague

London Bridge Hospital

Vinopolis City

Clink St

Southwark Cath

Tooley St

Hays Galleria

DUKE ST HL A200

Middle Yard

Hays Lane

London Dungeon

Battle Br Lane

Southw Crown

Winchester

Borough Market

Railway Ap

London Bridge Station

Winston Churchill's Britain at War Exp

TOOLEY STR

Bramah's Tea & Coffee Mus

PH

Hotel

Old Operating Theatre Museum

White Hart Yard

PO

London Bridge Station

St Thomas Hosp Operation Theatre

London Bridge Station

Morgans

Magdale

York Clinic

PH

Talbot Yard

Guys Hospital

ST THOMAS ST

BERMONDSEY

Providence square

A200

St

Holyrood

Maidstone Buildings Mews

ST A3

Bloomfield Clinic Guys

Greenwood Thtr

Mellior St

Davies's College

Mermaid Ct

Newcomen St

Snowsfields

City Banking College

Kirby Gv

CROS

Chapel Court

Tennis

Tabard Garden Estate

Crosby Row

Weston

Primary School

LA

Southwark Coroners Court

Baden Place

Guy St

St Hamlet

Leathermarket

Gate

PO

Plantain Pl

Porlock

Way

Tyers

Gardens

Leathermarket Street

Morocco

A

B

C

Dunsterville Way

Council Building

Leathermarket Court

Weston Street

Lamb

o|1 grid square represents 250 metres

he

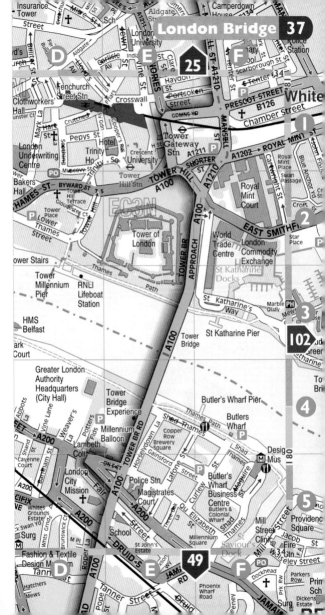

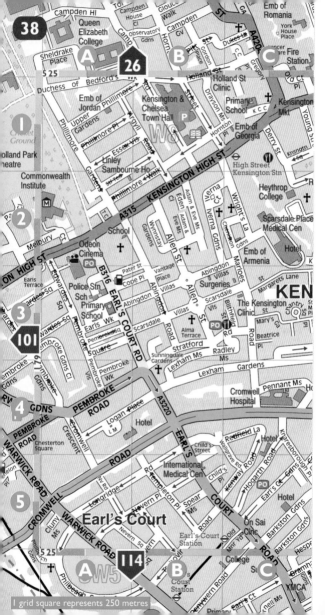

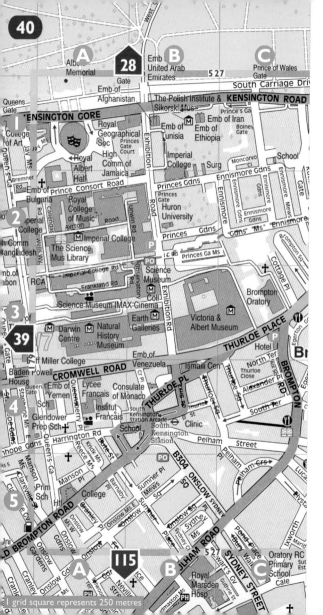

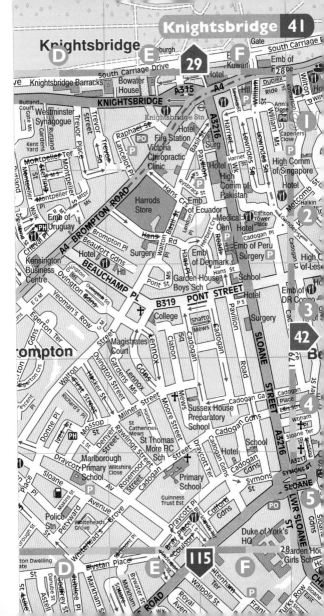

Grid references: 42, 30, 41, 116

Wellington Museum
Hyde Park
Corner Stn
HYDE PK CORNER
Wellington Arch
South Carriage Drive
A — B — C
DUKE OF WELLINGTON
Consti

Emb of Fran
528
DUPLEX
Ride
Kinnerton St
Ann's Close
PH
Capeners Close
High Comm of Singapore
Hotel
Motcomb St
Halkin Arcade
W. Halkin St
Peru
Cadogan Pl
High Comm of Lesotho
Emb of Finland
Emb of DR Congo
High Comm of Singapore
Cadogan Lane
Cadogan Place
Cadogan Place
Belgravia
Surgery
Emb of Iceland
Ebs street
Wbham
Sloane Ter
School
Emb Cottages
Surgery
Holy Trinity CE Primary School
Eaton Cl
Royal Court
Sloane Sq Stm
SLOANE
SO
LWR SLOANE
Symons St
York's
G.G.228 House Girls Sch
PIMLICO RD
CHELSEA
grid square represents 250 metres

Barrack Grosvenor Cts
Hotel
Wilton Pl
Wilton Rw
Emb of Luxembourg
Halkin St
Hotel
Emb of Turkey
Emb of Syria
High Comm of Malaysia
Chapel St
Emb of Portugal
BELGRAVE SQ
Wilton Ter
Wilton Crs
High Comm of Trinidad & Tobago
Emb of Cote d'Ivoire
High Comm of Brunei
Emb of Austria
Emb of Germany
Emb of Norway
Upr Belgrave St
Belgrave Ms South
Belgrave Ms
High Comm of Finland
Emb of Spain
Eaton Place
Eccleston Mews
Chesham Place
Lyall Mews
Lyall St
Emb of Hungary
Emb of Belgium
Emb of Bolivia
Lyall St
Surgery
Eaton Ms N
EATON SQUARE
Eaton Square
Eaton Ms
KING'S ROAD
Eaton Square
A3217
Eaton Square
Boscobel Place
Chester Sq
Eaton Ms
Minera Ms
ELIZABETH
Eaton Ms S
Gerald Rd
Ebury Mews
Caroline Terrace
Chester Terrace
Eaton Cl
Burton Ms
Graham Terrace
School
SW1W
Whittaker St
Holbein
PIMLICO ROAD
Council Building
St Barnabas CE Prim Sch
Ranelagh Grove
ROAD

CROSVENOR CRS
Headfort Pl
Emb of Ireland
European School of Economics
A302
CROSVENOR PLACE
Groom Place
Chester Street
Chester Cl
Chester Ms
Wilton St
Dorset
Wilton Street
London Tourist Board
B31
Eaton Rw
Mews N
Grosvenor Gdns Mew Nrth
HOBART PL
Eaton Square
ECCLESTON ST
Square
Ebury Ms E
Lwr Belgrave
Ebury Ms
Chester Sq
Preparatory School
Surg
Surgery
Eccleston Place
PO
BUCK
The Colonn Shopping Centre
Ebury Street
Victoria Coach Station
Semley Place
Cundy St
A3214
Police Station
Surgery
PO
Abb
Mano
Abb
Man
Esta

SW1X
SW1W

Districts: Belgravia, SW1X, SW1W

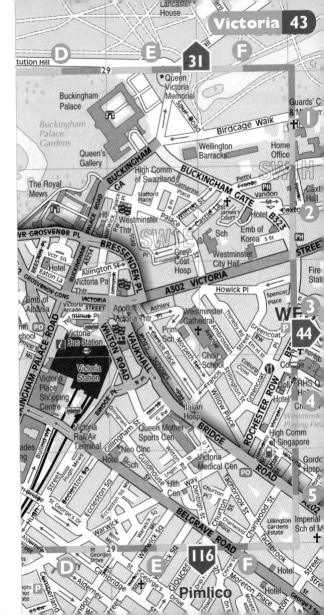

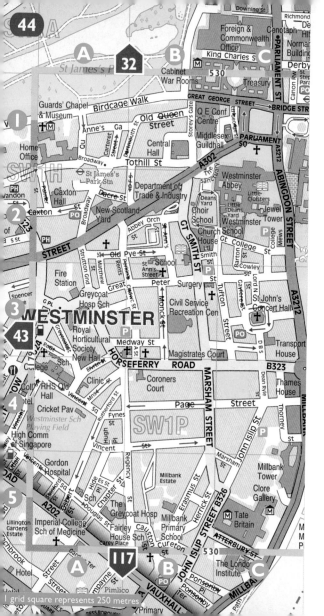

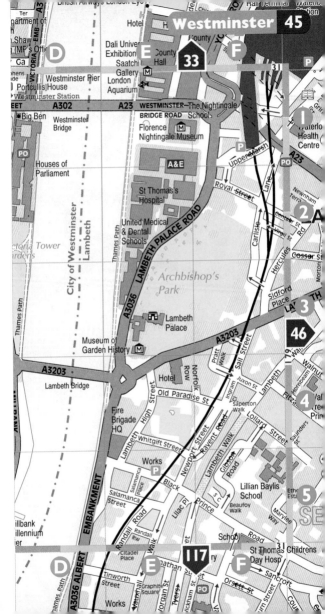

33

46

117

British Airways London Eye

Ter
epartment of
n-Shaw
g (MP's Offic
Ga
phens
de
Portcullis House
Westminster Station

VICTORIA EMB

Hotel

Dali Univers
Exhibition
Saatchi
Gallery
London
Aquarium

Westminster Pier

E County
Hall

County

YO

F

P

Hair Terminal Waterlo
tion

Grit

Waterlo
Health
Centre

A23

PO

Newnham
Terra

EET

A302

Big Ben

A23

Westminster
Bridge

Houses of
Parliament

PO

ctoria
Tower
ardens

Thames Path

City of Westminster

Lambeth

WESTMINSTER—The Nightingale
BRIDGE ROAD School

Florence
Nightingale Museum

A&E

St Thomas's
Hospital

United Medical
& Dental
Schools

Thames Path

LAMBETH PALACE ROAD

A3036

Upper Marsh

Royal Street

Lane

Carlisle

Archbishop's
Park

Lambeth
Palace

A3203

Museum of
Garden History

A3203

Lambeth Bridge

Fire
Brigade
HQ

Lambeth

High

Street

Whitgift Street

Hercules

Centaur
s Rd

Virgil

Cossar St

Sidford
Place

LA

Pratt
Walk

Sail Street

Norfolk
Row

Hotel

Old Paradise St

Newport Street

Ravent Road

Juxon St

Saperton
Walk

Ingram

Lambeth

Lollard Street

A

Morto

TH

Saunders

Fitzal

Wa

Walnut

Hornbeam

Wal
re
Prin

Works

P

EMBANKMENT

A3036 ALBERT

Salamanca
Street

Salamanca
place

Black

Randall
Road

Randall
RW

Randall
Walk

Lilac Pl

Prince

Gibson
Road

Lilian Baylis
School

Beaufoy
Walk

S C

Marylee
Way

Ethe
Esta

SE

Millbank
illennium
ier

Thames Path

D

Citadel
Place

Tinworth
Street

athan

Graphite
square

Morgan St

Works

E

Matthew

Wickham St

PO

hers

School

Prince
Road

St Thomas Childrens
Day Hosp

F

Sancroft

Orsett St

rn Ro

Cou

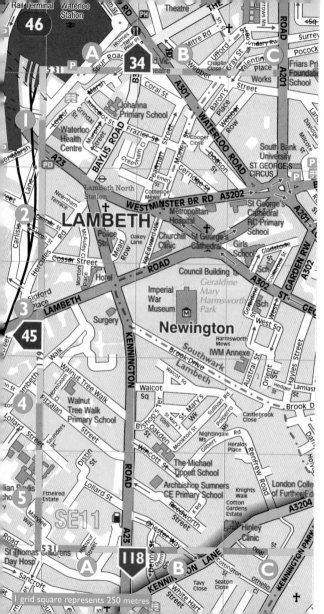

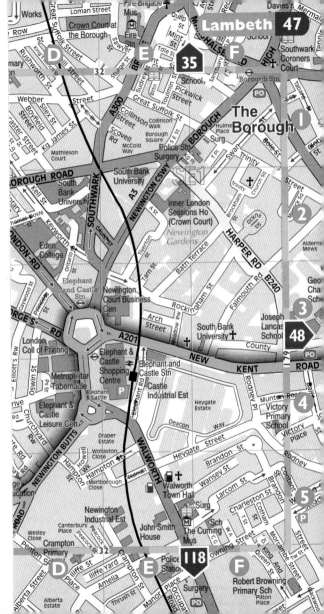

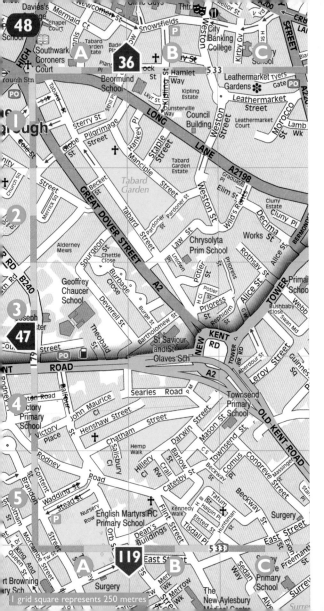

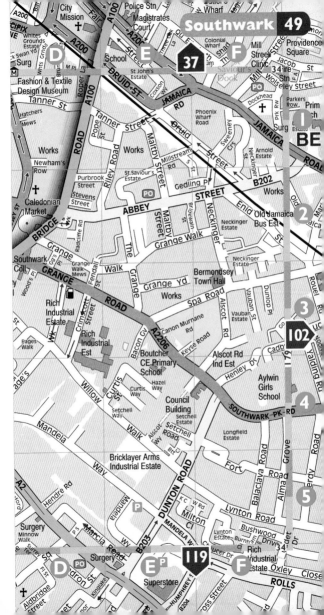

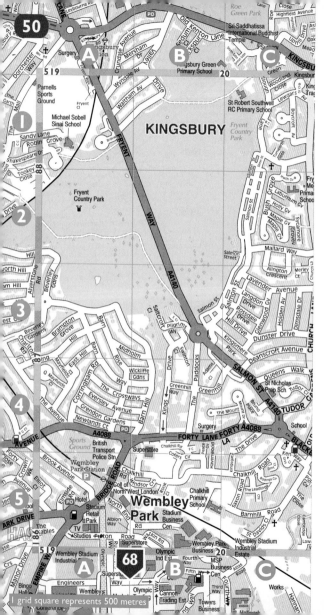

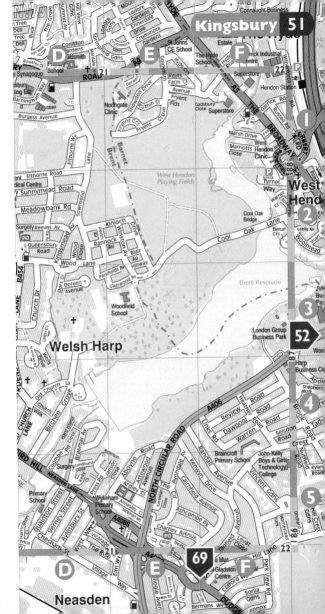

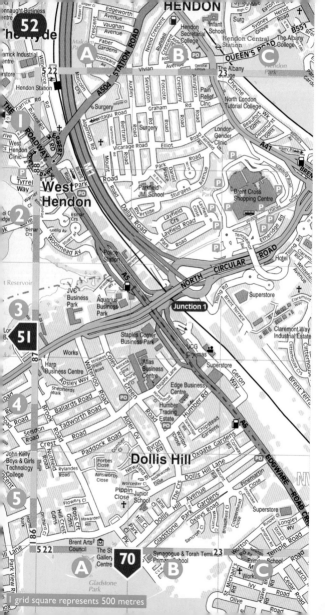

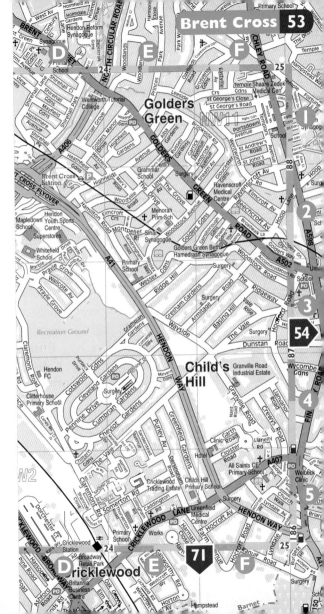

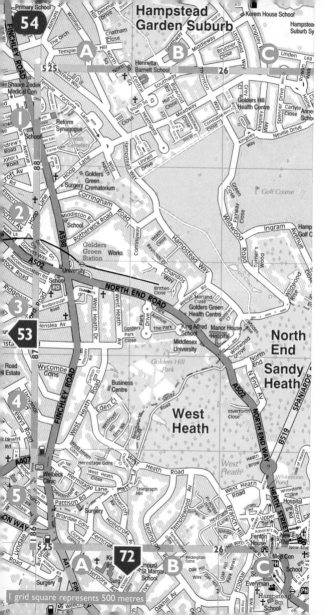

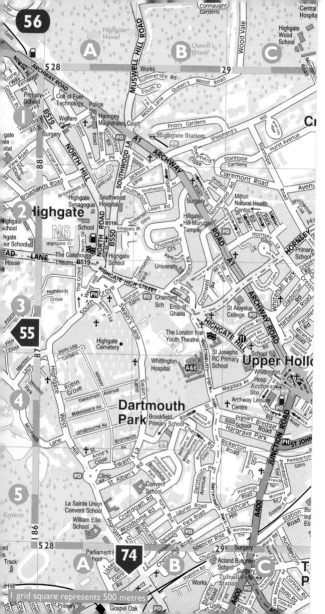

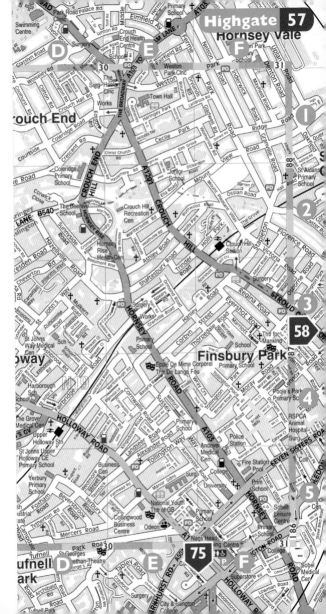

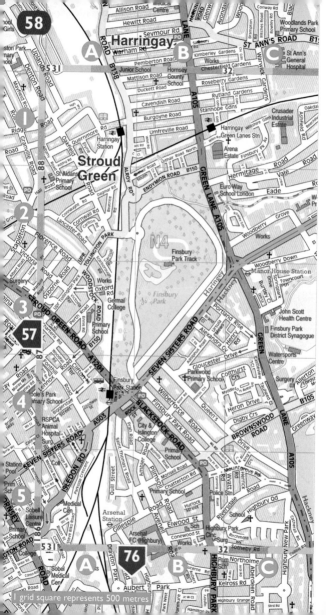

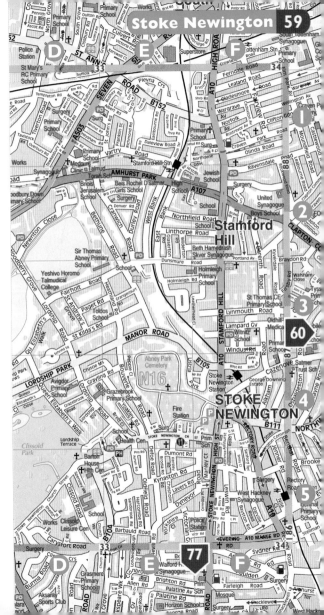

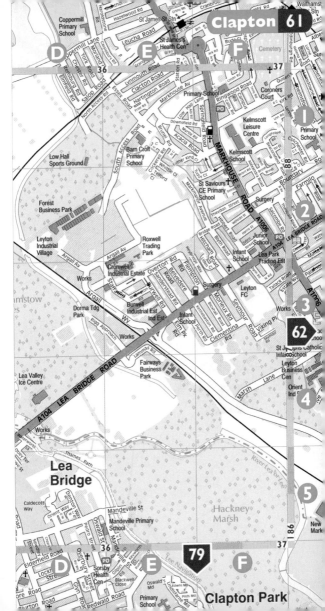

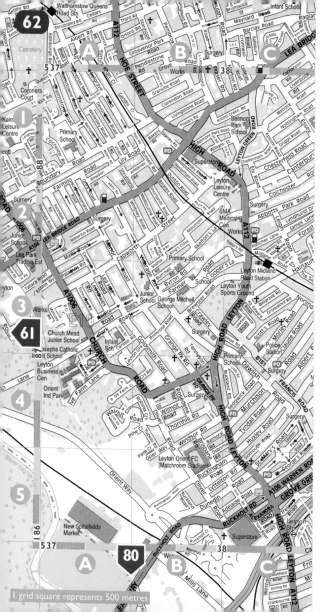

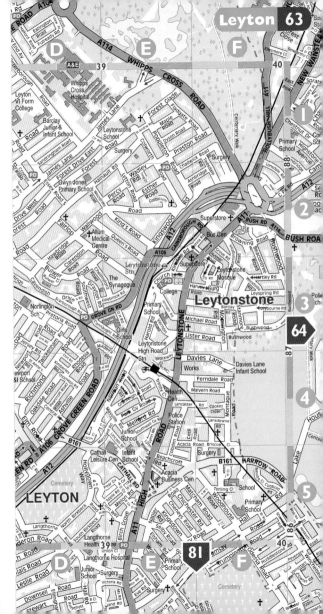

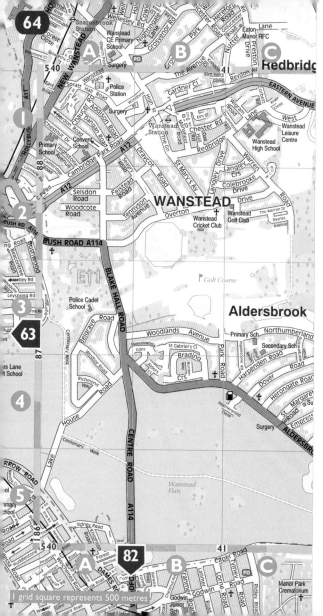

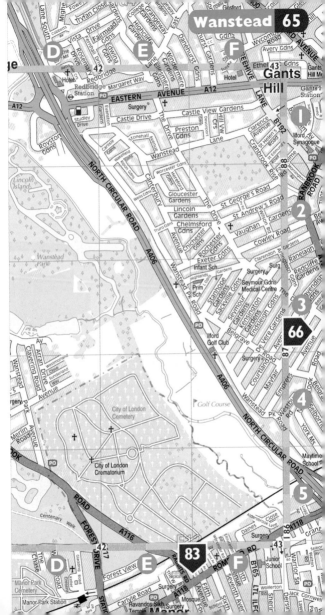

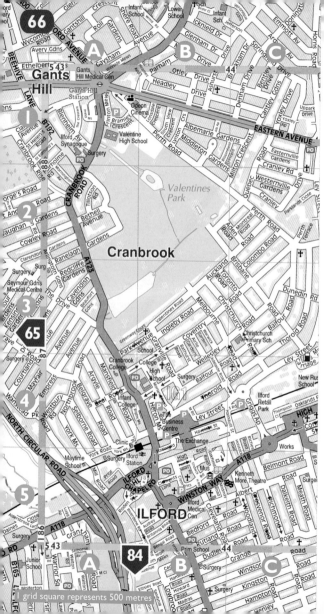

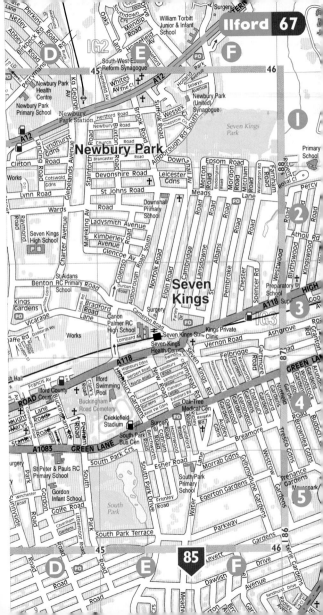

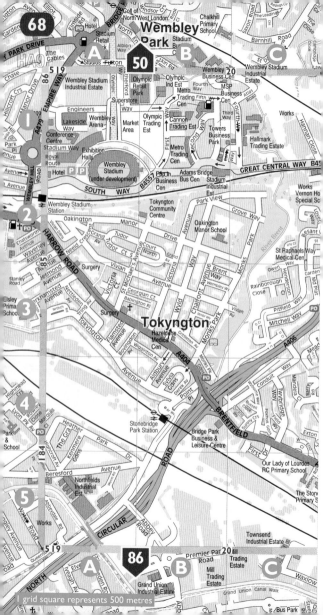

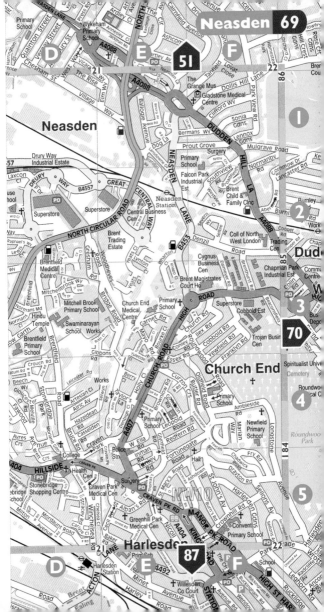

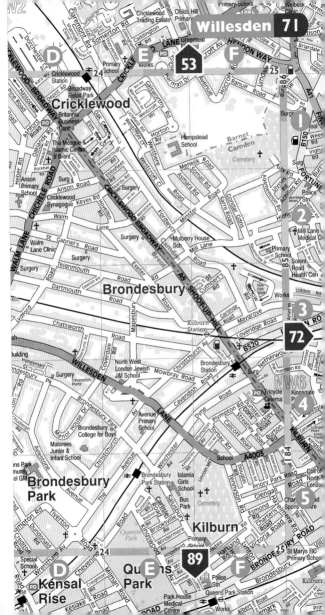

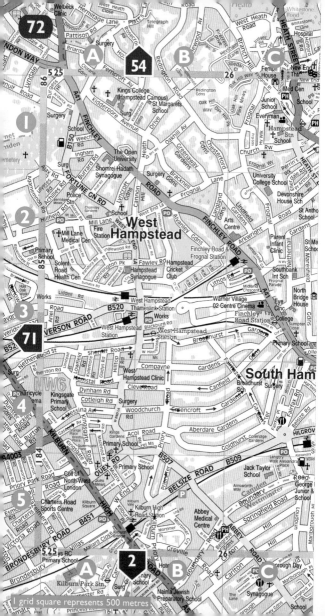

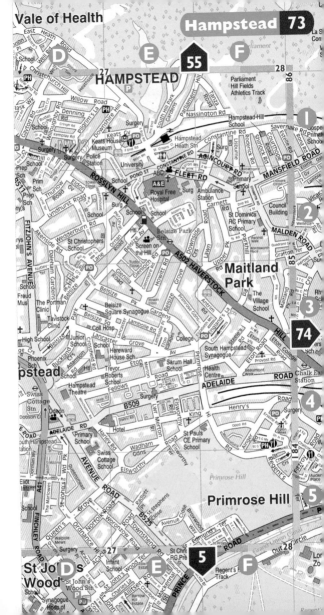

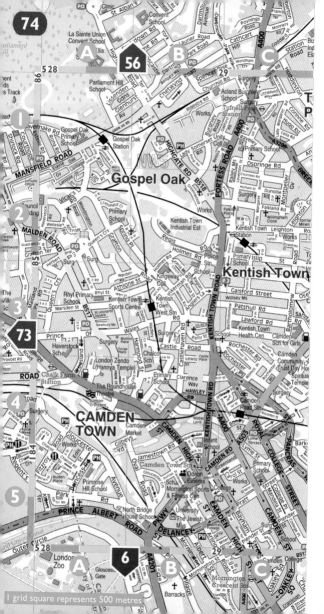

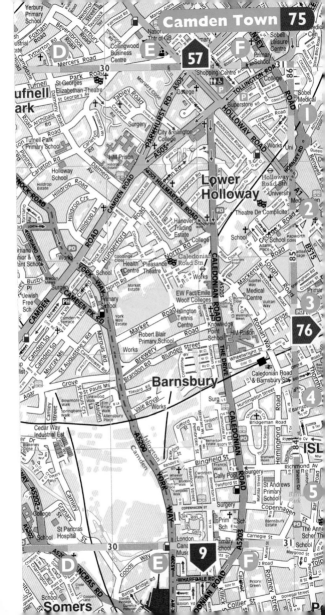

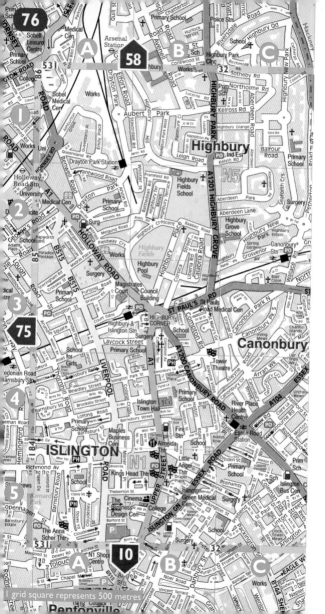

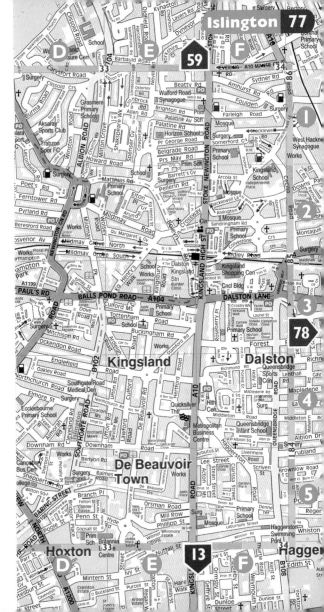

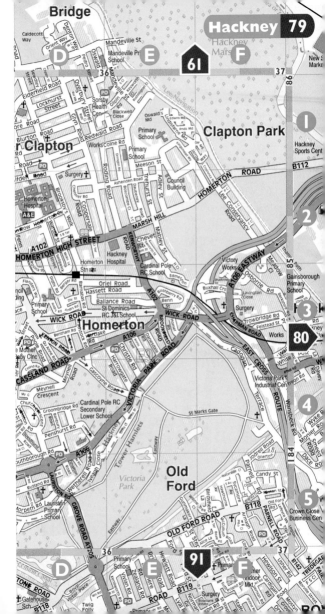

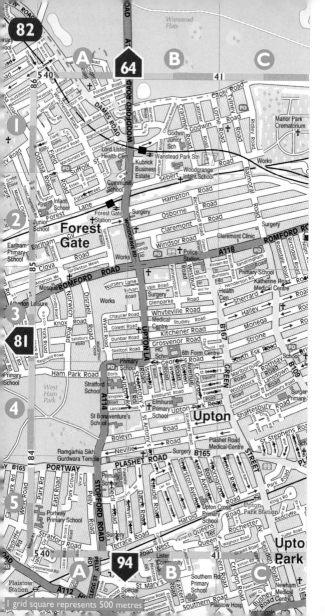

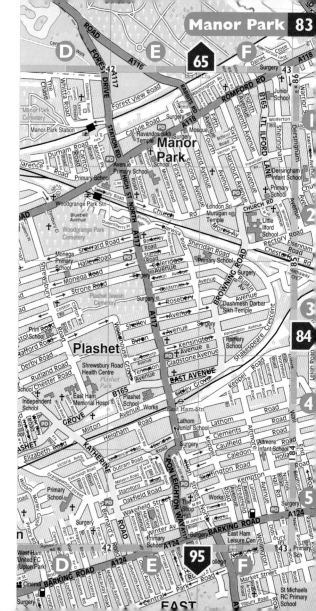

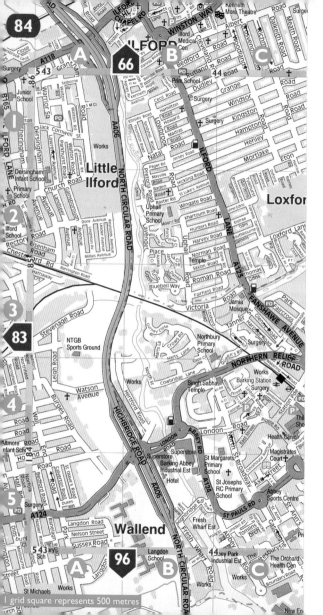

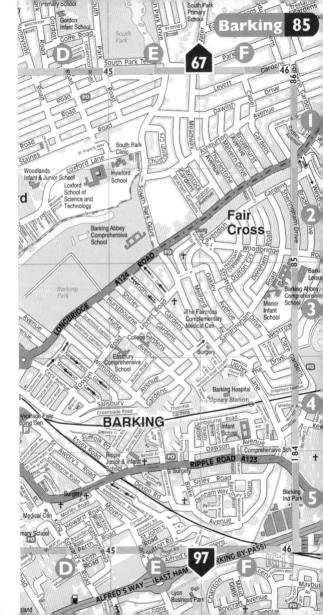

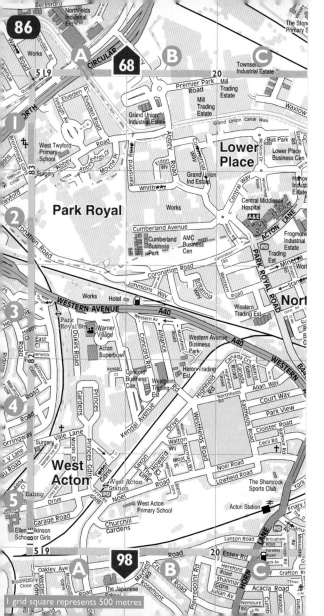

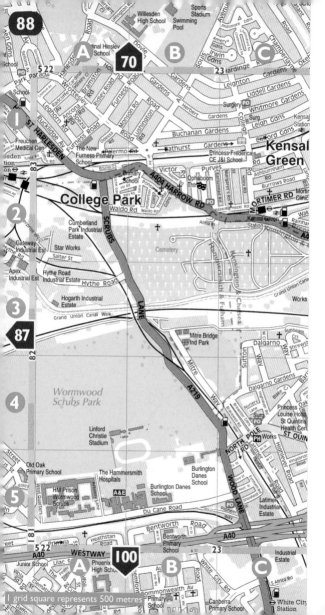

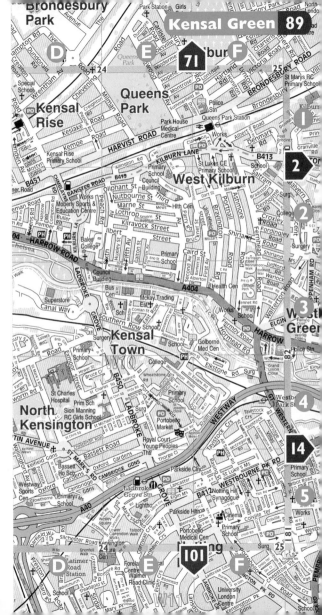

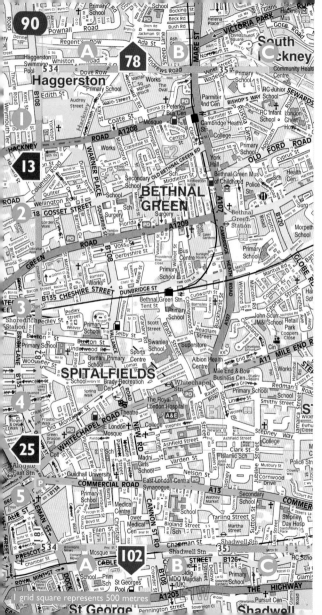

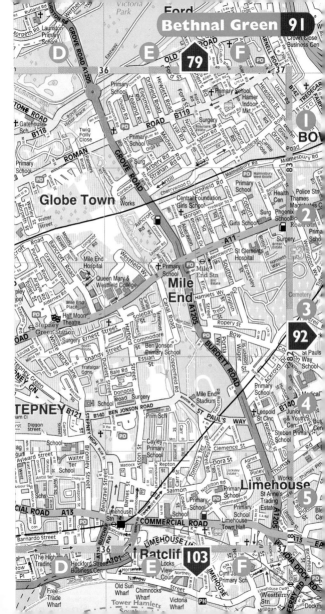

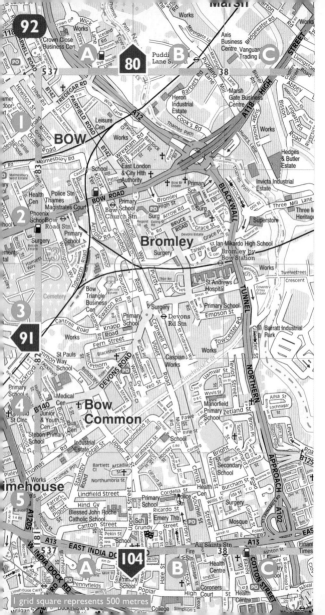

I grid square represents 500 metres

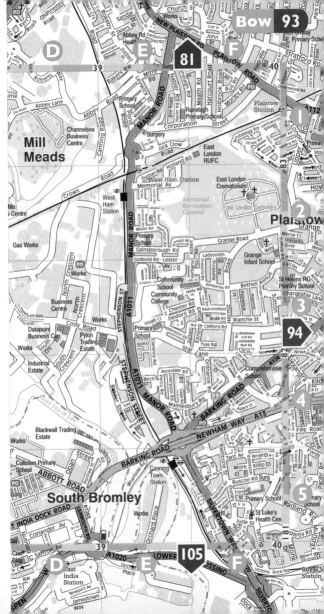

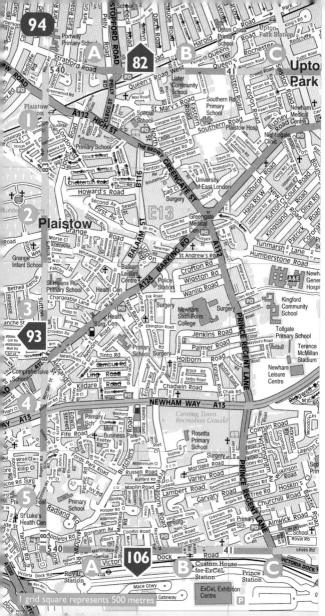

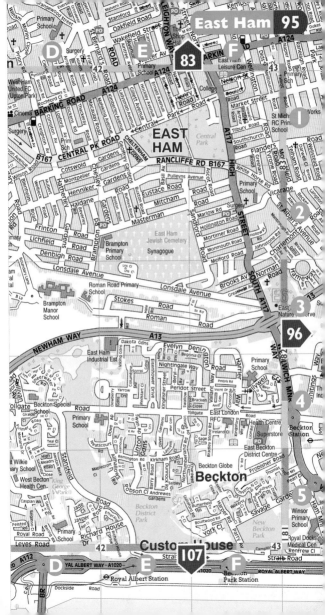

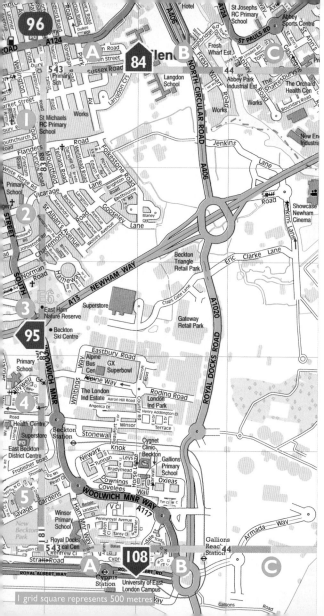

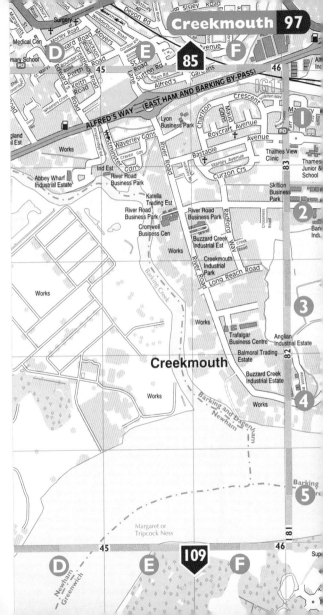

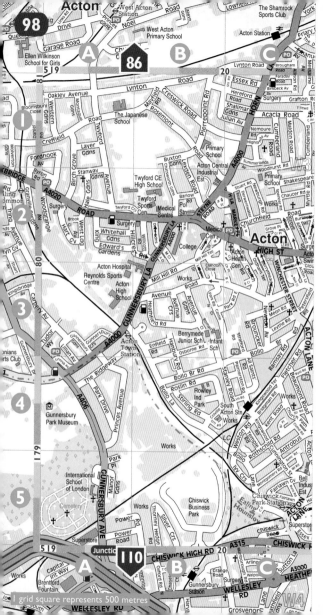

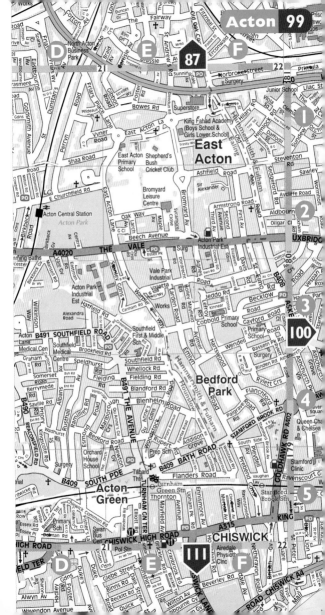

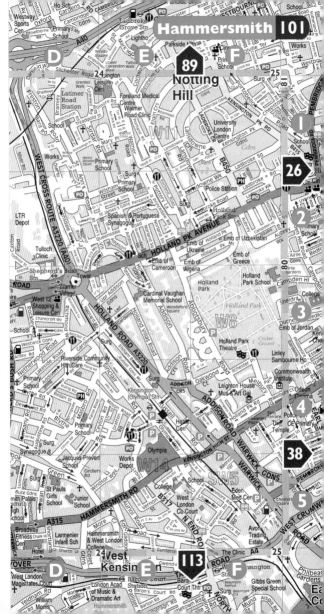

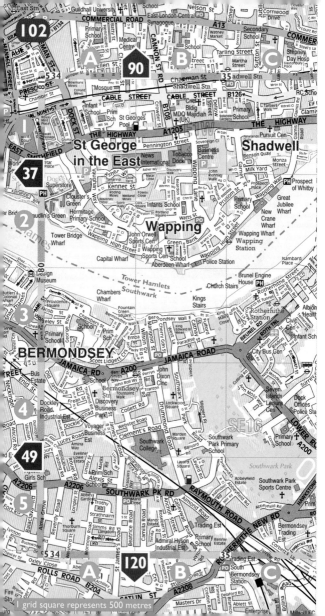

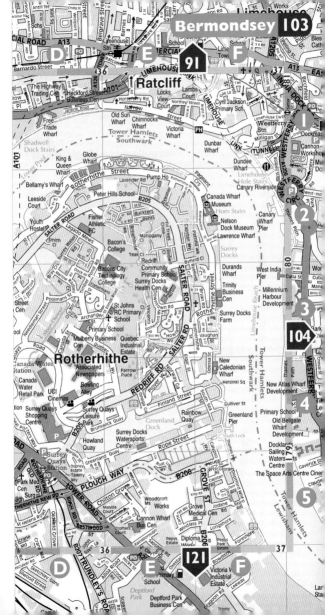

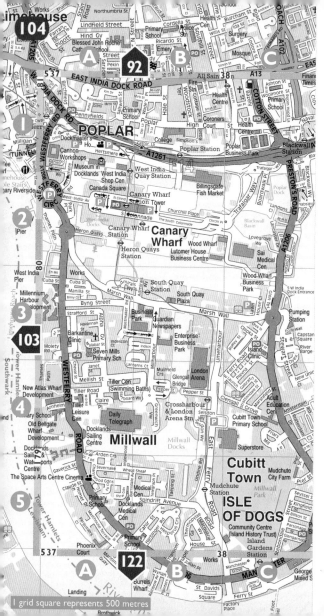

1 grid square represents 500 metres

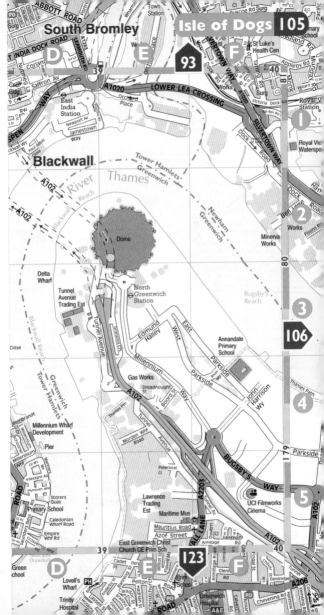

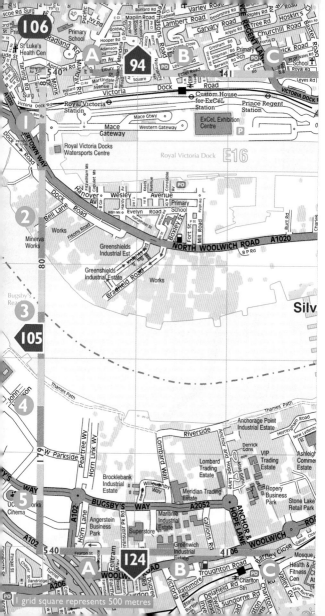

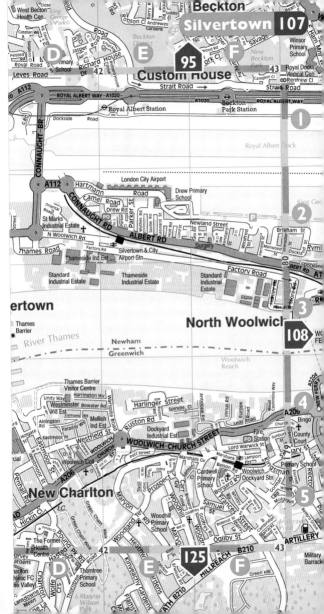

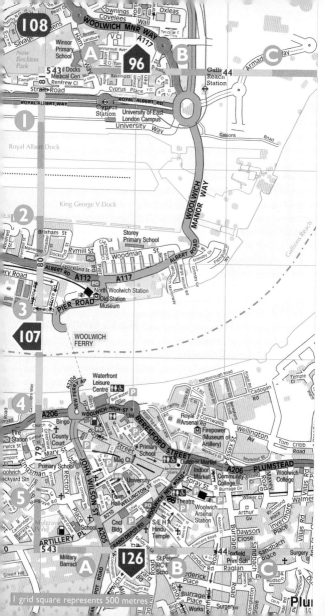

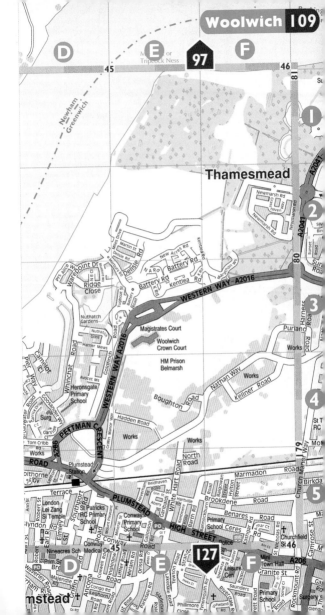

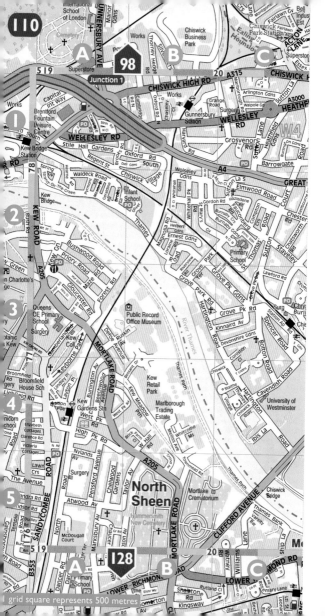

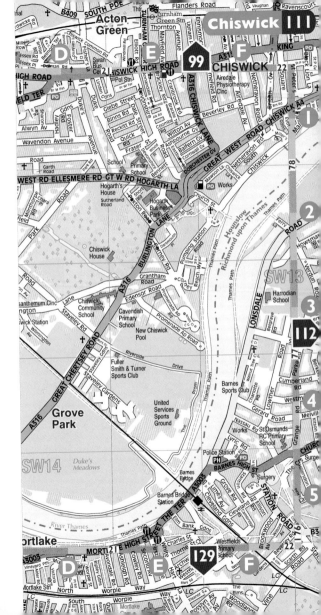

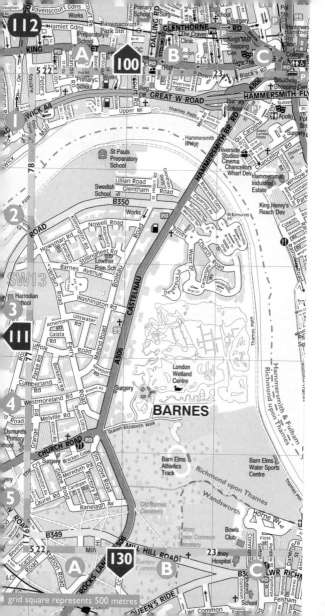

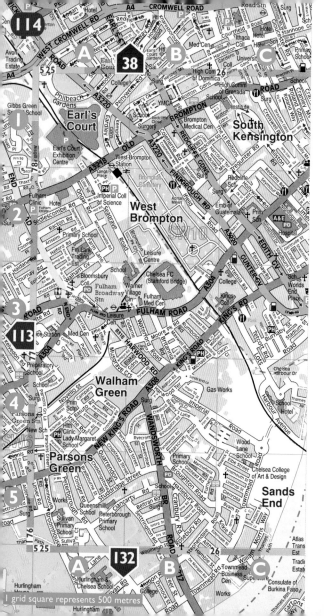

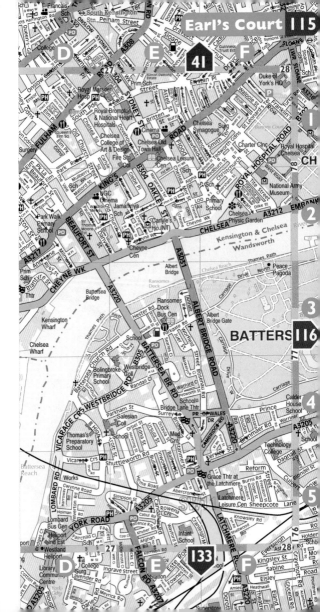

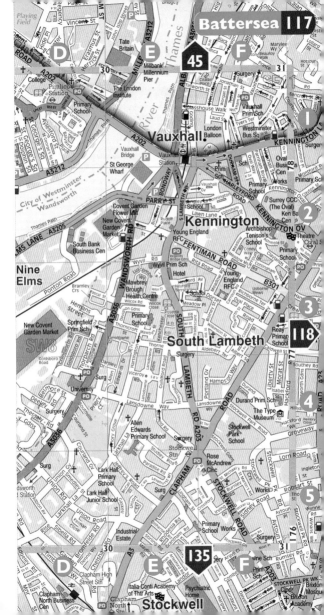

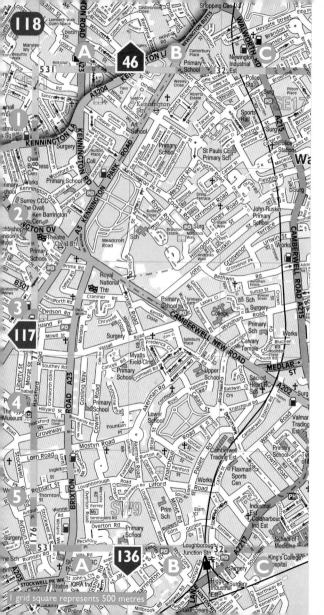

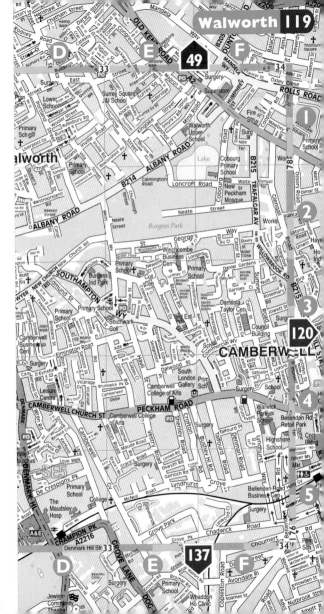

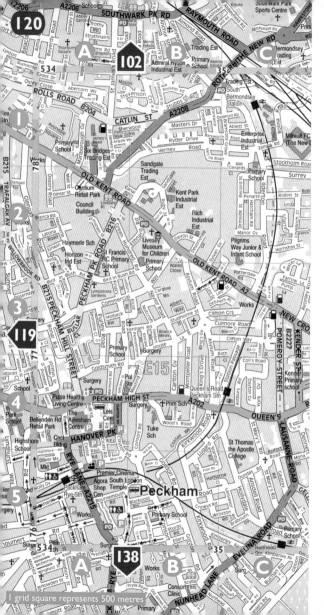

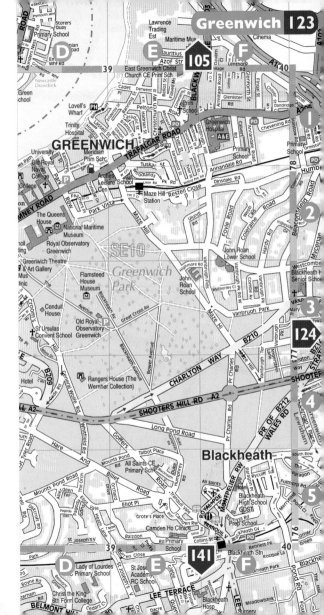

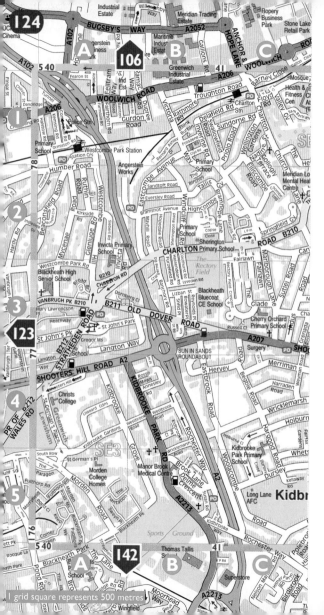

I grid square represents 500 metres

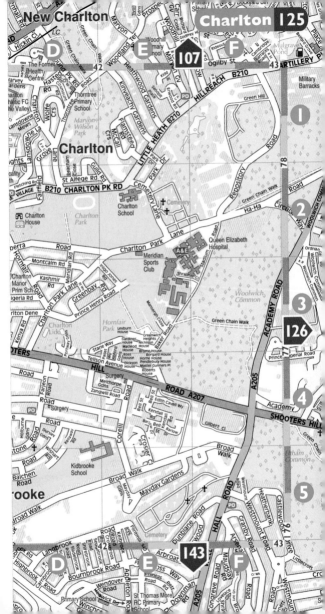

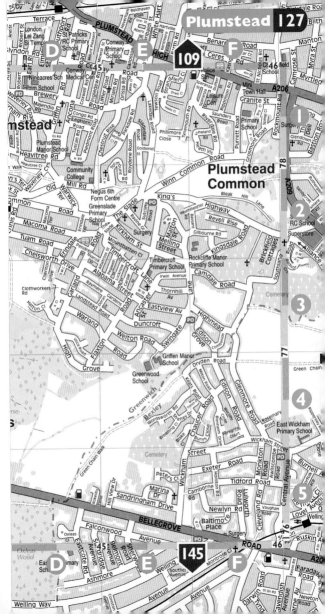

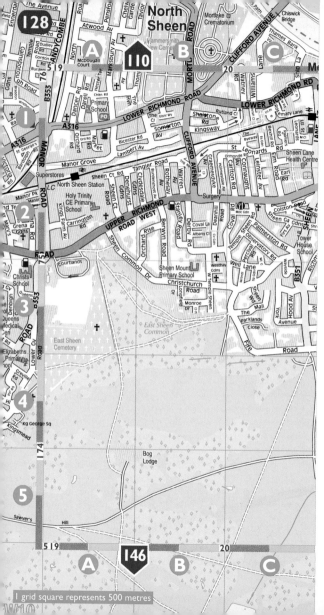

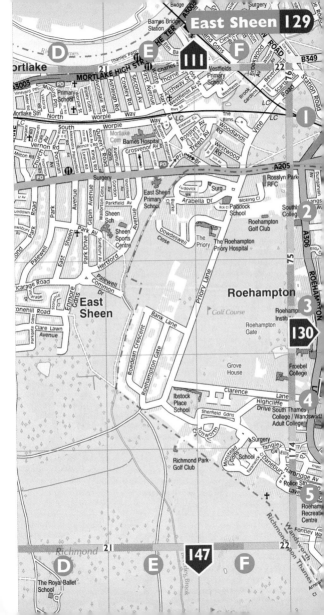

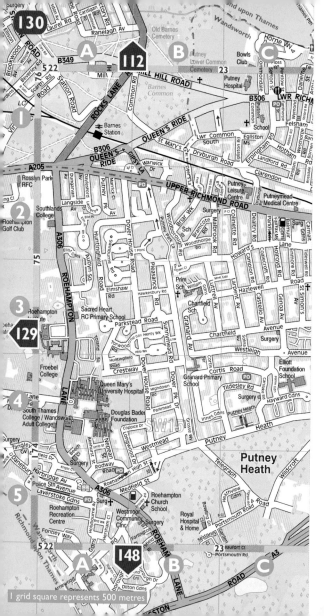

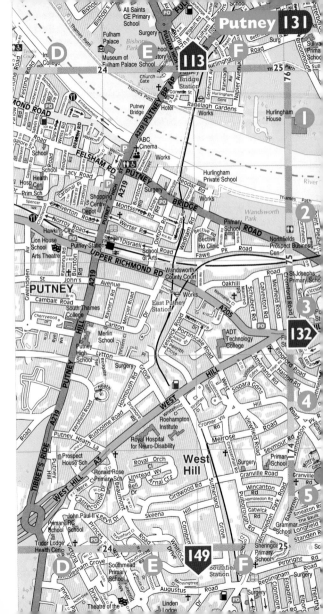

Sands End

132

114

A B C

132

114

Peterborough Rd
Coniger Rd
Studridge Street
School
Hazelbury Road
Furness
Lindrod St
Glenrosa St

Works
Queensmill
School
Clancarty
BR
Cranbury

Suliva Rd
Peterborough
Primary
School
Beltran St
Surg
Byam St
C

Road
Suliva
Prim
School
Suliva
Woolneigh St
Settrington Rd
Rosebury Rd
Hamble St
Edenhurst Av
M

Thames 5 25
76
A Sullivan Rd
B
A217
PO
Stephendale Road
A26
Townmead
Rd
Atlas
Trans
Est

Daisy Lane
Hurlingham &
Chelsea School
Sullivan Rd
Hugon Rd
Breer St
Dimock St
Townmead
Business
Superstore
Tradi
Estate

Hurlingham
House
College
Carnwath Road
Industrial Est
Consulate of
Burkina Faso

1

Hurlingham
Business Park
Carnwath
Carnwath Road
Industrial Est
Wandsworth
Bridge

Prim Sch

River Thames
Thames Pth
Pier
Ter

WANDSWORTH
The
Cswy
Smugglers Way
SWANDON WY
Charterhouse
Works
Nantes Clo

2

Thames
Northfields
Point Pleasant
Northfields
Enterprise Wy
Osiers Ind Est
Wandsworth
Stn
Ferrier
Industrial
Est
Ferrier St
PH
Surg
A214

Prospect Business
Cen
Frogmore
The Roche
School
ARMOURY WY
Ram Brewery
& Visitor
Centre
FAIRFIELD ST
RAM
Town
Hall
Tonsley
HUGUENOT PL

131

St Josephs
Primary School
Cranford Rd
Santos Rd
Giccson Ct
Police
Station
WANDSWORTH HIGH
Birch St
Primary
School
A3
WEST HILL
A3
College St
Cncl
Building
College School
A3

Mexfield Rd
Galve
Broomhill
BUCKHOLD
Hardwick's Wy
PO
P
P
Arndale
Health
Centre
The Wandsworth
Arndale Centre
Marcus
Ter
P
Rosehill Road

3

4

Haldon Rd
MERTON ROAD
The
Southfields Clinc
Mapleton
RD
Mapleton
A217
Wandle
Recreation
Centre
Sergeant
Industrial
Est
Iron Mill Rd
Vermont Rd
JMI School
On the
Road-Tours
Medical Cen

5

Seymo
Wimbledon Rd
A218
Surg
Brathway Rd
SW18
Wandsworth
Trading Estate
Della Rd
GARRATT LANE
Allfarthing
Primary
School

Prim
School
74
Granville
Rd
Camborne Rd
King
George's
Park
Furmage
Brocklebank
Health Cen
Swaffield Road
Bucharest
EARLSFIELD

Merton Rd
Kimber
Smeaton Rd
Merton Road
Industrial
Estate
Lydden Rd
Lydden Va
Bendon Va
Council
Building
Winna Road
ROAD

Grammar
School
Longfield St
Standen Road
School
Burr
Riverside
Business
tre
A26
Wandsworth
Cemetery

A
150
Southfields
B
St John's
Dr
Vanderbilt Rd
Cargill Rd
C sfield

1 grid square represents 500 metres

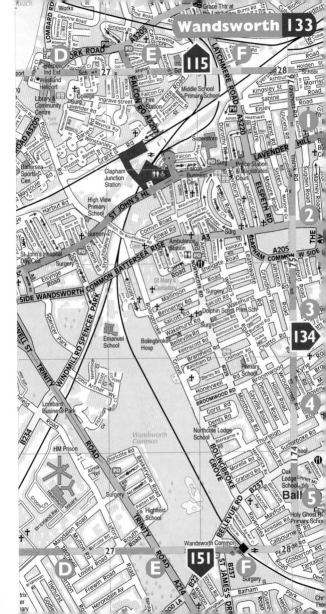

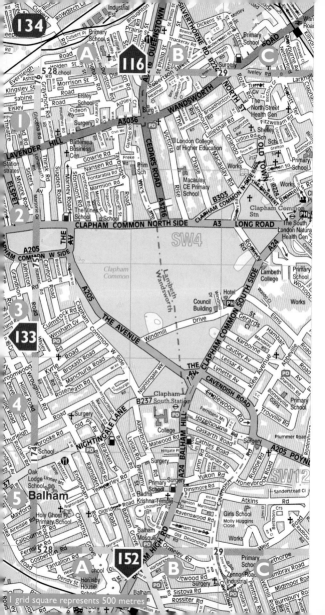

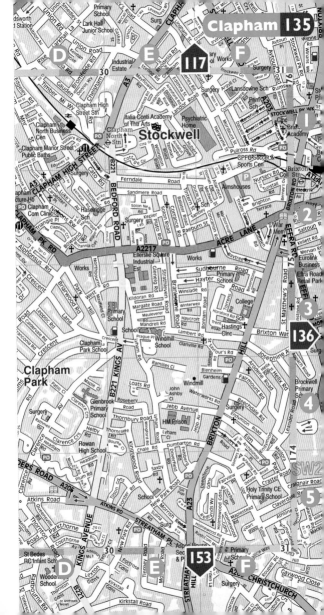

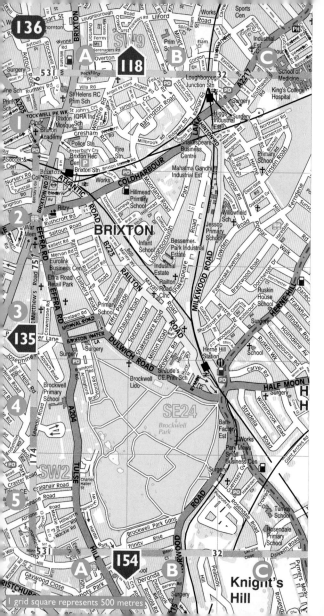

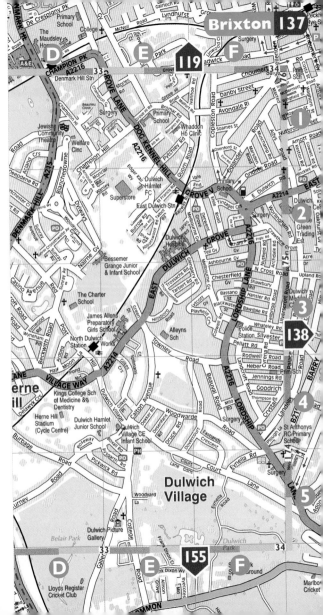

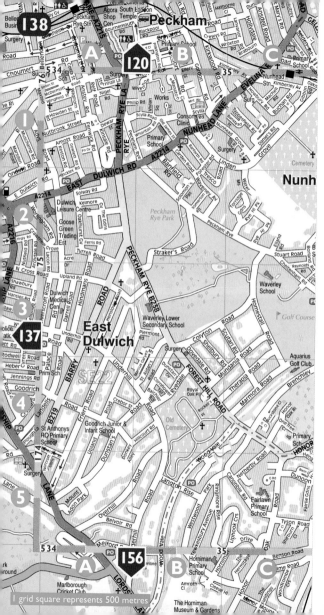

Peckham

138

120

137

East Dulwich

SE22

156

grid square represents 500 metres

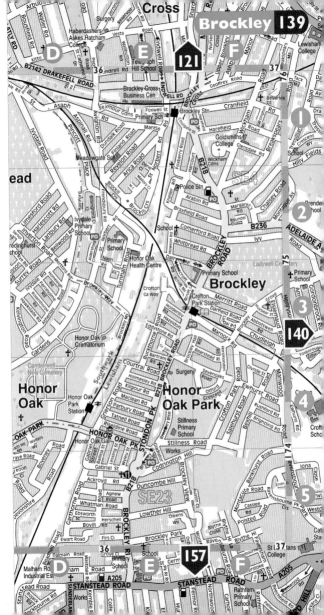

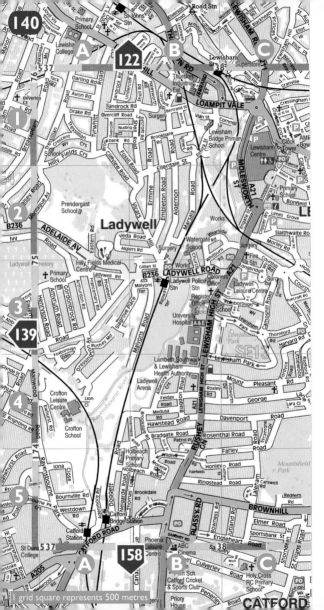

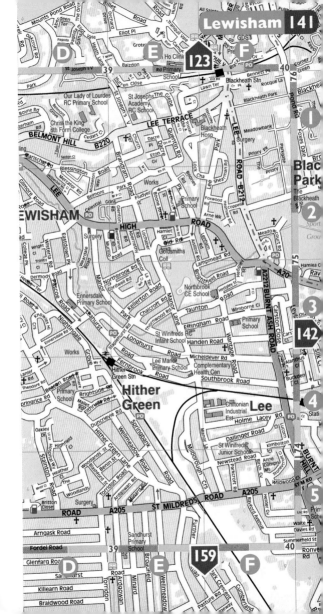

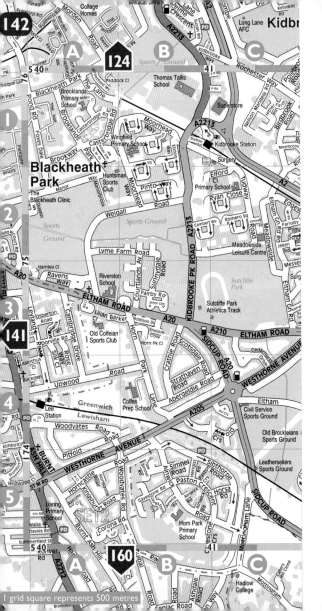

I grid square represents 500 metres

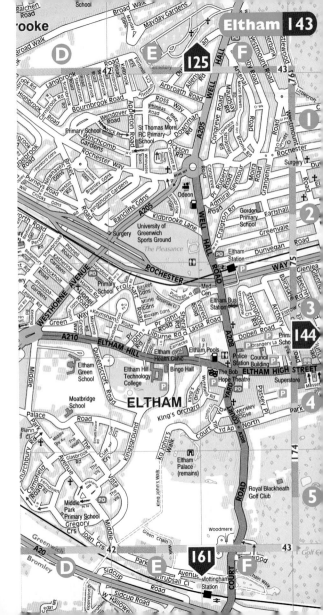

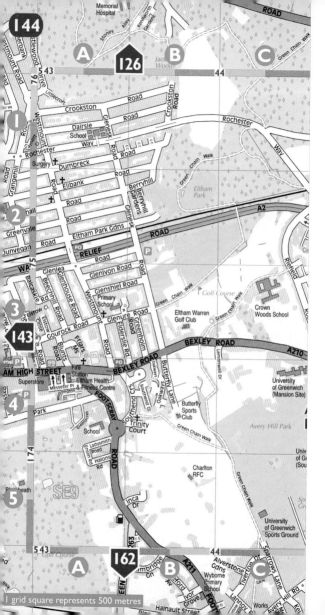

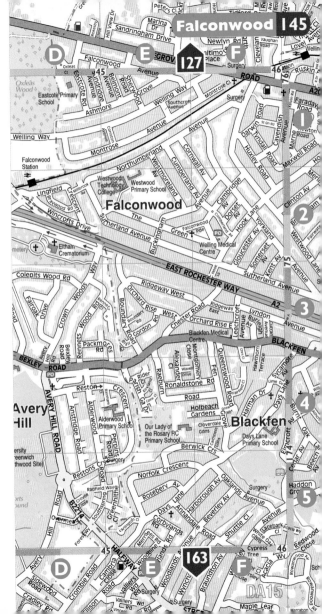

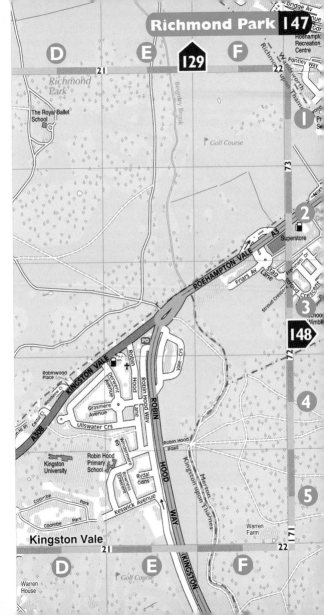

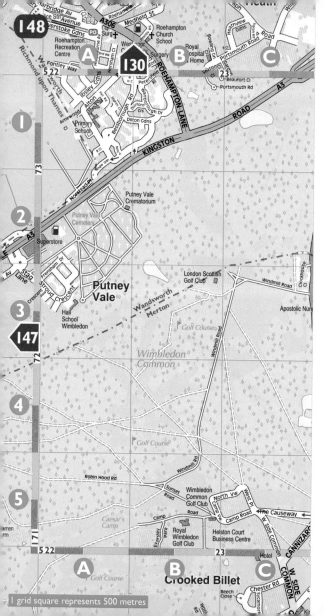

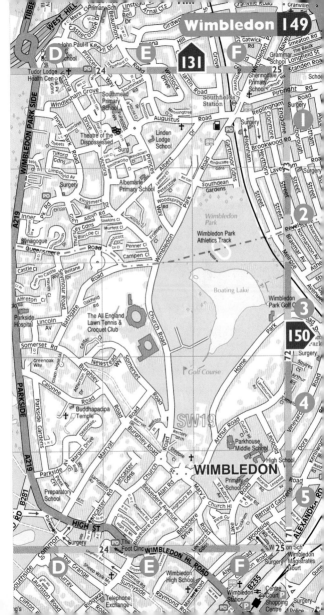

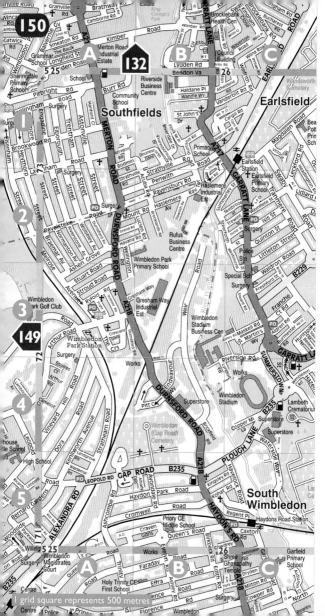

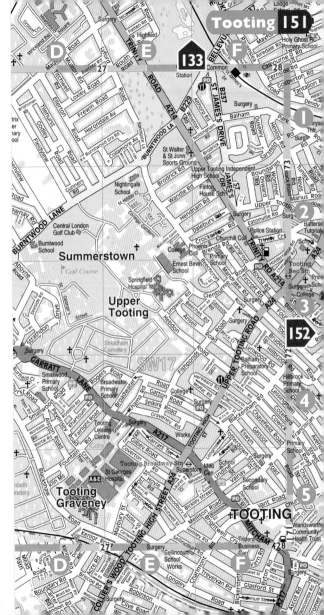

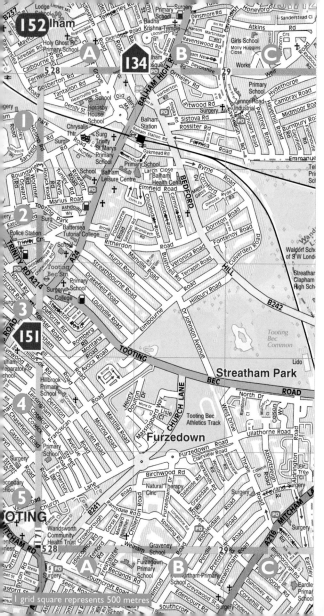

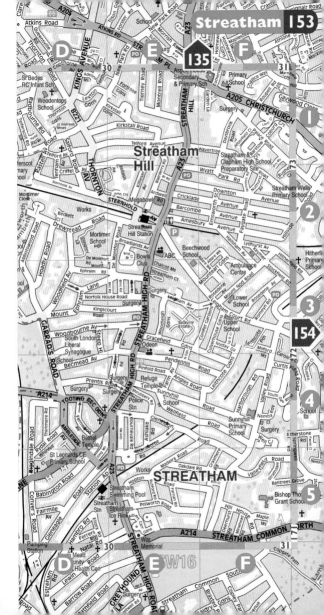

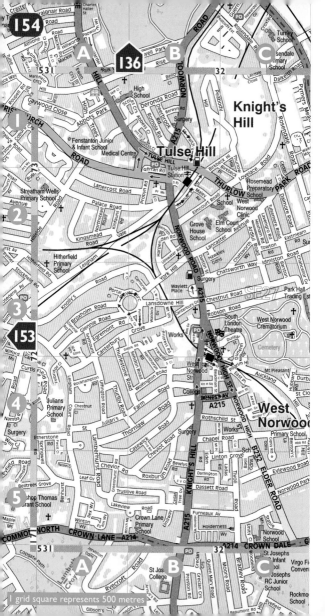

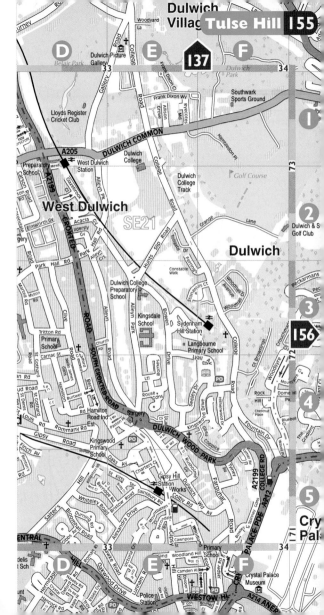

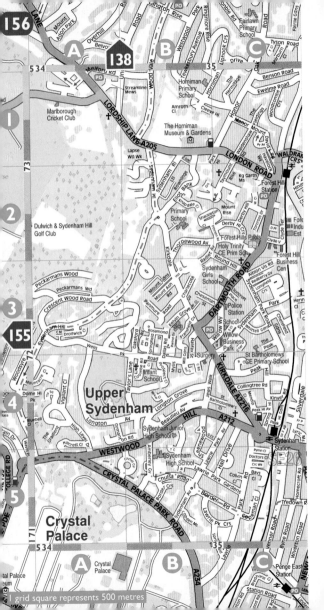

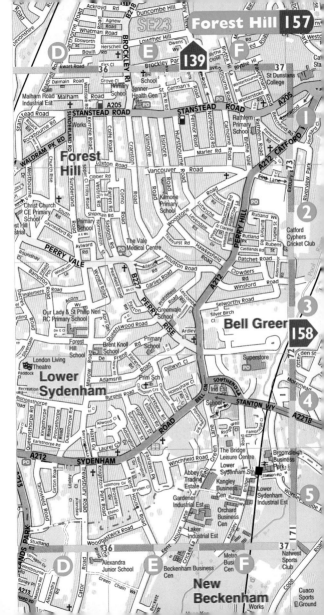

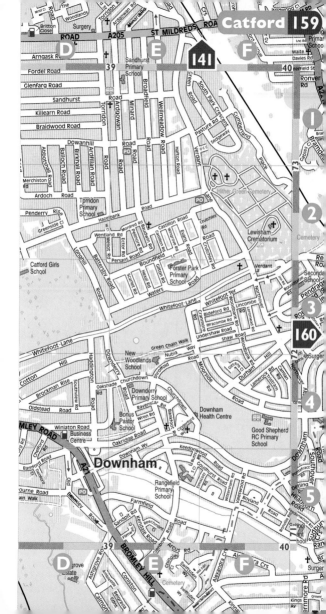

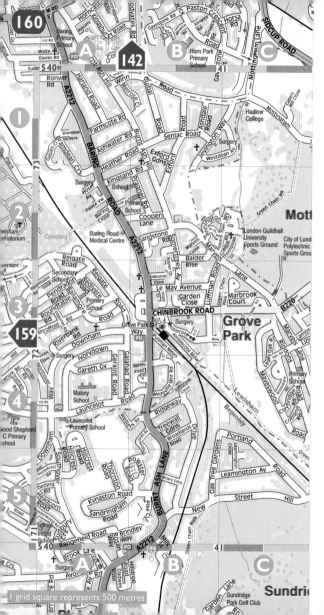

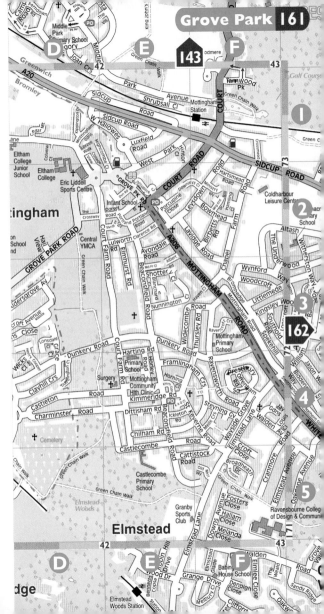

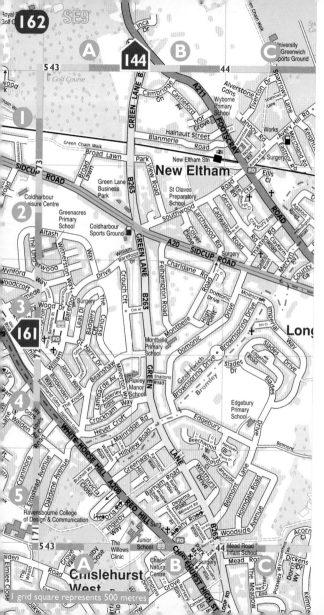

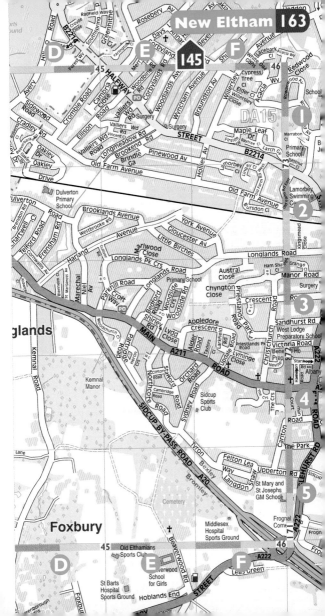

Acton	98	C2
Acton Green	99	D5
Aldersbrook	64	C3
Avery Hill	144	C4
Balham	133	F5
Barking	85	D4
Barnes	112	B4
Barnsbury	75	E4
Battersea	115	F3
Bayswater	27	D1
Beckton	95	F5
Bedford Park	99	F4
Belgravia	42	A4
Bell Green	157	F3
Bellingham	158	A4
Bethnal Green	90	B2
Blackfen	145	F4
Blackheath	123	F5
Blackheath Park	142	A2
Blackwall	105	D1
Bloomsbury	20	B2
The Borough	47	F1
Bow	92	A1
Bow Common	92	A4
Brixton	136	A2
Brockley	139	F3
Bromley	92	B2
Brompton	40	C3
Brondesbury	71	E3
Brondesbury Park	71	D5
Brook Green	100	C4
Camberwell	119	F4
Camden Town	74	A4
Canary Wharf	104	B2
Canonbury	76	C3
Catford	158	C1
Charlton	125	D1
Chelsea	116	A1
Child's Hill	53	E4
Chiswick	99	F5
Church End	69	F4
City of London	35	D1
Clapham	116	B5
Clapham Park	135	D4
Clapton Park	79	F1
Clerkenwell	10	A5
College Park	88	A2
Cranbrook	66	A2
Creekmouth	97	E4
Cricklewood	71	D1
Crouch End	56	C1
Crystal Palace	156	A5
Cubitt Town	104	C5
Custom House	107	E1
Dalston	77	F4
Dartmouth Park	56	A4
De Beauvoir Town	77	E5
Deptford	121	F2
Dollis Hill	52	B5
Downham	159	D5
Dudden Hill	70	A2
Dulwich	155	F2
Dulwich Village	137	E5
Earl's Court	38	A5
Earlsfield	150	C1
East Acton	99	E1
East Dulwich	138	A3
East Ham	95	E1
East Sheen	129	D3
Elmstead	161	E5
Eltham	143	E4
Fair Cross	85	F2
Falconwood	145	E2
Finsbury	10	A3
Finsbury Park	57	F4

Forest Gate	82	A2
Forest Hill	157	D1
Foxbury	163	D5
Fulham	113	D3
Furzedown	152	B4
Gants Hill	65	F1
Globe Town	91	D2
Golders Green	53	E1
Gospel Oak	74	A2
Greenwich	123	D1
Grove Park	111	D4
Grove Park	160	C3
Hackney	78	C3
Hackney Wick	80	A3
Haggerston	13	F1
Hammersmith	100	B5
Hampstead	73	D1
Harlesden	87	E1
Herne Hill	136	C4
Highbury	76	B1
Highgate	55	F2
Hither Green	141	E4
Holborn	21	E3
Homerton	79	D3
Honor Oak	139	D4
Honor Oak Park	139	E4
Hoxton	12	C2
Ilford	66	A5
Isle of Dogs	104	C5
Islington	76	A5
Kennington	117	E2
Kensal Green	88	C2
Kensal Rise	89	D1
Kensal Town	89	E3
Kensington	38	C3
Kentish Town	74	C3
Kidbrooke	124	C5
Kilburn	71	E5
Kingsbury	50	B1
Kingsland	77	E4
Kingston Vale	147	D5
Knightsbridge	29	C5
Knight's Hill	154	C1
Ladywell	140	A2
Lambeth	46	A2
Lea Bridge	61	D5
Lee	141	F4
Lewisham	140	C2
Leyton	63	D5
Leytonstone	63	F3
Limehouse	91	F5
Lisson Grove	17	F2
Little Ilford	84	A2
Longlands	162	C3
Lower Clapton	78	C1
Lower Holloway	75	F2
Lower Place	86	C1
Lower Sydenham	157	D4
Loxford	84	C2
Maida Vale	2	C3
Maitland Park	73	F3
Manor Park	83	E1
Marylebone	18	A3
Mayfair	30	C2
Mile End	91	E3
Mill Meads	93	D2
Millwall	104	A4
Mortlake	110	C5
Mottingham	160	C2
Neasden	69	D1
Newbury Park	67	D1
New Charlton	107	D5
New Cross	121	E5
New Cross Gate	121	E4
New Eltham	162	B2

Newington	46	B3
Nine Elms	117	D3
North Acton	86	C3
North End	54	C3
North Kensington	89	D4
North Sheen	110	B5
North Woolwich	107	E3
Notting Hill	101	E1
Nunhead	138	C2
Old Ford	79	E5
Old Oak Common	87	F3
Paddington	16	A3
Park Royal	86	A2
Parsons Green	114	A5
Peckham	120	B5
Pentonville	9	F1
Pimlico	116	C1
Plaistow	93	F2
Plashet	83	D3
Plumstead	126	C1
Plumstead Common	127	F2
Poplar	104	A1
Primrose Hill	73	F5
Putney	131	D3
Putney Heath	130	C5
Putney Vale	148	A3
Queens Park	89	F1
Ratcliff	103	E1
Regent's Park	7	D2
Roehampton	129	F3
Rotherhithe	103	D4
St George in the East	102	A1
St Giles	20	B4
St James	32	A4
St Johns	*122	A5
St Luke's	11	F5
St Pancras	9	D4
Sands End	114	C5
Seven Kings	67	E3
Shacklewell	78	A1
Shadwell	102	C1
Shepherd's Bush	100	B2
Shooters Hill	126	C4
Shoreditch	12	B4
Silvertown	106	C3
Soho	20	A5
Somers Town	8	A2
South Bromley	93	D5
Southend	158	C4
Southfields	150	A1
South Hackney	78	C5
South Hampstead	72	C4
South Kensington	39	E5
South Lambeth	117	E3
South Wimbledon	150	C5
Spitalfields	25	E2
Stamford Hill	59	F2
Stepney	90	C4
Stockwell	135	E1
Stoke Newington	59	F4
Strand	33	D1
Stratford	80	C4
Stratford Marsh	80	B5
Stratford New Town	80	C3
Streatham	153	E5
Streatham Hill	153	E1
Streatham Park	152	B4
Stroud Green	58	A1
Summerstown	151	D2
Temple Mills	80	B2
Thamesmead	109	F2
Tokyngton	68	B3
Tooting	151	F5
Tooting Graveney	151	D5
Tufnell Park	74	C1
Tulse Hill	154	B1
Upper Clapton	60	A3
Upper Holloway	56	C4
Upper Sydenham	156	A4
Upper Tooting	151	E3
Upton	82	B4
Upton Park	82	C5
Vale of Health	55	D5
Vauxhall	117	E1
Walham Green	114	A4
Wallend	84	A5
Walworth	118	C1
Wandsworth	132	A2
Wanstead	64	B2
Wapping	102	B2
Welsh Harp	51	D3
Wembley Park	50	A5
West Acton	86	A5
West Brompton	114	B2
West Dulwich	155	D2
West Hampstead	72	A2
West Heath	54	B4
West Hendon	52	A2
West Hill	131	E5
West Kensington	113	D1
West Kilburn	89	E2
Westminster	43	F3
West Norwood	154	C4
Whitechapel	37	F1
Willesden	70	A3
Willesden Green	70	B4
Wimbledon	149	E5
Woolwich	126	A2

USING THE STREET INDEX

Street names are listed alphabetically. Each street name is followed by its postal town or area locality, the Postcode District, the page number, and the reference to the square in which the name is found.

Standard index entries are shown as follows:

Aaron Hill Rd *EHAM* E6..........................**96** A4

Street names and selected addresses not shown on the map due to scale restrictions are shown in the index with an asterisk:

Abbeville Ms *CLAP* * SW4 ....**135** D3

GENERAL ABBREVIATIONS

ACC	ACCESS
ALY	ALLEY
AP	APPROACH
AR	ARCADE
ASS	ASSOCIATION
AV	AVENUE
BCH	BEACH
BLDS	BUILDINGS
BND	BEND
BNK	BANK
BR	BRIDGE
BRK	BROOK
BTM	BOTTOM
BUS	BUSINESS
BVD	BOULEVARD
BY	BYPASS
CATH	CATHEDRAL
CEM	CEMETERY
CEN	CENTRE
CFT	CROFT
CH	CHURCH
CHA	CHASE
CHYD	CHURCHYARD
CIR	CIRCLE
CIRC	CIRCUS
CL	CLOSE
CLFS	CLIFFS
CMP	CAMP
CNR	CORNER
CO	COUNTY
COLL	COLLEGE
COM	COMMON
COMM	COMMISSION
CON	CONVENT
COT	COTTAGE
COTS	COTTAGES
CP	CAPE
CPS	COPSE
CR	CREEK
CREM	CREMATORIUM
CRS	CRESCENT
CSWY	CAUSEWAY
CT	COURT
CTRL	CENTRAL
CTS	COURTS
CTYD	COURTYARD
CUTT	CUTTINGS
CV	COVE
CYN	CANYON
DEPT	DEPARTMENT
DL	DALE
DM	DAM
DR	DRIVE
DRO	DROVE
DRY	DRIVEWAY
DWGS	DWELLINGS
E	EAST
EMB	EMBANKMENT
EMBY	EMBASSY
ESP	ESPLANADE
EST	ESTATE
EX	EXCHANGE
EXPY	EXPRESSWAY
EXT	EXTENSION
F/O	FLYOVER
FC	FOOTBALL CLUB
FK	FORK
FLD	FIELD
FLDS	FIELDS
FLS	FALLS
FLS	FLATS

FM	FARM
FT	FORT
FWY	FREEWAY
FY	FERRY
GA	GATE
GAL	GALLERY
GDN	GARDEN
GDNS	GARDENS
GLD	GLADE
GLN	GLEN
GN	GREEN
GND	GROUND
GRA	GRANGE
GRG	GARAGE
GT	GREAT
GTWY	GATEWAY
GV	GROVE
HGR	HIGHER
HL	HILL
HLS	HILLS
HO	HOUSE
HOL	HOLLOW
HOSP	HOSPITAL
HRB	HARBOUR
HTH	HEATH
HTS	HEIGHTS
HVN	HAVEN
HWY	HIGHWAY
IMP	IMPERIAL
IN	INLET
IND EST	INDUSTRIAL ESTATE
INF	INFIRMARY
INFO	INFORMATION
INT	INTERCHANGE
IS	ISLAND
JCT	JUNCTION
JTY	JETTY
KG	KING
KNL	KNOLL
L	LAKE
LA	LANE
LDG	LODGE
LGT	LIGHT
LK	LOCK
LKS	LAKES
LNDG	LANDING
LTL	LITTLE
LWR	LOWER
MAG	MAGISTRATE
MAN	MANSIONS
MD	MEAD
MDW	MEADOWS
MEM	MEMORIAL
MKT	MARKET
MKTS	MARKETS
ML	MALL
ML	MILL
MNR	MANOR
MS	MEWS
MSN	MISSION
MT	MOUNT
MTN	MOUNTAIN
MTS	MOUNTAINS
MUS	MUSEUM
MWY	MOTORWAY
N	NORTH
NE	NORTH EAST
NW	NORTH WEST
O/P	OVERPASS
OFF	OFFICE
ORCH	ORCHARD

OV	OVAL	SHOP	SHOPPING
PAL	PALACE	SKWY	SKYWAY
PAS	PASSAGE	SMT	SUMMIT
PAV	PAVILION	SOC	SOCIETY
PDE	PARADE	SP	SPUR
PH	PUBLIC HOUSE	SPR	SPRING
PK	PARK	SQ	SQUARE
PKWY	PARKWAY	ST	STREET
PL	PLACE	STN	STATION
PLN	PLAIN	STR	STREAM
PLNS	PLAINS	STRD	STRAND
PLZ	PLAZA	SW	SOUTH WEST
POL	POLICE STATION	TDG	TRADING
PR	PRINCE	TER	TERRACE
PREC	PRECINCT	THWY	THROUGHWAY
PREP	PREPARATORY	TNL	TUNNEL
PRIM	PRIMARY	TOLL	TOLLWAY
PROM	PROMENADE	TPK	TURNPIKE
PRS	PRINCESS	TR	TRACK
PRT	PORT	TRL	TRAIL
PT	POINT	TWR	TOWER
PTH	PATH	U/P	UNDERPASS
PZ	PIAZZA	UNI	UNIVERSITY
QD	QUADRANT	UPR	UPPER
QU	QUEEN	V	VALE
QY	QUAY	VA	VALLEY
R.	RIVER	VIAD	VIADUCT
RBT	ROUNDABOUT	VIL	VILLA
RD	ROAD	VIS	VISTA
RDG	RIDGE	VLG	VILLAGE
REP	REPUBLIC	VLS	VILLAS
RES	RESERVOIR	VW	VIEW
RFC	RUGBY FOOTBALL CLUB	W	WEST
RI	RISE	WD	WOOD
RP	RAMP	WHF	WHARF
RW	ROW	WK	WALK
S	SOUTH	WKS	WALKS
SCH	SCHOOL	WLS	WELLS
SE	SOUTH EAST	WY	WAY
SER	SERVICE AREA	YD	YARD
SH	SHORE	YHA	YOUTH HOSTEL

POSTCODE TOWNS AND AREA ABBREVIATIONS

ABYW	Abbey Wood	CAMTN	Camden Town
ACT	Acton	CAN/RD	Canning Town/Royal Docks
ALP/SUD	Alperton/Sudbury	CANST	Cannon Street station
ARCH	Archway	CAT	Catford
BAL	Balham	CAVSQ/HST	Cavendish Square/ Harley Street
BANK	Bank		
BARB	Barbican	CDALE/KGS	Colindale/Kingsbury
BARK	Barking	CEND/HSY/T	Crouch End/Hornsey/ Turnpike Lane
BARN	Barnes		
BAY/PAD	Bayswater/Paddington	CHARL	Charlton
BECK	Beckenham	CHCR	Charing Cross
BERM/RHTH	Bermondsey/Rotherhithe	CHEL	Chelsea
BETH	Bethnal Green	CHST	Chislehurst
BFN/LL	Blackfen/Longlands	CHSWK	Chiswick
BGVA	Belgravia	CITYW	City of London west
BKHTH/KID	Blackheath/Kidbrooke	CLAP	Clapham
BLKFR	Blackfriars	CLKNW	Clerkenwell
BMLY	Bromley	CLPT	Clapton
BMSBY	Bloomsbury	CMBW	Camberwell
BOW	Bow	CONDST	Conduit Street
BROCKY	Brockley	COVGDN	Covent Garden
BRXN/ST	Brixton north/Stockwell	CRICK	Cricklewood
BRXS/STRHM	Brixton south/ Streatham Hill	DEPT	Deptford
		DUL	Dulwich
BTFD	Brentford	EA	Ealing
BTSEA	Battersea	ECT	Earl's Court

EDUL ....East Dulwich
EFNCH..............................East Finchley
EHAM ....East Ham
ELTH/MOT ....Eltham/Mottingham
EMB...................................Embankment
FARR....................................Farringdon
FENCHST........................Fenchurch Street
FITZ......................................Fitzrovia
FLST/FETLN...............Fleet Street/Fetter Lane
FSBYE...............................Finsbury east
FSBYPK.............................Finsbury Park
FSBYW.............................Finsbury west
FSTGT.................................Forest Gate
FSTH....................................Forest Hill
FUL/PGN.................Fulham/Parsons Green
GDMY/SEVK ....Goodmayes/Seven Kings
GINN....................................Gray's Inn
GLDGN................................Golders Green
GNTH/NBYPK............Gants Hill/Newbury Park
GNWCH................................Greenwich
GTPST.........................Great Portland Street
GWRST...............................Gower Street
HACK......................................Hackney
HAMP................................Hampstead
HBRY....................................Highbury
HCIRC.............................Holborn Circus
HDN..Hendon
HDTCH...............................Houndsditch
HGT......................................Highgate
HHOL.................................High Holborn
HMSMTH...........................Hammersmith
HNHL.................................Herne Hill
HOL/ALD......................Holborn/Aldwych
HOLWY.................................Holloway
HOM....................................Homerton
IL...Ilford
IS..Islington
KENS...................................Kensington
KIL/WHAMP.............Kilburn/West Hampstead
KTBR...............................Knightsbridge
KTN/HRWW/WS........Kenton/Harrow
                            Weald/Wealdstone
KTTN...............................Kentish Town
KUTN/CMB........................Kingston upon
                            Thames north/Coombe
LBTH......................................Lambeth
LEE/GVPK.....................Lee/Grove Park
LEW....................................Lewisham
LEY..Leyton
LINN................................Lincoln's Inn
LOTH....................................Lothbury
LSQ/SEVD ....Leicester Square/Seven Dials
LVPST.........................Liverpool Street
MANHO ....Mansion House
MBLAR................................Marble Arch
MHST.....................Marylebone High Street
MNPK..................................Manor Park
MON....................................Monument
MORT/ESHN............Mortlake/East Sheen
MUSWH..............................Muswell Hill
MV/WKIL ....Maida Vale/West Kilburn
MYFR/PICC.................Mayfair/Piccadilly

MYFR/PKLN ....Mayfair/Park Lane
NKENS...........................North Kensington
NOXST/BSQ..............New Oxford Street/
                            Bloomsbury Square
NRWD....................................Norwood
NTGHL...............................Notting Hill
NWCR..................................New Cross
OBST..........................Old Broad Street
OXSTW..........................Oxford Street west
PECK......................................Peckham
PIM.......................................Pimlico
PLSTW....................................Plaistow
POP/IOD.................Poplar/Isle of Dogs
PUT/ROE.................Putney/Roehampton
RCH/KEW.........................Richmond/Kew
RCHPK/HAM ....Richmond Park/Ham
REDBR................................Redbridge
REGST..............................Regent Street
RSQ..................................Russell Square
RYNPK..............................Raynes Park
SCUP..Sidcup
SDTCH................................Shoreditch
SEVS/STOTM...Seven Sisters/South Tottenham
SHB.............................Shepherd's Bush
SKENS...........................South Kensington
SOHO/CST............Soho/Carnaby Street
SOHO/SHAV...........Soho/Shaftesbury Avenue
SRTFD....................................Stratford
STBT....................................St Bart's
STHWK................................Southwark
STJS....................................St James's
STJSPK...........................St James's Park
STJWD..........................St John's Wood
STLK....................................St Luke's
STNW/STAM.............Stoke Newington/
                            Stamford Hill
STP......................................St Paul's
STPAN................................St Pancras
STRHM/NOR...........Streatham/Norbury
SYD....................................Sydenham
THMD..............................Thamesmead
TOOT......................................Tooting
TPL/STR.....................Temple/Strand
TWRH................................Tower Hill
VX/NE ....Vauxhall/Nine Elms
WALTH............................Walthamstow
WALW..................................Walworth
WAN....................................Wanstead
WAND/EARL............Wandsworth/Earlsfield
WAP......................................Wapping
WBLY....................................Wembley
WBPTN..........................West Brompton
WCHPL..............................Whitechapel
WELL.....................................Welling
WEST................................Westminster
WESTW....................Westminster west
WHALL..................................Whitehall
WIM/MER.................Wimbledon/Merton
WKENS..........................West Kensington
WLSDN................................Willesden
WNWD..........................West Norwood
WOOL/PLUM...............Woolwich/Plumstead

1

1 Av WOOL/PLUM SE18 ....**108** B4

A

Aaron Hill Rd EHAM E6 ....**96** A4
Abbess Cl BRXS/STRHM SW2 ....**154** B1
Abbeville Ms CLAP * SW4 ....**135** D3
Abbeville Rd CLAP SW4 ....**134** C4
Abbey Dr TOOT SW17 ....**152** A5
Abbeyfield Est BERM/RHTH SE16 ....**102** C5
Abbeyfield Rd BERM/RHTH SE16 ....**102** C5
Abbeyfields Cl WLSDN NW10 ....**86** A2
Abbey Gdns BERM/RHTH SE16 ....**102** A5
  HMSMTH W6 ....**113** E2
  STJWD NW8 ....**3** E2
Abbey La SRTFD E15 ....**92** C1
Abbey Orchard St WEST SW1P **44** B2
Abbey Rd BARK IG11 ....**84** B4
  KIL/WHAMP NW6 ....**72** B5
  SRTFD E15 ....**93** D1
  WLSDN NW10 ....**68** B5
Abbey St PLSTW E13 ....**94** A3
  STHWK SE1 ....**49** E2
Abbotsbury Cl SRTFD E15 ....**92** C1
  WKENS * W14 ....**101** E5
Abbotsbury Ms PECK SE15 ....**138** C1
Abbotsbury Rd WKENS W14 ....**101** E3
Abbotshade Rd BERM/RHTH * SE16 ....**103** D2
Abbotshall Rd CAT SE6 ....**159** D1
Abbots La STHWK SE1 ....**37** D4
Abbotsleigh Rd STRHM/NOR SW16 ....**152** C4
Abbots Mnr PIM * SW1V **116** B1
Abbots Pk BRXS/STRHM SW2 ....**154** A1
Abbot's Pl KIL/WHAMP NW6 ....**72** B5
Abbots Rd EHAM E6 ....**83** D5
Abbots Ter CEND/HSY/T N8 ....**57** E1
Abbotstone Rd PUT/ROE SW15 ....**130** C1
Abbott Rd POP/IOD E14 ....**92** C4
Abbotts Cl IS * N1 ....**76** C4
Abbotts Park Rd LEY E10 ....**62** C3
Abbotswell Rd BROCKY SE4 ....**139** E3
Abbotswood Rd EDUL SE22 ....**137** E2
  STRHM/NOR SW16 ....**153** D3
Abbott St POP/IOD E14 ....**92** C4
Abbotts Cl IS * N1 ....**76** C4
Abchurch La MANHO EC4N **36** B1
Abdale Rd SHB W12 ....**100** B3
Aberavon Rd BOW E3 ....**91** E2
Abercorn Cl STJWD NW8 ....**3** E2
Abercorn Pl STJWD NW8 ....**3** E3
Abercorn Wy STHWK SE1 ....**120** A1
Abercrombie St BTSEA SW11 ....**115** E5
Aberdare Gdns KIL/WHAMP NW6 ....**72** B4
Aberdeen La HBRY N5 ....**76** B2
Aberdeen Pk HBRY N5 ....**76** C1
Aberdeen Pl STJWD NW8 ....**16** A1
Aberdeen Rd HBRY N5 ....**76** C1
  WLSDN NW10 ....**69** F2
Aberdeen Ter BKHTH/KID SE3 ....**123** D5
Aberdour Rd IG11 IG11 ....**85** D5
Aberdour St STHWK SE1 ....**48** C5
Aberfeldy St POP/IOD E14 ....**92** C5
Aberford Gdns WOOL/PLUM SE18 ....**125** E4
Abergeldie Rd LEE/GVPK SE12 ....**142** B4
Abernethy Rd LEW SE13 ....**141** E2
Abersham Rd HACK E8 ....**77** F2
Abery St WOOL/PLUM SE18 ....**109** E5
Abingdon Cl STHWK * SW17 ....**49** F5
Abingdon Rd KENS W8 ....**38** B3
Abingdon St WEST SW1P **44** C2
Abingdon Vls KENS W8 ....**38** A3
Abinger Ms MV/WKIL W9 ....**2** A5

Abinger Rd CHSWK W4 ....**99** F4
Ablett St BERM/RHTH SE16 ....**120** C1
Abney Park Ter STNW/STAM * N16 ....**59** F4
Aboyne Rd TOOT SW17 ....**151** D3
  WLSDN NW10 ....**51** E5
Abyssinia Cl BTSEA SW11 ....**133** E2
Abyssinia Rd BTSEA * SW11 ....**133** E2
Acacia Cl DEPT SE8 ....**103** E5
Acacia Gdns STJWD NW8 ....**4** B1
Acacia Gv DUL SE21 ....**155** D2
Acacia Pl STJWD NW8 ....**4** B1
Acacia Rd ACT W3 ....**98** C1
  STJWD NW8 ....**4** B1
  WALTH E17 ....**61** E1
  WAN E11 ....**63** E4
Acacia Wy BFN/LL DA15 ....**145** F5
Academy Pl WOOL/PLUM SE18 ....**125** F4
Academy Rd WOOL/PLUM SE18 ....**125** F3
Acanthus Dr STHWK SE1 ....**120** A1
Acanthus Rd BTSEA SW11 ....**134** A1
Accommodation Rd GLDGN NW11 ....**53** F2
Acfold Rd FUL/PGN SW6 ....**114** B4
Achilles Cl STHWK SE1 ....**120** A1
Achilles Rd KIL/WHAMP NW6 ....**72** A2
Achilles St NWCR SE14 ....**121** E3
Acklam Rd NKENS W10 ....**89** F4
Ackmar Rd FUL/PGN SW6 ....**114** A4
Ackroyd Dr BOW E3 ....**91** F4
Ackroyd Rd FSTH SE23 ....**139** D5
Acland Rd WOOL/PLUM SE18 ....**127** D3
Acland Crs CMBW SE5 ....**137** D2
Acland Rd CRICK NW2 ....**70** B3
Acol Rd KIL/WHAMP NW6 ....**72** A4
Acorn Cl CHST BR7 ....**162** C5
Acorn Gdns ACT W3 ....**87** D4
Acorn Pde PECK * SE15 ....**120** B3
Acorn Wy FSTH SE23 ....**157** D3
Acre Dr EDUL SE22 ....**138** A2
Acre La BRXS/STRHM SW2 ....**135** F2
Acris St WAND/EARL SW18 ....**132** C3
Acton Hill Ms ACT * W3 ....**98** B2
Acton La ACT W3 ....**98** C2
  WLSDN NW10 ....**86** C2
Acton Ms HACK E8 ....**77** F5
Acton St FSBYW WC1X **9** E4
Acuba Rd WAND/EARL SW18 ....**150** B2
Ada Ct MV/WKIL W9 ....**3** F4
Ada Gdns POP/IOD E14 ....**93** D5
  SRTFD E15 ....**81** F5
Adair Rd NKENS W10 ....**89** E3
Adam & Eve Ms KENS * W8 ....**38** B2
Adams Cl WBLY HA9 ....**50** B4
Adamson Rd CAN/RD E16 ....**94** A5
  HAMP NW3 ....**73** D4
Adams Pl HOLWY N7 ....**75** F2
Adamsrill Rd SYD SE26 ....**157** D4
Adam's Rw MYFR/PKLN W1K **30** A2
Adam St TPL/STR WC2R **33** D2
Adam Wk FUL/PGN * SW6 ....**112** C3
Ada Pl BETH E2 ....**78** A5
Adare Wk STRHM/NOR SW16 ....**153** E2
Ada Rd CMBW SE5 ....**119** D3
Ada St HACK E8 ....**78** B5
Adderley Gdns ELTH/MOT SE9 ....**162** A4
Adderley Gv BTSEA SW11 ....**134** A3
Adderley St POP/IOD E14 ....**92** C5
Addington Gv SYD SE26 ....**157** E4
Addington Rd BOW E3 ....**92** A2
  CAN/RD E16 ....**93** E3
  FSBYPK N4 ....**58** A2
Addington Sq CMBW SE5 ....**118** C3
Addison Av NTGHL W11 ....**101** E2
Addison Bridge Pl WKENS W14 ....**101** E5
Addison Crs WKENS W14 ....**101** E4
Addison Dr LEE/GVPK SE12 ....**142** B3
Addison Gdns WKENS W14 ....**101** D4
Addison Gv CHSWK W4 ....**99** E4
Addison Pl NTGHL W11 ....**101** E2

Addison Rd *NTGHL* W11	101	E3
WAN E11	64	A1
Addison Ter *CHSWK* * W4	98	C5
Addle HI *BLKFR* EC4V	35	D1
Addle St *CITYW* * EC2V	23	F4
Adelaide Av *BROCKY* SE4	140	A2
Adelaide Gv *SHB* W12	100	A2
Adelaide Rd *CHST* BR7	162	B5
HAMP NW3	73	F4
IL IG1	66	B4
LEY E10	62	C5
WAND/EARL SW18	132	A3
Adelaide St *CHCR* * WC2N	32	C2
Adela St *NKENS* W10	89	E3
Adelina Gv *WCHPL* E1	90	C4
Adelina Ms *BAL* SW12	153	D1
Adeline PI *RSQ* WC1B	20	B3
Adeliza CI *BARK* IG11	84	C4
Adelphi Ter *CHCR* * WC2N	33	D2
Adeney Rd *HMSMTH* W6	113	D2
Aden Gv *STNW/STAM* N16	77	D1
Adenmore Rd *CAT* SE6	140	A5
Aden Rd *IL* IG1	66	B2
Adie Rd *HMSMTH* W6	100	C4
Adine Rd *PLSTW* E13	94	A3
Adler St *WCHPL* E1	90	A4
Adley St *CLPT* E5	79	E2
Admaston Rd *WOOL/PLUM* SE18	126	C3
Admiral Ms *NKENS* W10	89	D3
Admiral Seymour Rd *ELTH/MOT* SE9	143	F2
Admiral's Ga *GNWCH* SE10	122	B4
Admiral Sq *WBPTN* * SW10	114	C4
Admiral St *DEPT* SE8	122	A4
Admiral's Wk *HAMP* NW3	54	C3
Admirals Wy *POP/IOD* E14	104	B3
Admiral Wk *MV/WKIL* W9	14	B2
Adolf St *CAT* SE6	158	A4
Adolphus Rd *FSBYPK* N4	58	B4
Adolphus St *DEPT* SE8	121	F3
Adpar St *BAY/PAD* W2	16	A2
Adrian Ms *WBPTN* SW10	114	B2
Advance Rd *WNWD* SE27	154	C4
Adys Lawn *CRICK* NW2	70	B3
Adys Rd *PECK* SE15	137	F1
Affleck St *IS* * N1	9	F2
Afghan Rd *BTSEA* SW11	115	E5
Aftab Ter *WCHPL* * E1	90	B3
Agamemnon Rd *KIL/WHAMP* NW6	71	F2
Agar Gv *CAMTN* NW1	75	D4
Agar St *CHCR* WC2N	32	C2
Agate CI *CAN/RD* E16	95	D5
Agate Rd *HMSMTH* W6	100	C4
Agatha CI *WAP* E1W	102	B2
Agaton Rd *ELTH/MOT* SE9	162	C2
Agave Rd *CRICK* NW2	70	C1
Agdon St *FSBYE* EC1V	10	C5
Agincourt Rd *HAMP* NW3	73	F1
Agnes Av *IL* IG1	84	A1
Agnes CI *EHAM* E6	108	A1
Agnes Riley Gdns *CLAP* * SW4	134	C5
Agnes Rd *ACT* W3	99	F3
Agnes St *POP/IOD* E14	91	F5
Agnew Rd *FSTH* SE23	139	E5
Ainger Rd *HAMP* NW3	73	F4
Ainsdale Dr *STHWK* SE1	120	A1
Ainsley St *BETH* E2	90	B2
Ainsty St *BERM/RHTH* * SE16	102	C3
Ainsworth CI *CMBW* * SE5	119	D5
CRICK NW2	52	A5
Ainsworth Rd *HOM* E9	78	C4
Ainsworth Wy *STJWD* NW8	72	C5
Aintree Av *EHAM* E6	83	E5
Aintree St *FUL/PGN* SW6	113	E3
Airdrie CI *IS* * N1	75	F4
Airedale Av *CHSWK* W4	111	F1
Airedale Av South *CHSWK* * W4	111	F1
Airedale Rd *BAL* SW12	133	F5

Airlie Gdns *IL* IG1	66	B3
KENS W8	26	A4
Air St *REGST* W1B	31	F2
Aisgill Av *ECT* SW5	113	F1
Aislibie Rd *LEW* SE13	141	E2
Aitken CI *HACK* E8	78	A5
Aitken Rd *CAT* SE6	158	B2
Aitman Dr *CHSWK* * W4	110	A1
Ajax Rd *KIL/WHAMP* NW6	71	F1
Akehurst St *PUT/ROE* SW15	130	A4
Akenside Rd *HAMP* NW3	73	D2
Akerman Rd *CMBW* SE5	118	B4
Alabama St *WOOL/PLUM* SE18	127	D3
Alan Hocken Wy *SRTFD* E15	93	E1
Alan Rd *WIM/MER* SW19	149	E5
Alanthus CI *LEE/GVPK* SE12	141	F4
Alaska St *STHWK* SE1	34	A4
Albacore Crs *LEW* SE13	140	B4
Alba Gdns *GLDGN* NW11	53	E1
Albany Myfr *PICC* W1J	31	E2
Albany CI *MORT/ESHN* SW14	128	B2
Albany Ctyd *MYFR/PICC* * W1J	31	F2
Albany Ms *IS* * N1	76	A4
WALW SE17	118	C2
Albany PI *HOLWY* N7	76	A1
Albany Rd *CHST* BR7	162	B5
CMBW SE5	119	D2
FSBYPK N4	57	F1
MNPK E12	83	D1
WALTH E17	61	E1
WIM/MER SW19	150	B5
Albany St *CAMTN* NW1	7	D3
Alba PI *NTGHL* W11	89	F5
Albatross St *WOOL/PLUM* SE18	127	E3
Albemarle Ap *GNTH/NBYPK* IG2	66	B1
Albemarle Gdns *GNTH/NBYPK* IG2	66	B1
Albemarle St *CONDST* W1S	31	E2
Albemarle Wy *FARR* EC1M	22	C1
Alberta Est *WALW* SE17	118	C3
Alberta St *WALW* SE17	118	B3
Albert Av *VX/NE* SW8	117	F3
Albert Br *BTSEA* SW11	115	E3
Albert Bridge Ga *BTSEA* SW11	115	F3
Albert Bridge Rd *CHEL* SW3	115	E2
Albert Carr Gdns *STRHM/NOR* SW16	153	E5
Albert CI *HOM* E9	78	B5
Albert Cottages *WCHPL* * E1	90	A4
Albert Dr *WIM/MER* SW19	149	E2
Albert Gdns *WCHPL* E1	91	D5
Albert Ga *KTBR* SW1X	29	F5
Albert Ms *BROCKY* SE4	139	F2
FSBYPK * N4	57	F3
KENS W8	39	E2
POP/IOD * E14	103	E1
Albert PI *KENS* W8	39	D1
Albert Rd *CAN/RD* E16	107	D2
ELTH/MOT SE9	161	E3
FSBYPK N4	57	F3
IL IG1	66	C5
KIL/WHAMP NW6	89	F1
SEVS/STOTM N15	59	E1
WAN E11	62	C4
Albert Sq *SRTFD* E15	81	E2
VX/NE SW8	117	F3
Albert St *CAMTN* NW1	74	B5
Albert Ter *CAMTN* NW1	74	A5
WLSDN * NW10	69	D5
Albert Terrace Ms *CAMTN* NW1	74	A5
Albert Wy *PECK* SE15	120	B3
Albion Av *VX/NE* SW8	117	D5
Albion CI *BAY/PAD* W2	29	D1
Albion Dr *HACK* E8	77	F4
Albion Est *BERM/RHTH* * SE16	102	C3
Albion Gdns *HMSMTH* W6	100	B5
Albion Ga *BAY/PAD* W2	29	D1
Albion Gv *STNW/STAM* N16	77	E1

Albion Ms *BAY/PAD* W2 ....17 D5
   IS * N1 ....76 A4
Albion Pl *FARR* EC1M 22 C2
   HMSMTH W6 ....100 B5
Albion Sq *HACK* E8 ....77 F4
Albion St *BAY/PAD* W2 ....17 D5
   BERM/RHTH SE16 ....102 C3
Albion Ter *HACK* E8 ....77 F4
Albion Villas Rd *FSTH* SE23 ....156 C3
Albion Wy *LEW* SE13 ....140 C2
   STBT EC1A 23 E3
   WBLY HA9 ....50 A5
Albion Yd *IS* N1 ....9 D2
Albrighton Rd *CMBW* SE5 ....137 E1
Albury Ms *MNPK* E12 ....64 C3
Albury St *DEPT* SE8 ....122 A4
Albyn Rd *DEPT* SE8 ....122 A4
Alcester Cv *CLPT* E5 ....60 B4
Alconbury Rd *CLPT* E5 ....60 A4
Aldborough Rd South
   GDMY/SEVK IG3..67 E3
Aldbourne Rd *ACT* W3 ....99 F2
Aldbridge St *WALW* SE17 ....119 E1
Aldburgh Ms *MHST* W1U 18 B4
Aldbury Av *WBLY* HA9 ....68 B4
Aldebert Ter *VX/NE* SW8 ....117 F3
Aldeburgh St *GNWCH* SE10 ....124 A1
Alden Av *SRTFD* E15 ....93 F2
Aldenham St *CAMTN* NW1 ....7 F2
Aldensley Rd *HMSMTH* W6 ....100 B4
Alderbrook Rd *BAL* SW12 ....134 B4
Alderbury Rd *BARN* SW13 ....112 A2
Alder Cl *PECK* SE15 ....119 F2
Alder Cv *CRICK* NW2 ....52 A4
Alderholt Wy *PECK* * SE15 ....119 E3
Aldermanbury *CITYW* * EC2V 23 F4
Aldermanbury Sq *CITYW* EC2V 23 F3
Aldermoor Rd *CAT* SE6 ....157 F3
Alderney Ms *STHWK* SE1 ....48 A2
Alderney Rd *WCHPL* E1 ....91 D3
Alderney St *PIM* SW1V 42 C5
Alder Rd *MORT/ESHN* SW14 ....129 D1
   SCUP DA14..163 E3
The Alders *STRHM/NOR* * SW16 ....152 C4
Aldersbrook La *MNPK* E12 ....65 F5
Aldersbrook Rd *MNPK* E12........................64 C4
Alders Cl *WAN* E11 ....64 B4
Aldersey Gdns *BARK* IG11 ....85 D3
Aldersford Cl *BROCKY* SE4 ....139 D2
Aldersgate St *STBT* EC1A 23 E4
Aldersgrove Av *LEE/GVPK* SE12 ....160 C3
Aldershot Rd *KIL/WHAMP* NW6 ....71 F5
Aldershot Ter *WOOL/PLUM* * SE18 ....126 A3
Alderson St *NKENS* W10 ....89 E3
Alderton Cl *WLSDN* NW10 ....51 D4
Alderton Rd *HNHL* SE24 ....136 C1
Alderville Rd *FUL/PGN* SW6 ....113 F5
Alderwood Rd *ELTH/MOT* SE9 ....145 D4
Aldford St *MYFR/PKLN* W1K 30 A3
Aldgate *FENCHST* EC3M 25 D5
Aldgate Barrs *WCHPL* * E1 ....25 F4
Aldgate High St *TWRH* EC3N 25 E5
Aldine St *SHB* W12 ....100 C3
Aldington Rd *WOOL/PLUM* SE18 ....107 D4
Aldis Ms *TOOT* SW17 ....151 E3
Aldis St *TOOT* SW17 ....151 E3
Aldred Rd *KIL/WHAMP* NW6 ....72 A1
Aldren Rd *TOOT* SW17 ....150 C3
Aldrich Ter *WAND/EARL* SW18 ....150 C2
Aldridge Road Vls *NTGHL* W11 ....89 F4
Aldrington Rd *STRHM/NOR* SW16 ....14 C1
Aldsworth Cl *MV/WKIL* W9 ....14 C1
Aldwick Cl *CHST* BR7 ....163 D3
Aldworth Gv *LEW* SE13 ....140 C4
Aldworth Rd *SRTFD* E15 ....81 E4
Aldwych *TPL/STR* WC2R 33 E1
Alestan Beck Rd *CAN/RD* E16 ....95 D5

Alexander Av *WLSDN* NW10 ....70 B4
Alexander Cl *BFN/LL* DA15 ....145 E3
Alexander Evans Ms *FSTH* SE23 ....157 D2
Alexander Ms *BAY/PAD* W2 ....14 C4
Alexander Pl *SKENS* SW7 ....40 C4
Alexander Rd *ARCH* N19 ....57 E5
Alexander Sq *CHEL* SW3 ....40 C4
Alexander St *BAY/PAD* W2 ....14 B4
Alexandra Cl *BTSEA* * SW11 ....116 A4
Alexandra Cottages *NWCR* * SE14 ....121 F4
Alexandra Dr *NRWD* SE19 ....155 E5
Alexandra Ga *SKENS* SW7 ....28 A5
Alexandra Gv *FSBYPK* N4 ....58 B3
Alexandra Pl *STJWD* NW8 ....72 C5
Alexandra Rd *CHSWK* W4 ....99 D3
   EHAM E6 ....96 A2
   MORT/ESHN SW14 ....129 D1
   STJWD NW8 ....72 C4
   WALTH E17 ....61 F1
   WIM/MER SW19 ....150 A5
Alexandra St *CAN/RD* E16 ....94 A4
   NWCR SE14 ....121 E3
Alexis St *BERM/RHTH* SE16 ....102 A5
Alfearn Rd *CLPT* E5 ....78 C1
Alford Pl *IS* * N1 ....11 F2
Alfreda St *BTSEA* SW11 ....116 B4
Alfred Cl *CHSWK* W4 ....99 D5
Alfred Ms *FITZ* W1T 20 A2
Alfred Pl *FITZ* W1T 20 A2
Alfred Rd *ACT* W3 ....98 C2
   BAY/PAD W2 ....14 B2
   FSTGT E7 ....81 F2
Alfred's Gdns *BARK* IG11 ....97 E1
Alfred St *BOW* E3 ....91 F2
Alfred's Way
   (East Ham & Barking By-Pass)
   BARK IG11 ....97 D1
Alfreton Cl *WIM/MER* SW19 ....149 D3
Alfriston Rd *BTSEA* SW11 ....133 F3
Algarve Rd *WAND/EARL* SW18 ....150 B1
Algernon Rd *HDN* NW4 ....52 A1
   KIL/WHAMP NW6 ....72 A5
   LEW SE13 ....140 B2
Algiers Rd *LEW* SE13 ....140 A2
Alice La *BOW* E3 ....79 F5
Alice St *STHWK* SE1 ....48 C3
Alice Thompson Cl *LEE/GVPK* SE12 ......160 C2
Alice Walker Cl *HNHL* * SE24 ....136 C1
Alie St *WCHPL* E1 ....25 F5
Alington Crs *CDALE/KGS* NW9 ....50 C3
Alison Cl *EHAM* E6 ....96 A5
Aliwal Ms *BTSEA* * SW11 ....133 E2
Aliwal Rd *BTSEA* SW11 ....133 E2
Alkerden Rd *CHSWK* W4 ....111 E1
Alkham Rd *STNW/STAM* N16 ....59 F4
Allan Barclay Cl *STNW/STAM* N16 ....59 F1
Allan Wy *ACT* W3 ....98 C4
Allardyce St *CLAP* SW4 ....135 F2
Allcroft Rd *KTTN* NW5 ....74 A2
Allenby Rd *FSTH* SE23 ....157 E3
Allendale Cl *CMBW* SE5 ....119 D5
   SYD SE26 ....157 D5
Allen Edwards Dr *VX/NE* SW8 ....117 E4
Allen Rd *BOW* E3 ....91 F1
   STNW/STAM N16 ....75 D4
Allensbury Pl *HOLWY* N7 ....75 D4
Allen St *KENS* W8 ....38 B2
Allenswood Rd *ELTH/MOT* SE9 ....143 E1
Allerford Rd *CAT* SE6 ....158 B4
Allerton Rd *STNW/STAM* N16 ....58 C4
Allestree Rd *FUL/PGN* SW6 ....113 E3
Alleyn Crs *DUL* SE21 ....155 D2
Alleyn Pk *DUL* SE21 ....155 D3
Alleyn Rd *DUL* SE21 ....155 D3
Allfarthing La *WAND/EARL* SW18 ....132 C4
Allgood St *BETH* E2 ....13 F2
Allhallows La *CANST* EC4R 36 A1
Allhallows Rd *EHAM* E6...............................95 E5

Alliance Rd *ACT* W3 ....86 B3
  PLSTW E13 ....94 C3
Allied Wy *ACT* * W3 ....99 E3
Allington Cl *WIM/MER* SW19 ....149 D5
Allington Rd *NKENS* W10 ....89 E2
Allington St *WESTW* SW1E 43 D3
Allison Cl *GNWCH* SE10 ....122 C4
Allison Gv *DUL* SE21 ....155 E1
Allison Rd *ACT* W3 ....86 C5
Allitsen Rd *STJWD* NW8 ....4 C1
Allitson Rd *STJWD* NW8 ....4 C2
Allnutt Wy *CLAP* SW4 ....135 C3
Alloa Rd *DEPT* SE8 ....121 D1
Alloway Rd *BOW* E3 ....91 E2
Allport Ms *WCHPL* * E1 ....90 C4
All Saints Dr *BKHTH/KID* SE3 ....123 F5
All Saints Pas *WAND/EARL* * SW18 ..132 A3
All Saints' Rd *ACT* W3 ....98 C3
  NTGHL W11 ....89 F4
All Saints St *IS* N1 ....9 E1
Allsop Pl *CAMTN* NW1 ....17 F1
All Souls' Av *WLSDN* NW10 ....88 B3
All Souls' Pl *REGST* W1B 19 D3
Allwood Rd *SYD* SE26 ....157 D4
Almack Rd *CLPT* E5 ....78 C1
Alma Gv *STHWK* SE1 ....49 F5
Alma Pl *WLSDN* NW10 ....88 B2
Alma Rd *WAND/EARL* SW18 ....132 C3
Alma Sq *STJWD* NW8 ....3 F3
Alma St *KTTN* NW5 ....74 B3
  SRTFD E15 ....81 D3
Alma Ter *BOW* E3 ....79 F5
  KENS W8 ....38 B3
  WAND/EARL SW18 ....133 D5
Almeida St *IS* N1 ....76 B3
Almeric Rd *BTSEA* SW11 ....133 F2
Almington St *FSBYPK* * N4 ....57 E3
Almond Rd *BERM/RHTH* SE16 ....102 B5
Almorah Rd *IS* N1 ....77 D4
Alnwick Rd *CAN/RD* E16 ....94 C5
  LEE/GVPK SE12 ....142 B5
Alperton St *NKENS* W10 ....89 E3
Alpha Cl *CAMTN* NW1 ....5 D5
Alpha Gv *POP/IOD* E14 ....104 A3
Alpha Pl *CHEL* SW3 ....115 E2
  KIL/WHAMP NW6 ....2 B1
Alpha Rd *NWCR* SE14 ....121 F4
Alpha St *PECK* SE15 ....120 A5
Alpine Gv *HOM* * E9 ....78 C4
Alpine Rd *BERM/RHTH* SE16 ....102 C5
Alpine Wy *EHAM* E6 ....96 A4
Alric Av *WLSDN* NW10 ....69 D4
Alroy Rd *FSBYPK* N4 ....58 A2
Alsace Rd *WALW* SE17 ....119 E1
Alscot Rd *BERM/RHTH* SE16 ....49 F3
Alscot Wy *STHWK* SE1 ....49 E4
Alston Rd *TOOT* SW17 ....151 D4
Altash Wy *ELTH/MOT* SE9 ....161 F2
Altenburg Gdns *BTSEA* SW11 ....133 F2
Althea St *FUL/PGN* SW6 ....114 B5
Althorp Rd *TOOT* SW17 ....151 F1
Altmore Av *EHAM* E6 ....83 F4
Alton Rd *PUT/ROE* SW15 ....148 A1
Alton St *POP/IOD* E14 ....92 B4
Alvanley Gdns *KIL/WHAMP* NW6 ......2 B1
Alverstone Av *WAND/EARL* SW18 ..150 A2
Alverstone Gdns *ELTH/MOT* SE9 ...162 B1
Alverstone Rd *CRICK* NW2 ....70 C4
  MNPK E12 ....84 A1
Alverton St *DEPT* SE8 ....121 F1
Alvey St *WALW* SE17 ....119 E1
Alvington Crs *HACK* E8 ....77 F2
Alwold Crs *LEE/GVPK* SE12 ....142 C4
Alwyn Av *CHSWK* W4 ....111 D1
Alwyne La *IS* * N1 ....76 B4
Alwyne Pl *IS* * N1 ....76 C3
Alwyne Rd *IS* N1 ....76 C4
Alwyne Sq *IS* N1 ....76 C3

Alwyne Vls *IS* N1 ....76 B4
Alwyn Gdns *ACT* W3 ....86 B5
Alyn Bank *CEND/HSY/T* * N8 ....57 D1
Alyth Gdns *GLDGN* NW11 ....53 F1
Amar Ct *WOOL/PLUM* SE18 ....109 F5
Amardeep Ct *WOOL/PLUM* SE18 ...127 F5
Amazon St *WCHPL* E1 ....90 B5
Ambassador Gdns *EHAM* E6 ....95 F4
Ambassador Sq *POP/IOD* E14 ....104 B5
Ambergate St *WALW* SE17 ....118 B1
Amber Gv *CRICK* NW2 ....53 D3
Amberley Gv *SYD* SE26 ....156 B4
Amberley Rd *LEY* E10 ....62 A2
  MV/WKIL W9 ....14 B2
Amber St *SRTFD* * E15 ....81 D3
Amblecote Cl *LEE/GVPK* SE12 ......160 B3
Amblecote Meadow *LEE/GVPK* SE12 ..160 B3
Amblecote Rd *LEE/GVPK* SE12 .....160 B3
Ambler Rd *FSBYPK* N4 ....58 B5
Ambleside Av *STRHM/NOR* SW16 ..153 D4
Ambleside Cl *LEY* E10 ....62 B2
Ambleside Rd *WLSDN* NW10 ....69 F4
Ambrose Av *GLDGN* NW11 ....53 E2
Ambrosden Av *WEST1P* SW1P 43 F3
Ambrose Av *GLDGN* NW11 ....53 F1
Ambrose St *BERM/RHTH* SE16 ......102 B5
Amelia Cl *ACT* W3 ....98 B2
Amelia St *WALW* SE17 ....118 B1
Amen Cnr *STP* EC4M 23 D5
Amen Ct *STP* EC4M 23 D5
America Sq *TWRH* * EC3N 37 E1
America St *STHWK* SE1 ....35 E4
Amerland Rd *WAND/EARL* SW18 ...131 F4
Amersham Gv *NWCR* SE14 ....121 F3
Amersham Rd *NWCR* SE14 ....121 F4
Amersham V *NWCR* SE14 ....121 F3
Amery Gdns *WLSDN* NW10 ....70 B5
Amesbury Av *BRXS/STRHM* SW2 ...153 E2
Ames Cottages *POP/IOD* * E14 ....91 E4
Amethyst Rd *SRTFD* E15 ....81 D1
Amhurst Pde *STNW/STAM* * N16 .....59 F1
Amhurst Pk *STNW/STAM* N16 ....59 E2
Amhurst Rd *STNW/STAM* N16 ....59 F5
  STNW/STAM N16 ....78 B2
Amhurst Ter *HACK* E8 ....78 A1
Amiel St *WCHPL* E1 ....90 C3
Amies St *BTSEA* SW11 ....133 F1
Amina Wy *BERM/RHTH* SE16 ....102 A4
Amity Rd *SRTFD* E15 ....81 D5
Ammanford Gn *CDALE/KGS* * NW9 ...51 E1
Amner Rd *BTSEA* SW11 ....134 A1
Amor Rd *HMSMTH* W6 ....100 C4
Amott Rd *PECK* SE15 ....138 A1
Ampthill Est *CAMTN* NW1 ....7 E2
Ampthill Sq *CAMTN* NW1 ....7 E2
Ampton St *FSBYW* WC1X 9 E4
Amroth Cl *FSTH* SE23 ....156 B1
Amroth Gn *CDALE/KGS* * NW9 ....51 E1
Amsterdam Rd *POP/IOD* E14 ....104 C4
Amwell St *CLKNW* EC1R 10 A3
Amyruth Rd *BROCKY* SE4 ....140 A3
Amy Warne Cl *EHAM* E6 ....95 E4
Ancaster St *WOOL/PLUM* SE18 .....127 E3
Anchorage Cl *WIM/MER* SW19 ......150 A5
Anchor & Hope La *CHARL* SE7 ......106 B4
Anchor St *BERM/RHTH* SE16 ....102 B5
Anchor Ter *WCHPL* * E1 ....90 C3
Anchor Yd *FSBYE* * EC1V 11 E5
Ancill Cl *HMSMTH* W6 ....113 D2
Ancona Rd *WLSDN* NW10 ....88 A1
  WOOL/PLUM SE18 ....127 D1
Andalus Rd *BRXN/ST* SW9 ....135 E1
Anderson Cl *ACT* W3 ....87 D5
Anderson Rd *HOM* E9 ....79 D3
Anderson Sq *IS* * N1 ....76 B5
Anderson St *CHEL* SW3 ....115 F1
Andover Av *CAN/RD* E16 ....95 D5
Andover Pl *KIL/WHAMP* NW6 ....2 C2
Andover Rd *HOLWY* N7 ....57 F4

Andover Ter *HMSMTH* * W6 ....**100** B5
Andre St *HACK* E8..........**78** A2
Andrew Borde St *LSQ/SEVD* * WC2H..**20** B4
Andrewes Gdns *EHAM* E6..........**95** E5
Andrew Pl *VX/NE* SW8..........**117** D4
Andrews Rd *HACK* E8..........**78** B5
Andrews St *POP/IOD* E14..........**92** C5
Andrews Wk *WALW* SE17..........**118** D3
Anfield Cl *BAL* SW12..........**134** C5
Angel Ct *LOTH* EC2R..........**24** B4
Angelica Dr *EHAM* E6..........**96** A4
Angel La *SRTFD* E15..........**81** D3
Angell Park Gdns *BRXN/ST* SW9 ....**136** A1
Angell Rd *BRXN/ST* SW9..........**136** B1
Angell Town Est *BRXN/ST* * SW9 ....**118** A5
Angel Ms *WCHPL* E1..........**102** B1
Angel Pas *CANST* EC4R..........**36** A2
Angel Sq *FSBYE* * EC1V..........**10** C2
Angel St *STBT* EC1A..........**23** E4
Angel Wk *HMSMTH* W6..........**100** C5
Angerstein La *BKHTH/KID* SE3 ....**123** F3
Anglers La *KTTN* NW5..........**74** B3
Anglesea Av *WOOL/PLUM* SE18 ....**108** B5
Anglesea Rd *WOOL/PLUM* SE18 ....**108** B5
Angles Rd *STRHM/NOR* SW16........**153** E4
Anglian Rd *WAN* E11..........**63** D5
Anglo Rd *BOW* E3..........**91** F1
Angus Rd *PLSTW* E13..........**94** C2
Angus St *NWCR* SE14..........**121** E3
Anhalt Rd *BTSEA* SW11..........**115** E3
Ankerdine Crs *WOOL/PLUM* SE18 ..**126** B4
Anley Rd *HMSMTH* W6..........**101** D3
Annabel Cl *POP/IOD* E14..........**92** B5
Anna Cl *HACK* E8..........**77** F5
Annandale Rd *BFN/LL* DA15......**145** E5
 CHSWK W4..........**99** E5
 GNWCH SE10..........**123** F1
Anna Neagle Cl *FSTGT* E7..........**82** A1
Anne Compton Ms *LEE/GVPK* SE12....**141** E5
Annesley Cl *WLSDN* NW10..........**51** E5
Annesley Rd *BKHTH/KID* SE3 ....**124** B4
Anne St *PLSTW* E13..........**94** A3
Annette Rd *HOLWY* N7..........**75** F1
Annexe Market *WCHPL* * E1 ....**25** E2
Annie Besant Cl *BOW* * E3..........**79** F5
Anning St *SDTCH* EC2A..........**13** D5
Annis Rd *HOM* * E9..........**79** E3
Ann La *WBPTN* SW10..........**115** D3
Ann Moss Wy *BERM/RHTH* SE16 ....**102** C4
Ann's Cl *KTBR* SW1X..........**41** F1
Ann St *WOOL/PLUM* SE18..........**120** C5
Ansdell Rd *PECK* SE15..........**39** D2
Ansdell St *KENS* W8..........**39** D2
Ansdell Ter *KENS* W8..........**39** D2
Ansell Rd *TOOT* SW17..........**114** A2
Anselm Rd *FUL/PGN* SW6..........**158** C5
Ansford Rd *BMLY* BR1..........**101** D1
Ansleigh Pl *NTGHL* W11..........**70** B2
Anson Rd *CRICK* NW2..........**74** C1
 HOLWY N7..........**138** A1
Anstey Rd *PECK* SE15..........**138** A1
Anstice Cl *CHSWK* W4..........**111** E3
Anstridge Rd *ELTH/MOT* SE9 ....**145** D4
Antelope Rd *WOOL/PLUM* SE18......**107** F4
Anthony's Cl *WAP* E1W..........**90** B5
Anthony St *WCHPL* E1..........**91** E2
Antill Rd *BOW* E3..........**91** E1
Antill Ter *WCHPL* E1..........**91** D5
Anton St *HACK* E8..........**78** A2
Antrim Rd *HAMP* NW3..........**73** F3
Antrobus Rd *CHSWK* W4..........**98** C5
Apollo Pl *WAN* E11..........**63** E5
 WBPTN * SW10..........**115** D3
Apollo Wy *WOOL/PLUM* SE18......**109** D4
Apothecary St *BLKFR* * EC4V......**22** C5
Appach Rd *BRXS/STRHM* SW2 ....**136** A3
Apple Blossom Ct *VX/NE* * SW8....**117** D3
Appleby Rd *CAN/RD* E16..........**94** A5

 HACK E8..........**78** A4
Appleby St *BETH* E2..........**13** E1
Appledore Cl *TOOT* SW17..........**151** F2
Appledore Crs *BFN/LL* DA15......**163** E3
Appleford Rd *NKENS* W10..........**89** E3
Applegarth Rd *WKENS* * W14......**101** D4
Apple Rd *WAN* E11..........**63** E5
Appleton Rd *ELTH/MOT* SE9......**143** E1
Apple Tree Yd *STJS* SW1Y..........**31** F3
Applewood Cl *CRICK* NW2..........**52** B5
Appold St *SDTCH* EC2A..........**24** C2
Apprentice Wy *CLPT* E5..........**78** B1
The Approach *ACT* W3..........**87** D5
Approach Rd *BETH* E2..........**90** C1
April Gln *FSTH* SE23..........**157** D3
April St *STNW/STAM* N16..........**77** F1
Apsley Wy *CRICK* NW2..........**52** A4
 MYFR/PICC * W1J..........**30** C4
Aquila St *STJWD* NW8..........**4** B1
Aquinas St *STHWK* SE1..........**34** B4
Arabella Dr *PUT/ROE* SW15......**129** E2
Arabin Rd *BROCKY* SE4..........**139** E2
Arbery Rd *BOW* E3..........**91** E2
Arborfield Cl *BRXS/STRHM* SW2 ....**153** F1
Arbour Sq *WCHPL* E1..........**90** C5
Arbroath Rd *ELTH/MOT* SE9......**143** F3
Arbuthnot Rd *NWCR* SE14..........**121** D5
Arbutus St *HACK* E8..........**77** F5
The Arcade *ELTH/MOT* * SE9 ....**144** A4
 LVPST * EC2M..........**24** C3
Arcade Chambers *ELTH/MOT* * SE9 ..**144** A4
Arcadia St *POP/IOD* E14..........**92** A5
Archangel St *BERM/RHTH* SE16....**103** D3
Archbishop's Pl *BRXS/STRHM* SW2 ..**100** B2
Archdale Cl *SHB* W12..........**137** F3
Archdale Rd *EDUL* SE22..........**113** F2
Archel Rd *WKENS* W14..........**113** F2
Archer Sq *DEPT* SE8..........**121** E2
Archer St *SOHO/SHAV* W1D........**32** A1
Archery Cl *BAY/PAD* W2..........**12** E1
Archery Rd *ELTH/MOT* SE9......**143** F3
The Arches *CHCR* * WC2N..........**33** D3
Arch St *STHWK* SE1..........**47** E3
Archway Cl *ARCH* * N19..........**56** C4
 NKENS W10..........**89** D4
 WIM/MER SW19..........**150** B4
Archway Rd *ARCH* N19..........**56** C3
Archway St *BARN* SW13..........**129** E1
Arcola St *HACK* E8..........**77** F2
Arctic St *KTTN* NW5..........**74** B2
Ardbeg Rd *HNHL* SE24..........**137** D4
Arden Court Gdns *EFNCH* N2 ....**55** D1
Arden Crs *POP/IOD* E14..........**104** A5
Arden Est *IS* N1..........**12** C2
Ardfillan Rd *CAT* SE6..........**159** D1
Ardgowan Rd *CAT* SE6..........**141** E5
Ardilaun Rd *HBRY* N5..........**76** C1
Ardleigh Rd *IS* N1..........**77** E3
Ardley Cl *FSTH* SE23..........**157** E3
 WLSDN NW10..........**51** E5
Ardlui Rd *WNWD* SE27..........**154** C2
Ardmere Rd *LEW* SE13..........**141** D4
Ardoch Rd *CAT* SE6..........**159** D2
Ardshiel Cl *PUT/ROE* SW15......**131** D1
Ardwell Rd *BRXS/STRHM* SW2 ....**153** E2
Ardwick Rd *CRICK* NW2..........**72** A1
Arena Est *FSBYPK* * N4..........**58** B1
Argall Av *LEY* E10..........**61** D2
Argall Wy *LEY* E10..........**61** D3
Argenta Wy *WLSDN* NW10........**68** B4
Argon Ms *FUL/PGN* SW6..........**114** A3
Argyle Pl *HMSMTH* W6..........**100** B5
Argyle Rd *CAN/RD* E16..........**94** B5
 IL IG1..........**66** A4
 SRTFD E15..........**81** E1
 WCHPL E1..........**91** D3

Argyle Sq *STPAN* WC1H	9	D3
Argyle St *CAMTN* NW1	8	C3
Argyle Wk *STPAN* WC1H	8	C4
Argyll Cl *BRXN/ST* SW9	135	F1
Argyll Rd *KENS* W8	38	A1
WOOL/PLUM SE18	108	C4
Argyll St *REGST* W1B	19	E5
Arica Rd *BROCKY* SE4	139	E2
Ariel Rd *KIL/WHAMP* NW6	72	A3
Ariel Wy *SHB* W12	100	C2
Aristotle Rd *CLAP* SW4	135	D1
Arkindale Rd *CAT* SE6	158	C3
Arklow Rd *NWCR* SE14	121	F1
Arkwright Rd *HAMP* NW3	72	C2
Arlesford Rd *BRXN/ST* SW9	135	E1
Arlingford Rd *BRXS/STRHM* SW2	136	A4
Arlington Cl *BFN/LL* DA15	145	E3
LEW SE13	141	D3
Arlington Gdns *CHSWK* W4	110	C1
IL IG1	65	F2
Arlington Pde *BRXS/STRHM* * SW2	135	F2
Arlington Rd *CAMTN* NW1	74	B5
Arlington Sq *IS* N1	76	C5
Arlington St *MYFR/PICC* W1J	31	E3
Arlington Wy *CLKNW* EC1R	10	B3
Armadale Rd *FUL/PGN* SW6	114	A2
Armada St *DEPT* SE8	122	A2
Armada Wy *EHAM* E6	96	C5
Armagh Rd *BOW* E3	79	F5
Arminger Rd *SHB* W12	100	B2
Armitage Rd *GLDGN* NW11	53	E3
GNWCH SE10	105	F5
Armour Cl *HOLWY* N7	75	F3
Armoury Rd *DEPT* SE8	122	B5
Armoury Wy *WAND/EARL* SW18	132	A3
Armstrong Cl *EHAM* E6	95	F5
Armstrong Rd *ACT* W3	99	F2
Arnal Crs *WAND/EARL* SW18	131	E5
Arne St *LSQ/SEVD* WC2H	21	D5
Arne Wk *BKHTH/KID* SE3	141	F2
Arneway St *WEST* SW1P	44	B3
Arnewood Cl *PUT/ROE* SW15	148	A1
Arngask Rd *CAT* SE6	141	D5
Arnheim Pl *POP/IOD* E14	104	A4
Arnold Est *STHWK* SE1	49	F1
Arnold Rd *BOW* E3	92	A2
Arnott Cl *CHSWK* W4	99	D5
Arnould Av *CMBW* SE5	137	D2
Arnside St *WALW* SE17	118	C2
Arnulf St *CAT* SE6	158	B4
Arodene Rd *BRXS/STRHM* SW2	135	F4
Arragon Rd *EHAM* E6	83	D5
WAND/EARL SW18	150	A1
Arran Dr *MNPK* E12	65	D3
Arran Rd *CAT* SE6	158	B2
Arran Wk *IS* N1	76	C4
Arrow Rd *BOW* E3	92	B2
Arsenal Rd *ELTH/MOT* SE9	125	F5
Artesian Cl *WLSDN* NW10	69	D4
Artesian Houses *NTGHL* * W11	14	A5
Artesian Rd *NTGHL* W11	14	A5
Arthingworth St *SRTFD* E15	81	E5
Arthurdon Rd *LEW* SE13	140	A3
Arthur Gv *WOOL/PLUM* SE18	108	C5
Arthur Rd *EHAM* E6	95	F1
HOLWY N7	75	F1
WIM/MER SW19	149	F4
Arthur St *CANST* EC4R	36	B2
Artichoke Hl *WAP* E1W	102	B3
Artichoke Pl *CMBW* * SE5	119	D4
Artillery Cl *GNTH/NBYPK* IG2	66	C1
Artillery La *LVPST* EC2M	25	D3
SHB W12	88	A5
Artillery Pas *WCHPL* * E1	25	D3
Artillery Pl *WOOL/PLUM* SE18	108	C1
Artizan St *WCHPL* E1	25	D4
Arundel Cl *BTSEA* SW11	133	E3
Arundel Gdns *NTGHL* W11	101	F1
Arundel Gv *STNW/STAM* N16	77	E2
Arundel Pl *IS* N1	76	A3
Arundel Sq *HOLWY* N7	76	A3
Arundel St *TPL/STR* WC2R	33	F1
Arundel Ter *BARN* SW13	112	B2
Arvon Rd *HBRY* N5	76	A2
Asbaston Ter *IL* IG1	84	C2
Ascalon St *VX/NE* SW8	116	C3
Ascham St *KTTN* NW5	74	C2
Ascot Pde *CLAP* * SW4	135	E2
Ascot Rd *EHAM* E6	95	F2
Ashanti Ms *HACK* * E8	78	B3
Ashbourne Gv *CHSWK* W4	111	E1
EDUL SE22	137	F3
Ashbridge Rd *WAN* E11	63	E2
Ashbridge St *STJWD* NW8	16	C1
Ashbrook Rd *ARCH* N19	57	D3
Ashburn Gdns *SKENS* SW7	39	E4
Ashburnham Gv *CNWCH* SE10	122	B3
Ashburnham Pl *GNWCH* SE10	122	B3
Ashburnham Retreat *CNWCH* SE10	122	B3
Ashburnham Rd *WBPTN* * SW10	114	C3
WLSDN NW10	88	C2
Ashburn Pl *SKENS* SW7	39	E4
Ashburton Av *CNWCH/SEVK* IG3	85	F1
Ashburton Gv *HOLWY* N7	76	A1
Ashburton Rd *CAN/RD* E16	94	A5
Ashbury Rd *BTSEA* SW11	133	F1
Ashby Gv *IS* N1	76	C4
Ashby Ms *BROCKY* SE4	139	F1
Ashby Rd *BROCKY* SE4	121	F5
Ashby St *FSBYE* EC1V	11	D4
Ashchurch Gv *SHB* W12	100	A3
Ashchurch Park Vls *SHB* W12	100	A4
Ashchurch Ter *SHB* W12	99	F4
Ashcombe Pk *CRICK* NW2	51	E5
Ashcombe Rd *WIM/MER* SW19	150	A5
Ashcombe St *FUL/PGN* * SW6	114	B5
Ashcroft Rd *BOW* E3	91	E2
Ashdale Rd *LEE/GVPK* SE12	160	B1
Ashdown Crs *KTTN* * NW5	74	A2
Ashdown Rd *WLSDN* NW10	69	E5
Ashdown Wy *TOOT* SW17	152	A2
Ashenden Rd *CLPT* E5	79	E2
Ashen Gv *WIM/MER* SW19	150	A3
Asher Wy *WAP* E1W	102	A2
Ashfield Rd *ACT* W3	99	F2
FSBYPK N4	58	C1
Ashfield St *WCHPL* E1	90	B4
Ashfield Yd *WCHPL* * E1	90	C4
Ashford Cl *WALTH* E17	61	F1
Ashford Rd *CRICK* NW2	71	D1
EHAM E6	83	F3
Ashford St *IS* N1	12	C3
Ash Gv *CRICK* NW2	71	D1
HACK E8	78	B5
Ashgrove Rd *GDMY/SEVK* IG3	67	F3
Ashington Rd *FUL/PGN* * SW6	113	F5
Ashlake Rd *STRHM/NOR* SW16	153	E4
Ashland Pl *MHST* W1U	18	A2
Ashlar Pl *WOOL/PLUM* SE18	108	B5
Ashleigh Rd *MORT/ESHN* SW14	129	E1
Ashley Crs *BTSEA* SW11	134	A1
Ashley Pl *WEST* SW1P	43	E3
Ashley Rd *ARCH* N19	57	E3
FSTGT E7	82	C4
Ashlin Rd *SRTFD* E15	81	D1
Ashlone Rd *PUT/ROE* SW15	130	C1
Ashmead Ms *DEPT* * SE8	122	A4
Ashmead Rd *DEPT* SE8	122	A5
Ashmere Gv *BRXS/STRHM* SW2	135	E2
Ash Ms *KTTN* * NW5	74	C2
Ashmill St *CAMTN* NW1	16	C2
Ashmole St *VX/NE* SW8	117	F2
Ashmore Cl *PECK* SE15	120	A3
Ashmore Gv *WELL* DA16	145	D1

Ashmore Rd *MV/WKIL* W9 ....89 F2
Ashmount Rd *HCT* N6 ....56 C2
Ashness Rd *BTSEA* SW11 ....133 F3
Ashridge Crs *WOOL/PLUM* SE18 ....126 C3
Ash Rd *SRTFD* E15 ....81 E2
Ashtead Rd *CLPT* E5 ....60 A2
Ashton Rd *SRTFD* E15 ....81 D2
Ashton St *POP/IOD* E14 ....104 C1
Ashurst Dr *GNTH/NBYPK* IG2 ....66 B1
Ashurst Gdns *BRXS/STRHM* * SW2 ....154 A1
Ashvale Rd *TOOT* SW17 ....151 F5
Ashville Rd *WAN* E11 ....63 D4
Ashwater Rd *LEE/GVPK* SE12 ....160 A1
Ashwin St *HACK* E8 ....77 F3
Ashworth Cl *CMBW* SE5 ....119 D5
Ashworth Rd *MV/WKIL* W9 ....3 D3
Aske St *IS* N1 ....12 C3
Askew Crs *SHB* W12 ....99 F3
Askew Rd *SHB* W12 ....99 F3
Askham Rd *SHB* W12 ....100 A2
Askill Dr *PUT/ROE* SW15 ....131 E3
Asland Rd *SRTFD* E15 ....81 D5
Aslett St *WAND/EARL* SW18 ....132 B5
Asmara Rd *CRICK* NW2 ....71 E2
Aspenlea Rd *HMSMTH* W6 ....113 D2
Aspen Wy *POP/IOD* E14 ....104 C1
Aspern Gv *HAMP* NW3 ....73 E2
Aspinall Rd *BROCKY* SE4 ....139 D1
Aspinden Rd *BERM/RHTH* SE16 ......102 B5
Aspley Rd *WAND/EARL* SW18 ....132 B3
Assam St *WCHPL* E1 ....90 A5
Assata Ms *IS* N1 ....76 B3
Assembly Pas *WCHPL* E1 ....90 C4
Astbury Rd *PECK* SE15 ....120 C4
Astell St *CHEL* SW3 ....115 E1
Asteys Rw *IS* N1 ....76 B4
Astle St *BTSEA* SW11 ....116 A5
Astley Av *CRICK* NW2 ....70 C2
Aston St *WCHPL* E1 ....91 E5
Aston Ter *BAL* * SW12 ....134 B4
Astonville St *WAND/EARL* SW18 ......150 A1
Astoria Pde *STRHM/NOR* * SW16 ....153 E3
Astoria Wk *BRXN/ST* SW9 ....136 A1
Astrop Ms *HMSMTH* W6 ....100 C4
Astrop Ter *HMSMTH* W6 ....100 C4
Astwood Ms *SKENS* SW7 ....39 D4
Asylum Rd *PECK* SE15 ....120 B3
Atalanta St *FUL/PGN* SW6 ....113 D4
Atheldene Rd *WAND/EARL* SW18 ....150 B1
Athelney Rd *CAT* SE6 ....158 A3
Athelstane Gv *BOW* E3 ....91 F1
Athelstan Ms *FSBYPK* N4 ....58 A3
Athelstan Gdns *KIL/WHAMP* * NW6 ...71 E4
Athenlay Rd *PECK* SE15 ....139 D3
Athens Gdns *MV/WKIL* * W9 ....14 A1
Atherden Rd *CLPT* E5 ....78 C1
Atherfold Rd *BRXN/ST* SW9 ....135 E1
Atherstone Ms *SKENS* SW7 ....39 F4
Atherton Dr *WIM/MER* SW19 ....149 D4
Atherton Rd *BARN* SW13 ....112 A3
Atherton Rd *FSTGT* E7 ....81 F2
Atherton St *BTSEA* SW11 ....115 E5
Athlone Cl *CLPT* E5 ....78 B2
Athlone Rd *BRXS/STRHM* SW2 ....135 F5
Athlone St *KTTN* NW5 ....74 A3
Athol Sq *POP/IOD* E14 ....92 C5
Atkinson Rd *CAN/RD* E16 ....94 C4
Atkins Rd *BAL* SW12 ....134 C5
Atlantic Rd *BRXN/ST* SW9 ....136 C3
Atlas Gdns *CHARL* SE7 ....124 B5
Atlas Ms *HACK* E8 ....77 F3
Atlas Rd *PLSTW* E13 ....94 A1
Atley Rd *BOW* E3 ....80 A5
Atney Rd *PUT/ROE* SW15 ....131 E2

Atterbury Rd *FSBYPK* N4 ....58 A1
Atterbury St *WEST* SW1P 44 B5
Attewood Av *CRICK* NW2 ....51 E5
Attneave St *FSBYW* WC1X 10 A5
Atwell Rd *PECK* * SE15 ....120 A5
Atwood Av *RCH/KEW* TW9 ....110 A5
Atwood Rd *HMSMTH* W6 ....100 B5
Aubert Pk *HBRY* N5 ....76 A1
Aubert Rd *HBRY* N5 ....76 B1
Aubrey Pl *STJWD* NW8 ....3 E2
Aubrey Rd *KENS* W8 ....101 F2
Aubrey Wk *KENS* W8 ....101 F2
Auburn Cl *NWCR* SE14 ....121 E3
Aubyn Hl *WNWD* SE27 ....154 C4
Aubyn Sq *PUT/ROE* SW15 ....130 A2
Auckland Hl *WNWD* SE27 ....154 C4
Auckland Rd *BTSEA* SW11 ....133 E2
                  IL IG1 ....66 B3
                  LEY E10 ....62 B5
Auckland St *LBTH* SE11 ....117 F1
Auden Pl *CAMTN* NW1 ....74 A5
Audley Dr *CAN/RD* E16 ....106 A2
Audley Gdns *CDMY/SEVK* IG3 ....67 F4
Audley Rd *HDN* NW4 ....52 A3
Audley Sq *MYFR/PKLN* * W1K 30 B3
Audrey Rd *IL* IG1 ....66 B5
Audrey St *BETH* E2 ....90 A1
Augurs La *PLSTW* E13 ....94 B2
Augustine Rd *HMSMTH* W6 ....101 D4
Augustus Cl *SHB* W12 ....100 B3
Augustus Rd *WIM/MER* SW19 ....149 E1
Augustus St *CAMTN* NW1 ....7 D2
Aulton Pl *LBTH* SE11 ....118 A1
Auriga Ms *IS* N1 ....77 D2
Auriol Rd *WKENS* W14 ....101 E5
Austin Cl *CAT* SE6 ....139 E5
Austin Friars *OBST* EC2N 24 B4
Austin Friars Sq *OBST* * EC2N 24 B4
Austin Rd *BTSEA* SW11 ....116 A4
Austin St *BETH* E2 ....13 E4
Austral Cl *BFN/LL* DA15 ....163 F3
Australia Rd *SHB* W12 ....100 B1
Austral St *LBTH* SE11 ....46 C4
Autumn St *BOW* E3 ....79 F5
Avalon Rd *FUL/PGN* SW6 ....114 B4
Avebury Rd *WAN* E11 ....63 D3
Avebury St *IS* N1 ....77 D5
Aveline St *LBTH* SE11 ....117 F1
Avenell Rd *FSBYPK* N4 ....58 B5
Avening Rd *WAND/EARL* SW18 ......132 A4
Avening Ter *WAND/EARL* SW18 ......134 A3
The Avenue *BTSEA* SW11 ....99 E4
                  CHSWK W4 ....99 E4
                  GNWCH SE10 ....123 D3
                  KIL/WHAMP NW6 ....71 D5
                  WAN E11 ....64 B3
Avenue Rd *STJWD* NW8 ....73 E5
Avenue Crs *ACT* W3 ....98 B3
Avenue Gdns *ACT* W3 ....98 B3
                  MORT/ESHN SW14 ....129 E1
Avenue Park Rd *WNWD* SE27 ....154 B2
Avenue Rd *ACT* W3 ....98 B3
                  FSTGT E7 ....82 B2
                  HGT N6 ....56 C2
                  STJWD NW8 ....73 D5
                  WLSDN NW10 ....87 F1
Averill St *HMSMTH* W6 ....113 D2
Avery Farm Rw *BGVA* * SW1W 42 C5
Avery Hill Rd *ELTH/MOT* SE9 ....145 D4
                  ELTH/MOT SE9 ....162 C1
Avery Rw *MYFR/PKLN* W1K 30 C1
Aviary Cl *CAN/RD* E16 ....93 F4
Avignon Rd *BROCKY* SE4 ....139 D1
Avington Wy *PECK* * SE15 ....119 F3
Avis Sq *WCHPL* E1 ....91 D5
Avoca Rd *TOOT* SW17 ....152 A4
Avocet Cl *STHWK* SE1 ....119 F1
Avocet Ms *THMD* SE28 ....109 D4

Avondale Av CRICK NW2 ....51 E5
Avondale Park Gdns NTGHL * W11 .....101 E1
Avondale Park Rd NTGHL W11 ....101 E1
Avondale Pavement STHWK * SE1 ....120 C1
Avondale Ri PECK SE15 ....137 F1
Avondale Rd CAN/RD E16.....................93 E4
　ELTH/MOT SE9.......................................161 G2
　MORT/ESHN SW14................................129 D1
　WALTH E17..62 A2
　WIM/MER SW19 ....150 B5
Avondale Sq STHWK SE1 ....120 A1
Avonley Rd NWCR SE14 ....120 C3
Avonmore Gdns WKENS * W14 ....101 F5
Avonmore Pl WKENS W14 ....101 E5
Avonmore Rd WKENS W14 ....101 E5
Avonmouth St STHWK SE1 ....47 E2
Avon Rd BROCKY SE4 ....140 A1
Awliscombe Rd WELL DA16 ....127 F5
Axe St BARK IG11 ....84 C5
Axminster Rd HOLWY N7 ....57 E5
Aybrook St MHST W1U 18 A3
Aycliffe Rd SHB W12 ....99 F2
Aylesbury Cl FSTGT E7 ....81 F3
Aylesbury Rd WALW SE17 ....119 D1
Aylesbury St CLKNW EC1R 22 C1
　WLSDN NW10 ....51 D5
Aylesford St PIM SW1V 117 D1
Aylestone Av KIL/WHAMP NW6 ....71 G4
Aylmer Rd SHB W12 ....99 E3
　WAN E11..63 F2
Aylton Est BERM/RHTH * SE16 ....102 C3
Aylward Rd FSTH SE23 ....157 D2
Aylward St WCHPL * E1.........................90 C5
Aynhoe Rd HMSMTH * W6 ....101 D5
Ayres Cl PLSTW E13 ....94 A2
Ayres Crs WLSDN NW10........................69 D4
Ayres St STHWK SE1 ....35 F5
Ayrsome Rd STNW/STAM N16 ....59 E5
Ayrton Rd SKENS SW7 ....40 A2
Aysgarth Rd DUL SE21 ....137 D2
Aytoun Pl BRXN/ST SW9 ....117 F5
Aytoun Rd BRXN/ST SW9 ....117 F5
Azalea Cl IL IG1 ....84 B2
Azania Ms KTTN NW5 ....74 B2
Azenby Rd PECK SE15 ....119 F5
Azof St GNWCH SE10 ....105 E5

B

Baalbec Rd HBRY N5 ....76 B2
Babington Ri WBLY HA9 ....68 A3
Babington Rd STRHM/NOR SW16 ....153 D5
Babmaes St STJS SW1Y 32 A2
Bache's St IS N1 ....12 B4
Back Church La WCHPL E1 ....90 A5
Back HI CLKNW EC1R 22 B1
Back La HAMP NW3 ....72 C1
Bacon Gv STHWK SE1 ....49 E4
Bacon's La HGT N6..............................56 A3
Bacon St BETH E2 ....13 F5
Bacton St BETH E2 ....90 C2
Baden Pl STHWK SE1 ....36 A5
Baden Rd IL IG1 ....84 B2
Badgers Cft ELTH/MOT SE9 ....162 A3
Badminton Ms CAN/RD E16 ....106 A2
Badminton Rd BAL SW12 ....134 A4
Badsworth Rd CMBW SE5 ....118 C3
Bagley's La FUL/PGN SW6..................114 B4
Bagshot Ct WOOL/PLUM * SE18 ....114 B4
Bagshot St WALW SE17 ....119 E1
Baildon St DEPT SE8 ....121 F3
Bailey Cottages POP/IOD * E14...........91 E4
Bainbridge St NOXST/BSQ WC1A 20 B4
Baird Cl CDALE/KGS NW9 ....50 C1
　LEY E10...62 A3
Baird Gdns NRWD SE19......................155 F4

Baird St STLK EC1Y 11 F5
Baizdon Rd BKHTH/KID SE3 ....123 E5
Baker Rd WLSDN NW10.........................69 E5
　WOOL/PLUM SE18 ....125 E4
Bakers Av LEY E10 ....62 B1
Baker's Ms MHST W1U 18 A4
Bakers Rents BETH E2 ....13 E4
Baker's Rw CLKNW EC1R 22 A1
　SRTFD E15...93 E1
Baker St CAMTN NW1 ....17 F1
Baker's Yd CLKNW EC1R 22 A1
Bakery Cl BRXN/ST * SW9 ....117 F3
Balaam St PLSTW E13 ....94 A2
Balaclava Rd STHWK SE1 ....49 F5
Bala Gn CDALE/KGS * NW9 ....51 E3
Balcaskie Rd ELTH/MOT SE9 ....143 F3
Balchen Rd BKHTH/KID SE3 ....125 D5
Balchier Rd EDUL SE22 ....138 B4
Balcombe St CAMTN NW1 ....5 E1
Balcorne St HOM E9 ....78 C4
Balder Ri LEE/GVPK SE12 ....160 B2
Balderton St MYFR/PKLN W1K................18 B5
Baldock St BOW E3 ....92 B1
Baldwin Crs CMBW SE5 ....118 C4
Baldwin's Gdns FSBYW WC1X...............22 A2
Baldwin St FSBYE EC1V 12 A4
Baldwin Ter IS N1 ....11 E1
Baldwyn Gdns ACT W3 ....98 C1
Bale Rd WCHPL E1 ....91 E4
Balfern Gv CHSWK W4........................111 E1
Balfern St BTSEA SW11 ....115 E5
Balfe St IS N1 ....9 D2
Balfour Ms MYFR/PKLN W1K 30 B3
Balfour Pl MYFR/PKLN W1K 30 B2
Balfour Rd ACT W3 ....86 C4
　HBRY N5..76 C1
　IL IG1...66 B4
Balfour St STHWK SE1 ....48 A4
Balgowan St WOOL/PLUM SE18 ....109 F5
Balham Gv BAL SW12.........................134 A5
Balham High Rd BAL SW12 ....152 B1
Balham Hl BAL SW12 ....134 B5
Balham New Rd BAL SW12 ....134 B5
Balham Park Rd TOOT SW17 ....151 F1
Balham Station Rd BAL SW12 ....152 A1
Balkan Wk WAP * E1W 102 B1
Balladier Wk POP/IOD E14....................92 B4
Ballamore Rd BMLY BR1 ....160 A3
Ballance Rd HOM E9 ....79 D3
Ballantine St WAND/EARL SW18 ....132 C2
Ballards Rd CRICK NW2 ....52 A4
Ballast Quay GNWCH SE10 ....123 D1
Ballater Rd CLAP SW4 ....135 E2
Ballina St FSTH SE23 ....139 D5
Ballingdon Rd BTSEA SW11 ....134 A4
Balliol Rd NKENS W10 ....88 C5
Balloch Rd CAT SE6 ....159 D1
Ballogie Av WLSDN NW10.....................69 E1
Ballow Cl CMBW * SE5........................119 D3
Ball's Pond Pl IS * N1..........................77 D3
Balls Pond Rd IS N1 ....77 D3
Balmer Rd BOW E3 ....91 F1
Balmes Rd IS N1 ....77 D5
Balmoral Cl PUT/ROE * SW15 ....131 D4
Balmoral Gv HOLWY N7 ....75 F3
Balmoral Ms SHB W12........................99 F4
Balmoral Rd CRICK NW2 ....70 B3
　FSTGT E7..82 C1
　LEY E10...62 B4
Balmore St KTTN NW5.........................56 B4
Balmuir Gdns PUT/ROE SW15 ....130 C2
Balnacraig Av WLSDN NW10 ....69 E1
Baltie Ga PIM SW1V............................117 D1
Baltic Pl IS N1 ....77 E5
Baltic St East STLK EC1Y 23 E1
Baltic St West FARR EC1M 23 E1
Baltimore Pl WELL DA16 ....127 F5

Balvaird Pl *PIM* SW1V 117 D1
Balvernie Gv *WAND/EARL* SW18 ...131 F5
Bamborough Gdns *SHB* W12 ......100 C3
Bamford Rd *BMLY* BR1 ....159 D5
Bampton Rd *FSTH* SE23 ....32 C1
Banbury Ct *COVGDN* * WC2E 79 D4
Banbury Rd *HOM* E9 ....115 E3
Banbury St *BTSEA* * SW11 ....124 B3
Banchory Rd *BKHTH/KID* SE3 ....124 B3
Bancroft Rd *WCHPL* E1 ....91 D2
Banfield Rd *PECK* SE15 ....138 B1
Bangalore St *PUT/ROE* SW15 ....130 C1
Banim St *HMSMTH* W6 ....100 B4
Banister Rd *WLSDN* NW10 ....89 D2
The Bank *HGT* N6 ....56 B3
Bank End *STHWK* SE1 ....35 F3
Bankfoot Rd *BMLY* BR1 ....159 E4
Bankhurst Rd *CAT* SE6 ....139 E5
Bank La *PUT/ROE* SW15 ....129 E3
Bankside *STHWK* SE1 ....35 E2
Bankside *IL* IG1 ....84 C2
Bankton Rd *BRXS/STRHM* SW2 ..136 A2
Bankwell Rd *LEW* SE13 ....141 E2
Banner St *STLK* EC1Y 23 F1
Banning St *GNWCH* SE10 ....123 E1
Bannister Cl *BRXS/STRHM* SW2 ..154 A1
Bannockburn Rd *WOOL/PLUM* SE18 ...109 E5
Banstead St *PECK* SE15 ....138 C1
Bantry St *CMBW* SE5 ....119 D3
Banyard Rd *BERM/RHTH* SE16 ..102 B4
Baptist Gdns *HAMP* NW3 ....74 A3
Barandon Wk *NTGHL* * W11 ....101 D1
Barbauld Rd *STNW/STAM* N16 ....59 E5
Barbers Rd *SRTFD* E15 ....92 B1
Barbican *BARB* EC2Y 23 F2
Barb Ms *HMSMTH* W6 ....100 C4
Barbon Cl *BMSBY* WC1N 21 D2
Barchard St *WAND/EARL* SW18 ..132 B3
Barchester St *POP/IOD* E14 ....92 B4
Barclay Cl *FUL/PGN* * SW6 ....114 A3
Barclay Rd *FUL/PGN* SW6 ....114 A3
  PLSTW E13 ....94 C3
  WAN E11 ....63 F3
Barcombe Av *BRXS/STRHM* SW2 ..153 E2
Barden St *WOOL/PLUM* SE18 ....127 E3
Bardolph Rd *HOLWY* N7 ....75 E1
Bard Rd *NKENS* W10 ....101 D1
Bardsey Pl *WCHPL* E1 ....90 C4
Bardsey Wk *IS* * N1 ....76 C3
Bardsley La *BRXS/STRHM* SW2 ..136 A2
  GNWCH SE10 ....122 C2
Barfett St *NKENS* W10 ....89 F3
Barfield Rd *WAN* * E11 ....63 F3
Barford St *IS* N1 ....76 A5
Barforth Rd *PECK* SE15 ....138 B1
Bargate Cl *WOOL/PLUM* SE18 ..127 F1
Barge House Rd *CAN/RD* E16 ....108 B3
Barge House St *STHWK* SE1 ....34 B3
Bargery Rd *CAT* SE6 ....158 B1
Bargrove Crs *CAT* SE6 ....157 F2
Barham Cl *CHST* BR7 ....162 B5
Barham Rd *CHST* BR7 ....162 B5
Baring Cl *LEE/GVPK* SE12 ....160 A2
Baring Rd *BMLY* BR1 ....160 B4
Baring St *IS* N1 ....77 D5
Barker Dr *CAMTN* NW1 ....74 C4
Barking Rd *EHAM* E6 ....83 F5
  POP/IOD E14 ....93 E5
Bark Pl *BAY/PAD* W2 ....26 C1
Barkston Gdns *ECT* SW5 ....38 C5
Barkworth Rd *BERM/RHTH* SE16 ...120 B1
Barlborough St *NWCR* SE14 .....121 D3
Barlby Gdns *NKENS* W10 ....89 D3
Barlby Rd *NKENS* W10 ....88 C4
Barley Mow Pas *CHSWK* W4 .....111 D1
Barlow Dr *WOOL/PLUM* SE18 ...125 E4
Barlow Pl *MYFR/PICC* W1J 31 D2
Barlow Rd *ACT* W3 ....98 B2

Crick NW2 ....71 F3
Barlow St *WALW* SE17 ....48 B4
Barmeston Rd *CAT* SE6 ....158 B2
Barmouth Rd *WAND/EARL* SW18 ...132 C4
Barnabas Rd *HOM* E9 ....79 D3
Barnaby Pl *SKENS* SW7 ....40 A5
Barnard Ms *BTSEA* SW11 ....133 E2
Barnardo Gdns *WCHPL* * E1 ....91 D5
Barnardo St *WCHPL* E1 ....91 D5
Barnard Rd *BTSEA* SW11 ....133 E2
Barnby St *CAMTN* NW1 ....7 F2
  SRTFD E15 ....81 E5
Barn Cl *KTTN* * NW5 ....75 D2
Barnes Av *BARN* SW13 ....112 A3
Barnes Br *CHSWK* W4 ....111 E5
Barnes Cl *MNPK* E12 ....85 D1
Barnes High St *BARN* SW13 ......111 F5
Barnes Rd *IL* IG1 ....84 C2
Barnes St *POP/IOD* E14 ....91 E5
Barnes Ter *DEPT* SE8 ....121 F1
Barnet Gv *BETH* E2 ....90 A2
Barnett St *WCHPL* E1 ....90 B5
Barney Cl *CHARL* SE7 ....124 C1
Barn Fld *HAMP* * NW3 ....73 F2
Barnfield Gdns *WOOL/PLUM* * SE18 ...126 B2
Barnfield Rd *WOOL/PLUM* SE18 ...126 B2
Barnham St *STHWK* SE1 ....37 D3
Barn Hi *WBLY* HA9 ....50 B4
Barnhill Rd *WBLY* HA9 ....50 C5
Barningham Wy *CDALE/KGS* NW9 ...50 C1
Barn Ri *WBLY* HA9 ....50 B3
Barnsbury Est *IS* N1 ....75 F5
Barnsbury Gv *HOLWY* N7 ....75 F4
Barnsbury Pk *IS* N1 ....76 A4
Barnsbury Rd *IS* N1 ....10 A1
Barnsbury Sq *IS* N1 ....76 A4
Barnsbury St *IS* N1 ....76 A4
Barnsbury Ter *IS* N1 ....75 F4
Barnsdale Av *POP/IOD* E14 ......104 B5
Barnsdale Rd *MV/WKIL* W9 ....89 F3
Barnsley St *WCHPL* E1 ....90 B5
Barnsley St *WCHPL* E1 ....90 B3
Barnstaple La *LEW* SE13 ....140 C2
Barnston Wk *IS* * N1 ....76 C5
Barn St *STNW/STAM* N16 ....59 E4
Barn Wy *WBLY* HA9 ....50 A3
Barnwell Rd *BRXS/STRHM* SW2 ...136 A3
Barnwood Cl *MV/WKIL* W9 ....14 C1
Baroness Rd *BETH* E2 ....13 F3
Barons Cl *IS* * N1 ....10 A1
Barons Court Rd *WKENS* * W14 ...113 E1
Barons Keep *WKENS* * W14 ....113 E1
Baronsmead Rd *BARN* SW13 .....112 A4
Baron's Pl *STHWK* SE1 ....46 B1
Baron St *IS* N1 ....10 A2
Barque Ms *DEPT* SE8 ....122 A2
Barrett's Green Rd *WLSDN* NW10 ...86 C5
Barrett's Gv *STNW/STAM* N16 .....77 E2
Barrett St *MBLAR* W1H 18 B5
Barrhill Rd *BRXS/STRHM* SW2 ...153 E2
Barriedale *NWCR* SE14 ....121 E4
Barrier Point Rd *CAN/RD* E16 ...106 C3
Barringer Sq *TOOT* SW17 ....74 A2
Barrington Cl *KTTN* NW5 ....74 A2
Barrington Rd *BRXN/ST* SW9 ....136 B1
  MNPK E12 ....84 A3
Barrington Vls *WOOL/PLUM* SE18 ...126 A4
Barrowgate Rd *CHSWK* W4 ......110 C1
Barrow Hill Est *STJWD* NW8 ....4 C1
Barrow Hill Rd *STJWD* NW8 ....4 C1
Barrs Rd *WLSDN* NW10 ....69 D4
Barry Av *SEVS/STOTM* N15 ....59 F1
Barry Pde *EDUL* * SE22 ....138 A2
Barry Rd *EDUL* SE22 ....138 A4
  EHAM E6 ....95 E5
  WLSDN NW10 ....68 C2
Barset Rd *PECK* SE15 ....138 C1
Barston Rd *WNWD* SE27 ....154 C2
Barstow Crs *BRXS/STRHM* SW2 ...153 F1

Barter St *NOXST/BSQ* WC1A 21 D3
Bartholomew CI *STBT* EC1A 23 E3
   WAND/EARL SW18 ....132 C2
Bartholomew La *OBST* EC2N 24 B5
Bartholomew Rd *KTTN* NW5 ....74 C3
Bartholomew Sq *FSBYE* EC1V 11 F5
Bartholomew St *STHWK* SE1 ....48 B3
Bartholomew Vls *KTTN* NW5 ....74 C3
Barth Rd *WOOL/PLUM* SE18 ....109 E5
Bartle Av *EHAM* E6 ....95 E1
Bartle Rd *NTGHL* W11 ....89 D5
Bartlett CI *POP/IOD* E14 ....92 A5
Bartlett Ct *FLST/FETLN* * EC4A 22 B4
Barton CI *PECK* SE15 ....138 B1
Barton Rd *WKENS* W14 ....113 E4
Barton St *WEST* SW1P 44 C3
Bartram Rd *BROCKY* SE4 ....139 E3
Bartrip St *HOM* E9 ....79 E3
Barward CI *WOOL/PLUM* SE18 ....108 A5
Barwick Rd *FSTGT* E7 ....82 B1
Baseing CI *EHAM* E6 ....108 A1
Basevi Wy *DEPT* SE8 ....122 A2
Bashley Rd *WLSDN* NW10 ....87 D3
Basil Av *EHAM* E6 ....95 E2
Basil Gdns *WNWD* SE27 ....154 C5
Basil St *CHEL* SW3 ....41 E1
Basin App *POP/IOD* E14 ....91 E5
Basingdon Wy *CMBW* SE5 ....137 D2
Basinghall Av *CITYW* EC2V 24 A4
Basinghall St *CITYW* EC2V 24 A4
Basing HI *GLDGN* NW11 ....53 F3
Basing PI *BETH* E2 ....13 D3
Basing St *NTGHL* W11 ....89 F5
Basire St *IS* N1 ....76 C5
Baskerville Gdns *WLSDN* NW10 ....69 E1
Baskerville Rd *WAND/EARL* SW18 ....133 E5
Basket Gdns *ELTH/MOT* SE9 ....143 E3
Baslow Wk *CLPT* E5 ....79 D1
Basnett Rd *BTSEA* * SW11 ....134 A1
Bassano St *EDUL* SE22 ....137 D5
Bassant Rd *WOOL/PLUM* SE18 ....127 F2
Bassein Park Rd *SHB* W12 ....99 F5
Bassett Rd *NKENS* W10 ....89 D5
Bassett St *KTTN* NW5 ....74 A3
Bassingham Rd *WAND/EARL* SW18 ....132 C5
Basswood CI *PECK* SE15 ....138 B1
Bastwick St *FSBYE* EC1V 11 D5
Basuto Rd *FUL/PGN* SW6 ....114 A4
Batavia Rd *NWCR* SE14 ....121 E3
Batchelor St *IS* N1 ....10 B1
Bateman CI *BARK* IG11 ....84 C3
Batemans Cnr *CHSWK* * W4 ....99 D5
Bateman's Rw *SDTCH* EC2A 13 D5
Bateman St *SOHO/SHAV* W1D 20 A5
Bate St *POP/IOD* E14 ....103 F1
Bath CI *PECK* SE15 ....120 B3
Bathgate Rd *WIM/MER* SW19 ....149 D3
Bath Gv *BETH* E2 ....90 A1
Bath PI *IS* N1 ....12 C4
Bath Rd *CHSWK* W4 ....99 E5
   FSTGT E7 ....83 D3
Baths Ap *FUL/PGN* * SW6 ....113 F3
Bath St *FSBYE* EC1V 11 F4
Bath Ter *STHWK* SE1 ....47 E3
Bathurst Gdns *WLSDN* NW10 ....88 B1
Bathurst Ms *BAY/PAD* W2 ....28 B1
Bathurst Rd *IL* IG1 ....66 B3
Bathurst St *BAY/PAD* W2 ....28 B1
Bathway *WOOL/PLUM* SE18 ....108 A5
Batley PI *STNW/STAM* N16 ....59 F5
Batley Rd *STNW/STAM* N16 ....59 F5
Batman CI *SHB* W12 ....100 B2
Batoum Gdns *HMSMTH* W6 ....100 C4
Batson St *SHB* W12 ....100 A3
Batten Cottages *POP/IOD* * E14 ....91 E4
Batten St *BTSEA* SW11 ....133 E1
Battersby Rd *CAT* SE6 ....159 D2
Battersea Br *BTSEA* SW11 ....115 D3

Battersea Bridge Rd *BTSEA* SW11 ....115 E3
Battersea Church Rd *BTSEA* SW11 ....115 D4
Battersea High St *BTSEA* SW11 ....115 D4
Battersea Park Rd *BTSEA* SW11 ....116 A4
Battersea Ri *BTSEA* SW11 ....133 E3
Battersea Sq *BTSEA* * SW11 ....115 E3
Battery Rd *THMD* SE28 ....109 E3
Battishill St *IS* N1 ....76 B3
Battle Bridge La *STHWK* SE1 ....36 C4
Battle Bridge Rd *CAMTN* NW1 ....8 C2
Battledean Rd *HBRY* N5 ....76 B2
Batty St *WCHPL* E1 ....90 A5
Baudwin Rd *CAT* SE6 ....159 E2
The Baulk *WAND/EARL* SW18 ....132 A5
Bavaria Rd *ARCH* N19 ....57 E4
Bavent Rd *CMBW* SE5 ....118 C5
Bawdale Rd *EDUL* SE22 ....137 F3
Bawtree Rd *NWCR* SE14 ....121 E3
Baxendale St *BETH* E2 ....90 A2
Baxter Rd *CAN/RD* E16 ....94 C5
   IL IG1 ....84 B2
   IS N1 ....77 D3
Bayfield Rd *ELTH/MOT* SE9 ....143 D2
Bayford Ms *HACK* * E8 ....78 B4
Bayford Rd *WLSDN* NW10 ....89 D2
Bayford St *HACK* E8 ....78 B4
Bayham PI *CAMTN* NW1 ....74 C5
Bayham Rd *CHSWK* W4 ....99 D4
Bayham St *CAMTN* NW1 ....74 C5
Bayley St *FITZ* W1T 20 A3
Baylis Rd *STHWK* SE1 ....46 A2
Bayne CI *EHAM* E6 ....95 F5
Baynes Ms *HAMP* NW3 ....73 E3
Baynes St *CAMTN* NW1 ....74 C4
Bayonne Rd *FUL/PGN* SW6 ....113 E2
Bays CI *SYD* SE26 ....156 C5
Bayston Rd *STNW/STAM* N16 ....59 F5
Bayswater Rd *BAY/PAD* W2 ....27 D2
Baythorne St *BOW* E3 ....91 F4
Baytree CI *BFN/LL* DA15 ....163 F1
Baytree Rd *BRXS/STRHM* SW2 ....135 F2
Bazely St *POP/IOD* E14 ....104 C1
Beacham CI *CHARL* SE7 ....125 D2
Beachborough Rd *BMLY* BR1 ....158 C4
Beachcroft Rd *WAN* E11 ....63 E5
Beachy Rd *BOW* E3 ....80 A4
Beacon HI *HOLWY* N7 ....75 E2
Beacon Rd *LEW* SE13 ....141 D4
Beaconsfield CI *BKHTH/KID* SE3 ....124 A2
   CHSWK W4 ....110 C1
Beaconsfield Rd *BKHTH/KID* SE3 ....124 A2
   CAN/RD E16 ....93 F3
   CHSWK W4 ....99 D4
   ELTH/MOT SE9 ....161 E3
   LEY * E10 ....62 C5
   WALTH E17 ....61 F1
   WALW SE17 ....119 D2
   WLSDN NW10 ....69 F3
Beaconsfield Terrace Rd
   WKENS W14 ....101 E4
Beaconsfield Wk *FUL/PGN* SW6 ....113 F4
Beacontree Rd *WAN* E11 ....63 F2
Beadman PI *WNWD* * SE27 ....154 B4
Beadman St *WNWD* SE27 ....154 B4
Beadnell Rd *FSTH* SE23 ....157 D1
Beadon Rd *HMSMTH* W6 ....100 C5
Beak St *REGST* W1B 31 E1
Beale PI *BOW* E3 ....91 F1
Beale Rd *BOW* E3 ....79 F5
Beal Rd *IL* IG1 ....66 A4
Beanacre CI *HOM* * E9 ....79 F3
Beanshaw *ELTH/MOT* SE9 ....162 A4
Beardsfield *PLSTW* E13 ....82 A5
Beardsley Wy *ACT* W3 ....99 D3
Bear Gdns *STHWK* SE1 ....35 E3
Bear La *STHWK* SE1 ....35 D3
Bearstead Ri *BROCKY* SE4 ....139 F3
Bear St *LSQ/SEVD* WC2H 32 B1

Beatrice Cl PLSTW E13 ....94 A3
Beatrice Pl KENS W8 ....38 C3
Beatrice Rd FSBYPK N4 ....58 A2
   STHWK SE1 ....77 E1
Beatty Rd STNW/STAM N16 ....7 E1
Beatty St CAMTN * NW1 ....41 D2
Beauchamp Pl CHEL SW3 ....133 E2
Beauchamp Rd BTSEA SW11 ....82 B4
   FSTGT E7 ....22 A3
Beauchamp Ter PUT/ROE SW15 ....130 B1
Beauclerc Rd HMSMTH W6 ....96 A4
Beaufort EHAM E6 ....148 C1
Beaufort Cl PUT/ROE SW15 ....41 D2
Beaufort Gdns CHEL SW3 ....52 C1
   HDN NW4 ....66 A3
   IL IG1 ....66 A3
Beaufort St CHEL SW3 ....115 D2
Beaufoy Wk LBTH SE11 ....106 B2
Beaulieu Av CAN/RD E16 ....156 B4
   SYD SE26 ....156 B4
Beaulieu Cl CMBW SE5 ....137 D1
Beaulieu Pl CHSWK W4 ....98 A3
Beaumaris Gn CDALE/KGS * NW9 .....51 E1
Beaumont Av WKENS W14 ....113 F1
Beaumont Crs WKENS W14 ....113 F1
Beaumont Gdns HAMP NW3 ....54 A5
Beaumont Gv WCHPL E1 ....91 D3
Beaumont Ms MHST * W1U 18 B2
Beaumont Pl FITZ W1T 7 F5
Beaumont Ri ARCH N19 ....57 D3
Beaumont Rd CHSWK W4 ....98 C4
   LEY E10 ....62 B2
   PLSTW E13 ....94 B2
   WIM/MER SW19 ....131 E5
Beaumont Sq WCHPL E1 ....91 D4
Beaumont St W1U 18 B2
Beaumont Ter LEW * SE13 ....141 E5
Beaumont Wk HAMP NW3 ....73 F4
Beauval Rd EDUL SE22 ....137 F4
Beaverbank Rd ELTH/MOT SE9 ....163 D1
Beaverwood Rd CHST BR7 ....163 E5
Beavor La HMSMTH W6 ....100 A5
Bebbington Rd WOOL/PLUM * SE18 .109 E5
Beccles St POP/IOD E14 ....91 E5
Beck Cl LEW SE13 ....122 B4
Becket Av EHAM E6 ....96 A2
Becket St STHWK SE1 ....48 A2
Beckett Cl STRHM/NOR SW16 ....153 D2
   WLSDN NW10 ....69 D3
Beckford Cl WKENS W14 ....101 F5
Beckford Pl WALW * SE17 ....118 C1
Becklow Rd SHB W12 ....100 A3
Beck Rd HACK E8 ....78 B5
Beckton Rd CAN/RD E16 ....93 F4
Beckway St WALW SE17 ....48 B5
Beckwith Rd HNHL SE24 ....137 D4
Becmead Av STRHM/NOR SW16 ......153 D4
Becondale Rd NRWD SE19 ....155 E5
Bective Rd FSTGT E7 ....82 A1
   PUT/ROE SW15 ....131 F2
Bedale St STHWK * SE1 ....36 A4
Beddington Rd GDMY/SEVK IG3 ....67 F2
Bedford Av RSQ WC1B 20 B3
Bedfordbury CHCR WC2N 32 C1
Bedford Cl CHSWK W4 ....111 E2
Bedford Cnr CHSWK * W4 ....99 E5
Bedford Ct CHCR WC2N 32 C2
Bedford Gdns KENS W8 ....26 A4
Bedford Hl BAL SW12 ....152 B2
Bedford Pl RSQ WC1B 20 C2
Bedford Rd BFN/LL DA15 ....163 E3
   CEND/HSY/T N8 ....57 D1
   CHSWK W4 ....99 D4
   CLAP SW4 ....135 E2
   EHAM E6 ....84 A3
   IL IG1 ....66 B3
Bedford Rw FSBYW WC1X 21 F2

Bedford Sq RSQ WC1B 20 B3
Bedford St COVGDN WC2E 32 C1
Bedford Wy STPAN WC1H 20 B1
Bedgebury Gdns WIM/MER SW19 ....149 E2
Bedgebury Rd ELTH/MOT SE9 ....143 D2
Bedivere Rd BMLY BR1 ....160 A3
Bedser Cl VX/NE * SW8 ....117 F2
Beeby Rd CAN/RD E16 ....94 B4
Beech Av ACT W3 ....99 E2
Beech Cl DEPT SE8 ....121 F2
   PUT/ROE SW15 ....130 A5
Beech Ct ELTH/MOT * SE9 ....143 E4
Beechcroft Av GLDGN NW11 ....53 F2
Beechcroft Cl STRHM/NOR SW16 ....153 F5
Beechcroft Rd MORT/ESHN * SW14 .128 C1
   TOOT SW17 ....151 E5
Beechdale Rd BRXS/STRHM SW2 .....135 F4
Beechen Pl FSTH SE23 ....156 C2
Beeches Rd TOOT SW17 ....151 E3
Beechfield Rd CAT SE6 ....157 F1
   FSBYPK N4 ....58 C1
Beechhill Rd ELTH/MOT SE9 ....144 A3
Beechmont Cl BMLY BR1 ....159 E5
Beechmore Rd BTSEA SW11 ....115 E4
Beecholme Est CLPT * E5 ....60 C5
Beech St (Below) BARB EC2Y 23 E2
Beech Tree Cl IS N1 ....76 A4
Beech Wy WLSDN NW10 ....69 D4
Beechwood Av RCH/KEW TW9 ....110 A4
Beechwood Gv ACT W3 ....99 E1
Beechwood Rd CHST BR7 ....162 B4
   HACK E8 ....77 F3
Beechworth Cl HAMP NW3 ....54 B4
Beecroft La BROCKY SE4 ....139 E3
Beecroft Ms BROCKY SE4 ....139 E3
Beecroft Rd BROCKY SE4 ....139 E3
Beehive Cl HACK E8 ....77 F4
Beehive Rd BRXN/ST SW9 ....136 A1
Beeston Cl HACK E8 ....78 A2
Beeston Pl BGVA SW1W 43 D3
Beethoven St NKENS W10 ....89 E2
Begbie Rd BKHTH/KID SE3 ....124 C4
Begonia Cl EHAM E6 ....95 E4
Beira St BAL SW12 ....134 B5
Bekesbourne St POP/IOD * E14 ....91 E5
Belfast Rd STNW/STAM N16 ....59 F4
Belford Gv WOOL/PLUM SE18 ....108 A5
Belfort Rd PECK SE15 ....120 C5
Belfry Cl BERM/RHTH * SE16 ....120 B1
Belgrade Rd STNW/STAM N16 ....77 E1
Belgrave Cl ACT W3 ....98 C3
Belgrave Gdns STJWD NW8 ....72 B5
Belgrave Ms South KTBR SW1X 42 B2
Belgrave Ms West KTBR SW1X 42 A2
Belgrave Pl KTBR SW1X 42 B3
Belgrave Rd BARN SW13 ....111 F3
   IL IG1 ....66 A4
   PIM SW1V 43 E5
   PLSTW E13 ....94 C3
   WALTH E17 ....62 A1
   WAN E11 ....64 A3
Belgrave Sq KTBR SW1X 42 A2
Belgrave St WCHPL E1 ....91 D4
Belgrave Yd WCHPL E1 ....8 C5
Belgrove St CAMTN NW1 ....136 B1
Belinda Rd BRXN/ST SW9 ....136 B1
Belitha Vis IS N1 ....113 F1
Bellamy Cl ECT SW5 ....104 A3
   POP/IOD E14 ....91 E5
Bellamy St BAL SW12 ....134 B5
Bellasis Av BRXS/STRHM SW2 ....153 E1
Bell Dr WAND/EARL SW18 ....131 E5
Bellefields Rd BRXN/ST SW9 ....135 F1
Bellegrove Cl WELL DA16 ....127 F5
Bellegrove Rd WELL DA16 ....127 E5
Bellenden Rd PECK SE15 ....119 F5
Belleville Rd BTSEA SW11 ....133 E3
Bellevue Pl WCHPL * E1 ....90 C3
Bellevue Rd BARN SW13 ....112 A5

TOOT SW17 ....**133** F5
Bellew St TOOT SW17 ....**150** C3
Bell Gdns LEY * NE10 ....**62** A3
Bellgate Ms KTTN NW5 ....**74** B1
Bell Gn SYD SE26 ....**157** E4
Bell Green La SYD SE26 ....**157** F5
Bellina Ms KTTN NW5 ....**74** B1
Bellingham Gn CAT SE6 ....**158** A3
Bellingham Rd CAT SE6 ....**158** C3
Bell La CAN/RD E16 ....**106** A2
WCHPL E1 ....**25** E3
Bell Meadow NRWD SE19 ....**155** E4
Bello Cl BRXS/STRHM SW2 ....**154** B1
Bellot St GNWCH SE10 ....**123** E1
Bell St BAY/PAD W2 ....**16** C2
WOOL/PLUM SE18 ....**125** E4
Belltrees Gv STRHM/NOR SW16 ...**153** F5
Bell Water Ga WOOL/PLUM SE18 .**108** A4
Bell Wharf La CANST EC4R **35** F2
Bellwood Rd PECK SE15 ....**139** D2
Bell Yd LINN WC2A **22** A5
Belmont Av WELL DA16 ....**127** E5
Belmont Cl CLAP SW4 ....**134** C1
Belmont Gv CHSWK W4 ....**99** D5
LEW SE13 ....**141** D1
Belmont Hl LEW SE13 ....**141** D1
Belmont La CHST BR7 ....**162** C4
Belmont Pde CHST * BR7 ....**162** B5
Belmont Pk LEW SE13 ....**141** D2
Belmont Park Cl LEW SE13 ....**141** E2
Belmont Park Rd LEY E10 ....**62** B1
Belmont Rd CHST BR7 ....**162** B5
CLAP SW4 ....**134** C1
IL IG1 ....**66** C5
Belmont St CAMTN NW1 ....**74** A4
Belmont Ter CHSWK W4 ....**99** D5
Belmore La HOLWY * N7 ....**75** D2
Belmore St VX/NE SW8 ....**117** D4
Beloe Cl BARN SW13 ....**130** A2
Belsham St HOM E9 ....**78** C3
Belsize Av HAMP NW3 ....**73** E2
Belsize Ct Garages HAMP NW3 .....**73** D2
Belsize Crs HAMP NW3 ....**73** D2
Belsize Gdns HAMP NW3 ....**73** E3
Belsize La HAMP NW3 ....**73** D3
Belsize Ms HAMP * NW3 ....**73** D3
Belsize Pk HAMP NW3 ....**73** D3
Belsize Park Gdns HAMP NW3 ....**73** D3
Belsize Park Ms HAMP NW3 ....**73** D3
Belsize Pl HAMP NW3 ....**73** D2
Belsize Rd KIL/WHAMP NW6 ....**72** B5
Belsize Sq HAMP NW3 ....**73** D3
Belsize Ter HAMP NW3 ....**73** D3
Belson Rd WOOL/PLUM SE18 .....**107** F5
Beltane Dr WIM/MER SW19 ....**149** D3
Belthorn Crs BAL SW12 ....**134** C5
Belton Rd FSTGT E7 ....**82** B4
WLSDN NW10 ....**70** A3
Belton Wy BOW E3 ....**92** A4
Beltran Rd FUL/PGN SW6 ....**114** C4
The Belvedere WBPTN * SW10 ....**114** C5
Belvedere Av WIM/MER SW19 ....**149** E5
Belvedere Buildings STHWK SE1 ...**47** D1
Belvedere Dr WIM/MER SW19 ....**149** E5
Belvedere Gv WIM/MER SW19 ....**149** E5
Belvedere Ms PECK SE15 ....**138** C1
Belvedere Rd LEY E10 ....**61** E3
STHWK SE1 ....**33** E5
Belvedere Sq WIM/MER SW19 ....**149** E5
Belvoir Rd EDUL SE22 ....**138** A5
Bembridge Cl KIL/WHAMP NW6 .....**71** E4
Bemerton Est IS N1 ....**75** F4
Bemerton St IS N1 ....**75** F5
Bemish Rd PUT/ROE SW15 ....**131** D1
Benares Rd WOOL/PLUM SE18 ...**109** F5
Benbow Rd HMSMTH W6 ....**100** B4
Benbow St DEPT SE8 ....**122** A2
Benbury Cl BMLY BR1 ....**158** C5

Bendall Ms CAMTN NW1 ....**17** D2
Bendemeer Rd PUT/ROE SW15 ..**131** D1
Bendish Rd EHAM E6 ....**83** E4
Bendon Va WAND/EARL SW18 ....**132** B5
Benedict Rd BRXN/ST SW9 ....**135** F1
Bengal Rd IL IG1 ....**84** B1
Benham St CMBW SE5 ....**133** D1
Benhill Rd CMBW SE5 ....**119** D3
Benhurst La STRHM/NOR SW16 ..**154** A5
Benin St LEW SE13 ....**141** D5
Benjamin Cl HACK E8 ....**78** A5
Benjamin St FARR EC1M **22** C2
Ben Jonson Rd WCHPL E1 ....**91** D4
Benledi St POP/IOD E14 ....**93** D5
Bennelong Cl SHB W12 ....**100** B1
Bennerley Rd BTSEA SW11 ....**133** E3
Bennet's Hl BLKFR * EC4V **35** D1
BLKFR EC4V **35** D1
Bennett Gv LEW SE13 ....**122** B4
Bennett Pk BKHTH/KID SE3 ....**141** F1
Bennett Rd PLSTW E13 ....**94** C3
Bennett St CHSWK W4 ....**111** E2
WHALL SW1A **31** E3
Benn St HOM E9 ....**79** E3
Bensbury Cl PUT/ROE SW15 ....**130** B5
Benson Av PLSTW E13 ....**94** C1
Benson Quay WAP E1W **102** C1
Benson Rd FSTH SE23 ....**156** C1
Benthal Rd STNW/STAM N16 ....**59** F4
Bentham Rd HOM E9 ....**79** D3
Ben Tillet Cl CAN/RD * E16 ....**107** F2
Bentinck Ms MHST W1U **18** B4
Bentinck St MHST W1U **18** B4
Bentley Dr GNTH/NBYPK IG2 ....**66** C1
Bentley Rd IS N1 ....**77** E3
Benton Rd IL IG1 ....**67** D3
Benton's La WNWD SE27 ....**154** C4
Benton's Ri WNWD SE27 ....**155** D5
Bentworth Rd SHB W12 ....**88** B5
Benwell Rd HOLWY N7 ....**76** A1
Benwick Cl BERM/RHTH SE16 .....**102** B5
Benworth St BOW E3 ....**91** F2
Benyon Rd IS N1 ....**77** D5
Berber Rd BTSEA * SW11 ....**133** F3
Bercta Rd ELTH/MOT SE9 ....**162** C2
Berenger Wk WBPTN * SW10 ......**115** D3
Berens Rd WLSDN NW10 ....**89** D2
Beresford Av ALP/SUD HA0 ....**68** A5
Beresford Rd HBRY N5 ....**77** D2
Beresford Sq WOOL/PLUM SE18 .**108** B5
Beresford St WOOL/PLUM SE18 ..**108** B4
Beresford Ter HBRY N5 ....**76** C2
Berestede Rd HMSMTH W6 ....**111** F1
Bere St WAP E1W **103** D1
Berger Rd HOM E9 ....**79** D3
Bergham Ms WKENS W14 ....**101** D4
Bergholt Crs STNW/STAM N16 ......**59** E2
Bergholt Ms CAMTN NW1 ....**74** C4
Bering Wk CAN/RD E16 ....**95** D5
Berisford Ms WAND/EARL SW18 ..**132** C4
Berkeley Ms MBLAR W1H **17** F4
Berkeley Rd BARN SW13 ....**112** A4
MNPK E12 ....**83** A2
SEVS/STOTM N15 ....**59** D1
Berkeley Sq MYFR/PICC W1J **31** D2
Berkeley St MYFR/PICC W1J **31** D2
Berkley Rd CAMTN NW1 ....**73** F4
Berkshire Rd HOM E9 ....**79** F3
Bermans Wy WLSDN NW10 ....**69** E1
Bermondsey St STHWK SE1 ....**36** C4
Bermondsey Wall East
    BERM/RHTH SE16 ....**102** A3
Bermondsey Wall West
    BERM/RHTH SE16 ....**102** A3
Bernard Ashley Dr CHARL SE7 ....**124** B1
Bernard Cassidy St CAN/RD * E16 .**93** F4
Bernard Gdns WIM/MER SW19 ....**149** F5

Bernard St *BMSBY* WC1N 20 C1
Bernay's Gv *BRXN/ST* SW9 ....135 F2
Berners Ms *FITZ* W1T 19 F3
Berners Pl *FITZ* W1T 19 F4
Berners Rd *IS* N1 ....76 A5
Berners St *FITZ* W1T 19 F3
Berner Ter *WCHPL* E1 ....90 A5
Berridge Ms *KIL/WHAMP* NW6 ....72 A2
Berridge Rd *NRWD* SE19 ....155 D5
Berriman Rd *HOLWY* N7 ....57 F5
Berry Cl *WLSDN* NW10 ....69 E4
Berry Cottages *POP/IOD* * E14 ......91 E5
Berryfield Rd *WALW* SE17 ....118 B1
Berryhill *ELTH/MOT* SE9 ....144 B2
Berryhill Gdns *ELTH/MOT* SE9 ......144 B2
Berry La *DUL* SE21 ....155 D4
Berryman's La *SYD* SE26 ....157 D4
Berrymead Gdns *ACT* W3 ....98 C2
Berrymede Rd *CHSWK* W4 ....99 D4
Berry Pl *FSBYE* EC1V 11 D4
Berry St *FSBYE* EC1V 23 D1
Bertal Rd *TOOT* SW17 ....151 D4
Berthon St *DEPT* SE8....................122 A3
Bertie Rd *WLSDN* NW10 ....70 A3
Bertram Rd *HDN* NW4 ....52 A1
Bertram St *KTTN* NW5 ....56 B5
Bertrand St *LEW* SE13 ....140 B1
Berwick Crs *BFN/LL* DA15 ....145 E4
Berwick Rd *CAN/RD* E16 ....94 B5
Berwick St *SOHO/CST* W1F 19 F5
Berwyn Rd *HNHL* SE24 ....154 B1
    RCHPK/HAM TW10 ....128 B2
Beryl Av *EHAM* E6 ....95 E4
Beryl Rd *HMSMTH* W6 ....113 D1
Besant Cl *CRICK* * NW2 ....53 E5
Besant Rd *CRICK* NW2 ....71 E1
Besant Wy *WLSDN* NW10 ....68 C2
Bessant Dr *RCH/KEW* TW9 ....110 B4
Bessborough Rd *PIM* SW1V 117 D1
Bessborough Rd *PUT/ROE* SW15 ..148 A3
Bessborough St *PIM* SW1V 117 D1
Bessemer Rd *CMBW* SE5 ....118 C5
Bessie Lansbury Cl *EHAM* E6 ....96 A5
Besson St *NWCR* SE14 ....121 D4
Bessy St *BETH* * E2 ....90 C2
Bestwood St *DEPT* SE8 ....103 D5
Beswick Ms *KIL/WHAMP* NW6 ....72 B2
Betchworth Rd *GDMY/SEVK* IG3 ....67 E4
Bethell Av *CAN/RD* E16 ....93 F3
    IL IG1 ....66 A2
Bethnal Green Rd *BETH* E2 ....13 F5
Bethune Rd *STNW/STAM* N16 ....59 D2
    WLSDN NW10 ....87 D3
Bethwin Rd *CMBW* SE5 ....118 B3
Betterton St *LSQ/SEVD* WC2H 20 C5
Bettons Pk *SRTFD* E15 ....81 E5
Bettridge Rd *FUL/PGN* SW6 ....113 F5
Betts Rd *CAN/RD* E16 ....94 B5
Betts St *WCHPL* * E1 ....102 B1
Bevan St *IS* N1 ....76 C5
Bev Callender Cl *VX/NE* SW8 ......134 B1
Bevenden St *IS* N1 ....12 B3
Beveridge Rd *WLSDN* NW10 ....69 E4
Beverley Av *BFN/LL* DA15..............145 A5
Beverley Cl *BARN* SW13 ....112 A5
    BTSEA SW11 ....133 D2
Beverley Ct *BROCKY* SE4 ....139 F1
Beverley Gdns *BARN* SW13 ....129 F1
    GLDGN NW11 ....53 E2
    WBLY HA9 ....50 A3
Beverley Rd *BARN* SW13 ....129 F1
    CHSWK W4 ....111 F1
    EHAM E6 ....95 D2
Beversbrook Rd *ARCH* N19 ....57 D5
Beverstone Rd *BRXS/STRHM* SW2 ..135 F3
Beverston Ms *MBLAR* W1H..............17 E3
Bevin Cl *BERM/RHTH* SE16 ....103 E3
Bevington Rd *NKENS* * W10 ....89 E4

Bevington St *BERM/RHTH* SE16 ....102 A3
Bevin Sq *TOOT* SW17 ....151 F3
Bevin Wy *FSBYW* WC1X 10 A2
Bevis Marks *HDTCH* EC3A 25 D4
Bewdley St *IS* N1 ....76 A4
Bewick Ms *PECK* SE15 ....120 B3
Bewick St *VX/NE* SW8 ....116 B5
Bewley St *WCHPL* E1 ....102 B1
Bewlys Rd *WNWD* SE27 ....154 B5
Bexhill Rd *BROCKY* SE4 ....139 F4
    MORT/ESHN SW14 ....128 C1
Bexley Rd *ELTH/MOT* SE9 ....144 A4
Bianca Rd *PECK* SE15 ....119 F2
Bibury Cl *PECK* SE15 ....119 E2
Bicester Rd *RCH/KEW* TW9 ....128 A1
Bickenhall St *MHST* W1U 17 F2
Bickerton Rd *KTTN* NW5 ....56 B4
Bickley Rd *LEY* E10 ....62 B2
Bickley St *TOOT* SW17 ....151 E5
Bicknell Rd *CMBW* SE5 ....136 C1
Bidborough St *STPAN* WC1H 8 C4
Biddenden Wy *ELTH/MOT* SE9......162 A4
Bidder St *CAN/RD* E16 ....93 E4
Biddestone Rd *HOLWY* N7 ....75 F1
Biddulph Rd *MV/WKIL* W9 ....3 D4
Bideford Rd *BMLY* BR1 ....159 F3
Bidwell St *PECK* * SE15 ....120 B4
Biggerstaff Rd *SRTFD* E15 ....80 C5
Biggerstaff St *FSBYPK* N4 ....58 A4
Bigg's Rw *PUT/ROE* SW15 ....131 D1
Bigland St *WCHPL* E1 ....90 B5
Bignell Rd *WOOL/PLUM* SE18 ......126 B1
Bignold Rd *FSTGT* E7 ....82 A1
Bigwood Rd *GLDGN* NW11 ....54 B1
Bill Hamling Cl *ELTH/MOT* SE9 ....161 F2
Billingford Cl *BROCKY* SE4 ....139 D2
Billing Pl *WBPTN* * SW10 ....114 B3
Billing Rd *WBPTN* SW10 ....114 B3
Billing St *WBPTN* * SW10 ....114 B3
Billington Rd *NWCR* SE14 ....121 D3
Billiter Sq *FENCHST* * EC3M 25 D5
Billiter St *FENCHST* EC3M 25 D5
Billson St *POP/IOD* E14 ....104 C5
Bina Gdns *ECT* SW5 ....39 E5
Binden Rd *SHB* W12 ....99 F4
Binfield Rd *VX/NE* SW8 ....117 E4
Bingfield St *IS* N1 ....75 E5
Bingfield St *IS* N1 ....75 E5
Bingham Ct *IS* * N1 ....76 B4
Bingham Pl *MHST* W1U 18 A1
Bingham St *IS* N1 ....77 D3
Bingley Rd *CAN/RD* E16 ....94 C5
Binney St *MYFR/PKLN* W1K 30 B1
Binns Rd *CHSWK* W4 ....111 E1
Birbetts Rd *ELTH/MOT* SE9 ....161 F2
Birch Cl *CAN/RD* E16 ....93 E4
Birchdale Rd *FSTGT* E7 ....82 C2
Birchen Cl *CDALE/KGS* NW9 ....51 F3
Birchen Gv *CDALE/KGS* NW9 ....51 D4
Birchen La *BANK* EC3V 24 B5
The Birches *CHARL* SE7 ....124 B2
    CMBW * SE5 ....137 E1
Birchfield St *POP/IOD* E14 ....104 A1
Birch Gv *ACT* W3 ....98 A2
    LEE/GVPK SE12 ....141 F5
    WAN E11 ....63 E5
Birchington Rd *CEND/HSY/T* N8 ......57 D1
    KIL/WHAMP NW6 ....72 A5
Birchlands Av *BAL* SW12 ....133 F5
Birchmore Wk *HBRY* N5 ....58 C5
Birchwood Dr *HAMP* NW3 ....54 B5
Birchwood Rd *TOOT* SW17 ....152 B5
Birdbrook Rd *BKHTH/KID* SE3 ......142 C1
Birdcage Wk *STJSPK* SW1H 43 F1
Birdhurst Rd *WAND/EARL* SW18 ....132 C2
Bird in Bush Rd *PECK* SE15 ....120 A3
Bird-in-Hand Pas *FSTH* * SE23 ......156 C2
Birdlip Cl *PECK* SE15 ....119 E2

Birdsfield La *HOM* E9 ....**79** F5
Bird St *MHST* W1U **18** B5
Birkbeck Av *ACT* W3 ....**98** C1
Birkbeck Gv *ACT* W3 ....**99** D2
Birkbeck Hl *DUL* SE21 ....**154** B2
Birkbeck Ms *ACT* * W3 ....**99** D1
   HACK E8 ....**77** F2
Birkbeck Pl *DUL* SE21 ....**154** B1
Birkbeck Rd *ACT* W3 ....**99** D2
   HACK E8 ....**77** F2
   WIM/MER SW19 ....**150** B5
Birkbeck St *BETH* E2 ....**90** D2
Birkdale Cl *BERM/RHTH* * SE16 ....**120** B1
Birkenhead St *IS* N1 ....**9** D3
Birkhall Rd *CAT* SE6 ....**159** D1
Birkwood Cl *BAL* SW12 ....**135** D5
Birley St *BTSEA* SW11 ....**116** A5
Birnam Rd *HOLWY* N7 ....**57** F4
Birse Crs *WLSDN* NW10 ....**69** E1
Biscay Rd *HMSMTH* W6 ....**113** D1
Biscoe Wy *LEW* * SE13 ....**141** D2
Bisham Gdns *HGT* N6 ....**56** B5
Bishop King's Rd *WKENS* W14 ....**101** E5
   WKENS * W14 ....**101** E5
The Bishops Av *EFNCH* N2 ....**55** D1
Bishop's Av *FUL/PGN* SW6 ....**113** D5
   PLSTW E13 ....**82** B5
Bishop's Bridge Rd *BAY/PAD* W2... .....**15** D4
Bishops Cl *CHSWK* W4 ....**110** C1
   ELTH/MOT SE9 ....**162** C2
Bishop's Ct *STP* EC4M **22** C4
Bishopsgate *LVPST* EC2M **24** C3
Bishopsgate Ar *LVPST* EC2M **24** C3
Bishops Gv *EFNCH* N2 ....**55** D1
Bishops Md *CMBW* * SE5 ....**118** C3
Bishop's Park Rd *FUL/PGN* SW6 ....**113** D5
Bishops Rd *FUL/PGN* SW6 ....**113** F4
   HGT N6 ....**56** A1
Bishops Ter *LBTH* SE11 ....**46** B4
Bishopsthorpe Rd *SYD* SE26 ....**156** C4
Bishop St *IS* N1 ....**76** C5
Bishop's Wy *BETH* E2 ....**90** C1
Bishopswood Rd *HGT* N6 ....**55** F2
Bishop Wy *WLSDN* NW10 ....**69** E4
Bisson Rd *STRTFD* E15 ....**92** C1
Bittern St *STHWK* SE1 ....**47** E1
Blackall St *SDTCH* EC2A **12** C5
Blackbird Hl *CDALE/KGS* NW9 ....**50** C4
Blackbird Yd *BETH* E2 ....**13** F3
Blackburne's Ms *MYFR/PKLN* W1K **30** A1
Blackburn Rd *KIL/WHAMP* NW6 ....**72** B3
Blackdown Ter *WOOL/PLUM* * SE18 ...**125** F4
Blackenham Rd *TOOT* SW17 ....**151** F4
Blackett St *PUT/ROE* SW15 ....**131** D1
Blackfen Rd *BFN/LL* DA15 ....**145** F3
Blackfriars Br *EMB* EC4Y **34** C1
Black Friars La *BLKFR* EC4V **22** C5
Blackfriars Pas *BLKFR* EC4V **34** C1
Blackfriars Rd *STHWK* SE1 ....**34** C3
Blackfriars U/P *BLKFR* EC4V **35** D1
Blackheath Av *GNWCH* SE10 ....**123** E3
Blackheath Gv *BKHTH/KID* SE3 ....**123** F5
Blackheath Hl *GNWCH* SE10 ....**122** C4
Blackheath Pk *BKHTH/KID* SE3 ....**124** A5
   BKHTH/KID SE3 ....**141** F1
Blackheath Ri *LEW* SE13 ....**122** C5
Blackheath Rd *GNWCH* SE10 ....**122** B4
Blackheath V *BKHTH/KID* SE3 ....**123** E5
Black Horse Ct *STHWK* * SE1 ....**48** B3
Blackhorse Rd *DEPT* SE8 ....**121** E2
Blacklands Rd *CAT* SE6 ....**158** C4
Blacklands Ter *CHEL* SW3 ....**41** E5
Black Lion Ga *KENS* W8 ....**27** D2
Black Lion La *HMSMTH* W6 ....**100** A5
Blackmans Yd *BETH* * E2 ....**13** F5
Blackpool Rd *PECK* SE15 ....**120** B5
Black Prince Rd *LBTH* SE11 ....**45** E5
Blackshaw Rd *TOOT* SW17 ....**151** D5

Black's Rd *HMSMTH* W6 ....**112** C1
Blackstock Rd *FSBYPK* N4 ....**58** B4
Blackstone Est *HACK* E8 ....**78** A4
Blackstone Rd *CRICK* NW2 ....**70** C2
Black Swan Yd *STHWK* SE1 ....**36** C5
Blackthorn St *BOW* E3 ....**92** A3
Blacktree Ms *BRXN/ST* * SW9 ....**136** A1
Blackwall La *GNWCH* SE10 ....**123** E1
Blackwall Tunnel Northern Ap
   BOW E3 ....**92** B2
Blackwall Wy *POP/IOD* E14 ....**104** C1
Blackwater St *EDUL* SE22 ....**137** F3
Blackwood Cl *CLPT* E5 ....**79** E1
Blackwood St *WALW* SE17 ....**119** D1
Blagdon Rd *LEW* SE13 ....**140** B4
Blagrove Rd *NKENS* W10 ....**89** E4
Blair Av *CDALE/KGS* NW9 ....**51** E2
Blair Cl *BFN/LL* DA15 ....**145** E3
   IS N1 ....**76** C3
Blairderry Rd *BRXS/STRHM* SW2 ....**153** E2
Blair St *POP/IOD* E14 ....**92** C5
Blake Av *BARK* IG11 ....**85** E5
Blake Cl *NKENS* W10 ....**88** C4
   WELL DA16 ....**127** E4
Blake Gdns *FUL/PGN* SW6 ....**114** A4
Blake Hall Rd *WAN* E11 ....**64** A3
Blakemore Rd *STRHM/NOR* SW16 ......**153** E3
Blakeney Cl *CAMTN* NW1 ....**8** A1
   HACK E8 ....**78** A2
Blaker Ct *CHARL* * SE7 ....**124** C3
Blake Rd *CAN/RD* E16 ....**93** F3
Blaker Rd *SRTFD* E15 ....**80** C5
Blake's Rd *PECK* SE15 ....**119** E3
   PECK * SE15 ....**119** E3
Blanchard Cl *ELTH/MOT* SE9 ....**161** E3
Blanchard Wy *HACK* * E8 ....**78** A4
Blanch Cl *PECK* SE15 ....**120** C3
Blanchedowne *CMBW* SE5 ....**137** D2
Blanche St *CAN/RD* E16 ....**93** F3
Blandfield Rd *BAL* SW12 ....**134** A4
Blandford Rd *CHSWK* W4 ....**99** A4
   MHST W1U **17** F4
Blandford Sq *CAMTN* NW1 ....**17** D1
Blandford St *MHST* W1U **17** F4
Bland St *ELTH/MOT* SE9 ....**143** D2
Blaney Crs *EHAM* E6 ....**96** B3
Blanmerle Rd *ELTH/MOT* SE9 ....**162** B1
Blann Cl *ELTH/MOT* SE9 ....**143** D4
Blantyre St *WBPTN* SW10 ....**115** D3
Blantyre Wk *WBPTN* * SW10 ....**115** D3
Blashford St *LEW* SE13 ....**141** D5
Bleak Hill La *WOOL/PLUM* SE18 ....**127** F2
Blechynden St *NKENS* * W10 ....**101** D1
Bleeding Heart Yd *HCIRC* * EC1N **22** B3
Blendon Ter *WOOL/PLUM* SE18 ....**126** C1
Blendworth Wy *PECK* SE15 ....**119** E3
Blenheim Av *GNTH/NBYPK* IG2 ....**66** A1
Blenheim Crs *BRXS/STRHM* SW2 ....**135** F4
   CRICK NW2 ....**70** C2
Blenheim Gv *PECK* SE15 ....**119** E5
Blenheim Pas *STJWD* * NW8 ....**3** E1
Blenheim Rd *CHSWK* W4 ....**99** A4
   EHAM E6 ....**95** D2
   FSTGT E7 ....**81** E1
   STJWD NW8 ....**3** E1
Blenheim St *MYFR/PKLN* W1K **18** C5
Blenheim Ter *STJWD* NW8 ....**3** E1
Blenkarne Rd *BTSEA* SW11 ....**133** F4
Blessington Rd *LEW* SE13 ....**141** D2
Bletchley St *IS* N1 ....**11** F2
Bletsoe Wk *IS* N1 ....**11** F1
Blincoe Cl *WIM/MER* SW19 ....**149** D2
Blissett St *GNWCH* SE10 ....**122** C4
Bliss Ms *NKENS* W10 ....**89** E2
Blithfield St *KENS* W8 ....**38** C3
Bloemfontein Av *SHB* W12 ....**100** B2

Bloemfontein Rd *SHB* W12 ....**100** B1
Blomfield Rd *BAY/PAD* W2 ....**15** D2
Blomfield St *LVPST* EC2M **24** B5
Blomfield Vls *BAY/PAD* W2 ....**15** D3
Blondel St *BTSEA* SW11 ....**116** A5
Blondin St *BOW* E3 ....**92** A1
Bloomfield Crs *GNTH/NBYPK* IG2 ....**66** B1
Bloomfield Pl *MYFR/PKLN* W1K **31** D1
Bloomfield Rd *HGT* N6 ....**56** A1
    WOOL/PLUM SE18 ....**126** B1
Bloomfield Ter *BGVA* SW1W **116** A1
Bloom Gv *SYD* SE27 ....**154** B3
Bloomhall Rd *NRWD* SE19 ....**155** D5
Bloom Park Rd *FUL/PGN* SW6 ....**113** F3
Bloomsbury Pl *NOXST/BSQ* WC1A **21** D3
Bloomsbury Sq *NOXST/BSQ* WC1A **21** D3
Bloomsbury St *RSQ* WC1B **20** B3
Bloomsbury Wy *NOXST/BSQ* WC1A......**20** C3
Blore Cl *VX/NE* SW8 ....**117** D4
Blossom Cl *WCHPL* E1 ....**25** D2
Blount St *POP/IOD* E14 ....**91** E5
Bloxam Gdns *ELTH/MOT* SE9 ....**143** D3
Bloxhall Rd *LEY* E10 ....**61** F5
Blucher Rd *CMBW* SE5 ....**118** C3
Blue Anchor La *BERM/RHTH* SE16 ......**102** A5
Blue Anchor Yd *WCHPL* E1 ....**102** A1
Blue Ball Yd *WHALL* SW1A **31** E4
Bluebell Av *FSTGT* E7 ....**83** D2
Bluebell Cl *HOM* E9 ....**78** C5
    SYD SE26 ....**155** F4
Bluebell Wy *IL* IG1 ....**84** B3
Bluebird Wy *THMD* SE28 ....**109** D3
Blundell St *HOLWY* N7 ....**75** E4
Blunts Rd *ELTH/MOT* SE9 ....**144** A3
Blurton Rd *CLPT* E5 ....**79** D1
Blythe Cl *FSTH* SE23 ....**139** F5
Blythe Hill *FSTH* SE23 ....**139** F5
Blythe Hill La *FSTH* SE23 ....**139** F5
Blythe Hill Pl *FSTH* * SE23 ....**139** E5
Blythe Ms *WKENS* * W14 ....**101** D4
Blythe Rd *WKENS* W14 ....**101** D4
Blythe V *FSTH* SE23 ....**157** F1
Blyth Rd *WALTH* E17 ....**61** F2
Blyth's Whf *POP/IOD* * E14 ....**103** E1
Blythwood Rd *FSBYPK* N4 ....**57** E2
Boadicea St *IS* * N1 ....**75** F5
Boardwalk Pl *POP/IOD* E14 ....**104** C2
Boathouse Wk *PECK* SE15 ....**119** F3
Boat Lifter Wy *BERM/RHTH* SE16 ....**103** E5
Bob Anker Cl *PLSTW* E13 ....**94** A2
Bobbin Cl *CLAP* SW4 ....**134** C1
Bob Marley Wy *HNHL* SE24 ....**136** A2
Bocking St *HACK* E8 ....**78** B5
Boddicott Cl *WIM/MER* SW19 ....**149** E2
Bodmin St *WAND/EARL* SW18 ....**150** A1
Bodney Rd *CLPT* E5 ....**78** C3
Bohemia Pl *HACK* E8 ....**78** C3
Bohn Rd *WCHPL* E1 ....**91** E4
Boileau Rd *BARN* SW13 ....**112** A3
Bolden St *DEPT* SE8 ....**122** B5
Boldero Pl *STJWD* * NW8 ....**16** C1
Boleyn Rd *EHAM* E6 ....**95** D1
    FSTGT E7 ....**82** A4
    STNW/STAM N16 ....**77** E2
Bolina Rd *BERM/RHTH* SE16 ....**120** C1
Bolingbroke Gv *BTSEA* SW11 ....**133** E3
Bolingbroke Rd *WKENS* W14 ....**101** D4
Bolingbroke Wk *BTSEA* * SW11 ....**115** D3
Bollo Bridge Rd *ACT* W3 ....**98** B4
Bollo La *ACT* W3 ....**98** B4
Bolney Gdns *SKENS* SW7 ....**40** C1
Bolney St *VX/NE* SW8 ....**117** F3
Bolsover St *GTPST* W1W **19** D1
Bolt Ct *FLST/FETLN* * EC4A **22** B5
Bolton Crs *CMBW* SE5 ....**118** A2
Bolton Gdns *ECT* SW5 ....**114** B1
    WLSDN NW10 ....**89** D1
Bolton Gardens Ms *WBPTN* SW10 ......**114** B1

Bolton Rd *CHSWK* W4 ....**110** C3
    FSTGT E7 ....**81** F3
    KIL/WHAMP NW6 ....**72** B5
    WLSDN NW10 ....**69** E5
The Boltons *WBPTN* * SW10 ....**114** C1
Boltons Pl *WBPTN* SW10 ....**114** C1
Bolton St *MYFR/PICC* W1J **31** D1
Bombay St *BERM/RHTH* SE16 ....**102** B5
Bomore Rd *NTGHL* W11 ....**101** D1
Bonar Rd *PECK* SE15 ....**120** A3
Bonchurch Rd *NKENS* W10 ....**89** E4
Bond St *SRTFD* E15 ....**81** E2
Bondway *VX/NE* SW8 ....**117** E2
Boneta Rd *WOOL/PLUM* SE18 ....**107** F4
Bonfield Rd *LEW* SE13 ....**140** C2
Bonham Rd *BRXS/STRHM* SW2 ....**135** F3
Bonheur Rd *CHSWK* W4 ....**99** D3
Bonhill St *SDTCH* EC2A **24** B1
Bonita Ms *PECK* SE15 ....**139** D1
Bonner Rd *BETH* E2 ....**90** C1
Bonner St *BETH* * E2 ....**90** C1
Bonneville Gdns *CLAP* SW4 ....**134** C4
Bonnington Sq *VX/NE* SW8 ....**117** F2
Bonny St *CAMTN* NW1 ....**74** C4
Bonsor St *CMBW* SE5 ....**119** E3
Bonville Rd *BMLY* BR1 ....**159** F5
Boones Rd *LEW* SE13 ....**141** E2
Boone St *LEW* SE13 ....**141** E2
Boord St *GNWCH* SE10 ....**105** E4
Boothby Rd *ARCH* N19 ....**57** D4
Booth La *BLKFR* EC4V **35** E1
Boot St *IS* N1 ....**12** C1
Border Crs *SYD* SE26 ....**156** B5
Border Rd *SYD* SE26 ....**156** B5
Bordon Wk *PUT/ROE* SW15 ....**130** A3
Boreas Wk *IS* N1 ....**11** D2
Boreham Av *CAN/RD* E16 ....**94** A5
Borgard House *WOOL/PLUM* SE18 .....**125** E4
Borgard Rd *WOOL/PLUM* SE18 ....**107** F5
Borland Rd *PECK* SE15 ....**138** C2
Borneo St *PUT/ROE* SW15 ....**130** C1
Borough High St *STHWK* SE1 ....**47** F1
Borough Rd *STHWK* SE1 ....**46** C2
Borough Sq *STHWK* SE1 ....**47** E1
Borrett Cl *WALW* SE17 ....**118** C1
Borrodaile Rd *WAND/EARL* SW18 ......**132** B4
Borthwick Ms *SRTFD* * E15 ....**81** E1
Borthwick Rd *CDALE/KGS* NW9 ....**51** F1
    SRTFD E15 ....**122** A1
Borthwick St *DEPT* SE8 ....**122** B5
Bosbury Rd *CAT* SE6 ....**158** C3
Boscastle Rd *KTTN* NW5 ....**56** B5
Boscobel Pl *BGVA* SW1W **42** B4
Boscobel St *BAY/PAD* W2 ....**16** B2
Boscombe Av *LEY* E10 ....**63** D2
Boscombe Cl *CLPT* E5 ....**79** E2
Boscombe Rd *SHB* W12 ....**100** A3
Boss St *STHWK* * SE1 ....**37** E5
Boston Gdns *CHSWK* W4 ....**111** E2
Boston Pl *CAMTN* NW1 ....**17** E1
Boston Rd *EHAM* E6 ....**95** E2
Boswell Ct *BMSBY* WC1N **21** D2
Boswell St *BMSBY* WC1N **21** D2
Bosworth Rd *NKENS* W10 ....**89** E3
Botha Rd *PLSTW* E13 ....**94** B4
Bothwell Cl *CAN/RD* E16 ....**94** A4
Bothwell St *HMSMTH* W6 ....**113** D2
Botolph Aly *MON* EC3R **36** C3
Botolph La *MON* EC3R **36** C2
Bott's Ms *BAY/PAD* W2 ....**14** B5
Boughton Rd *THMD* SE28 ....**109** E4
Boulcott St *WCHPL* E1 ....**91** D5
Boultwood Rd *EHAM* E6 ....**95** F5
Boundaries Rd *BAL* SW12 ....**133** F3
Boundary Av *WALTH* E17 ....**61** F2
Boundary Cl *GDMY/SEVK* IG3 ....**85** E1
Boundary La *PLSTW* E13 ....**95** D2
    WALW SE17 ....**118** C2

Boundary Ms *STJWD* NW8 ....**72** C5
Boundary Rd *BARK* IG11 ....**96** C1
  BFN/LL DA15 ....**145** E3
  PLSTW E13 ....**94** C1
  STJWD NW8 ....**72** C5
  WALTH E17 ....**61** F2
Boundary Rw *STHWK* SE1 ....**34** C5
Boundfield Rd *CAT* SE6 ....**159** E3
Bourchier St *SOHO/CST* W1F **32** A1
Bourdon Pl *MYFR/PKLN* W1K **31** D1
Bourdon St *MYFR/PKLN* W1K **30** C2
Bourke Cl *CLAP* SW4 ....**135** E4
  WLSDN NW10 ....**69** E3
Bourlet Cl *FITZ* W1T **19** E3
Bournbrook Rd *BKHTH/KID* SE3 ....**143** D1
Bourne Est *HCIRC* EC1N **22** A2
Bournemouth Cl *PECK* SE15 ....**120** A5
Bournemouth Rd *PECK* SE15 ....**120** A5
Bourne Rd *CEND/HSY/T* N8 ....**57** E1
  FSTGT E7 ....**63** F5
Bourneside Gdns *CAT* SE6 ....**158** C5
Bourne St *BGVA* SW1W **42** A5
Bourne Ter *BAY/PAD* W2 ....**14** C2
Bournevale Rd *STRHM/NOR* SW16 ....**153** E4
Bournville Rd *CAT* SE6 ....**140** A5
Bousfield Rd *NWCR* SE14 ....**121** D5
Boutflower Rd *BTSEA* SW11 ....**133** E2
Boutique Hall *LEW* * SE13 ....**140** C2
Bouverie Ms *STNW/STAM* N16 ....**59** E4
Bouverie Pl *BAY/PAD* W2 ....**16** B4
Bouverie Rd *STNW/STAM* N16 ....**59** E4
Bouverie St *EMB* EC4Y **22** B5
Boveney Rd *FSTH* SE23 ....**139** D5
Bovill Rd *FSTH* SE23 ....**139** D5
Bovingdon Av *WBLY* HA9 ....**68** A3
Bovingdon Rd *FUL/PGN* SW6 ....**114** B4
Bowater Cl *CLAP* SW4 ....**135** E4
Bowater Pl *BKHTH/KID* SE3 ....**124** B3
Bowater Rd *WOOL/PLUM* SE18 ....**107** D4
Bow Bridge Est *BOW* E3 ....**92** B2
Bow Churchyard *STP* * EC4M **23** F5
Bow Common La *BOW* E3 ....**91** F3
Bowden St *LBTH* SE11 ....**118** A1
Bowditch *DEPT* SE8 ....**121** F1
Bowdon Rd *LEY* E10 ....**62** A2
Bowen Dr *DUL* SE21 ....**155** E3
Bowen St *POP/IOD* E14 ....**92** B5
Bower Av *GNWCH* SE10 ....**123** E4
Bowerdean St *FUL/PGN* SW6 ....**114** B4
Bowerman Av *NWCR* SE14 ....**121** E2
Bower St *WCHPL* * E1 ....**91** D5
Bowes Rd *ACT* W3 ....**99** E1
Bowfell Rd *HMSMTH* W6 ....**112** C2
Bowhill Cl *BRXN/ST* SW9 ....**118** A3
Bowie Cl *CLAP* SW4 ....**135** D5
Bowland Rd *CLAP* SW4 ....**135** D2
Bowland Yd *KTBR* * SW1X **41** F1
Bow La *STP* EC4M **23** F5
Bowley La *NRWD* SE19 ....**155** F5
Bowley St *POP/IOD* E14 ....**103** F1
Bowling Green Cl *PUT/ROE* SW15 ....**130** B5
Bowling Green La *CLKNW* EC1R **22** B1
Bowling Green Pl *STHWK* * SE1 ....**36** A5
Bowling Green Rw
  WOOL/PLUM * SE18 ....**107** F5
Bowling Green Wk *IS* N1 ....**12** C3
Bow Locks *BOW* * E3 ....**92** C3
Bowman Av *CAN/RD* E16 ....**93** F5
Bowman Ms *WAND/EARL* SW18 ....**149** F1
Bowmans Lea *FSTH* SE23 ....**138** C5
Bowman's Ms *HOLWY* N7 ....**57** F5
  WCHPL E1 ....**102** A1
Bowman's Pl *HOLWY* N7 ....**57** E5
Bowmead *ELTH/MOT* SE9 ....**161** F2
Bowmore Wk *CAMTN* NW1 ....**75** D4
Bowness Cl *HACK* * E8 ....**77** F3

Bowness Crs *PUT/ROE* SW15 ....**147** E5
Bowness Rd *CAT* SE6 ....**140** B5
Bowood Rd *BTSEA* SW11 ....**134** A2
Bow Rd *BOW* E3 ....**92** A2
Bow St *COVGDN* WC2E **21** D5
  SRTFD E15 ....**81** E2
Bowyer Cl *EHAM* E6 ....**95** F4
Bowyer Pl *CMBW* SE5 ....**118** C3
Bowyer St *CMBW* SE5 ....**118** C3
Boxall Rd *DUL* SE21 ....**137** E4
Boxley St *CAN/RD* E16 ....**106** B2
Boxworth Gv *IS* N1 ....**75** F5
Boyard Rd *WOOL/PLUM* SE18 ....**126** B1
Boyce Wy *PLSTW* E13 ....**94** A3
Boycroft Av *CDALE/KGS* NW9 ....**50** C1
Boydell Ct *STJWD* NW8 ....**73** D4
Boyd St *WCHPL* E1 ....**90** A5
Boyfield St *STHWK* SE1 ....**47** D1
Boyland Rd *BMLY* BR1 ....**159** F5
Boyne Rd *LEW* SE13 ....**141** D1
Boyne Terrace Ms *NTGHL* * W11 ....**101** F2
Boyson Rd *WALW* SE17 ....**118** C5
Boyton Cl *WCHPL* E1 ....**91** D3
Brabazon St *POP/IOD* E14 ....**92** B5
Brabourne Cl *NRWD* SE19 ....**155** E5
Brabourn Gv *PECK* SE15 ....**120** C5
Bracewell Rd *NKENS* W10 ....**88** C4
Bracey Rd *FSBYPK* * N4 ....**57** E3
Bracken Av *BAL* SW12 ....**134** A4
Brackenbury Gdns *HMSMTH* W6 ....**100** A3
Brackenbury Rd *HMSMTH* W6 ....**100** A3
Bracken Cl *EHAM* E6 ....**95** F4
Bracken Gdns *BARN* SW13 ....**112** A5
Brackley Rd *CHSWK* W4 ....**99** E5
Brackley St *BARB* EC2Y **23** F2
Brackley Ter *CHSWK* W4 ....**111** E1
Bracklyn St *IS* N1 ....**12** A1
Bracknell Gdns *HAMP* NW3 ....**72** B1
Bracknell Wy *HAMP* NW3 ....**72** B1
Bradbourne St *FUL/PGN* SW6 ....**114** A5
Bradbury St *STNW/STAM* N16 ....**77** E2
Braddyll St *GNWCH* SE10 ....**123** E1
Bradenham Cl *WALW* SE17 ....**119** D2
Braden St *MV/WKIL* * W9 ....**14** C1
Bradfield Rd *CAN/RD* E16 ....**106** A3
Bradford Cl *SYD* SE26 ....**156** B4
Bradford Rd *ACT* W3 ....**99** E3
  IL IG1 ....**67** D3
Bradgate Rd *CAT* SE6 ....**140** B4
Brading Crs *WAN* E11 ....**64** B4
Brading Rd *BRXS/STRHM* SW2 ....**135** F5
Brading Ter *SHB* W12 ....**100** A4
Bradiston Rd *MV/WKIL* W9 ....**89** F2
Bradley Cl *HOLWY* N7 ....**75** E4
Bradley's Cl *IS* N1 ....**10** A1
Bradley Stone Rd *EHAM* E6 ....**95** F5
Bradmead *VX/NE* * SW8 ....**116** B4
Bradmore Park Rd *HMSMTH* W6 ....**100** B4
Bradshaw Cottages *POP/IOD* * E14 ....**91** E5
Bradstock Rd *HOM* E9 ....**79** D3
Brad St *STHWK* SE1 ....**34** B4
Bradymead *EHAM* E6 ....**96** A5
Brady St *WCHPL* E1 ....**90** B3
Braemar Av *WIM/MER* SW19 ....**150** A2
  WLSDN NW10 ....**51** D5
Braemar Gdns *BFN/LL* DA15 ....**163** D3
Braemar Rd *PLSTW* E13 ....**94** A3
Braeside *BECK* BR3 ....**158** A5
Braes St *IS* N1 ....**76** B4
Braganza St *WALW* SE17 ....**118** B1
Braham St *WCHPL* E1 ....**25** F5
Braid Av *ACT* W3 ....**87** E5
Braidwood Rd *CAT* SE6 ....**159** D1
Brailsford Rd *BRXS/STRHM* SW2 ....**136** A4
Braintree St *BETH* * E2 ....**90** C2
Bramall Cl *FSTGT* E7 ....**81** F2
Bramber Rd *FUL/PGN* SW6 ....**113** F2
Bramblebury Rd *WOOL/PLUM* SE18 ....**127** D1

Bramble Gdns *SHB* W12 ....99 F1
The Brambles *WIM/MER* * SW19 ....149 F5
Bramcote Gv *BERM/RHTH* SE16 ....120 C1
Bramcote Rd *PUT/ROE* SW15 ....130 B2
Bramdean Crs *LEE/GVPK* SE12 ....160 A1
Bramdean Gdns *LEE/GVPK* SE12 ....160 A1
Bramerton St *CHEL* SW3 ....115 E2
Bramfield Rd *BTSEA* SW11 ....133 E4
Bramford Rd *WAND/EARL* SW18 ....132 C2
Bramham Gdns *ECT* SW5 ....114 B1
Bramhope La *CHARL* SE7 ....124 B2
Bramlands Cl *BTSEA* SW11 ....133 E1
Bramley Rd *GNTH/NBYPK* IG2 ....66 A1
   VX/NE SW8 ....117 D3
Bramley Rd *NKENS* W10 ....101 D1
Brampton Cl *CLPT* E5 ....60 B4
Brampton Gv *WBLY* HA9 ....50 A3
Brampton Rd *EHAM* E6 ....95 D3
Bramshaw Rd *HOM* E9 ....79 D3
Bramshill Gdns *KTTN* NW5 ....56 B5
Bramshill Rd *WLSDN* NW10 ....87 E1
Bramshot Av *CHARL* SE7 ....124 B2
Bramston Rd *WLSDN* NW10 ....88 A1
Bramwell Ms *IS* N1 ....75 F5
Brancaster Rd *GNTH/NBYPK* IG2 ....67 D1
   STRHM/NOR SW16 ....153 E3
Branch Hl *HAMP* NW3 ....54 C5
Branch Pl *IS* N1 ....77 D5
Branch Rd *POP/IOD* E14 ....91 E5
Branch St *CMBW* SE5 ....119 E3
Brand Cl *FSBYPK* N4 ....58 B3
Brandlehow Rd *PUT/ROE* SW15 ....131 F1
Brandon Est *WALW* SE17 ....118 B2
Brandon Ms *BARB* * EC2Y 24 A2
Brandon Rd *HOLWY* N7 ....75 E4
Brandon St *WALW* SE17 ....47 F5
Brandram Ms *LEW* * SE13 ....141 E2
Brandram Rd *LEW* SE13 ....141 E1
Brandreth Rd *EHAM* E6 ....95 F5
   TOOT SW17 ....152 B2
Brand St *GNWCH* SE10 ....122 C3
Brangbourne Rd *BMLY* BR1 ....158 C5
Brangton Rd *LBTH* SE11 ....117 F1
Branksea St *FUL/PGN* SW6 ....113 E3
Branksome Rd *BRXS/STRHM* SW2 ....135 E3
Branscombe St *LEW* SE13 ....140 B1
Bransdale Cl *KIL/WHAMP* NW6 ....72 A5
Brantwood Rd *HNHL* SE24 ....136 C5
Brasenose Dr *BARN* SW13 ....112 C2
Brassey Rd *KIL/WHAMP* NW6 ....71 F3
Brassey Sq *BTSEA* SW11 ....134 A1
Brassie Av *ACT* W3 ....87 D4
Brasted Cl *SYD* SE26 ....156 C4
Brathway Rd *WAND/EARL* SW18 ....132 A5
Bratley St *WCHPL* E1 ....90 A3
Braundton Av *BFN/LL* DA15 ....163 F1
Bravington Pl *MV/WKIL* W9 ....89 F3
Bravington Rd *MV/WKIL* W9 ....89 F2
Braxfield Rd *BROCKY* SE4 ....139 E2
Brayard's Rd *PECK* SE15 ....120 B5
Braybrook St *SHB* W12 ....87 F4
Brayburne Av *VX/NE* SW8 ....116 C5
Bray Crs *BERM/RHTH* SE16 ....103 D3
Braydon Rd *STNW/STAM* N16 ....59 F3
Bray Dr *CAN/RD* E16 ....105 F2
Brayfield Ter *IS* N1 ....76 A4
Brayford Sq *WCHPL* * E1 ....90 C5
Bray Pl *CHEL* SW3 ....115 F1
Braywood Rd *ELTH/MOT* SE9 ....145 D2
Bread St *BLKFR* EC4V 35 F1
   STP EC4M 23 F1
Breakspears Ms *BROCKY* SE4 ....122 A5
Breakspears Rd *BROCKY* SE4 ....139 F1
Bream Gdns *EHAM* E6 ....96 A2
Breamore Cl *PUT/ROE* SW15 ....148 A1
Breamore Rd *GDMY/SEVK* IG3 ....67 F4
Bream's Buildings *LINN* WC2A 22 A4
Bream St *BOW* E3 ....80 A4

Breasley Cl *PUT/ROE* SW15 ....130 B2
Brechin Pl *SKENS* SW7 ....114 C1
Brecknock Rd *ARCH* N19 ....74 C1
Brecknock Road Est *ARCH* * N19 ....75 D2
Brecon Gn *CDALE/KGS* * NW9 ....51 E1
Brecon Ms *KTTN* NW5 ....75 D3
Brecon Rd *HMSMTH* W6 ....113 E2
Brede Cl *EHAM* E6 ....96 A2
Bredgar Rd *ARCH* N19 ....56 C4
Breer St *FUL/PGN* SW6 ....132 B1
Breezer's HI *WAP* * E1W 102 A1
Bremner Rd *SKENS* SW7 ....39 F1
Brenchley Gdns *FSTH* SE23 ....138 C4
Brenda Rd *TOOT* SW17 ....151 F2
Brendon Av *WLSDN* NW10 ....69 E1
Brendon Rd *CHST* BR7 ....163 D3
Brendon St *MBLAR* W1H 17 D4
Brenley Gdns *ELTH/MOT* SE9 ....143 D2
Brent Cross F/O *HDN* NW4 ....52 C1
Brentfield *WLSDN* NW10 ....68 B4
Brentfield Cl *WLSDN* NW10 ....69 D3
Brentfield Gdns *CRICK* * NW2 ....53 D2
Brentfield Rd *WLSDN* NW10 ....69 D3
Brenthouse Rd *HACK* E8 ....78 B4
Brenthurst Rd *WLSDN* NW10 ....69 F3
Brenton St *POP/IOD* E14 ....91 E5
Brent Park Rd *CDALE/KGS* NW9 ....52 A3
Brent Rd *CAN/RD* E16 ....94 A5
   WOOL/PLUM SE18 ....126 B3
Brent Ter *CRICK* NW2 ....52 C3
Brent View Rd *CDALE/KGS* NW9 ....52 A1
Brent Wy *WBLY* HA9 ....68 B3
Brentwood Cl *ELTH/MOT* SE9 ....162 C1
Bressenden Pl *WESTW* SW1E 43 D2
Brett Cl *STNW/STAM* N16 ....59 E4
Brett Crs *WLSDN* NW10 ....69 D4
Brettell St *WALW* SE17 ....119 D1
Brett Pas *HACK* E8 ....78 B2
Brett Rd *HACK* E8 ....78 B2
Brett Vls *ACT* * W3 ....87 D4
Brewer St *REGST* W1B 31 F1
Brewery Rd *HOLWY* N7 ....75 E4
   WOOL/PLUM SE18 ....127 D1
Brewery Sq *STHWK* SE1 ....37 E4
Brewhouse La *WAP* E1W 102 B2
Brewhouse Rd *WOOL/PLUM* SE18 ....107 F5
Brewhouse St *PUT/ROE* SW15 ....131 E2
Brewhouse Wk *BERM/RHTH* SE16 ....103 E2
Brewhouse Yd *FSBYE* EC1V 10 C5
Brewster Gdns *NKENS* W10 ....88 C4
Brewster Rd *LEY* E10 ....62 B3
Briant St *NWCR* SE14 ....121 D4
Briardale Gdns *HAMP* NW3 ....54 A5
Briar Rd *CRICK* NW2 ....70 C1
Briar Wk *NKENS* * W10 ....89 E3
   PUT/ROE SW15 ....130 B2
Briarwood Cl *CDALE/KGS* * NW9 ....50 C1
Briarwood Rd *CLAP* SW4 ....135 D3
Briary Cl *HAMP* * NW3 ....73 E4
Briary Gdns *BMLY* BR1 ....160 B5
Brickbarn Cl *WBPTN* * SW10 ....114 C3
Brick Ct *EMB* * EC4Y 22 A5
Brickfield Rd *BOW* E3 ....92 B3
   WIM/MER SW19 ....150 B4
Brick La *BETH* E2 ....13 F4
   WCHPL E1 ....25 F1
Brick St *MYFR/PICC* W1J 30 C4
Brickwood Cl *SYD* SE26 ....156 B3
Bridale Cl *PECK* * SE15 ....119 F2
Bride Ct *BLKFR* * EC4Y 22 C5
Bride La *EMB* EC4Y 22 C5
Bridel Ms *FSBYE* EC1V 10 C2
Bridet St *HOLWY* N7 ....75 F3
Bridewain St *STHWK* SE1 ....49 E2
Bridewell Pl *BLKFR* EC4V 22 C5

WAP E1W	102	B2
Bridford Ms *REGST* W1B	19	D2
Bridge Av *HMSMTH* W6	112	C1
Bridge CI *NKENS* W10	89	D5
Bridge House Quay *POP/IOD* E14	104	C2
Bridgeland Rd *CAN/RD* E16	106	A1
Bridge La *BTSEA* SW11	115	E4
Bridgeman Rd *IS* N1	75	F4
Bridgeman St *STJWD* NW8	4	C2
Bridge Mdw *NWCR* SE14	121	D2
Bridge Pde *STRHM/NOR* * SW16	153	E5
Bridge PI *PIM* SW1V	43	D4
Bridgeport PI *WAP* * E1W	102	A2
Bridge Rd *EHAM* E6	83	F4
LEY E10	61	F2
SRTFD E15	81	D5
WBLY HA9	50	A5
WLSDN NW10	69	E3
Bridges Ct *BTSEA* SW11	133	D1
Bridge St *CHSWK* W4	99	D5
WEST SW1P	44	C1
Bridge Ter *LEW* * SE13	141	D2
SRTFD E15	81	D4
Bridgetown CI *NRWD* SE19	155	E5
Bridgeview *HMSMTH* W6	112	C1
Bridge Vls *WIM/MER* * SW19	150	A5
Bridgewater Rd *SRTFD* E15	80	C5
Bridgewater Sq *BARB* * EC2Y	23	E4
Bridgewater St *BARB* EC2Y	23	E2
Bridgeway *BARK* IG11	85	F4
Bridgeway St *CAMTN* NW1	7	F2
Bridgford St *WAND/EARL* SW18	150	C3
Bridgman Rd *CHSWK* W4	98	C4
Bridle La *SOHO/CST* W1F	31	F1
Bridport PI *IS* N1	12	B1
Bridstow PI *BAY/PAD* W2	14	B4
Brief St *CMBW* SE5	118	B4
Brierley Rd *BAL* SW12	152	C2
WAN E11	81	D1
Brierly Gdns *BETH* * E2	90	C1
Brigade St *BKHTH/KID* * SE3	123	F5
Briggeford CI *CLPT* E5	60	A4
Brightfield Rd *LEW* SE13	141	E3
Brightling Rd *BROCKY* SE4	139	F4
Brightlingsea Pl *POP/IOD* E14	103	F1
Brightman Rd *WAND/EARL* SW18	151	D1
Brighton Rd *EHAM* E6	96	A2
STNW/STAM N16	77	E1
Brighton Ter *BRXN/ST* SW9	135	F2
Brightside Rd *LEW* SE13	141	D4
Bright St *POP/IOD* E14	92	B5
Brightwell Crs *TOOT* SW17	151	F5
Brig Ms *DEPT* SE8	122	A2
Brill PI *CAMTN* NW1	8	B2
Brindle Ga *BFN/LL* DA15	163	E1
Brindley St *NWCR* SE14	121	F4
Brindley Wy *BMLY* BR1	160	A5
Brinklow Crs *WOOL/PLUM* SE18	126	B3
Brinkworth Wy *HOM* * E9	79	F3
Brinsley St *WCHPL* * E1	90	B5
Brinton Wk *STHWK* SE1	34	C4
Brion PI *POP/IOD* E14	92	C4
Brisbane Rd *IL* IG1	66	C2
LEY E10	62	B4
Brisbane St *CMBW* SE5	119	D3
Briscoe CI *WAN* E11	63	F4
Briset Rd *ELTH/MOT* SE9	143	D1
Briset St *FARR* EC1M	22	C2
Briset Wy *HOLWY* N7	57	F4
Bristol Gdns *MV/WKIL* W9	15	D1
Bristol Ms *MV/WKIL* W9	15	D1
Bristol Rd *FSTGT* E7	82	C3
Briston Gv *CEND/HSY/T* N8	57	E1
Bristow Rd *NRWD* SE19	155	E5
Britannia CI *CLAP* SW4	135	D2
Britannia Ga *CAN/RD* E16	106	A2
Britannia Rd *FUL/PGN* SW6	114	B3
IL IG1	66	B5
Britannia Rw *IS* N1	76	B5
Britannia St *FSBYW* WC1X	9	E3
Britannia Wk *IS* N1	12	A1
Britannia Wy *FUL/PGN* SW6	114	B3
WLSDN NW10	86	B3
British Est *BOW* E3	91	F2
British Gv *CHSWK* W4	111	F1
British Grove Pas *CHSWK* * W4	111	F1
British St *BOW* E3	91	F2
Britten CI *GLDGN* NW11	54	B3
Britten St *CHEL* SW3	115	E1
Britton CI *CAT* SE6	141	D5
Britton St *FARR* EC1M	22	C1
Brixham Gdns *GDMY/SEVK* IG3	85	E2
Brixham Rd *CAN/RD* E16	107	F2
Brixton HI *BRXS/STRHM* SW2	135	F4
Brixton Hill PI *BRXS/STRHM* SW2	135	E5
Brixton Ov *BRXN/ST* SW9	136	A2
Brixton Rd *LBTH* SE11	118	A2
Brixton Station Rd *BRXN/ST* SW9	136	A1
Brixton Water La *BRXS/STRHM* SW2	135	F3
Broadbent St *MYFR/PKLN* * W1K	30	C1
Broad Bridge CI *BKHTH/KID* SE3	124	A3
Broad Common Est		
STNW/STAM * N16	60	A3
Broad Ct *COVGDN* * WC2E	21	D5
Broadfield La *CRICK* NW2	52	C5
Broadfield La *HOLWY* N7	75	E4
Broadfield Rd *CAT* SE6	159	E1
Broadfields Wy *WLSDN* NW10	69	F1
Broadgates Rd *WAND/EARL* SW18	151	D1
Broadheath Dr *CHST* BR7	161	F5
Broadhinton Rd *CLAP* SW4	134	B1
Broadhurst Av *GDMY/SEVK* IG3	85	F1
Broadhurst CI *KIL/WHAMP* NW6	72	C3
Broadhurst Gdns *KIL/WHAMP* NW6	72	B3
Broadlands Av *STRHM/NOR* SW16	153	E2
Broadlands CI *HGT* N6	56	A2
STRHM/NOR SW16	153	E2
Broadlands Rd *BMLY* BR1	160	B4
HGT N6	55	F2
Broad Lawn *ELTH/MOT* SE9	162	A1
Broadley St *STJWD* NW8	16	C2
Broadley Ter *CAMTN* NW1	17	D1
Broadmead *CAT* SE6	158	A3
Broadstone PI *MHST* W1U	18	A3
Broad Street Av *LVPST* EC2M	24	C3
Broad Street PI *LVPST* EC2M	24	B3
Broadview *CDALE/KGS* NW9	50	A1
The Broad Wk *KENS* W8	27	D3
Broad Wk *BKHTH/KID* SE3	124	C5
Broadwalk La *GLDGN* NW11	53	F2
Broadwall *STHWK* SE1	34	B3
Broadwater Rd *TOOT* SW17	151	E4
WOOL/PLUM SE18	109	D4
The Broadway *ACT* * W3	98	A3
CDALE/KGS NW9	51	F1
CEND/HSY/T N8	57	E1
PLSTW E13	94	A1
Broadway *BARK* IG11	84	C5
SRTFD E15	81	D4
STJSPK SW1H	44	A1
Broadway Market *HACK* E8	78	B5
Broadway Market Ms *HACK* * E8	78	A5
Broadway Ms *STNW/STAM* N16	59	F2
Broadwell Pde *KIL/WHAMP* * NW6	72	C3
Broadwick St *SOHO/CST* W1F	19	F5
Broadwood Ter *WKENS* * W14	101	F5
Broad Yd *FARR* EC1M	22	C1
Brocas CI *HAMP* NW3	73	E4
Brockdish Av *BARK* IG11	85	F2
Brockenhurst Gdns *IL* IG1	84	C2
Brockham CI *WIM/MER* SW19	149	F5
Brockham Dr *BRXS/STRHM* SW2	135	F5
GNTH/NBYPK IG2	66	C1
Brockham St *STHWK* SE1	47	F2
Brockill Crs *BROCKY* SE4	139	E2

Brocklebank Rd CHARL SE7 ....106 B5
WAND/EARL SW18 ....132 C5
Brocklehurst St NWCR SE14 ....121 D3
Brockley Cross BROCKY SE4 ....139 E1
Brockley Gv BROCKY SE4 ....139 F3
Brockley Hall Rd BROCKY SE4 ....139 E4
Brockley Ms BROCKY SE4 ....139 E3
Brockley Pk FSTH SE23 ....139 E5
Brockley Ri FSTH SE23 ....139 E4
Brockley Rd BROCKY SE4 ....139 E4
Brockley Vw FSTH SE23 ....139 E5
Brockley Wy FSTH SE23 ....139 D3
Brockman Ri BMLY BR1 ....159 D4
Brock Pl BOW E3 ....92 B3
Brock Rd PLSTW E13 ....94 B4
Brock St PECK * SE15 ....138 C1
Brockway Cl WAN E11 ....63 E4
Brockwell Park Gdns HNHL SE24 ....136 B5
Brockworth Cl PECK SE15 ....119 E2
Brodia Rd STNW/STAM N16 ....59 E5
Brodie St STHWK SE1 ....119 F1
Brodlove La WAP E1W 103 D1
Brodrick Rd TOOT SW17 ....151 F1
TOOT SW17 ....151 E2
Brokesley St BOW E3 ....91 F3
Broke Wk HACK * E8 ....78 A5
Bromar Rd CMBW SE5 ....137 E1
Bromehead St WCHPL E1 ....90 C5
Brome House WOOL/PLUM SE18 ....125 E3
Bromell's Rd CLAP SW4 ....134 C2
Brome Rd ELTH/MOT SE9 ....143 F1
Bromfelde Rd CLAP SW4 ....135 D1
Bromfield St IS N1 ....10 B1
Bromhedge ELTH/MOT SE9 ....161 F3
Bromley Hall Rd POP/IOD E14 ....92 C4
Bromley High St BOW E3 ....92 B2
Bromley Rd CAT SE6 ....158 B2
LEY E10 ....62 B1
Bromley St WCHPL E1 ....91 D4
Brompton Ar KTBR * SW1X 41 E1
Brompton Cottages WBPTN * SW10 ....114 C2
Brompton Park Crs FUL/PGN SW6 ....114 B2
Brompton Pl CHEL SW3 ....41 D2
Brompton Rd CHEL SW3 ....40 C2
Brompton Sq CHEL SW3 ....40 C2
Brompton Ter WOOL/PLUM * SE18 ....126 A4
Bromwich Av HGT N6 ....56 A4
Bromyard Av ACT W3 ....99 E2
Brondesbury Ms KIL/WHAMP * NW6 ....72 A4
Brondesbury Pk CRICK NW2 ....70 C4
Brondesbury Rd KIL/WHAMP NW6 ....89 F1
Brondesbury Vls KIL/WHAMP NW6 ....89 F1
Bronsart Rd FUL/PGN SW6 ....113 E3
Bronte Cl FSTGT * E7 ....82 A1
Bronti Cl WALW SE17 ....118 C1
Bronze St DEPT SE8 ....122 A3
Brook Av WBLY HA9 ....50 A5
Brookbank Rd LEW SE13 ....140 A1
Brook Cl ACT W3 ....98 A2
TOOT SW17 ....152 A2
Brookdale Rd CAT SE6 ....140 B5
Brookdene Rd WOOL/PLUM SE18 ....109 E5
Brook Dr STHWK SE1 ....46 B3
Brookehowse Rd CAT SE6 ....158 B3
Brookend Rd BFN/LL DA15 ....163 E1
Brooke Rd CLPT E5 ....60 A5
Brooke's Market HCIRC * EC1N 22 C1
Brooke St HCIRC EC1N 22 A3
Brookfield Pk KTTN NW5 ....56 B3
Brookfield Rd CHSWK W4 ....99 D3
HOM E9 ....79 E3
Brook Gdns BARN SW13 ....129 F1
Brook Ga BAY/PAD W2 ....29 E2
Brook Gn HMSMTH W6 ....100 C4
Brook Hill Cl WOOL/PLUM SE18 ....126 B1
Brookhill Rd WOOL/PLUM SE18 ....126 B1
Brooking Rd FSTGT E7 ....82 A1
Brooklands Av BFN/LL DA15 ....163 D2

WAND/EARL SW18 ....150 B2
Brooklands Ct KIL/WHAMP * NW6 ....71 F4
Brooklands Pk BKHTH/KID SE3 ....142 A1
Brook La North BAY/PAD W2 ....27 F1
Brook Ms North BAY/PAD W2 ....27 F1
Brookmill Rd DEPT SE8 ....122 A4
Brook Rd CRICK NW2 ....52 A4
GNTH/NBYPK IG2 ....67 E1
Brooks Av EHAM E6 ....95 F3
Brooksbank St HOM * E9 ....79 D3
Brooksby Ms IS N1 ....76 A4
Brooksby St IS N1 ....76 A4
Brooksby's Wk HOM E9 ....79 D2
Brookside Rd GLDGN NW11 ....53 E1
Brooks La CHSWK W4 ....110 A2
Brooks Rd CHSWK W4 ....110 A1
PLSTW E13 ....82 A5
Brook St BAY/PAD W2 ....28 B1
MYFR/PKLN W1K 30 C1
Brooksville Av KIL/WHAMP NW6 ....71 E5
Brookview Rd STRHM/NOR SW16 ....152 C5
Brookville Rd FUL/PGN SW6 ....113 F5
Brookway BKHTH/KID SE3 ....142 A1
Brookwood Av BARN SW13 ....129 F1
Brookwood Rd WAND/EARL SW18 ....149 F1
Broome Wy CMBW SE5 ....119 D3
Broomfield WALTH E17 ....61 F2
Broomfield St POP/IOD E14 ....92 A4
Broomgrove Rd BRXN/ST SW9 ....117 F5
Broomhill Rd WAND/EARL SW18 ....132 A3
Broomhouse La FUL/PGN SW6 ....114 A5
Broomhouse Rd FUL/PGN SW6 ....114 A5
Broomsleigh St KIL/WHAMP * NW6 ....72 A2
Broomwood Rd BTSEA SW11 ....133 E4
Broseley Gv SYD SE26 ....157 E5
Brougham Rd ACT W3 ....86 C5
HACK E8 ....78 A5
Brougham St BTSEA SW11 ....115 F5
Brough Cl VX/NE SW8 ....117 E3
Broughton Dr HNHL SE24 ....136 A2
Broughton Gdns HGT N6 ....56 C1
Broughton Rd FUL/PGN SW6 ....114 B5
Broughton Road Ap FUL/PGN * SW6 ....114 B5
Broughton St VX/NE SW8 ....116 A5
Brouncker Rd ACT W3 ....98 C3
Brownfield St POP/IOD E14 ....92 A4
Brown Hart Gdns MYFR/PKLN W1K 30 B1
Brownhill Rd CAT SE6 ....140 C5
Browning Cl MV/WKIL * W9 ....15 F1
WELL DA16 ....127 F1
Browning Ms MNPK E12 ....83 F3
WAN E11 ....63 F2
Browning St WALW SE17 ....118 C1
Brownlow Ms FSBYW WC1X 9 F5
Brownlow Rd FSTGT E7 ....82 A1
HACK E8 ....77 F5
WLSDN NW10 ....69 E4
Brownlow St GINN WC1R 21 F5
Brownspring Dr ELTH/MOT SE9 ....162 B3
Brown St MBLAR W1H 17 E4
Brownswood Rd FSBYPK N4 ....58 C4
Broxash Rd BTSEA SW11 ....134 A4
Broxbourne House BOW E3 ....92 B3
Broxbourne Rd FSTGT E7 ....64 A5
Broxholm Rd WNWD SE27 ....154 A3
Broxted Rd FSTH SE23 ....157 F2
Broxwood Wy STJWD NW8 ....73 E5
Bruce Cl NKENS W10 ....89 D4
Bruce Rd BOW E3 ....92 B2
WLSDN NW10 ....69 D4
Bruckner St NKENS W10 ....89 E2
Brudenell Rd TOOT SW17 ....151 F3
Bruges Pl CAMTN NW1 ....74 C2
Brunel Cl WLSDN NW10 ....88 A2
Brunel Est BAY/PAD W2 ....14 A3
Brunel Rd ACT W3 ....87 E4

BERM/RHTH SE16 ....**102** C2
WALTH E17 ....**61** E1
Brunel St *CAN/RD* E16 ....**93** F5
Brune St *WCHPL* E1 ....**25** E3
Bruno Pl *WBLY* HA9 ....**50** C4
Brunswick Ct *STHWK* SE1 ....**49** D1
Brunswick Gdns *KENS* W8 ....**26** B4
Brunswick Ms *MBLAR* W1H **17** F3
Brunswick Pk *CMBW* SE5 ....**119** D4
Brunswick Pl *CAMTN* NW1 ....**18** D1
IS N1 ....**12** B4
Brunswick Quay *BERM/RHTH* SE16 ...**103** D4
Brunswick Rd *LEY* E10 ....**62** C3
Brunswick Sq *BMSBY* WC1N **9** D5
Brunswick Vls *CMBW* SE5 ....**119** E4
Brunton Pl *POP/IOD* E14 ....**91** F3
Brushfield St *WCHPL* E1 ....**25** D2
Brussels Rd *BTSEA* SW11 ....**133** D2
Bruton Av *MYFR/PICC* W1J **31** D2
Bruton Pl *MYFR/PKLN* W1K **31** D2
Bruton St *MYFR/PICC* W1J **31** D2
Bryan Av *WLSDN* NW10 ....**70** B3
Bryan Rd *BERM/RHTH* SE16 ....**103** F3
Bryanston Ms East *MBLAR* W1H ...**17** F3
Bryanston Ms West *MBLAR* W1H ...**17** F3
Bryanston Pl *MBLAR* W1H **17** F3
Bryanston Sq *MBLAR* W1H **17** F4
Bryanston St *MBLAR* W1H **17** F5
Bryant St *SRTFD* E15 ....**81** D4
Bryantwood Rd *HOLWY* N7 ....**76** A2
Bryden Cl *SYD* SE26 ....**157** E5
Brydges Pl *CHCR* WC2N **32** C3
Brydges Rd *SRTFD* E15 ....**81** D2
Brydon Wk *IS* N1 ....**75** E5
Bryett Rd *HOLWY* N7 ....**57** E5
Brymay Cl *BOW* E3 ....**92** A1
Brynmaer Rd *BTSEA* SW11 ....**115** F4
Bryony Rd *SHB* W12 ....**100** A1
Buchanan Gdns *WLSDN* NW10 ...**88** B3
Buchan Rd *PECK* SE15 ....**138** C1
Bucharest Rd *WAND/EARL* SW18 ...**132** C5
Buckden Cl *LEE/GVPK* SE12 ....**141** F4
Buckfast St *BETH* E2 ....**90** A2
Buckhold Rd *WAND/EARL* SW18 ...**132** A4
Buckhurst St *WCHPL* E1 ....**90** B3
Buckingham Av *WELL* DA16 ....**145** E2
Buckingham Dr *CHST* BR7 ....**162** B5
Buckland Crs *HAMP* NW3 ....**73** D4
Buckland Rd *LEY* E10 ....**62** C4
Buckland St *IS* N1 ....**12** B2
Bucklersbury *MANHO* * EC4N **24** A3
Buckle St *WCHPL* E1 ....**25** E2
Buckley Rd *KIL/WHAMP* NW6 ......**71** F4
Buckmaster Rd *BTSEA* SW11 .....**133** E2
Bucknall St *NOXST/BSQ* WC1A ...**20** C4
Buckner Rd *BRXS/STRHM* SW2 ...**135** D2
Buckstone Cl *FSTH* SE23 ....**138** C4
Buck St *CAMTN* NW1 ....**74** B5
Buckters Rents *BERM/RHTH* SE16 ...**103** E2
Buckthorne Rd *BROCKY* SE4 ....**139** E4
Buddings Cir *WBLY* HA9 ....**50** C5
Budge Wy *MANHO* EC4N **36** A1
Buer Rd *FUL/PGN* SW6 ....**113** E5
Bugsby's Wy *GNWCH* SE10 ....**105** F4
Bulinca St *WEST* * SW1P **44** C5
Bullace Rw *CMBW* SE5 ....**119** D4

Bullar Cl *PECK* SE15 ....**120** A3
Bullards Pl *BETH* E2 ....**91** D2
Bulleid Wy *PIM* SW1V **43** D5
Bullen St *BTSEA* SW11 ....**115** E5
Buller Rd *BARK* IG11 ....**85** E4
WLSDN NW10 ....**89** D2
Bullivant St *POP/IOD* E14 ....**104** C1
Bull Rd *SRTFD* E15 ....**93** F1
Bulls Aly *MORT/ESHN* * SW14 .....**129** D1
Bull Yd *PECK* SE15 ....**120** A4
Bulmer Ms *NTGHL* W11 ....**26** A3
Bulstrode Pl *MHST* W1U **18** B3
Bulstrode St *MHST* W1U **18** B4
Bulwer Court Rd *WAN* E11 ....**63** D3
Bulwer Rd *WAN* E11 ....**63** D3
Bulwer St *SHB* W12 ....**100** C2
Bunhill Rw *STLK* EC1Y **12** A5
Bunhouse Pl *BGVA* SW1W **116** A5
Bunning Wy *HOLWY* * N7 ....**75** E4
Bunsen St *BOW* E3 ....**91** E1
Bunton St *WOOL/PLUM* SE18 .....**108** A4
Buonaparte Ms *PIM* SW1V **117** D1
Burbage Cl *STHWK* SE1 ....**48** A3
Burbage Rd *HNHL* SE24 ....**137** D4
Burcham St *POP/IOD* E14 ....**92** B5
Burchell Rd *LEY* E10 ....**62** B3
PECK SE15 ....**120** B4
Burcote Rd *WAND/EARL* SW18 ...**151** D1
Burdenshott Av *RCHPK/HAM* TW10 ...**128** B2
Burden Wy *WAN* E11 ....**64** B4
Burder Cl *IS* N1 ....**77** E3
Burder Rd *IS* N1 ....**77** E3
Burdett Rd *BOW* E3 ....**91** F3
Burfield Cl *TOOT* SW17 ....**150** C4
Burford Rd *CAT* SE6 ....**157** F2
EHAM E6 ....**95** E2
SRTFD E15 ....**81** D4
Burford Wk *FUL/PGN* * SW6 ....**114** B3
Burges Gv *BARN* SW13 ....**112** B3
Burges Rd *EHAM* E6 ....**84** A4
Burgess Av *CDALE/KGS* NW9 .....**51** D1
Burgess Hl *CRICK* NW2 ....**72** A1
Burgess Rd *SRTFD* E15 ....**81** E1
Burgess St *POP/IOD* E14 ....**92** A4
Burge St *STHWK* SE1 ....**48** B3
Burghill Rd *SYD* SE26 ....**157** D4
Burghley Hall Cl *WIM/MER* * SW19 ...**149** E1
Burghley Rd *KTTN* NW5 ....**74** B1
WAN * E11 ....**63** E3
WIM/MER SW19 ....**149** D1
Burgh St *IS* N1 ....**11** D1
Burgon St *BLKFR* EC4V **23** D5
Burgon Street Hl *BLKFR* EC4V **23** D5
Burgos Gv *GNWCH* SE10 ....**122** B4
Burgoyne Rd *BRXN/ST* SW9 ......**135** F1
FSBYPK N4 ....**58** B1
Burke Cl *PUT/ROE* SW15 ....**129** E2
Burke St *CAN/RD* E16 ....**93** F4
Burland Rd *BTSEA* SW11 ....**133** F3
Burleigh Av *BFN/LL* DA15 ....**145** F3
Burleigh Pl *PUT/ROE* SW15 ....**131** D3
Burleigh St *COVGDN* WC2E **33** D1
Burleigh Wk *CAT* SE6 ....**158** C1
Burley Rd *CAN/RD* E16 ....**94** C5
Burlington Ar *CONDST* W1S **31** E2
Burlington Av *RCH/KEW* TW9 ......**110** A4
Burlington Cl *EHAM* E6 ....**95** E5
MV/WKIL W9 ....**2** A5
Burlington Gdns *ACT* W3 ....**98** C2
CHSWK W4 ....**110** C1
CONDST W1S **31** E2
Burlington La *CHSWK* W4 ....**110** C3
Burlington Ms *ACT* W3 ....**98** C2
Burlington Pde *CRICK* * NW2 .....**53** D5
Burlington Pl *FUL/PGN* SW6 ....**113** E5
Burlington Rd *CHSWK* * W4 ....**110** C1
FUL/PGN SW6 ....**113** E5
Burma Rd *STNW/STAM* N16 ....**77** D1

Burma Ter *NRWD* * SE19 ....155 E5
Burmester Rd *TOOT* SW17 ....150 C3
Burnaby Crs *CHSWK* W4 ....110 B2
Burnaby Gdns *CHSWK* W4 ....110 B2
Burnaby St *WBPTN* SW10 ....114 C3
Burnbury Rd *BAL* SW12 ....152 C1
Burnell Wk *STHWK* * SE1 ....119 F1
Burnels Av *EHAM* E6 ....96 A2
Burness Cl *HOLWY* N7 ....75 F3
Burne St *CAMTN* NW1 ....16 C2
Burney St *GNWCH* SE10 ....122 C3
Burnfoot Av *FUL/PGN* SW6 ....113 E4
Burnham Cl *STHWK* SE1 ....49 F5
Burnham St *BETH* E2 ....90 C2
Burnham Wy *SYD* SE26 ....157 F5
Burnley Rd *BRXN/ST* SW9 ....117 F3
    WLSDN NW10 ....69 F2
Burnsall St *CHEL* SW3 ....115 E1
Burns Cl *WELL* DA16 ....127 F4
Burnside Cl *BERM/RHTH* SE16 ....103 D2
Burns Rd *BTSEA* SW11 ....115 F5
    WLSDN NW10 ....69 F2
Burntwood Cl *WAND/EARL* * SW18 ...151 D1
Burntwood Grange Rd
    WAND/EARL SW18 ....151 D1
Burntwood La *TOOT* SW17 ....150 C3
Burntwood Vw *NRWD* * SE19 ....155 F5
Buross St *WCHPL* E1 ....90 B5
Burrage Gv *WOOL/PLUM* SE18 ....108 B5
Burrage Pl *WOOL/PLUM* SE18 ....126 B1
Burrage Rd *WOOL/PLUM* SE18 ....108 C5
Burrard Rd *CAN/RD* E16 ....94 A5
    KIL/WHAMP NW6 ....72 A2
Burr Cl *WAP* * E1W 102 A2
Burrell St *STHWK* SE1 ....34 C3
Burroughs Cottages *POP/IOD* * E14 ...91 E4
Burrow Rd *CMBW* SE5 ....137 E2
Burrows Ms *STHWK* SE1 ....34 C5
Burrows Rd *WLSDN* NW10 ....88 C2
Burr Rd *WAND/EARL* SW18 ....150 A1
Bursar St *STHWK* * SE1 ....36 C4
Bursdon Cl *BFN/LL* DA15 ....163 E3
Burslem St *WCHPL* E1 ....90 B5
Burstock Rd *PUT/ROE* SW15 ....131 F3
Burston Rd *PUT/ROE* SW15 ....131 D3
Burtley Cl *FSBYPK* N4 ....58 C3
Burton Bank *IS* * N1 ....77 D4
Burton Gv *WALW* SE17 ....119 F4
Burton La *BRXN/ST* * SW9 ....118 A5
Burton Ms *BGVA* SW1W 42 B5
Burton Pl *STPAN* WC1H 8 B5
Burton Rd *BRXN/ST* SW9 ....118 A5
    KIL/WHAMP NW6 ....71 F4
Burtons Ct *SRTFD* E15 ....81 D4
Burton St *STPAN* WC1H 8 B5
Burt Rd *CAN/RD* E16 ....106 C2
Burtwell La *WNWD* SE27 ....155 D4
Burwash Rd *WOOL/PLUM* SE18 ....127 D1
Burwell Cl *WCHPL* * E1 ....90 B5
Burwell Rd *LEY* E10 ....61 E3
Burwood Pl *BAY/PAD* W2 ....17 D4
Bury Cl *BERM/RHTH* SE16 ....103 D2
Bury Ct *HDTCH* EC3A 25 D4
Bury Pl *NOXST/BSQ* WC1A 20 C3
Bury St *HDTCH* EC3A 25 D5
    STJS SW1Y 31 E3
Bury Wk *CHEL* SW3 ....40 C5
Busby Pl *KTTN* NW5 ....75 D3
Bushbaby Cl *STHWK* SW1 ....48 C3
Bushberry Rd *HOM* E9 ....79 E3
Bush Cottages *WAND/EARL* SW18 ...132 A3
Bushell Cl *BRXS/STRHM* SW2 ....153 F2
Bushell Wy *CHST* BR7 ....162 A5
Bushey Hill Rd *CMBW* SE5 ....119 F4

Bushey Lees *BFN/LL* * DA15 ....145 F4
Bushey Rd *PLSTW* E13 ....94 C1
    SEVS/STOTM N15 ....59 E1
Bush Gv *CDALE/KGS* NW9 ....50 C2
Bush La *CANST* EC4R 36 A1
Bushmoor Crs *WOOL/PLUM* SE18 .....126 B3
Bushnell Rd *TOOT* SW17 ....152 B2
Bush Rd *BERM/RHTH* SE16 ....103 D5
    HACK E8 ....78 B5
    WAN E11 ....63 F2
Bushwood *WAN* E11 ....63 F2
Bushwood Dr *STHWK* SE1 ....49 F5
Bushwood Rd *RCH/KEW* TW9 ....110 A2
Butcher Rw *POP/IOD* E14 ....91 D5
Butchers Rd *CAN/RD* E16 ....94 A5
Bute Gdns *HMSMTH* W6 ....101 D3
Bute St *SKENS* SW7 ....40 A4
Bute Wk *IS* * N1 ....77 D3
Butler Rd *WLSDN* NW10 ....69 F4
Butlers & Colonial Whf *STHWK* SE1 ....37 F5
Butler St *BETH* * E2 ....90 C2
Butterfield Cl *BERM/RHTH* * SE16 ....102 A3
Butterfield Sq *EHAM* E6 ....95 F5
Butterfly La *ELTH/MOT* SE9 ....144 B4
Butterfly Wk *CMBW* * SE5 ....119 D4
Buttermere Cl *STHWK* SE1 ....49 E4
    WAN E11 ....81 D1
Buttermere Dr *PUT/ROE* SW15 ....131 E3
Buttermere Wk *HACK* * E8 ....77 F3
Butterwick *HMSMTH* W6 ....100 C5
Butterworth Ter *WALW* * SE17 ....118 C5
Buttesland St *IS* N1 ....12 B3
Buttmarsh Cl *WOOL/PLUM* SE18 .....126 B1
Buttsbury Rd *IL* IG1 ....84 C2
Butts Rd *BMLY* BR1 ....159 E5
Buxhall Crs *HOM* E9 ....79 F3
Buxted Rd *EDUL* SE22 ....137 E2
    HACK E8 ....77 F4
Buxton Gdns *ACT* W3 ....98 B1
Buxton Rd *ARCH* N19 ....57 D3
    CRICK NW2 ....70 B3
    EHAM E6 ....95 E2
    GNTH/NBYPK IG2 ....67 E1
    MORT/ESHN SW14 ....129 E1
    SRTFD E15 ....81 E2
Buxton St *WCHPL* E1 ....25 F1
Byam St *FUL/PGN* SW6 ....114 C5
The Bye *ACT* W3 ....87 E5
Byefield Cl *BERM/RHTH* SE16 ....103 E3
Byelands Cl *BERM/RHTH* SE16 ....103 D2
The Byeway *MORT/ESHN* SW14 ....128 C2
Byfeld Gdns *BARN* SW13 ....112 A4
Byfield Cl *BERM/RHTH* SE16 ....103 E3
Byford Cl *SRTFD* E15 ....81 E5
Bygrove St *POP/IOD* E14 ....92 B5
Byng Pl *GWRST* WC1E 20 B1
Byng St *POP/IOD* E14 ....104 A3
Byrne Rd *BAL* SW12 ....152 B1
Byron Av *MNPK* E12 ....83 E3
Byron Cl *HACK* E8 ....78 A5
    SYD * SE26 ....157 E4
Byron Dr *EFNCH* N2 ....55 D1
Byron Ms *HAMP* NW3 ....73 D2
Byron Rd *CRICK* NW2 ....52 B4
    LEY E10 ....62 B3
Byron St *POP/IOD* E14 ....92 C5
Bythorn St *BRXN/ST* SW9 ....135 F1
Byward St *MON* EC3R 37 D2
Bywater Pl *BERM/RHTH* SE16 ....103 E2
Bywater St *CHEL* SW3 ....115 F1
Bywell Pl *GTPST* * W1W 19 E3

C

Cabbell St *CAMTN* NW1 ....16 C3
Cable Pl *GNWCH* SE10 ....122 C4

Cable St *WCHPL* E1 ....102 A1
Cable Trade Pk *CHARL* * SE7 ...124 A1
Cabot Sq *POP/IOD* E14 ....104 A2
Cabot Wy *EHAM* E6 ....83 D5
Cabul Rd *BTSEA* SW11 ....115 E5
Cactus Cl *CMBW* * SE5 ....119 E5
Cadbury Wy *BERM/RHTH* SE16 ....49 F3
Caddington Rd *CRICK* NW2 ....53 E5
Cadell Cl *BETH* E2 ....13 F2
Cade Rd *GNWCH* SE10 ....123 D4
Cader Rd *WAND/EARL* SW18 .....132 C4
Cadet Dr *STHWK* SE1 ....119 F1
Cadet Pl *GNWCH* SE10 ....123 E1
Cadiz St *WALW* SE17 ....118 C1
Cadman Cl *BRXN/ST* SW9 ....118 B3
Cadogan Cl *HOM* * E9 ....79 F4
Cadogan Gdns *CHEL* SW3 ....41 F4
Cadogan Ga *KTBR* SW1X 41 F4
Cadogan La *KTBR* SW1X 42 A3
Cadogan Pl *KTBR* SW1X 41 F4
Cadogan Rd *WOOL/PLUM* SE18 ..108 C3
Cadogan Sq *KTBR* SW1X 41 E5
Cadogan St *CHEL* SW3 ....41 F5
Cadogan Ter *HOM* E9 ....79 F3
Cadoxton Av *SEVS/STOTM* N15 ...59 F1
Cadwallon Rd *ELTH/MOT* SE9 ....162 B2
Caedmon Rd *HOLWY* N7 ....75 F1
Cahill St *STLK* * EC1Y 23 F1
Cahir St *POP/IOD* E14 ....104 B5
Caird St *NKENS* W10 ....89 E2
Cairnfield Av *CRICK* NW2 ....51 E5
Cairns Rd *BTSEA* SW11 ....133 E3
Caistor Park Rd *SRTFD* E15 ....81 F5
Caistor Rd *BAL* SW12 ....134 B5
Caithness Gdns *BFN/LL* DA15 ...145 F4
Caithness Rd *HMSMTH* W6 ....101 D4
Calabria Rd *HBRY* N5 ....76 B3
Calais St *CMBW* SE5 ....118 B4
Calbourne Rd *BAL* SW12 ....133 F5
Caldecot Rd *CMBW* SE5 ....118 C5
Caldecott Wy *CLPT* E5 ....61 D5
Calderon Rd *WAN* E11 ....80 C1
Caldervale Rd *CLAP* SW4 ....135 D3
Calderwood St *WOOL/PLUM* SE18 ..108 A5
Caldicote Cl *CDALE/KGS* * NW9 ..51 E1
Caldwell St *BRXN/ST* SW9 ....117 F3
Caldy Wk *IS* * N1 ....76 C3
Caledonian Rd *HOLWY* N7 ....75 F2
Caledonian Wharf Rd *POP/IOD* E14 ..105 D3
Caledonia St *IS* N1 ....9 D2
Caledon Rd *EHAM* E6 ....83 F5
Cale St *CHEL* SW3 ....115 E1
Calidore Cl *BRXS/STRHM* * SW2 ..135 F4
Callaby Ter *IS* * N1 ....77 D3
Callaghan Cottages *WCHPL* * E1 ..90 C4
Callander Rd *CAT* SE6 ....158 A3
Callcott Rd *KIL/WHAMP* NW6 ......71 F4
Callcott St *KENS* W8 ....26 A3
Callendar Rd *SKENS* SW7 ....40 A2
Callingham Cl *POP/IOD* E14 ....91 F4
Callis Rd *WALTH* E17 ....61 F1
Callow St *CHEL* SW3 ....114 C2
Calmington Rd *CMBW* SE5 ....119 E2
Caionne Rd *WIM/MER* SW19 .....149 E5
Calshot St *IS* N1 ....9 E1
Calthorpe St *FSBYW* WC1X 9 F5
Calton Av *DUL* SE21 ....137 E4
Calverley Gv *ARCH* N19 ....57 D3
Calvert Av *BETH* E2 ....13 D4
Calverton Rd *EHAM* E6 ....84 A5
Calvert Rd *GNWCH* SE10 ....123 F1
Calvert St *CAMTN* NW1 ....74 A5
Calvin St *SPTL* E1 ....25 E1
Calydon Rd *CHARL* SE7 ....124 B1
Calypso Wy *BERM/RHTH* SE16 ...103 F4
Camarthen Gn *CDALE/KGS* * NW9 ..51 E1
Cambalt Rd *PUT/ROE* SW15 ....131 D3
Cambert Wy *ELTH/MOT* SE9 ......142 B3

Camberwell Church St *CMBW* SE5 ..119 D4
Camberwell Glebe *CMBW* SE5 ....119 D4
Camberwell Gn *CMBW* SE5 ....119 D4
Camberwell Gv *CMBW* SE5 ....119 D4
Camberwell New Rd *CMBW* SE5 ..118 B3
Camberwell Rd *CMBW* SE5 ....118 C2
Camberwell Station Rd *CMBW* SE5 ..118 C4
Camborne Rd *WAND/EARL* SW18 ..132 A5
WELL DA16 ....127 E5
Cambourne Ms *NTGHL* W11 ....89 E5
Cambray Rd *BAL* SW12 ....152 C1
Cambria Cl *BFN/LL* DA15 ....163 D1
Cambrian Cl *WNWD* SE27 ....154 B3
Cambrian Rd *LEY* E10 ....62 A2
Cambria Rd *CMBW* SE5 ....136 C1
Cambria St *FUL/PGN* SW6 ....114 B3
Cambridge Av *KIL/WHAMP* NW6 ...2 B1
WELL DA16 ....145 F2
Cambridge Barracks Rd
WOOL/PLUM SE18 ....107 F5
Cambridge Cl *WALTH* E17 ....61 F1
WLSDN NW10 ....50 C5
Cambridge Crs *BETH* E2 ....90 B1
Cambridge Dr *LEE/GVPK* SE12 ..142 A3
Cambridge Gdns *KIL/WHAMP* NW6 ..2 B1
NKENS W10 ....89 D5
Cambridge Ga *CAMTN* NW1 ....6 C4
Cambridge Gate Ms *CAMTN* NW1 ..7 D4
Cambridge Gn *ELTH/MOT* SE9 ...162 B1
Cambridge Gv *HMSMTH* W6 ......100 B5
Cambridge Heath Rd *BETH* E2 .....90 B2
Cambridge Pk *WAN* E11 ....64 A1
Cambridge Park Rd *WAN* E11 ....63 F2
Cambridge Pas *HOM* E9 ....78 C4
Cambridge Pl *KENS* * W8 ....39 D1
Cambridge Rd *BARK* IG11 ....84 C1
BARN SW13 ....111 F5
BTSEA SW11 ....115 E4
GDMY/SEVK IG3 ....67 E3
KIL/WHAMP NW6 ....2 B2
RCH/KEW TW9 ....110 A3
SCUP DA14 ....163 E4
WAN E11 ....64 A1
Cambridge Rd North *CHSWK* W4 ..110 B1
Cambridge Rd South *CHSWK* W4 ..110 B1
Cambridge Rw *WOOL/PLUM* SE18 ..126 B1
Cambridge Sq *BAY/PAD* W2 ....16 C4
Cambridge St *PIM* SW1V 116 B1
Cambridge Ter *CAMTN* NW1 ....7 D4
Cambridge Terrace Ms *CAMTN* * NW1 ..7 D4
Cambus Rd *CAN/RD* E16 ....94 A4
Camdale Rd *WOOL/PLUM* SE18 ..127 F3
Camden Gdns *CAMTN* * NW1 ....74 B4
Camden High St *CAMTN* NW1 ......74 B4
Camdenhurst St *POP/IOD* E14 .....91 E5
Camden Lock Pl *CAMTN* NW1 ......74 B4
Camden Ms *CAMTN* NW1 ....74 C4
Camden Park Rd *CAMTN* NW1 .....75 D3
Camden Pas *IS* N1 ....10 C1
Camden Rd *CAMTN* NW1 ....74 B5
WALTH E17 ....61 F1
WAN E11 ....64 B1
Camden Rd Permanent Wy
CAMTN * NW1 ....75 D5
Camden Rw *BKHTH/KID* SE3 ......123 E5
Camden Sq *CAMTN* NW1 ....75 D3
Camden St *CAMTN* NW1 ....74 B4
Camden Ter *CAMTN* NW1 ....75 D3
Camden Wk *IS* N1 ....76 B5
Camelford Wk *NTGHL* * W11 ....89 E5
Camellia St *VX/NE* SW8 ....117 E3
Camelot Cl *WIM/MER* SW19 ....149 F4
WOOL/PLUM SE18 ....109 D3
Camel Rd *CAN/RD* E16 ....107 D2
Camera Pl *WBPTN* SW10 ....115 D2
Cameron Rd *CAT* SE6 ....157 F2
GDMY/SEVK IG3 ....67 E3
Cameron Ter *LEE/GVPK* * SE12 ..160 B3

Camerton Cl HACK E8 ....77 F3
Camilla Rd BERM/RHTH SE16 ....102 B5
Camlan Rd BMLY BR1 ....159 F4
Camlet St BETH E2 ....13 E5
Camley St CAMTN NW1 ....75 D4
Camomile St LVPST EC2M 24 C4
Campana Rd FUL/PGN SW6 ....114 A4
Campbell Cl STRHM/NOR * SW16 ......153 D5
    WOOL/PLUM SE18 ....126 A4
Campbell Gordon Wy CRICK NW2 ....70 B1
Campbell Rd BOW E3 ....92 A2
    EHAM E6 ....83 E5
    FSTGT E7 ....81 E5
Campbell Wk IS N1 ....75 E5
Campdale Rd ARCH N19 ....57 D5
Campden Gv KENS W8 ....26 A5
Campden Hi KENS W8 ....26 A5
Campden Hill Gdns KENS W8 ....26 A3
Campden Hill PI KENS * W8 ....101 F2
Campden Hill Rd KENS W8 ....26 A3
Campden Hill Sq KENS W8 ....101 F2
Campden House Cl KENS W8 ....26 A5
Campden House Ter KENS * W8 ....26 B4
Campden St KENS W8 ....26 A4
Campden Ter CHSWK * W4 ....111 E1
Campen Cl WIM/MER SW19 ....149 E5
Camperdown St WCHPL E1 ....25 F5
Campfield Rd ELTH/MOT SE9 ....143 D5
Campion Cl EHAM E6 ....107 F1
Campion Rd PUT/ROE SW15 ....130 C2
Camplin St NWCR SE14 ....121 D3
Campshill PI LEW SE13 ....140 C3
Campshill Rd LEW SE13 ....140 C3
Campus Rd WALTH E17 ....61 F1
Camp Vw WIM/MER SW19 ....148 B5
Cam Rd SRTFD E15 ....81 D5
Canada Crs ACT W3 ....86 C4
Canada Rd ACT W3 ....86 C4
Canada St BERM/RHTH SE16 ....103 E3
Canada Wy SHB W12 ....100 B3
Canadian Av CAT SE6 ....158 B1
Canal Gdns DMNY SE8 ....121 E2
Canal Cl NKENS W10 ....89 D3
    WCHPL E1 ....91 E3
Canal Gv PECK SE15 ....120 A2
Canal Pth HACK E8 ....77 F5
Canal Rd WCHPL E1 ....91 E3
Canal St CMBW SE5 ....119 D2
Canal Wk IS N1 ....77 D3
    WLSDN * NW10 ....68 C4
Canal Wy NKENS W10 ....89 D3
Canberra Cl CHARL SE7 ....124 C2
    EHAM E6 ....83 F5
Canbury Ms SYD SE26 ....156 A3
Cancell Rd BRXN/ST SW9 ....118 A4
Candahar Rd BTSEA SW11 ....115 E5
Candler St SEVS/STOTM * N15 ....59 D1
Candover St GTPST * W1W 19 E3
Candy St BOW E3 ....79 F5
Caney Ms CRICK NW2 ....53 D4
Canfield Gdns KIL/WHAMP NW6 ....72 B4
Canfield PI HAMP NW6 ....72 C3
Canford Cl BTSEA SW11 ....134 A3
Canham Rd CHSWK W4 ....99 E3
Cann Hall Rd FSTGT E7 ....81 F1
Canning Cross CMBW SE5 ....119 E5
Canning PI KENS W8 ....39 E2
Canning Rd FSBYPK N4 ....58 B5
    SRTFD E15 ....93 E1
Cannon Dr POP/IOD E14 ....104 A1
Cannon La KIL/WHAMP NW6 ....72 A1
Cannon La HAMP NW3 ....55 D5
Cannon PI CHARL SE7 ....125 E1
    HAMP NW3 ....54 C5
Cannon St STP EC4M 23 E5
Cannon Street Rd WCHPL E1 ....90 B5
Canon Beck Rd BERM/RHTH SE16 ....102 C3

Canonbie Rd FSTH SE23 ....138 C5
Canonbury Crs IS N1 ....76 C4
Canonbury Gv IS N1 ....76 C4
Canonbury La IS N1 ....76 B4
Canonbury Pk North IS N1 ....76 C3
Canonbury Pk South IS N1 ....76 C3
Canonbury Rd IS N1 ....76 B3
Canonbury Sq IS N1 ....76 B4
Canonbury St IS N1 ....76 C4
Canonbury Vls IS N1 ....76 B4
Canon Murnane Rd STHWK SE1 ....49 E3
Canon Rw WHALL SW1A 44 C1
Canons Cl EFNCH N2 ....55 D2
Canon St IS N1 ....76 C5
Canrobert St BETH E2 ....90 B1
Cantelowes Rd CAMTN NW1 ....75 D3
Canterbury Av IL IG1 ....65 E2
Canterbury Cl CMBW * SE5 ....118 C5
    EHAM E6 ....95 F5
Canterbury Crs BRXN/ST SW9 ....136 A1
Canterbury Gv WNWD SE27 ....154 A3
Canterbury PI WALW SE17 ....47 D5
Canterbury Rd KIL/WHAMP NW6 ....2 A2
    LEY E10 ....62 C2
Canterbury Ter KIL/WHAMP NW6 ....2 A2
    LEY E10 ....62 C2
Cantley Gdns GNTH/NBYPK IG2 ....66 C1
Canton St POP/IOD E14 ....92 A5
Cantrell Rd BOW E3 ....92 A3
Cantwell Rd WOOL/PLUM SE18 ....126 B3
Canvey St STHWK SE1 ....35 E3
Cape Cl BARK IG11 ....84 B4
Capel Gdns GDMY/SEVK IG3 ....85 F1
Capel Rd FSTGT E7 ....82 B1
Capeners Cl KTBR SW1X 41 F1
    KTBR * SW1X 42 A1
Capern Rd WAND/EARL SW18 ....150 C1
Cape Yd WAP E1W 102 A2
Capital Interchange Wy CHSWK W4 .....110 A1
Capland St STJWD NW8 ....4 B5
Caple Pde WLSDN * NW10 ....87 F1
Caple Rd WLSDN NW10 ....87 F1
Capstan Rd DEPT SE8 ....103 F5
Capstan Sq POP/IOD E14 ....104 C3
Capstan Wy BERM/RHTH SE16 ....103 E2
Capstone Rd BMLY BR1 ....160 A4
Capulet Ms CAN/RD E16 ....106 A4
Capworth St LEY E10 ....62 A3
Caradoc St GNWCH SE10 ....123 E1
Caradon Ct WAN * E11 ....63 E3
Caravel Ms DEPT * SE8 ....122 A2
Caraway Cl PLSTW E13 ....94 B4
Carbis Rd POP/IOD E14 ....91 F5
Carburton St GTPST W1W 19 D2
Cardale St POP/IOD E14 ....104 C4
Carden Rd PECK SE15 ....138 B1
Cardiff St WOOL/PLUM SE18 ....127 E3
Cardigan PI BKHTH/KID * SE3 ....123 D5
Cardigan Rd BARN SW13 ....112 A3
    BOW E3 ....91 F1
Cardigan St LBTH SE11 ....118 A1
Cardigan Wk IS * N1 ....76 C4
Cardinal Bourne St STHWK * SE1 ....48 B3
Cardinal Hinsey Cl WLSDN NW10 ....88 A1
Cardinal PI PUT/ROE SW15 ....131 D2
Cardinals Wy ARCH N19 ....57 D3
Cardine Ms PECK SE15 ....120 B3
Cardington St CAMTN NW1 ....7 F3
Cardozo Rd HOLWY N7 ....75 E2
Cardross St HMSMTH W6 ....100 B4
Cardwell Rd HOLWY * N7 ....75 E1
Cardwell Ter HOLWY * N7 ....75 E1
Carew Cl HOLWY N7 ....57 F4
Carew St CMBW SE5 ....118 C5
Carey Gdns VX/NE SW8 ....116 A3
Carey La CITYW EC2V 23 E4
Carey PI WEST SW1P 44 A5
Carey St LINN WC2A 21 F5
Carey Wy WBLY HA9 ....68 B1

The Carfax *SYD* * SE26 ....156 C3
Carfax Pl *CLAP* SW4 ....135 D2
Carfree Cl *IS* N1 ....76 A4
Cargill Rd *WAND/EARL* SW18 ....150 C1
Carholme Rd *FSTH* SE23 ....157 F1
Carisbrooke Gdns *PECK* * SE15 ....119 F3
Carleton Gdns *ARCH* * N19 ....74 C2
Carleton Rd *HOLWY* N7 ....75 D1
Carleton Vls *KTTN* * NW5 ....74 C2
Carlile Cl *BOW* E3 ....91 F1
Carlingford Rd *HAMP* NW3 ....73 D1
Carlisle Av *ACT* W3 ....87 E5
  TWRH EC3N 25 D5
Carlisle Gdns *IL* IG1 ....65 E1
Carlisle La *STHWK* SE1 ....45 F2
Carlisle Pl *WEST* SW1P 43 E3
Carlisle Rd *FSBYPK* N4 ....58 A3
  KIL/WHAMP NW6 ....71 E5
  LEY E10 ....62 A3
Carlisle St *SOHO/CST* W1F 20 A5
Carlisle Wk *HACK* E8 ....77 F3
Carlisle Wy *TOOT* SW17 ....152 A5
Carlos Pl *MYFR/PKLN* W1K 30 B2
Carlow St *CAMTN* NW1 ....7 E1
Carlton Cl *HAMP* NW3 ....72 A2
Carlton Dr *PUT/ROE* SW15 ....131 D3
Carlton Gdns *STJS* SW1Y 32 A4
Carlton Gn *SCUP* * DA14 ....163 F4
Carlton Gv *PECK* SE15 ....120 B4
Carlton Hl *STJWD* NW8 ....3 D1
Carlton House Ter *STJS* SW1Y 32 A4
Carlton Ms *KIL/WHAMP* * NW6 ....72 A2
Carlton Rd *CHSWK* W4 ....99 D3
  FSBYPK N4 ....58 A2
  MNPK E12 ....83 D1
  MORT/ESHN SW14 ....128 C1
  SCUP DA14 ....163 F5
  WAN E11 ....63 F3
Carlton Sq *WCHPL* * E1 ....91 D3
Carlton St *STJS* SW1Y 32 A3
Carlton Ter *SYD* SE26 ....156 C3
Carlton Tower Pl *KTBR* SW1X 41 F3
Carlton V *KIL/WHAMP* NW6 ....2 A3
Carlwell St *TOOT* SW17 ....151 E5
Carlyle Cl *EFNCH* N2 ....54 C1
  WLSDN NW10 ....69 D5
Carlyle Ct *WBPTN* * SW10 ....114 C4
Carlyle Rd *MNPK* E12 ....83 F1
Carlyle Sq *CHEL* SW3 ....115 D1
Carmalt Gdns *PUT/ROE* SW15 ....130 C2
Carmel Cl *KENS* W8 ....26 C5
Carmelite St *EMB* EC4Y 34 B1
Carmen St *POP/IOD* E14 ....92 B5
Carmichael Cl *BTSEA* * SW11 ....133 D1
Carminia Rd *TOOT* SW17 ....152 B2
Carnaby St *REGST* W1B 31 E1
Carnac St *WNWD* SE27 ....155 D4
Carnarvon Rd *LEY* E10 ....62 C1
  SRTFD E15 ....81 F3
Carnbrook Rd *BKHTH/KID* SE3 ....143 D1
Carnecke Gdns *ELTH/MOT* SE9 ....143 E3
Carnegie Pl *WIM/MER* SW19 ....149 D3
Carnegie St *IS* N1 ....75 F5
Carnoustie Dr *IS* N1 ....75 F4
Carnwath Rd *FUL/PGN* SW6 ....132 A1
Carolina Cl *SRTFD* E15 ....81 D3
Caroline Cl *BAY/PAD* W2 ....27 D2
  STRHM/NOR SW16 ....153 F4
Caroline Gdns *BETH* E2 ....13 D3
  PECK * SE15 ....120 B3
Caroline Pl *BAY/PAD* W2 ....27 D1
  VX/NE SW8 ....116 A5
Caroline Place Ms *BAY/PAD* * W2 ....27 D2
Caroline St *WCHPL* E1 ....91 D5
Caroline Ter *BGVA* SW1W 42 A5
Caroline Wk *HMSMTH* W6 ....113 E3
Carol Cl *CAMTN* NW1 ....74 C5
Carpenters Ms *HOLWY* * N7 ....75 E2

Carpenter's Pl *CLAP* SW4 ....135 D2
Carpenters Rd *SRTFD* E15 ....80 B4
Carpenter St *MYFR/PKLN* W1K 30 C2
Carrara Ms *HACK* E8 ....78 A2
Carr Gv *WOOL/PLUM* SE18 ....107 E5
Carriage Dr East *BTSEA* SW11 ....116 A2
Carriage Dr North *BTSEA* SW11 ....115 F3
Carriage Dr South *BTSEA* SW11 ....115 F4
Carriage Dr West *BTSEA* SW11 ....115 F3
Carriage Ms *IL* IG1 ....66 C4
Carrick Ms *DEPT* SE8 ....122 A2
Carrington Gdns *FSTGT* E7 ....82 A1
Carrington Rd *RCHPK/HAM* TW10 ....128 B2
Carrington St *MYFR/PICC* W1J 30 C4
Carrol Cl *KTTN* NW5 ....74 B1
Carroll Cl *SRTFD* E15 ....81 F2
Carronade Pl *WOOL/PLUM* SE18 ....109 D4
Carron Cl *POP/IOD* E14 ....92 B5
Carroun Rd *VX/NE* SW8 ....117 F3
Carr St *POP/IOD* E14 ....91 E4
Carslake Rd *PUT/ROE* SW15 ....130 F3
Carson Rd *CAN/RD* E16 ....94 A4
  DUL SE21 ....154 C2
Carstairs Rd *CAT* SE6 ....158 C3
Carston Cl *LEE/GVPK* SE12 ....141 F3
Carswell Rd *CAT* SE6 ....140 C5
Carteret St *STJSPK* SW1H 44 A1
Carteret Wy *DEPT* SE8 ....103 E5
Carter La *BLKFR* EC4V 23 D5
Carter Pl *WALW* SE17 ....118 C1
Carter Rd *PLSTW* E13 ....82 A4
Carters Cl *KTTN* * NW5 ....75 D3
Carters Hill Cl *ELTH/MOT* SE9 ....160 C1
Carter St *WALW* SE17 ....118 C2
Carters Yd *WAND/EARL* * SW18 ....132 A3
Carthew Rd *HMSMTH* W6 ....100 B4
Carthew Vls *HMSMTH* W6 ....100 B4
Carthusian St *FARR* EC1M 23 E2
Carting La *TPL/STR* WC2E 33 D2
Cartwright Gdns *STPAN* WC1H 8 B4
Cartwright St *TWRH* EC3N 37 F1
Cartwright Wy *BARN* SW13 ....112 B3
Carver Rd *HNHL* SE24 ....136 C4
Cary Rd *WAN* E11 ....81 E1
Carysfort Rd *STNW/STAM* N16 ....59 D5
Casella Rd *NWCR* SE14 ....121 D3
Casewick Rd *WNWD* SE27 ....154 B5
Casey Cl *CAMTN* NW1 ....17 D1
  STJWD NW8 ....4 C4
Casimir Rd *CLPT* E5 ....60 B5
Casino Av *HNHL* SE24 ....136 C3
Caspian St *CMBW* SE5 ....119 D3
Caspian Wk *CAN/RD* E16 ....95 D5
Casselden Rd *WLSDN* NW10 ....69 D4
Cassidy Rd *FUL/PGN* SW6 ....114 A3
Cassland Rd *HOM* E9 ....79 D4
Casslee Rd *CAT* SE6 ....139 F5
Casson St *WCHPL* E1 ....90 A4
Castellain Rd *MV/WKIL* W9 ....2 C3
Castello Av *PUT/ROE* SW15 ....130 C3
Castelnau *BARN* SW13 ....112 B3
Casterbridge Rd *BKHTH/KID* SE3 ....142 A1
Casterton St *HACK* E8 ....78 B3
Castile Rd *WOOL/PLUM* SE18 ....108 A5
Castillon Rd *CAT* SE6 ....159 E2
Castlands Rd *CAT* SE6 ....157 F2
Castle Baynard St *BLKFR* EC4V 35 D1
Castlebrook Cl *LBTH* SE11 ....46 C4
Castle Cl *ACT* W3 ....98 B3
  WIM/MER SW19 ....149 D3
Castlecombe Dr *WIM/MER* SW19 ....131 D5
Castlecombe Rd *ELTH/MOT* SE9 ....161 E5
Castle Ct *BANK* * EC3V 24 B5
  SYD SE26 ....157 E4
Castle Dr *REDBR* IG4 ....65 E1
Castleford Av *ELTH/MOT* SE9 ....162 B1
Castlehaven Rd *CAMTN* NW1 ....74 B4
Castle La *WESTW* SW1E 43 E2

Castle Md *CMBW* * SE5 ....118 C3
Castle Ms *CAMTN* NW1 ....74 B3
Castle PI *CAMTN* NW1 ....74 B3
Castlereagh St *MBLAR* W1H 17 E4
Castle Rd *EHAM* E6 ....74 B3
Castle Rw *CHSWK* * W4 ....111 D1
Castle St *EHAM* E6 ....94 C1
Castleton Rd *LEE/GVPK* SE12 ....161 C3
Castletown Rd *WKENS* W14 ....113 E1
Castleview CI *FSBYPK* N4 ....58 C3
Castle View Gdns *IL* IG1 ....65 E1
Castle Vls *CRICK* * NW2 ....70 A3
Castle Wy *WIM/MER* SW19 ....149 D3
Castlewood Dr *ELTH/MOT* SE9 ....125 F5
Castlewood Rd *SEVS/STOTM* N15 .....60 A1
Castle Yd *HGT* N6 ....56 A2
     STHWK * SE1 ....35 D3
Castor La *POP/IOD* E14 ....104 B1
Caterham Rd *LEW* SE13 ....140 C1
Catesby St *WALW* SE17 ....48 B5
Catford Broadway *CAT* SE6 ....140 B5
Catford HI *CAT* SE6 ....157 F1
Catford Island *CAT* * SE6 ....140 B5
Catford Rd *CAT* SE6 ....158 A1
Cathall Rd *WAN* E11 ....63 D4
Cathay St *BERM/RHTH* SE16 ....102 B3
Cathcart HI *KTTN* NW5 ....56 C5
Cathcart Rd *WBPTN* * SW10 ....114 B2
Cathcart St *KTTN* NW5 ....74 B3
Cathedral St *STHWK* SE1 ....36 A3
Catherall Rd *HBRY* N5 ....58 C5
Catherine Griffiths Ct *CLKNW* * EC1R ...10 B5
Catherine Gv *GNWCH* SE10 ....122 B4
Catherine PI *WESTW* SW1E 43 E2
Catherine St *HOL/ALD* * WC2B 33 E1
Catherine Wheel Aly *LVPST* EC2M 25 D3
Catherine Wheel Yd *WHALL* SW1A 31 E4
Cathles Rd *BAL* SW12 ....134 B4
Cathnor Rd *SHB* W12 ....100 B3
Catling CI *FSTH* SE23 ....156 C3
Catlin St *BERM/RHTH* SE16 ....120 A1
Cato Rd *CLAP* SW4 ....135 D1
Cator St *PECK* SE15 ....119 F2
Cattistock Rd *ELTH/MOT* SE9 ....161 E5
Catton St *RSQ* WC1B 21 D1
Caudwell Ter *WAND/EARL* * SW18 ....133 D4
     PECK SE15 ....120 B5
Caulfield Rd *EHAM* E6 ....83 F4
     PECK SE15 ....120 B5
The Causeway *WAND/EARL* SW18 .....132 B2
     WIM/MER SW19 ....148 C5
Causton Cottages *POP/IOD* * E14 .....91 E4
Causton St *HGT* * N6 ....56 B2
Cautley Av *CLAP* SW4 ....134 C3
Cavalry Gdns *PUT/ROE* SW15 ....131 E3
Cavaye PI *WBPTN* SW10 ....114 C1
Cavell Rd *WCHPL* E1 ....90 B4
Cavendish Av *STJWD* NW8 ....4 B2
     WELL DA16 ....145 F1
Cavendish CI *KIL/WHAMP* NW6 ....71 F3
     STJWD NW8 ....4 B3
Cavendish Dr *WAN* E11 ....63 D3
Cavendish Gdns *BARK* IG11 ....85 F2
     CLAP * SW4 ....134 C4
     IL IG1 ....65 E1
Cavendish Ms North *REGST* W1B 19 D2
Cavendish Ms South *GTPST* * W1W 19 D3
Cavendish Pde *CLAP* * SW4 ....134 C4
Cavendish PI *KIL/WHAMP* NW6 ....71 F3
     MHST W1U 18 C4
Cavendish Rd *CHSWK* W4 ....110 C4
     CLAP SW4 ....134 B4
     FSBYPK N4 ....58 B1
     KIL/WHAMP NW6 ....71 E4
Cavendish Sq *CAVSQ/HST* * W1G 18 C4
Cavendish St *IS* N1 ....12 A2
Cavendish Ter *BOW* * E3 ....91 F2

Cavenham Gdns *IL* IG1 ....67 D5
Cave Rd *PLSTW* E13 ....94 B1
Caversham Flats *CHEL* * SW3 ....115 F2
Caversham Rd *KTTN* * NW5 ....74 C3
Caversham St *CHEL* SW3 ....115 F2
Caverswall St *SHB* W12 ....88 C5
Cawnpore St *NRWD* SE19 ....155 E5
Caxton Gv *BOW* E3 ....92 A2
Caxton Rd *SHB* W12 ....101 D2
     WIM/MER SW19 ....150 C5
The Caxtons *CMBW* * SE5 ....118 B3
Caxton St *STJSPK* SW1H 43 E2
Caxton St North *CAN/RD* E16 ....93 F5
Cayenne Ct *STHWK* SE1 ....37 D5
Cayton PI *FSBYE* EC1V 12 A4
Cayton St *FSBYE* EC1V 11 F3
Cazenove Rd *STNW/STAM* N16 ......59 F4
Cecil Av *BARK* IG11 ....85 D4
Cecil Ct *LSQ/SEVD* WC2H 32 B2
Cecile Pk *CEND/HSY/T* N8 ....57 E1
Cecilia Rd *HACK* E8 ....77 D1
Cecil Rd *ACT* W3 ....86 C4
     IL IG1 ....84 B1
     PLSTW E13 ....82 A5
     WAN E11 ....63 E4
     WLSDN NW10 ....69 C5
Cedar CI *BOW* E3 ....79 F5
     DUL SE21 ....154 C1
     KUTN/CMB KT2 ....147 D4
Cedar Ct *CHARL* * SE7 ....124 C2
     ELTH/MOT * SE9 ....143 E4
     WIM/MER SW19 ....149 D3
Cedar Gv *CRICK* NW2 ....70 C1
The Cedars *HOM* * E9 ....79 D4
     SRTFD E15 ....81 F5
Cedars CI *LEW* SE13 ....141 D1
Cedars Cottages *PUT/ROE* * SW15 ...130 A4
Cedars Ms *CLAP* * SW4 ....134 B2
Cedars Rd *BARN* SW13 ....111 F5
     CLAP SW4 ....134 B1
     SRTFD E15 ....81 E3
Cedar Tree Gv *WNWD* SE27 ....154 B5
Cedar Wy *CAMTN* NW1 ....75 D4
Cedric Rd *ELTH/MOT* SE9 ....162 C3
Celandine CI *POP/IOD* * E14 ....92 A4
Celandine Dr *HACK* E8 ....77 F4
Celandine Wy *SRTFD* E15 ....93 E2
Celbridge Ms *BAY/PAD* W2 ....15 D4
Celestial Gdns *LEW* SE13 ....141 D2
Celia Rd *ARCH* N19 ....74 C1
Celtic St *POP/IOD* E14 ....92 B4
Cemetery La *CHARL* SE7 ....125 E2
Cemetery Rd *FSTGT* E7 ....81 F2
Cenacle CI *HAMP* NW3 ....54 A5
Centaur St *STHWK* SE1 ....45 F2
Centenary Wk *WAN* E11 ....63 D4
Central Av *WAN* E11 ....63 D4
     WELL DA16 ....145 F1
Central Pde *ACT* * W3 ....98 A3
     STRHM/NOR * SW16 ....153 E4
Central Park Rd *EHAM* E6 ....95 D1
Central Sq *GLDGN* NW11 ....54 A1
Central St *FSBYE* EC1V 11 E3
Central Wy *WLSDN* NW10 ....86 C2
Centre Av *ACT* W3 ....99 D2
Centre Rd *WAN* E11 ....64 A4
Centre St *BETH* E2 ....78 B5
Centric CI *CAMTN* * NW1 ....74 B5
Centurion CI *HOLWY* N7 ....75 F4
Centurion La *BOW* E3 ....91 F1
Century Ms *CLPT* * E5 ....78 C2
Cephas Av *WCHPL* E1 ....90 C3
Cephas St *WCHPL* E1 ....90 C3
Ceres Rd *WOOL/PLUM* SE18 ....109 F5
Cerise Rd *PECK* SE15 ....120 A4

Cervantes Ct BAY/PAD W2 ....15 D5
Ceylon Rd WKENS W14 ....101 D4
Chadbourn St POP/IOD E14 ....92 B4
Chadwell St CLKNW EC1R 10 B3
Chadwick Rd CMBW SE5 ....119 C5
  IL IG1 ....66 B5
  WAN E11 ....63 E2
  WLSDN NW10 ....69 F5
Chadwick St WEST SW1P 44 B3
Chadwin Rd PLSTW E13 ....94 B4
Chagford St CAMTN NW1 ....17 E1
Chailey St CLPT E5 ....60 C5
Chalbury Wk IS N1 ....9 F1
Chalcot Crs CAMTN NW1 ....73 F5
Chalcot Gdns HAMP NW3 ....73 F3
Chalcot Ms STRHM/NOR SW16 ...153 D5
Chalcot Rd CAMTN NW1 ....74 A5
Chalcot Sq CAMTN NW1 ....74 A4
Chalcroft Rd LEW SE13 ....141 E3
Chaldon Rd FUL/PGN SW6 ....113 E3
Chale Rd BRXS/STRHM SW2 ....135 E4
Chalfont Av WBLY HA9 ....68 B3
Chalford Rd DUL SE21 ....155 D4
Chalgrove Rd HOM E9 ....78 A5
Chalk Farm Pde HAMP * NW3 ....74 A4
Chalk Hill Rd HMSMTH W6 ....101 D3
Chalkhill Rd WBLY HA9 ....50 A5
Chalklands WBLY HA9 ....50 A5
Chalk Rd PLSTW E13 ....94 B4
Challenge Cl WLSDN NW10 ....69 G5
Challice Wy BRXS/STRHM SW2 ......153 F1
Challoner Crs WKENS * W14 ....113 E3
Challoner St WKENS W14 ....113 F1
Chalmers Wk WALW * SE17 ....118 B2
Chalsey Rd BROCKY SE4 ....139 F2
Chalton Dr EFNCH N2 ....54 C1
Chalton St CAMTN NW1 ....8 A1
Chamberlain Cl WOOL/PLUM SE18 ..109 D4
Chamberlain Cottages CMBW * SE5 ..119 D4
Chamberlain St HAMP * NW3 ....73 F4
Chamberlayne Rd WLSDN NW10 ......70 C5
Chamberlens Garages
  HMSMTH * W6 ....100 B5
Chambers La WLSDN NW10 ....70 B4
Chambers Rd HOLWY N7 ....75 E1
Chambers St BERM/RHTH SE16 ....102 A3
Chamber St WCHPL E1 ....37 F1
Chambon Pl HMSMTH W6 ....100 A5
Chambord St BETH E2 ....13 F4
Champion Crs SYD SE26 ....157 E4
Champion Gv CMBW SE5 ....137 D5
Champion Hl CMBW SE5 ....137 D5
Champion Pk CMBW SE5 ....137 D5
Champion Rd SYD SE26 ....157 E4
Champness Cl WNWD SE27 ....155 D4
Champness Rd BARK IG11 ....85 F3
Chancellor Gv DUL SE21 ....154 C2
Chancellor's Rd HMSMTH W6 ....112 C1
Chancellors St HMSMTH W6 ....112 C1
Chancellors Whf HMSMTH * W6 ....112 C1
Chancel St STHWK SE1 ....34 C3
Chancery La LINN WC2A 21 F3
Chance St BETH E2 ....13 E5
Chanctonbury Cl ELTH/MOT SE9 ...162 B3
Chandler Av CAN/RD E16 ....94 A4
Chandlers Ct LEE/GVPK * SE12 ....160 B2
Chandlers Ms POP/IOD E14 ....104 A3
Chandler St WAP E1W 102 B2
Chandler Wy PECK SE15 ....119 F3
Chandos Pl CHCR WC2N 32 C2
Chandos Rd CRICK NW2 ....70 C2
  SRTFD E15 ....81 D3
  WLSDN NW10 ....87 D3
Chandos St CAVSQ/HST W1G 19 D3
Chandos Wy GLDGN NW11 ....54 B3
Channel Islands St IS N1 ....76 C3
Channelsea Rd SRTFD E15 ....81 D3
Chantrey Rd BRXN/ST SW9 ....135 F1

Chantry Cl MV/WKIL * W9 ....89 F3
Chantry Sq KENS W8 ....38 C3
Chantry St IS * N1 ....76 B5
Chant Sq SRTFD * E15 ....81 D4
Chant St SRTFD E15 ....81 D4
Chapel Ct STHWK SE1 ....36 A5
Chapel Farm Rd ELTH/MOT SE9 ...161 F3
Chapel House St POP/IOD E14 ......122 B1
Chapel Market IS N1 ....10 A1
Chapel Pl CAVSQ/HST W1G 18 C4
  IS N1 ....10 B1
Chapel Rd IL IG1 ....66 A5
  WNWD SE27 ....154 B4
Chapel Side BAY/PAD W2 ....26 C1
Chapel St BAY/PAD W2 ....16 C3
  KTBR SW1X 42 B2
Chaplin Cl STHWK SE1 ....34 B5
Chaplin Rd CRICK NW2 ....70 A3
  SRTFD E15 ....93 E1
Chapman Rd HOM E9 ....79 F3
Chapman Sq WIM/MER SW19 ....149 D2
Chapman St WCHPL E1 ....102 B1
Chapter Rd CRICK NW2 ....70 A2
  WALW SE17 ....118 B1
Chapter St WEST SW1P 44 A5
Chara Pl CHSWK W4 ....111 D2
Chardin Rd CHSWK * W4 ....99 E3
Chardmore Rd STNW/STAM N16 ......60 A3
Chardwell Cl EHAM E6 ....95 E5
Charecroft Wy WKENS W14 ....101 D3
Charford Rd CAN/RD E16 ....94 A4
Chargeable La PLSTW E13 ....94 A3
Chargeable St CAN/RD E16 ....93 F3
Charing Cross CHCR WC2N 32 B3
Charing Cross Rd SOHO/SHAV W1D ..20 B5
Charlbert St STJWD NW8 ....4 C1
Charlbury Gdns GDMY/SEVK IG3 ...67 F4
Charldane Rd ELTH/MOT SE9 ....162 B3
Charlecote Gv SYD SE26 ....156 B3
Charlemont Rd EHAM E6 ....95 F2
Charles Barry Cl CLAP * SW4 ....134 C1
Charles Coveney Rd PECK * SE15 ..119 F4
Charlesfield LEE/GVPK SE12 ....160 C3
Charles Flemwell Ms CAN/RD * E16 ..106 A2
Charles Grinling Wk
  WOOL/PLUM SE18 ....108 A5
Charles Haller St BRXS/STRHM SW2 ..136 A5
Charles II Pl CHEL * SW3 ....115 F1
Charles II St STJS SW1Y 32 A3
Charles La STJWD NW8 ....4 C2
Charles Pl CAMTN * NW1 ....7 F4
Charles Sq IS N1 ....12 B4
Charles Square Est IS N1 ....12 B4
Charles St BARN SW13 ....129 E1
  CAN/RD E16 ....106 C2
  MYFR/PICC W1J 30 C3
Charleston St WALW SE17 ....47 F5
Charleville Circ SYD SE26 ....156 A5
Charleville Rd WKENS W14 ....113 E1
Charlotte Despard Av BTSEA SW11 ..116 B2
Charlotte Ms FITZ W1T 19 F2
  NKENS W10 ....89 D5
Charlotte Pde FSTH * SE23 ....157 E2
Charlotte Pl FITZ W1T 19 F3
Charlotte Rd BARN SW13 ....111 F3
  IS N1 ....12 C4
Charlotte Rw CLAP SW4 ....134 C1
Charlotte St FITZ W1T 19 F2
Charlotte Ter IS * N1 ....75 F3
Charlow Cl FUL/PGN SW6 ....114 C5
Charlton Church La CHARL SE7 .....124 C1
Charlton Crs BARK IG11 ....97 F1
Charlton Dene CHARL SE7 ....124 C3
Charlton King's Rd KTTN NW5 ....75 D2
Charlton La CHARL SE7 ....125 D1
Charlton Park La CHARL SE7 ....125 D3
Charlton Park Rd CHARL SE7 ....125 D2

Charlton Pl *IS* N1 ....**10** C1
Charlton Rd *BKHTH/KID* SE3 ....**124** A3
  WLSDN NW10 ....**69** E5
Charlton Wy *BKHTH/KID* SE3 ....**123** E4
Charlwood Pl *PIM* SW1V **43** F5
Charlwood Rd *PUT/ROE* SW15 ......**131** D2
Charlwood St *PIM* SW1V **43** F5
Charlwood Ter *PUT/ROE* SW15 ......**131** D2
Charminster Rd *LEE/GVPK* SE12 ....**161** D4
Charnock Rd *CLPT* E5 ....**60** B5
Charnwood Gdns *POP/IOD* E14 ....**104** A5
Charnwood St *CLPT* E5 ....**60** A4
Charrington St *CAMTN* NW1 ....**8** A1
Charsley Rd *CAT* SE6 ....**158** B2
Charter Av *GNTH/NBYPK* IG2 ....**67** D3
The Charterhouse *FARR* * EC1M **23** D1
Charterhouse Buildings *FARR* EC1M ...**23** E1
Charterhouse Ms *FARR* EC1M **23** D2
Charterhouse Rd *HACK* E8 ....**78** A3
Charteris Rd *FSBYPK* N4 ....**57** F3
  KIL/WHAMP NW6 ....**71** F5
Charters Cl *NRWD* SE19 ....**155** E5
Chartfield Av *PUT/ROE* SW15 ....**130** B5
Chartfield Sq *PUT/ROE* SW15 ....**131** D3
Chartham Gv *WNWD* SE27 ....**154** A3
Chartley Av *CRICK* NW2 ....**51** E5
Chartley Pde *WLSDN* * NW10 ....**51** E5
Chart St *IS* N1 ....**12** B3
Chartwell Cl *CHST* BR7 ....**163** D2
Charwood *STRHM/NOR* * SW16 .....**154** A4
The Chase *CLAP* SW4 ....**134** B1
  MNPK E12 ....**83** D1
Chaseley Ct *CHSWK* W4 ....**110** B1
Chaseley St *POP/IOD* * E14 ....**91** E5
Chase Rd *ACT* W3 ....**87** D3
Chatfield Rd *BTSEA* SW11 ....**132** C1
Chatham Pl *HOM* E9 ....**78** C3
Chatham Rd *BTSEA* SW11 ....**133** D4
Chatham St *WALW* SE17 ....**48** A4
  WOOL/PLUM SE18 ....**108** B4
Chatsworth Av *BMLY* BR1 ....**160** B5
Chatsworth Cl *CHSWK* * W4 ....**110** C2
Chatsworth Est *CLPT* * E5 ....**79** D1
Chatsworth Gdns *ACT* W3 ....**98** B1
Chatsworth Rd *CHSWK* W4 ....**110** C2
  CLPT E5 ....**60** C5
  CRICK NW2 ....**71** D3
  FSTGT E7 ....**81** F2
Chatsworth Wy *WNWD* SE27 ....**154** B3
Chatterton Ms *FSBYPK* * N4 ....**58** B5
Chatterton Rd *FSBYPK* N4 ....**58** B5
Chatto Rd *BTSEA* SW11 ....**133** F4
Chaucer Av *RCH/KEW* TW9 ....**110** A5
Chaucer Dr *STHWK* SE1 ....**49** F5
Chaucer Rd *ACT* W3 ....**98** C2
  FSTGT E7 ....**82** A3
  HNHL SE24 ....**136** A3
  WAN E11 ....**64** A1
  WELL DA16 ....**127** F4
Chaundrye Cl *ELTH/MOT* SE9 ....**145** F4
Chauntler Rd *CAN/RD* E16 ....**106** B3
Cheam St *PECK* * SE15 ....**138** C1
Cheapside *CITYW* EC2V **23** F5
Cheesemans Ter *WKENS* * W14 .....**113** F1
Chelford Rd *BMLY* BR1 ....**159** D5
Chelmer Rd *HOM* E9 ....**79** D3
Chelmsford Cl *EHAM* E6 ....**95** F5
  HMSMTH W6 ....**113** D2
Chelmsford Gdns *IL* IG1 ....**65** E2
Chelmsford Rd *WALTH* E17 ....**62** A1
Chelmsford Sq *WLSDN* NW10 ....**70** C5
Chelsea Br *VX/NE* SW8 ....**116** B2
Chelsea Bridge Ga *BTSEA* SW11 ...**116** A2
Chelsea Bridge Rd *CHEL* SW3 ....**116** A1
Chelsea Cl *WLSDN* NW10 ....**69** D5
Chelsea Crs *CRICK* * NW2 ....**71** F3

  WBPTN * SW10 ....**114** C4
Chelsea Emb *CHEL* SW3 ....**115** F2
Chelsea Gdns *BGVA* * SW1W **116** A1
Chelsea Harbour Dr *WBPTN* SW10 ...**114** C4
Chelsea Manor Gdns *CHEL* * SW3 ..**115** E2
Chelsea Manor St *CHEL* SW3 ....**115** E1
Chelsea Park Gdns *WBPTN* SW10 ..**115** D2
Chelsea Sq *CHEL* SW3 ....**115** D1
Chelsea Towers *CHEL* * SW3 ....**115** E2
Chelsea Village *FUL/PGN* SW6 ....**114** B3
Chelsfield Gdns *SYD* SE26 ....**156** C5
Chelsham Rd *CLAP* SW4 ....**135** D1
Cheltenham Gdns *EHAM* E6 ....**95** E1
Cheltenham Pl *ACT* W3 ....**98** C3
Cheltenham Rd *LEY* E10 ....**62** C1
  PECK SE15 ....**138** C2
Cheltenham Ter *CHEL* SW3 ....**115** F1
Chelverton Rd *PUT/ROE* SW15 .....**131** D2
Chelwood Gdns *RCH/KEW* TW9 .....**110** A5
Chenappa Cl *PLSTW* E13 ....**94** A2
Cheney Rd *CAMTN* NW1 ....**8** C2
Cheneys Rd *WAN* E11 ....**63** E5
Chenies Ms *GWRST* WC1E **20** A1
Chenies Pl *CAMTN* NW1 ....**8** B1
Chenies St *FITZ* W1T **20** A2
Cheniston Gdns *KENS* W8 ....**38** B2
Chepstow Cl *PUT/ROE* SW15 ....**131** E3
Chepstow Cnr *BAY/PAD* * W2 ....**14** B5
Chepstow Crs *GDMY/SEVK* IG3 ......**67** E1
  NTGHL W11 ....**26** A1
Chepstow Pl *BAY/PAD* W2 ....**14** B5
Chepstow Rd *BAY/PAD* W2 ....**14** B4
Chepstow Vls *NTGHL* W11 ....**101** F1
Chepstow Wy *PECK* SE15 ....**119** F5
Chequer St *STLK* EC1Y **23** F1
Cherbury St *IS* N1 ....**12** C3
Cheriton Dr *WOOL/PLUM* SE18 ......**127** D3
Cheriton Sq *TOOT* SW17 ....**152** A2
Cherry Cl *BRXS/STRHM* * SW2 ......**136** A5
Cherry Garden St *BERM/RHTH* SE16 ...**102** B3
Cherrylands Cl *CDALE/KGS* * NW9 ....**50** C4
Cherry Orch *CHARL* SE7 ....**124** C2
Cherry Tree Cl *CHARL* * SE7 ....**124** C2
Cherry Tree Dr *STRHM/NOR* * SW16 ...**153** E3
Cherry Tree Rd *SRTFD* E15 ....**81** E2
Cherry Tree Wk *STLK* EC1Y **23** F1
Cherrywood Cl *BOW* E3 ....**91** E2
Cherrywood Dr *PUT/ROE* SW15 .....**131** D3
Chertsey Rd *IL* IG1 ....**85** D1
  WAN E11 ....**63** D4
Chertsey St *TOOT* SW17 ....**152** A5
Cheryls Cl *FUL/PGN* SW6 ....**114** B4
Cheseman St *SYD* SE26 ....**156** C5
Chesham Cl *KTBR* * SW1X **42** A3
Chesham Ms *KTBR* SW1X **42** A2
Chesham Pl *KTBR* SW1X **42** A2
Chesham St *KTBR* SW1X **42** A3
  WLSDN NW10 ....**51** D5
Cheshire St *BETH* E2 ....**90** A3
Chesholm Rd *STNW/STAM* N16 ....**59** E5
Cheshunt Rd *FSTGT* E7 ....**82** B1
Chesilton Rd *FUL/PGN* SW6 ....**113** F4
Chesley Gdns *EHAM* E6 ....**95** D1
Chesney St *BTSEA* SW11 ....**116** A4
Chesson Rd *WKENS* W14 ....**113** F2
Chester Cl *BARN* * SW13 ....**130** B1
  KTBR SW1X **42** B1
Chester Cl North *CAMTN* NW1 ....**7** D3
Chester Cl South *CAMTN* NW1 ....**7** D4
Chester Crs *HACK* E8 ....**77** F2
Chesterfield Gdns *GNWCH* * SE10 .**123** D3
  MYFR/PICC * W1J **30** C3
Chesterfield Gv *EDUL* SE22 ....**137** F3
Chesterfield Hl *MYFR/PICC* W1J **30** C2
Chesterfield Rd *CHSWK* W4 ....**110** C2
  LEY E10 ....**62** C2
Chesterfield St *MYFR/PICC* W1J **30** C3

Chesterfield Wy *PECK* SE15 ....120 C3
Chesterford Gdns *HAMP* NW3 ....72 B1
Chesterford Rd *MNPK* E12 ....83 F3
Chester Ga *CAMTN* NW1 ....6 C4
Chester Ms *KTBR* SW1X 42 C2
Chester Pl *CAMTN* NW1 ....6 B3
Chester Rd *BFN/LL* DA15 ....145 E3
  CAMTN NW1 ....6 B3
  CAN/RD E16 ....93 E3
  FSTGT E7 ....83 D4
  GDMY/SEVK IG3 ....67 F3
  KTTN NW5 ....56 B4
  WAN E11 ....64 B1
Chester Rw *BGVA* SW1W 42 A5
Chester Sq *BGVA* SW1W 42 B4
Chester Square Ms *BGVA* * SW1W 42 C3
Chester St *BETH* * E2 ....78 A5
  BETH E2 ....90 A3
  KTBR SW1X 42 B2
Chester Ter *CAMTN* NW1 ....6 C3
Chesterton Cl *WAND/EARL* SW18 ....132 A3
Chesterton Rd *NKENS* W10 ....89 D4
  PLSTW E13 ....94 A2
Chesterton Sq *WKENS* W14 ....101 F5
Chesterton Ter *PLSTW* E13 ....94 A2
Chester Wy *LBTH* SE11 ....46 B5
Chestnut Aly *FUL/PGN* * SW6 ....113 F2
Chestnut Av *FSTGT* E7 ....82 B1
  MORT/ESHN * SW14 ....129 D1
Chestnut Cl *CAT* SE6 ....158 C4
  NWCR SE14 ....121 F4
  STRHM/NOR SW16 ....154 A4
Chestnut Dr *WAN* E11 ....64 A1
Chestnut Gv *BAL* SW12 ....134 A5
Chestnut Pl *NRWD* SE19 ....155 F4
Chestnut Ri *WOOL/PLUM* SE18 ....127 E1
Chestnut Rd *WNWD* SE27 ....154 B3
Chettle Cl *STHWK* * SE1 ....48 A2
Chetwode Rd *TOOT* SW17 ....151 F3
Chetwynd Rd *KTTN* NW5 ....74 B1
Chetwynd Vls *KTTN* * NW5 ....74 B1
Cheval Pl *SKENS* SW7 ....41 D2
Cheval St *POP/IOD* E14 ....104 A4
Chevening Rd *GNWCH* SE10 ....123 F1
  KIL/WHAMP NW6 ....89 D1
Cheverton Rd *ARCH* N19 ....57 D3
Chevet St *HOM* E9 ....79 E2
Chevington *CRICK* * NW2 ....53 D4
Cheviot Rd *WNWD* SE27 ....154 A5
Chevron Cl *CAN/RD* E16 ....94 A5
Cheyne Gdns *CHEL* SW3 ....115 E2
Cheyne Ms *CHEL* SW3 ....115 E2
Cheyne Pl *CHEL* * SW3 ....115 E2
Cheyne Rw *CHEL* SW3 ....115 E2
Cheyne Wk *CHEL* SW3 ....115 E2
  HDN NW4 ....52 C1
Chichele Rd *CRICK* NW2 ....71 D2
Chicheley St *STHWK* SE1 ....33 F5
Chichester Cl *BKHTH/KID* SE3 ....124 C3
  EHAM E6 ....95 E5
Chichester Gdns *IL* IG1 ....65 E2
Chichester Rd *BAY/PAD* W2 ....15 D2
  KIL/WHAMP NW6 ....2 A2
  WAN E11 ....63 E4
Chichester St *PIM* SW1V 116 C1
Chichester Wy *POP/IOD* E14 ....105 D5
Chicksand St *WCHPL* E1 ....25 F3
Chiddingstone St *FUL/PGN* SW6 ....114 A5
Chigwell Hl *WAP* E1W 102 B1
Childeberth Rd *TOOT* SW17 ....152 B2
Childeric Rd *NWCR* SE14 ....121 E3
Childerley St *FUL/PGN* SW6 ....113 E4
Childers St *DEPT* SE8 ....121 E1
Child's Pl *ECT* SW5 ....38 B5
Chichester St *ECT* SW5 ....38 B4
Child's Wk *ECT* * SW5 ....38 B4
Chilham Rd *ELTH/MOT* SE9 ....161 E4

Chillerton Rd *TOOT* SW17 ....152 A5
Chillingworth Rd *HOLWY* N7 ....75 F2
Chiltern Gdns *CRICK* NW2 ....53 D5
Chiltern Rd *BOW* E3 ....92 A3
Chiltern St *MHST* W1U 18 A2
Chilthorne Cl *CAT* SE6 ....139 F5
Chilton Gv *DEPT* SE8 ....103 D5
Chilton Rd *RCH/KEW* TW9 ....128 A1
Chilton St *BETH* E2 ....13 F5
Chilver St *GNWCH* SE10 ....123 F1
Chilworth Ms *BAY/PAD* W2 ....15 F5
Chilworth St *BAY/PAD* W2 ....15 F5
Chinbrook Crs *LEE/GVPK* SE12 ....160 B3
Chinbrook Rd *LEE/GVPK* SE12 ....160 B3
Chipka St *POP/IOD* E14 ....104 C3
Chipley St *NWCR* SE14 ....121 E2
Chippendale St *CLPT* E5 ....61 D5
Chippenham Ms *MV/WKIL* W9 ....14 A1
Chippenham Rd *MV/WKIL* W9 ....2 A5
Chipstead Gdns *CRICK* NW2 ....52 B4
Chipstead St *FUL/PGN* SW6 ....114 A4
Chisenhale Rd *BOW* E3 ....91 E1
Chisley Rd *SEVS/STOTM* N15 ....59 E1
Chiswell Sq *BKHTH/KID* SE3 ....124 B5
Chiswell St *STLK* EC1Y 24 A3
Chiswick Br *MORT/ESHN* SW14 ....110 C5
Chiswick Common Rd *CHSWK* W4 ....99 D5
Chiswick High Rd *CHSWK* W4 ....110 B1
Chiswick House Grounds
  CHSWK * W4 ....111 D2
Chiswick La *CHSWK* W4 ....111 E1
Chiswick La South *CHSWK* W4 ....111 F2
Chiswick Ml *CHSWK* W4 ....111 F2
Chiswick Pk *CHSWK* * W4 ....98 C4
Chiswick Pier *CHSWK* W4 ....111 F3
Chiswick Quay *CHSWK* W4 ....110 C4
Chiswick Rd *CHSWK* W4 ....98 C5
Chiswick Sq *CHSWK* W4 ....111 E2
Chiswick Staithe *CHSWK* W4 ....110 B4
Chiswick Village *CHSWK* W4 ....110 A2
Chitty St *FITZ* W1T 19 F2
Chivalry Rd *BTSEA* SW11 ....133 E3
Chobham Gdns *WIM/MER* SW19 ....149 D2
Chobham Rd *SRTFD* E15 ....81 D2
Cholmeley Cl *HGT* * N6 ....56 B2
Cholmeley Crs *HGT* N6 ....56 B2
Cholmeley Pk *HGT* N6 ....56 B3
Cholmley Gdns *KIL/WHAMP* NW6 ....72 A2
Cholmondeley Av *WLSDN* NW10 ....88 A1
Chopwell Cl *SRTFD* * E15 ....81 D4
Choumert Gv *PECK* SE15 ....120 A5
Choumert Rd *PECK* SE15 ....137 F1
Chow Sq *HACK* * E8 ....77 F2
Chrisp St *POP/IOD* E14 ....92 B4
Christchurch Av *KIL/WHAMP* NW6 ....71 D5
Christchurch Hl *HAMP* NW3 ....55 D5
Christchurch Pas *HAMP* NW3 ....55 D5
Christchurch Rd *BFN/LL* DA15 ....163 F4
  BRXS/STRHM SW2 ....153 F1
Christ Church Rd *CEND/HSY/T* N8 ....57 E1
Christchurch Rd *IL* IG1 ....66 B3
  MORT/ESHN SW14 ....128 B3
Christchurch Sq *HOM* E9 ....78 C5
Christchurch St *CHEL* SW3 ....115 E2
Christchurch Ter *CHEL* * SW3 ....115 F2
Christchurch Wy *GNWCH* SE10 ....123 E1
Christian St *WCHPL* E1 ....90 A5
Christie Rd *HOM* E9 ....79 E3
Christina Sq *FSBYPK* N4 ....58 B3
Christina St *SDTCH* EC2A 12 C5
Christopher Cl *BFN/LL* DA15 ....145 F3
Christopher Pl *CAMTN* * NW1 ....8 B3
Christophers Ms *NTGHL* * W11 ....101 E2
Christopher St *SDTCH* EC2A 24 B1
Chryssell Rd *BRXN/ST* SW9 ....118 A3
Chubworthy St *NWCR* SE14 ....121 E2
Chudleigh Crs *GDMY/SEVK* IG3 ....85 E1
Chudleigh Rd *BROCKY* SE4 ....139 F3

KIL/WHAMP NW6	**70**	C4
Chudleigh St WCHPL E1	**91**	D5
Chulsa Rd SYD SE26	**156**	B5
Chumleigh Gdns CMBW * SE5	**119**	E2
Chumleigh St CMBW SE5	**119**	E2
Church Ap DUL SE21	**155**	D5
Church Av CAMTN NW1	**74**	B3
MORT/ESHN SW14	**129**	D2
Churchbury Rd ELTH/MOT SE9	**143**	D5
Church Crs HOM E9	**79**	D4
Churchcroft Cl BAL * SW12	**134**	A5
Churchdown BMLY BR1	**159**	E4
Church Dr CDALE/KGS NW9	**51**	D3
Churchfield Rd ACT W3	**98**	C2
Churchfields GNWCH SE10	**122**	C2
Church Garth ARCH * N19	**57**	D4
Church Ga FUL/PGN SW6	**131**	E1
Church Gn BRXN/ST * SW9	**118**	A5
Church Gv LEW SE13	**140**	B2
Church Hl WIM/MER SW19	**149**	F5
WOOL/PLUM SE18	**107**	F4
Church Hyde WOOL/PLUM SE18	**127**	E2
Churchill Gdns PIM SW1V	**116**	B1
Churchill Gardens Rd PIM SW1V	**116**	B1
Churchill Pl POP/IOD E14	**104**	B2
Churchill Rd CAN/RD E16	**94**	C5
CRICK NW2	**70**	B3
KTTN NW5	**74**	B1
Churchill Wk HOM E9	**78**	C2
Church La CDALE/KGS NW9	**50**	C3
TOOT SW17	**151**	F5
WAN E11	**63**	E3
Churchley Rd SYD SE26	**156**	B4
Church Md CMBW * SE5	**118**	C3
Churchmead Rd WLSDN NW10	**70**	A3
Church Pth CHSWK W4	**98**	A5
Church Ri FSTH SE23	**157**	D1
Church Rd ACT W3	**98**	C3
BARN SW13	**112**	A5
GNTH/NBYPK IG2	**67**	E1
IS N1	**76**	C3
LEY E10	**62**	A3
MNPK E12	**83**	F2
WIM/MER SW19	**149**	E4
WLSDN NW10	**69**	E5
Church Rw FUL/PGN * SW6	**114**	B3
HAMP NW3	**72**	C1
WAND/EARL * SW18	**132**	A3
Church St BAY/PAD W2	**16**	B2
CHSWK W4	**111**	E2
SRTFD E15	**81**	E5
Church Street Est STJWD NW8	**16**	B1
Church St North SRTFD E15	**81**	E5
Church Ter FUL/PGN * SW6	**114**	B5
LEW SE13	**141**	E1
Church V FSTH SE23	**156**	C2
Church Wk CDALE/KGS NW9	**51**	D4
CRICK NW2	**53**	F5
STNW/STAM N16	**59**	D5
Churchway CAMTN NW1	**8**	B3
Churchyard Rw LBTH SE11	**47**	D4
Churston Av PLSTW E13	**82**	B5
Churston Cl BRXS/STRHM * SW2	**154**	B1
Churton Pl CHSWK * W4	**110**	B2
PIM SW1V	**43**	F5
Churton St PIM SW1V	**43**	F5
Chyngton Cl BFN/LL DA15	**163**	F3
Cibber Rd FSTH SE23	**157**	D2
Cicada Rd WAND/EARL SW18	**132**	C4
Cicely Rd PECK SE15	**120**	A4
Cinderford Wy BMLY BR1	**159**	E4
Cinnamon St WAP E1W	**102**	B2
The Circle CRICK NW2	**52**	C3
Circular Wy WOOL/PLUM SE18	**51**	E5
Circus Ms MBLAR * W1H	**125**	F2
Circus Pl LVPST * EC2M	**17**	E2
Circus Rd STJWD NW8	**24**	B3
Circus St GNWCH SE10	**122**	C3

Cirencester St BAY/PAD W2	**14**	C2
Citadel Pl LBTH SE11	**117**	F1
Citizen Rd HOLWY N7	**58**	A5
Citron Ter PECK * SE15	**138**	B1
City Barracks SHB * W12	**100**	C2
City Garden Rw IS N1	**11**	D2
City Rd FSBYE EC1V	**10**	C2
SDTCH EC2A	**24**	B2
Clabon Ms KTBR SW1X	**41**	E3
Clack Cl BERM/RHTH SE16	**102**	C3
Clacton Rd WALTH E17	**61**	E1
Claire Pl POP/IOD E14	**104**	A4
Clairvale Rd TOOT SW17	**152**	B5
Clancarty Rd FUL/PGN SW6	**114**	A5
Clandon Cl ACT W3	**98**	B3
Clandon Rd GDMY/SEVK IG3	**67**	E4
Clandon St DEPT SE8	**122**	A5
Clanricarde Gdns BAY/PAD W2	**26**	B2
Clapham Common North Side CLAP SW4	**134**	A2
Clapham Common South Side CLAP SW4	**134**	B4
Clapham Common West Side BTSEA SW11	**133**	F2
Clapham Court Ter CLAP * SW4	**135**	E3
Clapham Crs CLAP SW4	**135**	D3
Clapham High St CLAP SW4	**135**	D2
Clapham Manor St CLAP SW4	**134**	C1
Clapham Park Est CLAP * SW4	**135**	D5
Clapham Park Rd CLAP SW4	**135**	D3
Clapham Park Ter CLAP * SW4	**134**	C2
Clapham Rd BRXN/ST SW9	**135**	E3
Clapham Rd South IS N1	**117**	E5
Claps Gate La EHAM E6	**77**	D3
Clapton Common CLPT E5	**96**	B3
Clapton Sq CLPT E5	**60**	A2
Clapton Ter STNW/STAM N16	**78**	C2
Clapton Wy CLPT E5	**60**	A2
Clara Pl WOOL/PLUM SE18	**78**	A1
Clare Cnr ELTH/MOT SE9	**108**	A5
Clare Gdns BARK IG11	**144**	B5
FSTGT E7	**85**	F3
NTGHL * W11	**82**	A1
Clare La IS N1	**89**	E5
Clare Lawn Av MORT/ESHN SW14	**76**	C3
Clare Ms FUL/PGN SW6	**129**	D3
Claremont Cl BRXS/STRHM SW2	**114**	B3
CAN/RD E16	**153**	F1
IS N1	**108**	A2
Claremont Gdns GDMY/SEVK IG3	**10**	B2
Claremont Gv CHSWK W4	**67**	E4
Claremont Rd CRICK NW2	**111**	E3
CRICK NW2	**52**	C2
FSTGT E7	**53**	D3
HGT N6	**82**	B2
MV/WKIL W9	**56**	B2
WAN E11	**89**	E1
Claremont Sq IS N1	**63**	D5
Claremont St GNWCH SE10	**10**	A3
Claremont Vls CMBW * SE5	**122**	B5
Claremont Wy CRICK NW2	**119**	D3
IL IG1	**52**	C3
Clarence Av CLAP SW4	**65**	F1
Clarence Crs CLAP SW4	**135**	D5
Clarence Gdns CAMTN NW1	**135**	D4
Clarence Ga CAMTN NW1	**7**	A4
Clarence La PUT/ROE SW15	**5**	F5
Clarence Ms CLPT E5	**129**	F4
Clarence Pas CAMTN * NW1	**78**	B2
Clarence Pl CLPT E5	**8**	C2
Clarence Rd CAN/RD E16	**78**	B2
CHSWK W4	**93**	E3
CLPT E5	**110**	A1
DEPT SE8	**78**	B1
ELTH/MOT SE9	**122**	B2
FSTGT E7	**161**	E2
KIL/WHAMP NW6	**82**	C1
	71	F4

Clarence Ter *CAMTN* NW1.................5 F5
Clarence Wk *CLAP* SW4.................117 E5
Clarence Wy *CAMTN* NW1.................74 B4
Clarendon Cl *BAY/PAD* * W2.................28 C1
HOM E9.................78 C4
Clarendon Cross *NTGHL* W11.................101 E1
Clarendon Dr *PUT/ROE* SW15.................130 C2
Clarendon Gdns *IL* IG1.................65 F3
MV/WKIL W9.................15 F1
Clarendon Ga *BAY/PAD* W2.................28 C1
Clarendon Ms *BAY/PAD* W2.................28 C1
Clarendon Pl *BAY/PAD* W2.................28 C1
Clarendon Ri *LEW* SE13.................140 C1
Clarendon Rd *LEY* E10.................62 B1
NTGHL W11.................101 E1
Clarendon St *PIM* SW1V.................116 B1
Clarendon Ter *MV/WKIL* W9.................3 F4
Clarens St *CAT* SE6.................157 F2
Clare Rd *NWCR* SE14.................121 F5
WAN E11.................63 D1
WLSDN NW10.................70 A4
Clare St *BETH* E2.................90 B1
Clareville Gv *SKENS* SW7.................39 F5
Clareville St *SKENS* SW7.................39 F5
Clarges Ms *MYFR/PICC* W1J.................30 C3
Clarges St *MYFR/PICC* W1J.................31 D3
Claribel Rd *BRXN/ST* SW9.................118 B5
Clarissa St *HACK* E8.................77 F5
Clarkes Ms *CAVSQ/HST* W1G.................18 B2
Clarkson Rd *CAN/RD* E16.................93 F5
Clarkson Rw *CAMTN* NW1.................7 D2
Clarkson St *BETH* * E2.................90 B2
Clark's Rd *IL* IG1.................67 D4
Clark St *WCHPL* E1.................90 C5
Claude Rd *LEY* E10.................62 C3
PECK SE15.................120 B5
PLSTW E13.................82 B5
Claude St *POP/IOD* E14.................104 A5
Claudia Pl *WIM/MER* SW19.................149 E1
Claughton Rd *PLSTW* E13.................94 C1
Clavell St *GNWCH* SE10.................122 C2
Claverdale Rd *BRXS/STRHM* SW2.................135 F1
Clavering Av *BARN* SW13.................112 B2
Clavering Rd *MNPK* E12.................65 D3
Claverton St *PIM* SW1V.................116 C1
Clave St *WAP* E1W.................102 C2
Claxton Gv *HMSMTH* W6.................113 D1
Claybank Gv *LEW* SE13.................140 B1
Claybridge Rd *LEE/GVPK* SE12.................160 C4
Claybrook Rd *HMSMTH* W6.................113 D2
Claydown Ms *WOOL/PLUM* SE18.................126 A4
Clayfarm Rd *ELTH/MOT* SE9.................162 C1
Clayhill Crs *LEE/GVPK* SE12.................161 D4
Claylands Pl *BRXN/ST* SW9.................118 A3
Claylands Rd *VX/NE* SW8.................117 F2
Claypole Rd *SRTFD* * E15.................92 C1
Clays La *SRTFD* E15.................80 B2
Clays Lane Cl *SRTFD* E15.................80 B2
Clay St *MHST* W1U.................17 F3
Clayton Cl *EHAM* E6.................95 F5
Clayton Dr *DEPT* SE8.................121 E1
Clayton Ms *GNWCH* SE10.................123 D4
Clayton Rd *PECK* SE15.................120 A4
Clayton St *LBTH* SE11.................118 A2
Cleanthus Cl *WOOL/PLUM* SE18.................126 B4
Cleanthus Rd *WOOL/PLUM* SE18.................126 B4
Clearbrook Wy *WCHPL* E1.................90 C5
Clearwater Ter *WKENS* W14.................101 D3
Clearwell Dr *MV/WKIL* W9.................14 C1
Cleaver Sq *LBTH* SE11.................118 A1
Cleaver St *LBTH* SE11.................118 A1
Cleeve Hl *FSTH* SE23.................156 B1
Clegg St *PLSTW* E13.................94 A1
WAP E1W.................102 B2
Clematis Cottages *SHB* * W12.................100 A1
Clematis St *SHB* W12.................99 F1
Clem Attlee Ct *FUL/PGN* * SW6.................113 F2
Clem Attlee Pde *FUL/PGN* * SW6.................113 F2

Clemence St *POP/IOD* E14.................91 F4
Clemence St *CLAP* SW4.................135 D2
Clement Av *CLAP* SW4.................135 D2
Clement Cl *CHSWK* W4.................99 D5
KIL/WHAMP NW6.................70 C4
Clementina Rd *LEY* E10.................61 F3
Clement Rd *WIM/MER* SW19.................149 E5
Clements Av *CAN/RD* E16.................106 A1
Clements Inn *LINN* WC2A.................21 F5
Clements La *IL* IG1.................66 B5
MANHO EC4N.................36 B1
Clements Rd *BERM/RHTH* SE16.................102 B4
BERM/RHTH SE16.................102 A4
EHAM E6.................83 F4
IL IG1.................66 B5
Clendon Wy *WOOL/PLUM* SE18.................109 D5
Clennam St *STHWK* * SE1.................35 H1
Clenston Ms *MBLAR* W1H.................17 E4
Clephane Rd *IS* N1.................76 C3
Clere Pl *SDTCH* EC2A.................12 B5
Clere St *SDTCH* EC2A.................12 B5
Clerkenwell Cl *CLKNW* EC1R.................10 B5
Clerkenwell Gn *CLKNW* EC1R.................22 C1
Clerkenwell Rd *CLKNW* EC1R.................22 A1
Clermont Rd *HOM* E9.................78 C5
Cleveland Av *CHSWK* W4.................99 F5
Cleveland Gdns *BARN* SW13.................111 F5
BAY/PAD W2.................15 E5
CRICK NW2.................53 D4
Cleveland Ms *FITZ* W1T.................19 E2
Cleveland Pl *STJS* SW1Y.................31 F3
Cleveland Rd *BARN* SW13.................111 F5
CHSWK W4.................98 C4
IL IG1.................66 B5
IS N1.................77 D4
WELL DA16.................127 F5
Cleveland Rw *WHALL* SW1A.................31 F4
Cleveland Sq *BAY/PAD* W2.................15 E5
Cleveland St *CAMTN* NW1.................19 D1
Cleveland Ter *BAY/PAD* W2.................15 E5
Cleveland Wy *WCHPL* E1.................90 C3
Cleveleys Rd *CLPT* E5.................60 B5
Clevely Cl *CHARL* SE7.................107 D5
Cleverly Est *SHB* * W12.................100 A2
Cleve Rd *KIL/WHAMP* NW6.................72 A4
Cleves Rd *EHAM* E6.................83 D5
Clifden Rd *CLPT* E5.................78 C2
Clifford Av *MORT/ESHN* SW14.................110 C5
RCH/KEW TW9.................128 B1
Clifford Cl *PLSTW* * E13.................94 B2
Clifford Dr *BRXN/ST* SW9.................136 B2
Clifford Gdns *WLSDN* NW10.................88 C1
Clifford Rd *CAN/RD* E16.................93 F3
CONDST W1S.................31 E2
Clifford Wy *WLSDN* NW10.................69 F1
Clifton Av *SHB* W12.................99 F3
Clifton Crs *PECK* SE15.................120 B3
Clifton Gdns *CHSWK* W4.................99 D5
GLDGN NW11.................53 F1
MV/WKIL W9.................15 E1
SEVS/STOTM N15.................59 F3
Clifton Ga *WBPTN* * SW10.................114 C2
Clifton Gv *HACK* E8.................78 A3
Clifton Hl *KIL/WHAMP* NW6.................3 E1
BERM/RHTH SE16.................102 C3
WBPTN * SW10.................114 C2
Clifton Ri *NWCR* SE14.................121 E3
Clifton Rd *CAN/RD* E16.................93 E4
CEND/HSY/T N8.................57 D1
FSTGT E7.................83 D3
GNTH/NBYPK IG2.................67 D1
MV/WKIL W9.................3 F5

SCUP DA14 ....163 E4
WLSDN NW10 ....88 A1
Clifton St SDTCH EC2A 24 C1
Clifton Ter FSBYPK N4 ....58 A4
Clifton Vls MV/WKIL W9 ....15 D2
Clifton Wy PECK SE15 ....120 C3
Clink St STHWK SE1 ....36 A3
Clinton Rd BOW E3 ....91 E2
FSTGT E7 ....82 A1
Clinton Ter DEPT * SE8 ....122 A2
Clipper Cl BERM/RHTH SE16 ....103 D3
Clipper Wy LEW SE13 ....140 C2
Clipstone Ms GTPST W1W 19 E2
Clipstone St GTPST W1W 19 D2
Clissold Crs STNW/STAM N16 ....77 D1
Clissold Rd STNW/STAM N16 ....59 D5
Clitheroe Rd BRXN/ST SW9 ....117 E5
Clitherow House CRICK NW2 ....52 C3
Clitterhouse Crs CRICK NW2 ....52 C3
Clitterhouse Rd CRICK NW2 ....52 C3
Clive Ct WLSDN * NW10 ....69 F4
Cliveden Pl BGVA SW1W 42 A4
Clive Rd DUL SE21 ....155 D3
Cloak La BLKFR EC4V 35 F1
Clockhouse Av BARK IG11 ....84 C5
Clockhouse Cl WIM/MER SW19 ....148 C3
Clockhouse Pl PUT/ROE SW15 ....131 E3
Clock Tower Ms IS N1 ....76 C5
Clock Tower Pl HOLWY * N7 ....75 E3
Cloister Pl ACT W3 ....86 C4
CRICK NW2 ....53 F5
Clonbrock Rd STNW/STAM N16 ....77 E1
Cloncurry St FUL/PGN SW6 ....113 D5
Clonmel Rd FUL/PGN SW6 ....113 F3
Clonmore St WAND/EARL SW18 ....149 F1
Ciorane Gdns HAMP NW3 ....54 A3
The Close GNTH/NBYPK IG2 ....67 E1
RCH/KEW TW9 ....128 B1
WBLY HA9 ....50 C5
Cloth Ct STBT EC1A 23 D3
Cloth Fair STBT EC1A 23 D3
Clothier St HDTCH * EC3A 25 D4
Cloth St STBT * EC1A 23 E2
Clothworkers Rd WOOL/PLUM SE18 ...127 D3
Cloudesdale Rd TOOT SW17 ....152 B1
Cloudesley Pl IS N1 ....76 A5
Cloudesley Rd IS N1 ....76 A5
Cloudesley Sq IS N1 ....76 A5
Cloudesley St IS N1 ....76 A5
Clova Rd FSTGT E7 ....82 A3
Clove Crs POP/IOD E14 ....104 C1
Clovelly Rd CHSWK * W4 ....99 D3
Clovelly Wy WCHPL E1 ....90 C5
Clover Cl WAN * E11 ....63 D4
Cloverdale Gdns BFN/LL DA15 ....145 F4
Clover Ms CHEL SW3 ....115 F2
Clove St PLSTW E13 ....94 B3
Clowders Rd CAT SE6 ....157 F3
Cloysters Gn WAP * E1W 102 A2
Club Rw BETH E2 ....13 E4
Cluny Est STHWK SE1 ....48 C2
Cluny Ms ECT SW5 ....38 A5
Cluny Pl STHWK SE1 ....48 C2
Clutton St POP/IOD E14 ....92 B4
Clyde Cl CAMTN NW1 ....8 B1
Clyde Flats FUL/PGN * SW6 ....113 F3
Clyde Pl LEY E10 ....62 B2
Clydesdale Gdns RCHPK/HAM TW10 ..128 B2
Clydesdale Rd NTGHL W11 ....89 F5
Clyde St DEPT SE8 ....121 F2
Clyde Ter FSTH SE23 ....156 C2
Clyde V FSTH SE23 ....156 C2
Clyston St VX/NE SW8 ....116 C5
Coach & Horses Yd CONDST * W1S ...31 E1
Coach House La HBRY * N5 ....76 B1
WIM/MER SW19 ....149 D4
Coach House Ms FSTH SE23 ....138 C4
NWCR * SE14 ....121 D4
Coach House Yd WAND/EARL * SW18 .132 B2

Coalecroft Rd PUT/ROE SW15 ....130 C2
Coates Av WAND/EARL SW18 ....133 E4
Coate St BETH E2 ....90 A1
Cobbett Rd ELTH/MOT SE9 ....143 F1
Cobbett St VX/NE SW8 ....117 F3
Cobble La IS N1 ....76 B4
Cobble Ms FSBYPK N4 ....58 C5
Cobbold Ms SHB * W12 ....99 F3
Cobbold Rd SHB W12 ....99 F3
WAN E11 ....63 F5
WLSDN NW10 ....69 F3
Cobb St WCHPL E1 ....25 E4
Cobden Ms SYD SE26 ....156 B5
Cobden Rd WAN E11 ....63 F5
Cobham Cl BTSEA * SW11 ....133 E4
Cobham Ms CAMTN NW1 ....75 D4
Cobham Rd GDMY/SEVK IG3 ....67 E4
Cobland Rd LEE/GVPK SE12 ....160 C4
Coborn Rd BOW E3 ....91 F2
Coborn St BOW E3 ....91 F2
Cobourg Rd CMBW SE5 ....119 F2
Cobourg St CAMTN NW1 ....7 F4
Coburg Cl WEST SW1P 43 F4
Coburg Crs BRXS/STRHM SW2 ....153 F1
Coburg Dwellings WCHPL * E1 ......102 C1
Cochrane Ms STJWD NW8 ....4 B2
Cochrane St STJWD NW8 ....4 B2
Cockerell Rd WALTH E17 ....61 E2
Cock La STBT EC1A 22 C3
Cockspur Ct STJS SW1Y 32 B3
Cockspur St STJS * SW1Y 32 B3
Code St WCHPL E1 ....25 F1
Codling Cl WAP E1W 102 A2
Codrington Hl FSTH SE23 ....139 E5
Codrington Ms NTGHL W11 ....89 E5
Cody Rd CAN/RD E16 ....93 D3
Cofers Cir WBLY HA9 ....50 B5
Coffey St DEPT SE8 ....122 A3
Coin St STHWK SE1 ....34 A3
Coity Rd KTTN NW5 ....74 A3
Cokers La DUL SE21 ....154 C1
Coke St WCHPL E1 ....90 A5
Colbeck Ms ECT SW5 ....39 D5
Colberg Pl STNW/STAM * N16 ....59 F2
Colby Rd NRWD SE19 ....155 E5
Colchester Rd WALTH E17 ....62 A1
Colchester St WCHPL E1 ....25 F4
Coldbath Sq CLKNW * EC1R 10 A5
Coldbath St LEW SE13 ....122 B4
Coldblow La NWCR SE14 ....121 D3
Coldharbour POP/IOD E14 ....104 C2
Coldharbour Crest ELTH/MOT * SE9 .162 A3
Coldharbour La BRXN/ST SW9 ....136 A2
Coldharbour Pl CMBW SE5 ....118 C5
Coldstream Gdns WAND/EARL SW18 ..131 F4
Colebeck Ms IS N1 ....76 B3
Colebert Av WCHPL E1 ....90 C3
Colebrooke Dr WAN E11 ....64 B2
Colebrooke Pl IS N1 ....76 B5
Colebrooke Rw IS N1 ....10 C2
Coleby Pth CMBW * SE5 ....119 D3
Coleford Rd WAND/EARL SW18 ......132 C3
Colegrave Rd SRTFD E15 ....81 D2
Colegrove Rd PECK SE15 ....119 F2
Coleherne Ms WBPTN SW10 ....114 B1
Coleherne Rd WBPTN SW10 ....114 B1
Colehill Gdns FUL/PGN * SW6 ....113 E4
Colehill La FUL/PGN SW6 ....113 E4
Coleman Flds IS N1 ....76 C5
Coleman Rd CMBW SE5 ....119 E3
Colemans Heath ELTH/MOT SE9 ......162 A3
Coleman St LOTH EC2R 24 A4
Colenso Rd CLPT E5 ....78 C1
GNTH/NBYPK IG2 ....67 E3
Colepits Wood Rd ELTH/MOT SE9 ...145 D3
Coleraine Rd BKHTH/KID SE3 ....123 F2
Coleridge Av MNPK E12 ....83 E3
Coleridge Cl VX/NE SW8 ....116 B5

Coleridge Gdns *KIL/WHAMP* NW6 ....**72** C4
Coleridge Rd *CEND/HSY/T* N8 ....**57** F1
  FSBYPK N4..........**58** A4
Coles Green Rd *CRICK* NW2 ....**52** A3
Colestown St *BTSEA* SW11 ....**115** E5
Cole St *STHWK* SE1 ....**47** F1
Colet Gdns *WKENS* W14 ....**113** D1
Coley St *FSBYW* WC1X **21** F1
Colfe & Hatcliffe Glebe *LEW* * SE13..........**140** B3
Colfe Rd *FSTH* SE23 ....**157** E1
Colinette Rd *PUT/ROE* SW15 ....**130** C2
Colin Rd *WLSDN* NW10 ....**70** A3
Coliston Rd *WAND/EARL* SW18..........**132** A5
Collamore Av *WAND/EARL* SW18 ....**151** E1
Collard Pl *CAMTN* NW1 ....**74** B4
College Ap *GNWCH* SE10 ....**122** C2
College Crs *KIL/WHAMP* NW6..........**72** C3
College Cross *IS* N1 ....**76** A4
College East *WCHPL* * E1 ....**25** F3
College Gdns *TOOT* SW17 ....**151** E2
College Gv *CAMTN* NW1 ....**75** D5
College M *CANST* * EC4R **35** F1
College Ms *IS* N1 * **76** A4
  WEST SW1P..........**44** C2
College Pde *KIL/WHAMP* * NW6 ....**71** E5
College Park Cl *LEW* SE13 ....**141** D2
College Pl *CAMTN* NW1 ....**74** C5
  WBPTN * SW10..........**114** C3
College Rd *DUL* SE21 ....**137** E5
  NRWD SE19..........**155** F5
  WLSDN NW10..........**88** C1
College Rw *CANST* * EC4R **35** F1
College Vw *ELTH/MOT* SE9 ....**161** D1
College Yd *KIL/WHAMP* * NW6 ....**71** E5
  KTTN * NW5..........**74** B2
Collent St *HOM* E9 ....**78** C3
Collett Rd *BERM/RHTH* SE16 ....**102** A4
Collier Cl *EHAM* E6 ....**108** B1
Collier St *IS* N1 ....**9** E2
Collingbourne Rd *SHB* W12 ....**100** B2
Collingham Gdns *ECT* SW5 ....**39** D5
Collingham Pl *ECT* SW5 ....**38** C5
Collingham Rd *ECT* SW5 ....**39** D4
Collington St *GNWCH* * SE10 ....**123** D1
Collingtree Rd *SYD* SE26 ....**156** C4
Collingwood St *WCHPL* E1 ....**90** B3
Collinson St *STHWK* SE1 ....**47** E1
Collinson Wk *STHWK* SE1 ....**47** E1
Collins Rd *HBRY* N5 ....**76** C1
Collins St *BKHTH/KID* SE3 ....**123** E5
Coll's Rd *PECK* SE15 ....**120** C4
Collyer Pl *PECK* SE15 ....**120** A4
Colman Rd *CAN/RD* E16 ....**94** C4
Colmar Cl *WCHPL* E1 ....**91** D3
Colmore Ms *PECK* SE15 ....**120** B4
Colnbrook St *STHWK* SE1 ....**46** C3
Colne Rd *CLPT* E5 ....**79** D1
Colne St *PLSTW* E13 ....**94** A2
Cologne Rd *BTSEA* SW11 ....**133** D2
Colombo Rd *IL* IG1 ....**66** C3
Colombo St *STHWK* SE1 ....**34** C4
Colomb St *GNWCH* SE10 ....**123** E1
Colonial Dr *CHSWK* W4 ....**98** C5
The Colonnade *DEPT* * SE8 ....**105** F5
Colonnade *BMSBY* WC1N **20** C1
Colosseum Ter *CAMTN* NW1..........**7** D5
Colson Wy *STRHM/NOR* SW16 ....**152** C4
Colston Rd *FSTGT* E7 ....**83** D3
  MORT/ESHN SW14..........**128** C2
Colthurst Crs *FSBYPK* N4 ....**58** B4
Columbas Dr *HAMP* * NW3 ....**55** D2
Columbia Rd *BETH* E2 ....**13** E3
  PLSTW * E13..........**93** F3
Columbine Av *EHAM* E6 ....**95** E4
Columbine Wy *LEW* * SE13 ....**122** C5
Colview Ct *ELTH/MOT* SE9 ....**161** D2
Colvestone Crs *HACK* E8 ....**77** F2
Colville Est *IS* N1 ....**77** D5

Colville Gdns *NTGHL* W11 ....**89** F5
Colville Houses *NTGHL* * W11 ....**89** F5
Colville Ms *NTGHL* W11 ....**89** F5
Colville Pl *FITZ* W1T **19** F3
Colville Rd *ACT* W3 ....**98** B4
  NTGHL W11..........**89** F5
  WAN E11..........**62** C5
Colville Sq *NTGHL* * W11 ....**89** F5
Colville Square Ms *NTGHL* * W11 ....**89** F5
Colville Ter *NTGHL* W11 ....**89** F5
Colvin Cl *SYD* SE26 ....**156** C5
Colvin Rd *EHAM* E6 ....**83** E4
Colwell Rd *EDUL* SE22 ....**137** E5
Colwick Cl *HGT* N6 ....**57** D2
Colwith Rd *HMSMTH* W6 ....**112** C2
Colworth Gv *WALW* SE17 ....**47** F5
Colworth Rd *WAN* E11 ....**63** E1
Colwyn Cl *STRHM/NOR* SW16 ....**152** C5
Colwyn Gn *CDALE/KGS* * NW9 ....**51** E1
Colwyn Rd *CRICK* NW2 ....**52** B5
Colyer Cl *ELTH/MOT* SE9 ....**162** B2
Colyton Rd *EDUL* SE22 ....**138** B3
Combe Av *BKHTH/KID* SE3 ....**123** F3
Combedale Rd *GNWCH* SE10 ....**124** A1
Combemartin Rd *WAND/EARL* SW18 ....**131** E5
Comber Cl *CRICK* NW2 ....**52** A5
Comber Gv *CMBW* SE5 ....**118** C3
Combermere Rd *BRXN/ST* SW9 ....**135** F1
Comberton Rd *CLPT* E5 ....**60** B4
Combeside *WOOL/PLUM* SE18 ....**127** F3
Comeragh Ms *WKENS* * W14 ....**113** E1
Comeragh Rd *WKENS* W14 ....**113** E1
Comerford Rd *BROCKY* SE4 ....**139** E2
Comet Cl *MNPK* E12 ....**83** D1
Comet Pl *DEPT* SE8 ....**122** A3
Comet St *DEPT* SE8 ....**122** A3
Commercial Rd *POP/IOD* E14 ....**91** E5
  WCHPL E1..........**25** F4
Commercial St *WCHPL* E1 ....**25** F1
Commercial Wy *PECK* SE15 ....**119** F4
  WLSDN NW10..........**86** B1
Commerell Pl *GNWCH* SE10 ....**123** F1
Commerell St *GNWCH* SE10 ....**123** E1
Commodore St *WCHPL* E1 ....**91** D4
Commondale *PUT/ROE* SW15 ....**112** C5
Common Rd *BARN* SW13 ....**130** A1
Commonwealth Av *SHB* W12 ....**100** B1
Community Rd *SRTFD* E15 ....**81** D2
Como Rd *FSTH* SE23..........**157** E2
Compayne Gdns *KIL/WHAMP* NW6 ....**72** B4
Compton Av *EHAM* E6 ....**95** D1
  HGT N6..........**55** E2
  IS N1..........**76** B3
Compton Cl *CAMTN* NW1 ....**7** D4
  CRICK NW2..........**53** D2
Compton Crs *CHSWK* W4 ....**110** C2
Compton Pas *FSBYE* EC1V **11** D5
Compton Pl *STPAN* WC1H **8** C5
Compton Rd *IS* N1 ....**76** B3
  WLSDN NW10..........**89** D2
Compton St *FSBYE* EC1V **10** C5
Compton Ter *IS* N1 ....**76** B3
Comus Pl *WALW* SE17 ....**48** C5
Comyn Rd *BTSEA* SW11 ....**133** E2
Comyns Cl *CAN/RD* E16 ....**93** F4
Conant Ms *WCHPL* E1 ....**102** A1
Concanon Rd *BRXS/STRHM* SW2 ....**135** F2
Concert Hall Ap *STHWK* SE1 ....**33** F4
Concorde Dr *EHAM* E6 ....**95** F4
Concord Rd *ACT* W3 ....**86** B3
Condell Rd *VX/NE* SW8 ....**116** C4
Conder St *POP/IOD* E14 ....**91** E5
Condover Crs *WOOL/PLUM* SE18 ....**126** B3
Condray Pl *BTSEA* SW11 ....**115** E3
Conduit Ct *COVGDN* * WC2E **32** C1
Conduit Ms *BAY/PAD* W2 ....**16** A5
Conduit Pas *BAY/PAD* W2 ....**16** A5
Conduit Pl *BAY/PAD* W2 ....**16** A5

Conduit Rd *WOOL/PLUM* SE18 ....126 B1
Conduit St *CONDST* W1S 31 D1
Conduit Wy *WLSDN* NW10 ....68 C4
Coney Acre *DUL* SE21 ....154 C1
Congleton Gv *WOOL/PLUM* SE18 ....126 C1
Congo Rd *WOOL/PLUM* SE18 ....127 D1
Congreve Rd *ELTH/MOT* SE9 ....143 F1
Congreve St *WALW* SE17 ....48 C5
Conifer Gdns *STRHM/NOR* SW16 ....153 F3
Coniger Rd *FUL/PGN* SW6 ....114 A5
Coningham Ms *SHB* W12 ....100 A2
Coningham Rd *SHB* W12 ....100 B3
Coningsby Rd *FSBYPK* N4 ....58 B2
Conington Rd *LEW* SE13 ....122 B5
Conisborough Crs *CAT* SE6 ....158 C3
Coniston Av *BARK* IG11 ....85 E4
    WELL DA16 ....145 E1
Coniston Cl *BARN* SW13 ....111 F3
Coniston Cl *BAY/PAD* * W2 ....17 D5
Conistone Wy *HOLWY* N7 ....75 E4
Conlan St *NKENS* W10 ....89 E3
Conley Rd *WLSDN* NW10 ....69 E1
Conley St *GNWCH* * SE10 ....123 E1
Connaught Av *MORT/ESHN* SW14 ....128 C1
Connaught Br *ELTH/MOT* SE16 ....16 C5
Connaught Cl *BAY/PAD* W2 ....107 D2
    LEY * E10 ....61 E4
Connaught La *IL* IG1 ....66 C4
Connaught Ms *FUL/PGN* * SW6 ....113 E4
    HAMP * NW3 ....73 E2
    WOOL/PLUM SE18 ....126 A1
Connaught Pl *BAY/PAD* W2 ....29 E1
Connaught Rd *CAN/RD* E16 ....107 D1
    FSBYPK N4 ....58 A2
    IL IG1 ....67 D4
    WAN E11 ....63 D3
    WLSDN NW10 ....87 E1
    WOOL/PLUM SE18 ....126 A1
Connaught Sq *BAY/PAD* W2 ....17 D5
Connaught St *BAY/PAD* W2 ....17 D5
Connor St *HOM* * E9 ....79 D5
Consort Rd *PECK* SE15 ....120 B5
Cons St *STHWK* * SE1 ....34 B5
Constable Av *CAN/RD* E16 ....106 B2
Constable Cl *GLDGN* NW11 ....54 B1
Constable Wk *DUL* SE21 ....155 E3
Constance Rd *CAN/RD* E16 ....107 E2
Constantine Rd *HAMP* NW3 ....73 E2
Constitution Hl *WHALL* SW1A 30 C5
Constitution Ri *WOOL/PLUM* SE18 ....126 A4
Content St *WALW* SE17 ....47 F5
Convent Gdns *NTGHL* W11 ....89 F5
Conway Gv *ACT* W3 ....87 D4
Conway Ms *FITZ* W1T 19 E2
Conway Rd *CRICK* NW2 ....52 C4
Conway St *FITZ* W1T 19 E1
Conybeare *HAMP* NW3 ....73 E4
Conyer's Rd *STRHM/NOR* SW16 ....153 D2
Conyer St *BOW* * E3 ....91 E1
Cookes Cl *WAN* E11 ....63 F4
Cook's Rd *SRTFD* E15 ....92 B1
    WALW * SE17 ....118 B2
Coolfin Rd *CAN/RD* E16 ....94 A5
Coolhurst Rd *CEND/HSY/T* N8 ....57 D1
Cool Oak Br *CDALE/KGS* NW9 ....51 F2
Cool Oak La *CDALE/KGS* NW9 ....51 F2
Coomassie Rd *MV/WKIL* W9 ....89 F3
Coombe Ldg *CHARL* SE7 ....124 C2
Coombe Pk *KUTN/CMB* KT2 ....146 C5
Coombe Ridings *KUTN/CMB* KT2 ....146 C4
Coombe Rd *CHSWK* W4 ....111 E1
    SYD SE26 ....156 B4
    WLSDN NW10 ....51 D5
Coombe Vls *WAND/EARL* * SW18 ....118 B4
Coombe Wood Rd *KUTN/CMB* KT2 ....146 C5
Coombs St *IS* N1 ....11 D2

Coomer Ms *FUL/PGN* * SW6 ....113 F2
Coomer Pl *FUL/PGN* SW6 ....113 F2
Cooper Cl *STHWK* SE1 ....46 B1
Cooper Rd *CRICK* NW2 ....70 A2
    HDN NW4 ....53 D1
Coopersale Rd *HOM* E9 ....79 D2
Coopers Cl *WCHPL* E1 ....90 C3
Coopers La *CAMTN* NW1 ....8 B2
    LEE/GVPK SE12 ....160 B2
    LEY E10 ....62 B3
Cooper's Rd *STHWK* SE1 ....119 F1
Cooper's Rw *TWRH* EC3N 37 E1
Cooper St *CAN/RD* E16 ....93 F4
Copeland Rd *PECK* SE15 ....120 A5
Copeman Cl *SYD* SE26 ....156 C5
Copenhagen Pl *POP/IOD* E14 ....91 F5
Copenhagen St *IS* N1 ....75 E5
Cope Pl *KENS* W8 ....38 A3
Cope St *BERM/RHTH* SE16 ....103 D5
Copford Wk *IS* * N1 ....76 C5
Coplestone Rd *PECK* SE15 ....137 F1
Copley Cl *WALW* SE17 ....118 B2
Coppelia Rd *BKHTH/KID* SE3 ....141 F2
Copperas St *DEPT* SE8 ....122 B2
Copperfield Rd *BOW* E3 ....91 E3
Copperfield St *STHWK* SE1 ....33 D5
Coppermead Cl *CRICK* NW2 ....52 C5
Copper Mill La *TOOT* SW17 ....150 C4
Coppermill La *WALTH* E17 ....60 C1
Copper Rw *STHWK* SE1 ....37 E4
Coppice Dr *PUT/ROE* SW15 ....130 A4
Coppock Cl *BTSEA* SW11 ....115 E5
Copse Cl *CHARL* SE7 ....124 B2
Copsewood Cl *BFN/LL* DA15 ....145 E4
Copthall Av *LOTH* EC2R 24 B4
Copthorne Av *BAL* SW12 ....135 D5
Coptic St *NOXST/BSQ* WC1A 20 C3
Copton Cl *BOW* E3 ....92 A4
Coral St *STHWK* SE1 ....46 B1
Coram St *STPAN* WC1H 20 C1
Corbet Pl *WCHPL* E1 ....25 E2
Corbett Rd *WAN* E11 ....64 C1
Corbett's La *BERM/RHTH* SE16 ....102 C5
Corbicum *WAN* E11 ....63 E2
Corbridge Crs *BETH* E2 ....90 B1
Corbylands Rd *BFN/LL* DA15 ....145 E5
    BFN/LL DA15 ....163 E1
Corbyn St *FSBYPK* N4 ....57 E3
Corby Rd *WLSDN* NW10 ....86 C1
Cordelia Cl *HNHL* SE24 ....136 B2
Cordelia St *POP/IOD* E14 ....92 B5
Cording St *POP/IOD* E14 ....92 B4
Cordova Rd *BOW* E3 ....91 E2
Cordwell Rd *LEW* SE13 ....141 D3
Corelli Rd *BKHTH/KID* SE3 ....125 E4
Corfield St *BETH* E2 ....90 B3
Coriander Av *POP/IOD* E14 ....93 D5
Corinne Rd *ARCH* N19 ....74 C1
Cork St Ms *CONDST* W1S 31 E2
Cork Sq *WAP* E1W 102 A2
Cork St *CONDST* W1S 31 E2
Corlett St *CAMTN* NW1 ....16 C2
Cormont Rd *CMBW* SE5 ....118 B4
Cormorant Rd *FSTGT* E7 ....81 F2
Cornelia St *HOLWY* N7 ....75 F3
Corner Fielde *BRXS/STRHM* * SW2 ....153 F1
Corner Gn *BKHTH/KID* SE3 ....124 A5
Corney Reach Wy *CHSWK* W4 ....111 E3
Corney Rd *CHSWK* W4 ....111 E2
Cornflower Ter *EDUL* SE22 ....138 B4
Cornford Gv *BAL* SW12 ....152 B2
Cornhill *BANK* EC3V 24 B5
Cornmill La *LEW* SE13 ....140 B1
Cornmow Dr *WLSDN* NW10 ....69 F2
Cornthwaite Rd *CLPT* E5 ....60 C5
Cornwall Av *BETH* E2 ....90 C2
    WELL DA16 ....145 E1
Cornwall Cl *BARK* IG11 ....85 F3

Cornwall Crs *NTGHL* W11 ....**101** E1
Cornwall Gdns *SKENS* SW7 ....**39** E3
   WLSDN NW10 ....**70** B3
Cornwall Gv *CHSWK* W4 ....**111** D1
Cornwallis Av *BFN/LL* DA15 ....**163** D2
Cornwallis Rd *ARCH* N19 ....**57** E4
   WOOL/PLUM SE18 ....**108** B4
Cornwallis Sq *ARCH* N19 ....**57** E4
Cornwallis Wk *ELTH/MOT* SE9 ....**143** F1
Cornwall Ms South *SKENS* SW7 ....**39** E3
Cornwall Ms West *SKENS* * SW7 .....**39** D3
Cornwall Rd *FSBYPK* N4 ....**58** A2
   STHWK SE1 ....**34** A3
Cornwall Sq *LBTH* * SE11 ....**118** C4
Cornwall St *WCHPL* * E1 ....**102** B1
Cornwall Ter *CAMTN* NW1 ....**17** F1
Cornwall Terrace Ms *CAMTN* NW1 .....**17** F1
Corn Wy *WAN* E11 ....**63** D5
Cornwood Dr *WCHPL* E1 ....**90** C5
Corona Rd *LEE/GVPK* SE12 ....**142** A5
Coronation Rd *PLSTW* E13 ....**94** C2
   WLSDN NW10 ....**86** B2
Coronation Vls *WLSDN* * NW10 ....**86** B3
Coronet St *IS* N1 ....**12** C4
Corporation Rw *CLKNW* EC1R **10** B5
Corporation St *HOLWY* N7 ....**75** E2
   SRTFD E15 ....**93** E1
Corrance Rd *BRXS/STRHM* SW2 ......**135** E2
Corringham Rd *GLDGN* NW11 ....**54** A2
   WBLY HA9 ....**50** A4
Corringway *GLDGN* NW11 ....**54** B2
Corris Gn *CDALE/KGS* * NW9 ....**51** E1
Corscombe Cl *KUTN/CMB* KT2 ......**146** C5
Corsham St *IS* N1 ....**12** B4
Corsica St *HBRY* N5 ....**76** B3
Cortayne Rd *FUL/PGN* * SW6 ....**113** F5
Cortis Rd *PUT/ROE* SW15 ....**130** B4
Cortis Ter *PUT/ROE* SW15 ....**130** B3
Corunna Rd *VX/NE* SW8 ....**116** C4
Corunna Ter *VX/NE* SW8 ....**116** C4
Coryton Ph *MV/WKIL* W9 ....**89** F3
Cosbycote Av *HNHL* SE24 ....**136** C3
Cosmo Pl *RSQ* WC1B **21** D2
Cosmur Cl *SHB* W12 ....**99** F4
Cossall Wk *PECK* SE15 ....**120** B4
Cosser St *STHWK* SE1 ....**46** A2
Costa St *PECK* SE15 ....**120** A5
Cosway St *CAMTN* NW1 ....**17** D2
Cotall St *POP/IOD* E14 ....**92** A5
Coteford St *TOOT* SW17 ....**151** F4
Cotesbach Rd *CLPT* E5 ....**60** C5
Cotham St *WALW* SE17 ....**47** F5
Cotherstone Rd *BRXS/STRHM* SW2 ..**153** F1
Cotleigh Rd *KIL/WHAMP* NW6 ....**72** A4
Cotman Ct *LFNCH* N2 ....**54** C1
Cotswold Gdns *CRICK* NW2 ....**53** D4
   EHAM E6 ....**95** D2
   CNTH/NBYPK IG2 ....**67** D2
Cotswold Ga *CRICK* NW2 ....**53** E3
Cotswold St *WNWD* SE27 ....**154** B4
Cottage Gn *CMBW* SE5 ....**119** D3
Cottage Gv *BRXN/ST* SW9 ....**135** E1
Cottage Pl *SKENS* SW7 ....**40** C2
Cottage St *POP/IOD* E14 ....**104** B1
Cottesbrook St *NWCR* SE14 ....**121** E3
Cottesloe Ms *STHWK* SE1 ....**46** B2
Cottesmore Gdns *KENS* W8 ....**39** D2
Cottingham Rd *VX/NE* SW8 ....**117** F3
Cottington St *LBTH* SE11 ....**118** A1
Cotton Av *ACT* W3 ....**87** D5
Cotton Gardens *LBTH* SE11 ....**46** C5
Cotton Hi *BMLY* BR1 ....**159** D4
Cotton Rw *BTSEA* SW11 ....**132** C1
Cottons Centre *STHWK* * SE1 ....**36** C3
Cotton's Gdns *BETH* E2 ....**13** D3
Cotton St *POP/IOD* E14 ....**104** C1
Coulgate St *BROCKY* SE4 ....**139** E1
Coulson St *CHEL* SW3 ....**115** F1

Coulter Rd *HMSMTH* W6 ....**100** B4
Councillor St *CMBW* SE5 ....**118** C3
Counter St *STHWK* SE1 ....**36** C3
Countess Rd *KTTN* NW5 ....**74** C2
County Ga *CHST* BR7 ....**162** C3
County Gv *CMBW* SE5 ....**118** C4
County Rd *EHAM* E6 ....**96** B4
County St *STHWK* SE1 ....**47** F3
Coupland Pl *WOOL/PLUM* SE18 ......**126** C1
Courland Gv *VX/NE* SW8 ....**117** D4
Courland St *VX/NE* SW8 ....**117** D4
The Course *ELTH/MOT* SE9 ....**162** A3
Courtauld Rd *ARCH* N19 ....**57** D3
Court Cl *HAMP* * NW3 ....**73** D4
Courtenay Av *HGT* N6 ....**55** E2
Courtenay Rd *WAN* * E11 ....**63** F5
Courtenay Sq *LBTH* * SE11 ....**118** A1
Courtenay St *LBTH* SE11 ....**117** F1
Court Farm Rd *ELTH/MOT* SE9 ....**161** D2
Courtfield Gdns *ECT* SW5 ....**39** D5
Courtfield Ms *SKENS* * SW7 ....**39** E5
Courtfield Rd *SKENS* SW7 ....**39** E5
Court Gdns *HOLWY* N7 ....**76** A3
Courthill Rd *LEW* SE13 ....**140** C2
Courthope Rd *HAMP* NW3 ....**73** F1
   WIM/MER SW19 ....**149** E5
Courtland Av *IL* IG1 ....**65** F4
Courtland Rd *EHAM* E6 ....**83** E5
Courtlands *RCHPK/HAM* TW10 ....**128** A3
Courtlands Av *LEE/GVPK* SE12 ....**142** B3
   RCH/KEW TW9 ....**110** B5
Court La *DUL* SE21 ....**137** E5
Court Lane Gdns *DUL* SE21 ....**137** E5
Courtmead Cl *HNHL* SE24 ....**136** C4
Courtnell St *BAY/PAD* W2 ....**14** A4
Courtney Rd *HOLWY* N7 ....**76** A2
Courtrai Rd *BROCKY* SE4 ....**139** E4
Court Rd *ELTH/MOT* SE9 ....**161** F1
Courtside *CEND/HSY/T* N8 ....**57** D1
   SYD * SE26 ....**156** C3
Court St *WCHPL* E1 ....**90** B4
Court Vw *HGT* * N6 ....**56** B4
Court Wy *ACT* W3 ....**86** C4
The Courtyard *IS* N1 ....**75** F4
Court Yd *ELTH/MOT* SE9 ....**143** E4
Cousin La *CANST* EC4R **36** A2
Couthurst Rd *BKHTH/KID* SE3 ....**124** B2
Coutts Crs *KTTN* * NW5 ....**56** A5
Coval Gdns *MORT/ESHN* SW14 ......**128** B2
Coval La *MORT/ESHN* SW14 ....**128** B2
Coval Rd *MORT/ESHN* SW14 ....**128** C2
Covelees Wall *EHAM* E6 ....**96** A5
Covent Gdn *COVGDN* WC2E **33** D1
Covent Garden Piazza *COVGDN* WC2E ..**33** D1
Coventry Cl *EHAM* E6 ....**95** F5
   KIL/WHAMP NW6 ....**2** B1
Coventry Cross Est *BOW* E3 ....**92** C3
Coventry Rd *IL* IG1 ....**66** B3
   WCHPL E1 ....**90** B3
Coventry St *MYFR/PICC* W1J **32** A2
Coverdale Rd *KIL/WHAMP* NW6 ....**71** E4
   SHB W12 ....**100** B2
The Coverdales *BARK* IG11 ....**97** D1
Coverley Cl *WCHPL* * E1 ....**90** A4
Coverton Rd *TOOT* SW17 ....**151** E4
Cowbridge La *BARK* IG11 ....**84** B4
Cowcross St *FARR* EC1M **22** C2
Cowdenbeath Pth *IS* N1 ....**75** E5
Cowden St *CAT* SE6 ....**158** A4
Cowick Rd *TOOT* SW17 ....**151** F4
Cow Leaze *EHAM* E6 ....**96** A5
Cowley La *WAN* * E11 ....**63** E5
Cowley Rd *ACT* W3 ....**99** F2
   BRXN/ST SW9 ....**118** A4
   IL IG1 ....**65** F2
   MORT/ESHN SW14 ....**129** E1
Cowley St *WEST* SW1P **44** C3
Cowling Cl *NTGHL* W11 ....**101** E1

Cowper Av EHAM E6 ....83 E4
Cowper Rd ACT W3 ....99 D2
  STNW/STAM N16 ....77 E1
Cowper St STLK EC1Y 12 B5
Cowper Ter NKENS * W10 ....89 D4
Cowthorpe Rd VX/NE SW8 ....117 D4
Coxmount Rd CHARL SE7 ....125 D1
Coxson Wy STHWK SE1 ....49 E1
Coxwell Rd WOOL/PLUM SE18 ....127 D1
Crabtree Cl BETH E2 ....15 E1
Crabtree La FUL/PGN SW6 ....113 D3
Craddock St CAMTN * NW1 ....74 A3
Cradley Rd ELTH/MOT SE9 ....163 D1
Craigerne Rd BKHTH/KID SE3 ....124 D5
Craigholm WOOL/PLUM SE18 ....126 A5
Craignair Rd BRXS/STRHM SW2 ....135 F5
Craig's Ct WHALL SW1A 32 C3
Craigton Rd ELTH/MOT SE9 ....143 F2
Crail Rw WALW SE17 ....48 B5
Cramer St MHST W1U 18 B1
Crammond Rd HMSMTH W6 ....113 E2
Cranberry La CAN/RD E16 ....93 E3
Cranborne Rd BARK IG11 ....85 D5
Cranbourne Rd MNPK E12 ....83 E2
  SRTFD E15 ....80 C1
Cranbourn St LSO/SEVD WC2H 32 B1
Cranbrook Ri IL IG1 ....65 F1
Cranbrook Rd CHSWK W4 ....111 E1
  DEPT SE8 ....122 A4
  IL IG1 ....66 A2
Cranbrook St BETH E2 ....91 D1
Cranbury Rd FUL/PGN SW6 ....114 B5
Crane Av ACT W3 ....98 C1
Crane Ct FLST/FETLN EC4A 22 C1
  MORT/ESHN * SW14 ....128 C2
Crane Gv HOLWY N7 ....76 A3
Crane Md BERM/RHTH SE16 ....103 D5
Crane St PECK SE15 ....119 F4
Cranfield Rd BROCKY SE4 ....139 F1
Cranford Cottages WAP * E1W 103 D1
Cranford St WAP E1W 103 D1
Cranhurst Rd CRICK NW2 ....70 C2
Cranleigh Gdns BARK IG11 ....85 D4
Cranleigh Ms BTSEA * SW11 ....115 E5
Cranleigh St CAMTN NW1 ....7 F2
Cranley Dr GNTH/NBYPK IG2 ....66 C2
Cranley Gdns SKENS SW7 ....114 C1
Cranley Ms SKENS SW7 ....114 C1
Cranley Pl SKENS SW7 ....40 A5
Cranley Rd GNTH/NBYPK IG2 ....66 C1
  PLSTW E13 ....94 B4
Cranmer Rd BRXN/ST SW9 ....118 A3
  FSTGT E7 ....82 B1
Cranmer Ter TOOT SW17 ....151 D5
Cranmore Rd BMLY BR1 ....159 E3
  CHST BR7 ....161 F5
Cranston Est IS N1 ....12 B1
Cranston Rd FSTH SE23 ....157 E1
Cranswick Rd BERM/RHTH SE16 ....120 B1
Crantock Rd CAT SE6 ....158 C2
Cranwell Cl BOW E3 ....92 B3
Cranwich Rd STNW/STAM N16 ....59 E2
Cranwood St FSBYE EC1V 12 B4
Cranworth Gdns BRXN/ST SW9 ....118 A4
Craster Rd BRXS/STRHM SW2 ....135 F5
Crathie Rd LEE/GVPK SE12 ....142 B4
Craven Cl CLPT * E5 ....60 A2
Craven Gdns BARK IG11 ....97 E1
  WIM/MER SW19 ....150 B5
Craven Hl BAY/PAD W2 ....27 F1
Craven Hill Gdns BAY/PAD W2 ....27 E1
Craven Hill Ms BAY/PAD W2 ....27 F1
Craven Ms BTSEA SW11 ....134 A1
Craven Pk WLSDN NW10 ....69 D4
Craven Park Ms WLSDN NW10 ....69 E4
Craven Park Rd STNW/STAM N16 ....77 E2
Craven Rd BAY/PAD W2 ....27 F1
  WLSDN NW10 ....69 D5

Craven St CHCR WC2N 32 C3
Craven Ter BAY/PAD W2 ....27 F1
Craven Wk CLPT E5 ....60 A2
Crawford Pas CLKNW EC1R 22 A1
Crawford Pl BAY/PAD W2 ....17 D4
Crawford Rd CMBW SE5 ....118 C5
Crawford St MBLAR W1H 17 E3
Crawley Rd LEY E10 ....62 B3
Crawthew Gv EDUL SE22 ....137 F2
Craybury End ELTH/MOT SE9 ....162 C1
Crayford Rd HOLWY N7 ....75 E1
Crealock St WAND/EARL SW18 ....132 B4
Crebor St EDUL SE22 ....138 A4
Crediton Hl KIL/WHAMP NW6 ....72 B2
Crediton Rd WLSDN NW10 ....71 D5
Credon Rd BERM/RHTH SE16 ....120 B1
  PLSTW E13 ....94 C1
Creechurch La HDTCH EC3A 25 D4
Creechurch Pl HDTCH * EC3A 25 D5
Creed La BLKFR EC4V 23 D5
Creek Rd BARK IG11 ....97 F2
  DEPT SE8 ....122 A2
Creekside DEPT SE8 ....122 A3
Creeland Gv CAT SE6 ....157 F1
Creffield Cl FUL/PGN SW6 ....113 D2
Creffield Rd ACT W3 ....98 A1
Creighton Av EHAM E6 ....95 D1
Creighton Cl SHB W12 ....100 B1
Creighton Rd KIL/WHAMP NW6 ....89 D1
Cremer St BETH E2 ....14 C5
Cremorne Est WBPTN * SW10 ....115 D2
Cremorne Rd WBPTN SW10 ....114 C3
The Crescent ACT W3 ....87 F5
  BARN SW13 ....111 F5
  CRICK NW2 ....52 B5
  GNTH/NBYPK IG2 ....66 A1
  SCUP DA14 ....163 F4
  WIM/MER SW19 ....150 A3
Crescent TWRH EC3N 37 E1
Crescent Arcade GNWCH SE10 ....122 C2
Crescent Gdns WIM/MER SW19 ....150 A3
Crescent Gv CLAP SW4 ....134 C2
Crescent La CLAP SW4 ....135 D3
Crescent Pl CHEL SW3 ....40 C4
Crescent Rd BFN/LL SE13 ....163 F3
  CEND/HSY/T N8 ....57 D1
  LEY E10 ....62 B4
  PLSTW E13 ....82 A5
  WOOL/PLUM SE18 ....126 B1
Crescent Rw STLK EC1Y 23 E1
Crescent St IS * N1 ....75 F4
Crescent Wy BROCKY SE4 ....140 A1
Crescent Wood Rd DUL SE21 ....156 A3
Cresford Rd FUL/PGN SW6 ....114 B4
Crespigny Rd HDN NW4 ....52 B1
Cresset Rd HOM E9 ....78 C3
Cresset St CLAP SW4 ....135 D1
Cressfield Cl KTTN NW5 ....74 A2
Cressida Rd ARCH N19 ....56 C3
Cressingham Rd LEW SE13 ....140 C1
Cressington Cl STNW/STAM N16 ....77 E2
Cresswell Pk BKHTH/KID SE3 ....141 F1
Cresswell Pl WBPTN SW10 ....114 C1
Cressy Ct HMSMTH W6 ....100 B4
Cressy Houses WCHPL * E1 ....90 C4
Cressy Pl WCHPL E1 ....90 C4
Cressy Rd HAMP NW3 ....73 F1
The Crest KTTN * NW5 ....75 D2
Crestfield St CAMTN NW1 ....9 D3
Crest Rd CRICK NW2 ....52 A4
Crestway PUT/ROE SW15 ....130 A4
Creswick Rd ACT W3 ....98 B1
Crewdson Rd BRXN/ST SW9 ....117 F3
Crewe Pl WLSDN NW10 ....87 F2
Crews St POP/IOD * E14 ....104 A5
Crewys Rd CRICK NW2 ....53 F4
  PECK SE15 ....120 B5
Crichton St VX/NE * SW8 ....116 C5

Cricketers Wk SYD SE26 ....156 C5
Cricketfield Rd CLPT E5 ....78 B1
Cricklade Av BRXS/STRHM SW2 ....153 E2
Cricklewood Broadway CRICK NW2 ....52 C5
Cricklewood La CRICK NW2 ....71 E1
Cridland St SRTFD E15 ....81 F5
Crieff Rd WAND/EARL SW18 ....132 C4
Criffel Av BRXS/STRHM SW2 ....153 D2
Crimscott St STHWK SE1 ....49 D3
Crimsworth Rd VX/NE SW8 ....117 D4
Crinan St IS N1 ....9 D1
Cringle St VX/NE SW8 ....116 C3
Cripplegate St BARB * EC2Y 23 E2
Crispian Cl WLSDN NW10 ....69 E1
Crispin St WCHPL E1 ....25 E3
Crisp Rd HMSMTH W6 ....112 C1
Cristowe Rd FUL/PGN * SW6 ....113 F5
Criterion Ms ARCH N19 ....57 D4
Cricketers Rd WAND/EARL SW18 ....132 B3
Crockerton Rd TOOT SW17 ....151 F2
Crockham Wy ELTH/MOT SE9 ....162 A4
The Croft WLSDN NW10 ....87 F1
Croft Cl CHST BR7 ....161 F5
Croftdown Rd KTTN NW5 ....56 A5
Crofters Ct DEPT SE8 ....103 E5
Crofters Wy CAMTN NW1 ....75 D3
Crofton Av CHSWK W4 ....110 C3
Crofton Gate Wy BROCKY SE4 ....139 E3
Crofton Park Rd BROCKY SE4 ....139 F4
Crofton Rd CMBW SE5 ....119 E5
    PLSTW E13 ....94 B3
Crofts St WCHPL E1 ....102 A1
Crofts St DEPT SE8 ....103 E5
    WCHPL E1 ....102 A1
Croft Wy BFN/LL DA15 ....163 E3
Crogsland Rd CAMTN NW1 ....74 A4
Cromartie Rd ARCH N19 ....57 D2
Cromarty Vls BAY/PAD * W2 ....27 E1
Crombie Ms BTSEA * SW11 ....115 E5
Crombie Rd BFN/LL DA15 ....163 D1
Cromer Rd LEY E10 ....63 D2
Cromer St STPAN WC1H 9 D3
Cromer Ter HACK E8 ....78 A2
Cromer Villas Rd WAND/EARL SW18 ...131 F4
Cromford Rd PUT/ROE SW15 ....131 F3
Crompton St BAY/PAD W2 ....16 A1
Cromwell Av HGT N6 ....56 B3
    HMSMTH W6 ....112 B1
Cromwell Cl CHSWK * W4 ....110 B1
Cromwell Crs ECT SW5 ....38 A4
Cromwell Gv HMSMTH W6 ....100 C4
Cromwell Ms SKENS * SW7 ....40 A4
Cromwell Pl ACT W3 ....98 C2
    HGT * N6 ....56 B3
    MORT/ESHN SW14 ....128 C1
    SKENS SW7 ....40 B4
Cromwell Rd BRXN/ST SW9 ....118 B4
    FSTGT E7 ....82 C4
    SKENS SW7 ....40 A4
    WIM/MER SW19 ....150 A5
Crondace Rd FUL/PGN SW6 ....114 A4
Crondall St IS N1 ....12 B1
Cronin St PECK SE15 ....119 F3
Crooke Rd DEPT SE8 ....121 E1
Crookham Rd FUL/PGN SW6 ....113 F4
Crookston Rd ELTH/MOT SE9 ....144 A1
Croombs Rd CAN/RD E16 ....94 C4
Croom's Hl GNWCH SE10 ....123 D3
Croom's Hill Gv GNWCH SE10 ....122 C3
Cropley St IS N1 ....12 A1
Cropthorne Ct MV/WKIL W9 ....3 F4
Crosby Rd FSTGT E7 ....82 A3
Crosby Rw STHWK SE1 ....48 A1
Crosby Wk HACK E8 ....77 F3
Crosier Cl WOOL/PLUM SE18 ....125 E4
Crossbrook Rd BKHTH/KID SE3 ....125 E5
Crossfield Est DEPT SE8 ....122 A3
Crossfield Rd HAMP NW3 ....73 D3

Crossfield St DEPT SE8 ....122 A3
Crossford St BRXN/ST SW9 ....117 F5
Cross Keys Cl MHST W1U 18 B3
Crosslet St WALW SE17 ....48 B4
Crosslet V GNWCH SE10 ....122 B4
Crossley St HOLWY N7 ....76 A3
Crossmead ELTH/MOT SE9 ....161 F1
Cross Rd CMBW SE5 ....119 E5
Cross St BARN SW13 ....111 E5
    IS N1 ....76 B5
Crossthwaite Av HNHL SE24 ....137 D2
Crosswall TWRH EC3N 37 E1
The Crossway ELTH/MOT SE9 ....161 D2
Crossway STNW/STAM N16 ....77 E2
The Crossways WBLY HA9 ....50 A4
Crossways Ter CLPT * E5 ....78 C1
Croston St HACK E8 ....78 A5
Crouch End HI ARCH N19 ....162 A3
Crouch HI ARCH N19 ....57 D2
Crouch Hall Rd CEND/HSY/T N8 ....57 D1
Crouch HI ARCH N19 ....57 E2
Crouchmans Cl DUL SE21 ....155 F3
Crouch Rd WLSDN NW10 ....69 D3
Crowborough Rd TOOT SW17 ....152 A5
Crowder St WCHPL E1 ....102 B1
Crowfoot Cl HOM E9 ....79 F2
Crowline Wk IS * N1 ....76 C3
Crown Cl BOW E3 ....80 A5
    KIL/WHAMP NW6 ....72 B3
Crown Ct HOL/ALD WC2B 21 D5
Crowndale Rd CAMTN NW1 ....7 F1
Crownfield Rd SRTFD E15 ....81 D2
Crownhill Rd WLSDN NW10 ....69 F5
Crown La STRHM/NOR SW16 ....154 A5
Crown Lane Gdns WNWD * SE27 ....154 A5
Crown Office Rw EMB EC4Y 34 A1
Crown Pas STJS SW1Y 31 F4
Crown Pl KTTN NW5 ....74 B3
    SDTCH EC2A 24 C1
Crownstone Rd BRXS/STRHM SW2 ......136 A3
Crown St ACT W3 ....98 A2
    CMBW SE5 ....118 C3
Crown Ter CRICK * NW2 ....98 C2
Crown Vls ACT * W3 ....98 C3
Crown Woods Wy ELTH/MOT SE9 ....145 D3
Crows Rd BARK IG11 ....84 B3
    SRTFD E15 ....93 D2
Crowthorne Cl WAND/EARL SW18 ....131 E5
Crowthorne Rd NKENS W10 ....89 D5
Croxley Rd MV/WKIL W9 ....89 F2
Croxted Cl DUL SE21 ....136 C5
Croxted Rd DUL SE21 ....155 D2
Croyde Cl ELTH/MOT SE9 ....145 D5
Croydon Rd PLSTW E13 ....94 A3
Crozier Ter HOM E9 ....79 D2
Crucifix La STHWK SE1 ....36 C5
Cruden St IS N1 ....76 B5
Cruickshank St FSBYW WC1X 10 A3
Cruikshank Rd SRTFD E15 ....81 E1
Crusoe Ms STNW/STAM N16 ....59 D4
Crutched Friars TWRH EC3N 37 D1
Crutchley Rd CAT SE6 ....159 E2
Crystal Palace Park Rd NRWD SE19 ....156 A5
Crystal Palace Rd EDUL SE22 ....137 F4
Cuba St POP/IOD E14 ....104 A3
Cubitt St FSBYW WC1X 9 F4
Cubitt Ter CLAP SW4 ....134 C1
Cudham St CAT SE6 ....140 B5
Cudworth St WCHPL E1 ....90 B3
Cuff Crs ELTH/MOT SE9 ....143 D5
Culford Gdns CHEL SW3 ....41 D5
Culford Gv IS N1 ....77 E3
Culford Ms IS N1 ....77 D3
Culford Rd IS N1 ....77 E4
Cullen Wy WLSDN NW10 ....86 C3

Culling Rd *BERM/RHTH* SE16 ....102 C4
Cullingworth Rd *WLSDN* NW10 ....70 A2
Culloden Cl *STHWK* SE1 ....120 A1
Culloden St *POP/IOD* E14 ....92 C5
Cullum St *FENCHST* EC3M 36 C1
Culmore Rd *PECK* SE15 ....120 B3
Culmstock Rd *BTSEA* SW11 ....134 A3
Culross St *MYFR/PKLN* W1K 30 A2
Culverden Rd *BAL* SW12 ....152 C3
Culverhouse Gdns
    STRHM/NOR SW16 ....153 F4
Culverley Rd *CAT* SE6 ....158 B1
Culvert Pl *BTSEA* SW11 ....116 A5
Culvert Rd *BTSEA* SW11 ....115 F5
Culworth St *STJWD* NW8 ....4 C2
Cumberland Av *WELL* DA16 ....145 E1
    WELL DA16 ....145 F2
    WLSDN NW10 ....86 B2
Cumberland Cl *HACK* E8 ....77 F3
Cumberland Gdns *FSBYW* WC1X 9 F3
Cumberland Ga *BAY/PAD* W2 ....29 E1
    CAMTN NW1 ....6 C5
Cumberland Market *CAMTN* NW1 ....7 D3
Cumberland Pk *ACT* W3 ....98 C1
Cumberland Pl *CAMTN* NW1 ....6 C3
    CAT SE6 ....159 F1
Cumberland Rd *ACT* W3 ....98 C1
    BARN SW13 ....111 F4
    MNPK E12 ....83 D1
    PLSTW E13 ....94 B4
    RCH/KEW TW9 ....110 A4
Cumberland St *PIM* SW1V 116 B1
Cumberland Ter *CAMTN* NW1 ....6 C2
Cumberland Terrace Ms *CAMTN* NW1 ..6 C2
Cumbrian Gdns *CRICK* NW2 ....53 D4
Cumming St *IS* N1 ....9 F2
Cumnor Cl *BRXN/ST* SW9 ....117 F5
Cunard Rd *WLSDN* NW10 ....87 D2
Cundy Rd *CAN/RD* E16 ....94 C5
Cundy St *BGVA* SW1W 42 B5
Cunningham Pl *STJWD* NW8 ....4 A5
Cunnington St *CHSWK* W4 ....98 C4
Cupar Rd *BTSEA* SW11 ....116 A4
Cupola Cl *BMLY* BR1 ....160 B5
Cureton St *WEST* SW1P 117 D1
Curlew St *STHWK* SE1 ....37 E5
Curnick's La *WALW* SE27 ....154 C4
Curran Av *BFN/LL* DA15 ....145 F3
Curricle St *ACT* W3 ....99 E2
Currie Hill Cl *WIM/MER* SW19 ....149 F4
Cursitor St *FLST/FETLN* EC4A 22 A4
Curtain Pl *SDTCH* EC2A 13 D5
Curtain Rd *IS* N1 ....13 D4
    SDTCH EC2A 24 C1
Curtis Dr *ACT* W3 ....87 D5
Curtis Field Rd *STRHM/NOR* SW16 ..153 F4
Curtis St *STHWK* SE1 ....49 E4
Curtis Wy *STHWK* SE1 ....49 E4
The Curve *SHB* W12 ....100 A1
Curwen Av *FSTGT* E7 ....82 B1
Curwen Rd *SHB* W12 ....100 A3
Curzon Crs *BARK* IG11 ....97 F2
Curzon Pl *MYFR/PKLN* W1K 30 B4
Curzon St *MYFR/PICC* W1J 31 D3
Custom House Reach
    BERM/RHTH SE16 ....103 F4
Cutcombe Rd *CMBW* SE5 ....118 C5
The Cut *STHWK* SE1 ....34 B5
Cuthberga Cl *BARK* IG11 ....84 C4
Cuthbert St *BAY/PAD* W2 ....16 A2
Cutlers Gardens Ar *LVPST* EC2M 25 D4
Cutler St *HDTCH* EC3A 25 D4
Cygnet Cl *WLSDN* NW10 ....69 D2
Cygnet St *WCHPL* E1 ....13 F5
Cynthia St *IS* N1 ....9 F2
Cypress Gdns *BROCKY* SE4 ....139 E3
Cypress Tree Cl *BFN/LL* DA15 ....163 F1

Cyprus Cl *FSBYPK* N4 ....58 A1
Cyprus Pl *BETH* E2 ....90 C1
    EHAM E6 ....108 A1
Cyprus St *BETH* E2 ....90 C1
Cyrena Rd *EDUL* SE22 ....137 F4
Cyrus St *FSBYE* EC1V 11 D5
Czar St *DEPT* SE8 ....122 A2

D

Dabin Crs *GNWCH* SE10 ....122 C4
Dacca St *DEPT* SE8 ....121 F2
Dace Rd *BOW* E3 ....80 A5
Dacre Gdns *LEW* * SE13 ....141 E2
Dacre Pk *LEW* SE13 ....141 E1
Dacre Pl *LEW* SE13 ....141 E1
Dacre Rd *PLSTW* E13 ....82 B5
    WAN E11 ....63 F3
Dacres Est *FSTH* * SE23 ....157 D3
Dacres Rd *FSTH* SE23 ....157 D3
Dacre St *STJSPK* SW1H 44 A2
Daffodil Gdns *IL* IG1 ....84 B2
Daffodil St *SHB* W12 ....99 F1
Dafforne Rd *TOOT* SW17 ....151 F3
Dagenham Rd *LEY* E10 ....61 F3
Dagmar Gdns *WLSDN* NW10 ....89 D1
Dagmar Pas *IS* * N1 ....76 B5
Dagmar Rd *BAL* SW12 ....134 B5
    FSBYPK N4 ....58 A2
Dagmar Ter *IS* * N1 ....76 B5
Dagnall St *BTSEA* SW11 ....115 F5
Dagnan Rd *BAL* SW12 ....134 B5
Dagonet Rd *BMLY* BR1 ....160 A3
Dahlia Gdns *IL* IG1 ....84 B3
Daines St *MNPK* E12 ....65 F5
Dainford Cl *BMLY* BR1 ....159 D5
Daintry Wy *HOM* E9 ....79 F3
Dairsie Rd *ELTH/MOT* SE9 ....144 A1
Dairy La *WOOL/PLUM* SE18 ....107 F5
Dairyman Cl *CRICK* * NW2 ....53 D5
Daisy La *FUL/PGN* SW6 ....132 A1
Dakota Gdns *EHAM* E6 ....95 E3
Dalberg Rd *BRXS/STRHM* SW2 ....136 A3
Dalby Rd *WAND/EARL* SW18 ....132 C2
Dalby St *KTTN* NW5 ....74 B3
Dalebury Rd *TOOT* SW17 ....151 F2
Dale Cl *BKHTH/KID* SE3 ....142 A1
Daleham Gdns *HAMP* NW3 ....73 D2
Daleham Ms *HAMP* * NW3 ....73 D3
Dale Rd *KTTN* NW5 ....74 A2
    WALW SE17 ....118 B2
Dale Rw *NTGHL* W11 ....89 E5
Daleside Rd *TOOT* SW17 ....152 B5
Dale St *CHSWK* W4 ....111 E1
Daleview Rd *SEVS/STOTM* N15 ....59 E1
Daley St *HOM* E9 ....79 D3
Daley Thompson Wy *VX/NE* SW8 ....116 B5
Dalgarno Gdns *NKENS* W10 ....88 B4
Dalgarno Wy *NKENS* W10 ....88 C3
Dalkeith Rd *DUL* SE21 ....154 C1
    IL IG1 ....66 C5
Dallas Rd *HDN* NW4 ....52 A2
    SYD SE26 ....156 B4
Dallinger Rd *LEE/GVPK* SE12 ....141 F4
Dalling Rd *HMSMTH* W6 ....100 B4
Dallington Sq *FSBYE* EC1V 11 D5
Dallington St *FSBYE* EC1V 11 D5
Dallin Rd *WOOL/PLUM* SE18 ....126 B3
Dalmain Rd *FSTH* SE23 ....157 D1
Dalmeny Av *HOLWY* N7 ....75 D1
Dalmeny Rd *HOLWY* N7 ....75 D1
Dalmeyer Rd *WLSDN* NW10 ....69 F3
Dalmore Rd *DUL* SE21 ....154 C2
Dalrymple Rd *BROCKY* SE4 ....139 E2
Dalston La *HACK* E8 ....77 F3
Dalton St *WNWD* SE27 ....154 B2

Dalwood St *CMBW* SE5 ....119 E4
Dalyell Rd *BRXN/ST* SW9 ....135 F1
Damask Crs *CAN/RD* E16 ....93 E3
Damer Ter *WBPTN* SW10 ....114 C3
Dames Rd *FSTGT* E7 ....82 A1
Dame St *IS* N1 ....11 E1
Damien St *WCHPL* E1 ....90 B4
Damsel Ct *BERM/RHTH* * SE16 ......102 A3
Danbury St *IS* N1 ....11 D1
Danby St *PECK* SE15 ....137 F3
Dancer Rd *FUL/PGN* SW6 ....113 F4
　RCH/KEW TW9 ....128 A1
Dando Crs *BKHTH/KID* SE3 ....142 B1
Dandridge Cl *GNWCH* SE10 ....123 F1
Danebury Av *PUT/ROE* SW15 ....129 F5
Daneby Rd *CAT* SE6 ....158 C3
Danecroft Rd *HNHL* SE24 ....136 C3
Danehurst St *FUL/PGN* SW6 ....113 E4
Danemere St *PUT/ROE* SW15 ......130 C1
Dane Pl *BOW* E3 ....91 E1
Dane Rd *IL* IG1 ....84 C2
Danescombe *LEE/GVPK* SE12 ....160 A1
Danesdale Rd *HOM* E9 ....79 E3
Dane St *GINN* WC1R 21 D3
Daneswood Av *CAT* SE6 ....158 C3
Daneville Rd *CMBW* SE5 ....119 D4
Dangan Rd *WAN* E11 ....64 A1
Daniel Bolt Cl *POP/IOD* E14 ....92 B4
Daniel Gdns *PECK* SE15 ....119 F3
Daniel Pl *HDN* NW4 ....52 B1
Daniel's Rd *PECK* SE15 ....138 C1
Dan Leno Wk *FUL/PGN* * SW6 ....114 B3
Dansey Pl *SOHO/SHAV* W1D 32 A1
Dante Rd *LBTH* SE11 ....46 C4
Danube St *CHEL* SW3 ....115 E1
Danvers St *CHEL* SW3 ....115 D2
Daphne St *WAND/EARL* SW18 ......132 C4
Daplyn St *WCHPL* E1 ....90 A4
D'arblay St *SOHO/CST* W1F 19 F5
Darell Rd *RCH/KEW* TW9 ....128 A1
Darenth Rd *STNW/STAM* N16 ....59 F3
Darfield Rd *BROCKY* SE4 ....139 F3
Darfield Wy *NKENS* W10 ....101 D1
Darfur St *PUT/ROE* SW15 ....131 D1
Darien Rd *BTSEA* SW11 ....133 D1
Darlan Rd *FUL/PGN* SW6 ....113 F3
Darley Rd *BTSEA* SW11 ....133 F4
Darling Rd *BROCKY* SE4 ....140 A1
Darling Rw *WCHPL* E1 ....90 B3
Darlington Rd *WNWD* SE27 ....154 B5
Darnley Rd *HACK* E8 ....78 B3
Darnley Ter *NTGHL* W11 ....101 D2
Darrell Rd *EDUL* SE22 ....138 A3
Darren Cl *FSBYPK* N4 ....57 F2
Darsley Dr *VX/NE* SW8 ....117 D4
Dartford St *WALW* SE17 ....118 C2
Dartmoor Wk *POP/IOD* * E14 ....104 A5
Dartmouth Cl *NTGHL* W11 ....89 F3
Dartmouth Gv *GNWCH* SE10 ....122 C4
Dartmouth Hl *GNWCH* SE10 ....122 C4
Dartmouth Park Av *KTTN* NW5 ....56 B5
Dartmouth Park Hl *ARCH* N19 ....56 B5
Dartmouth Park Rd *KTTN* NW5 ....56 B5
Dartmouth Pl *CHSWK* W4 ....111 E2
　FSTH SE23 ....156 C2
Dartmouth Rd *CRICK* NW2 ....71 D3
　HDN NW4 ....52 A1
　SYD SE26 ....156 B3
Dartmouth Rw *LEW* SE13 ....122 C5
Dartmouth St *STJSPK* SW1H 44 A1
Dartmouth Ter *GNWCH* SE10 ....123 D4
Dartrey Wk *WBPTN* * SW10 ....114 C3
Dart St *MV/WKIL* W9 ....89 F2
Darville Rd *STNW/STAM* N16 ....59 F5
Darwell Cl *EHAM* E6 ....96 A1
Darwin Rd *WELL* DA16 ....145 F1
Darwin St *WALW* SE17 ....48 B4
Dashwood Rd *CEND/HSY/T* N8 ....57 F1

Dassett Rd *WNWD* SE27 ....154 B5
Datchelor Pl *CMBW* * SE5 ....119 D4
Datchet Rd *CAT* SE6 ....157 F3
Date St *WALW* SE17 ....118 C1
Daubeney Rd *CLPT* E5 ....79 E2
Dault Rd *WAND/EARL* SW18 ....132 C4
Davenant Rd *ARCH* N19 ....57 D4
Davenant St *WCHPL* E1 ....90 A4
Davenport Rd *LEW* SE13 ....140 B4
Daventry Av *WALTH* E17 ....62 A1
Daventry St *CAMTN* NW1 ....16 C2
Davern Cl *GNWCH* SE10 ....105 F5
Davey Cl *HOLWY* N7 ....75 F3
Davey Rd *HOM* E9 ....80 A4
Davey St *PECK* SE15 ....119 F2
Davidge St *STHWK* SE1 ....46 C1
David Ms *MHST* W1U 17 F2
Davidson Gdns *VX/NE* SW8 ....117 E3
David's Rd *FSTH* SE23 ....156 C1
David St *SRTFD* E15 ....81 D3
Davies La *WAN* E11 ....63 E4
Davies Ms *MYFR/PKLN* * W1K 30 C1
Davies St *MYFR/PKLN* W1K 30 C1
Davis Rd *ACT* W3 ....99 F2
Davis St *PLSTW* E13 ....94 B1
Davisville Rd *SHB* W12 ....100 A3
Dawes Rd *FUL/PGN* SW6 ....113 F3
Dawes St *WALW* SE17 ....119 D1
Dawlish Av *WAND/EARL* SW18 ......150 B2
Dawlish Dr *GDMY/SEVK* IG3 ....85 F1
Dawlish Rd *CRICK* NW2 ....71 D3
　LEY E10 ....62 C4
Dawnay Gdns *WAND/EARL* SW18 .151 D2
Dawnay Rd *WAND/EARL* SW18 ......150 C2
Dawn Crs *SRTFD* E15 ....81 D5
Dawpool Rd *CRICK* NW2 ....51 F4
Dawson Av *BARK* IG11 ....85 F4
Dawson Cl *WOOL/PLUM* SE18 ......108 C5
Dawson Gdns *BARK* IG11 ....85 F4
Dawson Pl *BAY/PAD* W2 ....26 A1
Dawson Rd *CRICK* NW2 ....70 C2
Dawson St *BETH* E2 ....13 F2
Daylesford Av *PUT/ROE* SW15 ......130 A2
Daysbrook Rd *BRXS/STRHM* SW2 .153 F1
Days La *BFN/LL* DA15 ....145 E5
Dayton Gv *PECK* SE15 ....120 C4
Deacon Ms *IS* N1 ....77 D4
Deacon Rd *CRICK* NW2 ....70 A3
Deacons Ter *IS* * N1 ....76 C3
Deacon Wy *WALW* SE17 ....47 E4
Deal Porters Wy *BERM/RHTH* SE16 ..102 C4
Deal St *WCHPL* E1 ....90 A4
Dealtry Rd *PUT/ROE* SW15 ....130 C2
Deal Wk *BRXN/ST* SW9 ....118 A3
Dean Bradley St *WEST* SW1P 44 C3
Deancross St *WCHPL* E1 ....90 C5
Deanery Ms *MYFR/PKLN* * W1K 30 B3
Deanery Rd *SRTFD* E15 ....81 E3
Deanery St *MYFR/PKLN* W1K 30 B3
Dean Farrar St *STJSPK* SW1H 44 B2
Deanhill Ct *MORT/ESHN* * SW14 ...128 B2
Deanhill Rd *MORT/ESHN* SW14 .....128 B2
Dean Rd *CRICK* NW2 ....70 C3
Dean Ryle St *WEST* SW1P 44 C3
Deans Cl *CHSWK* W4 ....110 B2
Dean's Buildings *WALW* SE17 ....48 B5
Dean's Ct *BLKFR* EC4V 23 D5
Deanscroft Av *CDALE/KGS* NW9 ....50 C4
Deans Gate Cl *FSTH* SE23 ....157 D3
Dean's Ms *CAVSQ/HST* * W1G 19 D4
Dean Stanley St *WEST* SW1P 44 C3
Dean St *FSTGT* E7 ....82 A2
　SOHO/CST W1F 20 A1
Deans Yd *WEST* SW1P 44 B2
Dean Trench St *WEST* SW1P 44 C3
Deason St *SRTFD* * E15 ....80 C5
De Barowe Ms *HBRY* * N5 ....76 B1
De Beauvoir Crs *IS* N1 ....77 E5

De Beauvoir Est *IS* * N1 ....77 E5
De Beauvoir Rd *IS* N1 ....77 E4
De Beauvoir Sq *IS* N1 ....77 E4
Debnams Rd *BERM/RHTH* SE16..102 C5
Decima St *STHWK* SE1 ....48 C2
Deck Cl *BERM/RHTH* SE16..............103 D2
De Crespigny Pk *CMBW* SE5 ....119 D5
Deeley Rd *VX/NE* SW8 ....117 D4
Deepdale *WIM/MER* SW19 ....149 D4
Deepdene Gdns *BRXS/STRHM* SW2..135 F5
Deepdene Rd *HNHL* SE24 ....136 C2
Deerbrook Rd *BRXS/STRHM* SW2 ....154 B1
Deerdale Rd *HNHL* SE24 ....136 C2
Deerhurst Rd *KIL/WHAMP* NW6........71 D4
  STRHM/NOR SW16 ....153 F5
Deeside Rd *TOOT* SW17 ....151 D3
Dee St *POP/IOD* E14 ....92 C5
Defoe Av *RCH/KEW* TW9 ....110 A3
Defoe Rd *BERM/RHTH* SE16............103 F3
  STNW/STAM N16 ....59 E4
De Frene Rd *SYD* SE26 ....157 D4
Degema Rd *CHST* BR7 ....162 B5
Dehar Crs *CDALE/KGS* NW9 ....51 F2
Dekker Rd *DUL* SE21 ....137 E4
Delacourt Rd *BKHTH/KID* SE3........124 B3
Delafield Rd *CHARL* SE7 ....124 B1
Delaford Rd *BERM/RHTH* SE16 ....120 B1
Delaford St *FUL/PGN* SW6 ....113 E3
Delamere St *BAY/PAD* W2 ....15 E3
Delamere Ter *BAY/PAD* W2................15 D2
Delancey Pas *CAMTN* NW1 ....74 B5
Delancey St *CAMTN* NW1 ....74 B5
De Laune St *WALW* SE17 ....118 B2
Delaware Rd *MV/WKIL* W9 ....2 C5
Delawyk Crs *HNHL* SE24 ....137 D4
Delhi St *IS* N1 ....75 E5
Delia St *WAND/EARL* SW18 ....132 B5
Delisle Rd *THMD* SE28 ....109 E2
Dell Cl *STHWK* SE15 ....81 D5
Dellow Cl *GNTH/NBYPK* IG2............67 D2
Dellow St *WCHPL* E1 ....102 B1
Dell's Ms *PIM* * SW1V 43 F5
Delme Crs *BKHTH/KID* SE3............124 B5
Deloraine St *DEPT* SE8 ....122 A4
Delorme St *HMSMTH* W6 ....113 D2
Delta Est *BETH* * E2 ....90 A2
Delta St *BETH* * E2 ....90 A2
Delverton Rd *WALW* SE17 ....118 B1
Delvino Rd *FUL/PGN* SW6 ....114 A4
Demeta Cl *WBLY* HA9 ....50 C5
De Montfort Pde
  STRHM/NOR * SW16 ....153 E3
De Montfort Rd *STRHM/NOR* SW16..153 D2
De Morgan Rd *FUL/PGN* SW6..........132 B1
Dempster Rd *WAND/EARL* SW18......132 C3
Denbigh Cl *NTGHL* W11 ....101 F1
  WLSDN NW10 ....69 E4
Denbigh Pl *PIM* * SW1V 116 C1
Denbigh Rd *EHAM* E6 ....95 D2
  NTGHL W11 ....101 F1
Denbigh St *PIM* SW1V 43 E5
Denbigh Ter *NTGHL* W11 ....101 F1
Dendy St *BAL* SW12 ....152 A1
Dene Cl *BROCKY* SE4 ....139 E1
Denehurst Gdns *ACT* W3 ....98 B2
  HDN NW4 ....52 C1
  RCHPK/HAM TW10 ....128 A2
Denewood Rd *HGT* N6 ....55 E1
Dengie Wk *IS* * N1 ....76 C5
Dengil Crs *KTTN* NW5........................74 A2
Denham Dr *GNTH/NBYPK* IG2..........66 C1
Denham Wy *BARK* IG11 ....85 E5
Denholme Rd *MV/WKIL* W9 ....89 F2
Denman Rd *PECK* SE15 ....119 F4
Denman St *REGST* W1B......................31 F2
Denmark Gv *IS* N1 ....10 A1
Denmark Hl *CMBW* SE5 ....119 D4
  HNHL SE24 ....137 D2

Denmark Rd *CMBW* SE5 ....118 C4
  KIL/WHAMP NW6 ....89 F1
Denmark Sq *LSQ/SEVD* WC2H 20 B5
  PLSTW E13 ....94 B4
  WAN E11 ....63 E5
Denne Ter *HACK* E8 ....77 F5
Dennett's Gv *NWCR* SE14 ....121 D5
Dennett's Rd *NWCR* SE14 ....120 C4
Denning Cl *STJWD* NW8 ....3 F3
Denning Rd *HAMP* NW3 ....73 D1
Dennington Park Rd
  KIL/WHAMP NW6 ....72 A3
Dennis Wy *CLAP* SW4 ....135 D1
Denny Crs *LBTH* SE11 ....118 A1
Denny St *LBTH* SE11 ....118 A1
Densham Rd *SRTFD* E15 ....81 E5
Denton St *WAND/EARL* SW18........132 B4
Denton Wy *CLPT* E5 ....61 D5
Dents Rd *BTSEA* SW11 ....133 F4
Denver Rd *STNW/STAM* N16 ....59 E2
Denyer St *CHEL* SW3 ....41 D4
Denzil Rd *WLSDN* NW10 ....69 F2
Deodar Rd *PUT/ROE* SW15 ....131 E2
Depot Ap *CRICK* NW2........................71 D1
Depot St *CMBW* SE5 ....119 D2
Deptford Br *GNWCH* SE10 ....122 A4
Deptford Broadway *DEPT* SE8........122 A4
Deptford Church St *DEPT* SE8 ......122 A2
Deptford Gn *DEPT* SE8 ....122 A2
Deptford High St *DEPT* SE8 ....122 A2
Deptford Market *DEPT* * SE8..........122 A3
Deptford Whf *DEPT* SE8................103 F5
Derby Ga *WHALL* SW1A 32 C5
Derby Hl *FSTH* SE23 ....156 C2
Derby Hill Crs *FSTH* SE23 ....156 C2
Derby Rd *FSTGT* E7 ....83 D4
  HOM E9 ....79 D5
  MORT/ESHN SW14 ....128 B2
Derbyshire St *BETH* E2 ....90 A2
Derby St *MYFR/PICC* W1J 30 B4
Dereham Pl *SDTCH* EC2A 13 D5
Dereham Rd *BARK* IG11....................85 F3
Derek Av *WBLY* HA9 ....68 B4
Derek Walcott Cl *HNHL* * SE24......136 B3
Dericote St *HACK* E8 ....78 A5
Derifall Cl *EHAM* E6 ....95 F4
Dering St *CONDST* W1S 18 C3
Derinton Rd *TOOT* SW17 ....152 A4
Dermody Gdns *LEW* * SE13 ....141 D3
Dermody Rd *LEW* SE13 ....141 D3
Deronda Rd *BRXS/STRHM* SW2 ....154 B1
Derrick Gdns *CHARL* SE7 ....106 C3
Derry St *KENS* W8 ....38 C1
Dersingham Av *MNPK* E12................83 F1
Dersingham Rd *CRICK* NW2 ....53 E5
Derwent Av *PUT/ROE* SW15 ....147 E4
Derwent Gv *EDUL* SE22..................137 F2
Derwent Ri *CDALE/KGS* NW9 ....51 E1
Derwent St *GNWCH* SE10 ....123 E1
Derwentwater Rd *ACT* W3 ....98 C2
Desborough Cl *BAY/PAD* W2 ....15 D2
Desenfans Rd *DUL* SE21 ....137 E4
Desford Rd *CAN/RD* E16 ....93 E3
Desmond St *NWCR* SE14 ....121 E2
Despard Rd *ARCH* N19 ....56 C3
Detling Rd *BMLY* BR1 ....160 A5
Detmold Rd *CLPT* E5 ....60 B4
Devalls Cl *EHAM* E6 ....108 A1
Devas St *BOW* E3 ....92 B3
Devenay Rd *SRTFD* E15 ....81 F4
De Vere Gdns *IL* IG1 ....65 F4
  KENS W8 ....39 E1
Deverell St *STHWK* SE1 ....48 A3
De Vere Ms *KENS* W8 ....39 E2
Devereux Ct *TPL/STR* WC2R 22 A5
Devereux La *BARN* SW13 ....112 B3
Devereux Rd *BTSEA* SW11 ....133 E1
Devizes St *IS* N1 ....77 D5

Devon Gdns *FSBYPK* N4 ....58 B1
Devonhurst Pl *CHSWK* * W4 ....111 D1
Devonia Rd *IS* N1 ....11 D1
Devonport Gdns *IL* IG1 ....65 F1
Devonport Ms *SHB* * W12 ....100 B3
Devonport Rd *SHB* W12 ....100 C3
Devonport St *WCHPL* E1 ....90 C5
Devon Rd *BARK* IG11 ....85 E5
Devons Est *BOW* E3 ....92 B2
Devonshire Cl *CAVSQ/HST* W1G ...18 C2
  SRTFD E15 ....81 E1
Devonshire Dr *GNWCH* SE10 ....122 B4
Devonshire Gdns *CHSWK* W4 ......110 C3
Devonshire Gv *PECK* SE15 ....120 B2
Devonshire Ms South
  CAVSQ/HST W1G 18 C2
Devonshire Ms West *CAVSQ/HST* W1G ...18 B1
Devonshire Pl *CAVSQ/HST* W1G 18 B1
  CRICK NW2 ....54 A5
  KENS * W8 ....38 C3
Devonshire Place Ms *MHST* W1U ...18 B1
Devonshire Pl *CAN/RD* E16 ....94 B5
  CHSWK W4 ....111 E1
  ELTH/MOT SE9 ....161 E4
  FSTH SE23 ....139 D5
  GNTH/NBYPK IG2 ....67 D2
  WALTH E17 ....62 A1
Devonshire Rw *LVPST* EC2M 25 D3
Devonshire Sq *LVPST* EC2M 25 D4
Devonshire St *CAVSQ/HST* W1G 18 B2
  CHSWK W4 ....111 E1
Devonshire Ter *BAY/PAD* W2 ....15 F5
  EDUL * SE22 ....138 A2
Devons Rd *BOW* E3 ....92 A4
Devon St *PECK* SE15 ....120 B2
Devon St *PECK* SE15 ....120 B2
De Walden St *CAVSQ/HST* W1G 18 B3
Dewar St *PECK* SE15 ....138 A1
Dewberry Gdns *EHAM* E6 ....95 E4
Dewberry St *POP/IOD* E14 ....92 C5
Dewey Rd *IS* N1 ....10 A1
Dewey Rd *TOOT* SW17 ....151 F5
Dewhurst Rd *HMSMTH* W6 ....101 D4
Dewsbury Rd *WLSDN* NW10 ....70 A2
D'Eynsford Rd *CMBW* SE5 ....119 D4
Diadem Ct *SOHO/SHAV* * W1D 20 A4
Diamond St *PECK* SE15 ....119 E3
  WLSDN NW10 ....68 C4
Diana Cl *DEPT* SE8 ....121 F2
Diana Pl *CAMTN* NW1 ....7 D5
Dibden St *IS* N1 ....76 C5
Dicey Av *CRICK* NW2 ....70 C2
Dickens Est *BERM/RHTH* * SE16 ....102 A4
Dickens Ms *EC1M* 22 C1
Dickenson Rd *CEND/HSY/T* N8 ......57 E2
Dickens Rd *EHAM* E6 ....95 D1
Dickens Sq *STHWK* SE1 ....47 F2
Dickens St *VX/NE* SW8 ....116 B5
Dickson House *WOOL/PLUM* SE18 .125 E4
Dickson Rd *ELTH/MOT* SE9 ....143 E1
Didsbury Cl *EHAM* E6 ....83 F5
Digby Crs *FSBYPK* N4 ....58 C4
Digby Rd *BARK* IG11 ....85 F4
  HOM E9 ....79 D3
Digby St *BETH* E2 ....90 C2
Diggon St *WCHPL* E1 ....91 D4
Dighton Rd *WAND/EARL* SW18 ......132 C3
Dignum St *IS* * N1 ....10 A1
Digswell St *HOLWY* * N7 ....76 A3
Dilhorne Cl *LEE/GVPK* SE12 ....160 B3
Dilke St *CHEL* SW3 ....115 F2
Dillwyn St *SYD* SE26 ....157 E3
Dilton Gdns *PUT/ROE* SW15 ....148 A1
Dimes Pl *HMSMTH* W6 ....100 B5
Dimond Cl *FSTGT* E7 ....82 A1
Dimsdale Dr *CDALE/KGS* NW9 ....50 C3
Dimson Crs *BOW* E3 ....92 A3
Dingle Gdns *POP/IOD* * E14 ....104 A1
Dingley La *STRHM/NOR* SW16 ......153 D2

Dingley Pl *FSBYE* EC1V 11 F4
Dingley Rd *FSBYE* EC1V 11 E4
Dingwall Gdns *GLDGN* NW11 ....54 A1
Dingwall Rd *WAND/EARL* SW18 .....132 C5
Dinmont St *BETH* E2 ....90 B1
Dinsdale Rd *BKHTH/KID* SE3 ....123 F2
Dinsmore Rd *BAL* SW12 ....134 B5
Dirleton Rd *SRTFD* E15 ....81 F1
Disbrowe Rd *HMSMTH* W6 ....113 D2
Discovery Wk *WAP* E1W 102 B1
Disney Pl *STHWK* SE1 ....35 F5
Disney Pl *STHWK* SE1 ....35 F5
Disney St *STHWK* SE1 ....35 F5
Disraeli Rd *FSTGT* E7 ....82 A3
  PUT/ROE SW15 ....131 F2
  WLSDN NW10 ....86 C1
Diss St *BETH* E2 ....13 E3
Distaff La *BLKFR* EC4V 35 E1
Distillery La *HMSMTH* W6 ....112 C1
Distillery Rd *HMSMTH* W6 ....112 C1
Distin St *LBTH* SE11 ....46 A5
Ditchburn St *POP/IOD* E14 ....104 C1
Dittisham Rd *ELTH/MOT* SE9 ....161 E4
Dixon Cl *EHAM* E6 ....95 F5
Dixon Rd *NWCR* SE14 ....121 F4
Dobell Rd *ELTH/MOT* SE9 ....143 F3
Dobree Av *WLSDN* NW10 ....70 B4
Dobson Cl *KIL/WHAMP* NW6 ....73 D4
Dockers Tanner Rd *POP/IOD* E14 ...104 A5
Dockhead *STHWK* SE1 ....49 F1
Dock Hill Av *BERM/RHTH* SE16 .....103 D3
Dockland St *CAN/RD* E16 ....108 A2
Dockley Rd *BERM/RHTH* SE16 ....102 A4
Dock Rd *CAN/RD* E16 ....105 F1
Dockside Rd *CAN/RD* E16 ....107 D1
Dock St *WCHPL* E1 ....102 A1
Doctors Cl *SYD* SE26 ....156 C5
Dodbrooke Rd *WNWD* SE27 ....154 A3
Doddington Gv *WALW* SE17 ....118 B2
Doddington Pl *WALW* SE17 ....118 B2
Dodson St *STHWK* SE1 ....46 B1
Dog Kennel Hl *CMBW* SE5 ....137 E1
Dog La *WLSDN* NW10 ....69 E1
Doherty Rd *PLSTW* E13 ....94 A3
Dolben Ct *DEPT* * SE8 ....103 F5
Dolben St *STHWK* * SE1 ....35 D4
Dolby Rd *FUL/PGN* SW6 ....113 F5
Dolland St *LBTH* SE11 ....117 F1
Dollis Hill Av *CRICK* NW2 ....52 B5
Dollis Hill Est *CRICK* * NW2 ....52 A5
Dollis Hill La *CRICK* NW2 ....69 F1
Dolman Rd *CHSWK* W4 ....99 D5
Dolman St *CLAP* SW4 ....135 F2
Dolphin La *POP/IOD* E14 ....104 B1
Dolphin Sq *CHSWK* * W4 ....111 E3
  PIM SW1V 116 C1
Dombey St *BMSBY* WC1N 21 E2
Dome Hill Pk *SYD* SE26 ....155 F4
Domett Cl *CMBW* SE5 ....137 D2
Domingo St *FSBYE* EC1V 11 E5
Dominica Cl *PLSTW* E13 ....95 D2
Dominion St *LVPST* EC2M 24 B2
Domonic Dr *ELTH/MOT* SE9 ....162 B3
Donald Rd *PLSTW* E13 ....82 B5
Donaldson Rd *KIL/WHAMP* NW6 .....71 F5
  WOOL/PLUM SE18 ....126 A4
Doncaster Gdns *FSBYPK* * N4 ....58 C1
Donegal St *IS* N1 ....9 F2
Doneraile St *FUL/PGN* SW6 ....113 D5
Dongola Rd *PLSTW* E13 ....94 B3
  WCHPL E1 ....91 E4
Dongola Rd West *PLSTW* E13 ....94 B3
Donkey Aly *EDUL* SE22 ....138 A3
Donne Pl *CHEL* SW3 ....41 D4
Donnington Rd *WLSDN* NW10 ....70 B5
Donoghue Cottages *POP/IOD* * E14 ..91 E4
Don Phelan Cl *CMBW* SE5 ....119 D4

Doon St *STHWK* SE1 .... 34 A4
Dorando Cl *SHB* * W12 .... 100 B1
Doran Gv *WOOL/PLUM* SE18 .... 127 E3
Dora Rd *WIM/MER* SW19 .... 150 A5
Dora St *POP/IOD* E14 .... 91 F5
Dorchester Ct *CRICK* NW2 .... 53 D5
   HNHL SE24 .... 136 C3
Dorchester Dr *HNHL* SE24 .... 136 C3
Dorchester Gv *CHSWK* W4 .... 111 E2
Dorchester Pde *STRHM/NOR* * SW16 ... 153 D2
Dordrecht Rd *ACT* W3 .... 99 E2
Dore Av *MNPK* E12 .... 84 A2
Doreen Av *CDALE/KGS* NW9 .... 51 D3
Doria Rd *FUL/PGN* SW6 .... 113 F5
Doric Wy *CAMTN* NW1 .... 8 A3
Doris Rd *FSTGT* E7 .... 82 A4
Dorking Cl *DEPT* SE8 .... 121 F2
Doricote Rd *WAND/EARL* SW18 .... 133 D5
Dorman Wy *STJWD* NW8 .... 73 D5
Dormay St *WAND/EARL* SW18 .... 132 B3
Dormer Cl *SRTFD* E15 .... 81 F3
Dornberg Rd *BKHTH/KID* SE3 .... 124 A3
Dornberg Rd *BKHTH/KID* * SE3 .... 124 B3
Dorncliffe Rd *FUL/PGN* SW6 .... 113 E5
Dornfell St *KIL/WHAMP* NW6 .... 71 F2
Dornton Rd *BAL* SW12 .... 152 B2
Dorothy Rd *BTSEA* SW11 .... 133 F1
Dorrington St *HCIRC* EC1N 22 A2
Dorrit St *STHWK* * SE1 .... 35 F5
Dors Cl *CDALE/KGS* NW9 .... 51 D3
Dorset Av *DAGE* DA16 .... 145 F2
Dorset Buildings *EMB* * EC4Y 22 C5
Dorset Cl *CAMTN* NW1 .... 17 E2
Dorset Ms *KTBR* SW1X 42 C2
Dorset Pl *SRTFD* E15 .... 81 D3
Dorset Ri *EMB* EC4Y 22 C5
Dorset Rd *ELTH/MOT* SE9 .... 161 E2
   VX/NE SW8 .... 117 F3
Dorset Sq *CAMTN* NW1 .... 17 E1
Dorset St *MHST* W1U 17 F3
Dorton Cl *PECK* * SE15 .... 119 E3
Dorville Crs *HMSMTH* W6 .... 100 B4
Dorville Rd *LEE/GVPK* SE12 .... 142 A3
Dothill Rd *WOOL/PLUM* SE18 .... 126 C3
Doughty Ms *BMSBY* WC1N 21 E1
Doughty St *BMSBY* WC1N 9 E5
Douglas Est *IS* * N1 .... 76 C3
Douglas Ms *CRICK* NW2 .... 53 E5
Douglas Pl *POP/IOD* * E14 .... 122 C1
Douglas Rd *CAN/RD* E16 .... 94 A4
   IS N1 .... 76 C4
   KIL/WHAMP NW6 .... 71 F5
Douglas Rd North *IS* N1 .... 76 C3
Douglas Rd South *IS* * N1 .... 76 C3
Douglas St *WEST* SW1P 44 A5
Douglas Wy *NWCR* SE14 .... 121 F3
Doulton Ms *HAMP* NW3 .... 72 B3
Dounesforth Gdns
   WAND/EARL SW18 .... 150 B1
Douro Pl *KENS* W8 .... 39 D2
Douro St *BOW* E3 .... 92 A1
Douthwaite Sq *WAP* E1W 102 A1
Dove Ap *EHAM* E6 .... 95 E4
Dove Ct *LOTH* * EC2R 24 A5
Dovedale Rd *EDUL* SE22 .... 138 B3
Dovehouse Md *BARK* IG11 .... 97 D1
Dovehouse St *CHEL* SW3 .... 115 E1
Dove Ms *ECT* SW5 .... 39 E5
Dover Cl *CRICK* NW2 .... 53 D4
Dovercourt Est *IS* N1 .... 77 D3
Dovercourt Rd *DUL* SE21 .... 137 E4
Doverfield Rd *BRXS/STRHM* SW2 .... 135 E4
Dover House Rd *PUT/ROE* SW15 .... 130 A2
Dove Rd *IS* N1 .... 77 D3
Dove Rw *BETH* E2 .... 90 A1
Dover Park Dr *PUT/ROE* SW15 .... 130 B4
Dover Patrol *BKHTH/KID* SE3 .... 124 B5
Dover Rd *MNPK* E12 .... 64 C4

Wool/PLUM SE18 .... 126 B5
Dover St *MYFR/PICC* W1J 31 D2
Dover Ter *RCH/KEW* * TW9 .... 110 A5
Doves Yd *IS* N1 .... 76 A5
Doveton Cl *WCHPL* E1 .... 90 C3
Dowanhill Rd *CAT* SE6 .... 159 D1
Dowdeswell Cl *PUT/ROE* SW15 .... 129 E2
Dowdney Cl *KTTN* NW5 .... 74 C2
Dowgate Hl *CANST* EC4R 36 A1
Dowlas St *CMBW* SE5 .... 119 E3
Downderry Rd *BMLY* BR1 .... 159 D3
Downend *WOOL/PLUM* SE18 .... 126 B3
Downer's Cottages *CLAP* SW4 .... 134 C2
Downfield Cl *MV/WKIL* W9 .... 14 C1
Downham Rd *IS* N1 .... 77 D4
Downham Wy *BMLY* BR1 .... 159 E5
Downings *EHAM* E6 .... 96 A5
Downhills Av *GDMY/SEVK* IG3 .... 67 E5
Downham Hl *HAMP* NW3 .... 73 D1
Downside Crs *HAMP* NW3 .... 73 E2
Downs Av *CHST* BR7 .... 161 F5
Downs Court Pde *CLPT* * E5 .... 78 B2
Downsell Rd *WAN* E11 .... 81 D1
Downsfield Rd *WALTH* E17 .... 61 E1
Downshall Av *GDMY/SEVK* IG3 .... 67 E5
Downshire Hl *HAMP* NW3 .... 73 D1
Downs La *CLPT* * E5 .... 78 B1
Downs Park Rd *HACK* E8 .... 78 A2
Downs Rd *CLPT* E5 .... 78 A1
Down St *MYFR/PICC* W1J 30 C4
Down Street Ms *MYFR/PICC* W1J 30 C5
Downton Av *BRXS/STRHM* SW2 .... 153 F2
Downtown Rd *BERM/RHTH* SE16 .... 103 E3
Dowrey St *IS* N1 .... 76 A5
Dowson Cl *CMBW* * SE5 .... 137 D2
Doyce St *STHWK* * SE1 .... 35 E5
Doyle Gdns *WLSDN* NW10 .... 70 B5
D'Oyley St *KTBR* SW1X 42 A4
Doynton St *KTTN* * NW5 .... 56 B4
Draco Ga *PUT/ROE* * SW15 .... 130 C1
Draco St *WALW* SE17 .... 118 C2
Dragonfly Cl *PLSTW* E13 .... 94 B2
Dragon Rd *PECK* * SE15 .... 119 E2
Dragoon Rd *DEPT* SE8 .... 121 F1
Dragor Rd *WLSDN* NW10 .... 86 C2
Drake Cl *BERM/RHTH* SE16 .... 103 D3
Drakefell Rd *NWCR* SE14 .... 121 D5
Drakefield Rd *TOOT* SW17 .... 152 A3
Drake Rd *BROCKY* SE4 .... 140 A1
Drakes Ctyd *KIL/WHAMP* NW6 .... 71 F4
Drake St *BMSBY* WC1N 21 E3
Draper Est *WALW* SE17 .... 47 D4
Draper Pl *IS* N1 .... 76 B5
Drapers St *SRTFD* E15 .... 80 C1
Drapers Wy *BERM/RHTH* SE16 .... 102 A3
Drawell Cl *WOOL/PLUM* SE18 .... 127 E1
Draycot Rd *WAN* E11 .... 64 B1
Draycott Av *CHEL* SW3 .... 41 D5
Draycott Cl *CRICK* NW2 .... 53 D5
Draycott Pl *CHEL* SW3 .... 41 E5
Draycott Ter *CHEL* SW3 .... 41 E4
Drayford Cl *MV/WKIL* * W9 .... 89 F3
Drayson Ms *KENS* W8 .... 38 B1
Drayton Cl *IL* IG1 .... 67 D3
Drayton Gdns *WBPTN* SW10 .... 114 C1
Drayton Pk *HBRY* N5 .... 58 A5
Drayton Park Ms *HOLWY* * N7 .... 75 E1
Drayton Rd *WAN* E11 .... 63 D3
   WLSDN NW10 .... 69 E5
Dreadnought St *GNWCH* SE10 .... 105 E4
Dresden Cl *HAMP* NW3 .... 72 B3
Dresden Rd *ARCH* N19 .... 56 C3
Dressington Av *BROCKY* SE4 .... 140 A4
Drewery Ct *BKHTH/KID* * SE3 .... 141 E1
Drew Rd *CAN/RD* E16 .... 107 E2

Drews Cottages BAL * SW12 ....153 D2
Drewstead Rd STRHM/NOR SW16 .....153 D2
Driffield Rd BOW E3 ....91 E1
The Drive ACT W3 ....86 C5
  BARK IG11 ....85 F4
  GLDGN NW11 ....53 E2
  HOLWY N7 ....75 F3
  IL IG1 ....65 E1
  WBLY HA9 ....50 C4
Dr Johnson Av TOOT SW17 ....152 B3
Droitwich CI SYD SE26 ....156 A3
Dromore Rd PUT/ROE SW15 ....131 E4
Droop St NKENS W10 ....89 E3
Drovers PI PECK SE15 ....120 B3
Druce Rd DUL SE21 ....137 E4
Druid St STHWK SE1 ....37 F5
Drummond Crs CAMTN NW1 ....8 A3
Drummond Ga PIM SW1V 117 D1
Drummond Rd BERM/RHTH SE16 ....102 B4
  WAN E11 ....64 B1
Drummond St CAMTN NW1 ....7 E5
Drum St WCHPL E1 ....25 F4
Drury La HOL/ALD WC2B 21 D4
Drury Wy WLSDN NW10 ....69 D2
Dryad St PUT/ROE SW15 ....131 D1
Dryburgh Rd PUT/ROE SW15 ....130 B1
Dryden Rd WIM/MER SE18 ....127 F4
Dryden St COVGDN WC2E 21 D5
Dryfield CI WLSDN NW10 ....68 C3
Drylands Rd CEND/HSY/T N8 ....57 F3
Drysdale Dwellings HACK * E8 ....77 F2
Drysdale PI BETH E2 ....13 D3
Drysdale St IS N1 ....13 D4
Dublin Av HACK E8 ....78 A5
Ducal St BETH E2 ....13 F4
Du Cane CI SHB * W12 ....88 C5
Du Cane Rd SHB W12 ....88 B5
Duchess Ms CAVSQ/HST W1G 19 D3
Duchess of Bedford's Wk KENS W8 ....101 F3
Duchess St REGST W1B 19 D3
Duchy St STHWK SE1 ....34 B3
Ducie St CLAP SW4 ....135 E2
Duckett Rd FSBYPK N4 ....58 B1
Duckett St WCHPL E1 ....91 D4
Duck La SOHO/CST W1F 20 A5
Du Cros Rd ACT W3 ....99 E2
Dudden Hill La WLSDN NW10 ....69 F1
Dudden Hill Pde WLSDN * NW10 ....69 F1
Duddington CI ELTH/MOT SE9 ....161 D4
Dudley Av IL IG1 ....84 B1
  KIL/WHAMP NW6 ....89 E1
Dudley St BAY/PAD * W2 ....16 A3
Dudlington Rd CLPT E5 ....60 C4
Dudmaston Ms CHEL SW3 ....115 D1
Dufferin Av STLK EC1Y 24 A1
Dufferin St STLK EC1Y 23 F1
Duff St POP/IOD E14 ....92 B5
Dufour's PI SOHO/CST W1F 19 F5
Duke Humphrey Rd BKHTH/KID SE3 ....123 E4
Duke of Wellington PI WHALL SW1A 42 B1
Duke of York St STJS SW1Y 31 F3
Duke Rd CHSWK W4 ....111 D1
Duke's Av CHSWK W4 ....111 D1
Dukes Ga CHSWK * W4 ....98 C5
Dukes La KENS W8 ....26 C5
Duke's Ms MHST W1U 18 B4
Duke's PI HDTCH EC3A 25 E5
Dukes Rd ACT W3 ....86 A3
  CAMTN NW1 ....8 A3
  EHAM E6 ....84 A5
Dukesthorpe Rd SYD SE26 ....157 D4
Duke St MBLAR W1H 18 B4
Duke Street HI STHWK SE1 ....36 B3
Duke Street St James's
  MYFR/PICC W1J 31 F3
Duke's Yd MYFR/PKLN W1K 30 B1
Dulas St FSBYPK N4 ....57 F3
Dulford St NTGHL W11 ....101 E1

Dulka Rd BTSEA SW11 ....133 F3
Dulverton Rd ELTH/MOT SE9 ....162 C2
Dulwich Common DUL SE21 ....155 D1
The Dulwich Oaks DUL * SE21 ....155 F3
Dulwich Rd HNHL SE24 ....136 A3
Dulwich Village DUL SE21 ....137 D4
Dulwich Wood Av NRWD SE19 ....155 E5
Dulwich Wood Pk NRWD SE19 ....155 E4
Dumbarton Rd BRXS/STRHM SW2 ....135 E4
Dumont Rd STNW/STAM N16 ....59 E3
Dumpton PI CAMTN NW1 ....74 A4
Dunbar Rd FSTGT E7 ....82 A3
Dunbar St WNWD SE27 ....154 C3
Dunblane Rd ELTH/MOT SE9 ....143 F1
Dunboyne Rd HAMP NW3 ....73 F2
Dunbridge St BETH E2 ....90 A3
Duncan Gv ACT W3 ....87 E5
Duncannon St CHCR WC2N 32 C2
Duncan Rd HACK E8 ....78 B5
Duncan St IS N1 ....10 C1
Duncan Ter IS N1 ....10 C2
Dunch St WCHPL * E1 ....90 B5
Duncombe HI FSTH SE23 ....139 E5
Duncombe Rd ARCH N19 ....57 D3
Duncrievie Rd LEW SE13 ....141 D4
Duncroft WOOL/PLUM SE18 ....127 E3
Dundalk Rd BROCKY SE4 ....139 E1
Dundas Rd PECK SE15 ....120 C5
Dundee Rd PLSTW E13 ....94 B1
Dundee St WAP E1W 102 B2
Dundonald CI EHAM E6 ....95 E5
Dundonald Rd WLSDN NW10 ....71 D5
Dunedin Rd IL IG1 ....66 C3
  LEY E10 ....62 B5
Dunelm Gv WNWD SE27 ....154 C4
Dunelm St WCHPL E1 ....91 D5
Dunfield Rd CAT SE6 ....158 B5
Dunford Rd HOLWY N7 ....75 F1
Dungarvan Av PUT/ROE SW15 ....130 A2
Dunkery Rd ELTH/MOT SE9 ....161 D4
Dunkirk St WNWD * SE27 ....154 C4
Dunlace Rd CLPT E5 ....78 C2
Dunloe St BETH E2 ....13 E2
Dunlop PI BERM/RHTH SE16 ....49 F3
Dunmore Rd KIL/WHAMP NW6 ....71 E4
Dunmow Rd SRTFD E15 ....81 D1
Dunmow Wk IS * N1 ....76 C5
Dunnock Rd EHAM E6 ....95 E5
Dunn St HACK E8 ....77 F2
Dunollie PI KTTN NW5 ....74 C2
Dunollie Rd KTTN NW5 ....74 C2
Dunoon Gdns FSTH * SE23 ....139 D5
Dunoon Rd FSTH SE23 ....138 C5
Dunraven Rd SHB W12 ....100 A2
Dunraven St MYFR/PKLN W1K 29 F1
Dunsany Rd HMSMTH W6 ....101 D4
Dunsmure Rd STNW/STAM N16 ....59 E3
Dunstable Ms CAVSQ/HST W1G 18 B2
Dunstan Houses WCHPL * E1 ....90 C4
Dunstan Rd GLDGN NW11 ....53 F3
Dunstan's Gv EDUL SE22 ....138 B4
Dunstan's Rd EDUL SE22 ....138 A5
Dunster Ct FENCHST EC3M 36 C1
Dunster Dr CDALE/KGS NW9 ....50 C4
Dunster Gdns KIL/WHAMP NW6 ....71 F4
Dunsterville Wy STHWK SE1 ....48 B1
Dunston Rd BTSEA SW11 ....116 A5
  HACK E8 ....77 F5
Dunston St HACK E8 ....77 F5
Dunton Rd LEY E10 ....62 B2
  STHWK SE1 ....49 E5
Duntshill Rd WAND/EARL SW18 ....150 B1
Dunvegan Rd ELTH/MOT SE9 ....143 F2
Dunworth Ms NTGHL * W11 ....89 F5
Duplex Ride KTBR SW1X 41 F1
Dupont St POP/IOD E14 ....91 E5
Dupree Rd CHARL SE7 ....124 B1

Durand Gdns *BRXN/ST* SW9 ....117 F4
Durand Wy *WLSDN* NW10 ....68 C4
Durant St *BETH* E2 ....90 A1
Durban Rd *GNTH/NBYPK* IG2 ....67 E3
   SRTFD E15 ....93 E2
   WNWD SE27 ....154 C4
Durford Crs *PUT/ROE* SW15 ....148 A1
Durham Hl *BMLY* BR1 ....159 H4
Durham House St *CHCR* * WC2N 33 D2
Durham Ri *BETH* E2 ....115 F1
Durham Ri *WOOL/PLUM* SE18 ....126 C1
Durham Rd *CAN/RD* E16 ....93 E3
   HOLWY N7 ....57 F4
   MNPK E12 ....83 D1
Durham Rw *WCHPL* E1 ....91 D4
Durham St *LBTH* SE11 ....117 F1
Durham Ter *BAY/PAD* W2 ....14 C4
Durham Yd *BETH* * E2 ....90 B2
Durley Av *PIN* HA5 ....47 F3
Durley Rd *STNW/STAM* N16 ....59 E2
Durlston Rd *CLPT* E5 ....60 A4
Durning Rd *NRWD* SE19 ....155 D5
Durnsford Av *WAND/EARL* SW18 ....150 A3
Durnsford Rd *WAND/EARL* SW18 ....150 A2
Durrell Rd *FUL/PGN* SW6 ....113 E4
Durrington Rd *CLPT* E5 ....79 E1
Dursley Cl *BKHTH/KID* SE3 ....124 C5
Dursley Gdns *BKHTH/KID* SE3 ....125 D4
Dursley Rd *BKHTH/KID* SE3 ....124 C5
Durward St *WCHPL* E1 ....90 B4
Durweston Ms *MHST* * W1U 17 F2
Dutch Yd *WAND/EARL* SW18 ....132 A3
Duthie St *POP/IOD* E14 ....104 C1
Dutton St *GNWCH* SE10 ....122 C4
Dye House La *BOW* E3 ....80 A5
Dyer's Buildings *FLST/FETLN* EC4A 22 A3
Dyers Hall Rd *WAN* E11 ....63 E3
Dyer's La *PUT/ROE* SW15 ....130 B1
Dylways *CMBW* SE5 ....137 D2
Dymock St *FUL/PGN* SW6 ....132 B1
Dyneley Rd *LEE/GVPK* SE12 ....160 C4
Dyne Rd *KIL/WHAMP* NW6 ....71 F4
Dynevor Rd *STNW/STAM* N16 ....59 E5
Dynham Rd *KIL/WHAMP* NW6 ....72 A4
Dyott St *NOXST/BSQ* WC1A 20 C4
Dysart St *SDTCH* EC2A 24 B1
Dyson Rd *FSTGT* E7 ....81 F3
   WAN E11 ....63 E1

E

Eade Rd *FSBYPK* N4 ....58 C2
Eagle Ct *FARR* EC1M 22 C2
Eagle Ms *IS* N1 ....77 E3
Eagle Pl *WBPTN* SW10 ....114 C1
Eaglesfield Rd *WOOL/PLUM* SE18 ......126 B4
Eagle St *GINN* WC1R 21 E3
Eagle Wharf Rd *IS* N1 ....11 F1
Ealdham Sq *ELTH/MOT* SE9 ....142 C2
Ealing Rd *BOW* E3 ....92 B2
Eamont St *STJWD* NW8 ....4 C1
Eardley Crs *ECT* SW5 ....114 A1
Earldom Rd *PUT/ROE* SW15 ....130 C2
Earlham Gv *FSTGT* E7 ....81 F2
Earlham St *LSQ/SEVD* WC2H 20 B5
Earl Ri *WOOL/PLUM* SE18 ....127 D1
Earl Rd *MORT/ESHN* SW14 ....128 C2
Earl's Court Gdns *ECT* SW5 ....38 C5
Earl's Court Rd *KENS* W8 ....38 A3
Earl's Court Sq *ECT* SW5 ....114 B1
Earlsferry Wy *IS* N1 ....75 E4
Earlsfield Rd *WAND/EARL* SW18 ....150 C1
Earlshall Rd *ELTH/MOT* SE9 ....143 F2
Earlsmead Rd *WLSDN* NW10 ....88 B2
Earls Ter *KENS* W8 ....101 F4
Earlsthorpe Ms *BAL* SW12 ....134 A4
Earlsthorpe Rd *SYD* SE26 ....157 D4

Earlstoke Est *FSBYE* EC1V 10 C3
Earlstoke St *FSBYE* EC1V 10 C3
Earlston Gv *HOM* E9 ....78 B5
Earl St *SDTCH* EC2A 24 C2
Earls Wk *KENS* W8 ....38 A3
Earlswood St *GNWCH* SE10 ....123 E1
Early Ms *CAMTN* NW1 ....74 B5
Earnshaw St *NOXST/BSQ* WC1A 20 B4
Earsby St *WKENS* W14 ....101 E5
East Acton Ar *ACT* * W3 ....87 F5
East Acton La *ACT* W3 ....99 D2
East Arbour St *WCHPL* E1 ....91 D5
East Av *MNPK* E12 ....83 E4
East Bank *STNW/STAM* N16 ....59 E2
Eastbourne Av *ACT* W3 ....87 D5
Eastbourne Gdns *MORT/ESHN* SW14 ...128 C1
Eastbourne Ms *BAY/PAD* W2 ....15 F4
Eastbourne Rd *CHSWK* W4 ....110 C2
   EHAM E6 ....96 A2
   SEVS/STOTM N15 ....59 E1
   SRTFD E15 ....81 E5
Eastbourne Ter *BAY/PAD* W2 ....15 F4
Eastbrook Rd *BKHTH/KID* SE3 ....124 B4
Eastbury Av *BARK* IG11 ....85 E5
Eastbury Gv *CHSWK* W4 ....111 E1
Eastbury Rd *EHAM* E6 ....96 A3
Eastbury Sq *BARK* IG11 ....85 F5
Eastbury Ter *WCHPL* E1 ....91 D3
Eastcastle St *GTPST* W1W 19 E4
Eastcheap *FENCHST* EC3M 36 B1
East Churchfield Rd *ACT* W3 ....99 D2
East Cl *EA* W5 ....86 A3
Eastcombe Av *CHARL* SE7 ....124 B2
Eastcote Av *WELL* DA16 ....127 D5
Eastcote St *BRXN/ST* SW9 ....117 E5
East Cross Route *HOM* E9 ....79 F3
Eastdown Pk *LEW* SE13 ....141 D2
East Dulwich Gv *EDUL* SE22 ....137 E3
East Dulwich Rd *EDUL* SE22 ....137 F2
Eastern Av *WAN* E11 ....64 C1
Eastern Rd *BROCKY* SE4 ....140 A2
   PLSTW E13 ....94 B1
Easternville Gdns *GNTH/NBYPK* IG2 ....66 C1
East Ferry Rd *POP/IOD* E14 ....104 B4
Eastfields Rd *ACT* W3 ....86 C4
Eastfield St *POP/IOD* * E14 ....91 E4
East Ham Manor Wy *EHAM* E6 ....96 A5
East Harding St *FLST/FETLN* EC4A 22 B4
East Heath Rd *HAMP* NW3 ....55 D5
East Hl *WAND/EARL* SW18 ....132 C3
   WBLY HA9 ....50 A4
East India Dock Rd *POP/IOD* E14 ....92 A5
Eastlake Rd *CMBW* SE5 ....118 B5
Eastlands Crs *EDUL* SE22 ....137 F4
East La *BERM/RHTH* SE16 ....102 A3
Eastlea Ms *CAN/RD* E16 ....93 E3
Eastleigh Cl *CRICK* NW2 ....51 E5
Eastman Rd *ACT* W3 ....99 D3
Eastmearn Rd *DUL* SE21 ....154 C2
Eastmoor Pl *WOOL/PLUM* SE18 ....107 D4
Eastmoor St *CHARL* SE7 ....107 D4
East Mount St *WCHPL* * E1 ....90 B4
Eastney St *GNWCH* SE10 ....123 D1
Eastnor Rd *ELTH/MOT* SE9 ....162 C1
Easton St *FSBYW* WC1X 10 A5
East Parkside *GNWCH* SE10 ....105 E3
East Pl *WNWD* SE27 ....154 C4
East Poultry Av *FARR* EC1M 22 C3
East Rd *IS* N1 ....12 A4
   SRTFD E15 ....82 A5
East Rochester Wy *BFN/LL* DA15 ....145 E3
East Row *NKENS* W10 ....89 E3
   WAN E11 ....64 A1
East Sheen Av *MORT/ESHN* SW14 ......129 D3
East Side *SHB* * W12 ....100 C3
East Smithfield *WAP* E1W 37 F2
East St *BARK* IG11 ....84 C4
   WALW SE17 ....118 C1

East Surrey Gv *PECK* SE15 ....119 F3
East Tenter St *WCHPL* E1 ....25 F5
East Ter *BFN/LL* * DA15 ....163 E1
East V *ACT* W3 ....99 F2
Eastview Av *WOOL/PLUM* SE18 ....127 E3
Eastway *HOM* E9 ....79 G5
Eaton Cl *BGVA* SW1W 42 A4
Eaton Dr *BRXN/ST* SW9 ....136 B2
Eaton Ga *BGVA* SW1W 42 A4
Eaton La *BGVA* SW1W 43 D3
Eaton Ms North *KTBR* SW1X 42 B3
Eaton Ms South *BGVA* SW1W 42 B4
Eaton Ms West *BGVA* SW1W 42 B4
Eaton Pl *KTBR* SW1X 42 A3
Eaton Rw *BGVA* SW1W 42 C2
Eaton Sq *BGVA* SW1W 42 B3
Eaton Ter *BGVA* SW1W 42 A4
Eaton Ter *BOW* * E3 ....91 E2
Eaton Terrace Ms *KTBR* SW1X 42 A4
Eatonville Rd *TOOT* SW17 ....151 F1
Eatonville Vls *TOOT* SW17 ....151 F2
Ebbisham Dr *VX/NE* SW8 ....117 F2
Ebbsfleet Rd *CRICK* NW2 ....71 E2
Ebdon Wy *BKHTH/KID* SE3 ....142 B1
Ebenezer St *IS* N1 ....12 A3
Ebley Cl *PECK* SE15 ....119 F2
Ebner St *WAND/EARL* SW18 ....132 B3
Ebor St *BETH* E2 ....13 E5
Ebsworth St *FSTH* SE23 ....139 D5
Eburne Rd *HOLWY* N7 ....57 F5
Ebury Bridge Rd *BGVA* SW1W 116 A1
Ebury Br *BGVA* SW1W 42 B4
Ebury Ms East *BGVA* SW1W 42 C4
Ebury Ms *BGVA* SW1W 42 C4
Ebury Sq *BGVA* SW1W 42 C5
Ebury St *BGVA* SW1W 42 B5
Ecclesbourne Rd *IS* N1 ....76 C4
Eccles Rd *BTSEA* SW11 ....133 F2
Eccleston Ms *KTBR* SW1X 42 B3
Eccleston Pl *BGVA* SW1W 42 C4
Eccleston Sq *PIM* SW1V 43 D5
Eccleston Square Ms *PIM* SW1V 43 D5
Eccleston St *BGVA* SW1W 42 B3
Eckford St *IS* N1 ....10 A1
Eckstein Rd *BTSEA* SW11 ....133 F2
Eclipse Rd *PLSTW* E13 ....94 B4
Ector Rd *CAT* SE6 ....159 G2
Edans Ct *SHB* W12 ....99 F3
Edbrooke Rd *MV/WKIL* W9 ....14 A1
Eddiscombe Rd *FUL/PGN* SW6 ......13 F5
Eddystone Rd *BROCKY* SE4 ....139 E3
Edenbridge Cl *BERM/RHTH* * SE16 120 B1
Edenbridge Rd *HOM* * E9 ....79 D4
Eden Cl *HAMP* NW3 ....54 A4
Eden Cl *KENS* W8 ....38 B2
Eden Gv *HOLWY* N7 ....75 F2
Edenham Wy *NKENS* W10 ....89 F3
Edenhurst Av *FUL/PGN* SW6 ....131 F1
Eden Rd *WNWD* SE27 ....154 B5
Edensor Rd *CHSWK* W4 ....111 E3
Edenvale St *FUL/PGN* SW6 ....114 B5
Edgar Kail Wy *CMBW* SE5 ....137 E1
Edgarley Ter *FUL/PGN* * SW6 ......113 E4
Edgar Rd *BOW* E3 ....92 B2
Edgbury *CHST* BR7 ....162 B4
Edgecote Cl *ACT* W3 ....98 C2
Edgefield Av *BARK* IG11 ....85 F4
Edge Hl *WOOL/PLUM* SE18 ....126 B2
Edgehill Rd *CHST* BR7 ....162 C3
Edgeley La *CLAP* SW4 ....135 D1
Edgeley Rd *CLAP* SW4 ....135 D1
Edgel St *WAND/EARL* SW18 ....132 B2
Edgepoint Cl *WNWD* * SE27 ....154 B5
Edge St *KENS* W8 ....26 B3
Edgeworth Rd *ELTH/MOT* SE9 ....142 C2
Edgware Rd *BAY/PAD* W2 ....16 A1
Edgware Rd *CDALE/KGS* NW9 ......52 A3
Edinburgh Cl *BETH* E2 ....90 C1
Edinburgh Ga *BAY/PAD* W2 ....29 E5

Edinburgh Rd *PLSTW* E13 ....94 B1
Edison Gv *WOOL/PLUM* SE18 ......127 F3
Edison Rd *CEND/HSY/T* N8 ....57 D1
Edison Rd *WELL* DA16 ....127 F4
Edis St *CAMTN* NW1 ....74 A5
Edith Cavell Wy *WOOL/PLUM* SE18 125 E4
Edith Gv *WBPTN* SW10 ....114 C2
Edithna St *BRXN/ST* SW9 ....135 E1
Edith Rd *EHAM* E6 ....83 D4
Edith Rd *SRTFD* E15 ....81 D2
Edith Rd *WKENS* W14 ....101 E5
Edith Rw *FUL/PGN* SW6 ....114 A3
Edith St *BETH* E2 ....13 F1
Edith Ter *WBPTN* * SW10 ....114 C3
Edith Vls *WKENS* W14 ....101 F5
Edmeston Cl *HOM* E9 ....79 D3
Edmund Halley Wy *GNWCH* SE10 105 E3
Edmund Hurst Dr *EHAM* E6 ....96 B4
Edmund St *CMBW* SE5 ....119 D3
Edna St *BTSEA* SW11 ....115 E4
Edric Rd *NWCR* SE14 ....121 D3
Edwardes Pl *WKENS* W14 ....101 F4
Edwardes Sq *KENS* W8 ....38 A3
Edward Mann Cl East *WCHPL* * E1 91 D5
Edward Mann Cl West *WCHPL* * E1 91 D5
Edward Ms *CAMTN* * NW1 ....7 D3
Edward Pl *DEPT* SE8 ....121 F2
Edward Rd *CHST* BR7 ....162 B5
Edward's Cottages *IS* * N1 ....76 B4
Edward's La *STNW/STAM* N16 ......59 D4
Edwards Ms *IS* N1 ....76 B4
Edwards Ms *IS* W1H 18 A5
Edward Sq *IS* N1 ....75 F5
Edward St *CAN/RD* E16 ....94 A3
Edward St *NWCR* SE14 ....121 E3
Edward Temme Av *SRTFD* E15 ......81 F4
Edward Tyler Rd *LEE/GVPK* SE12 160 B2
Edwin Av *EHAM* E6 ....96 A1
Edwin Pl *FUL/PGN* SW6 ....114 A3
Edwin St *CAN/RD* E16 ....94 A4
Edwin St *WCHPL* E1 ....90 C3
Effie Pl *FUL/PGN* SW6 ....114 A3
Effie Rd *FUL/PGN* SW6 ....114 A3
Effingham Rd *LEW* SE13 ....141 E3
Effort St *TOOT* SW17 ....151 E5
Effra Pde *HNHL* SE24 ....136 A3
Effra Rd *BRXS/STRHM* SW2 ....135 F2
Egbert St *CAMTN* NW1 ....74 A5
Egeremont Rd *WAND/EARL* SW18 132 C3
Egerton Crs *CHEL* SW3 ....40 C4
Egerton Dr *GNWCH* SE10 ....122 B4
Egerton Gdns *CHEL* SW3 ....40 C3
Egerton Gdns *CDMY/SEVK* IG3......67 F5
Egerton Gdns *WLSDN* * NW10 ......70 C5
Egerton Gardens Ms *CHEL* SW3 ....41 D3
Egerton Pl *CHEL* * SW3 ....41 D3
Egerton Rd *STNW/STAM* * N16 ....59 F2
Egerton Ter *CHEL* SW3 ....41 D3
Egham Rd *PLSTW* E13 ....94 B4
Eglantine Rd *WAND/EARL* SW18 ..132 C3
Eglinton Hl *WOOL/PLUM* SE18 ....126 B3
Eglinton Rd *WOOL/PLUM* SE18 ....126 A2
Egliston Ms *PUT/ROE* SW15 ....130 C1
Egliston Rd *PUT/ROE* SW15 ....130 C1
Eglon Ms *CAMTN* NW1 ....73 F4
Egmont St *NWCR* SE14 ....121 D3
Egremont Rd *WNWD* SE27 ....154 A3
Eider Cl *FSTGT* E7 ....81 F2
Eighth Av *MNPK* E12 ....83 F1
Eisenhower Dr *EHAM* E6 ....95 E4
Elaine Gv *KTTN* NW5 ....74 A2
Elam Cl *CMBW* SE5 ....118 B5
Elam St *CMBW* SE5 ....118 B5
Eland Rd *BTSEA* SW11 ....133 F1
Elba Pl *WALW* * SE17 ....47 F4
Elbe St *FUL/PGN* SW6 ....114 C5
Elborough St *WAND/EARL* SW18 ..150 A1
Elbury Dr *CAN/RD* E16 ....94 A5

Elcho St *BTSEA* SW11 ....115 E3
Elcot Av *PECK* SE15 ....120 B3
Elder Cl *BFN/LL* DA15 ....163 F1
Elderfield Rd *CLPT* E5 ....79 D1
Elderflower Wy *SRTFD* E15 ....81 E4
Elder Rd *WNWD* SE27 ....154 C5
Elderslie Rd *ELTH/MOT* SE9 ....144 A3
Elder St *WCHPL* E1 ....25 E2
Elderton Rd *SYD* SE26 ....157 E4
Elder Wk *IS* N1 ....76 B5
Eldon Gv *HAMP* NW3 ....73 D2
Eldon Rd *KENS* W8 ....39 D3
Eldon St *LVPST* EC2M 24 B3
Eldon Wy *WLSDN* NW10 ....86 B1
Eleanor Gv *BARN* SW13 ....129 E1
Eleanor Rd *HACK* E8 ....78 B3
                 SRTFD E15 ....81 F3
Eleanor St *BOW* E3 ....92 A2
Electric Av *BRXN/ST* SW9 ....136 A2
Electric La *BRXN/ST* * SW9 ....136 A2
Elephant & Castle *STHWK* SE1 ......47 D4
Elephant La *BERM/RHTH* SE16 ......102 C3
Elephant Rd *WALW* SE17 ....47 E4
Elfindale Rd *HNHL* SE24 ....136 C5
Elford Cl *ELTH/MOT* SE9 ....142 C2
Elfort Rd *HBRY* N5 ....76 A1
Elfrida Crs *CAT* SE6 ....158 A4
Elf Rw *WAP* E1W 102 C1
Elgar Av *WLSDN* NW10 ....69 D3
Elgar Cl *DEPT* SE8 ....122 A3
   PLSTW E13 ....94 C1
Elgar St *BERM/RHTH* SE16 ....103 E3
Elgin Av *MV/WKIL* W9 ....14 A1
   SHB W12 ....100 A3
Elgin Crs *NTGHL* W11 ....101 E1
Elgin Est *MV/WKIL* W9 ....14 A1
Elgin Ms *NTGHL* W11 ....89 E5
Elgin Ms North *MV/WKIL* W9 ....3 D3
Elgin Ms South *MV/WKIL* W9 ....3 D4
Elgin Rd *GDMY/SEVK* IG3 ....67 E3
Elgood Cl *NTGHL* W11 ....101 E1
Elia Ms *IS* N1 ....10 C1
Elias Pl *LBTH* SE11 ....118 A2
Elia St *IS* N1 ....10 C2
Elibank Rd *ELTH/MOT* SE9 ....144 A2
Elim St *STHWK* SE1 ....48 B2
Elim Wy *PLSTW* E13 ....93 F2
Eliot Bank *FSTH* SE23 ....156 B2
Eliot Gdns *PUT/ROE* SW15 ....130 A2
Eliot Hl *BKHTH/KID* SE3 ....122 C5
Eliot Pk *LEW* SE13 ....122 C5
Eliot Pl *BKHTH/KID* SE3 ....123 E5
Eliot V *BKHTH/KID* SE3 ....123 D5
Elizabeth Av *IL* IG1 ....67 D4
   IS N1 ....76 C4
Elizabeth Barnes Ct *FUL/PGN* * SW6 ..114 B5
Elizabeth Br *BGVA* SW1W 42 C5
Elizabeth Cl *MV/WKIL* * W9 ....15 F1
Elizabeth Gdns *ACT* W3 ....99 F1
Elizabeth Ms *HAMP* NW3 ....73 E3
Elizabeth Sq *EHAM* E6 ....83 D5
Elizabeth Sq *BERM/RHTH* SE16 ....103 E1
Elizabeth St *BGVA* SW1W 42 B4
Elkington Rd *PLSTW* E13 ....94 B3
Elkstone Rd *NKENS* W10 ....89 F4
Ellaline Rd *HMSMTH* W6 ....113 D2
Ella Ms *HAMP* NW3 ....73 F1
Elland Rd *PECK* SE15 ....138 C2
Ella Rd *CEND/HSY/T* N8 ....57 E2
Ellenborough Pl *PUT/ROE* SW15 ...130 A2
Ellen St *WCHPL* E1 ....90 A5
Ellerby St *FUL/PGN* SW6 ....113 D4
Ellerdale Rd *HAMP* NW3 ....72 C3
Ellerdale St *LEW* SE13 ....140 B2
Ellerslie Rd *SHB* W12 ....100 B3
Ellerton Rd *BARN* SW13 ....112 A4
   WAND/EARL SW18 ....151 D1
Ellery St *PECK* SE15 ....120 B5

Ellesmere Rd *BOW* E3 ....91 E1
   WLSDN NW10 ....70 A2
Ellesmere St *POP/IOD* E14 ....92 B5
Ellingfort Rd *HACK* E8 ....78 B4
Ellingham Rd *SHB* W12 ....100 A3
   WAN E11 ....81 D1
Ellington St *HOLWY* N7 ....76 A3
Elliot Cl *SRTFD* E15 ....81 E4
Elliot Rd *HDN* NW4 ....52 B1
Elliott Rd *BRXN/ST* SW9 ....118 B3
   CHSWK W4 ....99 E5
Elliott's Pl *IS* N1 ....76 B5
Elliott Sq *HAMP* NW3 ....73 E4
Elliott's Rw *LBTH* SE11 ....47 D3
Ellis Cl *CRICK* NW2 ....70 C3
   ELTH/MOT SE9 ....162 C2
Elliscombe Mt *CHARL* * SE7 ....124 C2
Elliscombe Rd *CHARL* SE7 ....124 C1
Ellisfield Dr *PUT/ROE* SW15 ....129 F5
Ellison Rd *BARN* SW13 ....111 F5
   BFN/LL DA15 ....163 D1
Ellis St *KTBR* SW1X 41 F4
Ellora Rd *STRHM/NOR* SW16 ....153 D5
Ellsworth St *BETH* * E2 ....90 B2
Elm Bank Gdns *BARN* SW13 ....111 E5
Elmbourne Rd *TOOT* SW17 ....152 B3
Elmbridge Wk *HACK* * E8 ....78 A4
Elmbrook Gdns *ELTH/MOT* SE9 ....143 E2
Elm Cl *WAN* E11 ....64 B1
Elmcourt Rd *WNWD* SE27 ....154 B2
Elmcroft Av *BFN/LL* DA15 ....145 F5
   GLDGN NW11 ....53 F2
Elmcroft Crs *GLDGN* NW11 ....53 D2
Elmcroft St *CLPT* E5 ....78 C1
Elmdene Rd *WOOL/PLUM* SE18 ....126 B1
Elmer Rd *CAT* SE6 ....140 C5
Elmfield Rd *TOOT* SW17 ....152 B2
   WALTH E17 ....61 D1
Elmfield Wy *MV/WKIL* W9 ....14 A2
Elm Friars Wk *HOLWY* N7 ....75 D4
Elm Gn *ACT* W3 ....87 E5
Elmgreen Cl *SRTFD* E15 ....81 E5
Elm Gv *CEND/HSY/T* N8 ....57 E1
   CRICK NW2 ....71 D1
   PECK SE15 ....120 A5
Elm Grove Rd *BARN* SW13 ....112 A4
Elm Hall Gdns *WAN* E11 ....64 B1
Elmhurst Rd *ELTH/MOT* SE9 ....161 E2
   FSTGT E7 ....82 B4
Elmhurst St *CLAP* SW4 ....135 D1
Elmington Est *CMBW* SE5 ....118 C3
Elmington Rd *CMBW* SE5 ....119 D3
Elmira St *LEW* SE13 ....140 B1
Elm La *CAT* SE6 ....157 F2
Elmley Cl *WOOL/PLUM* SE18 ....109 D5
Elmore Rd *LEY* E10 ....62 D5
Elmore St *IS* N1 ....77 D4
Elm Pk *BRXS/STRHM* SW2 ....135 F4
Elm Park Gdns *WBPTN* SW10 ....115 D1
Elm Park La *CHEL* SW3 ....115 D2
Elm Park Rd *CHEL* SW3 ....115 D2
   LEY E10 ....61 E3
Elm Pl *SKENS* SW7 ....115 D1
Elm Rd *FSTGT* E7 ....81 F3
   MORT/ESHN SW14 ....128 C1
   WAN E11 ....63 D4
Elm Rw *HAMP* NW3 ....54 C5
The Elms *BARN* SW13 ....129 F3
   TOOT * SW17 ....152 A3
Elmscott Rd *BMLY* BR1 ....159 E5
Elms Crs *CLAP* SW4 ....134 C4
Elmshaw Rd *PUT/ROE* SW15 ....130 A3
Elmside Rd *WBLY* HA9 ....50 A5
Elms Ms *BAY/PAD* W2 ....28 A1
Elms Rd *CLAP* SW4 ....134 C3
Elmstead Av *CHST* BR7 ....161 F5
Elmstead Cl *GDMY/SEVK* IG3 ....67 E4
Elmstone Rd *FUL/PGN* SW6 ....114 A4

Elm St *FSBYW* WC1X 21 F1
Elm Ter *CRICK* NW2 .... 54 A5
  ELTH/MOT SE9 .... 144 A4
Elmton Wy *STNW/STAM* N16 .... 60 A5
Elm Tree CI *STJWD* NW8 .... 4 A3
Elm Tree Ct *CHARL* * SE7 .... 124 C2
Elm Tree Rd *STJWD* NW8 .... 4 A4
Elm Wk *HAMP* NW3 .... 54 E1
Elm Wy *WLSDN* NW10 .... 69 E1
Elmwood Rd *CHSWK* W4 .... 110 C2
  HNHL SE24 .... 137 D3
Elmworth Gv *DUL* SE21 .... 155 D2
Elnathan Ms *MV/WKIL* W9 .... 15 D1
Elphinstone St *HBRY* N5 .... 76 B1
Elrington Rd *HACK* E8 .... 78 A3
Elsa Cottages *POP/IOD* * E14 .... 91 E4
Elsa St *WCHPL* * E1 .... 91 E4
Elsdale St *HOM* E9 .... 78 C3
Elsden Ms *BETH* * E2 .... 90 C1
Elsenham St *MNPK* E12 .... 83 F2
Elsenham St *WIM/MER* SW19 .... 149 F1
Elsham Rd *WAN* E11 .... 63 E5
  WKENS W14 .... 101 E3
Elsham Ter *WKENS* * W14 .... 101 E3
Elsie Lane Ct *BAY/PAD* W2 .... 14 B3
Elsiemaud Rd *BROCKY* SE4 .... 139 F3
Elsie Rd *EDUL* SE22 .... 137 F2
Elsinore Gdns *CRICK* * NW2 .... 53 E5
Elsinore Rd *FSTH* SE23 .... 157 E1
Elsinore Wy *RCH/KEW* TW9 .... 128 B1
Elsley Rd *BTSEA* SW11 .... 133 F1
Elspeth Rd *BTSEA* SW11 .... 133 E2
Elsted St *WALW* SE17 .... 48 B5
Elstow CI *ELTH/MOT* SE9 .... 143 F3
Elstree Gdns *IL* IG1 .... 84 C2
Elswick Rd *LEW* SE13 .... 140 B1
Elswick St *FUL/PGN* SW6 .... 114 C5
Elsworthy Ri *HAMP* NW3 .... 73 E4
Elsworthy Rd *HAMP* NW3 .... 73 E5
Elsworthy Ter *HAMP* NW3 .... 73 E4
Elsynge Rd *WAND/EARL* SW18 .... 133 D3
Eltham Gn *ELTH/MOT* SE9 .... 142 C5
Eltham Green Rd *ELTH/MOT* SE9 .. 142 C3
Eltham High St *ELTH/MOT* SE9 .... 143 E5
Eltham HI *ELTH/MOT* SE9 .... 143 D3
Eltham Palace Rd *ELTH/MOT* SE9 . 142 C5
Eltham Park Gdns *ELTH/MOT* SE9 . 144 A2
Eltham Rd *ELTH/MOT* SE9 .... 142 C5
Elthiron Rd *FUL/PGN* SW6 .... 114 A4
Elthorne Rd *ARCH* N19 .... 57 D4
  CDALE/KGS NW9 .... 51 D2
Elthorne Wy *CDALE/KGS* NW9 ..... 51 D1
Elthruda Rd *LEW* SE13 .... 141 D4
Eltisley Rd *IL* IG1 .... 84 B1
Elton PI *STNW/STAM* N16 .... 77 E2
Eltringham St *WAND/EARL* SW18 . 132 C2
Elvaston Ms *SKENS* SW7 .... 39 F3
Elvaston PI *SKENS* SW7 .... 39 E3
Elveden PI *WLSDN* NW10 .... 86 A1
Elveden Rd *WLSDN* NW10 .... 86 A1
Elver Gdns *BETH* E2 .... 90 A2
Elverson Ms *DEPT* * SE8 .... 121 F3
Elverson Rd *DEPT* SE8 .... 122 B5
Elverton St *WEST* SW1P 44 A4
Elvino Rd *SYD* SE26 .... 157 D5
Elvis Rd *CRICK* NW2 .... 70 C3
Elwin St *BETH* E2 .... 90 A2
Elwood St *HBRY* N5 .... 58 B5
Elwyn Gdns *LEE/GVPK* SE12 ...... 142 A5
Ely Cottages *VX/NE* * SW8 .... 117 F3
Elyne Rd *FSBYPK* N4 .... 58 A1
Ely PI *HCIRC* EC1N 22 B3
Ely Rd *LEY* E10 .... 62 C1
Elysium PI *FUL/PGN* SW6 .... 113 F5
Elysium St *FUL/PGN* SW6 .... 113 F5
Elystan PI *CHEL* SW3 .... 115 E1
Elystan St *CHEL* SW3 .... 40 C5
Elystan Wk *IS* N1 .... 76 A5

Emanuel Av *ACT* W3 .... 86 C5
Embankment *PUT/ROE* SW15 .... 131 D1
Embankment Gdns *CHEL* SW3 ..... 115 F2
Embankment PI *CHCR* WC2N 33 D3
Emba St *BERM/RHTH* SE16 .... 102 A3
Embleton Rd *LEW* SE13 .... 140 B2
Emden St *FUL/PGN* SW6 .... 114 B4
Emerald CI *CAN/RD* E16 .... 95 F3
Emerald St *BMSBY* WC1N 21 E2
Emerson Rd *STHWK* SE1 .... 35 E3
Emerson St *STHWK* SE1 .... 35 E3
Emery Hill St *WEST* SW1P 43 F3
Emery St *STHWK* SE1 .... 46 B3
Emily PI *HOLWY* N7 .... 76 A1
Emily St *CAN/RD* E16 .... 93 F5
Emlyn Rd *SHB* W12 .... 99 E3
Emmanuel Rd *BAL* SW12 .... 152 C1
Emma Rd *PLSTW* E13 .... 93 F2
Emma St *BETH* E2 .... 90 B1
Emmott CI *EFNCH* N2 .... 54 C1
  WCHPL E1 .... 91 E3
Emperor's Ga *SKENS* SW7 .... 39 E4
Empire Pde *WBLY* * HA9 .... 50 A5
Empire Wharf Rd *POP/IOD* E14 .... 105 D5
Empress Av *IL* IG1 .... 65 F4
  MNPK E12 .... 64 C4
Empress PI *ECT* SW5 .... 114 A1
Empress St *WALW* SE17 .... 118 C2
Empson St *BOW* E3 .... 92 B3
Emsworth St *BRXS/STRHM* SW2 . 153 F2
Emu Rd *VX/NE* SW8 .... 116 B5
Enbrook St *NKENS* W10 .... 89 E2
Enclave Ct *FSBYE* EC1V 11 D5
Endeavour Wy *WIM/MER* SW19 ... 150 B4
Endell St *LSQ/SEVD* WC2H 20 C4
Enderby St *GNWCH* SE10 .... 123 E1
Endlesham Rd *BAL* SW12 .... 134 A5
Endsleigh Gdns *IL* IG1 .... 65 F3
  STPAN WC1H 8 A5
Endsleigh PI *STPAN* WC1H 8 B5
Endsleigh St *STPAN* WC1H 8 B5
Endwell Rd *BROCKY* SE4 .... 121 E5
Endymion Rd *BRXS/STRHM* SW2 . 135 F5
  FSBYPK N4 .... 58 B2
Energen CI *WLSDN* NW10 .... 69 E3
Enfield Rd *ACT* W3 .... 98 B3
  IS N1 .... 77 E4
Enford St *MBLAR* W1H 17 E2
Engadine CI *WAND/EARL* SW18 .. 149 F1
Engate St *LEW* SE13 .... 140 C2
Engineer CI *WOOL/PLUM* SE18 ... 126 A2
Engineers Wy *WBLY* HA9 .... 68 A1
Englefield Rd *IS* N1 .... 77 D4
Engleheart Rd *CAT* SE6 .... 140 B5
Englewood Rd *CLAP* SW4 .... 134 B4
English St *BOW* E3 .... 91 F3
Enid St *STHWK* SE1 .... 49 F2
Enmore Gdns *MORT/ESHN* SW14 . 129 D3
Enmore Rd *PUT/ROE* SW15 .... 130 C2
Ennersdale Rd *LEW* SE13 .... 141 D3
Ennismore Av *CHSWK* W4 .... 99 F5
Ennismore Gdns *SKENS* SW7 .... 40 B2
Ennismore Gardens Ms *SKENS* SW7 . 40 B2
Ennismore Ms *SKENS* SW7 .... 40 C1
Ennismore St *SKENS* SW7 .... 40 C2
Ennis Rd *FSBYPK* N4 .... 58 A3
  WOOL/PLUM SE18 .... 127 D2
Ensign St *WCHPL* E1 .... 102 A1
Enslin Rd *ELTH/MOT* SE9 .... 144 A4
Ensor Ms *SKENS* SW7 .... 115 D1
Enterprise Wy *WAND/EARL* SW18 . 132 A2
  WLSDN NW10 .... 87 F2
Enterprize Wy *DEPT* * SE8 .... 103 F5
Entrance to Strand U/P
  TPL/STR WC2R 33 F2
Epcot Ms *WLSDN* * NW10 .... 89 D2
Epirus Ms *FUL/PGN* SW6 .... 114 A3
Epirus Rd *FUL/PGN* SW6 .... 113 F3

Epping Cl *POP/IOD* E14 ....104 A5
Epping Pl *HOLWY* N7 ....76 A3
Epple Rd *FUL/PGN* SW6 ....113 F4
Epsom Rd *GDMY/SEVK* IG3 ....67 F1
   LEY E10 ....62 C1
Epworth St *SDTCH* EC2A 24 B1
Equity Sq *BETH* E2 ....13 F4
Erasmus St *WEST* SW1P 44 B5
Erconwald St *ACT* W3 ....87 F5
Eresby Pl *KIL/WHAMP* NW6 ....72 A4
Erica St *SHB* W12 ....100 A1
Eric Clarke La *BARK* IG11 ....96 B3
Ericcson Cl *WAND/EARL* SW18 ....132 A3
Eric Est *BOW* E3 ....91 F5
Eric Rd *FSTGT* E7 ....82 A1
   WLSDN NW10 ....69 F3
Eric St *BOW* E3 ....91 F5
Eridge Rd *CHSWK* W4 ....99 D4
Erindale *WOOL/PLUM* SE18 ....127 D2
Erindale Ter *WOOL/PLUM* SE18 ...127 D2
Erlanger Rd *NWCR* SE14 ....121 D4
Erlich Cottages *WCHPL* * E1 ....90 C1
Ermine Rd *LEW* SE13 ....140 B2
   SEVS/STOTM N15 ....59 F1
Ermington Rd *ELTH/MOT* SE9 ......162 C2
Ernald Av *EHAM* E6 ....95 E3
Ernest Av *WNWD* SE27 ....154 B4
Ernest Gdns *CHSWK* W4 ....110 B2
Ernest St *WCHPL* E1 ....91 D3
Ernshaw Pl *PUT/ROE* SW15 ....131 E3
Erpingham Rd *PUT/ROE* SW15 .....130 C1
Errington Rd *MV/WKIL* W9 ....89 F3
Errol St *STLK* EC1Y 23 F1
Erskine Ms *HAMP* * NW3 ....73 F4
Erskine Rd *HAMP* NW3 ....73 F4
Erwood Rd *CHARL* SE7 ....125 E1
Esam St *STRHM/NOR* SW16 ....154 A5
Escreet Gv *WOOL/PLUM* SE18 .....108 A5
Esher Rd *GDMY/SEVK* IG3 ....67 E5
Esk Rd *PLSTW* E13 ....94 B3
Esmar Crs *CDALE/KGS* NW9 ....52 A2
Esmeralda Rd *STHWK* SE1 ....102 A3
Esmond Gdns *CHSWK* * W4 ....99 D5
Esmond Rd *CHSWK* W4 ....99 D4
   KIL/WHAMP NW6 ....71 F5
Esmond St *PUT/ROE* SW15 ....131 E2
Esparto St *WAND/EARL* * SW18 ...132 B5
Essendine Rd *MV/WKIL* W9 ....2 B5
Essex Ct *BTSEA* SW13 ....111 F5
   TPL/STR * WC2R 22 C1
Essex Gdns *FSBYPK* N4 ....58 B1
Essex Park Ms *ACT* W3 ....99 E3
Essex Pl *CHSWK* W4 ....98 C5
Essex Place Sq *CHSWK* * W4 ....99 D5
Essex Rd *ACT* W3 ....98 C1
   BARK IG11 ....85 D4
   CHSWK W4 ....99 D5
   IS N1 ....76 B5
   LEY E10 ....62 C1
   WALTH E17 ....61 E1
   WLSDN NW10 ....69 E4
Essex Rd South *WAN* E11 ....63 E3
Essex St *FSTGT* E7 ....82 A2
   TPL/STR WC2R 22 A5
   WOOL/PLUM SE18 ....108 C5
Essex Vls *KENS* W8 ....38 A1
Essian St *WCHPL* E1 ....91 E4
Estate Wy *LEY* E10 ....61 F3
Estcourt Rd *FUL/PGN* SW6 ....113 F3
Estelle Rd *HAMP* NW3 ....73 F1
Esterbrooke St *WEST* SW1P 44 A5
Este Rd *BTSEA* SW11 ....133 E1
Esther Rd *WAN* E11 ....63 E2
Estoria Cl *BRXS/STRHM* SW2 .....136 A5
Eswyn Rd *TOOT* SW17 ....151 F4
Etchingham Rd *SRTFD* E15 ....80 C1
Ethelbert St *BAL* SW12 ....152 B1
Ethelburga St *BTSEA* * SW11 ......115 E4
Ethelden Rd *SHB* W12 ....100 B2
Etheldred St *LBTH* SE11 ....46 A5
Ethel Rd *CAN/RD* E16 ....106 B1
Ethel St *WALW* * SE17 ....47 F5
Etheridge Rd *CRICK* NW2 ....52 C2
Etherow St *EDUL* SE22 ....138 A4
Etherstone Rd *STRHM/NOR* SW16 .153 F4
Ethnard Rd *PECK* SE15 ....120 B2
Etloe Rd *LEY* E10 ....62 A4
Eton Av *HAMP* NW3 ....73 E4
Eton Cl *WAND/EARL* SW18 ....132 B5
Eton College Rd *HAMP* NW3 ......73 F3
Eton Garages *HAMP* NW3 ....73 E3
Eton Gv *LEW* SE13 ....141 E1
Eton Pl *HAMP* * NW3 ....74 A4
Eton Ri *HAMP* * NW3 ....73 F3
Eton Rd *HAMP* NW3 ....73 F3
   IL IG1 ....84 C1
Eton Vls *HAMP* NW3 ....73 F3
Etta St *DEPT* SE8 ....121 E2
Ettrick St *POP/IOD* E14 ....92 C5
Eugenia Rd *BERM/RHTH* SE16 ....120 C1
Europa Pl *FSBYE* EC1V 11 E4
Europe Rd *WOOL/PLUM* SE18 .....107 F4
Eustace Pl *WOOL/PLUM* SE18 .....107 F5
Eustace Rd *EHAM* E6 ....95 E2
   FUL/PGN SW6 ....114 A3
Euston Rd *CAMTN* NW1 ....7 E5
Euston Sq *CAMTN* NW1 ....8 A3
Euston St *CAMTN* NW1 ....7 F5
Evandale Rd *BRXN/ST* SW9 ....118 A5
Evangelist Rd *KTTN* NW5 ....74 B1
Evans Cl *HACK* E8 ....77 F3
Evans Rd *CAT* SE6 ....159 E2
Evanston Gdns *REDBR* IG4 ....65 E1
Evelina Rd *PECK* SE15 ....138 C1
Eveline Lowe Est *BERM/RHTH* SE16 .102 A4
Evelyn Denington Rd *EHAM* E6 ....95 E3
Evelyn Est *DEPT* SE8 ....121 E2
Evelyn Gdns *WBPTN* SW10 ....114 C1
Evelyn Rd *CAN/RD* E16 ....106 A2
   CHSWK W4 ....99 D4
   WIM/MER SW19 ....150 B5
Evelyn St *DEPT* SE8 ....121 F2
Evelyn Wk *IS* N1 ....12 A2
Evenwood Cl *PUT/ROE* * SW15 ...131 E3
Everatt Cl *WAND/EARL* * SW18 ...131 F4
Everdon Rd *BARN* SW13 ....112 A2
Everest Pl *POP/IOD* E14 ....92 C4
Everest Rd *ELTH/MOT* SE9 ....143 E5
Everett Cl *WLSDN* NW10 ....87 D2
Everilda St *IS* * N1 ....75 F5
Evering Rd *STNW/STAM* N16 .....113 D2
Everington St *HMSMTH* W6 ....113 D2
Everitt Rd *WLSDN* NW10 ....87 D2
Everleigh St *FSBYPK* N4 ....57 F3
Eve Rd *SRTFD* E15 ....81 E1
   SRTFD E15 ....93 E1
Eversholt St *CAMTN* NW1 ....7 F1
Evershot Rd *FSBYPK* N4 ....57 F3
Eversleigh Rd *BTSEA* SW11 ....133 F1
   EHAM E6 ....83 D5
Eversley Av *WBLY* HA9 ....50 A4
Eversley Pk *WIM/MER* SW19 .....148 A5
Eversley Rd *CHARL* SE7 ....124 B2
Everthorpe Rd *PECK* SE15 ....137 F1
Everton Buildings *CAMTN* NW1 .....7 E4
Evesham Av *WALTH* E17 ....101 D1
Evesham St *NTGHL* W11 ....101 D1
Evesham Wk *BRXN/ST* SW9 ......118 A5
Evesham Wy *BTSEA* SW11 ....134 A1
Ewald Rd *FUL/PGN* SW6 ....113 F5
Ewart Pl *BOW* * E3 ....91 F1
Ewart Rd *FSTH* SE23 ....139 D5
Ewe Cl *HOLWY* N7 ....75 E3
Ewelme Rd *FSTH* SE23 ....156 C1
Ewen Crs *BRXS/STRHM* SW2 .....136 A5

Ewer St *STHWK* SE1 .... 35 E4
Ewhurst Cl *WCHPL* E1 .... 90 C4
Ewhurst Rd *BROCKY* SE4 .... 139 F4
Exbury Rd *CAT* SE6 .... 158 A2
Excel Ct *LSQ/SEVD* WC2H 32 B2
Exchange Ar *LVPST* EC2M 24 C3
Exchange Ct *COVGDN* WC2E 33 D2
Exchange Sq *SDTCH* * EC2A 25 D2
Exeter Cl *EHAM* E6 .... 95 F5
Exeter Gdns *IL* IG1 .... 65 F3
Exeter Ms *FUL/PGN* SW6 .... 114 A3
Exeter Pde *CRICK* * NW2 .... 71 E3
Exeter Rd *CAN/RD* E16 .... 94 A4
    CRICK NW2 .... 71 E3
    WELL DA16 .... 127 F5
Exeter St *COVGDN* WC2E 33 D1
Exeter Wy *NWCR* SE14 .... 121 F3
Exford Gdns *LEE/GVPK* SE12 .... 160 B1
Exford Rd *LEE/GVPK* SE12 .... 160 B2
Exhibition Rd *SKENS* SW7 .... 40 C1
Exmoor St *NKENS* W10 .... 89 D3
Exmouth Ms *CAMTN* * NW1 .... 7 F4
Exmouth Pl *HACK* E8 .... 78 B5
Exmouth Pl *WCHPL* E1 .... 90 C5
Exning Rd *CAN/RD* E16 .... 93 F3
Exon St *WALW* SE17 .... 48 C5
Exton Crs *WLSDN* NW10 .... 68 C5
Exton St *EHAM* E6 .... 34 A4
Eyhurst Cl *CRICK* NW2 .... 52 A3
Eylewood Rd *WNWD* SE27 .... 154 C5
Eynella Rd *DUL* SE21 .... 137 F5
Eynham Rd *SHB* W12 .... 88 C5
Eynsford Rd *GDMY/SEVK* IG3 .... 67 E4
Eyot Gdns *HMSMTH* W6 .... 111 F3
Eyre Street HI *CLKNW* EC1R 22 A1
Eythorne Rd *BRXN/ST* SW9 .... 118 A4
Ezra St *BETH* E2 .... 13 F3

F

Fabian Rd *FUL/PGN* SW6 .... 113 F3
Fabian St *EHAM* E6 .... 95 F3
The Facade *FSTH* * SE23 .... 156 B5
Factory Rd *POP/IOD* E14 .... 122 C1
Factory Rd *CAN/RD* E16 .... 107 D2
Fairbank Est *IS* N1 .... 12 A2
Fairbridge Rd *ARCH* N19 .... 57 D4
Fairby Rd *LEE/GVPK* SE12 .... 142 B3
Fairchild Cl *BTSEA* SW11 .... 115 D5
Fairchild Pl *SDTCH* * EC2A 25 D1
Fairchild St *SDTCH* EC2A 25 D1
Fairclough St *WCHPL* E1 .... 90 A5
Faircross Av *BARK* IG11 .... 84 C3
Fairdale Gdns *PUT/ROE* SW15 ...... 130 B2
Fairfax Gdns *BKHTH/KID* SE3 .... 124 C4
Fairfax Ms *PUT/ROE* SW15 .... 130 C1
Fairfax Pl *KIL/WHAMP* NW6 .... 72 C4
Fairfax Rd *CHSWK* W4 .... 99 F4
    KIL/WHAMP NW6 .... 72 C4
Fairfield Av *HDN* NW4 .... 52 B1
Fairfield Cl *BFN/LL* DA15 .... 145 E4
Fairfield Ct *WAND/EARL* SW18 ...... 132 B3
Fairfield Gv *CHARL* SE7 .... 125 D2
Fairfield Rd *BOW* E3 .... 92 A1
    IL IG1 .... 84 B3
Fairfields *CAT* SE6 .... 140 B5
Fairfield St *WAND/EARL* SW18 ...... 132 B3
Fairfoot Rd *BOW* * E3 .... 92 A3
Fairhazel Gdns *KIL/WHAMP* NW6 .... 72 B3
Fairholme Rd *IL* IG1 .... 65 F2
    WKENS W14 .... 113 E3
Fairholt Rd *STNW/STAM* N16 .... 59 D3
Fairholt St *SKENS* SW7 .... 41 D3
Fairland Rd *SRTFD* E15 .... 81 F3
Fairlawn *CHARL* SE7 .... 124 C5

Fairlawn Av *CHSWK* W4 .... 98 C5
Fairlawn Ct *CHARL* * SE7 .... 124 C3
Fairlawn Gv *CHSWK* W4 .... 98 C5
Fairlawn Pk *SYD* SE26 .... 157 E5
Fairlie Gdns *FSTH* SE23 .... 138 C5
Fairlight Av *WLSDN* NW10 .... 87 E1
Fairlight Rd *TOOT* SW17 .... 151 D4
Fairlop Rd *WAN* E11 .... 63 D2
Fairmead Rd *HOLWY* N7 .... 57 E5
Fairmile Av *STRHM/NOR* SW16 ..... 153 D5
Fairmount Rd *BRXS/STRHM* SW2 .. 135 F4
Fairoak Dr *ELTH/MOT* SE9 .... 145 D3
Fairstead Wk *IS* * N1 .... 76 C3
Fair St *STHWK* SE1 .... 37 D5
Fairthorn Rd *CHARL* SE7 .... 124 A1
Fairview Cl *SYD* * SE26 .... 157 E4
Fairview Pl *BRXS/STRHM* SW2 ..... 135 F5
Fairview Rd *SEVS/STOTM* N15 .... 59 F1
The Fairway *ACT* W3 .... 87 E5
Fairway Cl *GLDGN* NW11 .... 54 C2
Fairway Gdns *IL* IG1 .... 84 C2
Fairweather Rd *STNW/STAM* N16 .. 60 A1
Fairwyn Rd *SYD* SE26 .... 157 E3
Fakruddin St *WCHPL* E1 .... 90 A3
Falaize Av *IL* IG1 .... 84 B1
Falconberg Ct *SOHO/SHAV* * W1D .. 20 A4
Falcon Cl *CHSWK* W4 .... 110 B2
    STHWK SE1 .... 35 D3
Falcon Ct *IS* N1 .... 11 D2
Falcon Gv *BTSEA* SW11 .... 133 E1
Falcon La *BTSEA* SW11 .... 133 E1
Falcon Rd *BTSEA* SW11 .... 133 E1
Falcon St *PLSTW* E13 .... 94 A3
Falcon Ter *BTSEA* * SW11 .... 133 E1
Falconwood Av *WELL* DA16 .... 127 D5
Falconwood Pde *WELL* DA16 .... 145 E1
Falkirk St *IS* N1 .... 13 D2
Falkland Pl *KTTN* NW5 .... 74 C2
Falkland Rd *KTTN* NW5 .... 74 C2
Fallow Ct *STHWK* * SE1 .... 120 A1
Falmouth Cl *LEE/GVPK* SE12 .... 141 F3
Falmouth Rd *STHWK* SE1 .... 47 F3
Falmouth St *SRTFD* E15 .... 81 D2
Fambridge Cl *SYD* SE26 .... 157 F4
Fane St *WKENS* W14 .... 113 F2
Fann St *FARR* EC1M 23 E1
Fanshawe Av *BARK* IG11 .... 84 C3
Fanshaw St *IS* N1 .... 12 C3
Fanthorpe St *PUT/ROE* SW15 ...... 130 C1
Faraday Cl *HOLWY* N7 .... 75 F3
    NKENS W10 .... 89 E4
Faraday Rd *ACT* W3 .... 98 C1
    SRTFD E15 .... 81 F3
Faraday Wy *WOOL/PLUM* SE18 ..... 107 D4
Fareham St *SOHO/CST* * W1F 20 A4
Faringford Rd *SRTFD* E15 .... 81 E5
Farjeon Rd *BKHTH/KID* SE3 .... 125 D4
Farleigh Pl *STNW/STAM* N16 .... 77 F1
Farleigh Rd *STNW/STAM* N16 .... 77 F1
Farley Dr *GDMY/SEVK* IG3 .... 67 E3
Farley Rd *CAT* SE6 .... 140 C5
Farlington Pl *PUT/ROE* SW15 .... 130 B5
Farlow Rd *PUT/ROE* SW15 .... 131 D1
Farlton Rd *WAND/EARL* SW18 ...... 132 B5
The Farm *WIM/MER* SW19 .... 131 D5
Farm Av *CRICK* NW2 .... 53 E5
    STRHM/NOR SW16 .... 153 E4
Farm Cl *FUL/PGN* * SW6 .... 114 A3
Farmcote Rd *LEE/GVPK* SE12 ...... 160 A1
Farmdale Rd *GNWCH* SE10 .... 124 A1
Farmer Rd *LEY* E10 .... 62 B3
Farmers Rd *CMBW* SE5 .... 118 A2
Farmer St *KENS* W8 .... 26 A3
Farmfield Rd *BMLY* BR1 .... 159 E5
Farmilo Rd *WALTH* E17 .... 62 A2
Farmland Wk *CHST* BR7 .... 162 B5
Farm La *FUL/PGN* SW6 .... 114 A2
Farm Pl *KENS* W8 .... 26 A3

Farm Rd *WLSDN* NW10 ....69 D5
Farmstead Rd *CAT* SE6 ....158 B4
Farm St *MYFR/PICC* W1J.........................30 C2
Farnaby Rd *ELTH/MOT* SE9 ....142 C2
Farnan Rd *STRHM/NOR* SW16 ....153 E5
Farnborough Cl *WBLY* HA9.....................50 B4
Farnborough Wy *PECK* SE15 ....119 E3
Farncombe St *BERM/RHTH* SE16 ....102 A3
Farnell Ms *ECT* SW5 ....114 B1
Farnham Pl *STHWK* SE1 ....35 D4
Farnham Rd *GDMY/SEVK* IG3 ....67 F1
Farnham Royal *LBTH* SE11 ....117 E1
Faroe Rd *WKENS* W14 ....101 D4
Farquhar Rd *NRWD* SE19 ....155 F5
WIM/MER SW19 ....150 A3
Farrance St *POP/IOD* E14 ....92 A5
Farren Rd *FSTH* SE23............................157 E2
Farrier St *CAMTN* NW1 ....74 B4
Farrier Wk *WBPTN* * SW10 ....114 C2
Farringdon La *CLKNW* EC1R 22 B1
Farringdon Rd *FARR* EC1M.......................22 C3
FSBYW WC1X 10 A5
Farringdon St *FLST/FETLN* EC4A 22 C4
Farrins Rents *BERM/RHTH* SE16 ....103 E2
Farrow La *PECK* SE15 ....120 C3
Farrow Pl *BERM/RHTH* SE16 ....103 E4
Farthing Aly *STHWK* * SE1 ....102 A3
Farthing Flds *WAP* E1W 102 B2
Fashion St *WCHPL* E1 ....25 E3
Fassett Rd *HACK* E8 ....78 A3
Fassett Sq *HACK* E8 ....78 A3
Fauconberg Rd *CHSWK* W4 ....110 C2
Faulkner St *NWCR* SE14 ....120 C4
Faunce St *WALW* SE17 ....118 B3
Favart Rd *FUL/PGN* SW6 ....114 A4
Faversham Rd *CAT* SE6 ....139 F5
Fawcett Cl *BTSEA* SW11 ....115 D5
Fawcett Est *CLPT* * E5 ....60 A1
Fawcett Rd *WLSDN* NW10 ....69 D5
Fawcett St *WBPTN* SW10 ....114 C3
Fawe Park Rd *PUT/ROE* SW15 ....131 F2
Fawe St *POP/IOD* E14 ....92 B4
Fawley Rd *KIL/WHAMP* NW6 ....72 B2
Fawnbrake Av *HNHL* SE24 ....136 B3
Fawn Rd *PLSTW* E13 ....94 C1
Fawood Av *WLSDN* NW10 ....69 D4
Faygate Rd *BRXS/STRHM* SW2 ....153 F2
Fayland Av *STRHM/NOR* SW16 ....152 C5
Fearon St *GNWCH* SE10 ....124 A1
Feathers Pl *GNWCH* SE10 ....123 D2
Featherstone Av *FSTH* SE23 ....156 B2
Featherstone St *STLK* EC1Y 12 A5
Featley Rd *BRXN/ST* SW9 ....136 B1
Felbridge Cl *STRHM/NOR* SW16 ....154 A4
Felbrigge Rd *GDMY/SEVK* IG3 ....67 F4
Felday Rd *LEW* SE13 ....140 B4
Felden St *FUL/PGN* SW6 ....113 F4
Feldman Cl *STNW/STAM* N16 ....60 A3
Felgate Ms *HMSMTH* W6 ....100 B5
Felhampton Rd *ELTH/MOT* SE9 ....162 B3
Felix Av *CEND/HSY/T* N8 ....57 E1
Felix St *BETH* * E2 ....90 B1
Felixstowe Rd *WLSDN* * NW10................88 B2
Fellbrigg Rd *EDUL* SE22 ....137 F3
Fellbrigg St *WCHPL* E1 ....90 B3
Fellows Rd *HAMP* NW3 ....73 D4
Felltram Wy *CHARL* SE7 ....124 A1
Felmersham Cl *CLAP* SW4.....................135 E2
Felsberg Rd *BRXS/STRHM* SW2 ....135 E4
Felsham Rd *PUT/ROE* SW15 ....130 C1
Felspar Cl *WOOL/PLUM* SE18 ....127 F1
Felstead Rd *HOM* E9 ....80 A3
WAN E11 ....64 A2
Felstead St *HOM* E9 ....79 F3
Felsted Rd *CAN/RD* E16 ....95 D3
Felton Lea *SCUP* DA14 ....163 F5
Felton Rd *BARK* IG11 ....97 E1

Felton St *IS* N1 ....77 D5
Fenchurch Av *FENCHST* EC3M 24 C5
Fenchurch Buildings *FENCHST* EC3M......25 D5
Fenchurch Pl *FENCHST* * EC3M 37 D1
Fenchurch St *FENCHST* EC3M 36 C1
Fendall St *STHWK* SE1 ....49 D3
Fendt Cl *CAN/RD* E16 ....93 F5
Fenelon Pl *WKENS* W14 ....101 F5
Fen Gv *BFN/LL* DA15 ....145 F4
Fenham Rd *PECK* SE15 ....120 A3
Fennel Cl *CAN/RD* E16 ....93 E3
Fennell Cl *WOOL/PLUM* SE18 ....126 A2
Fenner Cl *BERM/RHTH* SE16.................102 B5
Fenner Sq *BTSEA* * SW11 ....133 D1
Fenning St *STHWK* SE1 ....36 C5
Fen St *CAN/RD* E16 ....105 F1
Fentiman Rd *VX/NE* SW8 ....117 E2
Fenton Cl *BRXN/ST* * SW9 ....117 F5
CHST BR7 ....161 F5
HACK E8 ....77 F3
Fenton's Av *PLSTW* E13 ....94 B2
Fenwick Gv *PECK* SE15 ....138 A1
Fenwick Pl *BRXN/ST* SW9 ....135 E1
Fenwick Rd *PECK* SE15 ....138 A1
Ferdinand Pl *CAMTN* NW1 ....74 A4
Ferdinand St *CAMTN* NW1 ....74 A4
Ferguson Dr *ACT* W3 ....87 D5
Ferguson's Cl *POP/IOD* E14 ....104 A3
Fergus Rd *HBRY* N5 ....76 B2
Fermor Rd *FSTH* SE23 ....157 E1
Fermoy Rd *MV/WKIL* W9 ....89 F3
Fernbank Ms *CLAP* SW4 ....134 B4
Fernbrook Rd *LEW* SE13 ....141 E4
Ferncliff Rd *HACK* E8 ....78 A2
Fern Cl *IS* * N1 ....12 C1
Ferncroft Av *HAMP* NW3 ....54 A5
Ferndale Rd *CLAP* SW4 ....135 E2
FSTGT E7 ....82 B4
SEVS/STOTM N15 ....59 F1
WAN E11 ....63 F4
Ferndale St *EHAM* E6 ....108 B3
Ferndene Rd *HNHL* SE24 ....136 C2
Ferndown *ELTH/MOT* SE9.....................143 D5
Ferndown Rd *MV/WKIL* W9 ....89 F2
Fernhill St *CAN/RD* E16 ....107 F2
Fernholme Rd *PECK* SE15 ....139 D3
Fernhurst Rd *FUL/PGN* SW6 ....113 E4
Fernlea Rd *BAL* SW12 ....152 B1
Fernleigh Cl *MV/WKIL* W9.......................89 F3
Fernsbury St *FSBYW* WC1X 10 A4
Fernshaw Cl *WBPTN* * SW10 ....114 C2
Fernshaw Rd *WBPTN* SW10 ....151 F2
Fernside Rd *BAL* SW12 ....152 A1
Ferns Rd *SRTFD* E15 ....81 E3
Fern St *BOW* E3 ....92 A3
Ferntower Rd *HBRY* N5 ....77 D2
Fern Wk *STHWK* SE1 ....120 A1
Fenways *IL* IG1 ....66 B5
Fernwood Av *STRHM/NOR* SW16 ....153 D4
Ferranti Cl *WOOL/PLUM* SE18 ....107 D4
Ferrers Rd *STRHM/NOR* SW16 ....153 D5
Ferrey Ms *BRXN/ST* SW9 ....118 A5
Ferriby Cl *IS* N1 ....76 A4
Ferrier St *WAND/EARL* SW18 ....132 B2
Ferrings *DUL* SE21 ....155 E2
Ferris Rd *EDUL* SE22 ....138 A2
Ferron Rd *CLPT* * E5 ....60 B5
Ferry La *BARN* SW13 ....111 F2
Ferry Rd *BARN* SW13 ....112 A3
Ferry St *POP/IOD* E14 ....122 C1
Festing Rd *PUT/ROE* SW15 ....131 D1
Fetter La *FLST/FETLN* EC4A 22 B4
Ffinch St *DEPT* SE8 ....122 A3
Field Cottages *FUL/PGN* * SW6 ....113 F5
Field Ct *GINN* WC1R 21 F3
Fieldgate St *WCHPL* E1 ....90 A4
Fieldhouse Rd *BAL* SW12 ....152 C1

Fielding Rd *CHSWK* W4 ....99 D4
WKENS W14 ....101 D4
The Fieldings *FSTH* SE23 ....156 C1
Fielding St *WALW* SE17 ....118 C2
Field Rd *FSTGT* E7 ....82 A1
HMSMTH W6 ....113 E1
Fields Est *HACK* * E8 ....78 A4
Field St *FSBYW* WC1X 9 E3
Fieldview *WAND/EARL* SW18 ....151 D1
Field Wy *WLSDN* NW10 ....68 C4
Fieldway Crs *HBRY* N5 ....76 A2
Fife Rd *CAN/RD* E16 ....94 A4
MORT/ESHN SW14 ....128 C3
Fife Ter *IS* N1 ....9 F1
Fifield Pth *FSTH* SE23 ....157 D3
Fifth Av *MNPK* E12 ....83 F1
NKENS W10 ....89 E3
Fifth Wy *WBLY* HA9 ....68 B1
Filey Av *STNW/STAM* N16 ....60 A3
Fillebrook Rd *WAN* E11 ....63 D3
Filmer Chambers *FUL/PGN* * SW6 ....113 F4
Filmer Rd *FUL/PGN* SW6 ....113 F4
Finborough Rd *WBPTN* SW10 ....114 B2
Finch Av *WNWD* SE27 ....155 D4
Finch La *BANK* EC3V 24 B5
Finchley Pl *STJWD* NW8 ....4 A1
Finchley Rd *GLDGN* NW11 ....54 A4
KIL/WHAMP NW6 ....72 A1
Finch Ms *PECK* * SE15 ....119 F4
Finden Rd *FSTGT* E7 ....82 B2
Findhorn St *POP/IOD* E14 ....92 C5
Findon Cl *WAND/EARL* SW18 ....132 A4
Findon Rd *SHB* W12 ....100 A3
Fingal St *GNWCH* SE10 ....123 F1
Finland Rd *BROCKY* SE4 ....139 E1
Finland St *BERM/RHTH* SE16 ....103 E4
Finlay St *FUL/PGN* SW6 ....113 D4
Finnis St *BETH* E2 ....90 B2
Finsbury Av *LVPST* * EC2M 24 B3
Finsbury Circ *LVPST* EC2M 24 B3
Finsbury Est *CLKNW* EC1R 10 B4
Finsbury Market *SDTCH* EC2A 24 C1
Finsbury Park Av *FSBYPK* N4 ....58 C1
Finsbury Park Rd *FSBYPK* N4 ....58 A4
Finsbury Pavement *SDTCH* EC2A 24 B2
Finsbury Sq *SDTCH* EC2A 24 B1
Finsbury St *STLK* EC1Y 24 A2
Finsen Rd *HNHL* SE24 ....136 C2
Finstock Rd *NKENS* W10 ....89 D3
Firbank Cl *CAN/RD* E16 ....95 D4
Firbank Rd *PECK* SE15 ....120 B5
Fircroft Rd *TOOT* SW17 ....151 F3
Firecrest Dr *HAMP* NW3 ....54 B5
Firefly Gdns *EHAM* E6 ....95 E3
Firhill Rd *CAT* SE6 ....158 A3
Firs Av *MORT/ESHN* SW14 ....128 C3
Firsby Rd *STNW/STAM* N16 ....59 F3
Firs Cl *FSTH* SE23 ....139 D5
Firside Gv *BFN/LL* DA15 ....163 F1
First Av *ACT* W3 ....99 F2
MNPK E12 ....83 E1
MORT/ESHN SW14 ....111 E5
NKENS W10 ....89 F3
PLSTW E13 ....94 A2
First Dr *WLSDN* NW10 ....68 C4
First St *CHEL* SW3 ....41 D4
First Wy *WBLY* HA9 ....68 B1
Firth Gdns *FUL/PGN* SW6 ....113 D4
Fir Tree Cl *STRHM/NOR* SW16 ....152 C5
Fir Trees Cl *BERM/RHTH* SE16 ....103 E2
Fishermans Dr *BERM/RHTH* SE16 ....103 D3
Fishers Ct *NWCR* SE14 ....121 D4
Fisher's La *BANK* 99 D5
Fisher St *CAN/RD* E16 ....94 A4
RSQ WC1B 21 E3
Fisherton St *STJWD* NW8 ....16 A1
Fishguard Wy *CAN/RD* E16 ....108 B2
CAN/RD E16 ....108 B2

Fishponds Rd *TOOT* SW17 ....151 E4
Fish Street HI *MON* * EC3R 36 B1
Fisons Rd *CAN/RD* E16 ....106 A2
Fitzalan St *LBTH* SE11 ....45 F4
Fitz-George Av *WKENS* W14 ....101 E5
Fitzgerald Av *MORT/ESHN* SW14 ....129 E1
Fitzgerald Rd *MORT/ESHN* SW14 ....129 D1
Fitzhardinge St *MBLAR* W1H 18 A4
Fitzhugh Gv *WAND/EARL* SW18 ....133 D4
Fitz-James Av *WKENS* W14 ....101 E5
Fitzjohn's Av *HAMP* NW3 ....73 D3
Fitzmaurice Pl *MYFR/PICC* W1J 31 D3
Fitzneal St *ACT* W3 ....87 F5
Fitzroy Cl *HGT* N6 ....55 F3
Fitzroy Crs *CHSWK* * W4 ....111 D3
Fitzroy Ms *GTPST* W1W 19 E1
Fitzroy Pk *HGT* N6 ....55 F3
Fitzroy Rd *CAMTN* NW1 ....74 A5
Fitzroy Sq *FITZ* W1T 19 E1
Fitzroy St *CAMTN* NW1 ....19 E1
Fitzwarren Gdns *ARCH* N19 ....56 C3
Fitzwilliam Ms *CAN/RD* E16 ....106 A2
Fitzwilliam Rd *CLAP* SW4 ....134 C1
Fiveways Rd *BRXN/ST* SW9 ....118 A5
Fladbury Rd *SEVS/STOTM* N15 ....59 D1
Fladgate Rd *WAN* E11 ....63 E4
Flamborough St *POP/IOD* E14 ....91 E5
Flamsteed Av *WBLY* HA9 ....68 A3
Flamsteed Rd *CHARL* SE7 ....125 E1
Flanchford Rd *SHB* W12 ....99 F4
Flanders Rd *CHSWK* W4 ....99 E5
EHAM E6 ....95 F4
Flanders Wy *HOM* E9 ....79 D3
Flank St *WCHPL* E1 ....102 A1
Flask Wk *HAMP* NW3 ....72 C1
Flavell Ms *GNWCH* SE10 ....123 E1
Flaxman Rd *CMBW* SE5 ....118 B5
Flaxman Ter *STPAN* WC1H 8 B4
Flaxton Rd *WOOL/PLUM* SE18 ....127 D4
Fleece Wk *HOLWY* * N7 ....75 E3
Fleet Pl *STP* EC4M 22 C4
Fleet Rd *HAMP* NW3 ....73 E2
Fleet Sq *FSBYW* WC1X 9 E4
Fleet St *EMB* EC4Y 22 B5
Fleet Street HI *BETH* * E2 ....90 A3
Fleet Ter *CAT* * SE6 ....140 C5
Fleetwood Cl *CAN/RD* E16 ....95 D4
Fleetwood Rd *WLSDN* NW10 ....70 A2
Fleetwood St *STNW/STAM* N16 ....59 E4
Fleming Cl *MV/WKIL* W9 ....14 A1
WBPTN * SW10 ....114 C2
Fleming Rd *WALW* SE17 ....118 B2
Flempton Rd *LEY* E10 ....61 E3
Fletcher Cl *EHAM* E6 ....108 B1
Fletcher La *LEY* E10 ....62 C2
Fletcher Rd *CHSWK* W4 ....98 C4
Fletcher St *WCHPL* E1 ....102 A1
Fletching Rd *CHARL* SE7 ....125 D2
CLPT E5 ....60 C5
Fleur De Lis St *WCHPL* E1 ....25 E1
Flimwell Cl *BMLY* BR1 ....159 E5
Flintmill Crs *BKHTH/KID* SE3 ....125 E5
ELTH/MOT SE9 ....143 E1
Flinton St *WALW* SE17 ....119 E1
Flint St *WALW* SE17 ....48 B5
Flitcroft St *LSQ/SEVD* WC2H 20 B5
Flock Mill Pl *WAND/EARL* SW18 ....150 B1
Flockton St *BERM/RHTH* SE16 ....102 A3
Flodden Rd *CMBW* SE5 ....118 C4
Flood St *CHEL* SW3 ....115 E1
Flood Wk *CHEL* SW3 ....115 E2
Flora Cl *POP/IOD* E14 ....92 B3
Floral Pl *IS* N1 ....77 D2
Floral St *COVGDN* WC2E 33 D1
Florence Gdns *CHSWK* W4 ....110 C2
Florence Rd *CHSWK* W4 ....99 D4
EHAM E6 ....82 C5
FSBYPK N4 ....57 F2

NWCR SE14	121	F4
PLSTW E13	94	A1
Florence St CAN/RD E16	93	F3
IS N1	76	B4
Florence Ter NWCR SE14	121	F4
Florence Vls HGT * N6	56	B2
Florence Wy BAL SW12	151	F1
Florfield Rd HACK E8	78	B3
Florian Rd PUT/ROE SW15	131	E2
Florida St BETH E2	90	A2
Floss St PUT/ROE SW15	112	C5
Flower & Dean Wk WCHPL E1	25	F3
Flowers Cl CRICK NW2	52	A5
Flowers Ms ARCH N19	56	C4
Floyd Rd CHARL SE7	124	C1
Fludyer St LEW SE13	141	E2
Foley St GTPST W1W	19	E3
Folgate St WCHPL E1	25	D2
Foliot St ACT W3	87	F5
Folkestone Rd EHAM E6	96	A1
Follett St POP/IOD E14	92	C5
Folly Wall POP/IOD E14	104	C3
Fontarabia Rd BTSEA SW11	134	A2
Fontenoy Rd TOOT SW17	152	B2
Fonthill Ms FSBYPK N4	57	F4
Fonthill Rd FSBYPK N4	57	F4
Fontley Wy PUT/ROE SW15	130	A5
The Footpath PUT/ROE * SW15	130	A3
Footscray Rd ELTH/MOT SE9	144	A4
Forbes Cl CRICK NW2	52	A5
Forbes St WCHPL E1	90	A5
Forburg Rd STNW/STAM N16	60	A3
Fordel Rd CAT SE6	159	D1
Fordham St WCHPL E1	90	A5
Fordingley Rd MV/WKIL W9	89	F2
Fordmill Rd CAT SE6	158	A2
Ford Rd BOW E3	91	E1
Fords Park Rd CAN/RD E16	94	A5
Ford Sq WCHPL E1	90	B4
Ford St BOW E3	79	E5
CAN/RD E16	93	F5
Fordwych Rd CRICK NW2	71	E2
Fordyce Rd LEW SE13	140	C4
Foreland St WOOL/PLUM SE18	109	D5
Foreshore DEPT SE8	103	F5
Forest Dr MNPK E12	65	D5
Forest Dr East WAN E11	63	D2
Forest Dr West WAN E11	62	C2
Forester Rd PECK SE15	138	B2
Forest Gld WAN E11	63	E1
Forest Gv HACK E8	77	F3
Forest Hill Rd EDUL SE22	138	B4
Forestholme Cl FSTH * SE23	156	C2
Forest La FSTGT E7	82	A2
Fore St BARB EC2Y	24	A3
Forest Rd FSTGT E7	82	A1
HACK E8	77	F3
RCH/KEW TW9	110	A3
WAN E11	63	D2
Forest Side FSTGT E7	82	B1
Forest St FSTGT E7	82	A2
Forest Vw WAN E11	63	F2
Forest View Rd MNPK E12	83	E1
Forest Wy BFN/LL DA15	145	D5
Forfar Rd BTSEA SW11	116	A4
Forge Pl CAMTN NW1	74	A3
Forman Pl STNW/STAM N16	77	F1
Formosa St MV/WKIL W9	15	D1
Formunt Cl CAN/RD E16	93	F4
Forres Gdns GLDGN NW11	54	A1
Forrester Pth SYD SE26	156	C4
Forset St MBLAR W1H	17	D4
Forster Rd BRXS/STRHM SW2	135	E5
WALTH E17	61	E1
Forston St IS N1	11	F1
Forsyth Gdns WALW SE17	118	B2
Forsythia Cl IL IG1	84	B2
Fortess Gv KTTN NW5	74	C2
Fortess Rd KTTN NW5	74	B2
Fortess Wk KTTN NW5	74	B2
Forthbridge Rd BTSEA SW11	134	A2
Fortis Cl CAN/RD E16	94	C5
Fortnam Rd ARCH N19	57	D4
Fort Rd STHWK SE1	49	F5
Fortrose Gdns BRXS/STRHM SW2	153	E1
Fort St CAN/RD E16	106	B2
WCHPL * E1	25	D3
Fortuna Cl HOLWY * N7	75	F3
Fortunegate Rd WLSDN NW10	69	E1
Fortune Green Rd KIL/WHAMP NW6	72	A1
Fortune St STLK EC1Y	23	F1
Fortune Wy WLSDN NW10	88	A2
Forty Acre La CAN/RD E16	94	A4
Forty La WBLY HA9	50	B4
Forum Magnum Sq STHWK SE1	33	E5
Fosbury Ms BAY/PAD W2	27	D2
Foscote Ms MV/WKIL W9	14	B1
Foscote Rd HDN NW4	52	B1
Foskett Rd FUL/PGN SW6	115	F5
Fossdene Rd CHARL SE7	124	B1
Fossil Rd LEW SE13	140	A1
Foss Rd TOOT SW17	151	D4
Foster La CITYW EC2V	23	E4
Foster Rd ACT W3	99	E1
CHSWK W4	111	D1
PLSTW E13	94	A3
Fosters Cl CHST BR7	161	F5
Fothergill Cl PLSTW E13	82	A5
Foulden Rd STNW/STAM N16	77	F1
Foulden Ter STNW/STAM N16	77	F1
Foulis Ter SKENS SW7	40	A5
Foulser Rd TOOT SW17	151	F3
Foundry Cl BERM/RHTH SE16	103	E2
Foundry Ms CAMTN NW1	7	F5
Fountain Dr WAND/EARL * SW18	132	B5
Fountain Dr NRWD SE19	155	F4
Fountain Green Sq		
BERM/RHTH SE16	102	A3
Fountain Ms HAMP * NW3	73	F3
Fountain Pl BRXN/ST SW9	118	A4
Fountain Rd TOOT SW17	151	D5
Fountayne Rd STNW/STAM N16	60	A4
Fount St VX/NE SW8	117	D3
Fournier St WCHPL E1	25	F2
Four Seasons Cl BOW E3	92	A1
Fourth Av MNPK E12	83	F1
NKENS W10	89	E3
Fourth Wy WBLY HA9	68	B3
Fowey Cl WAP E1W	102	B2
Fowler Cl BTSEA SW11	133	D1
Fowler Rd FSTGT E7	82	A1
IS N1	76	B5
Fownes St BTSEA SW11	133	E1
Fox & Knot St FARR * EC1M	23	D2
Foxberry Rd BROCKY SE4	139	E2
Foxborough Gdns BROCKY SE4	140	A4
Foxbourne Rd TOOT SW17	152	A2
Fox Cl CAN/RD E16	94	A4
WCHPL E1	90	C3
Foxcroft Rd WOOL/PLUM SE18	126	B4
Foxes Dl BKHTH/KID SE3	142	A1
Foxglove St ACT W3	99	F1
Foxham Rd ARCH N19	57	D5
Foxhole Rd ELTH/MOT SE9	143	E3
Fox Hollow Cl WOOL/PLUM SE18	127	E1
Foxholt Gdns WLSDN NW10	68	C4
Foxley Cl HACK E8	78	A2
Foxley Rd CMBW SE5	118	A3
Foxley Sq BRXN/ST * SW9	118	B3
Foxmore St BTSEA SW11	115	F4
Fox Rd CAN/RD E16	93	F4
Foxwell St BROCKY SE4	139	E1
Foxwood Rd BKHTH/KID SE3	141	F2
Foyle Rd BKHTH/KID SE3	123	F2
Framfield Rd HBRY N5	76	B2
Framlingham Crs ELTH/MOT SE9	161	E4

Further Green Rd CAT SE6 ....141 E5
Furzedown Dr TOOT SW17.............152 B5
Furzedown Rd TOOT SW17.............152 B5
Furzefield Rd BKHTH/KID SE3 ....124 C3
Furze St BOW * E3...........................92 A4
Fye Foot La BLKFR * EC4V 35 E1
Fyfield Rd BRXN/ST SW9................136 A1
Fynes St WEST SW1P 44 A4

G

Gable Ct SYD SE26 ....156 B4
Gables Cl CMBW SE5 ....119 E4
LEE/GVPK SE12 ....160 A1
Gabriel St FSTH SE23 ....139 D5
Gabriel's Whf STHWK SE1 ....34 A3
Gad Cl PLSTW E13...........................94 B2
Gadsbury Cl CDALE/KGS NW9.........51 F1
Gadwall Cl CAN/RD E16...................94 B5
Gage Rd CAN/RD E16.......................93 E4
Gainford St IS N1............................76 A5
Gainsborough Av MNPK E12 ....84 C3
Gainsborough Ct SHB W12 ....100 C3
Gainsborough Gdns GLDGN NW11...53 F2
HAMP NW3 ....55 D5
Gainsborough Rd CHSWK W4 ....99 F5
SRTFD E15.....................................93 E2
WAN E11...63 E2
Gainsford St STHWK SE1 ....37 E4
Gairloch Rd CMBW SE5.................119 E5
Gaisford St KTTN NW5.....................74 C3
Gaitskell Rd ELTH/MOT SE9 ....162 C1
Galahad Rd BMLY BR1....................160 A3
Galata Rd BARN SW13 ....112 A3
Galatea Sq PECK SE15....................138 B1
Galbraith St POP/IOD E14..............104 C4
Galena Rd HMSMTH W6 ....100 B5
Galen Pl NOXST/BSQ WC1A.............20 C3
Galesbury Rd WAND/EARL SW18 ...132 C4
Gales Gdns BETH E2.........................90 B2
Gale St BOW E3................................92 A4
Galgate Cl WIM/MER SW19............149 D1
Galleon Cl BERM/RHTH SE16 ....102 C3
The Galleries IS * N1.......................10 C1
Gallery Rd DUL SE21......................155 D1
Galleywall Rd BERM/RHTH SE16 ...102 B5
Galilia Rd HBRY N5...........................76 B2
Gallions Rd CAN/RD E16.................108 B1
CHARL SE7 ....106 B5
Gallions View Rd THMD SE28 ....109 E3
Gallon Cl CHARL SE7......................106 C5
Galloosson Rd WOOL/PLUM SE18 .109 E5
Galloway Rd SHB W12....................100 A2
Gallus Sq BKHTH/KID SE3 ....142 B1
Galsworthy Crs BKHTH/KID * SE3 .124 C4
Galsworthy Rd CRICK NW2...............71 E1
Galton St NKENS W10.......................89 E3
Galveston Rd PUT/ROE SW15 ....131 F3
Galway Cl BERM/RHTH * SE16 ......120 B1
Galway St FSBYE EC1V.....................11 F4
Gambetta St VX/NE SW8................116 B5
Gambia St STHWK SE1......................35 D4
Gamble Rd TOOT SW17..................151 E4
Gamlen Rd PUT/ROE SW15............131 D2
Gamuel Cl WALTH E17......................62 A1
Gandhi Cl WALTH E17......................62 A1
Ganton St SOHO/CST * W1F.............19 F5
Gap Rd WIM/MER SW19.................150 A5
Garage Rd ACT W3............................86 A5
Garbutt Pl MHST * W1U....................18 B2
Garden Cl LEE/GVPK SE12 ....160 B3
PUT/ROE SW15............................130 B5
Garden Pl TPL/STR * WC2R..............34 A1
Garden Flats HMSMTH * W6 ....113 D2
Garden La BRXS/STRHM SW2..........153 D1
Garden Pl HACK E8...........................77 F5

Garden Rd RCH/KEW TW9.............128 A1
STJWD NW8 ....3 F3
Garden Rw STHWK SE1....................46 C3
The Gardens EDUL SE22.................138 A2
STNW/STAM * N16 ....59 F2
Garden St WCHPL E1........................91 D4
Garden Studios BAY/PAD * W2 ......15 E3
Garden Ter PIM * SW1V..................117 D1
Garden Wk SDTCH EC2A...................12 C5
Garden Wy WLSDN NW10.................68 C3
Gardiner Av CRICK * NW2.................70 C2
Gardiner House WOOL/PLUM SE18.125 E3
Gardner Cl WAN E11..........................64 B1
Gardner Rd PLSTW E13.....................94 B3
Gardners La BLKFR EC4V...................35 E1
Gardnor Rd HAMP NW3.....................73 D1
Gareth Gv BMLY BR1......................160 A4
Garfield Rd BTSEA SW11................134 A1
PLSTW E13.......................................93 F3
Garford St POP/IOD E14..................104 A1
Garibaldi St WOOL/PLUM SE18 .....109 E5
Garland Rd WOOL/PLUM SE18 ......127 D3
Garlick Hl BLKFR EC4V......................35 F1
Garlies Rd FSTH SE23 ....157 E3
Garlinge Rd CRICK NW2....................71 F3
Garnault Ms CLKNW EC1R................10 B4
Garnault Pl CLKNW EC1R..................10 B4
Garnham St STNW/STAM N16..........59 F4
Garnet Rd WLSDN NW10...................69 E3
Garnet St WAP E1W........................102 C1
Garnett Cl ELTH/MOT SE9...............143 F1
Garnett Rd HAMP NW3......................73 F2
Garnham St STNW/STAM N16..........59 F4
Garnies Cl PECK SE15.....................119 F3
Garrad's Rd STRHM/NOR SW16 .....153 D3
Garrard Cl CHST BR7......................162 B5
Garrard Wk WLSDN * NW10.............69 E3
Garratt La TOOT SW17...................150 C3
Garratt Ter TOOT SW17..................151 E4
Garrett Cl ACT W3............................87 D4
Garrett St STLK EC1Y.........................23 E1
Garrick Av GLDGN NW11..................53 E1
Garrick Cl BTSEA SW11..................132 C2
Garrick Dr WOOL/PLUM SE18 ....109 D4
Garrick Rd CDALE/KGS NW9............51 F1
RCH/KEW TW9..............................110 A5
Garrick St COVGDN WC2E................32 C1
Garrick Yd CHCR WC2N....................32 C1
Garrison Cl WOOL/PLUM SE18 ......126 A3
Garsdale Ter WKENS * W14............113 F1
Garside Cl WOOL/PLUM SE18 ....109 D4
Garsington Ms BROCKY SE4............139 F1
Garthorne Rd FSTH SE23................139 D5
Garth Rd CHSWK W4......................111 D1
CRICK NW2 ....53 F4
Gartmoor Gdns WIM/MER SW19...149 F1
Gartmore Rd GDMY/SEVK IG3.........67 F3
Garton Pl WAND/EARL SW18 ....132 C4
Gartons Wy BTSEA SW11...............132 C1
Garvary Rd CAN/RD E16...................94 B5
Garway Rd BAY/PAD W2...................14 C5
Gascoigne Pl BETH E2.......................13 E3
Gascoigne Rd BARK IG11.................84 C5
Gascony Av KIL/WHAMP NW6 ....72 A4
Gascoyne Rd HOM E9.......................79 D4
Gaselee St POP/IOD E14.................104 C1
Gasholder Pl LBTH SE11..................117 F1
Gaskarth Rd BAL SW12...................134 B4
Gaskell Rd HGT N6............................55 F1
Gaskell St CLAP SW4......................117 E5
Gaskin St IS N1.................................76 B5
Gaspar Cl ECT * SW5.........................39 D4
Gaspar Ms ECT SW5..........................39 D4
Gassiot Rd TOOT SW17..................151 F4
Gastein Rd HMSMTH W6................113 D2
Gataker St BERM/RHTH SE16.........102 B4

Gatcombe Rd ARCH N19.............57 D5
Gateforth St STJWD NW8.............16 C1
Gatehouse Sq STHWK SE1.............35 F3
Gateley Rd BRXN/ST SW9.............135 F1
Gate Ms SKENS SW7.............41 D1
Gates Ct WALW * SE17.............118 C5
Gateside Rd TOOT SW17.............151 F3
Gate St HHOL WC1V.............21 E4
Gateway WALW SE17.............118 C2
Gateway Ar IS * N1.............10 C1
Gateway Ms HACK * E8.............77 F2
Gathorne St BETH E2.............91 D1
Gatliff Cl BGVA * SW1V.............116 A1
Gatliff Rd BGVA SW1V.............116 B1
Gatonby St PECK SE15.............119 F4
Gatton Rd TOOT SW17.............151 E4
Gatwick Rd WAND/EARL SW18.............131 F5
Gauden Cl CLAP SW4.............135 D1
Gauden Rd CLAP SW4.............135 D1
Gaumont Ter SHB * W12.............100 C3
Gaunt St STHWK SE1.............47 D2
Gautrey Rd PECK SE15.............120 C5
Gavel St WALW * SE17.............48 B4
Gaverick St POP/IOD E14.............104 A5
Gavestone Crs LEE/GVPK SE12.............142 B5
Gavestone Rd LEE/GVPK SE12.............142 B5
Gawber St BETH E2.............90 C2
Gawsworth Cl SRTFD E15.............81 F2
Gay Cl CRICK NW2.............70 B2
Gayfere St WEST SW1P.............44 C3
Gayford Rd SHB W12.............99 F3
Gayhurst Rd HACK E8.............78 A4
Gaynesford Rd FSTH SE23.............157 D2
Gay Rd SRTFD E15.............93 D1
Gayton Crs HAMP NW3.............73 D1
Gayton Rd HAMP NW3.............73 D1
Gayville Rd BTSEA SW11.............133 F4
Gaywood Cl BRXS/STRHM SW2.............153 F1
Gaywood St STHWK SE1.............47 D3
Gaza St WALW SE17.............118 B1
Geary Rd WLSDN NW10.............70 A2
Geary St HOLWY N7.............75 F2
Gedling Pl STHWK SE1.............49 E2
Geere Rd SRTFD E15.............81 F5
Gees Ct MHST W1U.............18 B5
Gee St FSBYE EC1V.............11 E5
Geffrye Est IS N1.............13 D2
Geffrye St BETH E2.............13 E1
Geldart Rd PECK SE15.............120 B3
Geldeston Rd CLPT E5.............60 A4
Gellatly Rd PECK SE15.............120 C5
General Wolfe Rd GNWCH SE10.............123 D4
Genesta Rd WOOL/PLUM SE18.............126 B2
Geneva Dr HNHL SE24.............136 A2
Genoa Av PUT/ROE SW15.............130 C3
Geoffrey Cl CMBW SE5.............118 C5
Geoffrey Gdns EHAM E6.............95 E1
Geoffrey Rd BROCKY SE4.............139 F1
George Beard Rd DEPT SE8.............103 F5
George Downing Est
  STNW/STAM N16.............59 F4
George La LEW SE13.............140 C4
George Mathers Rd LBTH * SE11.............46 C4
George Ms CAMTN NW1.............7 E4
George Rw BERM/RHTH SE16.............102 A3
Georges Rd HOLWY N7.............75 F3
  HOLWY N7.............75 F2
George St BARK IG11.............84 C4
  CAN/RD E16.............93 F5
  MBLAR W1H.............17 F4
Georgetown Cl NRWD SE19.............155 D5
Georgette Pl GNWCH SE10.............122 C3
George Wyver Cl WIM/MER SW19.............131 E5
George Yd BANK EC3V.............24 B5
  MYFR/PKLN W1K.............30 B1
Georgiana St CAMTN NW1.............74 C5
Georgian Ct WBLY HA9.............68 A3
Georgina Gdns BETH * E2.............13 D1
Geraint Rd BMLY BR1.............160 A3
Geraldine Rd CHSWK W4.............110 A2
  WAND/EARL SW18.............132 C3
Geraldine St LBTH SE11.............46 C3
Gerald Rd BGVA SW1W.............42 B4
  CAN/RD E16.............93 F3
Gerard Rd BARN SW13.............111 F4
Gerards Cl BERM/RHTH SE16.............120 C2
Gerda Rd ELTH/MOT SE9.............162 B2
Germander Wy SRTFD E15.............93 E2
Gernon Rd BOW E3.............91 E1
Geron Wy CRICK NW2.............52 C4
Gerrard Pl SOHO/SHAV * W1D.............32 B1
Gerrard Rd IS N1.............10 C1
Gerrard St SOHO/SHAV W1D.............32 B1
Gerridge St STHWK SE1.............46 B1
Gertrude St WBPTN SW10.............114 C2
Gervase Cl WBLY HA9.............50 C5
Gervase St PECK SE15.............120 B3
Ghent St CAT SE6.............158 A2
Ghent Wy HACK E8.............77 F3
Giant Arches Rd HNHL SE24.............136 C5
Gibbins Rd SRTFD E15.............80 C4
Gibbon Rd ACT W3.............99 E1
  PECK SE15.............120 C5
Gibbons Rd WLSDN NW10.............69 D3
Gibbon Wk PUT/ROE * SW15.............130 A2
Gibbs Cl NRWD * SE19.............155 D5
Gibbs Gn WKENS * W14.............113 F1
Gibbs Sq NRWD * SE19.............155 D5
Gibraltar Wk BETH E2.............13 F4
Gibson Cl WCHPL E1.............90 C1
Gibson Gdns STNW/STAM * N16.............59 F4
Gibson Rd LBTH SE11.............45 F3
Gibson Sq IS N1.............76 A5
Gibson St GNWCH SE10.............123 E1
Gideon Rd BTSEA SW11.............134 A1
Giesbach Rd ARCH N19.............56 C4
Giffin St DEPT SE8.............122 A3
Gifford St IS N1.............75 E4
Gift La SRTFD E15.............81 E5
Gilbert Cl WOOL/PLUM SE18.............125 F4
Gilbert Pl NOXST/BSQ WC1A.............20 C3
Gilbert Rd LBTH SE11.............46 B4
Gilbert St MYFR/PKLN W1K.............18 B5
  SRTFD E15.............81 E1
Gilbey Rd TOOT SW17.............151 E4
Gilbeys Yd CAMTN NW1.............74 A4
Gilbourne Rd WOOL/PLUM SE18.............127 F2
Gilda Crs STNW/STAM N16.............60 A3
Gildea St REGST W1B.............19 D3
Gildersome St WOOL/PLUM SE18.............126 A2
Giles Coppice NRWD SE19.............155 F4
Gilkes Crs EDUL SE22.............137 E4
Gilkes Pl DUL SE21.............137 E4
Gill Av CAN/RD E16.............94 A5
Gillender St BOW E3.............92 C3
Gillespie Rd FSBYPK N4.............58 A5
Gillett Av EHAM E6.............95 E1
Gillett Pl HACK E8.............77 F2
Gillett St STNW/STAM N16.............77 E2
Gillian St LEW SE13.............140 B3
Gillingham Ms PIM SW1V.............43 D4
Gillingham Rd CRICK NW2.............53 E5
Gillingham Rw PIM * SW1V.............43 E4
Gillingham St PIM SW1V.............43 D5
Gillison Wk BERM/RHTH * SE16.............102 A4
Gillman Dr SRTFD E15.............81 E5
Gilmore Rd LEW SE13.............141 D2
Gilpin Av MORT/ESHN SW14.............129 D2
Gilpin Cl BAY/PAD W2.............15 F3
Gilpin Rd CLPT E5.............79 E1
Gilstead Rd FUL/PGN SW6.............114 B5
Gilston Rd WBPTN SW10.............114 C1
Gilton Rd CAT SE6.............159 E3
Giltspur St STBT EC1A.............23 D4
Gipsy Hl NRWD SE19.............155 E5

Gipsy La *BARN* SW13 .... 130 A1
Gipsy Rd *WNWD* SE27 .... 155 D4
Gipsy Road Gdns *WNWD* SE27 .... 154 C4
Giralda CI *CAN/RD* E16 .... 95 D3
Giraud St *POP/IOD* E14 .... 92 B5
Girdlers Rd *HMSMTH* W6 .... 101 D5
Girdwood Rd *WAND/EARL* SW18 .. 131 E5
Gironde Rd *FUL/PGN* SW6 .... 113 F3
Girton Rd *SYD* SE26 .... 157 D5
Gissing Wk *IS* * N1 .... 76 A4
Gittens CI *BMLY* BR1 .... 159 F4
Gladding Rd *MNPK* E12 .... 83 D1
The Glade *CHARL* SE7 .... 124 C3
    HACK * E8 .... 77 F3
    SHB * W12 .... 100 B3
Gladesmore Rd *SEVS/STOTM* N15 . 59 F1
Gladiator St *FSTH* SE23 .... 139 E4
Glading Ter *STNW/STAM* N16 .... 59 F5
Gladsmuir Rd *ARCH* N19 .... 56 C3
Gladstone Av *MNPK* E12 .... 83 E4
Gladstone Ms *KIL/WHAMP* NW6 ...... 71 F3
Gladstone Pde *CRICK* * NW2 .... 52 C5
Gladstone Park Gdns *CRICK* NW2 ... 52 B5
Gladstone Rd *CHSWK* * W4 .... 99 D3
Gladstone St *STHWK* SE1 .... 46 C2
Gladstone Ter *VX/NE* * SW8 .... 116 B4
    WNWD * SE27 .... 154 C4
Gladwell Rd *CEND/HSY/T* N8 .... 57 F1
Gladwyn Rd *PUT/ROE* SW15 .... 131 D1
Gladys Rd *KIL/WHAMP* NW6 .... 72 A4
Glaisher St *DEPT* SE8 .... 122 B2
Glamis PI *WAP* E1W 102 C1
Glamis Rd *WAP* E1W 102 C1
Glanville Rd *BRXS/STRHM* SW2 .... 135 E3
Glasbrook Rd *ELTH/MOT* SE9 ...... 143 D5
Glaserton Rd *STNW/STAM* N16 ...... 59 E2
Glasgow Rd *PLSTW* E13 .... 94 B1
Glasgow Ter *PIM* SW1V 116 C1
Glasshill St *STHWK* SE1 .... 35 D5
Glasshouse Flds *WAP* E1W 103 D1
Glasshouse St *REGST* W1B 31 F2
Glasshouse Wk *LBTH* SE11 .... 117 E1
Glasshouse Yd *STBT* EC1A 23 E1
Glass St *BETH* * E2 .... 90 B3
Glass Yd *WOOL/PLUM* SE18 .... 108 A4
Glastonbury PI *WCHPL* E1 .... 90 C5
Glastonbury St *KIL/WHAMP* NW6 ... 71 F2
Glaucus St *BOW* E3 .... 92 B4
Glazbury Rd *WKENS* W14 .... 101 E5
Glazebrook CI *DUL* SE21 .... 155 D2
The Glebe *BKHTH/KID* SE3 .... 141 E1
    STRHM/NOR * SW16 .... 153 D4
Glebe CI *CHSWK* * W4 .... 111 E1
Glebe Ct *BKHTH/KID* * SE3 .... 141 E1
Glebelands Av *CNTH/NBYPK* IG2 ... 67 D2
Glebelands CI *CMBW* * SE5 .... 137 E1
Glebe PI *CHEL* SW3 .... 115 E2
Glebe Rd *BARN* SW13 .... 112 A5
    HACK * E8 .... 77 F4
    WLSDN NW10 .... 70 A3
Glebe St *CHSWK* * W4 .... 111 D1
Glebe Ter *BOW* E3 .... 92 A1
Gledhow Gdns *ECT* SW5 .... 39 E5
Gledstanes Rd *WKENS* W14 .... 113 E1
Clegg PI *PUT/ROE* * SW15 .... 131 D2
Glenaffric Av *POP/IOD* E14 .... 104 C5
Glen Albyn Rd *WIM/MER* SW19 ... 149 D3
Glenalvon Wy *CHARL* SE7 .... 107 E5
Glenarm Rd *CLPT* E5 .... 78 C1
Glenavon Rd *SRTFD* E15 .... 81 E4
Glenbarr CI *ELTH/MOT* SE9 .... 144 B1
Glenbrook Rd *KIL/WHAMP* NW6 ..... 72 A2
Glenburnie Rd *TOOT* SW17 .... 151 F3
Glencairne CI *CAN/RD* E16 .... 95 D4
Glencoe Av *CNTH/NBYPK* IG2 ...... 67 E2
Glendale CI *ELTH/MOT* SE9 .... 144 A1
Glendall St *CLAP* SW4 .... 135 F1
Glendarvon St *PUT/ROE* SW15 .... 131 D1

Glendower Gdns *MORT/ESHN* SW14 . 129 D1
Glendower Rd *MORT/ESHN* SW14 . 129 D1
Glendun Rd *ACT* W3 .... 99 E1
Gleneagle Ms *STRHM/NOR* SW16 . 153 D5
Gleneagle Rd *STRHM/NOR* SW16 . 153 D5
Gleneagles CI *BERM/RHTH* * SE16 . 120 B1
Gleneldon Ms *STRHM/NOR* SW16 . 153 E4
Gleneldon Rd *STRHM/NOR* SW16 . 153 E4
Glenelg Rd *BRXS/STRHM* SW2 ..... 135 E3
Glenesk Rd *ELTH/MOT* SE9 .... 144 A1
Glenfarg Rd *CAT* SE6 .... 159 D1
Glenfield Rd *BAL* SW12 .... 152 C1
Glenfinlas Wy *CMBW* SE5 .... 118 B3
Glenforth St *GNWCH* SE10 .... 105 F5
Glengall Br *POP/IOD* E14 .... 104 B4
Glengall Gv *POP/IOD* E14 .... 104 B4
Glengall Rd *KIL/WHAMP* NW6 .... 71 F5
    PECK SE15 .... 119 F2
Glengall Ter *PECK* SE15 .... 119 F2
Glengarnock Av *POP/IOD* E14 ..... 104 C5
Glengarry Rd *EDUL* SE22 .... 137 E2
Glenhead CI *ELTH/MOT* SE9 .... 144 B1
Glenhouse Rd *ELTH/MOT* SE9 .... 144 A3
Glenhurst Av *KTTN* NW5 .... 74 A1
Glenilla Rd *HAMP* NW3 .... 73 E3
Glenister Rd *GNWCH* SE10 .... 123 F1
Glenlea Rd *ELTH/MOT* SE9 .... 144 A3
Glenloch Rd *HAMP* NW3 .... 73 E3
Glenluge Rd *BKHTH/KID* SE3 ..... 124 A2
Glenlyon Rd *ELTH/MOT* SE9 .... 144 A3
Glenmore Rd *HAMP* NW3 .... 73 E3
    WELL DA16 .... 127 F4
Glennie Rd *WNWD* SE27 .... 154 A3
Glenny Rd *BARK* IG11 .... 84 C3
Glenparke Rd *FSTGT* E7 .... 82 B3
Glen Rd *PLSTW* E13 .... 94 C3
Glenrosa St *FUL/PGN* SW6 .... 114 C5
Glenroy St *SHB* W12 .... 88 C5
Glensdale Rd *BROCKY* SE4 .... 139 F1
Glenshiel Rd *ELTH/MOT* SE9 ...... 144 A3
Glentanner Wy *TOOT* SW17 .... 151 D3
Glen Ter *POP/IOD* E14 .... 104 C3
Glentham Cottages *BARN* * SW13 . 112 A2
Glentham Gdns *BARN* SW13 .... 112 B1
Glentham Rd *BARN* SW13 .... 112 A2
Glenthorne Rd *HMSMTH* W6 .... 100 B5
Glenton Rd *LEW* SE13 .... 141 E2
Glentworth St *CAMTN* NW1 .... 17 F1
Glenure Rd *ELTH/MOT* SE9 .... 144 A3
Glenville Gv *DEPT* SE8 .... 121 F3
Glenwood Av *BFN/LL* DA15 .... 163 E2
    CAMTN NW1 .... 74 A4
    WELL DA16 .... 16 C5
Gloucester Circ *GNWCH* SE10 .... 122 C3
Gloucester CI *WLSDN* NW10 .... 69 D4
Gloucester Ct *MON* EC3R 37 D2
    RCH/KEW * TW9 .... 110 A3
Gloucester Crs *CAMTN* NW1 .... 74 B5
Gloucester Dr *FSBYPK* N4 .... 58 B4
Gloucester Gdns *BAY/PAD* W2 ...... 15 D4
    GLDGN NW11 .... 53 F2
    IL IG1 .... 65 E2
Gloucester Ga *CAMTN* NW1 .... 6 B1
Gloucester Gate Br *CAMTN* * NW1 . 74 B5
Gloucester Gate Ms *CAMTN* NW1 ... 6 C1
Gloucester Ms *BAY/PAD* W2 .... 15 E5
Gloucester Ms West *BAY/PAD* W2 . 15 E5
Gloucester PI *CAMTN* NW1 .... 17 E1

Gloucester Place Ms *MBLAR* W1H **17** F3
Gloucester Rd *ACT* W3 ....**98** C3
   LEY E10 ....**62** A2
   MNPK E12 ....**65** F5
   RCH/KEW TW9 ....**110** A3
   SKENS SW7 ....**39** E2
Gloucester Sq *BAY/PAD* W2 ....**16** B5
   BETH E2 ....**78** A5
Gloucester St *PIM* SW1V **116** C1
Gloucester Ter *BAY/PAD* W2 ....**15** D1
Gloucester Wk *KENS* W8 ....**26** B5
Gloucester Wy *CLKNW* EC1R **10** B4
Glycena Rd *BTSEA* SW11 ....**133** F1
Glynde Ms *CHEL* SW3 ....**41** D3
Glynde St *BROCKY* SE4 ....**139** F4
Glyndon Rd *WOOL/PLUM* SE18 ....**108** C5
Glynfield Rd *WLSDN* NW10 ....**69** E4
Glyn Rd *CLPT* E5 ....**79** D1
Glyn St *LBTH* SE11 ....**117** F1
Godalming Rd *POP/IOD* E14 ....**92** B4
Godbold Rd *SRTFD* E15 ....**93** E3
Goddard Pl *ARCH* N19 ....**56** C5
Goddards Wy *IL* IG1 ....**67** D3
Godfrey Hl *WOOL/PLUM* SE18 ....**107** E5
Godfrey Rd *WOOL/PLUM* SE18 ....**107** F5
Godfrey St *CHEL* SW3 ....**115** E1
   SRTFD E15 ....**92** C1
Goding St *LBTH* SE11 ....**117** E1
Godley Rd *WAND/EARL* SW18 ....**151** D1
Godliman St *BLKFR* * EC4V **23** D5
Godman Rd *PECK* * SE15 ....**120** B5
Godolphin Pl *ACT* W3 ....**99** D1
Godolphin Rd *SHB* W12 ....**100** B2
Godwin Cl *IS* N1 ....**11** F1
Godwin Rd *FSTGT* E7 ....**82** B1
Goffers Rd *BKHTH/KID* SE3 ....**123** E4
Golborne Gdns *NKENS* * W10 ....**89** E3
Golborne Ms *NKENS* W10 ....**89** E4
Golborne Rd *NKENS* W10 ....**89** C4
Goldcrest Cl *CAN/RD* E16 ....**95** D4
Golden Cross Ms *NTGHL* * W11 ....**89** F5
Golden Hind Pl *DEPT* * SE8 ....**103** F5
Golden La *STLK* EC1Y **11** C5
Golden Lane Est *STLK* EC1Y **23** E1
Golden Plover Cl *CAN/RD* E16 ....**94** A5
Golden Sq *SOHO/CST* W1F **31** F1
Golden Yd *HAMP* * NW3 ....**72** C1
Golders Gdns *GLDGN* NW11 ....**53** E2
Golders Green Crs *GLDGN* NW11 ....**53** E3
Golders Green Rd *GLDGN* NW11 ....**53** E1
Golders Hl *GLDGN* * NW11 ....**54** B4
Golderslea *GLDGN* * NW11 ....**54** A3
Golders Manor Dr *GLDGN* NW11 ....**53** D1
Golders Park Cl *GLDGN* NW11 ....**54** A3
Golders Wy *GLDGN* NW11 ....**53** F2
Goldfinch Rd *THMD* SE28 ....**109** D4
Goldhawk Ms *SHB* W12 ....**100** B3
Goldhawk Rd *HMSMTH* W6 ....**99** F5
Goldhurst Ter *KIL/WHAMP* NW6 ....**72** B4
Golding St *WCHPL* E1 ....**90** A5
Goldington Crs *CAMTN* NW1 ....**8** A1
Goldington St *CAMTN* NW1 ....**8** A1
Goldman Cl *BETH* E2 ....**90** A3
Goldney Rd *MV/WKIL* W9 ....**14** A1
Goldsboro Rd *VX/NE* SW8 ....**117** D4
Goldsmid St *WOOL/PLUM* SE18 ....**127** E1
Goldsmith Av *ACT* W3 ....**99** D1
   MNPK E12 ....**83** E3
Goldsmith Pl *KIL/WHAMP* * NW6 ....**72** B5
Goldsmith Rd *ACT* W3 ....**99** D2
   LEY E10 ....**62** A1
   PECK SE15 ....**120** A4
Goldsmiths Cl *ACT* * W3 ....**99** D2
Goldsmith's Rw *BETH* E2 ....**78** A5
Goldsmith St *CITYW* EC2V **23** F4
Goldsworthy Gdns
   BERM/RHTH SE16 ....**102** C5
Goldwing Cl *CAN/RD* E16 ....**94** A5

Golfe Rd *IL* IG1 ....**67** D5
Gollogly Ter *CHARL* SE7 ....**124** C1
Gomm Rd *BERM/RHTH* SE16 ....**102** C4
Gondar Gdns *CRICK* NW2 ....**71** F2
Gonson St *DEPT* SE8 ....**122** B2
Gonston Cl *WIM/MER* SW19 ....**149** E2
Conville St *FUL/PGN* SW6 ....**131** E1
Goodall Rd *WAN* E11 ....**62** C5
Goodey Rd *BARK* IG11 ....**85** F4
Goodge Pl *FITZ* W1T **19** F4
Goodge St *FITZ* W1T **19** F3
Goodhall St *WLSDN* NW10 ....**87** F2
Goodinge Cl *HOLWY* N7 ....**75** D2
Goodinge Rd *HOLWY* N7 ....**75** E3
Goodman Crs *BRXS/STRHM* SW2 ......**153** D2
Goodman Rd *LEY* E10 ....**62** C2
Goodman's Stile *WCHPL* E1 ....**90** A5
Goodman's Yd *TWRH* EC3N **37** E1
Goodrich Rd *EDUL* SE22 ....**137** F4
Goodson Rd *WLSDN* NW10 ....**69** E4
Goods Wy *CAMTN* NW1 ....**8** C1
Goodway Gdns *POP/IOD* E14 ....**93** D5
Goodwin Cl *BERM/RHTH* SE16 ....**49** F3
Goodwin Rd *SHB* W12 ....**100** A3
Goodwins Ct *CHCR* WC2N **32** C1
Goodwin St *FSBYPK* N4 ....**58** A4
Goodwood Rd *NWCR* SE14 ....**121** E3
Goosander Wy *WOOL/PLUM* SE18 ......**109** D4
Gooseley La *EHAM* E6 ....**96** A2
Gophir La *CANST* * EC4R **36** A1
Gopsall St *IS* N1 ....**77** D5
Gordon Av *MORT/ESHN* SW14 ....**129** E2
Gordonbrock Rd *BROCKY* SE4 ....**140** A3
Gordon Cl *WALTH* E17 ....**62** A1
Gordondale Rd *WIM/MER* SW19 ....**150** A2
Gordon Gv *CMBW* SE5 ....**118** B5
Gordon House Rd *KTTN* NW5 ....**74** A1
Gordon Pl *KENS* W8 ....**26** B5
Gordon Rd *BARK* IG11 ....**85** E5
   BFN/LL DA15 ....**145** E3
   CHSWK W4 ....**110** B2
   IL IG1 ....**67** D5
   PECK SE15 ....**120** B5
   SRTFD E15 ....**80** C1
   WAN E11 ....**64** A1
Gordon Sq *STPAN* WC1H **8** B5
Gordon St *PLSTW* E13 ....**94** A2
   STPAN WC1H **8** A5
Gorefield Pl *KIL/WHAMP* NW6 ....**2** A1
Gore Rd *HOM* E9 ....**78** C5
Gore St *SKENS* SW7 ....**39** F2
Gorham Pl *NTGHL* W11 ....**101** E1
Goring St *HDTCH* EC3A **25** D4
Gorleston St *WKENS* W14 ....**101** E5
Gorman Rd *WOOL/PLUM* SE18 ....**107** F5
Gorse Ri *TOOT* SW17 ....**152** A5
Gorst Rd *BTSEA* SW11 ....**133** F4
   WLSDN NW10 ....**86** C3
Gorsuch Pl *BETH* E2 ....**13** E3
Gorsuch St *BETH* E2 ....**13** E3
Gosberton Rd *BAL* SW12 ....**151** F1
Gosfield St *GTPST* W1W **19** D2
Goslett Yd *SOHO/SHAV* W1D **20** B4
Gosling Wy *BRXN/ST* SW9 ....**118** A4
Gosport Wy *PECK* SE15 ....**119** F3
Gossage Rd *WOOL/PLUM* SE18 ....**127** D1
Gosset St *BETH* E2 ....**90** A2
Gossington Cl *CHST* BR7 ....**162** B4
Gosterwood St *DEPT* SE8 ....**121** E2
Goswell Pl *FSBYE* EC1V **11** D4
Goswell Rd *FSBYE* EC1V **11** D3
Gottfried Ms *KTTN* NW5 ....**74** C1
Goudhurst Rd *BMLY* BR1 ....**159** E5
Gough Rd *FSTGT* E7 ....**81** F1
Gough Sq *FLST/FETLN* EC4A **22** B4
Gough St *FSBYW* WC1X **9** F5
Gould Ter *HACK* E8 ....**78** B2
Goulston St *WCHPL* E1 ....**25** E4

Goulton Rd CLPT E5 ....78 B2
Gourock Rd ELTH/MOT SE9 ....144 A3
Govan St BETH E2 ....78 A5
Govier Cl SRTFD E15 ....81 E4
Gowan Av FUL/PGN SW6 ....113 E4
Gowan Rd WLSDN NW10 ....70 B4
Gower Cl BAL SW12 ....134 C4
Gower Ms GWRST WC1E 20 B3
Gower Pl STPAN WC1H 7 F5
Gower Rd FSTGT E7 ....82 A3
Gower St GWRST WC1E 7 F5
Gower's Wk WCHPL E1 ....90 A5
Gowlett Rd PECK SE15 ....138 A1
Gowrie Rd BTSEA SW11 ....134 A1
Gracechurch St BANK EC3V 36 B1
Gracedale Rd TOOT SW17 ....152 B5
Grace Jones Cl HACK * E8 ....77 F3
Grace Pl BOW E3 ....92 B2
Grace's Ms CMBW SE5 ....119 D5
STJWD * NW8 ....3 F2
Grace's Ms CMBW SE5 ....119 E5
Grace St BOW E3 ....92 B2
The Gradient SYD SE26 ....156 A4
Graduate Pl STHWK SE1 ....48 C2
Graemesdyke Av MORT/ESHN SW14 ...128 B1
Grafton Crs CAMTN NW1 ....74 B3
Grafton Gdns FSBYPK N4 ....58 C1
Grafton Ms FITZ W1T 19 E1
Grafton Pl CAMTN NW1 ....8 A4
Grafton Rd ACT W3 ....98 C5
KTTN NW5 ....74 A2
Grafton Sq CLAP SW4 ....134 C1
Grafton St MYFR/PICC W1J 31 D1
Grafton Ter KTTN NW5 ....73 F2
Grafton Wy GTPST W1W 19 E2
Grafton Wy KTTN NW5 ....74 B3
Graham Rd CHSWK W4 ....99 D4
HACK E8 ....78 A5
HDN NW4 ....52 B1
PLSTW E13 ....94 A3
Graham St IS N1 ....11 D2
Graham Ter BGVA SW1W 42 B5
Cramer Cl WAN E11 ....63 D4
Grampian Gdns CRICK NW2 ....53 E3
Granada St TOOT SW17 ....151 F5
Granard Av PUT/ROE SW15 ....130 A3
Granard Rd BAL SW12 ....133 F5
Granary Rd WCHPL E1 ....90 B3
Granary Sq IS * N1 ....76 A3
Granary St CAMTN NW1 ....75 D5
Granby Rd ELTH/MOT SE9 ....125 F5
WOOL/PLUM SE18 ....108 B4
Granby St BETH E2 ....13 F5
Granby Ter CAMTN NW1 ....7 E2
Grand Av FARR EC1M 23 D2
WBLY HA9 ....68 B2
Grand Av East WBLY HA9 ....68 B2
Grand Depot Rd WOOL/PLUM SE18 .....126 A1
Grandison Rd BTSEA SW11 ....133 F3
Grand Junction Whf IS * N1 ....11 E2
Grand Pde FSBYPK * N4 ....58 B1
MORT/ESHN * SW14 ....128 C2
WBLY * HA9 ....68 B2
Grand Union Canal Wk BAY/PAD W2 .....14 B2
WLSDN NW10 ....86 B1
Grand Union Cl MV/WKIL W9 ....89 F4
Grand Union Crs HACK E8 ....78 A5
Grand Union Wk CAMTN * NW1 ....74 B4
Grand Wk WCHPL * E1 ....91 E3
Granfield St BTSEA * SW11 ....133 D1
The Grange ALP/SUD HA0 ....68 A4
STHWK SE1 ....49 E2
WKENS * W14 ....101 F5
Grangecourt Rd STNW/STAM N16 ....59 D3
Grange Gdns HAMP NW3 ....54 B5
Grange Gv IS N1 ....76 C3

Grangehill Pl ELTH/MOT SE9 ....143 F1
Grangehill Rd ELTH/MOT SE9 ....143 F2
Grange Houses HBRY * N5 ....76 C1
Grange La DUL SE21 ....155 F2
Grange Park Rd LEY E10 ....62 B3
Grange Pl KIL/WHAMP NW6 ....72 A4
Grange Rd BARN SW13 ....112 A4
CHSWK W4 ....110 B1
HGT N6 ....56 A1
IL IG1 ....84 C1
LEY E10 ....62 A3
PLSTW E13 ....93 F2
STHWK SE1 ....49 D3
WLSDN NW10 ....70 B3
Grange St IS * N1 ....77 D5
Grange Wk STHWK SE1 ....49 D5
Grange Walk Ms STHWK SE1 ....49 D5
Grangeway KIL/WHAMP NW6 ....72 A4
Grangewood St EHAM E6 ....83 D5
Grange Yd STHWK SE1 ....49 E3
Granite St WOOL/PLUM SE18 ....127 F1
Granleigh Rd WAN E11 ....63 E4
Gransden Av HACK E8 ....78 B4
Gransden Rd SHB W12 ....99 F3
Grantbridge St IS N1 ....11 D1
Grantham Pl MYFR/PICC W1J 30 C4
Grantham Rd BRXN/ST SW9 ....135 E1
CHSWK W4 ....111 E3
MNPK E12 ....66 A5
Grantley St WCHPL E1 ....91 D2
Grant Rd BTSEA SW11 ....133 D1
Grant St IS N1 ....10 A1
PLSTW E13 ....94 A2
Grant Ter CLPT * E5 ....60 A2
Grantully Rd MV/WKIL W9 ....2 C4
Granville Ar BRXN/ST * SW9 ....136 A1
Granville Gv LEW SE13 ....140 C1
Granville Pk LEW SE13 ....140 C1
Granville Pl FUL/PGN * SW6 ....114 B3
MBLAR W1H 18 A5
Granville Rd CRICK NW2 ....53 F4
FSBYPK N4 ....57 F1
IL IG1 ....66 B3
KIL/WHAMP NW6 ....2 A2
LEY E10 ....62 B1
WAND/EARL SW18 ....131 F5
Granville Sq PECK * SE15 ....119 D5
Granville St FSBYW WC1X 9 F4
Grape St LSQ/SEVD WC2H 20 C4
Graphite Sq LBTH * SE11 ....117 F1
Grasmere Av ACT W3 ....98 C1
PUT/ROE SW15 ....147 D4
Grasmere Rd PLSTW E13 ....94 A1
STRHM/NOR SW16 ....153 F5
Grasshaven Wy THMD SE28 ....109 F2
Grassmount FSTH SE23 ....156 B2
Grately Wy PECK * SE15 ....119 E3
Gratton Rd WKENS W14 ....101 E4
Gravel La WCHPL E1 ....25 E4
Gravelwood Cl CHST BR7 ....162 C3
Gravenel Gdns TOOT * SW17 ....151 E5
Graveney Rd TOOT SW17 ....151 E4
Gravesend Rd SHB W12 ....100 A1
Grayling Cl CAN/RD E16 ....93 E3
Grayling Rd STNW/STAM N16 ....59 D2
Grayling Sq BETH * E2 ....90 A2
Grayshott Rd BTSEA SW11 ....134 A1
Gray's Inn Rd FSBYW WC1X 9 D3
Gray's Inn Sq GINN WC1R 22 A2
Gray St STHWK SE1 ....34 C5
Gray's Yd MHST * W1U 18 B5
Grazebrook Rd STNW/STAM N16 ....59 D4
Great Brownings DUL SE21 ....155 F4
Great Castle St REGST W1B 19 E4
Great Central St CAMTN NW1 ....17 E2
Great Central Wy WBLY HA9 ....68 C2

Great Chapel St *SOHO/CST* W1F 20 A4
Great Chertsey Rd *CHSWK* W4.....111 D4
Great Church La *HMSMTH* W6.........113 D1
Great College St *WEST* SW1P.............44 C2
Great Cross Av *GNWCH* SE10............123 E3
Great Cumberland Ms *MBLAR* W1H.....17 E5
Great Cumberland Pl *MBLAR* W1H.....17 E4
Great Dover St *STHWK* SE1...............48 A2
Great Eastern Rd *SRTFD* E15.............81 D4
Great Eastern St *SDTCH* EC2A............12 C4
Great Eastern Whf *BTSEA* * SW11.....115 E3
Greatfield Av *EHAM* E6...................95 F3
Greatfield Cl *LEW* SE13................140 A2
Greatfields Rd *BARK* IG11...............85 D5
Great George St *STJSPK* SW1H............44 B1
Great Guildford St *STHWK* SE1............35 E4
Great Harry Dr *ELTH/MOT* SE9.........162 A3
Great James St *BMSBY* WC1N............21 E2
Great Marlborough St *SOHO/CST* W1F...19 E5
Great Maze Pond *STHWK* SE1.............36 B4
Great Newport St *LSQ/SEVD* * WC2H...32 C1
Great New St *FLST/FETLN* * EC4A.......22 B4
Greatorex St *WCHPL* E1..................90 A4
Great Ormond St *BMSBY* WC1N..........21 D2
Great Percy St *FSBYW* WC1X...............9 F3
Great Peter St *WEST* SW1P...............44 A3
Great Portland St *GTPST* * W1W.........19 D1
Great Pulteney St *SOHO/CST* W1F.......31 F1
Great Queen St *HOL/ALD* WC2B..........21 D4
Great Russell St *FITZ* W1T...............20 B4
Great St Helen's *HDTCH* EC3A............24 C5
Great St Thomas Apostle *BLKFR* EC4V...35 F1
Great Scotland Yd *WHALL* SW1A..........32 C4
Great Smith St *WEST* SW1P...............44 B2
Great Spilmans *EDUL* SE22..............137 E3
Great Suffolk St *STHWK* SE1.............35 D4
Great Sutton St *FSBYE* EC1V.............23 D1
Great Swan Aly *LOTH* EC2R...............24 A4
Great Titchfield St *GTPST* W1W..........19 D1
Great Tower St *MON* EC3R................36 C1
Great Trinity La *BLKFR* EC4V.............35 F1
Great Turnstile *HHOL* * WC1V............21 F3
Great Western Rd *MV/WKIL* W9.........89 F4
Great West Rd *CHSWK* W4...............110 C2
   HMSMTH W6.........................112 B1
Great West Rd Chiswick *CHSWK* W4...111 F2
Great West Rd Ellesmere Rd
   CHSWK W4...........................110 C2
Great West Rd Hogarth La
   CHSWK W4...........................111 D2
Great Winchester St *OBST* EC2N.........24 B4
Great Windmill St *SOHO/SHAV* W1D....32 A2
Greaves Cl *BARK* IG11....................85 D4
Greaves Cottages *POP/IOD* * E14.......91 E4
Greaves Pl *TOOT* SW17.................151 E4
Grebe Cl *FSTGT* E7.......................81 F2
Greek St *SOHO/SHAV* W1D...............20 B5
The Green *ACT* W3.......................87 E5
   SRTFD E15............................81 F3
   WAN E11...............................64 B1
   WELL DA16............................145 E2
Greenacres *ELTH/MOT* SE9.............144 B4
Green Acres *SCUP* * DA14..............163 F4
Greenacre Sq *BERM/RHTH* * SE16.....103 D3
Green Arbour Ct *STP* * EC4M.............22 C4
Greenaway Gdns *HAMP* NW3............72 B1
Green Bank *WAP* E1W...................102 B2
Greenbay Rd *CHARL* SE7...............125 D3
Greenberry St *STJWD* NW8................4 C2
Green Chain Wk *CHARL* SE7............107 D5
   ELTH/MOT SE9.......................144 B5
Greencoat Pl *WEST* SW1P................43 F4
Greencoat Rw *WEST* SW1P...............43 F3
Greencroft Gdns *KIL/WHAMP* NW6......72 B4
Green Dl *EDUL* SE22....................137 D3
Green Dragon Yd *WCHPL* E1.............90 A4

Greenend Rd *CHSWK* W4.................99 E3
Greenfell Man *DEPT* * SE8.............121 F1
Greenfield Gdns *CRICK* NW2............53 E4
Greenfield Rd *WCHPL* E1.................90 A4
Greengate St *PLSTW* E13.................94 B1
Greenham Cl *STHWK* SE1.................46 A1
Greenhill *HAMP* NW3....................73 D1
   WBLY HA9.............................50 B4
Green Hl *WOOL/PLUM* SE18............125 F1
Greenhill Gv *MNPK* E12..................83 E1
Greenhill Pk *WLSDN* NW10...............69 E5
Greenhill Rd *WLSDN* NW10..............69 E5
Greenhill's Rents *FARR* * EC1M..........22 C2
Greenhills Ter *IS* N1.....................77 D3
Greenhill Wy *WBLY* HA9.................50 B4
Greenhithe Cl *ELTH/MOT* SE9..........145 E5
Greenholm Rd *ELTH/MOT* SE9.........144 B3
Green Hundred Rd *PECK* SE15.........120 A2
Greenhurst Rd *WNWD* SE27...........154 A5
Greenland Ms *DEPT* * SE8.............121 D1
Greenland Pl *CAMTN* * NW1.............74 B5
Greenland Quay *BERM/RHTH* SE16....103 D5
Greenland Rd *CAMTN* NW1..............74 B5
Greenland St *CAMTN* NW1..............74 B5
Green La *ELTH/MOT* SE9...............162 A1
   IL IG1..................................67 D4
   FSBYPK N4............................58 B1
Greenlaw St *WOOL/PLUM* SE18.......108 A4
Greenleaf Cl *BRXS/STRHM* * SW2.....136 A5
Greenleaf Rd *EHAM* E6..................82 C5
Greenman St *IS* N1.......................76 C4
Greenoak Wy *WIM/MER* SW19.........149 D4
Greenock Rd *ACT* W3....................98 B4
Greens Ct *NTGHL* * W11................101 F2
   SOHO/CST W1F.......................32 A1
Greens End *WOOL/PLUM* SE18........108 B5
Greenside Cl *CAT* SE6...................159 D2
Greenside Rd *SHB* W12..................100 A4
Greenslade Rd *BARK* IG11...............85 D4
Greenstead Gdns *PUT/ROE* SW15.....130 A3
Greenstone Ms *WAN* E11.................64 A1
Green St *FSTGT* E7.......................82 B2
   MYFR/PKLN W1K......................29 F1
Greenstreet Hl *NWCR* * SE14...........139 D1
Green Ter *CLKNW* EC1R...................10 B4
Greenvale Rd *ELTH/MOT* SE9...........143 F2
Greenview Cl *ACT* W3....................99 E2
Green Wk *STHWK* SE1....................48 C3
Greenway *CHST* BR7....................162 A5
Green Wy *ELTH/MOT* SE9...............143 D3
Greenway Cl *FSBYPK* N4.................58 C4
Greenway Ct *IL* IG1......................66 A3
Greenwell St *GTPST* W1W................19 D1
Greenwich Church St
   GNWCH * SE10.......................122 C2
Greenwich Crs *EHAM* E6.................95 E4
Greenwich Foot Tnl *POP/IOD* E14.....122 C1
Greenwich High Rd *GNWCH* SE10......122 B3
Greenwich Park St *GNWCH* * SE10.....123 D2
Greenwich Quay *DEPT* SE8.............122 B2
Greenwich South St *GNWCH* SE10......122 B4
Greenwich Vw *POP/IOD* E14...........104 B4
Greenwood Pl *KTTN* NW5................74 B2
Greenwood Rd *HACK* E8...................78 A2
   PLSTW E13............................93 F1
Greenwood Rd *WLSDN* * NW10..........69 D5
Green Yd *FSBYW* WC1X.....................9 F5
Greet St *STHWK* SE1.....................34 B4
Greg Cl *LEY* E10..........................62 C1
Gregor Ms *BKHTH/KID* SE3.............124 A3
Gregory Crs *ELTH/MOT* SE9.............143 D5
Gregory Pl *KENS* W8.....................26 C5
Greig Ter *WALW* SE17...................118 B2
Grenada Rd *CHARL* SE7.................124 C3
Grenade St *POP/IOD* E14................103 F1
Grenadier St *CAN/RD* E16..............108 A2
Grenard Cl *PECK* SE15..................120 A3
Grendon Gdns *WBLY* HA9................50 A4

Grendon St *STJWD* NW8 ....**4** C5
Grenfell Rd *NTGHL* W11 ....**101** D1
Grenfell Wk *NTGHL* W11 ....**101** D1
Grenville Pl *SKENS* SW7 ....**39** E4
Grenville Rd *ARCH* N19 ....**57** E3
Grenville St *BMSBY* WC1N **21** D1
Gresham Gdns *CRICK* NW2 ....**53** E3
Gresham Rd *BRXN/ST* SW9 ....**136** A1
   CAN/RD E16 ....**94** B5
   EHAM E6 ....**95** F1
   WLSDN NW10 ....**69** D2
Gresham St *CITYW* EC2V **23** E4
Gresham Wy *WIM/MER* SW19 ....**150** A3
Gresley Cl *WALTH* E17 ....**61** E1
Gresley Rd *ARCH* N19 ....**56** C3
Gressenhall Rd *WAND/EARL* SW18 ....**131** F4
Gresse St *FITZ* W1T **20** A3
Greswell St *FUL/PGN* SW6 ....**113** D4
Greville Ms *KIL/WHAMP* NW6 ....**72** B5
Greville Pl *KIL/WHAMP* NW6 ....**72** B5
Greville St *HCIRC* EC1N **22** B3
Grey Cl *EFNCH* N2 ....**54** C1
Greycoat Pl *WEST* SW1P **44** A3
Greycoat St *WEST* SW1P **44** A3
Greycot Rd *BECK* BR3 ....**158** A5
Grey Eagle St *WCHPL* E1 ....**25** F2
Greyhound Rd *HMSMTH* W6 ....**113** D2
   WLSDN NW10 ....**88** B2
Greyladies Gdns *GNWCH* SE10 ....**122** C5
Greystead Rd *FSTH* SE23 ....**138** C5
Grierson Rd *FSTH* SE23 ....**139** D5
Griffin Cl *WLSDN* NW10 ....**70** B2
Griffin Manor Wy *THMD* SE28 ....**109** D4
Griffin Rd *WOOL/PLUM* SE18 ....**127** D1
Griggs Ap *IL* IG1 ....**66** C4
Grigg's Pl *STHWK* SE1 ....**49** D3
Griggs Rd *LEY* E10 ....**62** C1
Grimsby Gv *CAN/RD* E16 ....**108** B2
Grimsby St *WCHPL* E1 ....**25** F1
Grimsel Pth *CMBW* SE5 ....**118** B3
Grimshaw Cl *HGT* * N6 ....**56** A2
Grimston Rd *FUL/PGN* SW6 ....**113** F5
Grindal St *STHWK* SE1 ....**46** A1
Grinling Pl *DEPT* SE8 ....**122** A2
Grinstead Rd *DEPT* SE8 ....**121** E1
Grittleton Av *WBLY* HA9 ....**68** B3
Grittleton Rd *MV/WKIL* W9 ....**2** A5
Grocers' Hall Ct *LOTH* * EC2R **24** A5
Groombridge Rd *HOM* E9 ....**79** D4
Groom Crs *WAND/EARL* SW18 ....**133** D5
Groomfield Cl *TOOT* SW17 ....**152** A4
Groom Pl *KTBR* SW1X **42** B2
Grosmont Rd *WOOL/PLUM* SE18 ....**127** F1
Grosse Wy *PUT/ROE* SW15 ....**130** B4
The Grove *FSBYPK* N4 ....**57** F2
   GLDGN NW11 ....**53** E2
   HGT N6 ....**56** A3
Grosvenor Av *HBRY* N5 ....**76** C2
   MORT/ESHN SW14 ....**129** E1
Grosvenor Br *VX/NE* SW8 ....**116** B2
Grosvenor Cottages *KTBR* SW1X **42** A4
Grosvenor Crs *KTBR* SW1X **42** B1
Grosvenor Crescent Ms *KTBR* SW1X **42** A1
Grosvenor Gdns *BGVA* SW1W **42** C3
   CRICK NW2 ....**70** C3
   GLDGN NW11 ....**53** F1
   MORT/ESHN SW14 ....**129** E1
Grosvenor Gardens Ms East
   BGVA * SW1W **43** D2
Grosvenor Gardens Ms North
   BGVA SW1W **42** C3
Grosvenor Ga *BAY/PAD* W2 ....**29** F2
Grosvenor HI *MYFR/PKLN* W1K **30** C1
Grosvenor Pde *ACT* * W3 ....**98** A2
Grosvenor Pk *CMBW* SE5 ....**118** C3
Grosvenor Pl *KTBR* SW1X **30** B5
Grosvenor Rd *CHSWK* W4 ....**110** C1
   EHAM E6 ....**83** D5
   FSTGT E7 ....**82** D3

IL IG1 ....**66** C5
   LEY E10 ....**62** C3
   PIM SW1V **116** C2
Grosvenor Sq *MYFR/PKLN* W1K **30** B1
Grosvenor St *MYFR/PKLN* W1K **30** B1
Grosvenor Ter *CMBW* SE5 ....**118** C3
Grosvenor Wy *CLPT* E5 ....**60** C4
Grosvenor Wharf Rd *POP/IOD* E14 ....**105** D5
Grote's Buildings *BKHTH/KID* SE3 ....**123** E5
Grote's Pl *BKHTH/KID* SE3 ....**123** E5
Groton Rd *WAND/EARL* SW18 ....**150** B2
Grotto Ct *STHWK* * SE1 ....**35** E5
Grotto Pas *MHST* W1U **18** A2
Grove Cl *FSTH* SE23 ....**157** D1
Grove Cottages *CHSWK* * W4 ....**111** E2
Grove Crescent Rd *SRTFD* E15 ....**81** D3
Grovedale Rd *ARCH* N19 ....**57** D4
Grove Dwellings *WCHPL* * E1 ....**90** C4
Grove End *KTTN* NW5 ....**74** B1
Grove End Rd *STJWD* NW8 ....**4** A2
Grove Gdns *STJWD* NW8 ....**5** D4
Grove Green Rd *LEY* E10 ....**62** C5
Grove Hill Rd *CMBW* SE5 ....**137** E1
Groveland Ct *STP* EC4M **23** F5
Grovelands Cl *CMBW* SE5 ....**119** E5
Grovelands Rd *SEVS/STOTM* N15 ....**60** A1
Grove La *CMBW* SE5 ....**119** D4
Grove Market Pl *ELTH/MOT* * SE9 ....**143** F4
Grove Ms *HMSMTH* W6 ....**100** C4
Grove Pk *CMBW* SE5 ....**119** E5
Grove Park Av *CHSWK* W4 ....**110** C3
Grove Park Gdns *CHSWK* W4 ....**110** B3
Grove Park Rd *CHSWK* W4 ....**110** B3
   ELTH/MOT SE9 ....**161** E2
Grove Park Ter *CHSWK* W4 ....**110** B3
Grove Pl *ACT* W3 ....**98** C2
   BAL SW12 ....**134** B4
   HAMP NW3 ....**55** D5
Grove Rd *ACT* W3 ....**98** C2
   BARN SW13 ....**111** F5
   BOW E3 ....**91** E1
   CRICK NW2 ....**70** C3
   HOM E9 ....**79** D5
   WAN E11 ....**63** F2
Groveside Cl *ACT* W3 ....**86** A5
Grove St *BERM/RHTH* SE16 ....**103** F5
Grove Ter *KTTN* NW5 ....**56** A5
Grove V *EDUL* SE22 ....**137** E2
Groveway *BRXN/ST* SW9 ....**117** F4
Grove Wy *WBLY* HA9 ....**68** C2
Grummant Rd *PECK* SE15 ....**119** F4
Grundy St *POP/IOD* E14 ....**92** B5
Gubyon Av *HNHL* SE24 ....**136** B3
Guernsey Gv *HNHL* SE24 ....**136** C5
Guernsey Rd *IS* N1 ....**76** C3
   WAN E11 ....**63** D3
Guibal Rd *LEE/GVPK* SE12 ....**160** B1
Guildford Gv *GNWCH* SE10 ....**122** B4
Guildford Rd *EHAM* E6 ....**95** E5
   GDMY/SEVK IG3 ....**67** E4
   VX/NE SW8 ....**117** E4
Guildhall Buildings *CITYW* EC2V **23** F4
Guildhall Yd *CITYW* EC2V **23** F4
Guildhouse St *PIM* SW1V **43** E5
Guild Rd *CHARL* SE7 ....**125** D1
Guilford Pl *BMSBY* WC1N **21** E1
Guilford St *BMSBY* WC1N **21** E1
Guilsborough Cl *WLSDN* NW10 ....**69** E4
Guinness Cl *HOM* E9 ....**79** E4
Guinness Sq *STHWK* SE1 ....**48** C3
Guinness Trust Est *CHEL* SW3 ....**41** E5
   SRTFD * E15 ....**81** F5
   STNW/STAM * N16 ....**59** F3
Guion Rd *FUL/PGN* SW6 ....**113** F5
Gulland Wk *IS* * N1 ....**76** C3
Gulliver Rd *BFN/LL* DA15 ....**163** D2
Gulliver St *BERM/RHTH* SE16 ....**103** F4
Gunmakers La *HOM* E9 ....**79** E5

Gunnell Cl SYD * SE26 ....156 A4
Gunner La WOOL/PLUM SE18...126 A1
Gunnersbury Av ACT W3 ....98 A4
Gunnersbury Av (North Circular Rd)
ACT W3..98 A4
Gunnersbury Cl CHSWK * W4 .....110 B1
Gunnersbury Crs ACT W3 ....98 A3
Gunnersbury Gdns ACT W3 ....98 A3
Gunnersbury La ACT W3 ....98 A3
Gunners Rd WAND/EARL SW18...151 D2
Gunning St WOOL/PLUM SE18......109 E5
Gunstor Rd STNW/STAM * N16 .....77 E1
Gun St WCHPL E1 ....25 E3
Gunter Gv WBPTN SW10..............114 C2
Gunterstone Rd WKENS W14........113 E1
Gunthorpe St WCHPL E1.................25 F3
Gunton Rd CLPT E5 ....60 B5
Gunwhale Cl BERM/RHTH SE16....103 D2
Gurdon Rd CHARL SE7..................124 A1
Gurney Cl BARK IG11 ....84 B3
    SRTFD E15 ....81 E2
Gurney Rd FUL/PGN SW6 ....132 C1
    SRTFD E15 ....81 E2
Guthrie St CHEL SW3....................115 E1
Gutter La CITYW EC2V.....................23 E4
Guy Barnett Gv BKHTH/KID SE3 ...142 A4
Guyscliff Rd LEW SE13.................140 C3
Guy St STHWK SE1..........................36 B5
Gwalior Rd PUT/ROE SW15..........131 D2
Gwendolen Av PUT/ROE SW15 ....131 D3
Gwendoline Av PLSTW E13.............82 B5
Gwendwr Rd WKENS W14 ....113 E1
Gwyn Cl FUL/PGN SW6.................132 C1
Gwynne Av BTSEA SW11..............115 D5
Gwynne Whf CHSWK W4 ....111 F2
Gylcote Cl HNHL SE24..................137 D2
Gyllyngdune Gdns GDMY/SEVK IG3 ...67 F5

H

Haarlem Rd HMSMTH W6.............101 D4
Haberdasher Pl IS N1 ....12 B3
Haberdasher St IS N1 ....12 B3
Hackford Rd BRXN/ST SW9...........117 F4
Hackford Wk BRXN/ST SW9...........117 F4
Hackney Gv HACK E8........................78 B3
Hackney Rd BETH E2 ....13 E5
Hadden Rd THMD SE28..................109 E4
Haddington Rd BMLY BR1.............159 D3
Haddo St GNWCH SE10 ....122 B2
Hadleigh Cl WCHPL E1.....................90 C3
Hadleigh St BETH E2........................90 C3
Hadley Gdns CHSWK W4 ....111 D1
Hadley St KTTN NW5........................74 B3
Hadrian Est BETH * E2......................90 A2
Hadrian St GNWCH SE10...............123 E1
Hadyn Park Rd SHB W12 ....100 A3
Hafer Rd BTSEA SW11 ....133 F2
Hafton Rd CAT SE6.........................159 E1
Haggerston Rd HACK E8..................77 F4
Hague St BETH E2 ....90 A2
Ha-Ha Rd WOOL/PLUM SE18........125 F2
Haig Rd East PLSTW E13 ....94 C2
Haig Rd West PLSTW E13 ....94 C2
Hailsham Av BRXS/STRHM SW2.....153 F2
Haimo Rd ELTH/MOT SE9 ....143 D3
Hainault Buildings LEY * E10 ....62 C3
Hainault Rd WAN E11.......................62 C3
Hainault St ELTH/MOT SE9............162 B1
    IL IG1..66 B4
Hainford Cl PECK SE15..................139 D2
Haining Cl CHSWK W4...................110 A1
Hainthorpe Rd WNWD SE27..........154 B3
Hainton Cl WCHPL E1......................90 B5
Halcomb St IS N1.............................77 F5
Halcrow St WCHPL * E1...................90 B4

Haldane Pl WAND/EARL SW18.......150 B1
Haldane Rd EHAM E6........................95 D2
    FUL/PGN SW6 ....113 F3
Haldon Rd WAND/EARL SW18.......131 F4
Hale Gdns ACT W3 ....98 A2
Hale Rd EHAM E6.............................95 E3
Hales St DEPT SE8.........................122 A3
Hale St POP/IOD E14 ....104 B1
Halesworth Rd LEW SE13..............140 B1
Haley Rd HDN NW4...........................52 C1
Half Moon Crs IS N1...........................9 F1
Half Moon La HNHL SE24...............136 C4
Half Moon Pas WCHPL E1................25 F5
Half Moon St MYFR/PICC W1J........31 D3
Halford Rd FUL/PGN SW6 ....114 A2
Halfway St BFN/LL DA15.................163 E1
Haliday Wk IS N1...............................77 D3
Halifax St SYD SE26.......................156 C5
Halkin Ar KTBR SW1X 42 A2
Halkin Ms KTBR * SW1X...................42 A2
Halkin Pl KTBR SW1X.......................42 A2
Halkin St KTBR SW1X.......................42 B1
The Hall BKHTH/KID SE3 ....142 A1
Hallam Cl CHST BR7.......................161 F5
Hallam Ms REGST W1B....................19 D2
Hallam St GTPST W1W 19 D2
Hall Dr SYD SE26...........................156 C5
Halley Rd FSTGT E7.........................82 C3
Halley St POP/IOD E14 ....91 E4
Hallfield Est BAY/PAD W2.................15 D5
Hall Ga STJWD NW8 ....3 F4
Halliford St IS N1 ....76 C4
Halliwell Rd BRXS/STRHM SW2.....135 F4
Hall Oak Wk KIL/WHAMP NW6 ....71 F3
Hall Pl BAY/PAD W2 ....16 A1
Hall Rd EHAM E6.............................83 F5
    MV/WKIL W9 ....3 F4
    WAN E11......................................81 D1
Hall St FSBYE EC1V.........................11 D3
Hallsville Rd CAN/RD E16................93 F5
Hall Vw ELTH/MOT SE9..................161 D2
Hallywell Crs EHAM E6.....................95 F4
Halons Rd ELTH/MOT SE9..............144 A5
Halpin Pl WALW SE17.......................48 B5
Halsbrook Rd BKHTH/KID SE3 ......142 C1
Halsbury Rd SHB W12....................100 B2
Halsey St CHEL SW3.........................41 E4
Halsham Crs BARK IG11....................85 F3
Halsmere Rd CMBW SE5................118 B4
Halstow Rd GNWCH SE10...............124 A1
    WLSDN NW10 ....89 D2
Halton Cross St IS * N1......................76 B3
Halton Rd IS N1................................76 B4
Hambalt Rd CLAP SW4...................134 C3
Hambledon Av WALW * SE17.........119 D2
Hambledon Pl DUL SE21................155 F1
Hambledon Rd WAND/EARL SW18..131 F5
Hambledown Rd ELTH/MOT * SE9 ..145 D5
Hamble St FUL/PGN SW6 ....132 B1
Hameway EHAM E6...........................96 A3
Hamfrith Rd SRTFD E15 ....81 F3
Hamilton Cl BERM/RHTH SE16......103 E3
    STJWD NW8 ....4 A4
Hamilton Gdns STJWD NW8...............3 F3
Hamilton Pk HBRY N5 ....76 B1
Hamilton Pk West HBRY N5..............76 B1
Hamilton Rd MYFR/PKLN W1K.........30 A4
Hamilton Rd CHSWK W4 ....99 E4
    GLDGN NW11 ....53 D2
    IL IG1...84 B1
    SRTFD E15 ....93 E2
    WLSDN NW10 ....70 A2
    WNWD SE27................................155 D4
Hamilton St DEPT SE8....................122 A2
Hamilton Ter STJWD NW8...................3 E2
Hamlea Cl BKHTH/KID SE3 ....142 A3
The Hamlet CMBW SE5..................137 D1
Hamlet Cl LEW SE13.......................141 E2

Hamlet Gdns *HMSMTH* W6 ....**100** A5
Hamlet Sq *CRICK* NW2 ....**53** E5
Hamlets Wy *BOW* E3 ....**91** F5
Hamlet Wy *STHWK* SE1 ....**48** B1
Hammersmith Br *HMSMTH* W6 ....**112** B1
Hammersmith Bridge Rd
  BARN SW13 ....**112** B2
Hammersmith Broadway
  HMSMTH W6 ....**100** C5
Hammersmith Emb *BARN* * SW13 ......**112** C1
Hammersmith F/O *HMSMTH* W6 ....**112** C1
Hammersmith Gv *HMSMTH* W6 ....**100** C4
Hammersmith Rd *HMSMTH* W6 ....**100** C5
Hammersmith Ter *HMSMTH* * W6 ....**112** A1
Hammett St *TWRH* EC3N **37** E1
Hammond St *KTTN* NW5 ....**74** C3
Hamond Sq *IS* N1 ....**12** C1
Ham Park Rd *SRTFD* E15 ....**81** F4
Hampden Cl *CAMTN* NW1 ....**8** B2
Hampden Gurney St *MBLAR* W1H **17** E5
Hampden Rd *ARCH* N19 ....**57** D4
Hampshire Hog La *HMSMTH* * W6 ....**100** B5
Hampshire St *KTTN* * NW5 ....**75** D3
Hampson Wy *VX/NE* SW8 ....**117** F4
Hampstead Gdns *GLDGN* NW11 ....**54** A1
Hampstead Ga *HAMP* NW3 ....**72** C2
Hampstead Gn *HAMP* NW3 ....**73** E2
Hampstead Gv *HAMP* NW3 ....**72** C1
Hampstead Hill Gdns *HAMP* NW3 ....**73** E1
Hampstead La *HGT* N6 ....**55** F2
Hampstead Rd *CAMTN* NW1 ....**7** E2
Hampstead Sq *HAMP* NW3 ....**54** C5
Hampstead Wy *GLDGN* NW11 ....**54** B2
Hampton Cl *IS* N1 ....**76** B3
Hampton St *FSTGT* E7 ....**82** B2
  IL IG1 ....**84** C1
  WAN E11 ....**63** D3
Hampton St *WALW* SE17 ....**47** D5
Ham Shades Cl *BFN/LL* DA15 ....**163** F3
Ham Yd *SOHO/SHAV* * W1D **32** A1
Hanameel St *CAN/RD* E16 ....**106** A2
Hanbury Rd *ACT* W3 ....**98** B3
Hanbury St *WCHPL* E1 ....**90** A4
Hancock Rd *BOW* E3 ....**92** C2
Handa Wk *IS* N1 ....**76** C3
Hand Ct *HHOL* WC1V **21** F3
Handel Pl *WLSDN* NW10 ....**69** D3
Handel St *BMSBY* WC1N **8** C5
Handen Rd *LEW* SE13 ....**141** E3
Handforth Rd *BRXN/ST* SW9 ....**118** A3
  IL IG1 ....**66** B5
Handley Gv *CRICK* NW2 ....**53** D5
Handley Rd *HOM* E9 ....**78** C4
Handtrough Wy *BARK* IG11 ....**96** B1
Hanford Row *WAND/EARL* SW18 ....**150** A1
Hangar View Wy *ACT* W3 ....**86** A3
Hanger Gn *EA* W5 ....**86** B2
Hankey Pl *STHWK* SE1 ....**48** B1
Hanley Gdns *FSBYPK* N4 ....**57** E3
Hanley Rd *FSBYPK* N4 ....**57** E3
Hannah Cl *WLSDN* * NW10 ....**68** C1
Hannah Mary Wy *STHWK* * SE1 ....**102** A5
Hannan Cl *WLSDN* NW10 ....**68** C1
Hannay La *ARCH* N19 ....**57** D2
Hannell Rd *FUL/PGN* SW6 ....**113** E3
Hannen Rd *WNWD* * SE27 ....**154** B3
Hannibal Rd *WCHPL* E1 ....**90** C4
Hannington Rd *CLAP* SW4 ....**134** B1
Hanover Av *CAN/RD* E16 ....**106** A2
Hanover Cl *RCH/KEW* TW9 ....**110** A3
Hanover Dr *CHST* BR7 ....**162** C4
Hanover Gdns *LBTH* SE11 ....**118** A2
Hanover Pk *PECK* SE15 ....**120** A4
Hanover Pl *COVGDN* WC2E **21** D5
Hanover Rd *WLSDN* NW10 ....**70** C4
Hanover Sq *CONDST* W1S **19** D5
Hanover Steps *BAY/PAD* * W2 ....**17** D5

Hanover St *CONDST* W1S **19** D5
Hanover Ter *CAMTN* NW1 ....**5** D4
Hanover Terrace Ms *CAMTN* NW1 ....**5** D4
Hanover Yd *IS* * N1 ....**11** D1
Hansard Ms *WKENS* W14 ....**101** D3
Hans Crs *CHEL* SW3 ....**41** E2
Hansler Rd *EDUL* SE22 ....**137** F3
Hanson Cl *BAL* SW12 ....**134** B5
  MORT/ESHN SW14 ....**128** C1
Hanson St *GTPST* W1W **19** E2
Hans Pl *KTBR* SW1X **41** E2
Hans Rd *CHEL* SW3 ....**41** E2
Hans St *KTBR* SW1X **41** F3
Hanway Pl *FITZ* W1T **20** A4
Hanway St *FITZ* W1T **20** A4
Harben Pde *KIL/WHAMP* * NW6 ....**73** D4
Harben Rd *KIL/WHAMP* NW6 ....**72** C4
Harberson Rd *BAL* SW12 ....**152** B1
  SRTFD E15 ....**81** F5
Harberton Rd *ARCH* N19 ....**56** C3
Harbet Rd *BAY/PAD* W2 ....**16** B3
Harbinger Rd *POP/IOD* E14 ....**104** B5
Harbledown Rd *FUL/PGN* SW6 ....**114** A4
Harbord Cl *CMBW* SE5 ....**119** D5
Harbord St *FUL/PGN* SW6 ....**113** D4
Harborough Av *BFN/LL* DA15 ....**145** E5
Harborough Rd *STRHM/NOR* SW16 ......**153** F4
Harbour Av *WBPTN* SW10 ....**114** C4
Harbour Rd *CMBW* SE5 ....**136** C1
Harbour Yd *WBPTN* * SW10 ....**114** C4
Harbridge Av *PUT/ROE* SW15 ....**129** F5
Harbut Rd *BTSEA* SW11 ....**133** D2
Harcombe Rd *STNW/STAM* N16 ....**59** E5
Harcourt Av *MNPK* E12 ....**83** F1
Harcourt Buildings *EMB* * EC4Y **34** A1
Harcourt Rd *BROCKY* SE4 ....**139** F2
  SRTFD E15 ....**93** F1
Harcourt St *CAMTN* NW1 ....**17** D3
Harcourt Ter *WBPTN* SW10 ....**114** B1
Hardel Wk *BRXS/STRHM* SW2 ....**136** A5
Hardens Manorway
  WOOL/PLUM SE18 ....**107** D4
Harders Rd *PECK* SE15 ....**120** B5
Hardess St *HNHL* SE24 ....**136** C1
Hardie Cl *WLSDN* NW10 ....**69** D2
Harding Cl *WALW* SE17 ....**118** C2
Hardinge Rd *WLSDN* NW10 ....**70** C5
Hardinge St *WCHPL* E1 ....**90** C5
  WOOL/PLUM SE18 ....**124** B4
Hardman Rd *CHARL* SE7 ....**124** B1
Hardwicke Ms *FSBYW* * WC1X **9** F4
Hardwicke Rd *CHSWK* W4 ....**98** C5
Hardwicke St *BARK* IG11 ....**84** C5
Hardwick St *CLKNW* EC1R **10** B4
Hardwick's Wy *WAND/EARL* SW18 ....**132** A3
Hardwidge St *STHWK* SE1 ....**36** C5
Hardy Av *CAN/RD* E16 ....**106** A2
Hardy Cl *BERM/RHTH* SE16 ....**103** D3
Hardy Cottages *GNWCH* * SE10 ....**123** D2
Hardy Rd *BKHTH/KID* SE3 ....**123** F2
Harebell Dr *EHAM* E6 ....**96** A4
Hare & Billet Rd *BKHTH/KID* SE3 ....**123** D4
Hare Ct *EMB* * EC4Y **22** A5
Harecourt Rd *IS* N1 ....**76** C3
Haredale Rd *HNHL* SE24 ....**136** C2
Haredon Cl *FSTH* SE23 ....**138** C5
Harefield Ms *BROCKY* SE4 ....**139** F1
Harefield Rd *BROCKY* SE4 ....**139** F1
Hare Marsh *BETH* E2 ....**90** A3
Hare Rw *BETH* E2 ....**90** B1
Hare St *WOOL/PLUM* SE18 ....**108** A4
Hare Wk *IS* N1 ....**13** D2
Harewood Av *CAMTN* NW1 ....**5** D5
Harewood Pl *CONDST* W1S **19** D5
Harewood Rw *CAMTN* NW1 ....**17** D2
Harfield Gdns *CMBW* * SE5 ....**137** E1
Harford St *WCHPL* E1 ....**91** E3
Hargood Rd *BKHTH/KID* SE3 ....**124** C4

Hargrave Pk *KTTN* NW5 ....56 C4
Hargrave Rd *ARCH* N19 ....56 C5
Hargwyne St *BRXN/ST* SW9 ....135 F1
Haringey Pk *CEND/HSY/T* N8 ....57 E1
Harland Av *BFN/LL* DA15 ....163 D3
Harland Rd *LEE/GVPK* SE12 ....160 A1
Harlescott Rd *PECK* SE15 ....139 D2
Harlesden Gdns *WLSDN* NW10 .....69 F5
Harlesden Rd *WLSDN* NW10 ....70 A4
Harleyford Rd *LBTH* SE11 ....117 F2
Harley Gdns *WBPTN* SW10 ....114 C1
Harley Gv *BOW* E3 ....91 F2
Harley Pl *CAVSQ/HST* W1G 18 C3
Harley Rd *HAMP* NW3 ....73 D4
  WLSDN NW10 ....87 E1
Harley St *CAVSQ/HST* W1G 18 C3
Harley Vls *WLSDN* * NW10 ....87 E1
Harlinger St *WOOL/PLUM* SE18 ...107 E4
Harman Cl *CRICK* NW2 ....53 E5
  STHWK * SE1 ....120 A1
Harman Dr *BFN/LL* DA15 ....145 F4
  CRICK NW2 ....53 E5
Harmood Gv *CAMTN* NW1 ....74 B4
Harmood St *CAMTN* NW1 ....74 B3
Harmsworth Ms *STHWK* SE1 ....46 B3
Harmsworth St *WALW* SE17 ....118 B1
Harold Rd *PLSTW* E13 ....82 B5
  WAN E11 ....63 E3
  WLSDN NW10 ....87 D2
Harp Cross La *MON* EC3R 36 C2
Harpenden Rd *MNPK* E12 ....64 C4
  WNWD SE27 ....154 B2
Harper Rd *EHAM* E6 ....95 F5
  STHWK SE1 ....47 F2
Harp Island Cl *WLSDN* NW10 ....51 D4
Harpley Sq *WCHPL* E1 ....90 C3
Harpour Rd *BARK* IG11 ....84 C3
Harpsden St *BTSEA* SW11 ....116 A4
Harpur St *BMSBY* WC1N 21 E2
Harraden Rd *BKHTH/KID* SE3 ......124 C4
Harrier Ms *THMD* SE28 ....109 D3
Harrier Wy *EHAM* E6 ....95 F4
Harriet Cl *BRXS/STRHM* SW2 ......136 A5
  HACK E8 ....78 A5
Harriet St *KTBR* SW1X 41 F1
Harriet Wk *KTBR* SW1X 41 F1
Harrington Cl *WLSDN* NW10 ....51 D5
Harrington Ct *MV/WKIL* * W9 ....89 F2
Harrington Gdns *SKENS* SW7 ....39 E5
Harrington Hl *CLPT* E5 ....60 B3
Harrington Rd *SKENS* SW7 ....40 A4
  WAN E11 ....63 E3
Harrington Sq *CAMTN* NW1 ....7 E1
Harrington St *CAMTN* NW1 ....7 E2
Harrington Wy *WOOL/PLUM* SE18 ..107 D4
Harriott Cl *GNWCH* SE10 ....105 F5
Harrison Rd *STPAN* WC1H 9 D4
  WALTH E17 ....61 F2
Harrison St *CMBW* SE5 ....119 D3
Harrowgate Ho *HOM* E9 ....79 E3
Harroway Rd *BTSEA* SW11 ....115 D5
Harrowby St *MBLAR* W1H 17 D4
Harrowgate Rd *HOM* E9 ....79 E3
Harrow Gn *WAN* E11 ....63 E5
Harrow La *POP/IOD* E14 ....104 C1
Harrow Pl *WCHPL* E1 ....25 D4
Harrow Rd *BARK* IG11 ....85 E5
  EHAM * E6 ....83 E6
  IL IG1 ....84 C1
  WAN E11 ....63 F5
  WBLY HA9 ....68 B3
  WLSDN NW10 ....88 B2
Harrow Rd F/O *BAY/PAD* W2 ....16 B3
Harrow St *CAMTN* * NW1 ....17 D2
Hartfield Ter *BOW* E3 ....92 A1
Hart Gv *ACT* W3 ....98 A2
Hartham Cl *HOLWY* N7 ....75 E2
Hartham Rd *HOLWY* N7 ....75 E2
Harting Rd *ELTH/MOT* SE9 ....161 E4

Hartington Rd *CAN/RD* E16 ....94 B5
  CHSWK W4 ....110 B3
  VX/NE SW8 ....117 E4
  WALTH E17 ....61 E1
Hartismere Rd *FUL/PGN* SW6 .....113 F3
Hartlake Rd *HOM* E9 ....79 D3
Hartland Rd *CAMTN* * NW1 ....74 B4
  KIL/WHAMP NW6 ....89 F1
  SRTFD E15 ....81 F4
Hartland Rd Arches *CAMTN* * NW1 ..74 A4
Hartley Av *EHAM* E6 ....83 E5
Hartley Rd *WAN* E11 ....63 F3
Hartley St *BETH* E2 ....90 C2
Hartmann Rd *CAN/RD* E16 ....107 E2
Hartnoll St *HOLWY* N7 ....75 F2
Harton St *DEPT* SE8 ....122 A4
Hartshorn Gdns *EHAM* E6 ....96 A3
Harts La *BARK* IG11 ....84 B3
  NWCR SE14 ....121 E3
Hartsmead Rd *ELTH/MOT* SE9 ....161 F2
Hart St *MON* EC3R 37 D1
Hartswood Gdns *SHB* * W12 ....99 F4
Hartswood Rd *SHB* W12 ....99 F3
Hartsworth Cl *PLSTW* E13 ....93 F1
Hartville Rd *WOOL/PLUM* SE18 ...109 E5
Hartwell St *HACK* E8 ....77 F3
Harvard Hl *CHSWK* W4 ....110 B1
Harvard Rd *CHSWK* W4 ....110 B1
  LEW SE13 ....140 C3
Harvey Gdns *CHARL* SE7 ....124 C1
Harvey Rd *CMBW* SE5 ....119 D4
  IL IG1 ....84 B2
  WAN E11 ....63 E3
Harvey St *IS* N1 ....77 D5
Harvington Wk *HACK* * E8 ....78 A4
Harvist Rd *KIL/WHAMP* NW6 ....89 E1
Harwood Ms *FUL/PGN* SW6 ....114 B3
Harwood Rd *FUL/PGN* SW6 ....114 A3
Harwood Ter *FUL/PGN* SW6 ....114 B4
Hascombe Ter *CMBW* * SE5 ....119 D5
Haseley End *FSTH* * SE23 ....138 C5
Haselrigge Rd *CLAP* SW4 ....135 D2
Haseltine Rd *SYD* SE26 ....157 F4
Hasker St *CHEL* SW3 ....41 D4
Haslam Cl *IS* N1 ....76 A4
Haslam St *PECK* SE15 ....119 E4
Haslemere Av *HDN* NW4 ....53 D1
  WAND/EARL SW18 ....150 B2
Haslemere Rd *CEND/HSY/T* N8 .....57 E2
  GDMY/SEVK IG3 ....67 F4
Hassard St *BETH* E2 ....13 F2
Hassendean Rd *BKHTH/KID* SE3 ..124 B2
Hassett Rd *HOM* E9 ....79 D3
Hassocks Cl *SYD* SE26 ....156 B3
Hassop Rd *CRICK* NW2 ....71 D1
Hasted Rd *CHARL* SE7 ....125 D1
Hastings Cl *PECK* * SE15 ....120 A3
Hastings St *STPAN* WC1H 8 C4
Hatcham Park Ms *NWCR* SE14 ....121 D4
Hatcham Park Rd *NWCR* SE14 .....121 D4
Hatcham Rd *PECK* SE15 ....120 C2
Hatchard Rd *ARCH* N19 ....57 D4
Hatchers Ms *STHWK* SE1 ....49 D1
Hatcliffe Cl *BKHTH/KID* SE3 ....141 F1
Hatcliffe St *GNWCH* SE10 ....123 F1
Hatfield Ct *BKHTH/KID* * SE3 ....124 A3
Hatfield Rd *CHSWK* W4 ....99 D3
  SRTFD E15 ....81 E4
Hatfields *STHWK* SE1 ....34 B3
Hathaway Crs *MNPK* E12 ....83 F3
Hatherley Gdns *CEND/HSY/T* N8 ...57 E1
  EHAM E6 ....95 D2
Hatherley Gv *BAY/PAD* W2 ....14 C4
Hatherley St *WEST* SW1P 43 F5
Hathern Gdns *ELTH/MOT* SE9 .....162 A4
Hathorne Cl *PECK* SE15 ....120 B5
Hathorne Ter *ARCH* * N19 ....57 D3
Hathway St *PECK* SE15 ....120 C5

Hatley Rd *HOLWY* N7 ....57 F4
Hat & Mitre Ct *FARR* EC1M 23 D1
Hatteraick St *BERM/RHTH* SE16 ....102 C3
Hatton Cl *WOOL/PLUM* SE18 ....127 D3
Hatton Gdn *CLKNW* EC1R 22 B1
Hatton Pl *HCIRC* EC1N 22 B1
Hatton Rw *STJWD* * NW8 ....16 B1
Hatton St *STJWD* NW8 ....16 B1
Hatton Wall *HCIRC* EC1N 22 A2
Haunch of Venison Yd
    MYFR/PKLN W1S 18 C5
Havana Rd *WIM/MER* SW19 ....150 A5
Havannah St *POP/IOD* E14 ....104 A3
Havelock Cl *SHB* * W12 ....100 B1
Havelock Rd *WIM/MER* SW19 ....150 C5
Havelock St *IL* IG1 ....66 B4
    IS N1 ....75 E5
Havelock Ter *VX/NE* SW8 ....116 B3
Havelock Wk *FSTH* SE23 ....156 C1
The Haven *RCH/KEW* TW9 ....128 A1
Haven Cl *ELTH/MOT* SE9 ....161 F3
    WIM/MER SW19 ....149 D3
Haven St *CAMTN* NW1 ....74 B4
Havenwood *WBLY* HA9 ....50 B5
Haverfield Gdns *RCH/KEW* TW9 ....110 A3
Haverfield Rd *BOW* E3 ....91 D2
Haverhill Rd *BAL* SW12 ....152 C1
Havering St *WCHPL* E1 ....91 D5
Haverstock Hl *HAMP* NW3 ....73 E3
Haverstock Pl *IS* N1 ....10 B2
Haverstock Rd *KTTN* NW5 ....74 A2
Haverstock St *IS* N1 ....11 D1
Havil St *CMBW* SE5 ....119 E4
Hawarden Gv *HNHL* SE24 ....136 C5
Hawarden Hl *CRICK* NW2 ....52 A5
Hawbridge Rd *WAN* E11 ....63 D3
Hawes St *IS* N1 ....76 B4
Hawgood St *BOW* E3 ....92 A4
Hawke Rd *BERM/RHTH* * SE16 ....103 D3
Hawkesbury Rd *PUT/ROE* SW15 ....130 B3
Hawkesfield Rd *FSTH* SE23 ....157 E2
Hawkins Wy *CAT* SE6 ....158 A5
Hawkley Gdns *WNWD* SE27 ....154 B2
Hawkshead Rd *CHSWK* W4 ....99 E4
    WLSDN * NW10 ....69 F4
Hawkslade Rd *PECK* SE15 ....139 D3
Hawksley Rd *STNW/STAM* N16 ....59 D5
Hawks Ms *GNWCH* * SE10 ....122 C3
Hawksmoor Cl *EHAM* E6 ....95 E5
    WOOL/PLUM SE18 ....127 E1
Hawksmoor Ms *WCHPL* E1 ....102 B1
Hawksmoor St *HMSMTH* W6 ....113 D2
Hawkstone Rd *BERM/RHTH* SE16 ....102 C5
Hawkwell Wk *IS* * N1 ....76 C5
Hawkwood Mt *CLPT* E5 ....60 B3
Hawley Crs *CAMTN* NW1 ....74 B4
Hawley Ms *CAMTN* NW1 ....74 B4
Hawley Rd *CAMTN* NW1 ....74 B4
Hawley St *CAMTN* NW1 ....74 B4
Hawstead Rd *LEW* SE13 ....140 B4
Hawthorne Av *HOM* E9 ....79 F5
Hawthorne Cl *IS* N1 ....77 E3
Hawthorne Gv *CDALE/KGS* NW9 ....50 C2
Hawthorn Rd *WLSDN* NW10 ....70 A4
Hawthorn Ter *BFN/LL* DA15 ....145 F4
Hawthorn Wk *NKENS* W10 ....89 E3
Hawtrey Rd *HAMP* NW3 ....73 E4
Hay Cl *SRTFD* E15 ....81 E4
Haycroft Gdns *WLSDN* NW10 ....70 A5
Haycroft Rd *BRXS/STRHM* SW2 ....135 E3
Hay Currie St *POP/IOD* E14 ....92 B3
Hayday Rd *CAN/RD* E16 ....94 A3
Hayden's Pl *NTGHL* W11 ....89 F5
Haydon Park Rd *WIM/MER* SW19 ....150 A5
Haydon's Rd *WIM/MER* SW19 ....150 B5
Haydon St *TWRH* EC3N 37 E1
Haydon Wk *WCHPL* E1 ....25 E5
Haydon Wy *BTSEA* SW11 ....132 C2
Hayes Pl *CAMTN* NW1 ....17 D1

Hayfield Pas *WCHPL* E1 ....90 C3
Haygarth Pl *WIM/MER* SW19 ....149 D5
Hay Hl *MYFR/PICC* W1J 31 D2
Hayles St *LBTH* SE11 ....46 C4
Hayling Cl *STNW/STAM* N16 ....77 E2
Haymarket *STJS* SW1Y 32 A2
Haymerle Rd *STHWK* SE1 ....120 A2
Haynes Cl *BKHTH/KID* SE3 ....141 E1
Hayne St *STBT* EC1A 23 D2
Hays La *STHWK* SE1 ....36 C3
Hay's Ms *MYFR/PICC* W1J 30 C2
Hay St *BETH* E2 ....78 A5
Hayter Rd *BRXS/STRHM* SW2 ....135 E3
Hayton Cl *HACK* E8 ....77 F3
Hayward Gdns *PUT/ROE* SW15 ....130 C4
Hayward's Pl *CLKNW* * EC1R 22 C1
Hazelbank Rd *CAT* SE6 ....159 D2
Hazelbourne Rd *BAL* SW12 ....134 B4
Hazeldean Rd *WLSDN* NW10 ....69 D4
Hazeldon Rd *BROCKY* SE4 ....139 E3
Hazel Gv *SYD* SE26 ....157 D4
Hazelhurst Rd *TOOT* SW17 ....150 C4
Hazellville Rd *ARCH* N19 ....57 D2
Hazelmere Rd *KIL/WHAMP* NW6 ....71 F5
Hazel Rd *SRTFD* * E15 ....81 E2
    WLSDN NW10 ....88 B2
Hazel Wy *STHWK* SE1 ....49 E4
Hazelwood Cl *CLPT* E5 ....61 E5
Hazlebury Rd *FUL/PGN* SW6 ....114 B5
Hazledene Rd *CHSWK* W4 ....110 C2
Hazlewell Rd *PUT/ROE* SW15 ....130 C3
Hazlewood Crs *NKENS* W10 ....89 E3
Hazlitt Ms *WKENS* * W14 ....101 E4
Hazlitt Rd *WKENS* W14 ....101 E4
Headcorn Rd *BMLY* BR1 ....159 F5
Headfort Pl *KTBR* SW1X 42 B1
Headington Rd *WAND/EARL* SW18 ....150 C1
Headlam Rd *CLAP* SW4 ....135 D4
Headlam St *WCHPL* E1 ....90 B3
Headley Dr *GNTH/NBYPK* IG2 ....66 B1
Head St *WCHPL* E1 ....91 D5
Heald St *NWCR* SE14 ....121 F4
Healey St *CAMTN* * NW1 ....74 B3
Hearne Rd *CHSWK* W4 ....110 A1
Hearn's Buildings *WALW* SE17 ....48 B5
Hearn St *SDTCH* EC2A 25 D1
Hearnville Rd *BAL* SW12 ....152 A1
Heath Brow *HAMP* NW3 ....54 C5
Heath Cl *GLDGN* NW11 ....54 B2
Heathcote St *BMSBY* WC1N 9 E5
Heath Dr *HAMP* NW3 ....72 B1
Heatherbank *ELTH/MOT* SE9 ....125 F5
Heather Cl *EHAM* E6 ....96 A5
    LEW SE13 ....141 D5
    VX/NE SW8 ....134 B1
Heather Gdns *GLDGN* NW11 ....53 E1
Heather Park Dr *ALP/SUD* HA0 ....68 A3
Heather Rd *CRICK* NW2 ....51 F4
    LEE/GVPK SE12 ....160 A2
Heather Wk *NKENS* W10 ....89 E3
Heatherwood Cl *MNPK* E12 ....64 B4
Heathfield Av *WAND/EARL* SW18 ....133 D5
Heathfield Cl *CAN/RD* E16 ....95 D4
Heathfield Gdns *CHSWK* W4 ....110 C1
    GLDGN NW11 ....53 D1
    WAND/EARL SW18 ....133 D4
Heathfield Pk *CRICK* NW2 ....70 C3
Heathfield Rd *ACT* W3 ....98 B3
    WAND/EARL SW18 ....132 C4
Heathfield Sq *WAND/EARL* SW18 ....133 D5
Heathfield Ter *CHSWK* W4 ....110 C1
    WOOL/PLUM SE18 ....127 E2
Heathgate *GLDGN* NW11 ....54 B1
Heathgate Pl *HAMP* NW3 ....73 F2
Heathland Rd *STNW/STAM* N16 ....59 D3
Heath La *BKHTH/KID* SE3 ....123 D5
Heathlee Rd *BKHTH/KID* SE3 ....141 F2

Heathman's Rd *FUL/PGN* * SW6 ....113 F4
Heath Md *WIM/MER* SW19..............149 D3
Heath Ri *PUT/ROE* SW15..............131 D4
Heath Rd *VX/NE* SW8..............116 B5
Heathside *HAMP* NW3..............73 D1
Heathstan Rd *SHB* W12..............88 A5
Heath St *HAMP* NW3..............54 C5
Heathview Gdns *PUT/ROE* SW15..............130 C5
Heath Vls *WAND/EARL* * SW18..............150 C1
  WOOL/PLUM SE18..............127 F1
Heathville Rd *ARCH* N19..............57 E2
Heathwall St *BTSEA* SW11..............133 F1
Heathway *BKHTH/KID* SE3..............124 A3
Heathwood Gdns *CHARL* SE7..............107 E5
Heaton Rd *PECK* SE15..............138 B1
Heaver Rd *BTSEA* * SW11..............133 D1
Heavitree Cl *WOOL/PLUM* SE18..............127 D1
Heavitree Rd *WOOL/PLUM* SE18..............127 D1
Hebdon Rd *TOOT* SW17..............151 E3
Heber Rd *CRICK* NW2..............71 D2
  EDUL SE22..............137 F4
Hebron Rd *HMSMTH* W6..............100 B4
Heckfield Pl *FUL/PGN* SW6..............114 A3
Heckford St *WAP* E1W..............103 D1
Hector St *WOOL/PLUM* * SE18..............109 E5
Heddington Gv *HOLWY* N7..............75 F2
Heddon St *CONDST* W1S..............31 E2
Hedger's Gv *HOM* * E9..............79 E3
Hedger St *LBTH* SE11..............46 C4
Hedgley St *LEE/GVPK* SE12..............141 E4
Hedingham Cl *IS* N1..............76 C4
Hedley Rw *HBRY* N5..............77 D2
Heenan Cl *BARK* IG11..............84 C3
Heidegger Crs *BARN* SW13..............112 B3
Heigham Rd *EHAM* E6..............83 D4
The Heights *CHARL* SE7..............124 C1
Heiron St *WALW* SE17..............118 B2
Helby Rd *CLAP* SW4..............135 D4
Helder Gv *LEE/GVPK* SE12..............141 F5
Helena Pl *HOM* * E9..............78 B5
Helena Rd *PLSTW* E13..............93 F1
  WLSDN NW10..............70 B2
Helena Sq *BERM/RHTH* SE16..............103 E1
Helenslea Av *GLDGN* NW11..............53 F3
Helen's Pl *BETH* E2..............90 C2
Helen St *WOOL/PLUM* * SE18..............108 B5
Helix Gdns *BRXS/STRHM* SW2..............135 F4
Helix Rd *BRXS/STRHM* SW2..............135 F4
Hellings St *WAP* E1W..............102 A2
Helme Cl *WIM/MER* SW19..............149 F5
Helmet Rw *FSBYE* EC1V..............11 F5
Helmore Rd *BARK* IG11..............85 E4
Helmsley Pl *HACK* E8..............78 B4
Helmsley St *HACK* E8..............78 B4
Helperby Rd *WLSDN* NW10..............69 E4
Helsinki Sq *BERM/RHTH* SE16..............103 F4
Helvetia St *CAT* SE6..............157 F2
Hemans St *VX/NE* SW8..............117 D3
Hemingford Rd *IS* N1..............75 F5
Hemlock Rd *SHB* W12..............99 F5
Hemming St *WCHPL* E1..............90 A3
Hemmingway Ct *KTTN* NW5..............74 A1
Hemp Wk *WALW* SE17..............48 B4
Hemstal Rd *KIL/WHAMP* NW6..............72 A4
Hemsworth St *IS* N1..............12 C1
Henchman St *SHB* W12..............87 F5
Henderson Cl *WLSDN* NW10..............68 C3
Henderson Dr *STJWD* NW8..............4 A5
Henderson Rd *FSTGT* E7..............82 C3
  WAND/EARL SW18..............133 E5
Hendham Rd *TOOT* SW17..............151 E2
Hendon Park Wy *GLDGN* * NW11..............53 F1
Hendon Wy *HDN* NW2..............52 C1
Hendre Rd *STHWK* SE1..............49 D5
Hendrick Av *BAL* SW12..............133 F4
Heneage La *HDTCH* EC3A..............25 D5
Heneage St *WCHPL* E1..............25 F3
Henfield Cl *ARCH* N19..............56 C3

Hengist Rd *LEE/GVPK* SE12..............142 B5
Hengrave Rd *FSTH* SE23..............138 C5
Henley Cl *BERM/RHTH* * SE16..............102 C3
Henley Dr *BERM/RHTH* SE16..............49 F4
Henley Rd *CAN/RD* E16..............107 F3
  IL IG1..............84 C1
  WLSDN NW10..............70 C5
Henley St *BTSEA* SW11..............116 A5
Hennel Cl *FSTH* SE23..............156 C3
Henniker Gdns *EHAM* E6..............95 D5
Henniker Ms *CHEL* SW3..............115 D2
Henniker Rd *SRTFD* E15..............81 D2
Henning St *BTSEA* SW11..............115 E4
Henrietta Cl *DEPT* SE8..............122 A2
Henrietta Ms *BMSBY* WC1N..............9 D5
Henrietta Pl *CAVSQ/HST* W1G..............18 C4
Henrietta St *COVGDN* WC2E..............33 D1
  SRTFD E15..............80 C2
Henriques St *WCHPL* E1..............90 A5
Henry Addlington Cl *EHAM* E6..............96 B4
Henry Cooper Wy *LEE/GVPK* SE12..............161 D3
Henry Dickens Ct *NTGHL* W11..............101 D1
Henry Doulton Dr *TOOT* SW17..............152 A4
Henry Jackson Rd *PUT/ROE* SW15..............131 D1
Henry Rd *EHAM* E6..............95 E1
  FSBYPK N4..............58 C3
Henryson Rd *BROCKY* SE4..............140 A3
Hensford Gdns *SYD* SE26..............156 B4
Henshall St *IS* N1..............77 D3
Henshaw St *WALW* SE17..............48 A4
Henslowe Rd *EDUL* SE22..............138 A3
Henson Av *CRICK* NW2..............70 C2
Henstridge Pl *STJWD* NW8..............4 C1
Henty Cl *BTSEA* SW11..............115 E3
Henty Wk *PUT/ROE* SW15..............130 B3
Henwick Rd *ELTH/MOT* SE9..............143 D1
Hepscott Rd *HOM* E9..............80 A3
Heralds Pl *LBTH* SE11..............46 C4
Herald St *BETH* E2..............90 B3
Herbal Hl *CLKNW* EC1R..............22 B1
Herbert Crs *KTBR* SW1X..............41 F2
Herbert Gdns *CHSWK* W4..............110 B2
  WLSDN NW10..............88 B1
Herbert Pl *WOOL/PLUM* SE18..............126 B2
Herbert Rd *CDALE/KGS* NW9..............52 A1
  CDMY/SEVK IG3..............67 E4
  MNPK E12..............83 E1
  WALTH E17..............61 F2
  WOOL/PLUM SE18..............126 B3
Herbert St *KTTN* NW5..............74 A3
  PLSTW E13..............94 A1
Herbrand St *BMSBY* WC1N..............8 C3
Hercules Pl *HOLWY* N7..............57 E5
Hercules Rd *STHWK* SE1..............45 F3
Hercules St *HOLWY* N7..............57 E5
Hereford Gdns *IL* IG1..............65 E2
Hereford Ms *BAY/PAD* W2..............14 B4
Hereford Rd *NWCR* * SE14..............121 F3
Hereford Retreat *PECK* SE15..............120 A3
Hereford Rd *ACT* W3..............98 C1
  BAY/PAD W2..............14 B5
Hereford Sq *SKENS* SW7..............39 F5
Hereford St *BETH* E2..............90 A3
Hereward Rd *TOOT* SW17..............151 E4
Heritage Pl *WAND/EARL* * SW18..............133 D4
Herlwyn Gdns *TOOT* SW17..............151 F4
Hermes Cl *MV/WKIL* W9..............14 A1
Hermes St *IS* N1..............10 A2
The Hermitage *BARN* * SW13..............111 F4
  FSTH SE23..............156 C1
  LEW * SE13..............122 C5
Hermitage Gdns *HAMP* NW3..............54 A5
Hermitage La *CRICK* NW2..............54 A5
Hermitage Rd *FSBYPK* N4..............58 C2
Hermitage Rw *HACK* * E8..............78 A2
Hermitage St *BAY/PAD* W2..............16 A3
Hermitage Wall *WAP* E1W..............102 A2
Hermit Rd *CAN/RD* E16..............93 F3

Hermit St *FSBYE* EC1V 10 C3
Herndon Rd *WAND/EARL* SW18 ......132 C3
Herne Cl *WLSDN* NW10 ....69 D2
Herne Hl *HNHL* SE24........................136 C3
Herne Hill Rd *HNHL* SE24 ....136 C1
Herne Pl *HNHL* SE24..........................136 B4
Heron Cl *WLSDN* NW10 ....69 D2
Heron Crs *SCUP* DA14 ....163 E4
Herondale Av *WAND/EARL* SW18 ....151 D3
Heron Dr *FSBYPK* N4 ....58 C4
Herongate Rd *MNPK* E12 ....64 C4
Heron Ms *IL* IG1 ....66 B4
Heron Quays *POP/IOD* E14 ....104 A2
Heron Rd *HNHL* SE24 ....136 C2
Herons Lea *HGT* * N6 ....55 F1
Herrick Rd *FSBYPK* N4 ....58 C5
Herrick St *WEST* SW1P 44 B5
Herries St *NKENS* W10 ....89 E1
Herringham Rd *CHARL* SE7 ....106 C4
Hersant Cl *WLSDN* NW10 ....70 A5
Herschell Rd *FSTH* SE23 ....139 D5
Hersham Cl *PUT/ROE* SW15 ....130 A5
Hershell Ct *MORT/ESHN* * SW14 ....128 B2
Hertford Av *MORT/ESHN* SW14 ......129 D3
Hertford Rd *BARK* IG11 ....84 B4
  GNTH/NBYPK IG2 ....67 E1
  IS N1 ....77 E4
Hertford St *MYFR/PICC* W1J 30 C3
Hertslet Rd *HOLWY* N7 ....57 F5
Hertsmere Rd *POP/IOD* E14 ....104 A1
Hesewall Cl *VX/NE* SW8 ....116 C5
Hesketh Pl *NTGHL* W11 ....101 E5
Hesketh Rd *FSTGT* E7 ....64 A5
Heslop Rd *BAL* SW12 ....151 F1
Hesper Ms *ECT* SW5 ....114 B1
Hesperus Crs *POP/IOD* E14 ....104 A5
Hessel St *WCHPL* E1 ....90 B5
Hestercombe Av *FUL/PGN* SW6 ....113 E5
Hester Rd *BTSEA* SW11 ....115 E3
Hester Ter *RCH/KEW* TW9 ....128 A1
Heston St *DEPT* SE8 ....121 F4
Hetherington Rd *CLAP* SW4 ....135 E2
Hetley Rd *SHB* W12 ....100 B2
Hevelius Cl *GNWCH* SE10 ....123 F1
Hever Cft *ELTH/MOT* SE9 ....162 A4
Heverham Rd *WOOL/PLUM* SE18 ..109 E5
Hewer St *NKENS* W10 ....89 D4
Hewett Rd *SDTCH* EC2A 25 D1
Hewison St *BOW* E3............................91 F1
Hewlett Rd *BOW* E3 ....91 E1
The Hexagon *HGT* N6 ....159 E3
Hexal Rd *CAT* SE6 ....159 E3
Hexham Rd *WNWD* SE27 ....154 C2
Heybridge Wy *LEY* E10 ....61 E2
Heyford Av *VX/NE* SW8 ....117 E3
Heyford Ter *VX/NE* SW8 ....117 E3
Heygate Est *WALW* SE17 ....47 F4
Heygate St *WALW* SE17 ....47 E5
Heysham La *HAMP* NW3 ....54 B5
Heysham Rd *SEVS/STOTM* N15 ....59 D1
Heythorp St *WAND/EARL* SW18 ......149 F1
Heyworth Rd *CLPT* E5 ....78 B1
  FSTGT E7 ....81 F2
Hibbert Rd *WALTH* E17 ....61 F2
Hibbert St *BTSEA* SW11 ....132 C1
Hichisson Rd *PECK* SE15 ....138 C3
Hickin Cl *CHARL* SE7 ....107 D5
Hickin St *POP/IOD* E14 ....104 C4
Hickling Rd *IL* IG1 ....84 B2
Hickman Cl *CAN/RD* E16 ....95 D4
Hicks Cl *BTSEA* SW11 ....133 E1
Hicks St *DEPT* SE8 ....121 E1
Hide Pl *WEST* SW1P 44 A5
The High Pde *STRHM/NOR* * SW16 ..153 E3
Highbank Pl *WAND/EARL* * SW18 ....132 B5
Highbank Wy *CEND/HSY/T* N8 ....58 A1
Highbridge Rd *BARK* IG11 ....84 B5
Highbrook Rd *BKHTH/KID* SE3 ......143 D1

Highbury Cnr *HBRY* * N5 ....76 B3
Highbury Crs *HBRY* N5 ....76 B2
Highbury Est *HBRY* N5 ....76 C2
Highbury Gdns *IL* IG1 ....67 E4
Highbury Gra *HBRY* N5 ....76 B1
Highbury Gv *HBRY* N5 ....76 B2
Highbury Hl *HBRY* N5 ....76 B3
Highbury New Pk *HBRY* N5 ....76 B3
Highbury Pk *HBRY* N5 ....76 B1
Highbury Pl *HBRY* N5 ....76 B3
Highbury Qd *HBRY* N5 ....58 C5
Highbury Rd *WIM/MER* SW19 ....149 E5
Highbury Station Pde * N5 ....76 B3
Highbury Station Rd *IS* * N1 ....76 A3
Highbury Ter *HBRY* N5 ....76 B2
Highbury Terrace Ms *HBRY* N5 ....76 B2
Highclere St *SYD* SE26 ....157 E4
Highcliffe Dr *PUT/ROE* SW15 ....129 F4
Highcombe *CHARL* SE7 ....124 B2
Highcombe Cl *ELTH/MOT* SE9 ......161 D1
Highcroft Gdns *GLDGN* NW11 ....53 F1
Highcroft Rd *ARCH* N19 ....57 E2
Highdown Rd *PUT/ROE* SW15 ....130 B4
Highfield Av *GLDGN* NW11 ....53 D2
Highfield Cl *LEW* SE13 ....141 D4
Highfield Gdns *GLDGN* NW11 ....53 E1
Highfield Rd *ACT* W3 ....86 B4
  GLDGN * NW11 ....53 E1
Highfields Gv *HGT* N6 ....56 A3
Highgate Av *HGT* N6 ....56 B2
Highgate Cl *HGT* N6 ....56 A2
Highgate High St *HGT* N6 ....56 A3
Highgate Hl *ARCH* N19 ....56 B3
Highgate Rd *KTTN* NW5 ....56 A5
Highgate Spinney *CEND/HSY/T* * N8 ..57 D1
Highgate West Hl *HGT* N6 ....56 A4
High Gv *WOOL/PLUM* SE18 ....127 D3
High Hill Ferry *CLPT* E5 ....60 B3
High Holborn *HHOL* WC1V 21 D4
Highland Cft *BECK* BR3 ....158 B5
Highlands Av *ACT* W3 ....98 C1
Highlands Gdns *IL* IG1 ....65 F3
Highland Ter *LEW* * SE13 ....140 B1
High Level Dr *SYD* SE26 ....156 A4
Highlever Rd *NKENS* W10 ....88 C4
Highmead *WOOL/PLUM* SE18 ......127 F3
High Meads Rd *CAN/RD* E16 ....95 D5
Highmore Rd *BKHTH/KID* SE3 ......123 E3
Highshore Rd *PECK* SE15 ....119 F5
Highstone Av *WAN* E11 ....64 A1
High St *ACT* W3 ....98 C2
  PLSTW E13 ....94 A1
  SRTFD E15 ....81 D4
  WAN E11 ....64 D1
  WIM/MER SW19 ....149 D5
High St Harlesden *WLSDN* NW10 ....87 F1
High Street Ms *WIM/MER* SW19 ....149 E5
High St North *MNPK* E12 ....83 E2
High St South *EHAM* E6 ....95 F1
High Timber St *BLKFR* EC4V 35 E1
High Trees *BRXS/STRHM* SW2 ......154 A1
The Highway *WAP* E1W 102 A1
Highwood Rd *ARCH* N19 ....57 E5
Highworth St *CAMTN* * NW1 ....17 D2
Hilary Cl *FUL/PGN* * SW6 ....114 B3
Hilary Rd *ACT* W3 ....99 F1
  SHB * W12 ....87 F5
Hilborough Rd *HACK* E8 ....77 F4
Hilda Rd *CAN/RD* E16 ....93 E3
  EHAM E6 ....83 D4

Hilda Ter *BRXN/ST* * SW9..............118 A5
Hildreth St *BAL* SW12...................152 B1
Hildyard Rd *FUL/PGN* SW6...........114 A2
Hiley Rd *WLSDN* NW10...................88 C2
Hilgrove Rd *KIL/WHAMP* NW6.........72 C4
Hillbeck Cl *PECK* SE15.................120 C3
Hillbrook Rd *TOOT* SW17..............151 F3
Hillbury Rd *TOOT* SW17...............152 B3
Hill Cl *CHST* BR7.......................162 B5
  CRICK NW2...............................52 B5
  GLDGN NW11.............................54 A1
Hillcourt Rd *EDUL* SE22.............138 B4
Hillcrest *HGT* N6..........................56 A2
  HNHL * SE24............................137 D2
Hillcrest Cl *SYD* SE26................156 A4
Hill Crest Gdns *CRICK* NW2...........52 A5
Hillcrest Rd *ACT* W3......................98 A2
  BMLY BR1.................................160 A4
Hillcroft Rd *EHAM* E6....................96 B4
Hill Dr *CDALE/KGS* NW9.................50 C3
Hilldrop Crs *HOLWY* N7..................75 D2
Hilldrop Est *HOLWY* N7..................75 D2
Hilldrop La *HOLWY* N7....................75 D2
Hilldrop Rd *HOLWY* N7....................75 D2
Hill End *WOOL/PLUM* SE18............126 A4
Hillersdon Av *BARN* SW13............112 A5
Hillery Cl *WALW* SE17....................48 B5
Hill Farm Rd *NKENS* W10...............88 C4
Hillfield Rd *KIL/WHAMP* NW6..........71 F2
Hill Gdns Craven *BAY/PAD* * W2.....27 E1
Hillgate Pl *BAL* SW12..................134 B4
  KENS W8...................................26 A3
Hillgate St *KENS* W8.....................26 A3
Hill House Rd *STRHM/NOR* SW16...153 F5
Hilliard's Ct *WAP* E1W.................102 C2
Hillier Rd *BTSEA* SW11................133 F4
Hillingdon St *WALW* SE17.............118 B2
Hillman St *HACK* E8.......................78 B3
Hillmarton Rd *HOLWY* N7...............75 E2
Hillmarton Ter *HOLWY* * N7............75 E2
Hillmead Dr *BRXN/ST* SW9...........136 B2
Hillmore Gv *SYD* SE26.................157 D5
Hillreach *WOOL/PLUM* SE18.........125 F1
Hillrise Rd *ARCH* N19.....................57 F2
Hill Rd *STJWD* NW8..........................3 F2
Hillsboro Rd *EDUL* SE22..............137 E3
Hillside *WLSDN* NW10....................69 D5
Hillside Cl *MV/WKIL* W9....................3 D1
Hillside Rd *BRXS/STRHM* SW2.......154 A2
  HGT N6......................................56 A1
Hillside Rd *BRXS/STRHM* SW2.......153 F2
  SEVS/STOTM N15.........................59 E1
Hillsleigh Rd *KENS* W8.................101 F2
Hills Pl *SOHO/CST* W1F..................19 E5
Hillstowe St *CLPT* E5......................60 C4
Hill St *MYFR/PICC* W1J...................30 C5
Hilltop Cottages *SYD* * SE26..........156 B4
Hilltop Rd *KIL/WHAMP* NW6............72 A4
Hill View Crs *IL* IG1.......................65 F1
Hill View Dr *WELL* DA16...............127 E5
Hillview Rd *CHST* BR7...................162 A5
Hillway *CDALE/KGS* NW9................51 E3
  HGT N6......................................56 A4
Hillworth Rd *BRXS/STRHM* SW2....136 A5
Hillyard St *BRXN/ST* SW9.............118 A4
Hillyfield Cl *HOM* E9......................79 E2
Hilly Flds *BROCKY* * SE4..............140 A4
Hilly Fields Crs *BROCKY* SE4........140 A2
Hilsea St *CLPT* E5..........................78 C1
Himley Rd *TOOT* SW17.................151 E5
Hinckley Rd *EDUL* SE22...............138 A2
Hind Ct *FLST/FETLN* * EC4A...........22 B5
Hinde Ms *MHST* * W1U...................18 A4
Hinde St *MHST* W1U........................18 A4
Hind Gv *POP/IOD* E14.....................92 A5
Hindmans Rd *EDUL* SE22.............138 A3
Hindmarsh Cl *WCHPL* E1.............102 A1
Hindrey Rd *CLPT* E5........................78 B2

Hindsley's Pl *FSTH* SE23...............156 C2
Hinstock Rd *WOOL/PLUM* SE18.....126 C3
Hinton Cl *ELTH/MOT* SE9..............161 E1
Hinton Rd *BRXN/ST* SW9...............136 B1
Hippodrome Pl *NTGHL* W11...........101 E1
Hitcham Rd *LEY* E10........................61 F2
Hither Farm Rd *BKHTH/KID* SE3....142 C1
Hitherfield Rd *STRHM/NOR* SW16..153 F2
Hither Green La *LEW* SE13............140 C3
Hitherwood Dr *DUL* SE21..............155 F4
Hoadly Rd *STRHM/NOR* SW16.......153 D3
Hobart Pl *BCVA* SW1W.....................42 C3
Hobbes Wk *PUT/ROE* SW15...........130 B3
Hobbs Pl *IS* * N1.............................77 E5
Hobbs Place Est *IS* N1....................12 C1
Hobbs Rd *WNWD* SE27.................154 C4
Hobday St *POP/IOD* E14..................92 B5
Hobsons Pl *WCHPL* * E1.................13 E4
Hobury St *WBPTN* SW10...............114 C2
Hocker St *BETH* * E2........................13 E4
Hockley Av *EHAM* E6........................95 E1
Hockley Ms *BARK* IG11....................97 E1
Hocroft Av *CRICK* NW2....................53 F5
Hocroft Rd *CRICK* NW2....................71 F1
Hocroft Wk *CRICK* NW2...................53 F5
Hodford Rd *GLDGN* NW11................53 F3
Hodister Cl *CMBW* SE5.................118 C3
Hoffman Sq *IS* * N1.........................12 B3
Hofland Rd *WKENS* W14................101 H4
Hogan Ms *BAY/PAD* W2....................16 A2
Hogarth Cl *CAN/RD* E16...................95 D4
Hogarth Pl *ECT* * SW5......................38 C5
Hogarth Rd *ECT* SW5.......................38 C5
Hogarth Ter *CHSWK* * W4...............111 E2
Hogshead Pas *WAP* * E1W.............102 B1
Holbeach Gdns *BFN/LL* DA15........145 E4
Holbeach Rd *CAT* SE6...................140 A5
Holbeck Rw *PECK* SE15.................120 A3
Holbein Ms *BGVA* SW1W...............116 A1
Holbein Pl *BCVA* SW1W...................42 A5
Holberton Gdns *WLSDN* NW10.......88 B2
Holborn *HCIRC* EC1N.......................22 A3
Holborn Circ *HCIRC* EC1N...............22 B3
Holborn Pl *HHOL* WC1V....................21 E3
Holborn Rd *PLSTW* E13....................94 B4
Holborn Viad *STBT* EC1A.................22 C3
Holbrooke Ct *HOLWY* N7..................57 E5
Holbrook Rd *SRTFD* E15..................93 F1
Holburne Cl *BKHTH/KID* SE3.........124 C4
Holburne Gdns *BKHTH/KID* SE3....125 D4
Holburne Rd *BKHTH/KID* SE3........124 C4
Holcombe St *HMSMTH* W6............112 B1
Holcroft Rd *HOM* E9........................78 C4
Holden Av *CDALE/KGS* NW9............50 C4
Holdenby Rd *BROCKY* SE4............139 E3
Holden St *BTSEA* SW11................116 A5
Holdernesse Rd *TOOT* SW17.........151 F3
Holderness Wy *WNWD* SE27.........154 B5
Holford Ms *FSBYW* * WC1X...............9 E3
Holford Rd *HAMP* NW3.....................54 C5
Holford St *FSBYW* WC1X..................10 A3
Holford Yd *FSBYW* * WC1X...............10 A2
Holgate Av *BTSEA* SW11...............133 D1
Holgate St *CHARL* SE7..................107 D4
Holland Dr *FSTH* SE23...................157 E3
Holland Gdns *WKENS* W14............101 E4
Holland Gv *BRXN/ST* SW9.............118 A3
Holland Pk *KENS* W8.....................101 F3
Holland Park Av *GDMY/SEVK* IG3.....67 E1
  WKENS W14................................101 E2
Holland Park Gdns *WKENS* W14.....101 E2
Holland Park Ms *NTGHL* W11.........101 F2
Holland Park Rd *WKENS* W14.........101 F4
Holland Park Ter *NTGHL* * W11......101 E2
Holland Pas *IS* N1...........................76 C5
Holland Pl *KENS* * W8......................26 C5
Holland Rd *EHAM* E6.......................83 F5
  SRTFD E15.................................93 E2

WKENS W14 ....**101** D3
WLSDN NW10 ....**70** A5
Holland Cl KENS W8...........................**38** B1
STHWK SE1...............................**35** D1
Holland Villas Rd WKENS W14 .....**101** D3
Hollar Rd STNW/STAM N16 ....**59** F5
Hollen St SOHO/CST W1F **19** F5
Holles St CAVSQ/HST W1G **19** D4
Holley Rd ACT W3...........................**99** E3
Holliday Sq BTSEA SW11 ....**133** D1
Hollies Av BFN/LL DA15.................**163** F2
Hollies Wy BAL * SW12...................**134** A5
Hollingbourne Rd HNHL SE24 ......**136** C3
Hollington Rd EHAM E6 ....**95** F2
Holloway Rd ARCH N19 ....**57** D4
EHAM E6 ....**95** F2
HOLWY N7...................................**76** A2
WAN E11 ....**63** D5
Hollybush Gdns BETH E2 ....**90** B2
Hollybush Hl WAN E11 ....**63** F1
Hollybush Pl BETH E2 ....**90** B2
Hollybush Rd PLSTW E13.................**94** B2
Holly Bush V HAMP * NW3 ....**72** C1
Holly Cl WLSDN NW10......................**69** E4
Hollycroft Av HAMP NW3 ....**54** A5
Hollydale Rd PECK SE15 ....**120** C5
Hollydown Wy WAN E11...................**63** D5
Holly Gv CDALE/KGS NW9 ....**50** C2
PECK SE15................................**119** F5
Holly Hedge Ter LEW SE13 ....**140** C5
Holly Hl HAMP NW3 ....**72** C1
Holly Lodge Gdns HGT N6 ....**56** A4
Holly Ms WBPTN SW10 ....**114** C1
Holly Mt HAMP * NW3 ....**72** C1
Hollymount Cl GNWCH SE10..........**122** C4
Holly Pk FSBYPK N4.........................**57** E2
Holly Rd CHSWK * W4 ....**99** D5
Holly St HACK E8 ....**77** F4
Hollytree Cl WIM/MER SW19 ....**149** D1
Hollyview Cl HDN NW4 ....**52** A1
Holly Vls HMSMTH * W6 ....**100** B4
Holly Wk HAMP NW3 ....**72** C1
Hollywood Ms WBPTN SW10 ....**114** C2
Hollywood Rd WBPTN SW10 ....**114** C2
Holman Rd BTSEA SW11 ....**115** D5
Holmbury Vw CLPT E5 ....**60** B3
Holmbush Rd PUT/ROE SW15 ....**131** E4
Holmcote Gdns HBRY N5 ....**76** C1
Holmdale Rd CHST BR7 ....**162** C5
KIL/WHAMP NW6 ....**72** A2
Holmdale Ter SEVS/STOTM N15.....**59** E1
Holmdene Av HNHL SE24 ....**136** C3
Holmead Rd FUL/PGN SW6............**114** B3
Holme Rd EHAM E6 ....**83** E5
Holmesdale Av MORT/ESHN SW14 ...**128** B1
Holmesdale Rd HGT N6....................**56** B2
Holmesley Rd BROCKY SE4 ....**139** E4
Holmes Rd KTTN NW5 ....**74** B2
Holmes Ter STHWK SE1 ....**34** A5
Holmewood Gdns BRXS/STRHM SW2...**135** F5
Holmewood Rd BRXS/STRHM SW2 ...**135** E5
Holmleigh Rd STNW/STAM N16 ......**59** E3
Holm Oak Cl WAND/EARL SW18 .....**131** F4
Holmshaw Cl SYD SE26 ....**157** E4
Holmside Rd BAL SW12 ....**134** A4
Holmwood Rd GDMY/SEVK IG3 ....**67** C4
Holne Cha EFNCH N2........................**54** C1
Holness Rd SRTFD E15 ....**81** F3
Holroyd Rd PUT/ROE SW15 ....**130** C2
Holstock Rd IL IG1 ....**66** C4
Holsworthy Sq FSBYW WC1X **21** F1
Holton St WCHPL E1 ....**91** D3
Holt Rd CAN/RD E16 ....**107** E2
Holwood Pl CLAP SW4....................**135** D2
Holybourne Av PUT/ROE SW15 ....**130** A5
Holyhead Cl BOW E3 ....**92** A2
Holyoake Ct BERM/RHTH SE16 .....**103** E3
Holyoak Rd LBTH SE11 ....**46** C4
Holyport Rd FUL/PGN SW6 ....**112** C3
Holyrood St STHWK SE1 ....**36** C4
Holywell Cl BERM/RHTH * SE16 ....**120** B1
BKHTH/KID SE3 ....**124** A2
Holywell La SDTCH EC2A **13** D5
Holywell Rw SDTCH EC2A **24** C1
Homecroft Rd SYD SE26 ....**156** C5
Homefield Cl WLSDN NW10 ....**68** C3
Homefield Rd CHSWK W4 ....**99** F5
Homefield St IS * N1 ....**12** C2
Homeleigh Rd PECK SE15 ....**139** D3
Home Park Rd WIM/MER SW19 .....**149** F4
Homer Dr POP/IOD E14 ....**104** A5
Home Rd BTSEA SW11 ....**115** E5
Homer Rd HOM E9 ....**79** E3
Homer Rw CAMTN NW1 ....**17** D3
Homer St CAMTN NW1 ....**17** D3
Homerton Gv HOM E9 ....**79** D2
Homerton High St HOM E9 ....**79** D2
Homerton Rd HOM E9 ....**79** F1
Homerton Rw HOM E9 ....**78** C2
Homerton Ter HOM E9 ....**78** C2
Homestall Rd EDUL SE22 ....**138** C3
Homestead Pk CRICK NW2 ....**51** F5
Homestead Rd FUL/PGN SW6 ....**113** F3
Homewood Gdns PECK * SE15 ......**120** C5
Honduras St FSBYE EC1V **11** E5
Honeybourne Rd KIL/WHAMP NW6 ..**72** B2
Honeybrook Rd BAL SW12 ....**134** C5
Honeyman Cl CRICK NW2 ....**71** D4
Honeywell Rd BTSEA SW11 ....**133** E4
Honeywood Rd WLSDN NW10.........**87** F1
Honiton Gdns PECK * SE15 ....**120** C5
Honiton Rd KIL/WHAMP NW6 ....**89** F1
WELL DA16 ....**127** F5
Honley Rd CAT SE6 ....**140** B5
Honor Oak Pk FSTH SE23 ....**138** C5
Honor Oak Ri FSTH SE23 ....**138** C4
Honor Oak Rd FSTH SE23 ....**138** C1
Hood Av MORT/ESHN SW14 ....**128** C3
Hook La WELL DA16 ....**145** F2
Hooper Rd CAN/RD E16 ....**94** A5
Hooper's Ms ACT W3........................**98** C2
Hooper St WCHPL E1 ....**102** A1
Hoop La GLDGN NW11.......................**53** F2
Hope Cl IS N1 ....**76** C3
LEE/GVPK SE12 ....**160** B5
Hopedale Rd CHARL SE7 ....**124** B2
Hopefield Av KIL/WHAMP NW6 ......**89** E1
Hope St BTSEA SW11 ....**133** D1
Hopetown St WCHPL * E1 ....**25** F3
Hopewell St CMBW SE5 ....**119** D3
Hopewell Yd CMBW SE5 ....**119** D3
Hop Gdns CHCR WC2N.......................**32** C2
Hopgood St SHB W12 ....**100** C2
Hopkinsons Pl CAMTN * NW1 ....**73** F5
Hopkins St SOHO/CST W1F **19** F5
Hopping La IS * N1 ....**76** B3
Hopton Pde STRHM/NOR * SW16 ..**153** D5
Hopton Rd STRHM/NOR SW16 ......**153** E5
WOOL/PLUM SE18 ....**108** B4
Hoptons Gdns STHWK * SE1 ....**35** D3
Hopton St STHWK SE1 ....**35** D3
Hopwood Cl TOOT SW17 ....**150** C3
Hopwood Rd WALW SE17 ....**119** D2
Hopwood Wk HACK * E8 ....**78** A4
Horace Rd FSTGT E7 ....**82** B1
Horatio Pl POP/IOD E14 ....**104** C3
Horatio St BETH E2 ....**13** F2
Horbury Crs NTGHL W11 ....**26** A2
Horbury Ms NTGHL W11 ....**101** F1
Horder Rd FUL/PGN SW6 ....**113** E4
Hordle Prom East PECK SE15 ....**119** F3
Hordle Prom North PECK * SE15 ...**119** F3
Hordle Prom West PECK SE15 ....**119** E3
Horley Rd ELTH/MOT SE9 ....**161** E4
Hormead Rd NKENS W10 ....**89** F3
Hornbeam Cl IL IG1 ....**85** D2

LBTH SE11	**46**	A4
Hornby Cl *HAMP* NW3	**73**	D4
Horncastle Cl *LEE/GVPK* SE12	**142**	A5
Horncastle Rd *LEE/GVPK* SE12	**142**	A5
Horndean Cl *PUT/ROE* SW15	**148**	A1
Horne House *WOOL/PLUM* SE18	**125**	E4
Horne Wy *PUT/ROE* SW15	**112**	C5
Hornfair Rd *CHARL* SE7	**125**	D2
Horniman Dr *FSTH* SE23	**156**	B5
Horniman Gdns *FSTH* * SE23	**156**	B1
Horning Cl *ELTH/MOT* SE9	**161**	E4
Horn La *ACT* W3	**98**	C2
GNWCH SE10	**106**	A5
Horn Link Wy *GNWCH* SE10	**106**	A5
Horn Park Cl *LEE/GVPK* SE12	**142**	B3
Horn Park La *LEE/GVPK* SE12	**142**	B3
Hornsey Chambers *CLPT* * E5	**60**	B4
Hornsey La *ARCH* N19	**56**	C2
Hornsey Lane Est *ARCH* * N19	**57**	D2
Hornsey Lane Gdns *HGT* N6	**57**	D2
Hornsey Ri *ARCH* N19	**57**	D2
Hornsey Rise Gdns *ARCH* N19	**57**	D2
Hornsey Rd *ARCH* N19	**57**	E3
Hornsey St *HOLWY* N7	**75**	F2
Hornshay St *PECK* SE15	**120**	C2
Hornton Pl *KENS* W8	**38**	B1
Hornton St *KENS* W8	**26**	B5
Horsa Rd *LEE/GVPK* SE12	**142**	C5
Horseferry Pl *GNWCH* SE10	**122**	C2
Horseferry Rd *POP/IOD* E14	**103**	E1
WEST SW1P	**44**	A3
Horse Guards Av *WHALL* SW1A	**32**	C1
Horse Guards Rd *WHALL* SW1A	**32**	B4
Horse Leaze *EHAM* E6	**96**	B5
Horsell Rd *HBRY* N5	**76**	A2
Horselydown La *STHWK* SE1	**37**	E5
Horseshoe Cl *CRICK* NW2	**52**	B4
POP/IOD E14	**122**	C1
Horse Yd *IS* N1	**76**	B5
Horsfeld Gdns *ELTH/MOT* SE9	**143**	E3
Horsfeld Rd *ELTH/MOT* SE9	**143**	D3
Horsford Rd *BRXS/STRHM* SW2	**135**	F1
Horsley St *WALW* SE17	**119**	D2
Horsman St *CMBW* SE5	**118**	C2
Horsmonden Rd *BROCKY* SE4	**139**	F3
Hortensia Rd *WBPTN* SW10	**114**	C2
Horticultural Pl *CHSWK* W4	**111**	D1
Horton Av *CRICK* NW2	**71**	E1
Horton Rd *HACK* E8	**78**	B3
Horton St *LEW* SE13	**140**	B1
Hosack Rd *BAL* SW12	**151**	F2
Hoser Av *LEE/GVPK* SE12	**160**	A2
Hosier La *STBT* EC1A	**22**	C3
Hoskin's Cl *CAN/RD* E16	**94**	C5
Hoskins St *GNWCH* SE10	**123**	D1
Hospital Wy *LEW* SE13	**141**	D4
Hotham Rd *PUT/ROE* SW15	**130**	C1
Hotham St *SRTFD* E15	**81**	E5
Hothfield Pl *BERM/RHTH* SE16	**102**	C4
Houghton Cl *HACK* * E8	**77**	F3
Houghton St *HOL/ALD* * WC2B	**21**	F5
Houndsditch *HDTCH* EC3A	**25**	D4
Houseman Wy *CMBW* SE5	**119**	D3
Houston Rd *FSTH* SE23	**157**	E2
Hoveden Rd *CRICK* NW2	**71**	D2
Howard Cl *ACT* W3	**86**	B5
CRICK * NW2	**71**	E1
Howard Rd *CRICK* NW2	**71**	D1
EHAM E6	**95**	F1
IL IG1	**84**	B1
SEVS/STOTM N15	**59**	E1
STNW/STAM N16	**77**	D1
WAN E11	**63**	E5
Howard's La *PUT/ROE* SW15	**130**	C2
Howard's Rd *PLSTW* E13	**94**	A2
Howbury Rd *PECK* SE15	**138**	C1
Howden St *PECK* SE15	**138**	A1
Howell Wk *WALW* SE17	**47**	D5
Howgate Rd *MORT/ESHN* SW14	**129**	D1
Howick Pl *WEST* SW1P	**43**	F3
Howie St *BTSEA* SW11	**115**	E3
Howitt Cl *HAMP* NW3	**73**	E4
Howitt Rd *HAMP* NW3	**73**	E3
Howland Ms East *FITZ* W1T	**19**	F1
Howland St *FITZ* W1T	**19**	F2
Howland Wy *BERM/RHTH* SE16	**103**	E3
Howletts Rd *HNHL* SE24	**136**	C4
Howley Pl *BAY/PAD* W2	**15**	F2
Howsman Rd *BARN* SW13	**112**	A2
Howson Rd *BROCKY* SE4	**139**	E2
How's St *BETH* E2	**13**	E1
Hoxton Market *IS* N1	**12**	C4
Hoxton Sq *IS* N1	**12**	C4
Hoxton St *IS* N1	**12**	C2
Hoylake Rd *ACT* W3	**87**	E5
Hoyland Cl *PECK* * SE15	**120**	B3
Hoyle Rd *TOOT* SW17	**151**	E5
Hoy St *CAN/RD* E16	**93**	F5
Hubbard Rd *WNWD* SE27	**154**	C4
Hubbard St *SRTFD* E15	**81**	E5
Hubert Gv *BRXN/ST* SW9	**135**	E1
Hubert Rd *EHAM* E6	**95**	D2
Huddart St *BOW* E3	**91**	F4
Huddleston Cl *BETH* * E2	**90**	C1
Huddlestone Rd *CRICK* NW2	**70**	B3
FSTGT E7	**81**	F1
Huddleston Rd *ARCH* N19	**56**	C1
Hudson Cl *SHB* * W12	**100**	B1
Hudson Rd *WOOL/PLUM* SE18	**126**	C1
Huggin Hl *BLKFR* EC4V	**35**	F1
Huggins Pl *BRXS/STRHM* SW2	**153**	F1
Hughan Rd *SRTFD* E15	**81**	D2
Hugh Dalton Av *FUL/PGN* * SW6	**113**	F2
Hughes Ter *CAN/RD* * E16	**93**	F4
Hugh Gaitskell Cl *FUL/PGN* * SW6	**113**	F2
Hugh Ms *PIM* SW1V	**43**	D5
Hugh Pl *WEST* SW1P	**44**	A4
Hugh St *PIM* SW1V	**43**	D5
Hugon Rd *FUL/PGN* SW6	**132**	C1
Hugo Rd *ARCH* N19	**74**	C1
Huguenot Pl *WAND/EARL* SW18	**132**	C3
WCHPL E1	**25**	F2
Hullbridge Ms *IS* N1	**77**	D5
Hull Cl *BERM/RHTH* * SE16	**103**	D2
Hull St *FSBYE* EC1V	**11**	E4
Hulme Ter *STHWK* SE1	**47**	F1
Hulse Av *BARK* IG11	**85**	D3
Humber Dr *NKENS* W10	**89**	D3
Humber Rd *BKHTH/KID* SE3	**124**	A2
CRICK NW2	**52**	B4
Humberstone Rd *PLSTW* E13	**94**	C2
Humbolt Rd *HMSMTH* W6	**113**	E2
Humphrey St *STHWK* SE1	**119**	F1
Hungerford Br *STHWK* SE1	**33**	E3
Hungerford La *HOLWY* N7	**75**	D3
Hungerford St *WCHPL* * E1	**90**	B5
Hunsdon Rd *NWCR* SE14	**121**	D3
Hunslett St *BETH* * E2	**90**	C1
Hunt Cl *BKHTH/KID* * SE3	**124**	A5
Hunter Cl *BAL* SW12	**152**	A1
STHWK SE1	**48**	B3
Hunter Ct *CMBW* * SE5	**137**	D2
Hunters Meadow *NRWD* SE19	**155**	E4
Hunters Rd *IL* IG1	**84**	B2
Hunter St *BMSBY* WC1N	**9**	D5
Huntingdon Gdns *CHSWK* * W4	**110**	C3
Huntingdon St *CAN/RD* E16	**93**	F5
IS N1	**75**	F4
Huntingfield Rd *PUT/ROE* SW15	**130**	A4
Huntley St *GWRST* WC1E	**19**	F1
Hunton St *WCHPL* E1	**90**	A4
Hunt's La *SRTFD* E15	**92**	C1
Huntsman St *WALW* SE17	**48**	C5
Huntspill St *TOOT* SW17	**150**	C3
Hunts Slip Rd *DUL* SE21	**155**	E3
Huntsworth Ms *CAMTN* NW1	**5**	E5
Hurdwick Pl *CAMTN* * NW1	**7**	E1

Hurlingham Gdns *FUL/PGN* SW6 ....**131** F1
Hurlingham Pk *FUL/PGN* * SW6 ....**131** F1
Hurlingham Rd *FUL/PGN* SW6 ....**113** F5
Hurlingham Sq *FUL/PGN* SW6 ....**132** A1
Hurlock St *FSBYPK* N4 ....**58** B5
Huron Rd *TOOT* SW17 ....**152** A2
Hurren Cl *BKHTH/KID* SE3 ....**141** E1
Hurry Cl *SRTFD* E15 ....**81** E4
Hurst Av *HGT* N6 ....**56** C1
Hurstbourne Gdns *BARK* IG11 ....**85** D3
Hurstbourne Rd *FSTH* SE23 ....**157** E1
Hurst Cl *GLDGN* NW11 ....**54** B1
Hurstdene Gdns *SEVS/STOTM* N15 ....**59** E2
Hurst St *HNHL* SE24 ....**136** B4
Hurstway Wk *NKENS* * W10 ....**101** D1
Huson Cl *HAMP* * NW3 ....**73** E4
Hutching's St *POP/IOD* E14 ....**104** A3
Hutchins Cl *SRTFD* E15 ....**80** C4
Hutton St *EMB* EC4Y **22** B5
Huxbear St *BROCKY* SE4 ....**139** F3
Huxley Cl *LEY* E10 ....**62** C4
Huxley St *NKENS* W10 ....**89** E2
Hyacinth Rd *PUT/ROE* SW15 ....**148** A1
Hyde Cl *PLSTW* E13 ....**94** A1
Hyde Farm Ms *BAL* SW12 ....**153** D1
Hyde La *BTSEA* SW11 ....**115** E4
Hyde Park Cnr *MYFR/PICC* W1J **30** B5
Hyde Park Crs *BAY/PAD* W2 ....**16** C5
Hyde Park Gdns *BAY/PAD* W2 ....**28** B1
Hyde Park Gardens Ms *BAY/PAD* W2 ....**28** B1
Hyde Park Ga *KENS* W8 ....**39** E1
Hyde Park Gate Ms *SKENS* * SW7 ....**39** F1
Hyde Park Pl *BAY/PAD* W2 ....**29** D1
Hyde Park Sq *BAY/PAD* W2 ....**16** C5
Hyde Park St *BAY/PAD* W2 ....**28** C1
Hyderabad Wy *SRTFD* E15 ....**81** E4
Hyde Rd *IS* N1 ....**77** E5
Hyde's Pl *IS* * N1 ....**76** B4
Hyde St *DEPT* SE8 ....**122** A2
Hydethorpe Rd *BAL* SW12 ....**152** C1
Hyde V *GNWCH* SE10 ....**122** C3
Hylton St *WOOL/PLUM* SE18 ....**109** F5
Hyndewood *FSTH* * SE23 ....**157** D3
Hyndman St *PECK* SE15 ....**120** B2
Hyson Rd *BERM/RHTH* SE16 ....**120** B1
Hythe Rd *WLSDN* NW10 ....**87** F2

Ibbotson Av *CAN/RD* E16 ....**93** F5
Ibbott St *WCHPL* E1 ....**90** C3
Ibis La *CHSWK* W4 ....**110** C4
Iceland Rd *BOW* E3 ....**80** A5
Ickburgh Est *CLPT* * E5 ....**60** B4
Ickburgh Rd *CLPT* E5 ....**60** B5
Ickleton Rd *ELTH/MOT* SE9 ....**161** E4
Ida St *POP/IOD* E14 ....**92** C5
Idmiston Rd *FSTGT* E7 ....**81** F2
                    WNWD SE27 ....**154** C3
Idol La *MON* EC3R **36** C2
Idonia St *DEPT* SE8 ....**121** F3
Iffley Rd *HMSMTH* W6 ....**100** B4
Ifield Rd *WBPTN* SW10 ....**114** B2
Ilbert St *NKENS* W10 ....**89** E2
Ilchester Gdns *BAY/PAD* W2 ....**26** C1
Ilchester Pl *WKENS* W14 ....**101** F4
Ildersly Gv *DUL* SE21 ....**155** D2
Ilderton Rd *BERM/RHTH* SE16 ....**120** C2
Ilex Rd *WLSDN* NW10 ....**69** F2
Ilex Wy *STRHM/NOR* SW16 ....**154** A5
Ilford HI *IL* IG1 ....**66** A5
Ilford La *IL* IG1 ....**84** B3
Ilfracombe Rd *BMLY* BR1 ....**159** F3
Iliffe St *WALW* SE17 ....**118** B1

Iliffe Yd *WALW* SE17 ....**118** B1
Ilkley Rd *CAN/RD* E16 ....**94** C4
Ilminster Gdns *BTSEA* SW11 ....**133** E2
Imber St *IS* N1 ....**77** D5
Imperial Av *STNW/STAM* * N16 ....**77** E1
Imperial Rd *FUL/PGN* SW6 ....**114** B4
Imperial College Rd *SKENS* SW7 ....**40** A3
Imperial Sq *FUL/PGN* SW6 ....**114** B4
Imperial St *BOW* E3 ....**92** C2
Imperial Wy *CHST* BR7 ....**162** C3
Imre Cl *SHB* W12 ....**100** B2
Inca Dr *ELTH/MOT* SE9 ....**144** B5
Inchmery Rd *CAT* SE6 ....**158** B2
Independent Pl *HACK* E8 ....**77** F2
Independents Rd *BKHTH/KID* SE3 ....**141** F1
Inderwick Rd *CEND/HSY/T* N8 ....**57** F1
Indescon Ct *POP/IOD* E14 ....**104** A3
India St *TWRH* EC3N **25** E5
India Wy *SHB* W12 ....**100** B1
Indigo Ms *POP/IOD* * E14 ....**104** C1
                    STNW/STAM N16 ....**59** D5
Indus Rd *CHARL* SE7 ....**124** C3
Ingal Rd *PLSTW* E13 ....**94** A3
Ingate Pl *VX/NE* SW8 ....**116** B4
Ingatestone Rd *MNPK* E12 ....**64** C3
Ingelow St *VX/NE* SW8 ....**116** B5
Ingersoll Rd *SHB* W12 ....**100** B2
Ingestre Pl *SOHO/CST* W1F **19** F5
Ingestre Rd *FSTGT* E7 ....**82** A1
                    KTTN NW5 ....**74** B1
Ingham Rd *KIL/WHAMP* NW6 ....**72** A1
Ingledew Rd *WOOL/PLUM* SE18 ....**127** D1
Inglefield Sq *WAP* * E1W **102** B2
Inglemere Rd *FSTH* SE23 ....**157** D3
Ingleside Gv *BKHTH/KID* SE3 ....**123** F2
Inglethorpe St *FUL/PGN* SW6 ....**113** D4
Ingleton St *BRXN/ST* SW9 ....**118** A5
Ingleton Rd *BRXN/ST* SW9 ....**118** A5
Inglewood Cl *POP/IOD* E14 ....**104** A5
Inglewood Rd *KIL/WHAMP* NW6 ....**72** A2
Inglis St *CMBW* SE5 ....**54** C2
Ingram Av *EFNCH* N2 ....**55** F4
Ingram Cl *LBTH* SE11 ....**45** F4
Ingrave St *BTSEA* SW11 ....**133** D1
Ingress St *CHSWK* W4 ....**111** E1
Inigo Jones Rd *CHARL* SE7 ....**125** D3
Inkerman Rd *KTTN* NW5 ....**74** B3
Inman Rd *WAND/EARL* SW18 ....**132** C5
                    WLSDN NW10 ....**69** E5
Inner Cir *CAMTN* NW1 ....**6** A4
Inner Park Rd *WIM/MER* SW19 ....**149** D3
Innes Gdns *PUT/ROE* SW15 ....**130** B4
Innes St *PECK* SE15 ....**119** D4
Inniskilling Rd *PLSTW* E13 ....**94** C1
Inskip Cl *LEY* E10 ....**62** B4
Institute Pl *HACK* E8 ....**78** B2
Integer Gdns *WAN* * E11 ....**63** D2
Inver Ct *BAY/PAD* W2 ....**15** D5
Inverforth Cl *HAMP* NW3 ....**54** C4
Inverine Rd *CHARL* SE7 ....**124** B1
Invermore Pl *WOOL/PLUM* SE18 ....**108** C5
Inverness Gdns *KENS* W8 ....**26** C4
Inverness Ms *BAY/PAD* W2 ....**27** D1
Inverness Pl *BAY/PAD* W2 ....**27** D1
Inverness St *CAMTN* NW1 ....**74** B5
Inverness Ter *BAY/PAD* W2 ....**15** D5
Inverton Rd *PECK* SE15 ....**139** D2
Invicta Cl *CHST* BR7 ....**162** B5
Invicta Plaza *STHWK* SE1 ....**34** C3
Invicta Rd *BKHTH/KID* SE3 ....**124** A3
Inville Rd *WALW* SE17 ....**119** D1
Inworth St *BTSEA* SW11 ....**115** E5
Inworth Wk *IS* * N1 ....**76** C5
Iona Cl *CAT* SE6 ....**140** A5
Ion Sq *BETH* * E2 ....**90** A1

Ireland Cl *EHAM* E6 ....**95** F4
Irene Rd *FUL/PGN* SW6 ....**114** A4
Ireton St *BOW* E3 ....**92** A3
Iris Cl *EHAM* E6 ....**95** E4
Iron Bridge Cl *WLSDN* NW10 ....**69** E2
Iron Mill Pl *WAND/EARL* * SW18 ....**132** B4
Iron Mill Rd *WAND/EARL* SW18 ....**132** B4
Ironmonger La *CITYW* EC2V **24** C4
Ironmonger Rw *FSBYE* EC1V **11** F4
Ironside Cl *BERM/RHTH* SE16 ....**103** D3
Irving Gv *BRXN/ST* SW9 ....**117** F5
Irving Ms *IS* N1 ....**76** C3
Irving Rd *WKENS* W14 ....**101** D4
Irving St *LSQ/SEVD* WC2H **32** B2
Irwell Est *BERM/RHTH* * SE16 ....**102** C3
Irwin Av *WOOL/PLUM* SE18 ....**127** E3
Irwin Gdns *WLSDN* NW10 ....**70** B5
Isabella Rd *HOM* * E9 ....**78** C2
Isabella St *STHWK* SE1 ....**34** C4
Isabel St *BRXN/ST* SW9 ....**117** F4
Isambard Ms *POP/IOD* E14 ....**104** C4
Isambard Pl *BERM/RHTH* SE16 ....**102** C2
Isis St *WAND/EARL* SW18 ....**150** C2
Isla Rd *WOOL/PLUM* SE18 ....**126** C2
Islay Wk *IS* * N1 ....**76** C3
Islay Whf *POP/IOD* * E14 ....**92** C4
Isledon Rd *HOLWY* N7 ....**58** A5
Islington Gn *IS* N1 ....**76** B5
Islington High St *IS* N1 ....**10** C1
Islington Park Ms *IS* N1 ....**76** B4
Islington Park St *IS* N1 ....**76** A4
Islip St *KTTN* NW5 ....**74** C2
Ismailia Rd *FSTGT* E7 ....**82** B3
Isom Cl *PLSTW* E13 ....**94** B2
Ivanhoe Rd *CMBW* SE5 ....**137** F1
Ivatt Pl *WKENS* W14 ....**113** F1
Iveagh Av *WLSDN* NW10 ....**86** A1
Iveagh Cl *HOM* E9 ....**79** D5
  WLSDN NW10 ....**86** A1
Ive Farm Cl *LEY* E10 ....**62** A4
Ive Farm La *LEY* E10 ....**62** A4
Iveley Rd *CLAP* SW4 ....**116** C5
Iverna Ct *KENS* W8 ....**38** B2
Iverna Gdns *KENS* W8 ....**38** B2
Iverson Rd *KIL/WHAMP* NW6 ....**71** F3
Ives St *CHEL* SW3 ....**41** D4
Ivimey St *BETH* * E2 ....**90** A2
Ivor Gv *ELTH/MOT* SE9 ....**162** B1
Ivor Pl *CAMTN* NW1 ....**17** E1
Ivor St *CAMTN* NW1 ....**74** C1
Ivorydown *BMLY* BR1 ....**160** A4
Ivy Church La *STHWK* * SE1 ....**119** F1
Ivy Ct *STHWK* * SE1 ....**120** A1
Ivy Crs *CHSWK* W4 ....**98** C5
Ivydale Rd *PECK* SE15 ....**139** D1
Ivyday Gv *STRHM/NOR* SW16 ....**153** F3
Ivy Gdns *CEND/HSY/T* N8 ....**57** E1
Ivymount Rd *WNWD* SE27 ....**154** A3
Ivy Rd *BROCKY* SE4 ....**139** F2
  CAN/RD E16 ....**94** A5
  CRICK NW2 ....**53** D2
  LEY E10 ....**62** A1
  TOOT SW17 ....**151** E5
Ivy St *IS* N1 ....**12** C1
Ixworth Pl *CHEL* SW3 ....**40** C5

Jacaranda Gv *HACK* E8 ....**77** F4
Jack Clow Rd *SRTFD* E15 ....**93** E1
Jack Cornwell St *MNPK* E12 ....**84** A1
Jackman Ms *WLSDN* NW10 ....**51** E5
Jackman St *HACK* E8 ....**78** B5
Jackson Cl *HOM* E9 ....**79** D4

Jackson Rd *BARK* IG11 ....**85** D5
  HOLWY N7 ....**75** F1
Jackson's La *HGT* N6 ....**56** A2
Jackson St *WOOL/PLUM* SE18 ....**126** A2
Jack Walker Ct *HBRY* N5 ....**76** B1
Jacob St *STHWK* SE1 ....**37** F5
Jacob's Well Ms *MHST* W1U **18** B4
Jacqueline Creft Ter *HGT* * N6 ....**56** A1
Jade Cl *CAN/RD* E16 ....**95** D5
  CRICK NW2 ....**53** D2
Jade Ter *KIL/WHAMP* * NW6 ....**72** C4
Jaffe Rd *IL* IG1 ....**66** C3
Jaggard Wy *BAL* SW12 ....**133** F5
Jago Cl *WOOL/PLUM* SE18 ....**126** C2
Jago Wk *CMBW* SE5 ....**119** D3
Jamaica Rd *BERM/RHTH* SE16 ....**102** B4
  STHWK SE1 ....**49** E1
Jamaica St *WCHPL* E1 ....**90** C4
James Av *CRICK* NW2 ....**70** C2
James Cl *GLDGN* * NW11 ....**53** E1
  PLSTW E13 ....**94** A1
James Collins Cl *NKENS* W10 ....**89** F3
James Joyes Wk *HNHL* * SE24 ......**136** B2
James La *WAN* E11 ....**62** C2
Jameson St *KENS* W8 ....**26** A3
James St *BARK* IG11 ....**84** C4
  COVGDN WC2E **33** D1
  MHST W1U **18** B5
Jamestown Rd *CAMTN* NW1 ....**74** B5
Jamestown Wy *POP/IOD* E14 ....**105** D1
Jamuna Close *POP/IOD* * E14 ....**91** E4
Jane St *WCHPL* E1 ....**90** B5
Janet St *POP/IOD* E14 ....**104** A4
Janeway Pl *BERM/RHTH* SE16 ....**102** B3
Janeway St *BERM/RHTH* SE16 ....**102** A3
Janson Cl *SRTFD* E15 ....**81** E2
  WLSDN NW10 ....**51** D5
Janson Rd *SRTFD* E15 ....**81** E2
Japan Crs *FSBYPK* N4 ....**57** F3
Jardine Rd *WAP* E1W **103** D1
Jarrett Cl *BRXS/STRHM* SW2 ....**154** B1
Jarrow Rd *BERM/RHTH* SE16 ....**102** C5
Jarrow Wy *HOM* E9 ....**79** E1
Jarvis Rd *EDUL* SE22 ....**137** E2
Jasmine Cl *IL* IG1 ....**84** B2
Jasmine Ct *LEE/GVPK* SE12 ....**142** A4
Jason Wk *ELTH/MOT* SE9 ....**162** A4
Jasper Rd *CAN/RD* E16 ....**95** D5
Jay Gdns *CHST* BR7 ....**161** F4
Jay Ms *SKENS* SW7 ....**39** F1
Jebb Av *BRXS/STRHM* SW2 ....**135** E4
Jebb St *BOW* E3 ....**92** A1
Jedburgh Rd *PLSTW* E13 ....**94** C2
Jedburgh St *BTSEA* SW11 ....**134** A2
Jeddo Ms *SHB* * W12 ....**99** F3
Jeddo Rd *SHB* W12 ....**99** F3
Jeffrey's Pl *CAMTN* NW1 ....**74** C4
Jeffrey's Rd *CLAP* SW4 ....**117** E5
Jeffrey's St *CAMTN* NW1 ....**74** B4
Jeger Av *BETH* * E2 ....**77** F5
Jeken Rd *ELTH/MOT* SE9 ....**142** C2
Jelf Rd *BRXS/STRHM* SW2 ....**136** A3
Jenkins La *BARK* IG11 ....**96** B1
Jenkins Rd *PLSTW* E13 ....**94** B3
Jenner Av *ACT* W3 ....**87** D4
Jenner Rd *STNW/STAM* N16 ....**59** F4
Jennifer Rd *BMLY* BR1 ....**159** F3
Jennings Rd *EDUL* SE22 ....**137** F4
Jenny Hammond Cl *WAN* E11 ....**63** F5
Jephson Rd *FSTGT* E7 ....**82** C5
Jephson St *CMBW* SE5 ....**119** D4
Jephtha Rd *WAND/EARL* SW18 ......**132** A4
Jerdan Pl *FUL/PGN* SW6 ....**114** A3
Jeremiah St *POP/IOD* E14 ....**92** B5
Jermyn St *STJS* SW1Y **31** E3
Jerningham Rd *NWCR* SE14 ....**121** F5
Jerome Crs *STJWD* NW8 ....**4** C5
Jerome St *WCHPL* E1 ....**25** E2

Jerrard St LEW SE13 ....140 B1
Jerrold St IS * N1 ....13 D2
Jersey Rd CAN/RD E16 ....94 C4
  IL IG1 ....84 B1
  IS N1 ....76 C3
  WAN E11 ....63 D3
Jersey St BETH E2 ....90 B2
Jerusalem Pas CLKNW EC1R ...22 C1
Jesmond Dene HAMP * NW3 ...72 C3
Jessam Av STNW/STAM N16 ...60 B3
Jesse Rd LEY E10 ....62 C3
Jessica Rd WAND/EARL SW18 ..132 C4
Jessup Cl WOOL/PLUM SE18 ..108 C5
Jevington St LEE/GVPK SE12 ...160 B1
Jewry St TWRH EC3N 25 E5
Jews Rw WAND/EARL SW18 ....132 B2
Jews Wk SYD SE26 ....156 B4
Jeymer Av CRICK NW2 ....70 B2
Jeypore Rd WAND/EARL SW18 ..132 C4
Jim Bradley Cl WOOL/PLUM SE18 ..108 A5
Joan Crs ELTH/MOT SE9 ....143 D5
Joan St STHWK SE1 ....34 C4
Jocelyn St PECK SE15 ....120 A4
Jockey's Flds FSBYW WC1X 21 F2
Jodane Rd DEPT SE8 ....103 F5
Jodrell Rd HOM E9 ....79 F5
Johanna St STHWK * SE1 ....46 A1
John Adam St CHCR WC2N 33 D3
John Aird Ct BAY/PAD W2 ....15 F2
John Archer Wy WAND/EARL SW18 ..133 D4
John Ashby Cl BRXS/STRHM SW2 ..135 E4
John Burns Dr BARK IG11 ....85 E5
John Campbell Rd STNW/STAM N16 ..77 E2
John Carpenter St EMB EC4Y ...34 C1
John Felton Rd BERM/RHTH * SE16 ..102 A3
John Fisher St WCHPL E1 ....102 A1
John Harrison Wy GNWCH SE10 ..105 F4
John Islip St WEST SW1P 44 D4
John Maurice Cl WALW SE17 ....48 A1
John McKenna Wk
  BERM/RHTH * SE16 ....102 A4
John Parker Sq BTSEA * SW11 ..133 D1
John Penn St LEW SE13 ....122 B4
John Prince's St CAVSQ/HST W1G ..19 D4
John Rennie Wk WAP E1W 102 B1
John Roll Wy BERM/RHTH SE16 ..102 A4
John Ruskin St CMBW SE5 ......118 B3
John's Ms BMSBY WC1N 21 F1
John Silkin La DEPT SE8 ....121 D1
John Smith Av FUL/PGN SW6 ..113 F4
Johnson Cl HACK E8 ....78 A5
Johnson Rd WLSDN NW10 ....69 D5
Johnson's Pl PIM SW1V 116 C1
Johnson St WCHPL E1 ....90 C5
Johnsons Wy WLSDN NW10 .....86 B3
John Spencer Sq IS * N1 ....76 B3
Johns Pl WCHPL E1 ....90 B5
Johnston Cl BRXN/ST SW9 ......117 F4
Johnstone Rd EHAM E6 ....95 F2
John St BMSBY WC1N 21 F1
  SRTFD E15 ....81 F5
John Trundle Highwalk BARB * EC2Y ..23 E4
John Williams Cl PECK SE15 ....121 D2
John Wilson St WOOL/PLUM SE18 ..108 A5
John Wooley Cl LEW SE13 ......141 E2
Joiners Arms Yd CMBW * SE5 ..119 D4
Joiner St STHWK SE1 ....36 A4
Jonathan St LBTH SE11 ....117 F1
Jones Rd PLSTW E13 ....94 B3
Joseph Av ACT W3 ....87 D5
Josephine Av BRXS/STRHM SW2 ..135 E4
Joseph Powell Cl BAL SW12 ....134 C4
Joseph Ray Rd WAN E11 ....63 E4
Joseph St BOW E3 ....91 F4
Joseph Trotter Cl CLKNW EC1R ..10 B4
Joshua St POP/IOD E14 ....92 C5
Joslings Cl SHB W12 ....100 A1
Joubert St BTSEA SW11 ....115 F5

Jowett St PECK SE15 ....119 F3
The Jubilee GNWCH * SE10 .....122 B3
Jubilee Bridge STHWK SE1 ......35 F2
Jubilee Cl CDALE/KGS NW9 .....51 D1
Jubilee Gdns STHWK * SE1 .....33 F4
Jubilee Market COVGDN * WC2E ..33 D1
Jubilee Pl CHEL SW3 ....115 E1
Jubilee St WCHPL E1 ....90 C5
Jubilee Ter FUL/PGN * SW6 .....113 E5
Judd St STPAN WC1H 8 C4
Jude St CAN/RD E16 ....93 F5
Judges' Wk HAMP NW3 ....54 C5
Juer St BTSEA SW11 ....115 E3
Julian Av ACT W3 ....98 B1
Julian Pl POP/IOD E14 ....122 B1
Julian Tayler Pth SYD * SE26 ...156 B2
Juliette Rd PLSTW E13 ....94 A1
Julius Nyerere Cl IS * N1 ....75 F5
Junction Ap BTSEA SW11 ....133 C1
  LEW SE13 ....140 C1
Junction Ms BAY/PAD W2 ....16 C4
Junction Pl BAY/PAD * W2 ....16 B4
Junction Rd ARCH N19 ....56 C5
  PLSTW E13 ....82 B5
Juniper Crs CAMTN NW1 ....74 A4
Juniper La EHAM E6 ....95 E4
Juniper Rd IL IG1 ....84 A1
Juniper St WCHPL * E1 ....102 C1
Juno Wy NWCR SE14 ....121 D2
Jupiter Wy HOLWY N7 ....75 F3
Jupp Rd SRTFD E15 ....81 D4
Jupp Rd West SRTFD E15 ....80 C5
Justice Wk CHEL SW3 ....115 E2
Jutland Rd CAT SE6 ....140 C5
  PLSTW E13 ....94 A3
Juxon St LBTH SE11 ....45 F4

K

Kambala Rd BTSEA SW11 ....115 D5
Kangley Bridge Rd SYD SE26 ...157 F5
Kara Wy CRICK NW2 ....71 D1
Karen Ct ELTH/MOT SE9 ....142 C3
Kashgar Rd WOOL/PLUM SE18 ..127 F1
Kashmir Rd CHARL SE7 ....125 D3
Kassala Rd BTSEA SW11 ....115 F4
Katherine Cl BERM/RHTH SE16 ..103 D2
Katherine Gdns ELTH/MOT SE9 ..143 D2
Katherine Rd EHAM E6 ....83 D4
Katherine Sq NTGHL * W11 .....101 E2
Kathleen Av ACT W3 ....86 C4
Kathleen Rd BTSEA SW11 ....133 F1
Kay Rd BRXN/ST SW9 ....117 E5
Kay St BETH E2 ....90 A1
  SRTFD E15 ....81 D4
Kean St HOL/ALD WC2B 21 E5
Keats Av CAN/RD E16 ....106 B2
Keats Cl STHWK SE1 ....49 E5
Keats Est STNW/STAM * N16 ...59 F4
Keats Gv HAMP NW3 ....73 E1
Keats Rd WELL DA16 ....127 E4
Keble Pl BARN * SW13 ....112 B2
Keble St TOOT SW17 ....150 C4
Kedleston Wk BETH E2 ....90 B2
Keeble Cl WOOL/PLUM * SE18 ..126 B2
Keedonwood Rd BMLY BR1 .....159 E4
Keel Cl BERM/RHTH SE16 ....103 D2
Keeley Rd ELTH/MOT SE9 ....143 D3
Keeling Rd ELTH/MOT SE9 ......143 D1
Keemor Cl WOOL/PLUM * SE18 ..126 A3
Keens Cl STRHM/NOR SW16 ....153 D5
Keen's Yd IS N1 ....76 B3
The Keep BKHTH/KID SE3 ....124 A5
Keesey St WALW SE17 ....119 D2
Keetons Rd BERM/RHTH * SE16 ..102 B4
  BERM/RHTH SE16 ....102 B4

Keevil Dr WIM/MER SW19......131 D5
Keighley Cl HOLWY N7......75 E1
Keightley Dr ELTH/MOT SE9......162 C1
Keildon Rd BTSEA SW11......133 F2
Keir Hardie Est CLPT * E5......60 B3
Keith Connor Cl VX/NE SW8......134 B1
Keith Gv SHB W12......100 A3
Keith Rd BARK IG11......97 D1
Kelbrook Rd BKHTH/KID SE3......125 E5
Kelceda Cl CRICK NW2......52 A4
Kelfield Gdns WLSDN W10......89 D5
Kelfield Ms NKENS W10......89 D4
Kelland Rd PLSTW E13......94 A3
Kellaway Rd BKHTH/KID SE3......124 C5
Keller Crs MNPK E12......83 D1
Kellerton Rd LEW SE13......141 E3
Kellett Rd BRXS/STRHM SW2......136 A2
Kellino St TOOT SW17......151 F4
Kellner Rd THMD SE28......109 F4
Kell St STHWK SE1......47 D2
Kelly Av PECK SE15......119 F4
Kelly Cl WLSDN NW10......51 D5
Kelly Ms MV/WKIL * W9......89 F4
Kelly St CAMTN NW1......74 B3
Kelman Cl CLAP SW4......117 D5
Kelmore Gv EDUL SE22......138 A2
Kelmscott Gdns SHB W12......100 A4
Kelmscott Rd BTSEA SW11......133 E3
Kelross Rd HBRY N5......76 B1
Kelsall Cl BKHTH/KID SE3......124 B5
Kelsey St BETH E2......90 A3
Kelso Pl KENS W8......38 C2
Kelvedon Rd FUL/PGN SW6......113 F3
Kelvin Gv SYD SE26......156 B3
Kelvington Rd PECK SE15......139 D3
Kelvin Rd HBRY N5......76 B1
Kember St IS N1......75 F4
Kemble Rd FSTH SE23......157 D1
Kemble St HOL/ALD WC2B......21 C5
Kemerton Rd CMBW SE5......136 C1
Kemey's St HOM E9......79 E2
Kempe Rd KIL/WHAMP NW6......89 D1
Kemplay Rd HAMP NW3......73 D1
Kemps Dr POP/IOD E14......104 A1
Kempsford Gdns ECT SW5......114 A1
Kempsford Rd LBTH SE11......46 B5
Kempson Rd FUL/PGN SW6......114 A4
Kempthorne Rd DEPT SE8......103 E5
Kempton Rd EHAM E6......83 F5
Kempt St WOOL/PLUM SE18......126 A2
Kemsing Rd GNWCH SE10......124 A1
Kenbury St CMBW SE5......118 C5
Kenchester Cl VX/NE SW8......117 E3
Kendal Av BARK IG11......85 E5
Kendal Cl CMBW SE5......118 B3
Kendal Ct ACT W3......86 A4
Kendale Rd BMLY BR1......159 E5
Kendall Pl MHST W1U......18 A3
Kendale Rd WOOL/PLUM SE18......125 D3
Kendal Pl PUT/ROE SW15......131 F3
Kendal Rd WLSDN NW10......70 A1
Kendal Steps BAY/PAD * W2......17 D5
Kendal St BAY/PAD W2......17 D5
Kender St NWCR SE14......120 C3
Kendoa Rd CLAP SW4......135 D2
Kendrick Ms SKENS SW7......40 A4
Kendrick Pl SKENS * SW7......40 A5
Kenilford Rd BAL SW12......134 B5
Kenilworth Av WIM/MER SW19......150 A5
Kenilworth Gdns GDMY/SEVK IG3......67 F4
   WOOL/PLUM SE18......126 B5
Kenilworth Rd BOW E3......91 E1
   KIL/WHAMP NW6......71 F5
Kenley Wk NTGHL * W11......101 E2
Kenlor Rd TOOT SW17......151 D5
Kenmare Gdns ALP/SUD HA0......68 A5
Kenmont Gdns WLSDN NW10......88 B3
Kenmure Rd HACK * E8......78 B2

Kenmure Yd HACK * E8......78 B2
Kennard Rd SRTFD E15......81 D4
Kennard St BTSEA SW11......116 A4
   CAN/RD E16......107 F2
Kennedy Cl PLSTW E13......94 A1
Kennedy Rd BARK IG11......85 E5
Kennedy Wk WALW SE17......48 B5
Kennet Cl BTSEA SW11......133 D2
Kenneth Av IL IG1......84 B1
Kenneth Crs CRICK NW2......70 B2
Kenneth Moor Rd IL * IG1......66 B5
Kennet Rd MV/WKIL W9......89 F3
Kennet St WAP E1W......102 A2
Kennet Wharf La BLKFR EC4V......35 F1
Kenninghall Rd CLPT E5......60 B5
Kennings Wy LBTH SE11......118 A1
Kennington Gv LBTH SE11......117 F2
Kennington La LBTH SE11......117 F1
Kennington Ov LBTH SE11......117 F2
Kennington Park Gdns LBTH SE11......118 B2
Kennington Park Pl WALW SE17......118 A2
Kennington Park Rd LBTH SE11......118 A2
Kennington Rd LBTH SE11......46 A3
Kenrick Pl MHST W1U......18 A2
Kensal Rd NKENS W10......89 E3
Kensal Whf NKENS * W10......89 E3
Kensington Av MNPK E12......83 E3
Kensington Church Ct KENS W8......38 C1
Kensington Church St KENS W8......26 A5
Kensington Church Wk KENS * W8......26 B5
Kensington Ct KENS W8......39 D1
Kensington Court Gdns KENS * W8......39 D2
Kensington Court Ms KENS * W8......39 D2
Kensington Court Pl KENS W8......39 D2
Kensington Gdns IL IG1......65 F3
Kensington Gardens Sq BAY/PAD W2......14 C5
Kensington Ga SKENS SW7......39 E2
Kensington Gore SKENS SW7......39 F1
Kensington Hall Gdns WKENS SW14......113 F1
Kensington High St KENS W8......38 A2
   WKENS W14......101 E3
Kensington Palace KENS W8......27 D4
Kensington Palace Gdns KENS W8......26 A3
Kensington Park Gdns NTGHL W11......101 F1
Kensington Park Ms NTGHL W11......89 F5
Kensington Park Rd NTGHL W11......89 F5
Kensington Pl KENS W8......26 A4
Kensington Rd KENS W8......39 D1
   SKENS SW7......40 C1
Kensington Sq KENS W8......38 C1
Kent Av WELL DA16......145 F3
Kentish Town Rd CAMTN NW1......74 B3
Kentlea Rd THMD SE28......109 E3
Kentmere Rd WOOL/PLUM SE18......109 E5
Kenton Rd HOM E9......79 D3
Kenton St STPAN WC1H......8 C5
Kent Rd CHSWK W4......98 C4
   RCH/KEW TW9......110 A3
Kent St BETH E2......13 F1
   PLSTW E13......94 B2
Kent Ter CAMTN NW1......5 D4
Kent View Gdns GDMY/SEVK IG3......67 E4
Kentwell Cl BROCKY * SE4......139 E2
Kentwode Gn BARN SW13......112 A3
Kent Yd SKENS SW7......41 D1
Kenward Rd ELTH/MOT SE9......142 F3
Ken Wy WBLY HA9......50 C4
Kenway Rd ECT SW5......38 C5
Kenwood Cl GLDGN NW11......55 D3
Kenwood Rd HGT N6......55 F1
Kenworthy Rd HOM E9......79 E2
Kenwyn Dr CRICK NW2......51 E5
Kenwyn Rd CLAP SW4......135 D2
Kenya Rd CHARL SE7......125 D3
Kenyon St FUL/PGN SW6......113 D4
Keogh Rd SRTFD E15......81 E3
Kepler Rd CLAP SW4......135 E2

Keppel Rd *EHAM* E6.....................................83 F4
Keppel St *GWRST* WC1E.............................20 B2
Kerbela St *BETH* E2....................................90 A3
Kerbey St *POP/IOD* E14..............................92 B5
Kerfield Crs *CMBW* SE5..............................119 D4
Kerfield Pl *CMBW* SE5................................119 D4
Kerrison Rd *BTSEA* SW11...........................133 E1
  SRTFD E15...81 D5
Kerry Cl *CAN/RD* E16.................................94 B5
Kerry Pth *NWCR* SE14...............................121 F2
Kerry Rd *NWCR* SE14.................................121 F2
Kersfield Rd *PUT/ROE* SW15......................131 D4
Kersley Ms *BTSEA* SW11.............................115 F4
Kersley Rd *STNW/STAM* N16......................59 E3
Kersley St *BTSEA* SW11..............................115 F5
Kerwick Cl *HOLWY* N7.................................75 F2
Keslake Rd *KIL/WHAMP* NW6.....................89 D1
Keston Rd *PECK* SE15.................................138 A1
Kestrel Av *EHAM* E6...................................95 E4
  HNHL SE24.......................................136 B3
Kestrel Cl *WLSDN* NW10............................69 D2
Kestrel Pl *NWCR* * SE14............................121 E2
Keswick Av *KUTN/CMB* KT2.......................147 E5
Keswick Rd *PUT/ROE* SW15.......................131 E4
Kettlebaston Rd *LEY* E10............................61 F3
Kew Br *RCH/KEW* TW9................................110 A2
Kew Bridge Arches *CHSWK* * W4.............110 A2
Kew Meadow Pth *RCH/KEW* TW9..............110 B4
Key Cl *WCHPL* E1..90 B3
Keyes Rd *CRICK* NW2.................................71 D2
Keymer Rd *BRXS/STRHM* SW2....................153 F2
Keynsham Gdns *ELTH/MOT* SE9................143 D3
Keynsham Rd *ELTH/MOT* SE9.....................143 D3
Keyse Rd *STHWK* SE1..................................49 E3
Keystone Crs *IS* N1......................................9 D2
Keyworth Cl *CLPT* E5...................................79 E1
Keyworth St *STHWK* SE1.............................47 D2
Kezia St *DEPT* SE8.....................................121 E1
Khama Rd *TOOT* SW17................................151 E4
Khartoum Rd *IL* IG1....................................84 B2
  PLSTW E13.......................................94 B2
  TOOT SW17.....................................151 D4
Khyber Rd *BTSEA* SW11..............................115 E5
Kibworth St *VX/NE* SW8..............................117 F3
Kidbrooke Gdns *BKHTH/KID* SE3...............124 A5
Kidbrooke Gv *BKHTH/KID* SE3...................124 A4
Kidbrooke La *ELTH/MOT* SE9......................143 E2
Kidbrooke Park Cl *BKHTH/KID* SE3...........124 B4
Kidbrooke Park Rd *BKHTH/KID* SE3...........124 B4
Kidbrooke Wy *BKHTH/KID* SE3..................124 B5
Kidderpore Av *HAMP* NW3..........................72 A1
Kidderpore Gdns *HAMP* NW3......................72 A1
Kidd Pl *CHARL* SE7....................................125 E1
Kilburn Br *KIL/WHAMP* NW6.......................72 A5
Kilburn High Rd *KIL/WHAMP* NW6.............72 A4
Kilburn La *NKENS* W10...............................89 D2
Kilburn Park Rd *KIL/WHAMP* NW6..............2 A1
Kilburn Pl *KIL/WHAMP* NW6........................72 A5
Kilburn Priory *KIL/WHAMP* NW6.................72 A5
Kilburn Sq *KIL/WHAMP* NW6......................72 A5
Kilburn V *KIL/WHAMP* NW6........................72 B5
Kildare Gdns *BAY/PAD* W2.........................14 A3
Kildare Rd *CAN/RD* E16..............................94 A4
Kildare Ter *BAY/PAD* W2............................14 A4
Kildoran Rd *CLAP* SW4..............................135 E3
Kilgour Rd *FSTH* SE23...............................139 E4
Kilkie St *FUL/PGN* SW6..............................114 C5
Killarney Rd *WAND/EARL* SW18..................132 C4
Killearn Rd *CAT* SE6..................................159 D1
Killick St *IS* N1...9 E1
Killieser Av *BRXS/STRHM* SW2..................153 E2
Killip Cl *CAN/RD* E16.................................93 F5
Killowen Rd *HOM* * E9................................79 D3
Killyon Rd *VX/NE* SW8...............................116 C5
Kilmaine Rd *FUL/PGN* SW6........................113 C5
Kilmarsh Rd *HMSMTH* W6.........................100 C5
Kilmington Rd *BARN* SW13........................112 A2
Kilmorie Rd *FSTH* SE23............................157 E1

Kilner St *POP/IOD* E14................................92 A4
Kiln Ms *TOOT* SW17...................................151 D5
Kiln Pl *KTTN* NW5..74 A1
Kilravock St *NKENS* W10.............................89 E2
Kimbell Gdns *FUL/PGN* SW6.....................113 E4
Kimbell Pl *ELTH/MOT* SE9.........................142 C2
Kimberley Av *EHAM* E6................................95 E1
  GNTH/NBYPK IG2............................67 D2
  PECK SE15......................................120 B5
Kimberley Rd *BRXN/ST* SW9......................117 E5
  CAN/RD E16....................................93 F3
  KIL/WHAMP NW6.............................71 E5
  WAN E11...63 D4
Kimber Rd *WAND/EARL* SW18....................132 A5
Kimbolton Cl *LEE/GVPK* SE12....................141 F4
Kimmeridge Gdns *ELTH/MOT* SE9.............161 E4
Kimmeridge Rd *ELTH/MOT* SE9.................161 E4
Kimpton Rd *CMBW* SE5.............................119 D4
Kinburn St *BERM/RHTH* * SE16.................103 D3
Kincaid Rd *PECK* SE15...............................120 B3
Kincardine Gdns *MV/WKIL* * W9...............14 A1
Kinder St *WCHPL* E1...................................90 B5
Kinfauns Rd *BRXS/STRHM* SW2.................154 A2
King Alfred Av *CAT* SE6..............................158 A3
King Arthur Cl *PECK* SE15.........................120 C3
King Charles St *WHALL* SW1A....................32 B5
King Charles Ter *WAP* * E1W.....................102 B1
King Charles Wk *WIM/MER* * SW19............149 E1
King David La *WCHPL* E1...........................102 C1
Kingdon Rd *KIL/WHAMP* NW6.....................72 A3
King Edward Rd *LEY* E10............................62 C3
King Edward's Gdns *ACT* W3......................98 A2
King Edward's Rd *BARK* IG11......................85 D5
  HACK E8..78 B5
King Edward St *STBT* EC1A.........................23 E4
King Edward the Third Ms
  BERM/RHTH * SE16..........................102 B3
King Edward Wk *STHWK* SE1......................46 B3
Kingfield St *POP/IOD* E14.........................104 C5
Kingfisher St *EHAM* E6...............................95 E4
Kingfisher Wy *WLSDN* * NW10....................69 D3
King Garth Ms *FSTH* SE23........................156 C2
King George Av *CAN/RD* E16......................95 D5
  GNTH/NBYPK IG2............................67 D1
King George St *GNWCH* SE10...................122 C3
Kingham Cl *NTGHL* W11.............................101 E3
  WAND/EARL SW18..........................132 C5
King Henry's Rd *HAMP* NW3.......................73 E4
King Henry St *STNW/STAM* N16.................77 E3
King Henry's Wk *IS* N1...............................77 E3
King Henry Ter *WAP* * E1W.......................102 B1
Kinghorn St *STBT* * EC1A..........................23 E3
King James St *STHWK* SE1........................47 D1
King John Ct *SDTCH* EC2A.........................13 D5
King John St *WCHPL* E1..............................91 D4
King John's Wk *ELTH/MOT* SE9.................143 E5
Kinglake Est *WALW* * SE17.........................119 D5
Kinglake St *WALW* SE17.............................119 E5
Kingly Ct *REGST* * W1B...............................31 F1
Kingly St *REGST* W1B..................................19 E5
King & Queen Cl *ELTH/MOT* * SE9..............161 E4
King & Queen St *WALW* * SE17...................118 C1
King & Queen Whf
  BERM/RHTH * SE16..........................103 D2
Kingsand Rd *LEE/GVPK* SE12....................160 D2
King's Arms Yd *LOTH* EC2R.......................24 A4
Kings Av *BAL* SW12....................................153 D1
  CLAP SW4.......................................135 E4
King's Bench St *STHWK* SE1.......................35 D5
King's Bench Wk *EMB* * EC4Y....................34 B1
Kingsbridge Ct *POP/IOD* E14.....................104 A5
Kingsbridge Rd *BARK* IG11.........................97 D1
  NKENS W10.....................................88 C5
Kingsbury Rd *IS* N1.....................................77 E3
Kingsbury Ter *IS* N1....................................77 E3
Kingsclere Cl *PUT/ROE* SW15....................130 A5
Kingscliffe Gdns *WIM/MER* SW19..............149 F1
King's Cl *LEY* E10..62 B2

Kirton Gdns *BETH* E2 ....13 F4
Kirton Ldg *WAND/EARL* * SW18 ....132 B4
Kirton Rd *PLSTW* E13........................94 C1
Kirwyn Wy *CMBW* SE5 ....118 B3
Kitcat Ter *BOW* E3 ....92 A2
Kitchener Rd *FSTGT* E7 ....82 B3
Kite Pl *BETH* * E2 ....90 A2
Kite Yd *BTSEA* * SW11 ....115 F4
Kitson Rd *BARN* SW13 ....112 A4
    CMBW SE5.....................................118 C3
Kitto Rd *NWCR* SE14 ....121 D5
Kiver Rd *ARCH* N19 ....57 E4
Klea Av *BAL* SW4 ....134 C4
Knapdale Cl *FSTH* SE23 ....156 B2
Knapmill Rd *CAT* SE6 ....158 A2
Knapmill Wy *CAT* SE6.......................158 A2
Knapp Cl *WLSDN* NW10 ....69 E3
Knapp Rd *BOW* E3 ....92 A3
Knaresborough Dr
    WAND/EARL SW18..........................150 B1
Knaresborough Pl *ECT* SW5 ....38 C4
Knatchbull Rd *CMBW* SE5................118 B5
    WLSDN NW10 ....69 D5
Knebworth Rd *STNW/STAM* * N16 .....77 E1
Kneller Rd *BROCKY* SE4 ....139 E2
Knighten St *WAP* E1W 102 B2
Knighthead Point *POP/IOD* * E14 ...104 A3
Knightland Rd *CLPT* E5 ....60 B4
Knighton Park Rd *SYD* SE26 ....157 D5
Knighton Rd *FSTGT* E7 ....64 A5
Knightrider Ct *BLKFR* * EC4V 23 D5
Knightrider St *BLKFR* EC4V 35 D1
Knightsbridge *SKENS* SW7 ....41 D1
Knightsbridge Gn *KTBR* * SW1X 41 E1
Knight's Hl *WNWD* SE27 ....154 B5
Knight's Hill Sq *WNWD* SE27...........154 B4
Knights Rd *CAN/RD* E16 ....106 A2
Knights Wk *LBTH* SE11 ....46 C5
Knivet Rd *FUL/PGN* SW6 ....114 A2
Knobs Hill Rd *SRTFD* E15 ....80 B5
Knockholt Rd *ELTH/MOT* SE9 ....143 D3
The Knole *ELTH/MOT* SE9 ....162 A4
Knoll Rd *WAND/EARL* SW18 ....132 C3
Knolly's Cl *STRHM/NOR* SW16 ....154 A3
    WNWD * SE27 ....154 B3
Knolly's Rd *STRHM/NOR* SW16........154 A3
Knottisford St *BETH* E2 ....91 D2
Knotts Green Rd *LEY* E10 ....62 B1
Knowle Cl *BRXN/ST* SW9 ....136 A1
Knowles Hill Crs *LEW* SE13 ....141 D3
Knowsley Rd *BTSEA* SW11 ....115 F5
Knox Rd *FSTGT* E7 ....82 A3
Knox St *MBLAR* W1H 17 E2
Knoyle St *NWCR* SE14 ....121 E2
Kohat Rd *WIM/MER* SW19 ....150 B5
Kossuth St *GNWCH* SE10 ....123 E1
Kramer Ms *ECT* * SW5 ....114 A1
Kreedman Wk *HACK* * E8 ....78 A2
Kylemore Cl *EHAM* E6 ....95 D1
Kylemore Rd *KIL/WHAMP* NW6 ....72 A4
Kynance Ms *KENS* W8 ....39 D3
Kynance Pl *KENS* W8 ....39 E3
Kynaston Rd *BMLY* BR1 ....160 A5
    STNW/STAM N16..............................59 E5
Kyrle Rd *BTSEA* SW11 ....134 A4
Kyverdale Rd *STNW/STAM* N16 ....59 F2

L

Laburnum Gv *CDALE/KGS* NW9 ....50 C2
Laburnum Pl *ELTH/MOT* * SE9 ....144 A3
Laburnum St *BETH* E2 ....77 F5
Lacebark Cl *BFN/LL* DA15 ....145 F5
Lackington St *SDTCH* EC2A...............24 B2
Lacon Rd *EDUL* SE22 ....138 A2
Lacy Rd *PUT/ROE* SW15 ....131 D2

Ladas Rd *WNWD* SE27 ....154 C5
Ladbroke Crs *NTGHL* W11 ....89 E5
Ladbroke Gdns *NTGHL* W11 ....101 F1
Ladbroke Gv *NKENS* W10 ....89 D3
    NTGHL W11 ....101 F1
Ladbroke Ms *NTGHL* W11 ....101 E2
Ladbroke Rd *NTGHL* W11 ....101 F2
Ladbroke Sq *NTGHL* W11 ....101 F1
Ladbroke Ter *NTGHL* W11 ....101 F1
Ladbroke Wk *NTGHL* W11 ....101 F2
Ladderstile Ride *RCHPK/HAM* TW10 .146 B5
Ladycroft Rd *LEW* SE13 ....140 B1
Lady Margaret Rd *ARCH* N19 ....74 C1
Ladyship Ter *EDUL* * SE22 ....138 B5
Ladysmith Av *EHAM* E6......................95 E1
    GNTH/NBYPK IG2 ....67 D2
Ladysmith Rd *CAN/RD* E16 ....93 F2
    ELTH/MOT SE9................................144 A4
Lady Somerset Rd *KTTN* NW5 ....74 B1
Ladywell Rd *LEW* SE13 ....140 A3
Ladywell St *SRTFD* E15 ....81 F5
Ladywell Water Tower
    BROCKY * SE4 ....139 F1
Lafone St *STHWK* SE1 ....37 E5
Lagado Ms *BERM/RHTH* SE16 ....103 D2
Lainson St *WAND/EARL* SW18 ....132 A5
Lairdale Cl *DUL* SE21 ....154 C1
Lairs Cl *HOLWY* * N7 ....75 E3
Laitwood Rd *BAL* SW12 ....152 B1
Lakedale Rd *WOOL/PLUM* SE18 ......127 E1
Lake House Rd *WAN* E11.....................64 A5
Lake Rd *WIM/MER* SW19 ....149 F5
Lakeside Rd *WKENS* W14 ....101 D4
Lakeside Wy *WBLY* HA9 ....68 A1
Lake View Est *BOW* * E3 ....91 D1
Lakeview Rd *WNWD* SE27 ....154 A5
Lakis Cl *HAMP* NW3 ....72 C1
Lalor St *FUL/PGN* SW6 ....113 E5
Lambarde Av *ELTH/MOT* SE9 ....162 A4
Lamberhurst Rd *WNWD* SE27 ....154 A4
Lambert Av *RCH/KEW* TW9...............128 A1
Lambert Jones Ms *BARB* * EC2Y 23 E2
Lambert Rd *BRXS/STRHM* SW2 ....135 E3
    CAN/RD E16 ....94 B5
Lambert St *IS* N1 ....76 A4
Lambeth Br *WEST* SW1P 45 D4
Lambeth High St *STHWK* SE1 ....45 E5
Lambeth Hl *BLKFR* * EC4V 35 E1
Lambeth Palace Rd *STHWK* SE1 ....45 E3
Lambeth Rd *STHWK* SE1 ....46 A3
Lambeth Wk *LBTH* SE11 ....45 F4
Lamb La *HACK* E8 ....78 B4
Lamble St *KTTN* NW5.........................74 A1
Lambolle Pl *HAMP* NW3 ....73 E3
Lambolle Rd *HAMP* NW3 ....73 E3
Lambourn Cl *CLAP* SW4 ....134 B1
Lambourne Av *WIM/MER* SW19 ....149 F4
Lambourne Gdns *BARK* IG11 ....85 E4
Lambourne Pl *BKHTH/KID* SE3.........124 B4
Lambourne Rd *BARK* IG11 ....85 E4
    GDMY/SEVK IG3 ....67 E4
    WAN E11..62 C2
Lambourn Rd *CLAP* SW4 ....134 B1
Lambrook Ter *FUL/PGN* SW6 ....113 E4
Lamb's Conduit Pas *FSBYW* WC1X 21 E1
Lamb's Conduit St *BMSBY* WC1N 21 E1
Lambscroft Av *LEE/GVPK* SE12 ....160 C3
Lambs Ms *IS* N1 ....76 B5
Lamb's Pas *STLK* EC1Y 24 A1
Lamb St *WCHPL* E1 ....25 E2
Lambton Pl *NTGHL* * W11 ....101 F1
Lambton Rd *ARCH* N19 ....57 E3
Lamb Wk *STHWK* SE1 ....48 C1
Lamerock Rd *BMLY* BR1 ....159 F4
Lamerton St *DEPT* SE8 ....122 A2
Lamington St *HMSMTH* W6 ....100 B5
Lamlash St *LBTH* SE11 ....46 C4

Lammas Rd HOM E9 ....79 D4
  LEY E10 ....61 E4
Lammermoor Rd BAL * SW12 ....134 B5
Lamont Rd WBPTN SW10 ....115 D2
Lamont Road Pas WBPTN * SW10 ....115 D2
Lamorbey CI BFN/LL DA15 ....163 F2
Lampard Gv STNW/STAM N16 ....59 F3
Lampern Sq BETH * E2 ....90 A2
Lampeter Sq HMSMTH W6 ....113 E2
Lamplighter CI WCHPL E1 ....90 C3
Lampmead Rd LEW SE13 ....141 E3
Lamport CI WOOL/PLUM SE18 ....107 F5
Lampton House CI WIM/MER SW19 .....149 D4
Lanark PI MV/WKIL W9 ....3 F5
Lanark Rd MV/WKIL W9 ....3 D2
Lanbury Rd PECK SE15 ....139 D2
Lancashire Ct BAY/PAD W1K 30 C1
Lancaster Av BARK IG11 ....85 E4
  WIM/MER SW19 ....149 D5
  WNWD SE27 ....154 B2
Lancaster CI IS N1 ....77 E4
Lancaster Ct BAY/PAD W2 ....27 F1
Lancaster Dr HAMP NW3 ....73 E3
  POP/IOD E14 ....104 C3
Lancaster Gdns WIM/MER SW19 ....149 E5
Lancaster Gv HAMP NW3 ....73 D3
Lancaster Ms BAY/PAD W2 ....27 F1
  WAND/EARL * SW18 ....132 B3
Lancaster Rd TPL/STR WC2R 33 E2
  WIM/MER SW19 ....149 D5
Lancaster Rd FSBYPK N4 ....58 A2
  FSTGT E7 ....82 A4
  NTGHL W11 ....89 E5
  WAN E11 ....63 E4
  WIM/MER SW19 ....149 D5
  WLSDN NW10 ....69 F3
Lancaster Stables HAMP * NW3 ....73 E3
Lancaster St STHWK SE1 ....46 C1
Lancaster Ter BAY/PAD W2 ....28 A1
Lancaster West NTGHL * W11 ....89 E5
Lancefield St MV/WKIL W9 ....2 A5
Lancell St STNW/STAM N16 ....59 F3
Lancelot PI SKENS SW7 ....41 E1
Lancer Sq KENS W8 ....26 C5
Lancey CI CHARL SE7 ....107 D5
Lancing Rd GNTH/NBYPK IG2 ....67 D1
Lancing Rd CAMTN NW1 ....8 A4
Landcroft Rd EDUL SE22 ....137 F4
Landells Rd EDUL SE22 ....137 F4
Landford Rd PUT/ROE SW15 ....130 C1
Landgrove Rd WIM/MER SW19 ....150 A5
Landleys Flds KTTN * NW5 ....75 D2
Landmann Wy NWCR SE14 ....121 D2
Landon PI KTBR SW1X 41 E2
Landons CI POP/IOD E14 ....104 C2
Landor Rd BRXN/ST SW9 ....135 E1
Landor Wk SHB W12 ....100 A3
Landridge Rd FUL/PGN SW6 ....113 E5
Landrock Rd CEND/HSY/T N8 ....57 D2
Landseer Av MNPK E12 ....84 A2
Landseer Rd ARCH N19 ....57 E5
Landstead Rd WOOL/PLUM SE18 ....127 D3
The Lane BKHTH/KID SE3 ....142 A1
  STJWD NW8 ....3 E2
Lane CI CRICK NW2 ....52 B5
Lanercost Rd BRXS/STRHM SW2 ....154 A2
Laneside CHST BR7 ....162 B5
Laneway PUT/ROE SW15 ....130 B3
Lanfranc Rd BOW E3 ....91 E1
Lanfrey PI WKENS W14 ....113 F1
Langbourne Av HGT N6 ....56 A4
Langbrook Rd BKHTH/KID SE3 ....143 D1
Langdale CI MORT/ESHN SW14 ....128 B2
Langdale Rd GNWCH SE10 ....122 C3
Langdale St WCHPL * E1 ....90 B5
Langdon CI WLSDN NW10 ....69 E5
Langdon Dr CDALE/KGS NW9 ....50 C3
Langdon Park Rd HGT N6 ....56 B2

Langdon PI MORT/ESHN SW14 ....128 C1
Langdon Rd EHAM E6 ....84 A5
Langdon Shaw SCUP DA14 ....163 F5
Langdon Wy STHWK SE1 ....102 A3
Langford CI HACK E8 ....78 A2
  SEVS/STOTM N15 ....59 E1
Langford Gn CMBW SE5 ....137 E1
Langford PI STJWD NW8 ....3 F2
Langford Rd FUL/PGN SW6 ....114 B5
Langham PI CAVSQ/HST W1G 19 D3
  CHSWK W4 ....111 E2
Langham St GTPST W1W 19 E3
Langholm CI BAL SW12 ....135 D5
Langland Gdns HAMP NW3 ....72 B3
Langler Rd WLSDN NW10 ....88 C1
Langley Ct COVGDN WC2E 32 C1
Langley Crs WAN E11 ....64 B2
Langley Dr ACT W3 ....98 B3
  WAN E11 ....64 B2
Langley La VX/NE SW8 ....117 E2
Langley St LSQ/SEVD WC2H 20 C5
Langmead St WNWD SE27 ....154 B4
Langroyd Rd TOOT SW17 ....151 F2
Langside Av PUT/ROE SW15 ....130 A2
Langston Hughes CI HNHL * SE24 ....136 B2
Lang St WCHPL E1 ....90 C3
Langthorn Ct LOTH * EC2R 24 B4
Langthorne Rd WAN E11 ....63 D5
Langthorne St FUL/PGN SW6 ....113 D4
Langton Av EHAM E6 ....96 A2
Langton CI FSBYW WC1X 9 F4
Langton Ri EDUL SE22 ....138 B5
Langton Rd BRXN/ST SW9 ....118 B3
  CRICK NW2 ....52 C5
Langton St WBPTN SW10 ....114 C2
Langton Wy BKHTH/KID SE3 ....124 A3
Langtry PI FUL/PGN SW6 ....114 A2
Langtry Rd STJWD NW8 ....72 B5
Langtry Wk STJWD NW8 ....72 C5
Lanhill Rd MV/WKIL W9 ....2 A5
Lanier Rd LEW SE13 ....140 C4
Lannoy Rd ELTH/MOT SE9 ....162 C1
Lanrick Rd POP/IOD E14 ....93 D5
Lansbury Gdns POP/IOD * E14 ....93 D5
Lanscombe Wk VX/NE * SW8 ....117 E3
Lansdowne Crs NTGHL W11 ....101 E1
Lansdowne Dr HACK E8 ....78 B5
Lansdowne Gdns VX/NE SW8 ....117 E4
Lansdowne Gn VX/NE SW8 ....117 E3
Lansdowne Gv WLSDN NW10 ....69 E1
Lansdowne HI WNWD SE27 ....154 B3
Lansdowne La CHARL SE7 ....125 D1
Lansdowne Ms CHARL SE7 ....125 D1
  NTGHL W11 ....101 F2
Lansdowne PI STHWK SE1 ....48 B2
Lansdowne Ri NTGHL W11 ....101 E1
Lansdowne Rd GDMY/SEVK IG3 ....67 F3
  HACK E8 ....78 A4
  NTGHL W11 ....101 E1
  WALTH E17 ....62 A1
  WAN E11 ....63 F4
Lansdowne Ter BMSBY WC1N 21 D1
Lansdowne Wk NTGHL W11 ....101 E2
Lansdowne Wy VX/NE SW8 ....117 E4
Lansdowne Wood CI WNWD SE27 ....154 B3
Lansdown Rd FSTGT E7 ....82 C4
Lantern CI PUT/ROE SW15 ....130 A2
Lanterns Ct POP/IOD E14 ....104 A4
Lant St STHWK SE1 ....35 E5
Lanvanor Rd PECK SE15 ....120 C5
Lapford CI MV/WKIL * W9 ....89 F3
Lapse Wood Wk DUL SE21 ....156 B1
Lapworth Ct BAY/PAD W2 ....15 D2
Lara CI LEW SE13 ....140 C4
Larch Av ACT W3 ....99 E2
Larch CI BAL SW12 ....152 B2
  DEPT SE8 ....121 F2

Larch Dr CHSWK * W4.................**110** A1
Larches Av MORT/ESHN SW14.....**129** D2
Larch Gv BFN/LL DA15................**163** F1
Larch Rd CRICK NW2.....................**70** C5
 LEY E10...**62** A4
Larchwood Rd ELTH/MOT SE9.....**162** B2
Larcom St WALW SE17.................**47** F5
Larden Rd ACT W3..........................**99** E3
Larissa St WALW * SE17................**48** B5
Larkbere Rd SYD SE26.................**157** E4
Larkfield Rd SCUP DA14..............**163** F3
Larkhall La CLAP SW4..................**117** D5
Larkhall Ri CLAP SW4...................**134** C1
Larkhill Ter WOOL/PLUM * SE18..**126** A3
Lark Rw BETH E2.............................**78** C5
Larnach Rd HMSMTH W6..............**113** D2
Larpent Av PUT/ROE SW15..........**130** C3
Lascelles Cl WAN E11....................**63** D4
Lassa Rd ELTH/MOT SE9................**143** E3
Lassell St GNWCH SE10................**123** D1
Latchmere Rd BTSEA SW11..........**115** F5
Latchmere St BTSEA SW11...........**115** F5
Latham Cl EHAM E6.......................**95** E5
Lathom Rd EHAM E6......................**83** F4
Latimer Av EHAM E6......................**83** F5
Latimer Pl NKENS W10..................**88** C5
Latimer Pl FSTGT E7......................**82** B1
 NKENS W10.....................................**88** C4
 SEVS/STOTM N15..........................**59** E1
Latona Rd PECK SE15...................**120** A2
Lattimer Pl CHSWK W4................**111** E3
Lauderdale Pde MV/WKIL * W9......**2** C4
Lauderdale Pl BARB * EC2Y...........**23** F3
Lauderdale Rd MV/WKIL W9...........**3** D4
Laud St LBTH SE11.......................**117** F1
Launcelot Rd BMLY BR1...............**160** A4
Launcelot St STHWK SE1...............**46** A1
Launceston Pl KENS W8................**39** E2
Launch St POP/IOD E14................**104** C4
Launders Ga ACT * W3..................**98** B3
Laundress La CLPT * E5.................**60** A5
Laundry Rd HMSMTH W6.............**113** E2
Laura Pl CLPT E5...........................**78** C1
Laura Ter FSBYPK * N4...................**58** B4
Laurel Bank Gdns FUL/PGN SW6..**113** F5
Laurel Cl TOOT SW17...................**151** E5
Laurel Gv SYD SE26.....................**157** D5
Laurel Rd BARN SW13..................**112** A5
The Laurels CMBW * SE5.............**118** B3
Laurel St HACK E8........................**77** F3
Laurence Ms SHB W12.................**100** A3
Laurence Pountney HI CANST * EC4R..**36** A1
Laurence Pountney La CANST EC4R..**36** A2
Laurie Gv NWCR SE14..................**121** E4
Laurier Rd KTTN NW5.....................**56** B5
Lauriston Rd HOM E9.....................**79** D3
Lausanne Rd PECK SE15..............**120** C4
Lavender Av CDALE/KGS NW9.......**50** C5
Lavender Cl CHEL SW3.................**115** D2
Lavender Gdns BTSEA SW11........**133** F2
Lavender Gv HACK E8....................**78** A4
Lavender HI BTSEA SW11.............**133** F1
Lavender Pl IL IG1..........................**84** B2
Lavender Rd BERM/RHTH SE16....**103** E2
 BTSEA SW11.................................**133** D1
Lavender St SRTFD E15.................**81** E3
Lavender Sweep BTSEA SW11......**133** F2
Lavender Ter BTSEA * SW11.........**133** E1
Lavengro Rd WNWD SE27............**154** C2
Lavenham Rd WAND/EARL SW18..**149** F2
Lavers Rd STNW/STAM N16............**59** E5
Laverstoke Gdns PUT/ROE SW15..**129** F5
Laverton Ms ECT * SW5.................**39** D5
Laverton Pl ECT SW5......................**39** D5
Lavidge Rd ELTH/MOT SE9...........**161** E2
Lavina Gv IS N1.................................**9** E1
Lavington Cl HOM E9.....................**79** F3
Lavington St STHWK SE1...............**35** D4

Lawford Rd CHSWK W4................**110** C3
 IS N1...**77** E4
 KTTN NW5..**74** C3
Lawless St POP/IOD * E14............**104** B1
Lawley St CLPT E5.........................**78** C1
Lawn Crs RCH/KEW TW9...............**110** A5
Lawn House Cl POP/IOD E14........**104** C3
Lawn La VX/NE SW8.....................**117** E2
Lawn Rd HAMP NW3........................**73** F2
The Lawns BKHTH/KID * SE3.......**141** F1
Lawns Ct WBLY * HA9......................**50** A4
Lawn Ter BKHTH/KID SE3.............**141** F1
Lawrence Av MNPK E12.................**84** A1
Lawrence Buildings STNW/STAM N16..**59** F5
Lawrence Cl SHB * W12................**100** B1
Lawrence La CITYW EC2V..............**23** F5
Lawrence Pl IS * N1........................**75** E5
Lawrence Rd EHAM E6...................**83** E5
 PLSTW E13.....................................**82** B5
 CAN/RD E16....................................**93** F4
 CHEL SW3.....................................**115** E2
Lawrence Wy WLSDN NW10...........**50** C5
Lawrie Park Av SYD SE26............**156** B5
Lawrie Park Crs SYD SE26...........**156** B5
Lawrie Park Gdns SYD SE26........**156** B5
Lawson Cl CAN/RD E16...................**94** C4
 WIM/MER SW19.............................**149** D3
Law St STHWK SE1.........................**48** B2
Lawton Rd BOW E3..........................**91** E2
 LEY E10..**62** C3
Laxcon Cl WLSDN NW10.................**69** D2
Laxley Cl CMBW SE5....................**118** B3
Laxton Pl CAMTN NW1......................**7** D5
Layard Rd BERM/RHTH SE16.......**102** B3
Layard Sq BERM/RHTH SE16.......**102** B5
Laycock St IS N1.............................**76** A3
Layer Gdns ACT W3........................**98** A1
Layfield Cl HDN NW4.......................**52** A3
Layfield Crs HDN NW4.....................**52** B2
Layfield Rd HDN NW4......................**52** B2
Laystall St FSBYW WC1X...............**22** A1
Layton Pl RCH/KEW TW9..............**110** A4
Layzell Wk ELTH/MOT SE9...........**161** D1
Lazenby Ct COVGDN * WC2E.........**32** C1
Leabank Sq HOM E9........................**80** A3
Leabank Vw SEVS/STOTM N15.......**60** A1
Leabourne Rd STNW/STAM N16.....**60** A1
Lea Bridge Rd CLPT E5....................**61** D4
Leacroft Av BAL SW12...................**133** F5
Leadale Rd STNW/STAM N16..........**60** A1
Leadenhall Pl FENCHST EC3M........**24** C5
Leadenhall St BANK EC3V...............**24** C5
Leader Av MNPK E12.......................**84** A2
The Leadings WBLY HA9..................**51** A5
Leaf Gv STRHM/NOR SW16...........**154** A5
Leafy Oak Rd LEE/GVPK SE12......**160** C5
Leagrave St CLPT E5........................**60** C5
Lea Hall Gdns LEY * E10..................**62** A3
Lea Hall Rd LEY E10........................**62** A3
Leahurst Rd LEW SE13..................**141** D3
Leake St STHWK SE1........................**33** F5
Lealand Rd SEVS/STOTM N15........**59** F1
Leamington Av BMLY BR1.............**160** C5
 BMLY BR1......................................**160** C4
Leamington Gdns GDMY/SEVK IG3..**67** F4
Leamington Pk ACT W3...................**87** D4
Leamington Road Vls NTGHL W11..**89** F3
Leamore St HMSMTH W6...............**100** B5
Leamouth Rd EHAM E6....................**95** E4
 POP/IOD E14...................................**93** D5
Leander Rd BRXS/STRHM SW2.....**135** F4
Learoyd Gdns EHAM E6.................**108** A1
Leas Dl ELTH/MOT SE9................**162** A3
Leaside Rd CLPT E5.........................**60** C3
Leasowes Rd LEY E10......................**62** A3
Leatherdale St WCHPL * E1............**91** D2
Leather Gdns SRTFD E15................**81** E5
Leatherhead Cl STNW/STAM N16....**59** E3

Leather La *CLKNW* EC1R 22 A1
Leathermarket Ct *STHWK* SE1 .....48 C1
Leathermarket St *STHWK* SE1 ......48 C1
Leathwaite Rd *BTSEA* SW11 ....133 F2
Leathwell Rd *DEPT* SE8 ....122 B5
Lea Valley Wk *CLPT* E5 ....60 B2
Leaway *CLPT* * E5 ....60 C3
Lebanon Gdns *WAND/EARL* SW18 ...132 A4
Lebanon Rd *WAND/EARL* SW18 ....132 A3
Lebrun Sq *BKHTH/KID* SE3 ....142 B2
Lechmere Rd *CRICK* NW2 ....70 B3
Leckford Rd *WAND/EARL* SW18 ...150 C2
Lecky St *SKENS* SW7 ....115 D1
Leconfield Av *BARN* SW13 ....129 F1
Leconfield Rd *HBRY* N5 ....77 D1
Leda Rd *WOOL/PLUM* SE18 ....107 F4
Ledbury Ms North *NTGHL* W11 .....26 A1
Ledbury Ms West *NTGHL* * W11 ....26 A1
Ledbury Rd *NTGHL* W11 ....89 F5
Ledbury St *PECK* SE15 ....120 A3
Leechcroft Av *BFN/LL* DA15 ....145 F3
Lee Church St *LEW* SE13 ....141 E2
Lee Conservancy Rd *HOM* E9 ....79 F1
Leeds Rd *IL* IG1 ....67 D3
Lee High Rd *LEW* SE13 ....141 D2
Leeke St *FSBYW* WC1X 9 E3
Leeland Wy *WLSDN* NW10 ....69 E1
Lee Pk *BKHTH/KID* SE3 ....141 F2
Lee Rd *BKHTH/KID* SE3 ....141 F1
Leeside Crs *GLDGN* NW11 ....53 E2
Leeson Rd *HNHL* * SE24 ....136 A3
Lees Pl *MYFR/PKLN* W1K 30 A3
Lee St *HACK* E8 ....77 F5
Lee Ter *BKHTH/KID* SE3 ....141 E1
Leeway *DEPT* SE8 ....121 F1
Leewood Cl *LEE/GVPK* * SE12 .....141 F4
Lefevre Wk *BOW* E3 ....79 F5
Leffern Rd *SHB* W12 ....100 A3
Lefroy Rd *SHB* W12 ....99 F3
Legard Rd *HBRY* N5 ....58 B5
Legatt Rd *ELTH/MOT* SE9 ....143 D3
Leggatt Rd *SRTFD* E15 ....92 C1
Legge St *LEW* SE13 ....140 C3
Leghorn Rd *WLSDN* NW10 ....88 A3
    WOOL/PLUM SE18 ....127 D1
Legion Cl *IS* N1 ....76 A3
Legion Ter *BOW* E3 ....80 A5
Leicester Gdns *GDMY/SEVK* IG3 ...67 E2
Leicester Pl *LSQ/SEVD* * WC2H 32 B1
Leicester Rd *WLSDN* NW10 ....69 D4
Leicester Sq *LSQ/SEVD* WC2H 32 B2
Leicester St *SOHO/SHAV* W1D 32 B1
Leigham Av *STRHM/NOR* SW16 ....153 E3
Leigham Court Rd *STRHM/NOR* SW16 .153 E3
Leigham Hall Pde *STRHM/NOR* * SW16 ..153 E3
Leigham V *STRHM/NOR* SW16 .....154 A3
Leigh Gdns *WLSDN* NW10 ....88 C1
Leigh Orchard Cl *STRHM/NOR* SW16 .153 F3
Leigh Rd *EHAM* E6 ....84 A4
    HBRY N5 ....76 B1
    LEY E10 ....62 C2
Leigh St *STPAN* WC1H 8 C5
Leighton Av *MNPK* E12 ....84 A2
Leighton Gdns *WLSDN* NW10 ....88 C1
Leighton Gv *KTTN* NW5 ....74 C2
Leighton Pl *KTTN* NW5 ....74 C2
Leighton Rd *KTTN* NW5 ....74 C2
Leila Parnell Pl *CHARL* SE7 ....124 C2
Leinster Av *MORT/ESHN* SW14 ....128 C1
Leinster Gdns *BAY/PAD* W2 ....15 E5
Leinster Ms *BAY/PAD* W2 ....27 E2
Leinster Pl *BAY/PAD* W2 ....15 E5
Leinster Sq *BAY/PAD* W2 ....26 B1
Leinster Ter *BAY/PAD* W2 ....27 E1
Leith Cl *CDALE/KGS* NW9 ....51 D3
Leithcote Gdns *STRHM/NOR* SW16 .153 F3
Leithcote Pth *STRHM/NOR* SW16 ..153 F3

Leith Yd *KIL/WHAMP* * NW6 ....72 A5
Lelitia Cl *HACK* E8 ....78 A5
Leman St *WCHPL* E1 ....25 F5
Le May Av *LEE/GVPK* SE12 ....160 B3
Lemmon Rd *GNWCH* SE10 ....123 E2
Lemna Rd *WAN* E11 ....63 E2
Lemonwell Dr *ELTH/MOT* SE9 ....144 B3
Lemsford Cl *SEVS/STOTM* N15 .....60 A1
Lena Gdns *HMSMTH* W6 ....100 C4
Lendal Ter *CLAP* * SW4 ....135 D1
Len Freeman Pl *FUL/PGN* SW6 ...113 F2
Lenham Rd *LEW* SE13 ....141 F2
Lennon Rd *CRICK* NW2 ....70 C2
Lennox Gdns *IL* IG1 ....65 F3
    KTBR SW1X 41 E3
    WLSDN NW10 ....69 F1
Lennox Gardens Ms *CHEL* SW3 ....41 E4
Lennox Rd *FSBYPK* N4 ....57 F4
    WALTH E17 ....61 F1
Lens Rd *FSTGT* E7 ....82 C4
Lenthall Rd *HACK* E8 ....77 F4
Lenthorp Rd *GNWCH* SE10 ....105 F5
Lentmead Rd *BMLY* BR1 ....159 F3
Lenton St *WOOL/PLUM* SE18 .....109 D5
Lenton Ter *FSBYPK* * N4 ....58 A4
Leof Crs *CAT* SE6 ....158 B5
Leonard Ct *KENS* * W8 ....38 A2
Leonard Pl *STNW/STAM* * N16 .....77 E1
Leonard Rd *FSTGT* E7 ....82 A1
Leonard St *CAN/RD* E16 ....107 E2
    SDTCH EC2A 12 B5
Leontine Cl *PECK* SE15 ....120 A3
Leopold Av *WIM/MER* SW19 ....149 F5
Leopold Ms *HOM* E9 ....78 C5
Leopold Rd *WIM/MER* SW19 ....149 F4
    WLSDN NW10 ....69 F4
Leopold St *BOW* E3 ....91 F4
Leo St *PECK* SE15 ....120 B3
Leppoc Rd *CLAP* SW4 ....135 D3
Leroy St *STHWK* SE1 ....48 C1
Lerry Cl *WKENS* W14 ....113 F2
Lescombe Cl *FSTH* SE23 ....157 E3
Lescombe Rd *FSTH* SE23 ....157 E3
Leslie Rd *CAN/RD* E16 ....94 B5
    WAN E11 ....81 D1
Lessar Av *CLAP* SW4 ....134 C3
Lessingham Av *TOOT* SW17 ......151 F4
Lessing St *FSTH* SE23 ....139 E5
Lester Av *SRTFD* E15 ....93 E3
Leswin Pl *STNW/STAM* N16 ....59 F5
Leswin Rd *STNW/STAM* N16 ....59 F5
Letchford Gdns *WLSDN* NW10 .....88 A2
Letchford Ms *WLSDN* * NW10 ......88 A2
Letchworth St *TOOT* SW17 ....151 F4
Letterstone Rd *FUL/PGN* SW6 ....113 F3
Lettice St *FUL/PGN* SW6 ....113 F5
Lett Rd *SRTFD* E15 ....81 D4
Levana Cl *WIM/MER* SW19 ....149 D1
Levehurst Wy *CLAP* SW4 ....117 E5
Levendale Rd *FSTH* SE23 ....157 E2
Leven Rd *POP/IOD* E14 ....92 C4
Leverett St *CHEL* SW3 ....41 D4
Leverholme Gdns *ELTH/MOT* SE9 .162 A4
Lever St *FSBYE* EC1V 11 E4
Leverton Pl *KTTN* NW5 ....74 C2
Leverton St *KTTN* NW5 ....74 C2
Levett Gdns *GDMY/SEVK* IG3 ....85 F1
Levett Rd *BARK* IG11 ....85 E3
Lewesdon Cl *WIM/MER* SW19 .....149 D1
Leweston Pl *STNW/STAM* N16 .....59 F2
Lewgars Av *CDALE/KGS* NW9 ......50 C1
Lewin Rd *MORT/ESHN* SW14 ......129 D1
Lewis Crs *WLSDN* NW10 ....69 D2
Lewis Gv *LEW* SE13 ....140 C2
Lewisham High St *LEW* SE13 ......140 B4
Lewisham Hl *LEW* SE13 ....122 C5
Lewisham Pk *LEW* SE13 ....140 B4
Lewisham Rd *LEW* SE13 ....122 C5

Lewisham Wy *BROCKY* SE4 ....121 F5
Lewis Pl *HACK* E8 ....78 A2
Lewis St *CAMTN* NW1 ....74 B4
Lexden Rd *ACT* W3 ....98 B1
Lexham Gdns *KENS* W8 ....38 B4
Lexham Ms *KENS* W8 ....38 B4
Lexington St *SOHO/CST* W1F 19 F5
Lexton Gdns *BAL* SW12 ....153 D1
Leyborne Pk *RCH/KEW* TW9 ....110 A4
Leybourne Rd *CAMTN* ' NW1 ....74 B4
WAN E11 ....63 F3
Leybourne St *CAMTN* NW1 ....74 B4
Leyburn House *WOOL/PLUM* SE18 ....125 E3
Leyden St *WCHPL* E1 ....25 E3
Leyes Rd *CAN/RD* E16 ....106 C1
Leyland Rd *LEE/GVPK* SE12 ....141 F5
Leylang Rd *NWCR* SE14 ....121 D3
Leysdown Rd *ELTH/MOT* SE9 ....161 E3
Leysfield Rd *SHB* W12 ....100 A3
Leyspring Rd *WAN* E11 ....63 F3
Ley St *IL* IG1 ....66 B4
Leythe Rd *ACT* W3 ....98 C3
Leyton Gra *LEY* E10 ....62 A4
Leyton Green Rd *LEY* E10 ....62 C1
Leyton Park Rd *LEY* E10 ....62 C4
Leyton Rd *SRTFD* E15 ....80 C2
Leytonstone Rd *SRTFD* E15 ....81 E2
Leywick St *SRTFD* E15 ....93 E1
Liardet St *NWCR* SE14 ....121 E2
Liberia Rd *HBRY* N5 ....76 B3
Liberty St *BRXN/ST* SW9 ....117 F4
Libra Rd *BOW* E3 ....79 F5
PLSTW E13 ....94 A1
Library Pde *WLSDN* ' NW10 ....69 E5
Library St *STHWK* SE1 ....47 D1
Lichfield Rd *BOW* E3 ....91 E2
CRICK NW2 ....71 E1
EHAM E6 ....95 D2
Lidcote Gdns *BRXN/ST* ' SW9 ....118 A5
Liddell Gdns *WLSDN* NW10 ....88 C1
Liddell Rd *KIL/WHAMP* NW6 ....72 A3
Liddington Rd *SRTFD* E15 ....81 F5
Liddon Rd *PLSTW* E13 ....94 B2
Liden Cl *LEY* E10 ....61 F2
Lidfield Rd *STNW/STAM* N16 ....77 D1
Lidgate Rd *PECK* ' SE15 ....119 F3
Lidiard Rd *WAND/EARL* SW18 ....150 C2
Lidyard Rd *ARCH* N19 ....56 C3
Liffler Rd *WOOL/PLUM* SE18 ....127 E1
Lifford St *PUT/ROE* SW15 ....131 D2
Lighterman Ms *WCHPL* E1 ....91 D5
Lighterman's Rd *POP/IOD* E14 ....104 A3
Ligonier St *BETH* E2 ....13 E5
Lilac Pl *LBTH* SE11 ....45 E5
Lilac St *SHB* W12 ....100 A1
Lilburne Gdns *ELTH/MOT* SE9 ....143 E3
Lilburne Rd *ELTH/MOT* SE9 ....143 E3
Lilestone St *CAMTN* NW1 ....4 C5
Lilford Rd *BRXN/ST* SW9 ....118 B5
Lilian Barker Cl *LEE/GVPK* SE12 ....142 A3
Lilley Cl *WAP* E1W 102 A2
Lillian Av *ACT* W3 ....98 A3
Lillian Rd *BARN* SW13 ....112 A2
Lillie Rd *FUL/PGN* SW6 ....113 D2
Lillieshall Rd *CLAP* SW4 ....134 B1
Lillie Yd *FUL/PGN* SW6 ....114 A2
Lillington Gardens Est *PIM* SW1V 43 F5
Lily Cl *WKENS* ' W14 ....101 E5
Lily Pl *HCIRC* EC1N 22 B2
Lily Rd *LEY* E10 ....62 A1
Lilyville Rd *FUL/PGN* SW6 ....113 F4
Limburg Rd *BTSEA* SW11 ....133 E2
Limeburner La *STP* EC4M 22 C4
Lime Cl *WAP* E1W 102 A2
Lime Gv *BFN/LL* DA15 ....145 F4
SHB W12 ....100 C3
Limeharbour *POP/IOD* E14 ....104 A4
Limehouse *POP/IOD* ' E14 ....104 A1

Limehouse Cswy *POP/IOD* E14 ....103 F1
Limehouse Link *POP/IOD* E14 ....103 E1
Lime Kiln Dr *CHARL* SE7 ....124 B2
Limerick Cl *BAL* SW12 ....134 C5
Limerston St *WBPTN* SW10 ....114 C2
The Limes *CMBW* ' SE5 ....137 E1
WAND/EARL ' SW18 ....132 A4
Limes Av *BARN* SW13 ....111 F5
GLDGN NW11 ....53 E2
Limes Field Rd *BARN* SW13 ....129 E1
Limesford Rd *PECK* SE15 ....139 D2
Limes Gdns *WAND/EARL* SW18 ....132 A4
Limes Gv *LEW* SE13 ....140 C2
Lime St *FENCHST* EC3M 36 C1
Lime Street Pas *BANK* ' EC3V 24 C5
Limes Wk *PECK* ' SE15 ....138 C2
Limetree Cl *BRXS/STRHM* SW2 ....153 F1
Lime Tree Ter *FSTH* ' SE23 ....157 F1
Lime Wk *SRTFD* ' E15 ....81 E5
Limpsfield Av *WIM/MER* SW19 ....149 D2
Linacre Rd *CRICK* NW2 ....70 B3
Linchmere Rd *LEE/GVPK* SE12 ....142 A5
Lincoln Av *WIM/MER* SW19 ....149 D3
Lincoln Est *BOW* E3 ....92 A3
Lincoln Gdns *IL* IG1 ....65 E2
Lincoln Ms *KIL/WHAMP* NW6 ....71 F5
Lincoln Rd *PLSTW* E13 ....94 B3
Lincoln's Inn Flds *LINN* WC2A 21 E4
Lincoln St *CHEL* SW3 ....41 E5
WAN E11 ....63 E4
Lincombe Rd *BMLY* BR1 ....159 F5
Lindal Rd *BROCKY* SE4 ....139 F5
Linden Av *WLSDN* NW10 ....89 D1
Linden Gdns *BAY/PAD* W2 ....26 B2
CHSWK W4 ....111 D1
Linden Gv *PECK* SE15 ....138 B1
Linden Ms *BAY/PAD* W2 ....26 B2
IS N1 ....77 D2
The Lindens *CHSWK* W4 ....110 C4
Lindfield Gdns *HAMP* NW3 ....72 C2
Lindfield St *POP/IOD* E14 ....92 A5
Lindisfarne Md *HOM* E9 ....79 E1
Lindley Est *PECK* ' SE15 ....120 A3
Lindley Pl *RCH/KEW* TW9 ....110 A4
Lindley Rd *LEY* E10 ....62 C4
Lindley St *WCHPL* E1 ....90 C4
Lindore Rd *BTSEA* SW11 ....133 F2
Lindo St *PECK* SE15 ....120 C5
Lindrop St *FUL/PGN* SW6 ....114 C5
Lindsay Sq *PIM* SW1V 117 D1
Lindsell St *GNWCH* SE10 ....122 C4
Lindsey Ms *IS* N1 ....76 C4
Lindsey St *STBT* EC1A 23 D2
Lind St *DEPT* SE8 ....122 B5
Lindway *WNWD* SE27 ....154 B5
Linford St *VX/NE* SW8 ....116 C4
Lingards Rd *LEW* SE13 ....140 C2
Lingey Cl *BFN/LL* DA15 ....163 F2
Lingfield Crs *ELTH/MOT* SE9 ....145 D2
Lingham St *BRXN/ST* SW9 ....117 E5
Ling Rd *CAN/RD* E16 ....94 A4
Lingwell Rd *TOOT* SW17 ....151 E3
Lingwood Rd *CLPT* E5 ....60 B2
Linhope St *CAMTN* NW1 ....5 E5
The Link *ACT* W3 ....86 B5
Links Rd *ACT* W3 ....86 A5
CRICK NW2 ....51 F4
Link St *HOM* E9 ....79 E3
Links Yd *WCHPL* E1 ....25 F3
Linkway *FSBYPK* N4 ....58 C2
Linkwood Wk *CAMTN* NW1 ....75 D4
Linnell Cl *GLDGN* NW11 ....54 B1
Linnell Dr *GLDGN* NW11 ....54 B1
Linnell Rd *CMBW* SE5 ....119 E5
Linnet Ms *BAL* SW12 ....134 A5
Linom Rd *CLAP* SW4 ....135 E2
Linscott Rd *CLPT* E5 ....78 C1
Linsdell Rd *BARK* IG11 ....84 C5

Linsey St BERM/RHTH SE16	102	A4
Linstead St KIL/WHAMP NW6	72	A4
Linstead Wy WAND/EARL SW18	131	E5
Lintaine Cl FUL/PGN * SW6	113	E2
Linthorpe Rd STNW/STAM N16	59	E2
Linton Cl CHARL SE7	124	C1
Linton Gdns EHAM E6	95	E5
Linton Gv WNWD SE27	154	B5
Linton Rd BARK IG11	84	C4
Linton St IS N1	76	A3
Linver Rd FUL/PGN SW6	113	F5
Linwood Cl CMBW SE5	119	F5
Lion Cl BROCKY SE4	140	A4
Lionel Gdns ELTH/MOT SE9	143	D3
Lionel Ms NKENS * W10	89	E4
Lionel Rd ELTH/MOT SE9	143	D3
Lion Mills BETH * E2	90	A1
Lion Rd EHAM E6	95	F4
Lions Cl LEE/GVPK SE12	160	C3
Liphook Crs FSTH SE23	138	C5
Lisburne Rd HAMP NW3	73	F1
Lisford St PECK SE15	119	F4
Lisgar Ter WKENS W14	101	F5
Liskeard Gdns BKHTH/KID SE3	124	C4
Lisle Cl TOOT SW17	152	B4
Lisle St SOHO/SHAV W1D	32	A1
Lismore WIM/MER * SW19	149	F5
Lismore Circ HAMP NW3	73	F2
Lismore Wk IS N1	74	A1
Lissenden Gdns KTTN NW5	16	C1
Lisson Gv CAMTN NW1	16	C1
STJWD NW8	4	B5
Lisson St CAMTN NW1	16	C2
Lister Cl ACT W3	87	D4
Lister Ms HOLWY N7	75	F1
Lister Rd WAN E11	63	E3
Liston Rd CLAP SW4	134	C1
Listowel Cl BRXN/ST SW9	118	A3
Listria Pk STNW/STAM N16	59	E4
Litchfield Av SRTFD * E15	81	E3
Litchfield Gdns WLSDN NW10	70	A3
Litchfield St LSQ/SEVD * WC2H	32	B1
Lithos Rd HAMP NW3	72	B3
Little Albany St CAMTN NW1	7	D5
Little Birches BFN/LL DA15	163	E2
The Little Boltons WBPTN SW10	114	B1
Little Bornes DUL SE21	155	E4
Little Britain STBT EC1A	23	D3
Littlebury Rd CLAP * SW4	135	D1
Little Chester St KTBR SW1X	42	C2
Little Cloisters WEST SW1P	44	C2
Littlecombe Cl PUT/ROE * SW15	131	D4
Littlecote Cl WIM/MER SW19	131	D5
Littlecroft ELTH/MOT SE9	144	A1
Little Deans Yd WEST SW1P	44	C2
Little Dimocks BAL SW12	152	B2
Little Dorrit Ct STHWK SE1	35	F5
Little Edward St CAMTN * NW1	7	D3
Little Essex St TPL/STR * WC2R	34	A1
Littlefield Cl ARCH N19	74	C1
Littlemoor Rd IL IG1	67	D5
Little Newport St LSQ/SEVD WC2H	32	B1
Little New St FLST/FETLN EC4A	22	B4
Little Portland St REGST W1B	19	D4
Little Rownings FSTH SE23	156	B2
Little Russell St NOXST/BSQ WC1A	20	C3
Little St James's St WHALL SW1A	31	E4
Little St Leonards MORT/ESHN SW14	128	C1
Little Smith St WEST SW1P	44	B2
Little Titchfield St GTPST W1W	19	E3
Littleton St WAND/EARL SW18	150	C2

Little Trinity La BLKFR EC4V	35	F1
Little Turnstile LINN WC2A	21	E3
Littlewood LEW SE13	140	C3
Livermere Rd HACK E8	77	F5
Liverpool Gv WALW SE17	119	D1
Liverpool Rd CAN/RD E16	93	E4
IS N1	76	A4
LEY E10	62	C1
Liverpool St LVPST EC2M	24	C3
Livesey Pl PECK SE15	120	A2
Livingstone Rd BTSEA SW11	133	D1
LEY E10	62	B1
SRTFD E15	80	C5
Lizard St FSBYE EC1V	11	F4
Lizban St BKHTH/KID SE3	124	B3
Llanelly Rd CRICK NW2	53	F4
Llanover Rd WOOL/PLUM SE18	126	A3
Llanvanor Rd CRICK NW2	53	F4
Llewellyn St BERM/RHTH SE16	102	A3
Lloyd Baker St FSBYW WC1X	10	A4
Lloyd Rd EHAM E6	83	F5
Lloyd's Av TWRH EC3N	25	D5
Lloyd's Pl BKHTH/KID * SE3	123	E5
Lloyd Sq FSBYW WC1X	10	A3
Lloyd's Rw CLKNW EC1R	10	B4
Lloyd St FSBYW WC1X	10	A3
Lloyd Vls BROCKY SE4	122	A5
Loampit Hl LEW SE13	122	A5
Loampit V LEW SE13	140	B1
Loanda Cl HACK E8	77	F5
Loats Rd CLAP SW4	135	E4
Locarno Rd ACT W3	98	C2
Lochaber Rd LEW SE13	141	E2
Lochaline St HMSMTH W6	112	C2
Lochinvar St BAL SW12	134	B5
Lochnagar St POP/IOD E14	92	C4
Lock Cha LEW SE13	141	E1
Lockgate Cl HOM E9	79	F2
Lockhart Cl HOLWY N7	75	F3
Lockhart St BOW E3	91	F3
Lockhurst St CLPT E5	79	D1
Lockington Rd VX/NE SW8	116	B4
Lockmead Rd LEW SE13	140	C1
SEVS/STOTM N15	60	A1
Locksley Est POP/IOD E14	91	F4
Locksley St POP/IOD E14	91	F4
Lockwood Cl SYD SE26	157	D4
Lockwood Sq BERM/RHTH SE16	102	B4
Lockyer St STHWK SE1	48	B1
Locton Gn BOW * E3	79	F5
Loddiges Rd HOM E9	78	C4
Loder St PECK SE15	120	C3
The Lodge SHB * W12	101	D3
Lodge Ms HBRY * N5	76	C1
Lodge Rd STJWD NW8	4	B3
Lodore St POP/IOD E14	92	C5
Loftie St BERM/RHTH SE16	102	A3
Lofting Rd IS N1	76	A4
Loftus Rd SHB W12	100	B2
Loftus Vls SHB * W12	100	B2
Logan Ms KENS W8	38	A4
Logan Pl KENS W8	38	A4
Lolesworth Cl WCHPL * E1	25	F3
Lollard St LBTH SE11	45	F4
Loman St STHWK SE1	35	D5
Lomas St WCHPL E1	90	A4
Lombard Av GDMY/SEVK IG3	67	E3
Lombard Rd BTSEA SW11	115	D5
Lombard St BANK EC3V	24	B5
Lombard Wall CHARL SE7	106	B4
Lombardy Pl BAY/PAD W2	26	C2
Lomond Gv CMBW SE5	119	D3
Loncroft Rd CMBW SE5	119	E2
Londesborough Rd STNW/STAM N16	77	E1
London Br CANST EC4R	36	B2
London Bridge St STHWK * SE1	36	B3
London Flds HACK * E8	78	B4
London Fields East Side HACK E8	78	B4

London Fields West Side *HACK* E8 ....**78** A4
London La *HACK* E8 ....**78** B4
London Ms *BAY/PAD* W2 ....**16** B5
London Rd *BARK* IG11 ....**84** B4
   FSTH SE23 ....**156** C1
   PLSTW E13 ....**94** A1
   STHWK SE1 ....**46** C2
London Stile *CHSWK* W4 ....**110** A1
London St *BAY/PAD* W2 ....**16** A5
   FENCHST EC3M **37** D1
London Ter *BETH* E2 ....**90** A1
London Wall *BARB* EC2Y **23** F3
London Wall Buildings *LVPST* EC2M **24** B3
Long Acre *COVGDN* WC2E **20** C5
Longbeach Rd *BTSEA* SW11 ....**133** F1
Longbridge Rd *BARK* IG11 ....**85** D3
Longbridge Wy *LEW* SE13 ....**140** C5
Longcroft *ELTH/MOT* SE9 ....**162** A3
Longdown Rd *CAT* SE6 ....**158** A4
Long Dr *ACT* W3 ....**87** E5
Longfellow Rd *BOW* E3 ....**91** E2
   WALTH E17 ....**61** F1
Longfellow Wy *STHWK* SE1 ....**49** F5
Longfield Crs *SYD* SE26 ....**156** C3
Longfield Dr *MORT/ESHN* SW14 ....**128** B3
Longfield Est *STHWK* SE1 ....**49** F4
Longfield St *WAND/EARL* SW18 ....**132** A5
Longford St *CAMTN* NW1 ....**7** D5
Longhedge St *BTSEA* SW11 ....**116** A5
Longhill Rd *CAT* SE6 ....**159** D2
Longhope Cl *PECK* SE15 ....**119** E2
Longhurst Rd *LEW* SE13 ....**141** E3
Longlands Park Crs *BFN/LL* DA15 ....**163** E3
Longlands Rd *BFN/LL* DA15 ....**163** E3
Long La *STBT* EC1A **23** D2
   STHWK SE1 ....**48** B1
Longley St *STHWK* SE1 ....**102** A5
Longley Wy *CRICK* NW2 ....**52** C5
Long Mark Rd *CAN/RD* E16 ....**95** D5
Long Meadow *KTTN* NW5 * **75** D3
Longmeadow Rd *BFN/LL* DA15 ....**163** E1
Longmoore St *PIM* SW1V **43** E5
Longnor Rd *WCHPL* E1 ....**91** D2
Long Pond Rd *BKHTH/KID* SE3 ....**123** E4
Long Reach Rd *BARK* IG11 ....**97** F3
Longridge Rd *ECT* SW5 ....**38** A3
Longshore *DEPT* SE8 ....**103** F5
Longstaff Crs *WAND/EARL* SW18 ....**132** A4
Longstaff Rd *WAND/EARL* SW18 ....**132** A4
Longstone Av *WLSDN* NW10 ....**69** F4
Longstone Rd *TOOT* SW17 ....**152** B5
Long St *BETH* E2 ....**13** E2
Longton Av *SYD* SE26 ....**156** A4
Longton Gv *SYD* SE26 ....**156** A4
Longville Rd *LBTH* SE11 ....**46** C4
Long Wk *STHWK* SE1 ....**49** D2
Longwood Dr *PUT/ROE* SW15 ....**130** A4
Long Yd *BMSBY* WC1N **21** E1
Lonsdale Av *EHAM* E6 ....**95** D4
Lonsdale Cl *EHAM* E6 ....**95** E3
   LEE/GVPK SE12 ....**161** D3
Lonsdale Crs *GNTH/NBYPK* IG2 ....**66** B3
Lonsdale Ms *RCH/KEW* * TW9 ....**110** A4
Lonsdale Pl *IS* N1 ....**76** A4
Lonsdale Rd *BARN* SW13 ....**111** F3
   CHSWK W4 ....**99** F5
   KIL/WHAMP NW6 ....**89** D1
   NTGHL W11 ....**89** F5
   WAN E11 ....**63** F2
Lonsdale Sq *IS* * N1 ....**76** A4
Loop Rd *CHST* BR7 ....**162** B5
Loraine Cottages *HOLWY* * N7 ....**75** F1
Loraine Rd *CHSWK* W4 ....**110** B2
   HOLWY N7 ....**75** F1
Lord Hills Rd *BAY/PAD* W2 ....**15** E3
Lord Holland La *BRXN/ST* * SW9 ....**118** A5

Lord Napier Pl *HMSMTH* W6 ....**112** A1
Lord North St *WEST* SW1P **44** C3
Lord Roberts Ms *FUL/PGN* * SW6 ....**114** B3
Lords Cl *DUL* SE21 ....**154** C2
Lordship Gv *STNW/STAM* N16 ....**59** D4
Lordship La *DUL* SE21 ....**156** A1
   EDUL SE22 ....**137** F4
Lordship Pk *STNW/STAM* N16 ....**59** D4
Lordship Park Ms *STNW/STAM* N16 ....**58** C4
Lordship Pl *CHEL* SW3 ....**115** E2
Lordship Rd *STNW/STAM* N16 ....**59** D3
Lordship Ter *STNW/STAM* N16 ....**59** D3
Lord St *CAN/RD* E16 ....**107** E2
Lords Vw *STJWD* NW8 ....**4** C4
Lord Warwick St *WOOL/PLUM* SE18 ....**107** F4
Lorenzo St *FSBYW* WC1X **9** E3
Loris Rd *HMSMTH* W6 ....**100** C4
Lorn Ct *BRXN/ST* SW9 ....**118** A5
Lorne Cl *STJWD* NW8 ....**5** D4
Lorne Gdns *WKENS* W14 ....**101** D3
Lorne Rd *FSBYPK* N4 ....**57** F3
   FSTGT E7 ....**82** B1
Lorn Rd *BRXN/ST* SW9 ....**117** F5
Lorrimore Rd *WALW* SE17 ....**118** B2
Lorrimore Sq *WALW* SE17 ....**118** B2
Lothair Rd North *FSBYPK* N4 ....**58** B1
Lothair Rd South *FSBYPK* N4 ....**58** A2
Lothbury *LOTH* EC2R **24** A4
Lothian Rd *BRXN/ST* SW9 ....**118** B4
Lothrop St *NKENS* W10 ....**89** E2
Lots Rd *WBPTN* SW10 ....**114** C3
Loudoun Rd *STJWD* NW8 ....**72** C5
Loughborough Pk *HNHL* SE24 ....**136** B2
Loughborough Rd *BRXN/ST* SW9 ....**118** A5
Loughborough St *LBTH* SE11 ....**117** F1
Lough Rd *HOLWY* N7 ....**75** F2
Louisa Cl *HOM* E9 ....**78** C4
Louisa St *WCHPL* E1 ....**91** D4
Louis Cl *CHST* BR7 ....**161** F4
Louise Bennett Cl *HNHL* * SE24 ....**136** B2
Louise Rd *SRTFD* E15 ....**81** E3
Louisville Rd *TOOT* SW17 ....**152** A3
Louvaine Rd *BTSEA* SW11 ....**133** D2
Lovage Ap *EHAM* E6 ....**95** E4
Lovat Cl *CRICK* NW2 ....**51** F5
Lovat La *FENCHST* EC3M **24** C1
Lovegrove St *STHWK* SE1 ....**120** A1
Lovegrove Wk *POP/IOD* E14 ....**104** C2
Lovelace Gn *ELTH/MOT* SE9 ....**143** F1
Lovelace Rd *DUL* SE21 ....**154** C2
Love La *CITYW* EC2V **23** F4
   WOOL/PLUM SE18 ....**108** A5
Lovelinch Cl *PECK* SE15 ....**120** C2
Lovell Pl *BERM/RHTH* SE16 ....**103** E4
Loveridge Ms *KIL/WHAMP* NW6 ....**71** F3
Loveridge Rd *KIL/WHAMP* NW6 ....**71** F3
Lovett Wy *WLSDN* NW10 ....**68** C2
Love Wk *CMBW* SE5 ....**119** D5
Lowbrook Rd *IL* IG1 ....**84** B1
Lowden Rd *HNHL* SE24 ....**136** B2
Lowe Av *CAN/RD* E16 ....**94** A4
Lowell St *POP/IOD* E14 ....**91** E5
Lower Addison Gdns *WKENS* W14 ....**101** E3
Lower Belgrave St *BGVA* SW1W **42** C3
Lower Clapton Rd *CLPT* E5 ....**78** B1
Lower Clarendon Wk *NTGHL* W11 ....**89** E5
Lower Common South
   PUT/ROE SW15 ....**130** B1
Lower Grosvenor Pl *KTBR* SW1X **42** C2
Lower James St *SOHO/CST* * W1F **31** F1
Lower John St *SOHO/CST* W1F **31** F1
Lower Lea Crossing *POP/IOD* E14 ....**105** E1
Lower Marsh *STHWK* SE1 ....**46** A1
Lower Merton Ri *HAMP* NW3 ....**73** E4
Lower Richmond Rd *PUT/ROE* SW15 ....**130** C1
   RCH/KEW TW9 ....**128** A1
Lower Rd *BERM/RHTH* SE16 ....**102** C3
Lower Sloane St *BGVA* SW1W **41** F5

Lower Ter *HAMP* NW3 ....54 C5
Lower Thames St *MON* EC3R 36 C2
Lowfield Rd *ACT* W3 ....86 C5
   KIL/WHAMP NW6 ....72 A4
Low Hall La *WALTH* E17 ....61 E1
Lowman Rd *HOLWY* N7 ....75 F1
Lowndes Cl *KTBR* SW1X 42 B3
Lowndes Ct *REGST* W1B 19 E5
Lowndes Pl *KTBR* SW1X 42 A3
Lowndes Sq *KTBR* SW1X 41 F1
Lowndes St *KTBR* SW1X 41 F2
Lowood St *WCHPL* E1 ....102 B1
Lowther Hl *FSTH* SE23 ....139 E5
Lowther Man *BARN* SW13 ....112 A4
Lowther Rd *BARN* SW13 ....111 F4
   HOLWY N7 ....76 A2
Lowth Rd *CMBW* SE5 ....118 C5
Loxford Av *EHAM* E6 ....95 D1
Loxford La *IL* IG1 ....84 C2
Loxford Rd *BARK* IG11 ....84 B3
Loxham St *STPAN* WC1H 9 D4
Loxley Cl *SYD* SE26 ....157 F5
Loxley Rd *WAND/EARL* SW18 ......151 D1
Loxton Rd *FSTH* SE23 ....157 D1
Lubbock St *NWCR* SE14 ....120 C3
Lucan Pl *CHEL* SW3 ....40 C5
Lucas Av *PLSTW* E13 ....82 B5
Lucas Sq *GLDGN* NW11 ....54 A1
Lucas St *DEPT* SE8 ....122 A5
Lucerne Ms *KENS* W8 ....26 B3
Lucerne Rd *HBRY* N5 ....76 B1
Lucey Rd *BERM/RHTH* SE16 ....102 A4
Lucey Wy *BERM/RHTH* SE16 ....102 A4
Lucien Rd *TOOT* SW17 ....152 A4
   WAND/EARL SW18 ....150 B2
Lucknow St *WOOL/PLUM* SE18 .....127 E3
Lucorn Cl *LEE/GVPK* SE12 ....141 F4
Ludgate Broadway *BLKFR* EC4V ...23 D5
Ludgate Circ *STP* EC4M 22 C5
Ludgate Hl *STP* EC4M 22 C5
Ludgate Sq *BLKFR* EC4V 23 D5
Ludlow St *FSBYE* EC1V 11 E5
Ludovick Wk *PUT/ROE* SW15 ......129 E2
Luffman Rd *LEE/GVPK* SE12 ......160 B3
Lugard Rd *PECK* SE15 ....120 B5
Lugg Ap *MNPK* E12 ....66 A5
Luke St *SDTCH* EC2A 12 C5
Lukin St *WCHPL* E1 ....102 C1
Lullingstone La *LEW* SE13 ......141 D4
Lulworth Rd *ELTH/MOT* SE9 ......161 E4
   PECK SE15 ....120 B5
   WELL DA16 ....127 F5
Lumley Flats *BCVA* SW1W 116 A1
Lumley Rd *MYFR/PKLN* W1K 18 B5
Lundy Wk *IS* N1 ....76 C3
Lupin Cl *BRXS/STRHM* SW2 ....154 B2
Lupton Cl *LEE/GVPK* SE12 ....160 B4
Lupton St *KTTN* NW5 ....74 C1
Lupus St *PIM* SW1V 116 B1
Lurgan Av *HMSMTH* W6 ....113 D2
Lurline Gdns *BTSEA* SW11 ....116 A4
Luscombe Wy *VX/NE* SW8 ....117 F3
Lushington Rd *CAT* SE6 ....158 B5
   WLSDN NW10 ....88 B1
Lushington Ter *HACK* E8 ....78 A2
Luther King Cl *WALTH* E17 ......61 E1
Luton Pl *GNWCH* SE10 ....122 C3
Luton Rd *PLSTW* E13 ....94 A3
Luton St *STJWD* NW8 ....16 B1
Luttrell Av *PUT/ROE* SW15 ......130 B3
Lutwyche Rd *FSTH* SE23 ....157 F2
Luxborough St *MHST* W1U 18 A1
Luxemburg Gdns *HMSMTH* W6 ......101 D5
Luxfield Rd *ELTH/MOT* SE9 ......161 E1
Luxford St *BERM/RHTH* SE16 .....103 D5
Luxmore St *BROCKY* SE4 ....121 F4
Luxor St *CMBW* SE5 ....118 B5
Lyall Av *DUL* SE21 ....155 E4

Lyall Ms *KTBR* SW1X 42 A3
Lyall Ms West *KTBR* SW1X 42 A3
Lyall St *KTBR* SW1X 42 A3
Lyal Rd *BOW* E3 ....91 E1
Lycett Pl *SHB* W12 ....100 A3
Lydd Cl *BFN/LL* DA15 ....163 E3
Lydden Gv *WAND/EARL* SW18 ......132 B5
Lydden Rd *WAND/EARL* SW18 ......132 B5
Lydeard Rd *EHAM* E6 ....83 F4
Lydford Cl *STNW/STAM* N16 .....77 E2
   MV/WKIL W9 ....89 F3
Lydford Rd *CRICK* NW2 ....71 D3
   MV/WKIL W9 ....89 F3
Lydhurst Av *BRXS/STRHM* SW2 ....153 F2
Lydney Cl *PECK* SE15 ....119 E3
   WIM/MER SW19 ....149 E2
Lydon Rd *CLAP* SW4 ....134 C1
Lydstep Rd *CHST* BR7 ....162 A4
Lyford Rd *WAND/EARL* SW18 .....133 D5
Lyford St *CHARL* SE7 ....107 E5
Lygon Pl *BCVA* SW1W 42 C3
Lyham Cl *CLAP* SW4 ....135 E4
Lyham Rd *BRXS/STRHM* SW2 ......135 E3
Lyme Farm Rd *LEE/GVPK* SE12 ...142 A2
Lyme Gv *HOM* E9 ....78 C4
Lymer Av *NRWD* SE19 ....155 F5
Lyme St *CAMTN* NW1 ....74 C4
Lyme Ter *CAMTN* NW1 ....74 C4
Lyminge Cl *SCUP* DA14 ....163 F4
Lyminge Gdns *WAND/EARL* SW18 ..151 E1
Lymington Rd *KIL/WHAMP* * NW6 ..72 B3
Lympstone Gdns *PECK* SE15 .....120 A3
Lynbrook Cl *PECK* SE15 ....119 E3
Lyncourt *BKHTH/KID* * SE3 .....123 D5
Lyncroft Gdns *KIL/WHAMP* NW6 ..72 A2
Lyndale *CRICK* NW2 ....53 F5
Lyndale Av *CRICK* NW2 ....53 F5
Lyndale Cl *BKHTH/KID* SE3 .....123 F2
Lyndhurst Cl *WLSDN* NW10 ......51 E5
Lyndhurst Dr *WAN* E11 ....62 C2
Lyndhurst Gdns *BARK* IG11 .....85 E3
   GNTH/NBYPK IG2 ....67 D1
   HAMP NW3 ....73 D2
Lyndhurst Gv *CMBW* SE5 ....119 E5
Lyndhurst Rd *HAMP* NW3 ....73 D2
Lyndhurst Sq *PECK* SE15 ....119 F4
Lyndhurst Ter *HAMP* NW3 ....73 D2
Lyndhurst Wy *PECK* SE15 ....119 F4
Lyndon Av *BFN/LL* DA15 ....145 F3
Lyndon Yd *TOOT* SW17 ....150 B4
Lyneham Wk *CLPT* * E5 ....79 D2
Lynette Av *CLAP* SW4 ....134 B4
Lynford Gdns *GDMY/SEVK* IG3 ...67 F4
Lyn Ms *STNW/STAM* * N16 ....77 F1
Lynmouth Rd *STNW/STAM* N16 ....59 F3
   WALTH E17 ....61 E1
Lynne Wy *WLSDN* NW10 ....69 E3
Lynn Ms *WAN* E11 ....63 E4
Lynn Rd *BAL* SW12 ....134 B5
   GNTH/NBYPK IG2 ....67 D2
   WAN E11 ....63 E4
Lynsted Gdns *ELTH/MOT* SE9 ....143 D2
Lynton Av *ACT* W3 ....86 C5
Lynton Cl *WLSDN* NW10 ....69 E2
Lynton Crs *GNTH/NBYPK* IG2 ....66 B1
Lynton Est *STHWK* SE1 ....49 F5
Lynton Rd *ACT* W3 ....98 A1
   KIL/WHAMP NW6 ....71 F5
   STHWK SE1 ....49 F5
Lynton Ter *ACT* * W3 ....86 C5
Lynwood Rd *TOOT* SW17 ....151 F3
Lyons Pl *STJWD* NW8 ....16 A1
Lyon St *IS* N1 ....75 F4
Lyons Wk *WKENS* W14 ....101 E5
Lyric Ms *SYD* SE26 ....156 C4
Lyric Rd *BARN* SW13 ....111 F4
Lysander Gv *ARCH* N19 ....57 D3
Lysander Ms *ARCH* * N19 ....57 E3
Lysias Rd *BAL* SW12 ....134 A4

Lysia St *FUL/PGN* SW6 ....113 D3
Lysons Wk *PUT/ROE* * SW15 ....130 A3
Lytcott Gv *EDUL* SE22 ....137 F3
Lytham St *WALW* SE17 ....119 D1
Lyttelton Rd *LEY* E10 ....62 B5
Lyttleton Cl *HAMP* NW3 ....73 E4
Lytton Gv *PUT/ROE* SW15 ....131 D3
Lytton Rd *WAN* E11 ....63 E2
Lyveden Rd *BKHTH/KID* SE3 ....124 B3

M

Mabledon Pl *CAMTN* NW1...................8 B4
Mablethorpe Rd *FUL/PGN* SW6 ....113 E3
Mabley St *HOM* E9 ....79 E2
Macarthur Rd *FSTGT* E7 ....82 A3
Macarthur Ter *CHARL* * SE7 ....125 D2
Macaulay Rd *CLAP* SW4 ....134 B1
    EHAM E6 ....95 D1
Macbean St *WOOL/PLUM* SE18 .....108 A4
Macbeth St *HMSMTH* W6 ....112 B1
Macclesfield Br *STJWD* NW8 ....5 D1
Macclesfield Rd *FSBYE* EC1V 11 E3
Macclesfield St *SOHO/SHAV* W1D 32 B5
Macdonald Rd *ARCH* N19 ....56 C4
    FSTGT E7 ....82 A1
Macduff Rd *BTSEA* SW11 ....116 A4
Mace Cl *WAP* E1W 102 B2
Mace Gtwy *CAN/RD* E16 ....106 A1
Mace St *BETH* E2 ....91 D1
Macfarlane Rd *SHB* W12 ....100 C2
Mac Farren Pl *CAMTN* NW1 ....18 B1
Macgregor Rd *CAN/RD* E16 ....94 C4
Machell Rd *PECK* SE15 ....138 C5
Mackay Rd *CLAP* SW4 ....134 B1
Mackennal St *STJWD* NW8 ....5 D2
Mackenzie Cl *SHB* * W12 ....100 B1
Mackenzie Rd *HOLWY* N7 ....75 F3
Mackeson Rd *HAMP* * NW3 ....73 F1
Mackie Rd *BRXS/STRHM* SW2 ....136 A5
Mackintosh La *HOM* E9 ....79 D2
Macklin St *HOL/ALD* WC2B 21 D4
Macks Rd *BERM/RHTH* SE16 ....102 A5
Mackworth St *CAMTN* NW1 ....7 E3
Maclean Rd *FSTH* SE23 ....139 E4
Macleod House *WOOL/PLUM* SE18 ...125 E3
Macleod St *WALW* SE17 ....118 C1
Maclise Rd *WKENS* W14 ....101 E4
Macoma Rd *WOOL/PLUM* SE18 ....127 D2
Macoma Ter *WOOL/PLUM* SE18 ......127 D2
Maconochies Rd *POP/IOD* * E14 ....122 B1
Macquarie Wy *POP/IOD* E14 ....104 B5
Macroom Rd *MV/WKIL* W9 ....89 F2
Maddams St *BOW* E3 ....92 B3
Maddock Wy *WALW* SE17 ....118 B2
Maddox St *MYFR/PKLN* W1K 31 D1
Madeira Rd *STRHM/NOR* SW16 ....153 E5
    WAN E11 ....63 D3
Madeline Gv *IL* IG1 ....85 D2
Madge Gill Wy *EHAM* E6 ....83 E5
Madinah Rd *HACK* E8 ....78 A3
Madras Pl *HOLWY* N7 ....76 A3
Madras Rd *IL* IG1 ....84 B1
Madrid Rd *BARN* SW13 ....112 A4
Madron St *STHWK* SE1 ....119 E1
Mafeking Av *EHAM* E6 ....95 D1
    GNTH/NBYPK IG2 ....67 D2
Mafeking Rd *CAN/RD* E16 ....93 F3
Magazine Ga *BAY/PAD* * W2 ....29 D3
Magdala Av *KTTN* NW5 ....56 C4
Magdalene Gdns *EHAM* E6 ....96 A3
Magdalen Rd *WAND/EARL* SW18 .....150 C1
Magdalen St *STHWK* SE1 ....36 C4
Magee St *LBTH* SE11 ....118 A2
Magnin Cl *HACK* E8 ....78 A5
Magnolia Cl *LEY* E10 ....62 A4

Magnolia Pl *CLAP* * SW4 ....135 E3
Magnolia Rd *CHSWK* W4 ....110 B2
Magnolia Whf *CHSWK* * W4 ....110 B2
Magpie Cl *FSTGT* E7 ....81 F2
Magpie Pl *NWCR* * SE14 ....121 E2
Magri Wk *WCHPL* E1 ....90 C4
Mahogany Cl *BERM/RHTH* SE16 .....103 E2
Maida Av *BAY/PAD* W2 ....15 F2
Maida V *KIL/WHAMP* NW6 ....3 D2
Maiden La *CAMTN* NW1 ....75 D4
    COVGDN WC2E 33 D2
    STHWK SE1 ....35 F4
Maiden Rd *SRTFD* E15 ....81 E4
Maidenstone HI *GNWCH* SE10 ....122 C4
Maidstone Buildings Ms *STHWK* SE1 ...35 F4
Main Barracks *WOOL/PLUM* * SE18 ...125 F1
Mainridge Rd *CHST* BR7 ....162 A4
Main Rd *BFN/LL* DA15 ....163 E3
Maismore St *PECK* SE15 ....120 A2
Maitland Cl *GNWCH* SE10 ....122 B3
Maitland Park Rd *HAMP* NW3 ....73 F3
Maitland Park Vls *HAMP* NW3 ....73 F3
Maitland Rd *SRTFD* * E15 ....81 F3
Majendie Rd *WOOL/PLUM* SE18 .....127 D1
Major Rd *BERM/RHTH* * SE16 ....102 A4
    SRTFD E15 ....80 C2
Makepeace Av *HGT* N6 ....56 A4
Makins St *CHEL* SW3 ....41 D5
Malabar St *POP/IOD* E14 ....104 A3
Malam Gdns *POP/IOD* E14 ....104 B1
Malbrook Rd *PUT/ROE* SW15 ....130 B2
Malcolm Gavin Cl *TOOT* SW17 ....151 E2
Malcolm Pl *BETH* E2 ....90 C3
Malcolm Rd *WCHPL* E1 ....90 C3
Malden Pl *KTTN* NW5 ....74 A2
Malden Rd *KTTN* NW5 ....73 F2
Maldon Cl *CMBW* * SE5 ....137 E1
    IS N1 ....76 C5
Maldon Rd *ACT* W3 ....98 C1
Malet Pl *GWRST* WC1E 20 A1
Maley Av *WNWD* SE27 ....154 B2
Malfort Rd *CMBW* SE5 ....137 E1
Malham Rd *FSTH* SE23 ....157 D1
The Mall *MORT/ESHN* SW14 ....128 C3
    WHALL SW1A 31 E5
Mallams Ms *BRXN/ST* SW9 ....136 A1
Mallard Wy *CDALE/KGS* NW9 ....50 C2
Mall Chambers *KENS* * W8 ....26 B3
Mallet Rd *LEW* SE13 ....141 D4
Mallinson Rd *BTSEA* SW11 ....133 E3
Mallord St *CHEL* SW3 ....115 D2
Mallory Cl *BROCKY* SE4 ....139 E2
Mallory St *CAMTN* NW1 ....17 D1
Mallow St *FSBYE* EC1V 12 A5
Mall Rd *HMSMTH* W6 ....112 B1
Mall Vls *HMSMTH* * W6 ....112 B1
Malmesbury Rd *BOW* E3 ....91 F1
    CAN/RD E16 ....93 E4
Malmesbury Ter *CAN/RD* E16 ....93 E4
Malmesbury West Est *BOW* E3 ....91 F2
Malpas Rd *BROCKY* SE4 ....121 F5
    HACK E8 ....78 B3
Malta Rd *LEY* E10 ....62 A3
Malta St *FSBYE* EC1V 10 C5
Maltby St *STHWK* SE1 ....49 E1
Maltings Pl *FUL/PGN* SW6 ....114 B3
    STHWK SE1 ....37 D5
Malton Ms *NKENS* * W10 ....89 E5
    WOOL/PLUM SE18 ....127 E5
Malton Rd *NKENS* W10 ....89 E5
Malton St *WOOL/PLUM* SE18 ....127 E5
Maltravers St *TPL/STR* WC2R 33 F1
Malt St *STHWK* SE1 ....120 A2
Malva Cl *WAND/EARL* SW18 ....132 B3
Malvern Cl *NKENS* W10 ....89 F4
Malvern Dr *GDMY/SEVK* IG3 ....85 F1
Malvern Gdns *CRICK* NW2 ....53 E4
Malvern Ms *KIL/WHAMP* NW6 ....2 A4

Malvern Pl *MV/WKIL* * W9 ....89 F2
Malvern Rd *EHAM* E6 ....83 E5
   HACK E8 ....78 A4
   KIL/WHAMP NW6 * 2 A3
   MV/WKIL * W9 ....89 F2
   WAN E11 ....63 E4
Malvern Ter *IS* N1 ....76 A5
Malwood Rd *BAL* SW12 ....134 B1
Malyons Rd *LEW* SE13 ....140 E3
Malyons Ter *BROCKY* SE4 ....140 E3
Managers Gv *POP/IOD* * E14 ....104 C2
Manaton Cl *PECK* SE15 ....138 B1
Manbey Gv *SRTFD* E15 ....81 E3
Manbey Park Rd *SRTFD* E15 ....81 E3
Manbey Rd *SRTFD* * E15 ....81 E3
Manbey St *SRTFD* E15 ....81 E3
Manbre Rd *HMSMTH* W6 ....112 C2
Manbrough Av *EHAM* E6 ....95 F2
Manchester Gv *POP/IOD* * W10 ....89 E3
Manchester Ms *MHST* W1U 18 A3
Manchester Rd *POP/IOD* E14 ....122 C1
   SEVS/STOTM N15 ....59 D1
Manchester Sq *MBLAR* W1H 18 B4
Manchester St *MHST* W1U 18 A3
Manchuria Rd *BTSEA* SW11 ....134 A4
Manciple St *STHWK* SE1 ....48 B1
Mandalay Rd *CLAP* SW4 ....134 C3
Mandela Rd *WLSDN* NW10 ....68 C4
Mandela St *CAN/RD* E16 ....94 A5
Mandela St *BRXN/ST* SW9 ....118 A3
   CAMTN NW1 ....74 C5
Mandela Wy *STHWK* SE1 ....49 D4
Mandeville Pl *MHST* W1U 18 A4
Mandeville St *CLPT* E5 ....61 E5
Mandrake Rd *TOOT* SW17 ....151 F1
Mandrake Wy *SRTFD* * E15 ....81 E4
Mandrell Rd *BRXS/STRHM* SW2 ....135 E4
Manette St *SOHO/SHAV* W1D 20 B5
Manfred Rd *PUT/ROE* SW15 ....131 F3
Manger Rd *HOLWY* N7 ....75 E3
Manilla St *POP/IOD* E14 ....104 A3
Manley Ct *STNW/STAM* N16 ....59 F5
Manley St *CAMTN* NW1 ....74 A5
Manningford Cl *FSBYE* * EC1V 10 C3
Manningtree Cl *WIM/MER* SW19 ....149 E1
Manningtree St *WCHPL* E1 ....90 A5
Manor Av *BROCKY* SE4 ....121 F5
Manorbrook *BKHTH/KID* SE3 ....142 A2
Manor Ct *ACT* * W3 ....98 C5
Manor Est *BERM/RHTH* SE16 ....102 B5
Manor Gdns *ACT* W3 ....98 A5
   HOLWY N7 ....57 E5
   VX/NE * SW8 ....116 C5
Manor Gv *PECK* SE15 ....120 C2
   RCH/KEW TW9 ....128 B3
Manor Hall Gdns *LEY* E10 ....62 A3
Manor House Dr *KIL/WHAMP* NW6 ....71 D4
Manor La *LEW* SE13 ....141 E3
Manor Lane Ter *LEW* SE13 ....141 E2
Manor Ms *KIL/WHAMP* NW6 ....2 B1
Manor Mt *FSTH* SE23 ....156 C1
Manor Pde *STNW/STAM* * N16 ....59 F4
Manor Pk *LEW* SE13 ....141 D3
Manor Park Rd *MNPK* E12 ....83 D1
   WLSDN NW10 ....69 E5
Manor Pl *WALW* SE17 ....118 B1
Manor Rd *BFN/LL* DA15 ....163 F3
   CAN/RD E16 ....94 A5
   LEY E10 ....62 A2
   STNW/STAM N16 ....59 E3
Manor Wy *BKHTH/KID* SE3 ....142 A2
Manresa Rd *CHEL* * SW3 ....115 D1
Mansard Beeches *TOOT* SW17 ....152 A5
Mansell Rd *ACT* W3 ....99 D2
Mansell St *TWRH* EC3N 37 F2
   WCHPL E1 ....25 F5
Mansergh Cl *WOOL/PLUM* SE18 ....125 E3

Manse Rd *STNW/STAM* N16 ....59 F5
Mansfield Ms *CAVSQ/HST* W1G 18 C3
Mansfield Rd *ACT* W3 ....86 B3
   HAMP NW3 ....73 F2
   IL IG1 ....66 A4
   WAN E11 ....64 B1
Mansfield St *CAVSQ/HST* W1G 18 C3
Mansford St *BETH* E2 ....90 A1
Mansion House Pl *MANHO* * EC4N 24 A5
The Mansions *ECT* * SW5 ....114 B1
Manson Ms *SKENS* SW7 ....39 F5
Manson Pl *SKENS* SW7 ....40 A5
Manstone Rd *CRICK* NW2 ....71 E2
Manthorpe Rd *WOOL/PLUM* SE18 ....126 C1
Mantilla Rd *TOOT* SW17 ....152 A4
Mantle Rd *BROCKY* SE4 ....139 E1
Mantle Wy *SRTFD* E15 ....81 E4
Mantua St *BTSEA* SW11 ....133 D1
Mantus Cl *WCHPL* E1 ....90 C3
Mantus Rd *WCHPL* E1 ....90 C3
Manville Gdns *TOOT* SW17 ....152 B3
Manville Rd *TOOT* SW17 ....152 A2
Manwood Rd *BROCKY* SE4 ....139 F4
Manwood St *CAN/RD* E16 ....107 E3
Many Gates *BAL* SW12 ....152 B2
Mapesbury Rd *CRICK* NW2 ....71 E3
Mapeshill Pl *CRICK* NW2 ....70 C3
Mape St *BETH* E2 ....90 B3
Maple Av *ACT* W3 ....99 E2
Maple Cl *CLAP* SW4 ....135 D4
   STNW/STAM N16 ....60 A1
Maplecroft Cl *EHAM* E6 ....95 D5
Mapledene Est *HACK* * E8 ....78 A4
Mapledene Rd *HACK* E8 ....77 F4
Maple Gv *CDALE/KGS* NW9 ....50 C2
Maple Leaf Dr *BFN/LL* DA15 ....163 F1
Maple Leaf Sq *BERM/RHTH* * SE16 ....103 D3
Maple Ms *KIL/WHAMP* * NW6 ....2 C1
   STRHM/NOR SW16 ....153 F5
Maple Pl *FITZ* W1T 19 F2
Maple Rd *WAN* E11 ....63 E1
Maples Pl *WCHPL* * E1 ....90 B4
Maplestead Rd *BRXS/STRHM* SW2 ....135 F5
Maple St *FITZ* W1T 19 E2
Mapleton Crs *WAND/EARL* SW18 ....132 B4
Mapleton Rd *WAND/EARL* SW18 ....132 A4
Maple Wk *NKENS* * W10 ....89 D3
Maplin Rd *CAN/RD* E16 ....94 A5
Maplin St *BOW* E3 ....91 F2
Marathon Wy *THMD* SE28 ....109 F4
Marban Rd *MV/WKIL* W9 ....89 F2
Marble Cl *ACT* W3 ....98 A5
Marble Dr *CRICK* NW2 ....53 D3
Marble Quay *WAP* E1W 37 F3
Marbrook Ct *LEE/GVPK* SE12 ....160 C5
Marcella Rd *BRXN/ST* SW9 ....118 A5
Marchant Rd *WAN* E11 ....63 D4
Marchant St *NWCR* SE14 ....121 E2
Marchbank Rd *WKENS* W14 ....113 F2
Marchmont St *BMSBY* WC1N 8 C5
Marchwood Cl *CMBW* SE5 ....119 E3
Marcia Rd *STHWK* SE1 ....49 D5
Marcilly Rd *WAND/EARL* SW18 ....133 D3
Marconi Rd *LEY* E10 ....62 A3
Marcon Pl *HACK* E8 ....78 B3
Marco Rd *HMSMTH* W6 ....100 B4
Marcus Garvey Ms *EDUL* SE22 ....138 B4
Marcus Garvey Wy *HNHL* SE24 ....136 A2
Marcus St *SRTFD* E15 ....81 E5
   WAND/EARL SW18 ....132 B4
Marcus Ter *WAND/EARL* SW18 ....132 B4
Marden Sq *BERM/RHTH* SE16 ....102 B4
Marechal Niel Av *BFN/LL* DA15 ....163 D3
Marechal Niel Pde *BFN/LL* * DA15 ....163 D3
Maresfield Gdns *HAMP* NW3 ....72 C2
Mare St *HACK* E8 ....78 B4
Margaret Gardiner Dr *ELTH/MOT* SE9 ....161 F2
Margaret Ingram Cl *FUL/PGN* * SW6 ....113 F2

Margaret Rd *STNW/STAM* * N16 ....59 F3
Margaret St *GTPST* W1W 19 E4
Margaretta Ter *CHEL* SW3 ....115 E2
Margaretting Rd *MNPK* E12 ....64 C4
Margaret Wy *REDBR* IG4 ....65 E1
Margate Rd *CLAP* SW4 ....135 E3
Margery St *FSBYW* WC1X 10 A4
Margin Dr *WIM/MER* SW19 ....149 D5
Margravine Gdns *HMSMTH* W6 ....113 D1
Margravine Rd *HMSMTH* W6 ....113 D2
Marham Gdns *WAND/EARL* SW18 ....151 E1
Maria Cl *BERM/RHTH* SE16 ....102 A5
Marian Pl *BETH* E2 ....90 B1
Marian Sq *BETH* E2 ....90 A1
Marian St *BETH* * E2 ....90 B1
Marian Wy *WLSDN* NW10 ....69 F4
Maria Ter *WCHPL* E1 ....91 D4
Marie Curie *CMBW* * SE5 ....119 E4
Marie Lloyd Wk *HACK* * E8 ....78 A3
Marigold Aly *STHWK* SE1 ....34 C2
Marigold St *BERM/RHTH* SE16 ....102 B3
Marina Dr *WELL* DA16 ....127 E5
Marine Dr *WOOL/PLUM* SE18 ....107 F5
Marinefield Rd *FUL/PGN* SW6 ....114 B5
Mariner Rd *MNPK* E12 ....84 A1
Mariners Ms *POP/IOD* E14 ....105 E3
Marine St *BERM/RHTH* SE16 ....102 A4
Marischal Rd *LEW* SE13 ....141 D1
Maritime Quay *POP/IOD* E14 ....122 A1
Maritime St *BOW* E3 ....91 F3
Marius Rd *TOOT* SW17 ....152 A2
Marjorie Gv *BTSEA* SW11 ....133 F2
The Market *COVGDN* * WC2E 33 D1
  PECK * SE15 ....120 A5
Market Est *HOLWY* N7 ....75 E3
Market Ms *MYFR/PICC* W1J 30 C4
Market Pde *LEY* * E10 ....62 B1
  STNW/STAM * N16 ....60 A3
Market Pl *ACT* W3 ....98 C2
  BERM/RHTH * SE16 ....102 A5
  SOHO/SHAV W1D 19 E4
Market Rd *HOLWY* N1 ....75 E3
  RCH/KEW TW9 ....128 A1
Market St *EHAM* E6 ....95 F1
  WOOL/PLUM SE18 ....108 A5
Markham Pl *CHEL* SW3 ....115 F1
Markham Sq *CHEL* SW3 ....115 F1
Markham St *CHEL* SW3 ....115 E1
Markhouse Av *WALTH* E17 ....61 E1
Markhouse Rd *WALTH* E17 ....61 F1
Mark La *MON* EC3R 37 D1
Markmanor Av *WALTH* E17 ....61 E2
Marksbury Av *RCH/KEW* TW9 ....128 A1
Mark St *SDTCH* EC2A 12 C5
  SRTFD E15 ....81 E4
Markwell Cl *SYD* SE26 ....156 B4
Marlborough Av *HACK* * E8 ....78 A5
Marlborough Cl *WALW* SE17 ....47 D5
Marlborough Ct *REGST* W1B 19 E5
Marlborough Crs *CHSWK* W4 ....99 D4
Marlborough Ga *BAY/PAD* W2 ....28 A2
Marlborough Gv *STHWK* SE1 ....120 A1
Marlborough Hi *STJWD* NW8 ....72 C5
Marlborough La *CHARL* SE7 ....124 C2
Marlborough Ms *BRXS/STRHM* SW2 ....135 F2
Marlborough Pde *FSBYPK* * N4 ....58 C3
Marlborough Pl *STJWD* NW8 ....3 E2
Marlborough Rd *ARCH* N19 ....57 E4
  CHSWK W4 ....110 C1
  FSTGT E7 ....82 C4
  SRTFD * E15 ....81 E1
  WHALL SW1A 31 F4
  WOOL/PLUM SE18 ....108 B4
Marlborough St *CHEL* SW3 ....40 C5
Marlborough Yd *ARCH* N19 ....57 D4
Marler Rd *FSTH* SE23 ....157 F1
Marloes Rd *KENS* W8 ....38 C2
The Marlowes *STJWD* NW8 ....73 D5

Marlow Rd *EHAM* E6 ....95 F2
Marlow Wy *BERM/RHTH* SE16 ....103 D3
Marl Rd *WAND/EARL* SW18 ....132 B2
Marlton St *GNWCH* SE10 ....123 F1
Marlwood Cl *BFN/LL* DA15 ....163 E2
Marmadon Rd *WOOL/PLUM* SE18 ....109 F5
Marmion Ms *BTSEA* * SW11 ....134 A1
Marmion Rd *BTSEA* SW11 ....134 A2
Marmont Rd *PECK* SE15 ....120 A4
Marmora Rd *EDUL* SE22 ....138 C4
Marne St *NKENS* W10 ....89 E2
Marney Rd *BTSEA* SW11 ....134 A2
Marnfield Crs *BRXS/STRHM* SW2 ....153 F1
Marnham Av *CRICK* NW2 ....71 E1
Marnock Rd *BROCKY* SE4 ....139 F3
Maroon St *POP/IOD* E14 ....91 E4
Maroons Wy *CAT* SE6 ....158 A5
Marquess Rd *IS* N1 ....77 D3
Marquess Rd North *IS* N1 ....76 C3
Marquess Rd South *IS* * N1 ....76 C3
Marquis Rd *CAMTN* NW1 ....75 D3
  FSBYPK N4 ....57 F3
Marrick Cl *PUT/ROE* SW15 ....130 A2
Marriott Rd *FSBYPK* N4 ....57 F3
  SRTFD E15 ....81 E5
Marriotts Cl *CDALE/KGS* NW9 ....51 F1
Marryat Pl *WIM/MER* SW19 ....149 E4
Marryat Rd *WIM/MER* SW19 ....149 D5
Marryat Sq *FUL/PGN* * SW6 ....113 E4
Marsala Rd *LEW* SE13 ....140 B2
Marsden Rd *PECK* SE15 ....137 F1
Marsden St *KTTN* NW5 ....74 A3
Marshall Cl *WAND/EARL* SW18 ....132 C4
Marshall Rd *LEY* E10 ....80 B1
Marshalls Gv *WOOL/PLUM* SE18 ....107 E5
Marshall St *SOHO/CST* W1F 19 F5
Marshalsea Rd *STHWK* SE1 ....35 F5
Marsham Cl *CHST* * BR7 ....162 B5
Marsham St *WEST* SW1P 44 B4
Marshbrook Cl *BKHTH/KID* SE3 ....143 D1
Marsh Dr *CDALE/KGS* NW9 ....51 F1
Marshfield St *POP/IOD* E14 ....104 C4
Marshgate La *SRTFD* E15 ....80 B4
Marsh Hi *HOM* E9 ....79 E2
Marsh La *LEY* E10 ....61 F4
Marsh Rd *POP/IOD* E14 ....104 B5
Marsh Wall *POP/IOD* E14 ....104 A3
Marsland Cl *WALW* SE17 ....118 A2
Marston Cl *KIL/WHAMP* NW6 ....72 C4
Martaban Rd *STNW/STAM* N16 ....59 E4
Martello St *HACK* E8 ....78 B4
Martell Rd *DUL* SE21 ....155 D3
Martel Pl *HACK* E8 ....77 F3
Martha Rd *SRTFD* E15 ....81 E3
Martha's Buildings *FSBYE* EC1V 12 A5
Martha St *WCHPL* E1 ....90 C5
Martin Bowes Rd *ELTH/MOT* SE9 ....143 F1
Martindale *MORT/ESHN* SW14 ....128 C3
Martindale Av *CAN/RD* E16 ....106 A1
Martindale Rd *BAL* SW12 ....134 B1
Martineau Rd *HBRY* N5 ....76 B1
Martineau St *WCHPL* E1 ....102 C1
Martin La *CANST* EC4R 36 B1
The Martins *SYD* SE26 ....156 B5
Martin St *THMD* SE28 ....109 E2
Martlett Ct *HOL/ALD* WC2B 21 D5
Marton Cl *CAT* SE6 ....158 A3
Marton Rd *STNW/STAM* * N16 ....59 E4
Martys Yd *HAMP* * NW3 ....73 D1
Marvels Cl *LEE/GVPK* SE12 ....160 B2
Marvels La *LEE/GVPK* SE12 ....160 B2
Marville Rd *FUL/PGN* SW6 ....113 F3
Marvin St *HACK* * E8 ....78 B3
Mary Adelaide Cl *PUT/ROE* SW15 ....147 E3
Mary Ann Buildings *DEPT* SE8 ....122 A2
Marybank *WOOL/PLUM* SE18 ....107 F5
Mary Datchelor Cl *CMBW* SE5 ....119 D4
Mary Gn *STJWD* * NW8 ....72 B5

Maryland Pk *SRTFD* E15 ....**81** E2
Maryland Rd *MV/WKIL* W9 ....**14** B1
  SRTFD E15 ....**81** D2
Maryland Sq *SRTFD* E15 ....**81** E2
Marylands Rd *MV/WKIL* W9 ....**14** B1
Maryland St *SRTFD* E15..........................**81** D2
Maryland Wk *IS* * N1 ....**76** C5
Mary Lawrencson Pl *BKHTH/KID* SE3 ..**123** F1
Marylebone High St *MHST* W1U **18** B2
Marylebone La *MHST* W1U **18** B4
Marylebone Ms *CAVSQ/HST* W1G............**18** B3
Marylebone Pas *GTPST* W1W **19** F4
Marylebone Rd *CAMTN* NW1 ....**17** D2
Marylebone St *MHST* W1U **18** B3
Marylee Wy *LBTH* SE11 ....**45** F5
Maryon Gv *CHARL* SE7.............................**107** E5
Maryon Ms *HAMP* NW3 ....**73** E1
Maryon Rd *CHARL* SE7.............................**107** E5
Mary Pl *NTGHL* W11 ....**101** E1
Mary Seacole Cl *HACK* * E8 ....**77** F5
Mary Secole Cl *HACK* E8 ....**77** F5
Mary St *CAN/RD* E16 ....**93** F4
  IS N1 ....**76** C5
Mary Ter *CAMTN* NW1 ....**74** C5
Masbro' Rd *WKENS* W14 ....**101** D4
Mascalls Rd *CHARL* SE7..........................**124** C2
Mascotts Cl *CRICK* NW2............................**52** B5
Masefield Gdns *EHAM* E6 ....**96** A3
Mashie Rd *ACT* W3 ....**87** E5
Maskall Cl *BRXS/STRHM* * SW2.............**154** A1
Maskell Rd *TOOT* SW17 ....**150** C3
Maskelyne Cl *BTSEA* SW11 ....**115** E4
Mason Cl *BERM/RHTH* SE16 ....**120** A1
Mason Ct *WBLY* * HA9 ....**50** A4
Mason's Arms Ms *CONDST* * W1S **19** D5
Mason's Av *CITYW* EC2V **24** A4
Masons Hl *WOOL/PLUM* SE18.................**108** B5
Mason's Pl *FSBYE* EC1V **11** D3
Mason St *WALW* SE17 ....**48** B4
Masons Yd *FSBYE* EC1V **11** E5
  STJS SW1Y **31** F3
Massie Rd *HACK* E8 ....**78** A3
Massingberd Wy *TOOT* SW17 ....**152** B4
Massinger St *WALW* SE17 ....**48** C5
Massingham St *WCHPL* E1 ....**91** D3
Master Gunners Pl *WOOL/PLUM* SE18 ..**125** E4
Masterman Rd *EHAM* E6 ....**95** E2
Masters Dr *BERM/RHTH* SE16 ....**120** B1
Master's St *WCHPL* E1 ....**91** D4
Mast House Ter *POP/IOD* * E14 ....**104** A5
Masthouse Ter *POP/IOD* E14 ....**104** A5
Mastmaker Rd *POP/IOD* E14 ....**104** A3
Matcham Rd *WAN* E11 ....**63** E5
Matchless Dr *WOOL/PLUM* SE18 ....**126** A3
Matham Gv *EDUL* SE22 ....**137** F2
Matheson Rd *WKENS* W14 ....**101** F5
Mathews Av *EHAM* E6 ....**96** A1
Mathews Park Av *SRTFD* E15.....................**81** F3
Mathews Yd *LSQ/SEVD* * WC2H **20** C5
Mathieson Ct *STHWK* SE1 ....**47** D1
Matilda St *IS* N1 ....**75** F5
Matlock Rd *LEY* E10.....................................**62** C1
Matlock St *WCHPL* E1 ....**91** E5
Matthew Cl *NKENS* * W10 ....**89** D3
Matthews St *BTSEA* * SW11 ....**115** F5
Matthias Rd *STNW/STAM* N16...................**77** D2
Mattingley Wy *PECK* * SE15 ....**119** F3
Mattingly Wy *PECK* SE15 ....**119** F3
Mattison Rd *FSBYPK* N4 ....**58** A1
Maud Cashmore Wy
  WOOL/PLUM SE18 ....**107** F4
Maude Rd *CMBW* SE5 ....**119** E5
Maud Gdns *BARK* IG11 ....**97** F1
  PLSTW E13 ....**93** F1
Maudlins Gn *WAP* * E1W **102** A2
Maud Rd *LEY* E10...**62** C5
  PLSTW E13 ....**81** F5
Maudslay Rd *ELTH/MOT* SE9 ....**143** F1

Maud St *CAN/RD* E16 ....**93** F4
Maud Wilkes Cl *KTTN* NW5 ....**74** C2
Mauleverer Rd *BRXS/STRHM* SW2........**135** E3
Maundeby Wk *WLSDN* * NW10 ....**69** E2
Maunsel St *WEST* SW1P **44** A4
Maurice St *SHB* W12 ....**88** B5
Mauritius Rd *GNWCH* SE10 ....**105** E5
Maury Rd *STNW/STAM* N16 ....**60** A4
Maverton Rd *BOW* * E3................................**80** A5
Mawbey Pl *STHWK* SE1 ....**119** F1
Mawbey Rd *STHWK* SE1 ....**119** F1
Mawbey St *VX/NE* SW8 ....**117** E3
Mawson La *CHSWK* W4 ....**111** F2
Maxey Rd *WOOL/PLUM* SE18 ....**108** C5
Maxted Rd *PECK* SE15...............................**137** F1
Maxwell Rd *FUL/PGN* SW6 ....**114** B3
Maya Cl *PECK* SE15....................................**120** B5
Mayall Rd *HNHL* SE24 ....**136** B3
Maybury Gdns *WLSDN* NW10 ....**70** A4
Maybury Rd *PLSTW* E13 ....**94** C3
Maybury St *TOOT* SW17 ....**151** E5
Mayday Gdns *BKHTH/KID* SE3 ....**125** E5
Mayerne Rd *ELTH/MOT* SE9 ....**143** D3
Mayesbrook Rd *BARK* IG11 ....**85** F5
Mayeswood Rd *LEE/GVPK* SE12 ....**160** C4
Mayfair Av *IL* IG1 ....**65** F4
Mayfair Ms *HAMP* * NW3 ....**73** F4
Mayfair Pl *MYFR/PICC* * W1J......................**31** D3
Mayfield Av *CHSWK* W4...............................**99** E5
Mayfield Cl *CLAP* SW4 ....**135** E3
  HACK E8 ....**77** F3
Mayfield Gdns *HDN* NW4 ....**53** D1
Mayfield Rd *ACT* W3 ....**98** B1
  CEND/HSY/T N8 ....**57** F1
  HACK * E8 ....**77** F4
  PLSTW E13 ....**93** F3
  SHB W12 ....**99** E3
Mayfields *WBLY* HA9 ....**50** A4
Mayfields Cl *WBLY* HA9 ....**50** A4
Mayflower Cl *BERM/RHTH* SE16 ....**103** D5
Mayflower Rd *BRXN/ST* SW9 ....**135** E1
Mayflower St *BERM/RHTH* SE16 ....**102** C3
Mayford Cl *BAL* SW12 ....**133** F5
Mayford Rd *BAL* SW12...............................**133** F5
Maygood St *IS* N1 ....**9** F1
Maygrove Rd *KIL/WHAMP* NW6 ....**71** F3
Mayhill Rd *CHARL* SE7..............................**124** B2
Maynard Cl *FUL/PGN* SW6 ....**114** B3
Maynards Quay *WAP* * E1W **102** C1
Mayola Rd *CLPT* E5 ....**78** C1
Mayo Rd *WLSDN* NW10 ....**69** E3
Mayow Rd *SYD* SE26 ....**157** D4
Mayplace La *WOOL/PLUM* SE18.............**126** B2
May Rd *PLSTW* E13 ....**94** A1
May's Buildings Ms *GNWCH* SE10 ....**123** D3
Mays Ct *CHCR* WC2N **32** C2
Maysoule Rd *BTSEA* SW11 ....**133** D2
May St *WKENS* W14 ....**113** F1
Maythorne Cottages *LEW* SE13..............**141** D4
Mayton St *HOLWY* N7 ....**57** F5
Maytree Wk *BRXS/STRHM* * SW2 ....**154** A2
Mayville Est *STNW/STAM* * N16...............**77** E2
Mayville Rd *IL* IG1...**84** B2
  WAN E11...**63** E4
Maze Hl *GNWCH* SE10 ....**123** E2
Mazenod Av *KIL/WHAMP* NW6...................**72** A4
Maze Rd *RCH/KEW* TW9 ....**110** A3
McAuley Cl *ELTH/MOT* SE9 ....**144** A3
  STHWK SE1 ....**46** A2
McCall Cl *CLAP* SW4 ....**117** E5
McCall Crs *CHARL* SE7 ....**125** E1
McCoid Wy *STHWK* SE1 ....**47** E1
McCrone Ms *HAMP* NW3 ....**73** D3
McCullum Rd *BOW* E3 ....**79** F5
McDermott Cl *BTSEA* SW11.....................**115** E5
McDermott Rd *PECK* SE15 ....**138** A1
McDougall Ct *RCH/KEW* TW9 ....**110** A5
McDowall Cl *CAN/RD* E16 ....**94** A4

McEwan Wy SRTFD * E15 ....81 D5
McGrath Rd FSTGT E7 ....81 F2
McGregor Rd NTCHL W11 ....89 F5
McKerrell Rd PECK SE15 ....120 A4
McLeod's Ms SKENS SW7 ....39 D3
McMillan St DEPT * SE8 ....122 A2
McNeil Rd CMBW SE5 ....119 D6
McNicol Dr WLSDN NW10 ....86 C1
Mead Cl CAMTN * NW1 ....74 A4
Meadcroft Rd LBTH SE11 ....118 A2
Meade Cl CHSWK W4 ....110 A2
Meadowbank BKHTH/KID SE3 ....141 F1
  HAMP NW3 ....73 F4
Meadowbank Cl FUL/PGN SW6 ....112 C3
Meadowbank Rd CDALE/KGS NW9 ....51 D2
Meadow Cl CAT SE6 ....158 A5
  CHST BR7 ....162 B5
  HOM E9 ....79 F2
Meadowcourt Rd BKHTH/KID SE3 ...141 F2
Meadow Garth WLSDN NW10 ....68 C3
Meadow La LEE/GVPK SE12 ....160 B3
Meadow Ms VX/NE SW8 ....117 E3
Meadow Pl CHSWK * W4 ....111 E3
  VX/NE SW8 ....117 E3
Meadow Rd BARK IG11 ....85 F4
  VX/NE SW8 ....117 E3
Meadow Rw STHWK SE1 ....47 E3
Meadows Cl LEY E10 ....62 A4
Meadowside ELTH/MOT SE9 ....142 C2
Meadowsweet Cl CAN/RD E16 ....95 D4
Meadowview Rd CAT SE6 ....158 A4
Mead Pl HOM E9 ....78 C3
Mead Plat WLSDN NW10 ....68 C3
Mead Rw STHWK SE1 ....46 A2
Meads La GDMY/SEVK IG3 ....67 F2
The Meadway BKHTH/KID SE3 ....123 D5
Meadway GDMY/SEVK IG3 ....85 E1
  GLDGN NW11 ....54 B1
Meadway Cl GLDGN NW11 ....54 B1
Meanley Rd MNPK E12 ....83 E2
Meard St SOHO/CST W1F 20 A5
Meath Rd IL IG1 ....66 C5
  SRTFD E15 ....93 F1
Meath St BTSEA SW11 ....116 B4
Mecklenburgh Pl BMSBY WC1N 9 E5
Mecklenburgh Sq BMSBY WC1N 9 E5
Mecklenburgh St BMSBY WC1N 9 E5
Medburn St CAMTN NW1 ....8 A1
Medcroft Gdns MORT/ESHN SW14 ...108 A2
Medebourne Cl BKHTH/KID SE3 .....142 C1
Medfield St PUT/ROE SW15 ....130 A5
Medhurst Cl BOW E3 ....91 E1
Median Rd CLPT E5 ....78 C2
Medina Rd HOLWY N7 ....58 A5
Medlar St CMBW SE5 ....118 C4
Medley Rd KIL/WHAMP NW6 ....72 A3
Medora Rd BRXS/STRHM SW2 ....135 F4
Medusa Rd LEW SE13 ....140 B4
Medway Cl IL IG1 ....84 C2
Medway Rd BOW E3 ....91 E1
Medway St WEST SW1P 44 A3
Medwin St BRXS/STRHM SW2 ....135 F2
Meerbrook Rd ELTH/MOT SE9 ....142 C1
Meeson Rd SRTFD E15 ....81 F4
Meeson St CLPT E5 ....79 E1
Meesons Whf SRTFD * E15 ....92 C1
Meeting Pth HOM * E9 ....78 C3
Meeting House Aly WAP * E1W 102 B2
Meeting House La PECK SE15 ....120 B4
Mehetabel Rd HACK E8 ....78 C3
Meister Cl IL IG1 ....67 D3
Melanda Cl CHST BR7 ....161 F5
Melaris Ms KIL/WHAMP NW6 ....72 A2
Melbourne Gv EDUL SE22 ....137 D2
Melbourne Ms BRXN/ST SW9 ....118 A4
  CAT SE6 ....140 C5
Melbourne Pl HOL/ALD WC2B 21 E5
Melbourne Rd EHAM E6 ....95 F1

IL IG1 ....66 B3
LEY E10 ....62 B2
Melbourne Sq BRXN/ST SW9 ....118 A4
Melbourne Ter EDUL * SE22 ....137 E2
  FUL/PGN * SW6 ....114 B3
Melbury Ct WKENS W14 ....101 F4
Melbury Dr CMBW SE5 ....119 E3
Melbury Rd WKENS W14 ....101 F4
Melbury Ter CAMTN NW1 ....17 D1
Melcombe Pl CAMTN NW1 ....17 E2
Melcombe St CAMTN NW1 ....17 F1
Meldon Cl FUL/PGN * SW6 ....114 B4
Melfield Gdns CAT SE6 ....158 B4
Melford Av BARK IG11 ....85 E3
Melford Rd DUL SE21 ....156 A1
  EHAM E6 ....95 F3
  IL IG1 ....67 D4
  WAN E11 ....63 E4
Melgund Rd HBRY N5 ....76 A2
Melina Pl STJWD NW8 ....4 A4
Melina Rd SHB W12 ....100 B3
Melior Pl STHWK * SE1 ....36 C5
Melior St STHWK SE1 ....36 B5
Meliot Rd CAT SE6 ....159 D2
Melling St WOOL/PLUM SE18 ....127 E2
Mellish St POP/IOD E14 ....104 A4
Mellison Rd TOOT SW17 ....151 E5
Melliss Av RCH/KEW TW9 ....110 B4
Mellitus St SHB W12 ....87 F5
Mells Crs ELTH/MOT SE9 ....161 E4
Mell St GNWCH SE10 ....123 E1
Melody Rd WAND/EARL SW18 ....132 C3
Melon Pl KENS * W8 ....26 B5
Melon Rd PECK SE15 ....120 A4
  WAN E11 ....63 E5
Melrose Av CRICK NW2 ....70 C2
  WIM/MER SW19 ....149 F2
Melrose Cl LEE/GVPK SE12 ....160 A1
Melrose Gdns HMSMTH W6 ....100 C3
Melrose Rd BARN SW13 ....111 F5
  WAND/EARL SW18 ....131 F4
Melrose Ter HMSMTH W6 ....100 C3
Melthorpe Gdns WOOL/PLUM SE18 ...125 D4
Melton Ct CAMTN NW1 ....7 F4
Melville Ct DEPT SE8 ....103 D5
Melville Pl IS * N1 ....76 C4
Melville Rd BARN SW13 ....112 A4
  WLSDN NW10 ....69 D4
Melville Villas Rd ACT * W3 ....99 D2
Memel St STLK EC1Y 23 E1
Memorial Av SRTFD E15 ....93 E2
Mendip Cl SYD SE26 ....156 C1
Mendip Dr GLDGN NW11 ....53 E4
Mendip Houses BETH * E2 ....90 C2
Mendip Rd BTSEA SW11 ....132 C1
Mendora Rd FUL/PGN SW6 ....113 E3
Menelik Rd CRICK NW2 ....71 E1
Menotti St BETH * E2 ....90 A3
Mentmore Ter HACK E8 ....78 B4
Meon Rd ACT W3 ....98 C3
Mepham St STHWK SE1 ....34 A4
Merbury Cl LEW SE13 ....140 C3
Merbury Rd THMD SE28 ....109 D2
Merbury St WOOL/PLUM SE18 ....108 B4
Mercator Pl POP/IOD E14 ....122 A1
Mercator Rd LEW SE13 ....141 D2
Merceron Houses BETH * E2 ....90 C2
Merceron St WCHPL E1 ....90 B3
Mercers Cl GNWCH SE10 ....105 F5
Mercers Cottages WCHPL * E1 ....91 E5
Mercers Pl HMSMTH W6 ....100 C3
Mercers Rd ARCH N19 ....57 D5
Mercer St LSQ/SEVD WC2H 20 C5
Merchant St BOW * E3 ....91 F2
Merchiston Rd CAT SE6 ....159 D2
Merchland Rd ELTH/MOT SE9 ....162 C1
Mercia Gv LEW SE13 ....140 C1
Mercier Rd PUT/ROE SW15 ....131 E3

Mercury Wy *NWCR* SE14.................**121** D2
Mercy Ter *LEW* SE13.......................**140** B3
Mere Cl *WIM/MER* SW19................**131** D5
Meredith Av *CRICK* NW2.................**70** C2
Meredith Ms *BROCKY* SE4...............**139** F2
Meredith St *CLKNW* EC1R................**10** C4
  PLSTW E13......................................**94** A2
Meredyth Rd *BARN* SW13.................**112** A5
Meretone Cl *BROCKY* SE4.................**139** E2
Mereworth Dr *WOOL/PLUM* SE18.....**126** B3
Meridian Rd *CHARL* SE7..................**125** D3
Meridian Sq *SRTFD* E15...................**81** D4
Merifield Rd *ELTH/MOT* SE9............**142** C2
Merivale Rd *PUT/ROE* SW15.............**131** E2
Merley Ct *CDALE/KGS* NW9..............**50** C3
Merlin Rd *MNPK* E12........................**65** D4
Merlin St *FSBYW* WC1X....................**10** A1
Mermaid Ct *STHWK* SE1...................**36** A5
Merredene St *BRXS/STRHM* SW2......**135** F4
Merrick Sq *STHWK* SE1.....................**48** A2
Merrilees Rd *BFN/LL* DA15...............**145** E5
Merriman Rd *BKHTH/KID* SE3...........**124** C4
Merrington Rd *FUL/PGN* SW6...........**114** A2
Merritt Rd *BROCKY* SE4....................**139** F3
Merrow St *WALW* SE17......................**119** D1
Merrow Wk *WALW* SE17.....................**119** D1
Merryfield *BKHTH/KID* SE3...............**123** F5
Merthyr Ter *BARN* SW13....................**112** B2
Merton Av *CHSWK* W4........................**99** F5
Merton La *HGT* N6.............................**55** F4
Merton Ri *HAMP* NW3........................**73** E4
Merton Rd *BARK* IG11.........................**85** E4
  GDMY/SEVK IG3...............................**67** F2
  WAND/EARL SW18............................**132** A5
Mertoun Ter *MBLAR* * W1H................**17** E4
Merttins Rd *PECK* SE15......................**139** D2
Meru Cl *KTTN* NW5............................**74** A2
Mervan Rd *BRXS/STRHM* SW2...........**136** A2
Mervyn Av *ELTH/MOT* SE9.................**162** C3
Messaline Av *ACT* W3........................**86** C5
Messent Rd *ELTH/MOT* SE9...............**142** C3
Messeter Pl *ELTH/MOT* SE9...............**144** A4
Messina Av *KIL/WHAMP* NW6............**72** A4
Meteor St *BTSEA* SW11.....................**134** A2
Methley St *LBTH* SE11.......................**118** A1
Methwold Rd *NKENS* W10..................**89** D4
Metropolitan Cl *POP/IOD* E14............**92** A4
Metropolitan Whf *WAP* * E1W............**102** C2
Mews North *BGVA* SW1W...................**42** C3
Mews South *PIM* SW1V......................**116** C1
Mews St *WAP* E1W.............................**37** F3
Mexfield Rd *PUT/ROE* SW15..............**131** F3
Meymott St *STHWK* SE1.....................**34** C4
Meynell Crs *HOM* E9.........................**79** D4
Meynell Gdns *HOM* E9......................**79** D4
Meynell Rd *HOM* E9..........................**79** D4
Meyrick Rd *BTSEA* SW11...................**133** D1
  WLSDN NW10..................................**70** A3
Miah Ter *WAP* * E1W..........................**102** A2
Micawber St *IS* N1............................**11** E3
Michael Rd *FUL/PGN* SW6.................**114** B4
  WAN E11...**63** E3
Michaels Cl *LEW* SE13.......................**141** E1
Micheldever Rd *LEW* SE13.................**141** E4
Michigan Av *MNPK* E12......................**83** E1
Micklethwaite Rd *FUL/PGN* SW6........**114** A2
Middle Dartrey Wk *WBPTN* * SW10....**114** C3
Middlefield *STJWD* NW8.....................**73** D5
Middle Park Av *ELTH/MOT* SE9..........**143** D4
Middle Rd *PLSTW* E13.........................**94** A1
Middle Rw *NKENS* W10.......................**89** E3
Middlesex Pl *HOM* E9.........................**78** C3
Middlesex St *WCHPL* E1......................**25** D3
Middle St *STBT* EC1A..........................**23** E2
Middle Temple La *TPL/STR* WC2R......**22** C4
Middleton Buildings *GTPST* W1W.......**19** E3
Middleton Dr *BERM/RHTH* SE16.........**103** D3
Middleton Gdns *GNTH/NBYPK* IG2......**66** B1

Middleton Gv *HOLWY* N7....................**75** E2
Middleton Pl *GTPST* W1W...................**19** E3
Middleton Rd *GLDGN* NW11...............**54** A3
  HACK E8..**77** F4
Middleton St *BETH* E2........................**90** B2
Middleton Wy *LEW* SE13....................**141** D2
Middle Yd *STHWK* SE1.......................**36** B3
Midford Pl *FITZ* * W1T........................**19** F1
Midholm *WBLY* HA9...........................**50** A3
Midhope St *STPAN* WC1H....................**9** D4
Midland Arches *CRICK* * NW2.............**52** B4
Midland Crs *HAMP* NW3.....................**72** C3
Midland Rd *CAMTN* NW1......................**8** B2
  LEY E10..**62** C2
Midland Ter *WLSDN* NW10..................**87** E3
Midlothian Rd *BOW* E3.......................**91** F3
Midmoor Rd *BAL* SW12......................**152** C1
Midship Cl *BERM/RHTH* * SE16..........**103** D2
Midship Point *POP/IOD* * E14.............**104** A3
Midstrath Rd *WLSDN* NW10................**69** E1
Milborne Gv *WBPTN* SW10.................**114** C1
Milborne St *HOM* E9..........................**78** C3
Milborough Crs *LEE/GVPK* SE12.........**141** E4
Milcote St *STHWK* SE1.......................**46** C1
Mildenhall Rd *CLPT* E5.......................**78** C1
Mildmay Av *IS* N1..............................**77** D3
Mildmay Gv North *IS* N1....................**77** D2
Mildmay Gv South *IS* N1....................**77** D2
Mildmay Pk *IS* N1..............................**77** D2
Mildmay Pl *STNW/STAM* * N16...........**77** E2
Mildmay Rd *IL* IG1..............................**66** B5
  IS N1..**77** D2
Mildmay St *IS* N1..............................**77** D3
Mile End Pl *WCHPL* E1.......................**91** D3
Mile End Rd *WCHPL* E1......................**90** C4
Miles Dr *THMD* SE28.........................**109** E2
Miles St *VX/NE* SW8...........................**117** E2
Milfoil St *SHB* W12.............................**100** A1
Milford La *TPL/STR* WC2R....................**34** A1
Milford Ms *STRHM/NOR* SW16............**153** F3
Milk St *BMLY* BR1..............................**160** B5
  CAN/RD E16....................................**108** B2
  CITYW EC2V.......................................**23** F4
Milkwell Yd *CMBW* SE5......................**118** C4
Milkwood Rd *HNHL* SE24...................**136** B3
Milk Yd *WAP* E1W................................**102** C1
Millais Av *MNPK* E12..........................**84** A2
Millais Rd *WAN* E11............................**80** C1
Millard Cl *STNW/STAM* N16...............**77** E2
Millbank *WEST* SW1P..........................**44** C4
Millbank Est *WEST* SW1P....................**44** B5
Millbank Wy *LEE/GVPK* SE12.............**142** A3
Millbrook Av *WELL* DA16....................**145** D2
Millbrook Rd *BRXN/ST* SW9...............**136** B1
Millennium Br *STHWK* SE1..................**35** E2
Millennium Cl *CAN/RD* E16.................**94** A5
Millennium Dr *POP/IOD* E14...............**105** D4
Millennium Pl *BETH* * E2....................**90** B1
Millennium Sq *STHWK* SE1.................**37** E5
Millennium Wy *GNWCH* SE10.............**105** E3
Millennium Whf *POP/IOD* E14............**105** D5
Miller's Av *HACK* E8...........................**77** F2
Miller's Ct *CHSWK* W4........................**111** F1
Miller's Ter *HACK* E8..........................**77** F2
Miller St *CAMTN* NW1...........................**7** E1
Miller's Wy *HMSMTH* W6....................**100** C3
Miller Wk *STHWK* SE1........................**34** B4
Millfield La *HGT* N6............................**55** F4
Millfields Rd *CLPT* E5.........................**78** C1
Mill Gdns *SYD* SE26..........................**156** B4
Millgrove St *BTSEA* SW11..................**116** A4
Millharbour *POP/IOD* E14...................**104** B4
Mill Hl *BARN* SW13............................**130** A1
Mill Hill Gv *ACT* * W3..........................**98** B2
Mill Hill Rd *ACT* W3...........................**98** B3
  BARN SW13.......................................**130** B1
Mill Hill Ter *ACT* W3...........................**98** B2
Millhouse Pl *WNWD* SE27..................**154** B4

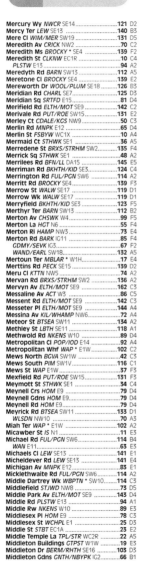

Millicent Rd *LEY* * E10 ....61 F3
Milligan St *POP/IOD* E14 ....103 F1
Mill La *CRICK* NW2 ....71 E2
   WOOL/PLUM SE18 ....126 A1
Millman Ms *BMSBY* * WC1N 21 E1
Millman Pl *BMSBY* WC1N 21 E1
Millman St *BMSBY* WC1N 21 E1
Millmark Gv *NWCR* SE14 ....121 E5
Mill Pl *POP/IOD* E14 ....91 E5
Millpond Est *BERM/RHTH* * SE16 ...102 B3
Mill Rd *CAN/RD* E16 ....106 B2
   IL IG1 ....66 A5
Mill Rw *IS* N1 ....77 E5
Mills Gv *POP/IOD* E14 ....92 A3
Millshot Cl *FUL/PGN* SW6 ....112 C4
Mills Rw *CHSWK* W4 ....99 D5
Millstream Rd *STHWK* SE1 ....49 E1
Mill St *CONDST* W1S 31 D1
   STHWK SE1 ....49 F1
Millwall Dock Rd *POP/IOD* E14 ....104 A4
Millwood St *NKENS* W10 ....89 E4
Milman Rd *KIL/WHAMP* NW6 ....89 D1
Milman's St *WBPTN* SW10 ....115 D2
   WBPTN * SW10 ....115 D2
Milne Ms *ELTH/MOT* SE9 ....143 E3
Milner Pl *IS* N1 ....76 A5
Milner Rd *SRTFD* E15 ....93 E2
Milner Sq *IS* * N1 ....76 A4
Milner St *CHEL* SW3 ....41 E4
Milnthorpe Rd *CHSWK* W4 ....111 D2
Milo Rd *EDUL* SE22 ....137 F4
Milroy Wk *STHWK* SE1 ....34 B3
Milson Rd *WKENS* W14 ....101 E4
Milton Av *EHAM* E6 ....83 D4
   HGT N6 ....56 C2
   WLSDN NW10 ....69 D5
Milton Cl *EFNCH* N2 ....54 C1
   STHWK SE1 ....49 E5
Milton Ct *BARB* EC2Y 24 A2
Milton Court Rd *NWCR* SE14 ....121 E2
Milton Crs *GNTH/NBYPK* IG2 ....66 C2
Milton Gv *STNW/STAM* N16 ....77 D1
Milton Pk *HGT* N6 ....56 C2
Milton Rd *ACT* W3 ....99 D2
   CDALE/KGS * NW9 ....52 A2
   HGT N6 ....56 C2
   HNHL SE24 ....136 B3
   MORT/ESHN SW14 ....129 D1
   WELL DA16 ....127 F4
Milton St *BARB* EC2Y 24 A2
Milverton Gdns *GDMY/SEVK* IG3 .....67 F4
Milverton Rd *KIL/WHAMP* NW6 ....70 C4
Milverton St *LBTH* SE11 ....118 A1
Milverton Wy *ELTH/MOT* SE9 ....162 A4
Milward St *WCHPL* E1 ....90 B4
Mimosa St *FUL/PGN* SW6 ....113 F4
Minard Rd *CAT* SE6 ....141 E5
Mina Rd *WALW* SE17 ....119 E1
Mincing La *MON* EC3R 36 C1
Minehead Rd *STRHM/NOR* SW16 ....153 F5
Mineral St *WOOL/PLUM* SE18 ....109 E5
Minera Ms *BGVA* SW1W 42 B4
Minerva Cl *BRXN/ST* SW9 ....118 A3
   SCUP DA14 ....163 E4
Minerva Rd *WLSDN* NW10 ....86 C3
Minerva St *BETH* E2 ....90 B1
Minet Av *WLSDN* NW10 ....87 E1
Minet Gdns *WLSDN* NW10 ....87 E1
Minet Rd *CMBW* SE5 ....118 B5
Minford Gdns *WKENS* W14 ....101 D3
Ming St *POP/IOD* E14 ....104 A1
Ministry Wy *ELTH/MOT* SE9 ....161 F2
Minnow Wk *WALW* SE17 ....49 D5
Minories *TWRH* EC3N 25 F1
Minshull St *VX/NE* * SW8 ....117 D4
Minson Rd *HOM* E9 ....79 D5
Minstead Gdns *PUT/ROE* SW15 ....129 F5
Minster Ct *MON* * EC3R 36 C1

Minster Rd *CRICK* NW2 ....71 E2
Mintern St *IS* N1 ....12 B1
Minton Ms *KIL/WHAMP* NW6 ....72 B3
Mint St *STHWK* SE1 ....35 E5
Mirabel Rd *FUL/PGN* SW6 ....113 F3
Miranda Cl *WCHPL* E1 ....90 C4
Miranda Rd *ARCH* N19 ....56 C3
Mirfield St *CHARL* SE7 ....107 D4
Miriam Rd *WOOL/PLUM* SE18 ....127 E1
Mission Pl *PECK* SE15 ....120 A4
Mitali Pas *WCHPL* E1 ....90 A5
Mitcham La *STRHM/NOR* SW16 ....152 C5
Mitcham Rd *EHAM* E6 ....95 E2
   GDMY/SEVK IG3 ....67 F2
   TOOT SW17 ....151 F5
Mitchellbrook Wy *WLSDN* NW10 ....69 D3
Mitchell St *FSBYE* EC1V 11 E5
Mitchell Wy *WLSDN* NW10 ....68 C3
Mitchison Rd *IS* N1 ....77 D3
Mitford Rd *ARCH* N19 ....57 E4
The Mitre *POP/IOD* E14 ....103 F1
Mitre Rd *SRTFD* E15 ....93 E1
   STHWK SE1 ....34 B5
Mitre Sq *HDTCH* EC3A 25 D5
Mitre St *HDTCH* EC3A 25 D5
Mitre Wy *WLSDN* NW10 ....88 B4
Moat Ct *ELTH/MOT* * SE9 ....143 F4
Moat Pl *ACT* W3 ....86 B5
   BRXN/ST SW9 ....135 F1
Moberly Rd *CLAP* SW4 ....135 D5
Modbury Gdns *HAMP* NW3 ....74 A3
Model Farm Cl *ELTH/MOT* SE9 ....161 F3
Moffat Rd *TOOT* SW17 ....151 E4
Mohammad Khan Rd *WAN* * E11 ....63 F3
Moiety Rd *POP/IOD* E14 ....104 A3
Moira Rd *ELTH/MOT* SE9 ....143 F2
Molescroft *ELTH/MOT* SE9 ....162 C3
Molesford Rd *FUL/PGN* * SW6 ....114 A4
Molesworth St *LEW* SE13 ....140 C1
Molly Huggins Cl *BAL* SW12 ....134 C5
Molyneux Dr *TOOT* SW17 ....152 B4
Molyneux St *MBLAR* W1H 17 D3
Monarch Dr *CAN/RD* E16 ....95 D4
Monarch Ms *WNWD* SE27 ....154 A5
Mona Rd *PECK* SE15 ....120 C5
Mona St *CAN/RD* E16 ....93 F4
Monck's Rw *WAND/EARL* * SW18 .....131 F4
Monck St *WEST* SW1P 44 B3
Monclar Rd *CMBW* SE5 ....137 D2
Moncorvo Cl *SKENS* SW7 ....40 C1
Moncrieff St *PECK* SE15 ....120 A5
Monega Rd *FSTGT* E7 ....82 C3
Monier Rd *BOW* E3 ....80 A4
Monk Dr *CAN/RD* E16 ....94 A4
Monks Dr *ACT* W3 ....86 A4
Monks Pk *WBLY* HA9 ....68 B3
Monks Park Gdns *WBLY* HA9 ....68 B3
Monk St *WOOL/PLUM* SE18 ....108 A5
Monkton Rd *WELL* DA16 ....46 B4
Monkton St *LBTH* SE11 ....49 F4
Monkwell Sq *BARB* EC2Y 23 F3
Monmouth Cl *CHSWK* W4 ....99 D4
Monmouth Pl *BAY/PAD* W2 ....14 B5
Monmouth Rd *BAY/PAD* W2 ....14 B5
   EHAM E6 ....95 F2
Monmouth St *LSQ/SEVD* WC2H 20 C5
Monnery Rd *ARCH* N19 ....56 C5
Monnow Rd *STHWK* SE1 ....120 A1
Monroe Dr *MORT/ESHN* SW14 ....128 B3
Monsell Rd *FSBYPK* N4 ....58 B5
Monson Rd *NWCR* SE14 ....121 D3
   WLSDN NW10 ....88 A1
Montacute Rd *CAT* SE6 ....139 F5
Montague Av *BROCKY* SE4 ....139 E1
Montague Cl *STHWK* SE1 ....36 A3
Montague Gdns *ACT* W3 ....85 E1
Montague Pl *GWRST* WC1E 20 B2
Montague Rd *HACK* E8 ....78 A2

WAN E11...63 F4
Montague Sq *NWCR* SE14.....................120 C3
Montague St *RSO* WC1B..........................20 C2
STBT EC1A..23 E3
Montagu Man *MHST* W1U........................17 F3
Montagu Ms North *MBLAR* W1H..............17 F3
Montagu Ms South *MBLAR* W1H...............17 F4
Montagu Ms West *MBLAR* W1H.................17 F4
Montagu Pl *MBLAR* W1H...........................17 E3
Montagu Rd *HDN* NW4.............................52 A1
Montagu Rw *MHST* W1U...........................17 F3
Montagu Sq *MBLAR* W1H..........................17 F3
Montagu St *MBLAR* W1H...........................17 F4
Montana Gdns *CAT* SE6..........................157 F5
Montana Rd *TOOT* SW17........................152 A3
Montbelle Rd *ELTH/MOT* SE9.................162 B3
Montcalm Rd *CHARL* SE7........................125 D3
Montclare St *BETH* E2...............................13 E4
Monteagle Av *BARK* IG11..........................84 C3
Monteagle Wy *PECK* SE15.......................138 B1
Montefiore St *VX/NE* SW8.......................116 B5
Montem Rd *FSTH* SE23...........................139 F5
Montem St *FSBYPK* N4.............................57 F3
Montesquieu Av *CAN/RD* * E16................93 F3
Montford Pl *LBTH* SE11............................118 A2
Montfort Pl *WIM/MER* SW19....................149 D1
Montgomery Cl *BFN/LL* DA15...................145 E3
Montgomery Rd *CHSWK* W4.......................98 C5
Montholme Rd *BTSEA* SW11....................133 F4
Monthorpe Rd *WCHPL* E1...........................90 A4
Montolieu Gdns *PUT/ROE* SW15.............130 B3
Montpelier Gdns *EHAM* E6........................95 D2
Montpelier Gv *KTTN* NW5..........................74 C2
Montpelier Ms *SKENS* SW7.........................41 D1
Montpelier Pl *SKENS* SW7..........................41 D1
WCHPL E1...90 C5
Montpelier Ri *GLDGN* NW11........................53 E2
Montpelier Rd *PECK* SE15.......................120 B4
Montpelier Rw *BKHTH/KID* SE3...............123 F5
Montpelier Sq *SKENS* SW7.........................41 D1
Montpelier St *SKENS* SW7...........................41 D1
Montpelier Ter *SKENS* SW7.........................41 D1
Montpelier V *BKHTH/KID* * SE3...............123 F5
Montpelier Wk *SKENS* SW7.........................41 D1
Montpelier Wy *GLDGN* NW11......................53 E2
Montreal Pl *HOL/ALD* WC2B.......................33 E1
Montreal Rd *IL* IG1....................................66 C2
Montrell Rd *BRXS/STRHM* SW2.................153 E1
Montrose Av *KIL/WHAMP* NW6....................89 E1
WELL DA16...145 D1
Montrose Cl *WELL* DA16...........................145 F1
Montrose Pl *KTBR* SW1X............................42 B1
Montrose Vls *HMSMTH* * W6....................112 A1
Montrose Wy *FSTH* SE23..........................157 D1
Montserrat Cl *NRWD* SE19.......................155 D5
Montserrat Rd *PUT/ROE* SW15................131 E2
Monument St *MON* EC3R............................36 B2
Monza St *WAP* E1W.................................102 C1
Moodkee St *BERM/RHTH* SE16................102 C4
Moody St *WCHPL* E1...................................91 D2
Moon Ct *LEE/GVPK* * SE12......................142 A2
Moon St *IS* N1..76 B5
Moorcroft Rd *STRHM/NOR* SW16.............153 E3
Moordown *WOOL/PLUM* SE18..................126 A4
Moore Cl *MORT/ESHN* SW14....................128 C1
Moore Park Rd *FUL/PGN* SW6..................114 B5
Moore St *CHEL* SW3...................................41 E4
Moorey Cl *SRTFD* E15................................81 F5
Moorfields *LVPST* EC2M.............................24 A3
Moorfields Highwalk *BARB* EC2Y...............24 A3
Moorgate *LOTH* EC2R.................................24 A4
Moorgate Pl *LOTH* * EC2R..........................24 A4
Moorhead Wy *BKHTH/KID* SE3.................142 B1
Moorhouse Rd *BAY/PAD* W2......................14 A4
The Moorings *CHSWK* * W4......................110 A2
Moorland Rd *BRXN/ST* SW9.....................136 B2
Moor La *BARB* EC2Y....................................24 A3
Mooreside Rd *BMLY* BR1..........................159 E4

Moor St *SOHO/SHAV* W1D..........................20 B5
Morant St *POP/IOD* E14...........................104 A1
Mora Rd *CRICK* NW2...................................70 C1
Mora St *FSBYE* EC1V..................................11 F4
Morat St *BRXN/ST* SW9.............................117 F4
Moravian Pl *WBPTN* SW10........................115 D2
Moravian St *BETH* E2..................................90 C1
Moray Ms *HOLWY* N7.................................57 F4
Moray Rd *HOLWY* N7..................................57 F4
Mordaunt Rd *WLSDN* NW10.......................69 D5
Mordaunt St *BRXN/ST* SW9......................135 F1
Morden Hl *LEW* SE13................................122 C5
Morden La *LEW* SE13................................122 C5
Morden Rd *BKHTH/KID* SE3......................124 A5
Morden Road Ms *BKHTH/KID* SE3............124 A5
Morden St *LEW* SE13................................122 B4
Morden Wharf Rd *GNWCH* SE10...............105 D2
Mordon Rd *GDMY/SEVK* IG3.......................67 F2
Mordred Rd *CAT* SE6................................159 F2
Morecambe Cl *WCHPL* * E1........................91 D4
Morecambe St *WALW* SE17........................47 F5
More Cl *CAN/RD* E16...................................93 F5
WKENS W14...101 D5
Moreland Cottages *BOW* * E3.....................92 A1
Moreland St *FSBYE* EC1V............................11 D3
Morella Rd *BAL* SW12...............................133 F5
Moremead Rd *CAT* SE6.............................157 F4
Morena St *CAT* SE6..................................140 B5
Moresby Rd *CLPT* E5..................................60 B3
Mores Gdn *CHEL* * SW3...........................115 D2
SEVS/STOTM N15......................................59 D1
Moreton Cl *CLPT* E5....................................60 C4
SEVS/STOTM N15......................................59 D1
Moreton Pl *PIM* SW1V..............................116 C1
Moreton Rd *SEVS/STOTM* N15....................59 D1
Moreton St *PIM* SW1V..............................116 C1
Moreton Ter *PIM* SW1V.............................116 C1
Moreton Terrace Ms North
PIM SW1V...116 C1
Moreton Terrace Ms South
PIM * SW1V..116 C1
Morgan Rd *HOLWY* N7................................76 A2
NKENS W10..89 F4
Morgans La *STHWK* SE1.............................36 C4
Morgan St *BOW* E3.....................................91 E2
CAN/RD E16...93 F4
Moriatry Cl *HOLWY* N7................................75 E1
Morie St *WAND/EARL* SW18......................132 B2
Morieux Rd *LEY* E10....................................61 F3
Moring Rd *TOOT* SW17.............................152 A4
Morkyns Wk *DUL* * SE21...........................155 E3
Morland Cl *GLDGN* NW11............................54 B3
Morland Est *HACK* * E8...............................78 A4
Morland Gdns *WLSDN* NW10........................69 D4
Morland Ms *IS* N1.......................................76 A4
Morland Rd *IL* IG1......................................66 B4
Morley Rd *BARK* IG11.................................85 D5
LEW SE13...140 C2
LEY E10..62 C3
SRTFD E15..93 F1
Morley St *STHWK* SE1................................46 B1
Morna Rd *CMBW* SE5................................118 C5
Morning La *HOM* E9....................................78 C3
Mornington Av *IL* IG1..................................66 A2
WKENS W14...101 F5
Mornington Crs *CAMTN* NW1........................7 E1
Mornington Gv *BOW* E3...............................92 A2
Mornington Ms *CMBW* SE5.........................118 C4
Mornington Pl *CAMTN* NW1..........................7 D1
Mornington Rd *DEPT* SE8..........................121 F3
WAN E11..63 D2
Mornington St *CAMTN* NW1...........................7 D1
Mornington Ter *CAMTN* NW1.......................74 B5
Morocco St *STHWK* SE1.............................48 C1
Morpeth Gv *HOM* E9...................................79 D5
Morpeth Rd *HOM* E9...................................78 C5
Morpeth St *BETH* E2...................................91 D2
Morpeth Ter *WEST* SW1P.............................43 E3
Morrab Gdns *GDMY/SEVK* IG3....................67 F5

Morris Av MNPK E12 ....83 F2
Morris Bishop Ter HCT * N6 ....56 A1
Morris Gdns STNW/EARL SW18 ....132 A5
Morrish Rd BRXS/STRHM SW2 ....135 E5
Morrison St BTSEA SW11 ....134 A1
Morris Pl FSBYPK N4 ....58 A4
Morris Rd POP/IOD E14 ....92 B4
   WAN E11 ....81 E1
Morris St WCHPL E1 ....90 B5
Morse Cl PLSTW E13 ....94 A2
Morshead Rd MV/WKIL W9 ....2 B4
Mortham St SRTFD E15 ....81 D5
Mortimer Cl BAL SW12 ....153 D2
   CRICK NW2 ....53 F5
Mortimer Crs KIL/WHAMP NW6 ....72 B5
Mortimer Pl KIL/WHAMP NW6 ....72 B5
Mortimer Rd EHAM E6 ....95 F2
   IS N1 ....77 E4
   WLSDN NW10 ....88 C2
Mortimer Sq NTGHL W11 ....101 D1
Mortimer St REGST W1B 19 D4
Mortimer Ter KTTN * NW5 ....74 B1
Mortlake High St MORT/ESHN SW14 ......129 D1
Mortlake Rd CAN/RD E16 ....94 B5
   IL IG1 ....84 C1
   MORT/ESHN SW14 ....128 B3
   RCH/KEW TW9 ....110 A3
Morton Ms ECT * SW5 ....38 C5
Morton St STHWK SE1 ....46 A3
Morton Rd IS N1 ....76 C3
   SRTFD E15 ....81 F4
Morval Rd BRXS/STRHM SW2 ....136 A3
Morven St TOOT SW17 ....151 F3
Morville St BOW E3 ....92 A1
Morwell St FITZ W1T 20 A3
Moscow Pl BAY/PAD W2 ....26 C1
Moscow Rd BAY/PAD W2 ....26 C1
Mossbury Rd BTSEA SW11 ....133 E1
Moss Cl WCHPL E1 ....90 A4
Mossford St BOW E3 ....91 F3
Mossop St CHEL SW3 ....41 D4
Mostyn Gdns WLSDN NW10 ....89 D2
Mostyn Gv BOW E3 ....91 F1
Mostyn Rd BRXN/ST SW9 ....118 A3
Motcomb St KTBR SW1X 42 A2
The Mothers Sq CLPT * E5 ....78 B1
Motley St VX/NE SW8 ....116 C5
Mottingham Gdns ELTH/MOT SE9 ....161 D2
Mottingham La ELTH/MOT SE9 ....160 C1
Mottingham Rd ELTH/MOT SE9 ....161 E3
Moulins Rd HOM E9 ....78 C4
Moundfield Rd STNW/STAM N16 ....60 C1
The Mount CLPT * E5 ....60 B4
   HAMP NW3 ....72 C1
   WBLY HA9 ....50 B4
Mountacre Cl SYD SE26 ....155 F4
Mount Adon Pk DUL SE21 ....138 A5
Mountague Pl POP/IOD E14 ....104 C1
Mount Angelus Rd PUT/ROE SW15 ....129 F5
Mount Ash Rd SYD SE26 ....156 B3
Mountbatten Cl NRWD SE19 ....155 E5
   WOOL/PLUM SE18 ....127 E2
Mount Dr WBLY HA9 ....50 C4
Mountearl Gdns STRHM/NOR SW16 ....153 F3
Mount Ephraim La
   STRHM/NOR SW16 ....153 D3
Mount Ephraim Rd
   STRHM/NOR SW16 ....153 D3
Mountfield Cl LEW SE13 ....141 D5
Mountfield Rd EHAM E6 ....95 F1
Mountford St WCHPL E1 ....90 A5
Mountfort Crs IS N1 ....76 A4
Mountfort Ter IS N1 ....76 A4
Mount Gdns SYD SE26 ....156 B3
Mountgrove Rd FSBYPK N4 ....58 C3
Mount Mills FSBYE EC1V 11 D4
Mount Nod Rd STRHM/NOR SW16 ....153 F3
Mount Pl ACT W3 ....98 B2

Mount Pleasant FSBYW WC1X 21 F2
   WNWD SE27 ....154 C4
Mount Pleasant Crs FSBYPK * N4 ....57 F2
Mount Pleasant HI CLPT E5 ....60 B4
Mount Pleasant La CLPT E5 ....60 B3
Mount Pleasant Pl
   WOOL/PLUM SE18 ....109 D5
Mount Pleasant Rd LEW SE13 ....140 C4
   WLSDN NW10 ....70 C4
Mount Pleasant Vls FSBYPK N4 ....57 F2
Mount Ri FSTH SE23 ....156 C2
Mount Rd CRICK NW2 ....52 B5
   HDN NW4 ....52 A1
   IL IG1 ....84 B2
   WAND/EARL SW18 ....150 A2
Mount Rw MYFR/PKLN W1K 30 C2
Mounts Pond Rd BKHTH/KID SE3 ....123 D5
The Mount Sq HAMP * NW3 ....54 C5
Mount St MYFR/PKLN W1K 30 A2
Mount Ter WCHPL E1 ....90 B4
Mount View Rd FSBYPK N4 ....57 F2
Mount Vls WNWD SE27 ....154 B3
Movers La BARK IG11 ....85 D5
Mowatt Cl ARCH N19 ....57 D3
Mowbray Rd KIL/WHAMP NW6 ....71 E4
Mowlem St BETH E2 ....90 B1
Mowll St BRXN/ST SW9 ....118 A3
Moxon Cl PLSTW E13 ....93 F1
Moxon St MHST W1U 18 A3
Moye Cl BETH * E2 ....90 A1
Moyers Rd WAN E11 ....62 C3
Moylan Rd HMSMTH W6 ....113 E2
Moyne Pl WLSDN NW10 ....86 A2
Moyser Rd TOOT SW17 ....152 B5
Mozart St NKENS W10 ....89 F2
Muir Cl WAND/EARL SW18 ....133 E4
Muirdown Av MORT/ESHN SW14 ....128 C2
Muirfield ACT W3 ....87 E5
Muirfield Cl BERM/RHTH * SE16 ....120 B1
Muirfield Crs POP/IOD E14 ....104 B4
Muirkirk Rd CAT SE6 ....158 C1
Muir Rd CLPT E5 ....78 A1
Muir St CAN/RD E16 ....107 F2
Mulberry Cl CHEL * SW3 ....115 D2
   STRHM/NOR SW16 ....152 C4
Mulberry Ms NWCR SE14 ....121 F4
Mulberry Pl HMSMTH W6 ....112 A1
Mulberry Rd HACK E8 ....77 F4
Mulberry St WCHPL E1 ....90 A5
Mulberry Wk CHEL SW3 ....115 D2
Mulgrave Rd WKENS W14 ....113 F2
   WLSDN NW10 ....69 F1
   WOOL/PLUM SE18 ....107 F5
Mulkern Rd ARCH N19 ....57 D3
Mullet Gdns BETH E2 ....90 A2
Mullins Pth MORT/ESHN SW14 ....129 D1
Mull Wk IS N1 ....76 C3
Mulready St STJWD NW8 ....16 C1
Multi Wy ACT W3 ....99 E3
Multon Rd WAND/EARL SW18 ....133 D5
Mumford Ct CITYW EC2V 23 F4
Mumford Rd HNHL SE24 ....136 B3
Muncaster Rd BTSEA SW11 ....133 F2
Muncies Ms CAT SE6 ....158 C2
Mundania Rd EDUL SE22 ....138 B4
Mundania Rd CAN/RD E16 ....94 A5
Munden St WKENS W14 ....101 E5
Mundford Rd CLPT E5 ....60 C2
Mundon Gdns IL IG1 ....67 D3
Mund St WKENS W14 ....113 F1
Mundy St IS N1 ....12 C3
Munro Ms NKENS W10 ....89 E4
Munster Ms FUL/PGN * SW6 ....113 F5
Munster Rd FUL/PGN SW6 ....113 E5
Munster Sq CAMTN NW1 ....7 D4
Munton Rd WALW SE17 ....47 F4
Murchison Rd LEY E10 ....62 C4
Murdock Cl CAN/RD E16 ....93 F5

Murdock St PECK SE15 ....120 B2
Murfett Cl WIM/MER SW19 ....149 E2
Muriel St IS N1 ....9 F1
Murillo Rd LEW SE13 ....141 D2
Murphy St STHWK SE1 ....46 A1
Murray Gv IS N1 ....12 A2
Murray Ms CAMTN NW1 ....75 D4
Murray Sq CAN/RD E16 ....94 A5
Murray St CAMTN NW1 ....75 D4
Murray Ter HAMP NW3 ....72 C1
Musard Rd HMSMTH W6 ....113 E2
Musbury St WCHPL E1 ....90 C5
Muscatel Pl CMBW SE5 ....119 E4
Muschamp Rd PECK SE15 ....137 F1
Muscovy St TWRH EC3N 37 D2
Museum St NOXST/BSQ WC1A 20 C3
Musgrave Crs FUL/PGN SW6 ....114 A3
Musgrove Rd NWCR SE14 ....121 D4
Musjid Rd BTSEA SW11 ....115 D5
Muston Rd CLPT E5 ....60 B4
Muswell Hill Rd HGT N6 ....56 A1
Mutrix Rd KIL/WHAMP NW6 ....72 A5
Mutton Pl CAMTN NW1 ....74 A3
Myatt Rd BRXN/ST SW9 ....118 B4
Mycenae Rd BKHTH/KID SE3 ....124 A2
Myddelton Pas CLKNW EC1R 10 B3
Myddelton Sq CLKNW EC1R 10 B3
Myddelton St CLKNW EC1R 10 B3
Myddleton Av FSBYPK N4 ....58 B4
Myers La NWCR SE14 ....121 D2
Mylis Cl SYD SE26 ....156 B4
Mylne Cl HMSMTH * W6 ....112 A1
Mylne St CLKNW EC1R 10 A2
Myrdle St WCHPL E1 ....90 A4
Myron Pl LEW SE13 ....140 C1
Myrtle Aly WOOL/PLUM SE18 ....108 A4
Myrtleberry Cl HACK * E8 ....77 F3
Myrtle Rd ACT W3 ....98 C2
   EHAM E6 ....83 E5
   IL IG1 ....66 B4
   WALTH E17 ....61 E1
Myrtle St IS N1 ....12 C2
Myrtle Wk IS N1 ....12 C2
Mysore Rd BTSEA SW11 ....133 F2
Myton Rd DUL SE21 ....155 D3

N

Nadine St CHARL SE7 ....124 C1
Nairne Gv HNHL SE24 ....137 D3
Nairn St POP/IOD E14 ....92 C4
Namba Roy Cl STRHM/NOR SW16 ....153 F4
Nankin St POP/IOD E14 ....92 A5
Nansen Rd BTSEA SW11 ....134 A2
Nantes Cl WAND/EARL SW18 ....132 C2
Nant Rd CRICK NW2 ....53 F4
Nant St BETH E2 ....90 B2
Naoroji St FSBYW WC1X 10 A4
Napier Av FUL/PGN SW6 ....131 F1
   POP/IOD E14 ....122 A1
Napier Cl DEPT SE8 ....121 F3
Napier Ct LEE/GVPK SE12 ....160 B3
Napier Gv IS N1 ....11 F2
Napier Pl WKENS W14 ....101 F1
Napier Rd EHAM E6 ....84 A5
   SRTFD E15 ....93 E1
   WAN E11 ....33 E5
   WKENS W14 ....101 F1
   WLSDN NW10 ....88 B2
Napier Ter IS N1 ....76 B4
Napoleon Cl CLPT E5 ....60 B5
Narbonne Av CLAP SW4 ....134 C4
Narborough St FUL/PGN SW6 ....114 B5
Narcissus Rd KIL/WHAMP NW6 ....72 A2
Narford Rd CLPT E5 ....60 A5
Narrow Boat Cl THMD SE28 ....109 D3

Narrow St ACT W3 ....98 B2
   POP/IOD E14 ....103 E1
Nascot St SHB W12 ....88 C5
Naseby Cl KIL/WHAMP * NW6 ....72 C4
Nash Rd BROCKY SE4 ....139 E2
Nash St CAMTN NW1 ....7 D3
Nasmyth St HMSMTH W6 ....100 B4
Nassau Rd BARN SW13 ....111 F4
Nassau St GTPST W1W 19 E3
Nassington Rd HAMP NW3 ....73 E1
Natal Rd IL IG1 ....84 B1
Nathaniel Cl WCHPL E1 ....25 F3
Nathan Wy THMD SE28 ....109 F4
National Ter BERM/RHTH * SE16 ....102 B3
Naval Rw POP/IOD E14 ....104 C1
Navarino Gv HACK E8 ....78 A3
Navarino Rd HACK E8 ....78 A3
Navarre Rd EHAM E6 ....95 E1
Navarre St BETH E2 ....13 E5
Navy St CLAP SW4 ....135 D1
Nayim Pl HACK E8 ....78 B3
Naylor Rd PECK SE15 ....120 B3
Nazareth Cl PECK SE15 ....120 B5
Nealden St BRXN/ST SW9 ....135 F1
Neal St LSQ/SEVD WC2H 20 C5
Neal Ter FSTH * SE23 ....157 D1
Neal Yd LSQ/SEVD WC2H 20 C5
Neasden Cl WLSDN NW10 ....69 E2
Neasden La WLSDN NW10 ....51 D5
Neasden La North WLSDN NW10 ....51 E5
Neate St CMBW SE5 ....119 E2
Neathouse Pl PIM SW1V 43 E4
Neatscourt Rd EHAM E6 ....95 D4
Nebraska St STHWK SE1 ....48 A1
Neckinger STHWK SE1 ....49 F2
Neckinger Est BERM/RHTH SE16 ....49 F2
Neckinger St STHWK SE1 ....49 F1
Nectarine Wy LEW SE13 ....122 B5
Needham Rd NTGHL W11 ....14 A5
Needleman St BERM/RHTH SE16 ....103 D3
Neeld Crs WBLY HA9 ....68 A2
Neils Yd LSQ/SEVD * WC2H 20 C5
Nelgarde Rd CAT SE6 ....140 A5
Nella Rd HMSMTH W6 ....113 D2
Nelldale Rd BERM/RHTH SE16 ....102 B5
Nello James Gdns WNWD SE27 ....155 D4
Nelson Cl KIL/WHAMP NW6 ....2 A3
Nelson Gdns BETH E2 ....90 A2
Nelson Mandela Rd BKHTH/KID SE3 ......142 C1
Nelson Pl IS N1 ....11 D2
Nelson Rd GNWCH SE10 ....122 C2
Nelson Sq STHWK SE1 ....34 C5
Nelsons Rw CLAP SW4 ....135 D2
Nelson St CAN/RD E16 ....105 F1
   EHAM E6 ....95 F1
   WCHPL E1 ....90 B5
Nelsons Yd CAMTN NW1 ....7 E1
Nelson Ter FSBYE EC1V 11 D2
Nemoure Rd ACT W3 ....98 C1
Nepaul Rd BTSEA SW11 ....115 E5
Nepean St PUT/ROE SW15 ....130 A4
Neptune St BERM/RHTH SE16 ....102 C4
Nesbit Cl BKHTH/KID SE3 ....141 E1
Nesbit Rd ELTH/MOT SE9 ....143 D2
Nesham St WAP E1W 102 A2
Ness St BERM/RHTH SE16 ....102 A4
Netheravon Rd CHSWK W4 ....111 F1
Netheravon Rd South CHSWK W4 ....111 F2
Netherby Rd FSTH SE23 ....138 C5
Netherfield Gdns BARK IG11 ....85 D3
Netherfield Rd TOOT SW17 ....152 A3
Netherford Rd CLAP SW4 ....116 C5
Netherhall Gdns HAMP NW3 ....72 C3
Netherhall Wy HAMP NW3 ....72 C2
Netherleigh Cl ARCH * N19 ....56 B3
Netherton Gv WBPTN SW10 ....114 C2
Netherton Rd SEVS/STOTM N15 ....59 D1
Netherwood Pl HMSMTH * W6 ....101 D4

Netherwood Rd HMSMTH W6 ...... 101 D4
Netherwood St KIL/WHAMP NW6 ...... 71 F4
Netley St CAMTN NW1 ...... 7 E4
Nettleden Av WBLY HA9 ...... 68 A3
Nettlefold PI WNWD SE27 ...... 154 B3
Nettleton Rd NWCR SE14 ...... 121 D3
Nevada St GNWCH SE10 ...... 122 C3
Nevern PI ECT SW5 ...... 38 B5
Nevern Rd ECT SW5 ...... 98 A5
Neville CI ACT W3 ...... 98 C3
    BFN/LL DA15 ...... 163 F4
    KIL/WHAMP NW6 ...... 89 F1
    PECK SE15 ...... 120 A3
    WAN E11 ...... 63 F5
Neville Dr EFNCH N2 ...... 54 C1
Neville Gill CI WAND/EARL SW18 ...... 132 A4
Neville Rd FSTGT E7 ...... 82 A4
    KIL/WHAMP * NW6 ...... 89 F1
Neville St SKENS SW7 ...... 115 D1
Neville Ter SKENS * SW7 ...... 115 D1
Nevill Rd STNW/STAM N16 ...... 77 E1
Nevinson CI WAND/EARL SW18 ...... 133 D4
Nevis Rd TOOT SW17 ...... 152 A2
New Acres Rd THMD SE28 ...... 109 E2
Newark Crs WLSDN NW10 ...... 87 D2
Newark Knok EHAM E6 ...... 96 A5
Newark St WCHPL E1 ...... 90 B4
New Barn St PLSTW E13 ...... 94 A3
Newbold Cottages WCHPL * E1 ...... 90 C5
New Bond St MYFR/PKLN W1J 31 D1
    MYFR/PKLN W1K 19 D5
New Bridge St EC4M 22 C5
New Broad St LVPST EC2M 24 B3
Newburgh Rd ACT W3 ...... 98 C2
Newburgh St SOHO/CST W1F 19 E5
New Burlington Ms CONDST W1S 31 E1
New Burlington PI CONDST W1S 31 E1
New Burlington St CONDST W1S 31 E1
Newburn St LBTH SE11 ...... 117 F1
Newbury Ms KTTN NW5 ...... 74 A3
Newbury Rd GNTH/NBYPK IG2 ...... 67 D1
Newbury St STBT EC1A 23 E3
New Butt La DEPT * SE8 ...... 122 A3
Newby PI POP/IOD E14 ...... 104 C1
Newby St VX/NE SW8 ...... 134 B1
Newcastle CI STP EC4M 22 C4
Newcastle PI BAY/PAD W2 ...... 16 B3
Newcastle Rw CLKNW EC1R 22 B1
New Cavendish St MHST W1U 18 B3
New Change STP EC4M 23 E5
New Charles St FSBYE EC1V 11 D3
New Church Rd CMBW SE5 ...... 118 C3
New City Rd PLSTW E13 ...... 94 C2
New College Ms IS * N1 ...... 76 A4
New College Pde HAMP * NW3 ...... 72 C3
Newcombe St KENS * W8 ...... 26 B3
Newcome Gdns STRHM/NOR SW16 ...... 153 E4
Newcomen Rd BTSEA SW11 ...... 133 D1
    WAN * E11 ...... 63 F5
Newcomen St STHWK SE1 ...... 36 A4
New Compton St LSQ/SEVD * WC2H 20 B5
New Ct TPL/STR * WC2R 34 A1
Newcourt St STJWD NW8 ...... 4 C2
New Crane PI WAP * E1W 102 C2
New Crescent Yd WLSDN * NW10 ...... 87 F1
New Cross Rd NWCR SE14 ...... 120 C3
Newdigate St STRHM/NOR * SW16 ...... 154 A4
Newell St POP/IOD E14 ...... 103 F1
New End HAMP NW3 ...... 72 C1
New End Sq HAMP NW3 ...... 73 D1
Newent CI PECK SE15 ...... 119 E3
New Era Est IS * N1 ...... 77 E5
New Ferry Ap WOOL/PLUM SE18 ...... 108 A4
New Fetter La FLST/FETLN EC4A 22 B4
Newfield Ri CRICK NW2 ...... 52 A5
Newgate St STBT EC1A 23 D4
New Globe Wk STHWK SE1 ...... 35 E3

New Goulston St WCHPL E1 ...... 25 E4
Newham's Rw STHWK SE1 ...... 49 D1
Newham Wy CAN/RD E16 ...... 93 F4
Newhaven Gdns ELTH/MOT SE9 ...... 143 D2
Newhaven La PLSTW E13 ...... 93 F4
Newick Rd CLPT E5 ...... 60 B5
Newington Barrow Wy HOLWY N7 ...... 57 F5
Newington Butts LBTH SE11 ...... 47 D5
Newington Cswy STHWK SE1 ...... 47 E2
Newington Gn STNW/STAM N16 ...... 77 D2
Newington Green Rd IS N1 ...... 77 D2
New Inn Broadway SDTCH * EC2A 13 D5
New Inn Sq SDTCH * EC2A 13 D5
New Inn St SDTCH * EC2A 13 D5
New Inn Yd SDTCH EC2A 13 D5
New Kent Rd STHWK SE1 ...... 47 E4
New Kings Rd FUL/PGN SW6 ...... 113 F5
    FUL/PGN SW6 ...... 114 A5
New King St DEPT SE8 ...... 122 A2
Newland Ct WBLY HA9 ...... 50 A4
Newlands Quay WAP E1W 102 C1
Newland St CAN/RD E16 ...... 107 E2
Newling CI EHAM E6 ...... 95 F5
Newling Est BETH * E2 ...... 13 F3
New London St MON * EC3R 37 D1
New Lydenburg St CHARL SE7 ...... 106 C4
Newlyn Rd WELL DA16 ...... 127 F5
Newman Rd PLSTW E13 ...... 94 B2
Newman's Rw LINN WC2A 21 F3
Newman St FITZ W1T 19 F3
Newmarsh Rd THMD SE28 ...... 109 F2
New Mount St SRTFD E15 ...... 81 D5
Newnham Ter STHWK SE1 ...... 46 A2
New North PI SDTCH EC2A 12 C5
New North Rd IS N1 ...... 12 B2
New North St BMSBY WC1N 21 E2
Newnton CI FSBYPK N4 ...... 59 D2
New Oxford St NOXST/BSQ WC1A 20 B4
New Park Rd BAL SW12 ...... 153 E1
    BRXS/STRHM SW2 ...... 135 E5
New Place Sq BERM/RHTH * SE16 ...... 102 B4
New Plaistow Rd SRTFD E15 ...... 81 E5
Newport Av POP/IOD E14 ...... 105 D1
Newport Ct SOHO/SHAV W1D 32 B1
Newport PI SOHO/SHAV * W1D 32 B1
Newport Rd BARN SW13 ...... 112 A4
    WAN E11 ...... 63 D4
Newport St LBTH SE11 ...... 45 E4
Newquay Rd CAT SE6 ...... 158 B2
New Quebec St MBLAR W1H 17 F5
New River Wy FSBYPK N4 ...... 59 D2
New Rd GDMY/SEVK IG3 ...... 67 E4
    WCHPL E1 ...... 90 B4
New Rw CHCR WC2N 32 C1
New Spring Gardens Wk
    LBTH * SE11 ...... 117 E1
New Sq LINN WC2A 21 F4
Newstead Rd LEE/GVPK SE12 ...... 141 F5
Newstead Wy WIM/MER SW19 ...... 149 D4
New St LVPST EC2M 25 D3
New Street HI BMLY BR1 ...... 160 B5
New Street Sq FLST/FETLN EC4A 22 B4
Newton Av ACT W3 ...... 98 C3
Newton CI WALTH E17 ...... 61 E1
Newton Gv CHSWK W4 ...... 99 E4
Newton Rd BAY/PAD W2 ...... 14 B5
    CRICK NW2 ...... 70 C1
    SRTFD * E15 ...... 81 D2
Newton St HOL/ALD WC2B 21 D4
Newton's Yd WAND/EARL SW18 ...... 132 A3
New Tower Buildings WAP * E1W 102 B2
Newtown St BTSEA SW11 ...... 116 B4
New Union CI POP/IOD E14 ...... 104 C4
New Union St BARB EC2Y 24 A3
New Wanstead WAN E11 ...... 64 A1
New Wharf Rd IS N1 ...... 9 D1
Niagara CI IS N1 ...... 11 F1
Nicholas La MANHO EC4N 36 B1

Nicholas Rd *WCHPL* E1 ....90 C3
Nicholay Rd *ARCH* N19 ....57 D3
Nichollsfield Wk *HOLWY* N7 ....75 E2
Nicholl St *BETH* E2 ....78 A5
Nichols Cl *FSBYPK* * N4 ....58 A3
Nicholson St *STHWK* SE1 ....34 C4
Nicoll Pl *HDN* NW4 ....52 B1
Nicoll Rd *WLSDN* NW10 ....69 D3
Nicosia Rd *WAND/EARL* SW18 ....133 G5
Niederwald Rd *SYD* SE26 ....157 E4
Nigel Ms *IL* IG1 ....84 B1
Nigel Playfair Av *HMSMTH* W6 ....112 B1
Nigel Rd *FSTGT* E7 ....82 C2
   PECK SE15 ....138 A1
Nigeria Rd *CHARL* SE7 ....124 C3
Nightingale Cl *CHSWK* W4 ....110 C2
Nightingale La *LEW* SE13 ....141 D3
Nightingale La *BAL* SW12 ....133 F5
Nightingale Ms *LBTH* SE11 ....46 B4
Nightingale Pl *WBPTN* SW10 ....114 C2
   WOOL/PLUM SE18 ....126 A3
Nightingale Rd *CLPT* E5 ....60 B5
   WLSDN NW10 ....87 F1
Nightingale Sq *BAL* SW12 ....134 A5
Nightingale V *WOOL/PLUM* SE18 ....126 A2
Nightingale Wk *BAL* SW12 ....134 B4
Nightingale Wy *EHAM* E6 ....95 E4
Nile Cl *STNW/STAM* N16 ....59 F5
Nile Rd *PLSTW* E13 ....94 C1
Nile St *IS* N1 ....12 A3
Nile Ter *PECK* SE15 ....119 F1
Nimrod Pas *IS* N1 ....77 F3
Nina Mackay Cl *SRTFD* * E15 ....81 E3
Nine Acres Cl *MNPK* E12 ....83 E2
Nine Elms La *VX/NE* SW8 ....116 C3
Nithdale Rd *WOOL/PLUM* SE18 ....126 B3
Niton Rd *RCH/KEW* * TW9 ....128 A1
Niton St *FUL/PGN* SW6 ....113 D3
No1 St *WOOL/PLUM* SE18 ....108 A5
No2 St *WOOL/PLUM* SE18 ....108 A5
Noble St *CITYW* EC2V 23 E4
Noel Rd *ACT* W3 ....86 A5
   EHAM E6 ....95 E3
   IS N1 ....10 C1
Noel St *SOHO/CST* * W1F 19 F5
Nolan Wy *CLPT* E5 ....78 A1
Norbiton Rd *POP/IOD* E14 ....91 F5
Norbroke St *ACT* W3 ....99 F1
Norburn St *NKENS* W10 ....89 E4
Norcott Rd *STNW/STAM* N16 ....60 A4
Norcroft Gdns *EDUL* SE22 ....138 A5
Norfolk Av *SEVS/STOTM* N15 ....59 F1
Norfolk Crs *BAY/PAD* W2 ....16 B4
   BFN/LL DA15 ....145 E1
Norfolk House Rd
   STRHM/NOR SW16 ....153 D3
Norfolk Ms *NKENS* W10 ....89 E4
Norfolk Pl *BAY/PAD* W2 ....16 B4
Norfolk Rd *BARK* IG11 ....85 E4
   EHAM E6 ....83 F5
   CDMY/SEVK IG3 ....67 E3
   STJWD NW8 ....3 D5
   WLSDN NW10 ....69 E4
Norfolk Rw *STHWK* SE1 ....45 E4
Norfolk Sq *BAY/PAD* W2 ....16 B4
Norfolk Square Ms *BAY/PAD* W2 ....16 B5
Norfolk St *FSTGT* E7 ....82 A2
Norgrove St *BAL* SW12 ....152 A1
Norland Pl *NTGHL* W11 ....101 E2
Norland Rd *NTGHL* W11 ....101 D2
Norland Sq *NTGHL* W11 ....101 E2
Norley V *PUT/ROE* SW15 ....148 A1
Norlington Rd *LEY* E10 ....62 C3
Normanby Cl *PUT/ROE* SW15 ....131 F3
Normanby Rd *WLSDN* NW10 ....69 E2
Normand Gdns *WKENS* * W14 ....113 E2
Normand Ms *WKENS* W14 ....113 E2
Normand Rd *WKENS* W14 ....113 F2
Normandy Cl *SYD* SE26 ....157 E3
Normandy Rd *BRXN/ST* SW9 ....118 A4
Normandy Ter *CAN/RD* E16 ....94 B5
Norman Gv *BOW* E3 ....91 E1
Normanhurst Rd *BRXS/STRHM* SW2 ..153 F2
Norman Rd *EHAM* E6 ....95 F3
   GNWCH SE10 ....122 B3
   IL IG1 ....84 B2
   WAN E11 ....63 E4
Normans Cl *WLSDN* NW10 ....69 D3
Normans Md *WLSDN* NW10 ....69 D3
Norman St *FSBYE* EC1V 11 E4
Norman Ter *KIL/WHAMP* * NW6 ....71 F3
Normanton Av *WIM/MER* SW19 ....150 A2
Normanton St *FSTH* SE23 ....157 D2
Norman Wy *ACT* W3 ....86 B4
Normington Cl *STRHM/NOR* SW16 ....154 A5
Norris St *STJS* SW1Y 32 A1
Norroy Rd *PUT/ROE* SW15 ....131 D2
Norstead Pl *PUT/ROE* SW15 ....148 A2
North Access Rd *WALTH* E17 ....61 D1
North Acton Rd *WLSDN* NW10 ....87 D1
Northampton Gv *IS* N1 ....76 C2
Northampton Pk *IS* N1 ....76 C3
Northampton Rd *CLKNW* EC1R 10 B5
Northampton Rw *CLKNW* * EC1R 10 B5
Northampton Sq *FSBYE* EC1V 10 C4
Northampton St *IS* * N1 ....76 C4
North Audley St *MYFR/PKLN* W1K 18 A5
North Av *RCH/KEW* TW9 ....110 A4
North Bank *STJWD* NW8 ....4 C4
North Birkbeck Rd *WAN* E11 ....63 D5
Northbourne Rd *CLAP* SW4 ....135 D2
Northbrook Rd *IL* IG1 ....66 A4
   LEW SE13 ....141 D3
Northburgh St *FSBYE* EC1V 23 D1
North Carriage Dr *BAY/PAD* W2 ....29 D1
Northchurch Rd *IS* N1 ....76 C5
   WBLY HA9 ....68 A3
Northchurch Ter *IS* N1 ....77 E4
North Circular Rd *CRICK* NW2 ....51 E5
   WLSDN NW10 ....69 D2
North Colonnade *POP/IOD* E14 ....104 A2
Northcote Rd *BTSEA* SW11 ....133 E2
   SCUP DA14 ....163 E4
   WLSDN NW10 ....69 E4
North Crs *CAN/RD* E16 ....93 D2
   FITZ W1T 20 A2
North Cross Rd *EDUL* SE22 ....137 F3
Northdene Gdns *SEVS/STOTM* N15 ....59 F1
Northdown St *IS* N1 ....9 E2
North Dr *STRHM/NOR* SW16 ....152 C4
North End *GLDGN* NW11 ....54 A4
North End Av *HAMP* NW3 ....54 A4
North End Crs *WKENS* W14 ....101 F5
North End Rd *FUL/PGN* SW6 ....114 A3
   GLDGN NW11 ....54 A3
   WBLY HA9 ....50 A5
North End Wy *HAMP* NW3 ....54 A4
Northern Relief Rd *BARK* IG11 ....84 C1
North Eyot Gdns *HMSMTH* * W6 ....111 F1
Northey St *POP/IOD* E14 ....103 E1
Northfield Rd *EHAM* E6 ....83 F3
   STNW/STAM N16 ....59 F2
Northfields *WAND/EARL* SW18 ....132 A3
Northfields Rd *ACT* W3 ....86 C4
Northgate Dr *CDALE/KGS* NW9 ....51 E1
North Gower St *CAMTN* NW1 ....7 E4
North Gv *HGT* N6 ....56 A2
North Hl *HGT* N6 ....55 F1
North Hill Av *HGT* N6 ....55 F1
Northiam St *HACK* E8 ....78 B5
Northington St *BMSBY* WC1N 21 E2
Northlands St *CMBW* SE5 ....118 C5
North Lodge Cl *PUT/ROE* * SW15 ......131 D3
North Ms *BMSBY* WC1N 21 F1
Northolme Rd *HBRY* N5 ....76 B1
Northover *BMLY* BR1 ....159 F3

North Pk ELTH/MOT SE9 ....143 F4
North Pas WAND/EARL SW18 ....132 A3
North Pole Rd SHB W12 ....88 C5
Northport St IS N1 ....77 D5
North Ri FUL/PAD * W2 ....17 D5
North Rd GDMY/SEVK IG3 ....67 E4
  HGT N6 ....56 A2
  HOLWY N7 ....75 D3
  WOOL/PLUM SE18 ....109 E5
North Rw MYFR/PKLN W1K 30 A1
North Several BKHTH/KID * SE3 ....123 D5
North Side Wandsworth Common
  WAND/EARL SW18 ....132 C3
North Sq GLDGN NW11 ....54 A1
Northstead Rd BRXS/STRHM SW2 ......154 A2
North St BARK IG11 ....84 B4
  PLSTW E13 ....94 B1
  VX/NE SW8 ....134 B1
North Tenter St WCHPL E1 ....25 F5
North Ter CHEL SW3 ....40 C4
Northumberland Aly TWRH * EC3N 25 D5
Northumberland Av CHCR WC2N 32 C3
  MNPK E12 ....64 C3
  WELL DA16 ....145 E2
Northumberland Pl BAY/PAD W2 ....14 A4
Northumberland Rd EHAM E6 ....95 E5
  WALTH E17 ....62 A2
Northumbria St POP/IOD E14 ....92 A5
North Verbena Gdns HMSMTH * W6 ....112 A1
North Vw WIM/MER SW19 ....148 B5
Northview Crs WLSDN NW10 ....69 F1
Northview Pde HOLWY * N7 ....57 E5
North Vls CAMTN NW1 ....75 D3
Northway Rd CMBW SE5 ....136 C1
Northways Pde KIL/WHAMP * NW6 ......73 D4
North Wharf Rd BAY/PAD W2 ....16 A3
Northwick Cl STJWD NW8 ....4 A5
Northwick Ter STJWD NW8 ....4 A5
Northwold Rd STNW/STAM N16 ....59 F4
Northwood Rd FSTH SE23 ....157 F1
  HGT N6 ....56 B2
North Woolwich Rd CAN/RD E16 ....106 B2
North Worple Wy MORT/ESHN SW14 ...129 D1
Norton Folgate WCHPL E1 ....25 D1
Norton Rd LEY E10 ....61 F3
Norval Gn BRXN/ST * SW9 ....118 A5
Norway Ga BERM/RHTH SE16 ....103 E4
Norway Pl POP/IOD E14 ....91 E5
Norway St GNWCH SE10 ....122 B2
Norwich St FSTGT E7 ....82 A2
Norwich St FLST/FETLN EC4A 22 A4
Norwood High St WNWD SE27 ....154 B3
Norwood Park Rd WNWD SE27 ....154 C5
Norwood Rd HNHL SE24 ....154 B1
Notley St CMBW SE5 ....119 D3
Notting Barn Rd NKENS W10 ....89 D4
Nottingdale Sq NTGHL * W11 ....101 E2
Nottingham Av CAN/RD E16 ....94 C4
Nottingham Ct LSQ/SEVD * WC2H 20 C5
Nottingham Pl MHST W1U 18 A1
Nottingham Rd LEY E10 ....62 C1
  TOOT SW17 ....151 F1
Nottingham St MHST W1U 18 A2
Nottingham Ter CAMTN NW1 ....18 A1
Notting Hill Ga KENS W8 ....26 B3
Novar Rd ELTH/MOT SE9 ....162 C1
Novello St FUL/PCN SW6 ....114 A4
Nowell Rd BARN SW13 ....112 A2
Noyna Rd TOOT SW17 ....151 F3
Nubia Wy BMLY BR1 ....159 E4
Nuding Cl LEW SE13 ....140 A1
Nugent Rd ARCH N19 ....3 F2
Nugent Ter STJWD NW8 ....3 F2
Nunhead Gv PECK SE15 ....138 B1
Nunhead La PECK SE15 ....138 B1
Nunnington Cl ELTH/MOT SE9 ....161 E3
Nursery Cl BROCKY SE4 ....121 F5
Nursery La BETH E2 ....77 F5

FSTGT E7 ....82 A3
NKENS W10 ....88 C4
Nursery Rd BRXN/ST SW9 ....135 F2
  HACK E8 ....78 C3
Nursery Rw WALW SE17 ....48 A5
Nutbourne St NKENS W10 ....89 F1
Nutbrook St PECK SE15 ....137 F1
Nutcroft Rd PECK SE15 ....120 B3
Nutfield Gdns GDMY/SEVK IG3 ....67 F4
Nutfield Rd CRICK NW2 ....52 A4
  EDUL SE22 ....137 F3
  SRTFD E15 ....80 C1
Nutford Pl BAY/PAD W2 ....17 D4
Nuthatch Gdns THMD SE28 ....109 D3
Nuthurst Av BRXS/STRHM SW2 ....153 F2
Nutley Ter HAMP NW3 ....73 D3
Nutmeg Cl CAN/RD E16 ....93 E3
Nutmeg La POP/IOD E14 ....93 D5
Nuttall St IS N1 ....13 D1
Nutt St PECK SE15 ....119 F3
Nutwell St TOOT SW17 ....151 E5
Nyanza St WOOL/PLUM SE18 ....127 D2
Nylands Av RCH/KEW TW9 ....110 A5
Nynehead St NWCR SE14 ....121 F3
Nyon Gv FSTH SE23 ....157 F2

Oakbank Gv HNHL SE24 ....136 C2
Oakbrook Cl BMLY BR1 ....160 B4
Oakbury Rd FUL/PCN SW6 ....114 B5
Oak Cottage Cl CAT SE6 ....159 E1
Oak Crs CAN/RD E16 ....93 E4
Oakcroft Rd BKHTH/KID SE3 ....123 D3
Oakdale Rd FSBYPK N4 ....58 C1
  FSTGT E7 ....82 B4
  PECK SE15 ....138 C1
  STRHM/NOR SW16 ....153 E5
  WAN E11 ....63 D4
Oakdene Av CHST BR7 ....162 A5
Oakden St LBTH SE11 ....46 B4
Oakeshott Av HGT N6 ....56 A4
Oakey La STHWK SE1 ....46 A2
Oakfield EHAM E6 ....83 E5
  FSBYPK N4 ....58 A1
  IL IG1 ....66 B5
  WIM/MER SW19 ....149 D3
Oakfield St WBPTN SW10 ....114 C2
Oakford Rd KTTN NW5 ....74 C1
Oak Gv CRICK NW2 ....71 D1
Oak Hall Rd WAN E11 ....64 C1
Oakham Cl CAT * SE6 ....157 F2
Oakhill Av HAMP NW3 ....72 C1
Oak Hill Pk HAMP NW3 ....72 B1
Oak Hill Park Ms HAMP NW3 ....72 C1
Oakhill Pl PUT/ROE SW15 ....132 A3
Oakhill Rd PUT/ROE SW15 ....131 F3
Oak Hill Wy HAMP NW3 ....72 B1
Oakhurst Gv EDUL SE22 ....138 A2
Oakington Manor Dr WBLY HA9 ....68 A2
Oakington Rd MV/WKIL W9 ....2 B5
Oakington Wy CEND/HSY/T N8 ....57 E1
Oakland Rd SRTFD E15 ....81 E1
Oaklands Av BFN/LL DA15 ....145 F5
Oaklands Gv SHB W12 ....100 A3
Oaklands Ms CRICK NW2 ....71 D1
Oaklands Park Av IL IG1 ....66 C4
Oaklands Pl CLAP SW4 ....134 C2
Oaklands Rd CRICK NW2 ....71 D1
  MORT/ESHN SW14 ....129 D1
Oak La POP/IOD E14 ....91 D1
Oakley Av ACT W3 ....98 A1
  BARK IG11 ....85 F3
Oakley Crs FSBYE * EC1V 11 D3
Oakley Dr BFN/LL DA15 ....163 D1

LEW SE13 ....**141** D4
Oakley Gdns *CHEL* SW3 ....**115** E2
Oakley Pl *STHWK* SE1 ....**119** F1
Oakley Rd *IS* N1 ....**77** D4
Oakley Sq *CAMTN* NW1 ....**7** F1
Oakley St *CHEL* SW3 ....**115** E1
Oakley Yd *BETH* * E2 ....**13** F5
Oakmead Rd *BAL* SW12 ....**152** B1
Oak Park Gdns *WIM/MER* SW19 ..**149** D1
Oakridge Rd *BMLY* BR1 ....**159** E4
The Oaks *WOOL/PLUM* SE18 ....**126** C1
Oaks Av *NRWD* SE19 ....**155** E5
Oaksford Av *SYD* SE26 ....**156** B3
Oakshade Rd *BMLY* BR1 ....**159** D4
Oakshaw Rd *WAND/EARL* SW18 ..**132** B5
Oak Tree Gdns *BMLY* BR1 ....**160** B5
Oaktree Gv *IL* IG1 ....**85** D2
Oak Tree Rd *STJWD* NW8 ....**4** B4
Oakview Rd *CAT* SE6 ....**158** B5
Oak Village *HAMP* NW3 ....**74** A1
Oak Vls *GLDGN* * N11 ....**53** F1
Oak Wy *ACT* W3 ....**99** E2
Oakways *ELTH/MOT* SE9 ....**144** B4
Oakwood Cl *WKENS* W14 ....**101** F4
Oakwood Gdns *GDMY/SEVK* IG3 ..**67** F4
Oakwood La *WKENS* W14 ....**101** F4
Oakworth Rd *NKENS* W10 ....**88** C4
Oat La *CITYW* EC2V **23** E4
Oban Cl *PLSTW* E13 ....**94** C3
Oban Rd *PLSTW* E13 ....**94** C2
Oban St *POP/IOD* E14 ....**93** D5
Oberstein Rd *BTSEA* SW11 .....**133** D2
Oborne Cl *HNHL* SE24 ....**136** B3
Observatory Gdns *KENS* W8 ....**26** A5
Observatory Rd *MORT/ESHN* SW14 ..**128** C2
SKENS SW7 ....**40** B2
Occupation La *WOOL/PLUM* SE18 ..**126** B4
Occupation Rd *WALW* SE17 ....**118** C1
Ocean Est *WCHPL* E1 ....**91** D3
Ocean St *WCHPL* E1 ....**91** D4
Ockendon Ms *IS* * N1 ....**77** D3
Ockendon Rd *IS* N1 ....**77** D3
Ockley Rd *STRHM/NOR* SW16 ..**153** E3
Octagon Ar *LVPST* * EC2M **24** C3
Octavia Ms *CRICK* * NW2 ....**70** B3
Octavia Rd *BTSEA* SW11 ....**115** E4
Octavius St *DEPT* SE8 ....**122** A3
Odeon Pde *ELTH/MOT* * SE9 ...**143** E2
HOLWY * N7 ....**57** E5
Odessa Rd *FSTGT* E7 ....**81** F1
WLSDN NW10 ....**88** A1
Odessa St *BERM/RHTH* SE16 ..**103** F4
Odger St *BTSEA* SW11 ....**115** F5
Odhams Wk *LSQ/SEVD* WC2H **20** C5
Odsey Vls *FSBYPK* * N4 ....**58** A1
Offa's Md *HOM* E9 ....**79** E1
Offenham Rd *ELTH/MOT* SE9 ..**161** F4
Offerton Rd *CLAP* SW4 ....**134** C1
Offley Rd *BRXN/ST* SW9 ....**118** A3
Offord Rd *IS* N1 ....**76** A4
Offord St *IS* N1 ....**75** F4
Ogilby St *WOOL/PLUM* SE18 ...**107** F5
Oglander Rd *PECK* SE15 ....**137** F2
Ogle St *GTPST* W1W **19** E2
Ohio Rd *PLSTW* E13 ....**93** F3
Oil Mill La *HMSMTH* W6 ....**112** A1
Okeburn Rd *TOOT* SW17 ....**152** A5
Okehampton Rd *WLSDN* NW10 ..**70** C5
Olaf St *NTGHL* W11 ....**101** D1
Old Bailey *STP* EC4M **23** D5
Old Barrack Yd *KTBR* SW1X **30** A5
Old Bond St *CONDST* W1S **31** E2
Old Brewery Ms *HAMP* NW3 ....**73** D1
Old Broad St *LVPST* EC2M **24** C4
Old Bromley Rd *BMLY* BR1 .....**159** D5
Old Brompton Rd *ECT* SW5 .....**114** A1
Old Buildings *LINN* WC2A **22** A4

Old Burlington St *CONDST* W1S ..**31** E1
Oldbury Pl *MHST* W1U **18** B2
Old Castle St *WCHPL* E1 ....**25** E4
Old Cavendish St *CAVSQ/HST* W1G ..**18** C4
Old Church La *CDALE/KGS* NW9 ..**50** C4
Old Church Rd *WCHPL* * E1 ....**91** D5
Old Church St *CHEL* SW3 ....**115** D1
Old Compton St *SOHO/SHAV* W1D ..**32** A1
Old Court Pl *KENS* W8 ....**26** C5
Old Dairy Ms *BAL* SW12 ....**152** A1
KTTN * NW5 ....**74** B3
Old Devonshire Rd *BAL* SW12 ..**134** B5
Old Dock Cl *RCH/KEW* TW9 .....**110** A2
Old Dover Rd *BKHTH/KID* SE3 ..**124** A3
Old Farm Av *BFN/LL* DA15 ......**163** D1
Old Farm Rd West *BFN/LL* DA15 ..**163** F2
Oldfield Gv *DEPT* SE8 ....**103** D5
Oldfield Ms *HGT* N6 ....**56** C2
Oldfield Rd *ACT* W3 ....**99** F3
STNW/STAM N16 ....**59** E5
WLSDN NW10 ....**69** F4
Old Fish Street Hl *BLKFR* * EC4V ..**35** E1
Old Fleet La *STP* EC4M **22** C4
Old Ford Lock *BOW* * E3 ....**80** A4
Old Ford Rd *BETH* E2 ....**90** C1
BOW E3 ....**79** E5
Old Gloucester St *BMSBY* WC1N ..**21** D2
Oldham Ter *ACT* W3 ....**98** C2
Oldhill St *STNW/STAM* N16 ....**60** A3
Old Hospital Cl *TOOT* * SW17 ..**151** F1
Old House Cl *WIM/MER* SW19 ..**149** E5
Old Jamaica Rd *STHWK* SE1 ....**102** A4
Old James St *PECK* SE15 ....**138** B1
Old Jewry *LOTH* * EC2R **24** A5
Old Kent Rd *STHWK* SE1 ....**119** E1
Old Manor Wy *ELTH/MOT* SE9 ..**161** F5
Old Manor Yd *ECT* SW5 ....**38** C5
Old Market Sq *BETH* E2 ....**13** E3
Old Marylebone Rd *CAMTN* NW1 ..**17** D3
Old Mill Rd *WOOL/PLUM* SE18 ..**127** D2
Old Mitre Ct *EMB* * EC4Y **22** B5
Old Montague St *WCHPL* E1 .....**90** A4
Old Nichol St *BETH* E2 ....**13** E5
Old North St *FSBYW* * WC1X **21** E2
Old Oak Common La *WLSDN* NW10 ..**87** E3
Old Oak La *WLSDN* NW10 ....**87** F2
Old Oak Rd *ACT* W3 ....**99** F1
The Old Orch *HAMP* * NW3 ....**73** F1
Old Paradise St *LBTH* SE11 ....**45** E4
Old Park Av *BAL* SW12 ....**134** A4
Old Park La *MYFR/PICC* W1J **30** B4
Old Pye St *WEST* SW1P **44** A2
Old Quebec St *MBLAR* W1H **17** F5
Old Queen St *STJSPK* SW1H **44** B1
Oldridge Rd *BAL* SW12 ....**134** A5
Old Rd *LEW* SE13 ....**141** E2
Old Royal Free Pl *IS* * N1 ....**76** A5
Old Royal Free Sq *IS* * N1 ....**76** A5
Old School Crs *FSTGT* E7 ....**82** A3
Old Seacoal La *STP* * EC4M **22** C5
Old South Lambeth Rd *VX/NE* * SW8 ..**117** E3
Old Sq *LINN* WC2A **21** F4
Old Stable Ms *FSBYPK* * N4 ....**58** C5
Oldstead Rd *BMLY* BR1 ....**159** D4
Old St *FSBYE* EC1V **11** E5
PLSTW E13 ....**94** B1
Old Town *CLAP* SW4 ....**134** C1
Old Tramyard *WOOL/PLUM* SE18 ..**109** E5
Old Woolwich Rd *GNWCH* SE10 ..**123** D2
Old York Rd *WAND/EARL* SW18 ..**132** B3
O'Leary Sq *WCHPL* E1 ....**90** C4
Olga St *BOW* E3 ....**91** E1
Olinda Rd *STNW/STAM* N16 ....**59** F1
Oliphant St *NKENS* W10 ....**89** E2
Oliver Cl *CHSWK* W4 ....**110** B2
Oliver Gdns *EHAM* E6 ....**95** E4
Oliver Ms *PECK* SE15 ....**120** A5
Olive Rd *CRICK* NW2 ....**70** C1

PLSTW E13 ....94 C2
Oliver Rd *LEY* E10 ....62 B4
Oliver's Yd *STLK* EC1Y 12 B5
Ollerton Gn *BOW* E3 ....79 F5
Ollgar Cl *ACT* W3 ....99 F2
Olliffe St *POP/IOD* E14 ....104 C4
Olmar St *STHWK* SE1 ....120 A2
Olney Rd *WALW* SE17 ....118 B2
Olven Rd *WOOL/PLUM* SE18 ......126 C3
Olympia Wy *WKENS* W14 ....101 E4
Olympic Wy *WBLY* HA9 ....68 A1
Oman Av *CRICK* NW2 ....70 C2
O'Meara St *STHWK* SE1 ....35 F4
Omega Pl *IS* N1 ....9 D2
Omega St *NWCR* SE14 ....121 F4
Ommaney Rd *NWCR* SE14 ....121 D4
Ondine Rd *EDUL* SE22 ....137 F2
Onega Ga *BERM/RHTH* SE16 ....103 E4
One Tree Cl *FSTH* SE23 ....138 C4
Ongar Rd *FUL/PGN* SW6 ....114 A2
Onra Rd *LEY* E10 ....62 A2
Onslow Gdns *SKENS* SW7 ....40 A5
Onslow Ms East *SKENS* SW7 ....40 A5
Onslow Ms West *SKENS* SW7 ....40 A5
Onslow Sq *SKENS* SW7 ....40 A5
Onslow St *FARR* EC1M 22 B1
Ontario St *STHWK* SE1 ....47 D3
Ontario Wy *POP/IOD* E14 ....104 A1
Opal Cl *CAN/RD* E16 ....95 D5
Openview *WAND/EARL* SW18 ......150 C1
Ophir Ter *PECK* SE15 ....120 A4
Oppenheim Rd *LEW* SE13 ....122 C5
Oppidans Rd *HAMP* NW3 ....73 F4
Orange Gv *WAN* E11 ....63 E5
Orange Pl *BERM/RHTH* SE16 ....102 C4
Orangery La *ELTH/MOT* SE9 ....145 F3
Orange St *LSQ/SEVD* WC2H 32 B2
WAP E1W 102 A2
Oransay Rd *IS* N1 ....76 C3
Oratory La *CHEL* * SW3 ....115 D1
Orbain Rd *FUL/PGN* SW6 ....113 E3
Orbel St *BTSEA* SW11 ....115 E4
Orb St *WALW* SE17 ....48 A5
The Orchard *BKHTH/KID* SE3 ......123 D5
CHSWK W4 ....52 A5
Orchard Cl *CRICK* NW2 ....138 C4
FSTH SE23 ....138 C4
NKENS W10 ....89 E4
Orchard Dr *BKHTH/KID* SE3 ....123 E5
Orchard Hl *LEW* SE13 ....122 B5
Orchard Ms *IS* N1 ....77 D4
Orchard Pl *POP/IOD* E14 ....105 E1
Orchard Ri *RCHPK/HAM* TW10 ....128 B3
Orchard Ri East *BFN/LL* DA15 .....145 E3
Orchard Ri West *BFN/LL* DA15 ....145 E3
Orchard Rd *HGT* N6 ....56 B2
RCH/KEW TW9 ....128 A1
SCUP DA14 ....163 E4
Orchardson St *STJWD* NW8 ....16 A1
Orchard Sq *WKENS* * W14 ....113 F1
Orchard St *MBLAR* W1H 18 A5
Orchard Ter *WLSDN* * NW10 ....69 F1
Orchid St *SHB* W12 ....100 A1
Orde Hall St *BMSBY* * WC1N 21 E2
Ordell Rd *BOW* E3 ....91 F1
Ordnance Crs *GNWCH* SE10 ....105 E3
Ordnance Hl *STJWD* NW8 ....73 D5
Ordnance Ms *STJWD* NW8 ....4 B1
Ordnance Rd *CAN/RD* E16 ....93 F4
WOOL/PLUM SE18 ....126 A2
Oregon Av *MNPK* E12 ....83 F2
Orestes Ms *KIL/WHAMP* * NW6 .....72 A2
Orford Rd *CAT* SE6 ....158 B3
Oriel Ct *HAMP* NW3 ....72 C1
Oriel Dr *BARN* SW13 ....112 C2
Oriel Rd *HOM* E9 ....79 D3
Oriental Rd *CAN/RD* E16 ....107 D3
Orient St *LBTH* SE11 ....46 C4

Orient Wy *CLPT* E5 ....61 D5
LEY E10 ....62 A5
Orissa Rd *WOOL/PLUM* SE18 ......127 E1
Orkney St *BTSEA* SW11 ....116 A5
Orlando Rd *CLAP* SW4 ....134 C1
Orleston Ms *HOLWY* N7 ....76 A3
Orleston Rd *HOLWY* N7 ....76 A3
Ormanton Rd *SYD* SE26 ....156 A4
Orme Ct *BAY/PAD* W2 ....26 C2
Orme Court Ms *BAY/PAD* * W2 ......27 D2
Orme La *BAY/PAD* W2 ....26 C2
Ormeley Rd *BAL* SW12 ....134 B5
Orme Sq *BAY/PAD* W2 ....26 C2
Orme Square Ga *KENS* W8 ....26 C2
Ormiston Gv *SHB* W12 ....100 B2
Ormiston Rd *GNWCH* SE10 ....124 A1
Ormond Cl *BMSBY* WC1N 21 D2
Ormonde Ct *STJWD* * NW8 ....73 F5
Ormonde Ga *CHEL* * SW3 ....115 F1
Ormonde Rd *MORT/ESHN* SW14 ...128 B3
Ormonde Ter *STJWD* NW8 ....73 F5
Ormond Rd *ARCH* N19 ....57 E3
Ormond Yd *STJS* SW1Y 31 F3
Ormsby Pl *STNW/STAM* N16 ....59 F5
Ormsby St *BETH* E2 ....13 E1
Ormside St *PECK* SE15 ....120 C2
Ornan Rd *HAMP* NW3 ....73 E2
Oronsay Wk *IS* * N1 ....119 D4
Orpheus St *CMBW* SE5 ....15 E4
Orsett Ms *BAY/PAD* W2 ....15 E4
Orsett St *LBTH* SE11 ....117 F1
Orsett Ter *BAY/PAD* W2 ....15 E4
Orsman Rd *IS* N1 ....77 E5
Orton St *WAP* E1W 102 A2
Orville Rd *BTSEA* SW11 ....115 D5
Orwell Rd *PLSTW* E13 ....94 C1
Osbaldeston Rd *STNW/STAM* N16 ...60 A4
Osberton Rd *LEE/GVPK* SE12 ....142 A3
Osbert St *WEST* SW1P 44 A5
Osborn Cl *HACK* E8 ....78 A5
Osborne Rd *ACT* W3 ....98 B3
CRICK NW2 ....70 B3
FSBYPK N4 ....58 A3
FSTGT E7 ....82 B2
HOM E9 ....79 F3
LEY E10 ....62 B5
Osborne Ter *TOOT* * SW17 ....152 A5
Osborn La *FSTH* SE23 ....139 E5
Osborn Sq *WCHPL* E1 ....25 F3
Osborn Ter *BKHTH/KID* SE3 ....141 F2
Oscar Faber Pl *IS* * N1 ....77 E4
Oscar St *DEPT* SE8 ....122 A4
Oseney Crs *KTTN* NW5 ....74 C3
O'Shea Gv *BOW* E3 ....79 F5
Osiers Rd *WAND/EARL* SW18 ......132 A3
Osier St *WCHPL* E1 ....90 C3
Osier Wy *LEY* E10 ....62 B5
Oslac Rd *CAT* SE6 ....158 B5
Osman Rd *HMSMTH* * W6 ....100 C4
Osmund St *SHB* W12 ....87 F5
Osnaburgh St *CAMTN* NW1 ....19 D1
Osnaburgh Ter *CAMTN* NW1 ....7 D5
Osprey Cl *EHAM* E6 ....95 E4
Osprey Est *BERM/RHTH* SE16 .....103 D5
Ospringe Rd *KTTN* NW5 ....74 C1
Ossian Rd *FSBYPK* N4 ....57 F2
Ossington Buildings *MHST* * W1U ...18 A2
Ossington Cl *BAY/PAD* * W2 ....26 B2
Ossington St *BAY/PAD* W2 ....26 B1
Ossory Rd *STHWK* SE1 ....120 A2
Ossulston St *CAMTN* NW1 ....8 B2
Ostade Rd *BRXS/STRHM* SW2 .....135 F5
Osten Ms *SKENS* SW7 ....39 D3
Osterley Rd *STNW/STAM* N16 ....77 E1
Oswald's Md *CLPT* E5 ....79 E5
Oswald St *CLPT* E5 ....61 D5
Oswald Ter *CRICK* * NW2 ....52 C5
Osward Rd *BAL* SW12 ....151 F2

Oswin St LBTH SE11 ....47 D4
Oswyth Rd CMBW SE5 ....119 E5
Otford Crs BROCKY SE4 ....139 F4
Othello Cl LBTH SE11 ....118 B1
Otis St BOW E3 ....92 C2
Otley Dr GNTH/NBYPK IG2 ....66 B1
Otley Rd CAN/RD E16 ....94 C5
Otley Ter CLPT E5 ....60 C4
Ottaway St CLPT E5 ....60 A5
Otterden St CAT SE6 ....158 A4
Otto Cl SYD * SE26 ....156 B2
Otto St WALW SE17 ....118 B2
Oulton Crs BARK IG11 ....85 F3
Ouseley Rd BAL SW12 ....151 F1
Outer Cir CAMTN NW1 ....5 F1
Outgate Rd WLSDN NW10 ....69 F4
Outram Pl IS N1 ....75 D5
Outram Rd EHAM E6 ....83 E5
Outwich St HDTCH * EC3A 25 D4
The Oval BETH E3 ....90 B1
Oval Pl VX/NE SW8 ....117 F3
Oval Rd CAMTN NW1 ....74 B5
Oval Wy LBTH SE11 ....117 F1
Overbury Rd FSBYPK N4 ....59 D1
Overbury St CLPT E5 ....79 D1
Overcliff Rd LEW SE13 ....140 A1
Overdown Rd CAT SE6 ....158 A4
Overhill Rd EDUL SE22 ....138 A5
Overlea Rd CLPT E5 ....60 A2
Overmead ELTH/MOT SE9 ....145 D5
Overstone Rd HMSMTH W6 ....100 C5
Overton Cl WLSDN NW10 ....68 C3
Overton Dr WAN E11 ....64 B2
Overton Rd BRXN/ST SW9 ....118 A5
    LEY E10 ....61 E3
Ovex Cl POP/IOD E14 ....104 C4
Ovington Gdns CHEL SW3 ....41 D3
Ovington Ms CHEL SW3 ....41 D3
Ovington Sq CHEL SW3 ....41 D3
Ovington St CHEL SW3 ....41 D3
Owen's Rw FSBYE EC1V 10 C3
Owen St FSBYE EC1V 10 C2
Owens Wy FSTH SE23 ....139 E1
Owen Wy WLSDN NW10 ....68 C3
Owgan Cl CMBW SE5 ....119 D3
Oxberry Av FUL/PGN SW6 ....113 E5
Oxendon St SOHO/SHAV * W1D 32 A2
Oxenford St PECK SE15 ....137 F1
Oxestalls Rd DEPT SE8 ....121 E1
Oxford Ct MANHO EC4N 36 A1
Oxford Gdns CHSWK W4 ....110 A1
    NKENS W10 ....89 D5
Oxford Ga HMSMTH * W6 ....101 D5
Oxford Rd FSBYPK N4 ....58 A3
    IL IG1 ....84 C1
    KIL/WHAMP NW6 ....2 B1
    PUT/ROE SW15 ....131 E2
    SRTFD E15 ....81 D3
Oxford Rd North CHSWK W4 ....110 A1
Oxford Rd South CHSWK W4 ....110 A1
Oxford Sq BAY/PAD W2 ....16 C5
Oxford St MYFR/PKLN W1K 18 A5
Oxgate Court Pde CRICK * NW2 ....52 B4
Oxgate Gdns CRICK NW2 ....52 B5
Oxgate La CRICK NW2 ....52 B4
Oxleas EHAM E6 ....96 B5
Oxleas Cl WELL DA16 ....127 D5
Oxley Cl STHWK SE1 ....119 F1
Oxleys Rd CRICK NW2 ....52 B5
Oxonian St EDUL SE22 ....137 F2
Oyster Catchers Cl CAN/RD E16 ....94 B5
Oyster Rw WCHPL E1 ....90 C5
Ozolins Wy CAN/RD E16 ....93 F5

P

Pace Pl WCHPL E1 ....90 B5
Pacific Rd CAN/RD E16 ....94 A5
Packington Sq IS N1 ....76 C5
Packington St IS N1 ....76 B5
Packmores Rd ELTH/MOT SE9 ....145 D3
Padbury Ct BETH E2 ....13 F4
Paddenswick Rd HMSMTH W6 ....100 A4
Paddington Gn BAY/PAD W2 ....16 A3
Paddington St MHST W1U 18 A2
Paddock Cl BKHTH/KID SE3 ....142 A1
    SYD SE26 ....157 D4
Paddock Rd CRICK NW2 ....52 A5
The Paddocks WBLY HA9 ....50 B4
Padfield Rd CMBW SE5 ....136 C1
Pagden St VX/NE SW8 ....116 B4
Pageant Crs BERM/RHTH SE16 ....103 F2
Page St WEST SW1P 44 B4
Page's Wk STHWK SE1 ....48 C4
Pages Yd CHSWK * W4 ....111 E2
Paget Ri WOOL/PLUM SE18 ....126 A3
Paget Rd IL IG1 ....84 D1
    STNW/STAM N16 ....59 D5
Paget St FSBYE EC1V 10 C3
Paget Ter WOOL/PLUM SE18 ....126 B2
Pagnell St NWCR SE14 ....121 F3
Pagoda Gdns BKHTH/KID SE3 ....123 D5
Paignton Rd SEVS/STOTM N15 ....59 E1
Painsthorpe Rd STNW/STAM N16 ....59 E5
Pakeman St HOLWY N7 ....57 F5
Pakenham Cl BAL SW12 ....152 A1
Pakenham St FSBYW WC1X 9 F4
Palace Av KENS W8 ....27 D4
Palace Ct BAY/PAD W2 ....26 C1
Palace Garden Ms KENS W8 ....26 B3
Palace Gardens Ter KENS W8 ....26 B3
Palace Ga KENS W8 ....39 E1
Palace Gn KENS W8 ....26 C4
Palace Ms FUL/PGN * SW6 ....113 F3
Palace Pl WESTW SW1E 43 E2
Palace Rd BRXS/STRHM SW2 ....153 F1
Palace St WESTW SW1E 43 E2
Palace Vw LEE/GVPK SE12 ....160 A2
Palamos Rd LEY E10 ....62 A3
Palatine Av STNW/STAM N16 ....77 E1
Palatine Rd STNW/STAM N16 ....77 E1
Palemead Cl FUL/PGN SW6 ....113 D4
Palermo Rd WLSDN NW10 ....88 A1
Palewell Common Dr
    MORT/ESHN SW14 ....129 D3
Palewell Pk MORT/ESHN SW14 ....129 D3
Palfrey Pl BRXN/ST SW9 ....117 F3
Palgrave Gdns CAMTN NW1 ....5 D5
Palgrave Rd SHB W12 ....99 F4
Palissy St BETH E2 ....13 E4
Pall Ml STJS SW1Y 32 A4
Pall Ml East STJS SW1Y 32 A3
Pall Mall Pl STJS SW1Y 31 F4
Palm Cl LEY E10 ....62 B5
Palmer Pl HOLWY N7 ....76 B2
Palmer Rd PLSTW E13 ....94 B3
Palmers Rd BETH E2 ....91 D1
    MORT/ESHN SW14 ....128 C1
Palmerston Crs WOOL/PLUM SE18 ....126 C2
Palmerston Rd ACT W3 ....98 C4
    FSTGT E7 ....82 C2
    KIL/WHAMP NW6 ....71 F4
    MORT/ESHN SW14 ....128 C2
Palmerston Wy VX/NE * SW8 ....116 B3
Palmer St STJSPK SW1H 44 A2
Pancras La MANHO EC4N 23 F5
Pancras Rd CAMTN NW1 ....8 A1
Pandora Rd KIL/WHAMP NW6 ....72 A3
Panfield Ms GNTH/NBYPK IG2 ....66 A1

Pangbourne Av NKENS * W10 ....88 C4
Panmure Cl HBRY N5 ....76 B1
Panmure Rd SYD SE26 ....156 B3
Pansy Gdns SHB W12 ....100 A1
Panther Dr WLSDN NW10 ....69 D2
Panton St LSQ/SEVD WC2H 32 B2
Paper Buildings EMB * EC4Y 34 B1
Papillons Wk BKHTH/KID SE3 ....124 A5
Papworth Gdns HOLWY N7 ....75 F2
Papworth Wy BRXS/STRHM SW2 ....136 A5
The Parade BROCKY * SE4 ....121 F4
   BTSEA * SW11 ....133 D2
   CMBW * SE5 ....137 E1
   FSBYPK * N4 ....58 A4
   RCH/KEW * TW9 ....128 A1
   SYD * SE26 ....156 B4
Parade Ms BRXS/STRHM SW2 ....154 B2
Parade Ter CDALE/KGS * NW9 ....52 A1
Paradise Pas HOLWY N7 ....76 A2
Paradise Rd CLAP SW4 ....117 E5
Paradise Rw BETH * E2 ....90 B2
Paradise Rd BERM/RHTH SE16 ....102 B3
Paradise Wk CHEL SW3 ....115 F2
The Paragon BKHTH/KID SE3 ....124 A5
Paragon Cl CAN/RD E16 ....94 A5
Paragon Ms WALW SE17 ....48 B4
Paragon Pl BKHTH/KID SE3 ....123 F5
Paragon Rd HACK E8 ....78 B3
Parbury Rd FSTH SE23 ....139 E4
Pardoner St STHWK SE1 ....48 B2
Pardon St FSBYE EC1V 11 D5
Parfett St WCHPL E1 ....90 A4
Parfrey St HMSMTH W6 ....112 C2
Parham Dr GNTH/NBYPK IG2 ....66 B1
Paris Gdn STHWK SE1 ....34 C3
Parish Gate Dr BFN/LL DA15 ....145 E4
Parish Whf WOOL/PLUM SE18 ....107 E5
The Park GLDGN NW11 ....54 B3
   HGT N6 ....56 A2
   SCUP DA14 ....163 F5
Park Ap BERM/RHTH * SE16 ....102 C4
Park Av CRICK NW2 ....70 C3
   EHAM E6 ....84 A5
   GLDGN NW11 ....54 B3
   IL IG1 ....66 A4
   MORT/ESHN SW14 ....129 D2
   SRTFD E15 ....81 E3
Park Av North WLSDN NW10 ....70 A5
Park Cl CRICK NW2 ....52 A5
   HOM E9 ....78 C5
   SKENS * SW7 ....41 E1
   WKENS W14 ....101 F4
Park Crs DUL * SE21 ....155 D3
Park Crs REGST W1B 18 C1
Park Crescent Ms East REGST W1B 18 C1
Park Crescent Ms West
   CAVSO/HST W1G 18 C1
Parkcroft Rd LEE/GVPK SE12 ....141 F5
Parkdale Rd WOOL/PLUM SE18 ....127 E1
Park Dr ACT W3 ....98 A4
   CHARL SE7 ....125 E1
   GLDGN NW11 ....54 B3
   MORT/ESHN SW14 ....129 D3
Park End HAMP NW3 ....73 E1
Parker Cl CAN/RD E16 ....107 E2
Parker Ms HOL/ALD * WC2B 21 D4
Parke Rd BARN SW13 ....112 A4
Parker's Rw STHWK SE1 ....49 F1
Parker St CAN/RD E16 ....107 E2
   HOL/ALD WC2B 21 D4
Parkfield Av MORT/ESHN SW14 ....129 E2
Parkfield Rd NWCR SE14 ....121 F4
   WLSDN NW10 ....70 A4
Parkfields PUT/ROE SW15 ....130 C2
Parkfields Av CDALE/KGS NW9 ....51 D3
Parkfield St IS N1 ....10 B2
Parkgate BKHTH/KID SE3 ....141 F1
Parkgate Gdns MORT/ESHN SW14 ....129 D3
Parkgate Rd BTSEA SW11 ....115 E3
Park Gv SRTFD E15 ....82 A5
Park Grove Rd WAN E11 ....63 E4
Park Hall Rd DUL SE21 ....155 D2
Parkham St BTSEA SW11 ....115 D3
Park Hl CLAP SW4 ....135 D3
   FSTH SE23 ....156 B2
Parkhill Rd BFN/LL DA15 ....163 E3
   HAMP NW3 ....73 F2
Parkhill Wk HAMP NW3 ....73 F2
Parkholme Rd HACK E8 ....78 A3
Parkhouse St CMBW SE5 ....119 D3
Parkhurst Rd HOLWY N7 ....75 E1
   MNPK E12 ....84 A1
Parklands HGT N6 ....56 B2
Parklands Cl GNTH/NBYPK IG2 ....66 C2
   MORT/ESHN SW14 ....128 C3
Parklands Rd TOOT SW17 ....152 B5
Park La MBLAR W1H 29 F1
   SRTFD * E15 ....80 C5
Parkmead PUT/ROE SW15 ....130 B4
Park Ms NKENS W10 ....89 E1
Park Pde ACT * W3 ....98 A4
   WLSDN NW10 ....87 F1
Park Pl ACT W3 ....98 A5
   POP/IOD E14 ....104 A2
   WHALL SW1A 31 E4
Park Place Vis BAY/PAD W2 ....15 F2
Park Rise FSTH SE23 ....157 E1
Park Rd CAMTN NW1 ....17 F1
   CDALE/KGS NW9 ....51 D2
   CDALE/KGS NW9 ....52 A2
   CHSWK W4 ....111 D2
   EHAM E6 ....82 C5
   IL IG1 ....67 D5
   LEY E10 ....62 A3
   MNPK E12 ....83 D1
   SRTFD E15 ....82 A5
   STJWD NW8 ....5 D4
   WAN E11 ....64 B3
   WLSDN * NW10 ....69 E5
Park Rd East ACT W3 ....98 C3
Park Rd North ACT W3 ....98 B3
   CHSWK W4 ....111 D2
Park Rw GNWCH SE10 ....123 D2
Park Royal Rd WLSDN NW10 ....86 C2
Park Side CRICK NW2 ....52 A5
Parkside BKHTH/KID * SE3 ....123 F5
   WIM/MER SW19 ....149 D4
Parkside Av WIM/MER SW19 ....149 D5
Parkside Crs HOLWY N7 ....58 A5
Parkside Est HOM * E9 ....79 D5
Parkside Gdns WIM/MER SW19 ....149 D4
Parkside St BTSEA SW11 ....116 A4
Park Sq East CAMTN NW1 ....6 C5
Park Square Ms CAMTN NW1 ....18 C1
Park Sq West CAMTN NW1 ....6 C5
Parkstead Rd PUT/ROE SW15 ....130 A3
Park Steps BAY/PAD * W2 ....29 D1
Parkstone Rd PECK * SE15 ....120 A5
Park St MYFR/PKLN W1K 30 A1
   STHWK SE1 ....35 E3
Parkthorne Rd BAL SW12 ....135 D5
Park Vw ACT W3 ....86 C4
   WBLY HA9 ....68 B2
Park View Est HBRY * N5 ....76 C1
Park View Rd CRICK NW2 ....69 F1
   ELTH/MOT SE9 ....162 B1
Park Village East CAMTN NW1 ....6 C1
Park Village West CAMTN NW1 ....6 C1
Park Vis TOOT * SW17 ....151 E5
Parkville Rd FUL/PGN SW6 ....113 F3
Park Vis GNWCH SE10 ....123 D2
Park Wk WBPTN SW10 ....114 C2
Parkway CAMTN NW1 ....74 B5
   GDMY/SEVK IG3 ....67 F5
Park West BAY/PAD W2 ....17 D4
Park West Pl BAY/PAD W2 ....17 D4

Parkwood Ms *HGT* N6......56 B1
Parkwood Rd *WIM/MER* SW19 149 F5
Parliament Ct *WCHPL* * E1......25 D3
Parliament Hl *HAMP* NW3......73 H1
Parliament Hill Flds *KTTN* * NW5..56 A5
Parliament Sq *WEST* SW1P......44 A4
Parliament St *WHALL* SW1A......32 C5
Parma Crs *BTSEA* SW11......133 F2
Parmiter St *BETH* E2......90 B1
Parnell Cl *SHB* W12......100 B4
Parnell Rd *BOW* E3......79 F5
Parnham St *POP/IOD* * E14......91 E5
Parolles Rd *ARCH* N19......56 C3
Parr Rd *EHAM* E6......83 D5
Parr St *IS* N1......12 A1
Parry Av *EHAM* E6......95 F5
Parry Pl *WOOL/PLUM* SE18......108 B5
Parry Rd *NKENS* W10......89 E2
Parry St *VX/NE* SW8......117 E2
Parsifal Rd *KIL/WHAMP* NW6......72 A2
Parsonage St *POP/IOD* E14......104 C5
Parsons Gn *FUL/PGN* SW6......114 A4
Parsons Green La *FUL/PGN* SW6 114 A4
Parsons Rd *PLSTW* E13......94 C1
Parthenia Rd *FUL/PGN* SW6......114 A4
Partridge Cl *CAN/RD* E16......95 D4
Partridge Gn *ELTH/MOT* SE9......162 A3
Partridge Rd *SCUP* DA14......163 E3
Partridge Sq *EHAM* E6......95 E4
Pascal St *VX/NE* SW8......117 D3
Pascoe Rd *LEW* SE13......141 D3
Pasley Cl *WALW* SE17......118 B3
Passey Pl *ELTH/MOT* SE9......143 F4
Passfield Dr *POP/IOD* E14......92 B4
Passmore St *BCVA* SW1W......42 A5
Paston Crs *LEE/GVPK* SE12......142 C5
Pastor St *LBTH* SE11......47 D4
Pasture Rd *CAT* SE6......159 E1
Patcham Ter *VX/NE* SW8......116 B4
Paternoster Rw *STP* EC4M......23 D5
Pater St *KENS* W8......38 A3
Patience Rd *BTSEA* SW11......115 E5
Patio Cl *CLAP* SW4......135 D4
Patmore St *VX/NE* SW8......116 C4
Patmos Rd *BRXN/ST* SW9......118 B3
Paton Cl *BOW* E3......92 A2
Patrick Rd *PLSTW* E13......94 C2
Patriot Sq *BETH* E2......90 B1
Patrol Pl *CAT* SE6......140 B4
Patshull Pl *KTTN* NW5......74 C3
Patshull Rd *KTTN* NW5......74 C3
Pattenden Rd *FSTH* SE23......157 F1
Patten Rd *WAND/EARL* SW18......133 D5
Patterdale Rd *PECK* SE15......120 C3
Pattina Wk *BERM/RHTH* SE16......103 E2
Pattison Rd *CRICK* NW2......54 A5
Paul Cl *SRTFD* E15......81 E4
Paulet Rd *CMBW* SE5......118 B5
Paul Julius Cl *POP/IOD* E14......105 D1
Paul Robeson Cl *EHAM* E6......96 A2
Paul St *SDTCH* EC2A......13 E5
  SRTFD E15......81 E5
Paultons Sq *CHEL* SW3......115 D2
Paultons St *CHEL* SW3......115 D2
Pauntley St *ARCH* N19......56 C3
Paveley Dr *BTSEA* SW11......115 E3
Paveley St *CAMTN* NW1......5 D1
The Pavement *CLAP* SW4......134 C2
  WAN * E11......62 C3
  WNWD * SE27......154 C4
The Pavilion *VX/NE* * SW8......117 D3
Pavilion Pde *SHB* * W12......88 C3
Pavilion Rd *IL* IG1......65 F2
  KTBR SW1X......41 F1
Pavilion St *KTBR* SW1X......41 F1
Pavillion Ter *SHB* * W12......88 C3
Pawsey Cl *PLSTW* E13......82 A3
Paxton Pl *WNWD* SE27......155 E4

Paxton Rd *CHSWK* W4......111 E2
  FSTH SE23......157 E3
Paxton Ter *PIM* SW1V......116 B2
Payne Cl *BARK* IG11......85 E4
Paynell Ct *BKHTH/KID* SE3......141 E1
Payne Rd *BOW* E3......92 B1
Paynesfield Av *MORT/ESHN* SW14 129 D1
Payne St *DEPT* SE8......121 F2
Paynes Wk *HMSMTH* W6......113 E2
Peabody Av *PIM* * SW1V......116 B1
Peabody Cl *GNWCH* * SE10......122 B4
  PIM SW1V......116 B1
Peabody Cottages *HNHL* * SE24......136 C5
Peabody Est *BTSEA* * SW11......133 E2
  CHEL * SW3......115 E2
  CLKNW * EC1R......22 B1
  CMBW * SE5......119 D4
  FUL/PGN SW6......114 A2
  HMSMTH * W6......112 C1
  HNHL SE24......136 B5
  NKENS * W10......88 C4
  STHWK * SE1......34 B3
  STHWK * SE1......35 E3
  STLK * EC1Y......23 F1
Peabody Hl *DUL* SE21......154 B1
Peabody Sq *IS* * N1......76 C5
Peabody Ter *CLKNW* * EC1R......22 B1
Peace Gv *WBLY* HA9......50 B5
Peace St *WOOL/PLUM* SE18......126 A2
Peach Rd *NKENS* W10......89 D2
Peachum Rd *BKHTH/KID* SE3......123 F2
Peacock St *WALW* SE17......47 D5
Peacock Yd *WALW* SE17......47 D5
The Peak *SYD* SE26......156 C3
Peak Hl *SYD* SE26......156 C4
Peak Hill Av *SYD* SE26......156 C4
Peak Hill Gdns *SYD* SE26......156 C4
Pearcefield Av *FSTH* SE23......156 C1
Pearl Cl *NWCR* SE14......121 E3
Pearcroft Rd *WAN* E11......63 D4
Peardon St *VX/NE* SW8......116 B5
Pearfield Rd *FSTH* SE23......157 E3
Pear Gv *WAN* E11......63 D5
Pearl Cl *CRICK* NW2......53 D2
  EHAM E6......96 A3
Pearl St *WAP* E1W......102 B3
Pearman St *STHWK* SE1......46 B2
Pear Pl *STHWK* SE1......34 A5
Pearscroft Ct *FUL/PGN* SW6......114 B4
Pearscroft Rd *FUL/PGN* SW6......114 B5
Pearson's Av *NWCR* SE14......122 A4
Pearson St *BETH* E2......13 E1
Pear Tree Cl *BETH* E2......77 F5
Pear Tree Ct *CLKNW* EC1R......22 B1
Peartree La *WAP* * E1W......102 C1
Peartree St *FSBYE* EC1V......11 D5
Peartree Wy *GNWCH* SE10......106 A3
Peary Pl *BETH* E2......90 C2
Peatfield Cl *BFN/LL* DA15......163 E3
Peckarmans Wd *DUL* SE21......156 A3
Peckett Sq *HBRY* * N5......76 C1
Peckford Pl *BRXN/ST* SW9......118 A3
Peckham Gv *PECK* SE15......119 E3
Peckham High St *PECK* SE15......120 A4
Peckham Hill St *PECK* SE15......120 A3
Peckham Park Rd *PECK* SE15......120 A3
Peckham Rd *CMBW* SE5......119 E4
Peckham Rye *EDUL* SE22......138 A3
Pecks Yd *WCHPL* * E1......25 E2
Peckwater St *KTTN* NW5......74 C2
Pedlars Wk *HOLWY* * N7......75 E2
Pedley St *BETH* E2......90 A3
  WCHPL E1......25 F1
Pedro St *CLPT* E5......61 D5
Peek Crs *WIM/MER* SW19......149 D5
Peel Gv *BETH* E2......90 C1
Peel Pas *KENS* * W8......26 A4
Peel Prec *KIL/WHAMP* NW6......89 F1

Peel St *KENS* W8..............................26 A4
Peerless St *FSBYE* EC1V...................12 A4
Pegasus Cl *STNW/STAM* * N16...........77 D1
Pegasus Pl *FUL/PGN* * SW6..............114 A4
  LBTH SE11.................................118 A2
Pegley Gdns *LEE/GVPK* SE12.............160 A2
Pegwell St *WOOL/PLUM* SE18............127 E3
Pekin St *POP/IOD* E14........................92 A5
Peldon Wk *IS* * N1.............................76 B5
Pelham Av *BARK* IG11.........................85 F5
Pelham Cl *CMBW* SE5.......................137 E1
Pelham Crs *SKENS* SW7.....................40 C5
Pelham Pl *SKENS* SW7........................40 C4
Pelham Rd *IL* IG1...............................67 D4
Pelham St *SKENS* SW7........................40 B4
Pelier St *WALW* SE17.......................118 C2
Pelinore Rd *CAT* SE6........................159 E2
Pellant Rd *FUL/PGN* SW6..................113 E3
Pellatt Rd *EDUL* SE22.......................137 F3
Pellerin Rd *STNW/STAM* N16.............77 D3
Pelling St *POP/IOD* E14......................91 F5
Pellipar Rd *WOOL/PLUM* SE18...........125 F1
Pelly Rd *PLSTW* E13..........................82 A5
Pelter St *BETH* E2..............................13 E3
Pelton Rd *GNWCH* SE10....................123 E1
Pember Rd *WLSDN* NW10....................89 D2
Pemberton Gdns *ARCH* N19................56 C5
Pemberton Pl *HACK* E8.......................78 B4
Pemberton Rd *FLST/FETLN* EC4A.........22 B4
Pemberton Ter *ARCH* N19...................56 C5
Pembridge Crs *NTGHL* W11...............101 F1
Pembridge Gdns *BAY/PAD* W2............26 A2
Pembridge Ms *NTGHL* W11.................26 A1
Pembridge Pl *BAY/PAD* W2.................26 A2
Pembridge Rd *NTGHL* W11..................26 A2
Pembridge Sq *BAY/PAD* W2.................26 A2
Pembridge Vls *NTGHL* W11..................26 A1
Pembroke Cl *KTBR* SW1X....................42 B1
Pembroke Cl *KENS* W8......................101 F4
Pembroke Gardens Cl *KENS* W8.........101 F4
Pembroke Ms *KENS* * W8....................38 A3
Pembroke St *IS* N1.............................75 E4
Pembroke Pl *KENS* * W8.....................38 A3
Pembroke Rd *ECT* SW5........................38 A4
  EHAM E6......................................95 F4
  GDMY/SEVK IG3..............................67 F3
Pembroke Sq *KENS* W8.......................38 A3
Pembroke St *IS* N1.............................75 E4
Pembroke Ter *STJWD* * NW8................73 D5
Pembroke Vls *KENS* W8.......................38 A3
Pembroke Wk *KENS* W8.......................38 A4
Pembrook Ms *BTSEA* * SW11.............133 D2
Pembry Cl *CLPT* * E5...........................78 B2
Pembury Cl *BRXN/ST* SW9................118 A4
Pembury Rd *CLPT* E5...........................78 B2
Pemell Cl *WCHPL* E1...........................90 C3
Penally Pl *IS* N1..................................77 D5
Penang St *WAP* E1W.........................102 B2
Penarth Rd *PECK* SE15......................120 C2
Penberth Rd *CAT* SE6........................158 C2
Pencombe Ms *NTGHL* W11................101 F1
Pencraig Wy *PECK* * SE15...................79 E1
Penda's Md *HOM* E9...........................79 F1
Pendennis Rd *STRHM/NOR* SW16......153 E4
Penderry Ri *CAT* SE6.........................159 D3
Penderyn Wy *HOLWY* N7.....................75 D1
Pendlebury House
  WOOL/PLUM SE18...........................125 E4
Pendragon Rd *BMLY* BR1...................160 A3
Pendrell Rd *BROCKY* SE4..................139 E1
Pendrell Rd *WOOL/PLUM* SE18..........127 D2
Pendulum Ms *HACK* * E8....................77 F2
Penerley Rd *CAT* SE6........................158 B1
Penfold Pl *BAY/PAD* W2.....................16 B1
Penfold St *STJWD* NW8......................16 B1
Penford Gdns *ELTH/MOT* SE9............143 D2
Penford St *CMBW* SE5.......................118 B5
Penge Rd *PLSTW* E13.........................82 C4
Penhall Rd *CHARL* SE7......................107 D5

Peninsular Park Rd *CHARL* SE7...........124 A1
Pennack Rd *PECK* SE15......................119 F2
Pennant Ms *KENS* W8..........................38 C4
Pennard Rd *SHB* W12........................100 C3
Penner Cl *WIM/MER* SW19.................149 E2
Pennethorne Cl *HOM* E9......................78 C5
Pennethorne Rd *PECK* SE15...............120 B3
Pennine Dr *CRICK* NW2.......................53 D4
Pennine La *CRICK* NW2.......................53 E4
Pennine Pde *CRICK* * NW2..................53 E4
Pennington St *WAP* E1W....................102 B1
Pennington Wy *LEE/GVPK* SE12.........160 B2
Penn Rd *HOLWY* N7............................75 D2
Penn St *IS* N1.....................................77 D5
Pennyfields *POP/IOD* E14..................104 A1
Pennymoor Wk *MV/WKIL* W9...............89 F3
Pennyroyal Av *EHAM* E6......................96 A5
Penpoll Rd *HACK* E8...........................78 B3
Penrhyn Crs *MORT/ESHN* SW14.........128 C2
Penrith Cl *PUT/ROE* SW15.................131 E3
Penrith Pl *STRHM/NOR* SW16............154 B2
Penrose Gv *WALW* SE17....................118 C1
Penrose St *WALW* SE17.....................118 C1
Penryn St *CAMTN* NW1..........................8 A1
Pensbury Pl *VX/NE* SW8....................116 C5
Pensbury St *VX/NE* SW8....................116 C5
Pensford Av *RCH/KEW* TW9...............110 A5
Penshurst Rd *HOM* E9.........................79 D4
Pentland Cl *CRICK* NW2......................53 E4
Pentland St *WAND/EARL* SW18..........132 C4
Pentlow St *PUT/ROE* SW15................112 C5
Pentney Rd *BAL* SW12.......................152 C1
Penton Gv *IS* N1.................................10 A2
Penton Pl *WALW* SE17........................47 D5
Penton Ri *FSBYW* WC1X.......................9 F3
Penton St *IS* N1..................................10 A1
Pentonville Rd *IS* N1...........................9 E2
Pentridge St *PECK* SE15...................119 F3
Penwith Rd *WAND/EARL* SW18..........150 B2
Penwortham Rd *ECT* SW5...................114 A1
Penzance Pl *NTGHL* W11...................101 E2
Penzance St *NTGHL* W11....................100 A1
Peony Gdns *SHB* W12..........................89 D1
Peploe Rd *KIL/WHAMP* NW6................95 F4
Pepper Cl *EHAM* E6...........................140 A3
Peppermead Sq *BROCKY* * SE4............63 E5
Peppermint Pl *WAN* E11.....................104 B4
Pepper St *POP/IOD* E14......................35 E5
  STHWK SE1.....................................
Peppie Cl *STNW/STAM* N16................103 E5
Pepys Est *DEPT* SE8..........................103 F5
Pepys Park Est *DEPT* SE8..................103 F5
Pepys Rd *NWCR* SE14........................121 D4
Pepys St *TWRH* EC3N..........................37 D1
Perceval Av *HAMP* NW3.......................73 E2
Perch St *HACK* E8..............................77 F1
Percival Rd *MORT/ESHN* SW14..........128 C3
Percival St *FSBYE* EC1V......................10 C5
Percy Ms *FITZ* W1T............................20 A3
Percy Rd *CAN/RD* E16..........................93 E4
  SHB W12......................................100 A3
  WAN E11...63 E2
Percy St *FITZ* W1T..............................20 A3
Peregrine Ct *WLSDN* NW10.................69 D2
Peregrine Ct *WELL* DA16...................127 F4
Perham Rd *WKENS* W14.....................113 E1
Peridot St *EHAM* E6............................95 E4
Perifield *DUL* SE21............................154 C1
Periton Rd *ELTH/MOT* SE9.................143 D2
Perkin's Rents *WEST* SW1P..................44 A2
Perkins Sq *STHWK* SE1.......................35 F3
Perks Cl *BKHTH/KID* SE3...................123 E5
Perpins Rd *ELTH/MOT* SE9.................145 E4
Perran Rd *BRXS/STRHM* SW2..............154 B2
Perrers Rd *HMSMTH* W6......................100 B4
Perrin's Ct *HAMP* * NW3......................72 C1
Perrin's Wk *HAMP* NW3.......................72 C1

Perry Av *ACT* W3 ....87 D5
Perry Ct *SEVS/STOTM* * N15 ....59 E1
Perryfield Wy *CDALE/KGS* NW9 ......51 F1
Perry Hl *CAT* SE6.........................157 F2
Perrymans Farm Rd *GNTH/NBYPK* IG2 ....67 D1
Perrymead St *FUL/PGN* SW6 ....114 A4
Perryn Rd *ACT* W3 ....99 D1
  BERM/RHTH SE16 ....102 B4
Perry Ri *FSTH* SE23 ....157 E3
Perry V *FSTH* SE23 ....156 C1
Persant Rd *CAT* SE6 ....159 E3
Perseverance Pl *BRXN/ST* * SW9 ...118 A3
Perth Av *CDALE/KGS* NW9 ....51 D2
Perth Rd *BARK* IG11 ....97 D1
  FSBYPK N4 ....58 A3
  GNTH/NBYPK IG2 ....66 B1
  LEY E10 ....61 E3
  PLSTW E13 ....94 B1
Perth Ter *GNTH/NBYPK* IG2 ....66 C2
Peter Av *WLSDN* NW10 ....70 B4
Peterboat Cl *GNWCH* SE10 ....105 E5
Peterborough Ms *FUL/PGN* SW6 ....114 A5
Peterborough Rd *FUL/PGN* SW6 ....114 A5
Peterborough Vls *FUL/PGN* SW6 ....114 B4
Petergate *BTSEA* SW11 ....132 C2
Peters Cl *WELL* DA16 ....127 E5
Petersfield Rd *PUT/ROE* SW15 .....148 B3
Petersfield Rd *ACT* W3 ....98 C3
Petersham La *SKENS* SW7 ....39 E2
Petersham Ms *SKENS* SW7 ....39 E3
Petersham Pl *SKENS* SW7 ....39 E3
Peter's Hl *BLKFR* EC4V 35 C1
Peterstow Cl *WIM/MER* SW19 ......149 E2
Peter St *SOHO/CST* W1F 32 A1
Petherton Rd *HBRY* N5 ....76 C2
Petiver Cl *HOM* * E9 ....78 C4
Petley Rd *HMSMTH* W6 ....112 C2
Peto Pl *CAMTN* NW1 ....7 D1
Petrie Cl *CRICK* * NW2 ....71 E3
Petros Gdns *HAMP* * NW3 ....72 B2
Petro St South *CAN/RD* E16 ....105 F1
Petticoat Sq *WCHPL* E1 ....25 E4
Petticoat Tower *WCHPL* * E1 ....25 E4
Pettiward Cl *PUT/ROE* SW15 ....130 E2
Pettman Crs *THMD* SE28 ....109 D4
Pett St *CHARL* SE7 ....107 E5
Petty France *STJSPK* SW1H 43 F2
Petworth St *BTSEA* SW11 ....115 F5
Petyt Pl *CHEL* * SW3 ....115 E2
Petyward *CHEL* SW3 ....41 D5
Pevensey Rd *FSTGT* E7 ....82 A1
  TOOT SW17 ....151 D4
Peyton Pl *GNWCH* SE10 ....122 C3
Pheasant Cl *CAN/RD* E16 ....94 B5
Phelp St *WALW* SE17 ....119 D2
Phene St *CHEL* SW3 ....115 E2
Philbeach Gdns *ECT* SW5 ....114 A1
Philchurch Pl *WCHPL* E1 ....90 A5
Philimore Cl *WOOL/PLUM* SE18 ...127 E1
Philippa Gdns *ELTH/MOT* SE9 ......143 D3
Philip Rd *PECK* SE15.....................138 A1
Philip St *PLSTW* E13 ....94 A3
Phillimore Gdns *KENS* W8 ....38 A1
  WLSDN NW10 ....70 C5
Phillimore Gardens Cl *KENS* * W8 ...38 A2
Phillimore Pl *KENS* W8 ....38 A1
Phillimore Wk *KENS* W8 ....38 A2
Phillipp St *IS* N1 ....77 E5
Philpot La *FENCHST* EC3M 36 C1
Philpot St *WCHPL* * E1 ....90 B5
Phineas Pett Rd *ELTH/MOT* SE9 ...143 E1
Phipp's Ms *BGVA* SW1W 43 D3
Phipp St *SDTCH* EC2A 12 C5
Phoebeth Rd *LEW* SE13 ....140 A3
Phoenix Cl *HACK* * E8 ....77 F5
Phoenix Pl *FSBYW* WC1X 9 F5
Phoenix Rd *CAMTN* NW1 ....8 A3
Phoenix St *LSQ/SEVD* WC2H 20 B5

Phoenix Wharf Rd *STHWK* SE1 ....49 F1
Physic Pl *CHEL* SW3 ....115 F2
Piccadilly *MYFR/PICC* W1J 30 C4
Piccadilly Ar *MYFR/PICC* W1J 31 E3
Piccadilly Circ *MYFR/PICC* W1J 32 A2
Pickard St *FSBYE* EC1V 11 D3
Pickering Av *EHAM* E6 ....96 A1
Pickering Pl *STJS* * SW1Y 31 F4
Pickering St *IS* N1 ....76 B5
Pickets St *BAL* SW12 ....134 A5
Pickfords Whf *IS* * N1 ....11 E2
Pickwick Rd *DUL* SE21..................137 D5
Pickwick St *STHWK* SE1 ....47 E1
Pickworth Cl *VX/NE* * SW8 ....117 E3
Picton Pl *MBLAR* W1H 18 B5
Picton St *CMBW* SE5 ....119 D3
Piedmont Rd *WOOL/PLUM* SE18 ...127 D1
Pier Head *WAP* * E1W 102 B2
Piermont Rd *EDUL* SE22 ....138 B3
Pierrepoint Ar *IS* * N1 ....10 C1
Pierrepoint Rd *ACT* W3 ....98 B1
Pierrepoint Rw *IS* N1 ....10 C1
Pier Rd *CAN/RD* E16 ....107 F3
Pier St *POP/IOD* E14 ....104 C5
Pier Ter *WAND/EARL* SW18 ....132 B2
Pier Wy *WOOL/PLUM* SE18 ....109 D4
Pigott St *POP/IOD* E14 ....92 A5
Pike Cl *BMLY* BR1 ....160 B5
Pilgrimage St *STHWK* SE1 ....48 A1
Pilgrim Hl *WNWD* SE27 ....154 C4
Pilgrim's La *HAMP* NW3 ....73 D1
Pilgrims Ms *POP/IOD* E14 ....105 D1
Pilgrim St *BLKFR* EC4V 22 C5
Pilgrims Wy *ARCH* N19 ....57 D3
  WBLY HA9 ....50 B3
Pilkington Rd *PECK* SE15 ....120 B5
Pilot Cl *DEPT* SE8 ....121 F2
Pilsden Cl *WIM/MER* SW19 ....149 E1
Pilton Pl *WALW* SE17 ....118 C1
Pimlico Rd *BGVA* SW1W 116 A1
Pinchin & Johnsons Yd *WCHPL* * E1 ...102 A1
Pinchin St *WCHPL* E1 ....102 A1
Pincott Pl *BROCKY* SE4 ....139 D1
Pindar St *SDTCH* EC2A 24 C2
Pindock Ms *MV/WKIL* W9 ....15 D1
Pine Apple Ct *WESTW* * SW1E 43 E2
Pine Av *SRTFD* E15 ....81 D2
Pine Cl *LEY* E10 ....62 A4
Pinefield Cl *POP/IOD* * E14 ....104 A1
Pine Gv *FSBYPK* N4 ....57 E4
  WIM/MER SW19 ....149 F5
Pinelands Cl *BKHTH/KID* * SE3 ....123 F3
Pinelees Ct *MORT/ESHN* * SW14 ...128 C2
Pinemartin Cl *CRICK* NW2 ....52 C5
Pine Rd *CRICK* NW2 ....70 C1
Pine St *CLKNW* EC1R 10 A5
Pinewood Av *BFN/LL* DA15 ....163 E1
Pinfold Rd *STRHM/NOR* SW16 ......153 E4
Pinnell Rd *ELTH/MOT* SE9 ....143 D2
Pintail Cl *EHAM* E6 ....95 D4
Pinto Wy *BKHTH/KID* SE3 ....142 B2
Pioneer Cl *SHB* W12 ....88 B5
Pioneer St *PECK* SE15 ....120 A4
Pioneer Wy *SHB* W12 ....88 C5
Piper Cl *HOLWY* N7 ....75 F2
Pippin Cl *CRICK* NW2 ....52 A5
Pirbright Rd *WAND/EARL* SW18 .....149 F1
Pirie St *CAN/RD* E16 ....106 B2
Pitchford St *SRTFD* E15 ....81 D4
Pitfield St *IS* N1 ....12 C1
Pitfield Wy *WLSDN* NW10 ....68 C3
Pitfold Rd *LEE/GVPK* SE12 ....142 A5
Pitman St *CMBW* SE5 ....118 C3
Pitsea Pl *WCHPL* E1 ....91 D5
Pitsea St *WCHPL* E1 ....91 D5
Pitt Crs *WIM/MER* SW19 ....150 B4
Pittman Gdns *IL* IG1 ....84 C2
Pitt's Head Ms *MYFR/PKLN* W1K 30 B4

Pitt St *KENS* W8 ....26 B5
Pixley St *POP/IOD* E14 ....91 F5
Plaistow Gv *SRTFD* E15 ....81 F5
Plaistow Park Rd *PLSTW* E13 ....94 B1
Plaistow Rd *PLSTW* E13 ....94 A1
  SRTFD E15 ....81 F5
Plane St *SYD* SE26 ....156 B3
Plantain Gdns *WAN* * E11 ....63 D5
Plantain Pl *STHWK* SE1 ....36 A5
The Plantation *BKHTH/KID* SE3 ....124 A5
Plashet Gv *EHAM* E6 ....82 C5
Plashet Rd *PLSTW* E13 ....82 A5
Plassy Rd *CAT* SE6 ....140 B5
Platina St *SDTCH* EC2A 12 B5
Plato Rd *CLAP* SW4 ....135 E2
Platt's La *HAMP* NW3 ....54 A5
Platt St *CAMTN* NW1 ....8 A1
Playfair St *HMSMTH* * W6 ....112 C1
Playfield Crs *EDUL* SE22 ....137 E3
Playford Rd *FSBYPK* N4 ....57 F4
Playgreen Wy *CAT* SE6 ....158 A4
Playhouse Yd *BLKFR* EC4V 22 C5
The Pleasance *PUT/ROE* SW15 ....130 B2
Pleasance Rd *PUT/ROE* SW15 ....130 B3
Pleasant Pl *IS* N1 ....76 B4
Plender St *CAMTN* NW1 ....74 C5
Pleshey Rd *HOLWY* N7 ....75 D1
Plevna Crs *SEVS/STOTM* N15 ....59 E1
Plevna St *POP/IOD* E14 ....104 C4
Pleydell Av *HMSMTH* W6 ....99 F4
Pleydell Est *FSBYE* * EC1V 11 F4
Pleydell St *EMB* EC4Y 22 B5
Plimsoll Cl *POP/IOD* E14 ....92 B5
Plimsoll Rd *FSBYPK* N4 ....58 B5
Plough La *EDUL* SE22 ....137 F4
  WIM/MER SW19 ....150 B5
Ploughmans Cl *CAMTN* NW1 ....75 D5
Plough Pl *FLST/FETLN* EC4A 22 B4
Plough Rd *BTSEA* SW11 ....133 D1
Plough St *WCHPL* * E1 ....90 A5
Plough Ter *BTSEA* SW11 ....133 D2
Plough Wy *BERM/RHTH* SE16 ....105 D5
Plough Yd *SDTCH* EC2A 25 D1
Plover Wy *BERM/RHTH* SE16 ....103 E4
Plowden Buildings *EMB* * EC4Y 34 A1
Plumbers Rw *WCHPL* E1 ....90 A4
Plumbridge St *GNWCH* * SE10 ....122 C4
Plum La *WOOL/PLUM* SE18 ....126 B3
Plummer Rd *CLAP* SW4 ....134 C4
Plumstead Common Rd
  WOOL/PLUM SE18 ....126 C2
Plumstead High St
  WOOL/PLUM SE18 ....109 D5
Plumstead Rd *WOOL/PLUM* SE18 ....108 C5
Plumtree Ct *FLST/FETLN* EC4A 22 B4
Plymouth Rd *CAN/RD* E16 ....94 A4
Plymouth Whf *POP/IOD* E14 ....105 D5
Plympton Av *KIL/WHAMP* NW6 ....71 F4
Plympton Pl *STJWD* * NW8 ....16 C1
Plympton Rd *KIL/WHAMP* NW6 ....71 F4
Plympton St *STJWD* NW8 ....16 C1
Pocock St *STHWK* SE1 ....34 C5
Podmore Rd *WAND/EARL* SW18 ....132 C2
Poet's Rd *HBRY* N5 ....77 D2
Point Cl *GNWCH* SE10 ....122 C4
Pointers Cl *POP/IOD* E14 ....122 B1
Point Hl *GNWCH* SE10 ....122 C4
Point Pl *WBLY* HA9 ....68 B4
Point Pleasant *WAND/EARL* SW18 ....132 A2
Poland St *SOHO/CST* W1F 19 F4
Polebrook Rd *BKHTH/KID* SE3 ....142 C1
Polecroft La *CAT* SE6 ....157 F2
Pollard Cl *CAN/RD* E16 ....106 A1
  HOLWY N7 ....75 F1
Pollard Rw *BETH* E2 ....90 A5
Pollard St *BETH* * E2 ....90 A2
Pollen St *CONDST* W1S 19 D5
Pollitt Dr *STJWD* NW8 ....4 A5

Polperro Ms *LBTH* SE11 ....46 C4
Polsted Rd *CAT* SE6 ....139 F5
Polthorne Gv *WOOL/PLUM* SE18 ....108 C5
Polworth Rd *STRHM/NOR* SW16 ....153 E5
The Polygon *CLAP* * SW4 ....134 C2
Polygon Rd *CAMTN* NW1 ....8 A3
Polytechnic St *WOOL/PLUM* SE18 ....108 A5
Pomell Wy *WCHPL* E1 ....25 F4
Pomeroy St *NWCR* SE14 ....120 C3
Pomfret Rd *CMBW* SE5 ....136 B1
Pomoja La *ARCH* N19 ....57 E4
Pond Cl *BKHTH/KID* SE3 ....124 A5
Ponder St *HOLWY* * N7 ....75 F4
Pond Farm Est *CLPT* * E5 ....60 C5
Pond Md *DUL* SE21 ....137 D4
Pond Pl *CHEL* SW3 ....40 C5
Pond Rd *BKHTH/KID* SE3 ....141 F1
  SRTFD E15 ....93 E1
Pond St *HAMP* NW3 ....73 E2
Ponler St *WCHPL* E1 ....90 B5
Ponsard Rd *WLSDN* NW10 ....88 B2
Ponsford St *HOM* E9 ....78 C3
Ponsonby Pl *WEST* SW1P 117 D1
Ponsonby Rd *PUT/ROE* SW15 ....130 B5
Ponsonby Ter *WEST* SW1P 117 D1
Pontefract Rd *BMLY* BR1 ....160 A5
Ponton Rd *VX/NE* SW8 ....41 E3
Pont St *KTBR* SW1X 41 E3
Pont Street Ms *CHEL* SW3 ....41 E3
Pool Cl *BECK* BR3 ....158 A5
Pool St *CAT* SE6 ....158 A2
Poole Rd *HOM* E9 ....79 D3
Pooles Buildings *FSBYW* WC1X 22 A1
Pooles La *WBPTN* * SW10 ....114 C3
Pooles Pk *FSBYPK* N4 ....58 A4
Poole St *IS* N1 ....77 D5
Poolmans St *BERM/RHTH* SE16 ....103 D3
Poonah St *WCHPL* E1 ....90 C5
Pope's Rd *BRXN/ST* * SW9 ....136 A2
Pope St *STHWK* SE1 ....49 D1
Popham Gdns *RCH/KEW* * TW9 ....128 B1
Popham Rd *IS* N1 ....76 B5
Popham St *IS* N1 ....76 B5
Poplar Bath St *POP/IOD* E14 ....104 B1
Poplar Cl *HOM* E9 ....79 F2
Poplar Crs *HMSMTH* W6 ....100 C3
Poplar Gv *WBLY* HA9 ....50 C5
Poplar High St *POP/IOD* E14 ....104 B1
Poplar Ms *SHB* W12 ....100 C2
Poplar Pl *BAY/PAD* W2 ....26 C1
Poplars Rd *LEY* E10 ....62 B1
Poplar Wk *HNHL* SE24 ....136 C2
Poppins Ct *FLST/FETLN* EC4A 22 C5
Poppleton Rd *WAN* E11 ....63 E1
Porchester Garden Ms *BAY/PAD* * W2 ...15 D5
Porchester Gdns *BAY/PAD* W2 ....27 D1
Porchester Ga *BAY/PAD* * W2 ....27 E2
Porchester Pl *BAY/PAD* W2 ....17 D5
Porchester Rd *BAY/PAD* W2 ....15 D4
Porchester Sq *BAY/PAD* W2 ....15 D4
Porchester Square Ms *BAY/PAD* W2 ......15 E4
Porchester Ter *BAY/PAD* W2 ....15 E5
Porchester Ter North *BAY/PAD* W2 ....15 D4
Porcupine Cl *ELTH/MOT* SE9 ....161 E2
Porden Rd *BRXN/ST* SW9 ....135 F2
Porlock St *STHWK* SE1 ....36 B5
Porlock St *WNWD* SE27 ....154 A3
Portbury Cl *PECK* SE15 ....120 A4
Portchester Cl *CMBW* SE5 ....136 C2
Portchester Ga *BAY/PAD* W2 ....27 E2
Portelet Rd *WCHPL* E1 ....91 D2
Porten Houses *WKENS* * W14 ....101 E4
Porten Rd *WKENS* W14 ....101 E4
Porter Rd *EHAM* E6 ....95 F5
Porter St *MHST* W1U 17 F2
  STHWK SE1 ....35 F3
Porters Wk *WAP* * E1W 102 B1

Porteus Rd *BAY/PAD* W2 ....15 F3
Portgate Cl *MV/WKIL* W9 ....89 F3
Porthcawe Rd *SYD* SE26..............157 E4
Portia Wy *BOW* E3........................91 F3
The Porticos *WBPTN* * SW10 ....115 D2
Portinscale Rd *PUT/ROE* SW15 ....131 F5
Portland Av *STNW/STAM* N16 ....59 F3
Portland Gdns *FSBYPK* N4 ....58 B1
Portland Gv *VX/NE* SW8 ....117 F4
Portland Ms *SOHO/CST* W1F 19 F5
Portland Pl *CAVSQ/HST* W1G 18 C1
Portland Ri *FSBYPK* N4 ....58 B3
Portland Rd *BMLY* BR1.................160 C4
  NTGHL W11 ....101 E1
Portland Sq *WAP* E1W.................102 A3
Portland St *WALW* SE17 ....119 D1
Portman Av *MORT/ESHN* SW14 ....129 C5
Portman Cl *W1H* 18 A4
Portman Ga *CAMTN* NW1 ....17 D1
Portman Ms *MBLAR* W1H 18 A5
Portman Pl *BETH* E2.....................90 C2
Portman Sq *MBLAR* W1H 17 F4
Portman St *MBLAR* W1H 18 A5
Portman Towers *MBLAR* W1H 17 F4
Portmeers Cl *WALTH* * E17 ....61 E1
Portnall Rd *MV/WKIL* W9 ....89 F2
Portobello Ct *NTGHL* * W11 ....101 F1
Portobello Ms *NTGHL* * W11 ....26 A3
Portobello Rd *NKENS* W10 ....89 E4
  NTGHL W11 ....101 F1
Portpool La *FSBYW* WC1X 22 A1
Portree St *POP/IOD* E14................93 D5
Portsdown Av *GLDGN* NW11 ....53 F1
Portsdown Ms *GLDGN* NW11 ....53 F1
Portsea Ms *BAY/PAD* W2 ....17 D5
Portsea Pl *BAY/PAD* W2 ....17 D5
Portslade Rd *VX/NE* SW8 ....116 A5
Portsmouth Rd *PUT/ROE* SW15 ...130 B5
Portsmouth St *LINN* WC2A 21 D4
Portsoken St *TWRH* EC3N 37 E1
Portugal St *LINN* WC2A 21 D3
Portway *SRTFD* E15......................81 F5
Portway Gdns *WOOL/PLUM* SE18 ..125 D4
The Postern *BARB* * EC2Y 23 F3
Post Office Ap *FSTGT* E7...............82 B2
Postway Ms *IL* IG1 ....66 B5
Potier St *STHWK* SE1 ....48 B3
Potterne Cl *WIM/MER* SW19 ....131 D5
Potters Flds *STHWK* SE1 ....37 D4
Pottery La *FUL/PGN* SW6 ....114 C5
Pottery La *NTGHL* W11 ....101 E2
Pottery St *BERM/RHTH* * SE16 .....102 B3
Pott St *BETH* E2...........................90 B2
Poulett Rd *EHAM* E6 ....95 F1
Poulton Cl *HACK* E8......................78 B3
Poultry *LOTH* EC2R 24 A5
Pound La *WLSDN* NW10 ....70 A3
Pound Park Rd *CHARL* SE7.............70 A3
Pound Pl *ELTH/MOT* SE9 ....107 D5
Pountney Rd *BTSEA* SW11 ....144 A4
Powell Rd *CLPT* E5........................60 B5
Power Rd *CHSWK* W4 ....98 A5
Powerscroft Rd *CLPT* E5 ....78 C1
Powis Gdns *GLDGN* NW11 ....53 F2
  NTGHL W11 ....89 F5
Powis Ms *NTGHL* W11 ....89 F5
Powis Pl *BMSBY* WC1N 21 D1
Powis Rd *BOW* E3 ....92 B2
Powis Sq *NTGHL* W11 ....89 F5
Powis Sq *WOOL/PLUM* SE18 ....108 A4
Powis Ter *NTGHL* W11 ....89 F5
Powlett Pl *CAMTN* * NW1 ....74 B4
Pownall Rd *HACK* E8 ....78 A5
Pownsett Ter *IL* IG1 ....84 C2
Powster Rd *BMLY* BR1 ....160 A5
Poynders Rd *CLAP* SW4 ....134 C5
Poynings Rd *ARCH* N19 ....56 C5

Poyntz Rd *BTSEA* SW11 ....115 F5
Poyser St *BETH* E2 ....90 B2
Praed Ms *BAY/PAD* W2 ....16 B4
Praed St *BAY/PAD* W2 ....16 B4
Pragel St *PLSTW* E13 ....94 B1
Pragnell Rd *LEE/GVPK* SE12 ....160 B2
Prague Pl *BRXS/STRHM* SW2 ....135 E3
Prah Rd *FSBYPK* N4 ....58 A4
Prairie St *VX/NE* SW8 ....116 A5
Pratt Ms *CAMTN* NW1 ....74 C5
Pratt St *CAMTN* NW1 ....74 C5
Pratt Wk *LBTH* SE11 ....45 F4
Prayle Gv *CRICK* NW2 ....53 D3
Prebend Gdns *CHSWK* W4 ....99 F5
Prebend St *IS* N1 ....76 C5
The Precinct *IS* * N1 ....11 E1
Premiere Pl *POP/IOD* E14.............104 A1
Premier Park Rd *WLSDN* NW10 .....86 B5
Prentis Rd *STRHM/NOR* SW16 .....153 D4
Prentiss Ct *CHARL* SE7.................107 D5
Prescot St *WCHPL* E1 ....37 F1
Prescott Pl *CLAP* SW4 ....135 D1
Presentation Ms *BRXS/STRHM* SW2 ...153 F2
Presidents Dr *WAP* E1W 102 A2
President St *FSBYE* * EC1V 11 E3
Press Rd *WLSDN* NW10 ....51 D5
Prestage Wy *POP/IOD* E14 ....104 C1
Prestbury Rd *FSTGT* E7 ....82 C4
Prestbury Sq *ELTH/MOT* SE9 ....161 F4
Prested Rd *BTSEA* SW11 ....133 E4
Preston Cl *STHWK* * SE1 ....48 C4
Preston Gdns *IL* IG1 ....65 E1
  WLSDN * NW10 ....69 E3
Preston Pl *WLSDN* NW10 ....70 A3
Preston Rd *WAN* E11 ....63 E1
Preston's Rd *POP/IOD* E14...........104 C1
Prestwich Ter *CLAP* * SW4 ....135 D3
Prestwood Cl *IS* * N1 ....11 F2
Pretoria Pde *LEW* * SE13 ....122 A5
Pretoria Rd *CAN/RD* E16 ....93 F2
  IL IG1 ....84 B1
  WAN E11 ....63 D1
Price Cl *TOOT* SW17 ....151 F3
Price's St *STHWK* SE1 ....35 D4
Prideaux Pl *ACT* W3 ....99 D1
  FSBYW WC1X 9 F3
Prideaux Rd *BRXN/ST* SW9 ....135 E1
Priestfield Rd *FSTH* SE23 ....157 E3
Priestlands Park Rd *BFN/LL* DA15...163 F3
Priestley Cl *STNW/STAM* * N16 .....59 F2
Priestley Wy *CRICK* NW2 ....52 A3
Prima Rd *BRXN/ST* SW9 ....118 A3
Primrose Cl *CAT* SE6 ....158 C5
Primrose Gdns *HAMP* NW3 ....73 E3
Primrose Hl *EMB* EC4Y 22 B5
Primrose Hill Rd *HAMP* NW3 ....73 E3
Primrose Hill Studios *CAMTN* NW1 ...74 A5
Primrose Ms *CAMTN* * NW1 ....73 F4
Primrose Rd *LEY* E10 ....62 B3
Primrose Sq *HOM* E9 ....78 C4
Primrose Wk *NWCR* SE14 ....121 E3
Primula St *SHB* W12 ....100 A1
Prince Albert Rd *STJWD* NW8 ....5 D1
Prince Albert Rd *STJWD* NW8 ....4 C1
Prince Arthur Rd *HAMP* NW3 ....72 C1
Prince Charles Dr *HDN* NW4 ....52 C2
Prince Charles Rd *BKHTH/KID* SE3 ...123 F4
Prince Consort Rd *SKENS* SW7 ......40 A2
Princedale Rd *NTGHL* W11 ....101 E2
Prince Edward Rd *HOM* E9 ....79 F3
Prince George Rd *STNW/STAM* N16 ...77 E1
Prince Henry Rd *CHARL* SE7........125 D3
Prince Imperial Rd
  WOOL/PLUM SE18 ....125 F4
Prince John Rd *ELTH/MOT* SE9 ....143 E3
Princelet St *WCHPL* E1 ....25 F2

Prince of Orange La *GNWCH* * SE10 ......**122** C3
Prince of Wales Dr *BTSEA* SW11 ......**115** E4
Prince of Wales Ga *SKENS* SW7 ......**28** C5
Prince of Wales Pas *CAMTN* * NW1 ......**7** E4
Prince of Wales Rd *BKHTH/KID* SE3 ....**123** F4
   CAN/RD E16 ......**94** C5
   KTTN NW5 ......**74** A3
Prince of Wales Ter *CHSWK* W4 ......**111** E1
   KENS W8 ......**39** D1
Prince Regent La *PLSTW* E13 ......**94** C3
Prince Regent Ms *CAMTN* NW1 ......**7** E4
Prince Rupert Rd *ELTH/MOT* SE9 ......**143** F2
Princes Av *MYFR/PICC* W1J.....**31** F3
Princes Av *ACT* W3 ......**98** A4
Princes Gdns *ACT* W3 ......**86** A4
   SKENS SW7......**40** B2
Princes Ga *SKENS* SW7 ......**40** B2
   SKENS SW7......**40** C1
Princes Gate Ct *SKENS* SW7 ......**40** A1
Princes Gate Ms *SKENS* SW7 ......**40** A1
Prince's Ms *BAY/PAD* W2 ......**26** B1
   HMSMTH * W6......**112** B1
Princes Pde *GLDGN* * NW11 ......**53** E1
Princes Park Av *GLDGN* NW11 ......**53** E1
Princes Pl *NTGHL* W11 ......**101** E2
Princes Ri *LEW* SE13 ......**122** C5
Princes Riverside Rd
   BERM/RHTH SE16.....**103** D2
Prince's Ms *STRHM/ESHN* SW14.....**129** D1
Princess Alice Wy *THMD* SE28 ......**109** D3
Princess Crs *FSBYPK* N4 ......**58** B4
Princess Louise Cl *BAY/PAD* W2......**16** B2
Princess May Rd *STNW/STAM* N16 ....**77** E1
Princess Ms *HAMP* **73** D3
Prince's Sq *BAY/PAD* W2 ......**26** B1
Princess Rd *CAMTN* NW1 ......**74** A5
   KIL/WHAMP NW6 ......**2** A1
Princess St *STHWK* SE1 ......**47** D3
Princes St *CONDST* W1S **19** D5
   LOTH EC2R **24** A5
Prince's St *PLSTW* E13.....**82** B5
Prince St *GNWCH* SE10.....**122** C3
Princethorpe Rd *SYD* SE26.....**157** D4
Princeton St *GINN* WC1R.....**21** E3
Priolo Rd *CHARL* SE7 ......**124** C1
Prior Bolton St *IS* N1 ......**76** B3
Prioress Rd *WNWD* SE27......**154** B3
Prioress St *STHWK* SE1 ......**48** B3
Prior Rd *IL* IG1.....**66** A5
Prior St *GNWCH* SE10 ......**122** C3
The Priory *BKHTH/KID* SE3 ......**141** F1
Priory Av *CHSWK* W4 ......**99** E4
Priory Ct *BLKFR* * EC4V **23** D5
   VX/NE SW8 ......**117** D4
Priory Gdns *BARN* SW13 ......**129** F1
   CHSWK * W4 ......**99** E5
   HGT N6......**55** D3
Priory Green Est *IS* N1 ......**9** E1
Priory La *CLAP* SW4.....**117** E4
Priory La *PUT/ROE* SW15 ......**129** F3
Priory Leas *ELTH/MOT* * SE9 ......**161** E1
Priory Pk *BKHTH/KID* SE3 ......**141** F1
Priory Park Av *KIL/WHAMP* NW6 ......**85** D4
Priory Rd *BARK* IG11 ......**99** D4
   CHSWK W4 ......**83** D5
   EHAM E6 ......**72** B4
   KIL/WHAMP NW6 ......**110** A2
   RCH/KEW TW9......**110** A2
Priory St *BOW* E3.....**92** B2
Priory Ter *KIL/WHAMP* NW6 ......**72** B5
Priory Wk *WBPTN* SW10 ......**114** C1
Pritchard's Rd *BETH* E2......**90** A1
Priter Rd *BERM/RHTH* * SE16.....**102** A4

Probert Rd *BRXS/STRHM* SW2 .....**136** A3
Probyn Rd *BRXS/STRHM* SW2 ......**154** B2
Procter St *GINN* WC1R.....**21** E3
The Promenade *CHSWK* W4.....**111** E4
Promenade Approach Rd
   CHSWK W4.....**111** E3
Prospect Cl *SYD* SE26.....**156** B3
Prospect Cottages
   WAND/EARL SW18.....**132** A2
Prospect Pl *CHSWK* W4 ......**111** D1
   CRICK NW2.....**53** F5
   WAP E1W.....**102** C2
Prospect Rd *CRICK* NW2 .....**53** F5
Prospect St *BERM/RHTH* SE16.....**102** B3
Prospect V *CHARL* SE7.....**107** E5
Prospero Rd *ARCH* N19.....**57** D3
Prothero Rd *FUL/PGN* SW6 ......**113** E3
Prout Gv *WLSDN* NW10.....**69** E1
Prout Rd *CLPT* E5.....**60** B5
Providence Cl *HOM* * E9.....**79** D5
Providence Ct *MYFR/PKLN* W1K **30** B1
Providence Pl *IS* * N1 ......**76** B1
Providence Row Cl *BETH* E2 .....**90** B2
Providence Sq *STHWK* SE1 ......**36** C5
Providence Yd *BETH* * E2.....**90** A2
Provost Est *IS* N1.....**12** A3
Provost Rd *HAMP* NW3.....**73** F4
Provost St *IS* N1.....**12** A2
Prowse Pl *CAMTN* NW1.....**74** C4
Prusom St *WAP* E1W.....**102** B2
Pudding La *MON* EC3R **36** B1
Pudding Mill La *SRTFD* E15.....**80** D5
Puddle Dock *BLKFR* EC4V **35** D1
Pulborough Rd *WAND/EARL* SW18 ..**131** F5
Pulford St *SEVS/STOTM* N15.....**95** E2
Pulleyns Av *EHAM* E6.....**130** C4
Pullman Gdns *PUT/ROE* SW15 ......**130** C4
Pullman Ms *LEE/GVPK* SE12 ......**160** B3
Pullman Pl *ELTH/MOT* SE9 ......**143** E3
Pulross Rd *BRXN/ST* SW9 ......**135** F1
Pulteney Cl *BOW* E3.....**79** F5
Pulton Pl *FUL/PGN* SW6 ......**114** A3
Puma Ct *WCHPL* E1 .....**25** E2
Pump Ct *EMB* * EC4Y.....**22** A5
Pumping Station Rd *CHSWK* W4 ...**111** E3
Pump La *NWCR* SE14.....**120** C3
Punderson's Gdns *BETH* E2 .....**90** B2
Purbeck Dr *CRICK* NW2.....**53** D4
Purbrook St *STHWK* SE1 ......**49** D2
Purcell Crs *FUL/PGN* * SW6.....**113** D2
Purcell Ms *WLSDN* * NW10 ......**69** E4
Purcell St *IS* N1.....**12** C1
Purchese St *CAMTN* NW1 ......**8** A1
Purdy St *BOW* E3.....**92** B3
Purelake Ms *LEW* * SE13 ......**141** D1
Purland Rd *THMD* SE28.....**109** F3
Purley Av *CRICK* NW2.....**53** E4
Purley Pl *IS* N1.....**76** B4
Purneys Rd *ELTH/MOT* SE9.....**143** D2
Pursers Cross Rd *FUL/PGN* * SW6 ..**113** F4
Purves Rd *WLSDN* NW10.....**88** B2
Putney Br *PUT/ROE* SW15 ......**131** E1
Putney Bridge Ap *PUT/ROE* SW15 ...**131** E1
Putney Bridge Rd *PUT/ROE* SW15 ...**131** E2
Putney Common *PUT/ROE* SW15 ...**130** C1
Putney Ex *PUT/ROE* * SW15 ......**131** D2
Putney Heath *PUT/ROE* SW15 ......**130** B4
Putney Heath La *PUT/ROE* SW15 ...**131** D4
Putney High St *PUT/ROE* SW15 ......**131** E2
Putney HI *PUT/ROE* SW15.....**131** D4
Putney Park Av *PUT/ROE* SW15 ......**130** A2
Putney Park La *PUT/ROE* SW15.....**130** B2
Pymers Md *DUL* SE21.....**154** C1
Pyrland Rd *HBRY* N5.....**77** D2
Pyrmont Gv *WNWD* SE27.....**154** B3
Pyrmont Rd *CHSWK* W4.....**110** A2
Pytchley Rd *CMBW* SE5 ......**137** E1

Q

The Quadrangle BAY/PAD W2	16	C4
HNHL * SE24	136	C4
WBPTN * SW18	114	C4
The Quadrant NKENS * W10	89	D3
Quadrant Ar REGST W1B	31	F2
Quadrant Gv HAMP NW3	73	F2
Quaggy Wk BKHTH/KID SE3	142	A2
Quainton St WLSDN NW10	51	D5
Quakers Pl FSTGT E7	83	D2
Quaker St WCHPL E1	25	E1
Quality Ct LINN WC2A	22	A4
Quantock Gdns CRICK * NW2	53	D4
Quarrendon St FUL/PGN SW6	114	A4
Quarry Rd WAND/EARL SW18	132	C4
Quartermile La LEY E10	80	B1
Quay House POP/IOD * E14	104	A3
Quebec Ms MBLAR W1H	17	F5
Quebec Rd GNTH/NBYPK IG2	66	C2
Quebec Wy BERM/RHTH SE16	103	D3
Queen Anne Ms CAVSQ/HST W1G	19	D3
Queen Anne Rd HOM E9	79	D3
Queen Anne's Gdns CHSWK W4	99	E4
Queen Anne's Ga STJSPK SW1H	44	A1
Queen Anne's Gv CHSWK W4	99	E4
Queen Anne's St CAVSQ/HST W1G	18	C3
Queen Anne Ter WAP * E1W	102	B1
Queen Caroline St HMSMTH W6	112	C1
Queen Caroline St HMSMTH W6	112	C1
Queen Elizabeth Buildings		
EMB * EC4Y	34	A1
Queen Elizabeth's Cl STNW/STAM N16	59	D4
Queen Elizabeth St STHWK SE1	37	D5
Queen Elizabeth's Wk		
STNW/STAM N16	59	D3
Queen Elizabeth Wk BARN SW13	112	A4
Queenhithe BLKFR EC4V	35	F2
Queen Margaret's Gv IS N1	77	E2
Queen Mother Ga BAY/PAD W2	30	B4
Queensberry Ms West SKENS * SW7	40	A4
Queensberry Pl FSTGT E7	83	D2
SKENS SW7	40	A4
Queensberry Wy SKENS * SW7	40	A4
Queensborough Ms BAY/PAD * W2	27	E1
Queensborough Pas BAY/PAD W2	27	E1
Queensborough Studios		
BAY/PAD W2	27	E1
Queensborough Ter BAY/PAD W2	27	D1
Queensbridge Rd HACK E8	77	F3
Queensbury Rd CDALE/KGS NW9	51	D2
Queensbury St IS N1	76	C4
Queens Circ VX/NE SW8	116	B3
Queen's Club Gdns WKENS W14	113	E2
WKENS * W14	113	E2
Queens Club Ter WKENS * W14	113	E2
Queen's Crs KTTN NW5	74	A2
Queenscroft Rd ELTH/MOT SE9	143	D3
Queensdale Crs NTGHL W11	101	D2
Queensdale Pl NTGHL W11	101	D2
Queensdale Rd NTGHL W11	101	D2
Queensdale Wk NTGHL W11	101	D2
Queens Down Rd CLPT E5	78	B1
Queen's Dr FSBYPK N4	58	B4
LEY E10	62	A2
Queen's Elm Sq CHEL SW3	115	D3
Queen's Gdns BAY/PAD W2	27	E1
Queens Garth SE23	156	C2
Queens Ga SKENS SW7	39	F1
Queensgate Gdns PUT/ROE SW15	130	B2
Queen's Gate Gdns SKENS SW7	39	E3
Queens Gate Ms SKENS SW7	39	E2
Queensgate Pl KIL/WHAMP NW6	72	A4
Queen's Gate Pl SKENS SW7	39	F3
Queen's Gate Place Ms SKENS SW7	39	F3
Queen's Gate Ter SKENS SW7	39	E2
Queen's Gv STJWD NW8	73	E1
Queen's Head St IS N1	76	B5
Queensland Pl HOLWY N7	76	A1
Queensland Rd HOLWY N7	76	A1
Queensmead STJWD NW8	73	D5
Queensmere Cl WIM/MER SW19	149	D2
Queensmere Rd WIM/MER SW19	149	D2
Queen's Ms BAY/PAD W2	26	C1
Queensmill Rd FUL/PGN SW6	113	D3
Queens Pde CRICK * NW2	70	C3
Queen's Ride BARN SW13	130	A1
Queen's Rd BARK IG11	84	C4
MORT/ESHN SW14	129	D1
PECK SE15	120	C4
PLSTW E13	82	B5
WALTH E17	61	F1
WAN E11	63	E2
WIM/MER SW19	150	B5
Queen's Rd West PLSTW E13	94	A1
Queen's Rw WALW SE17	119	D2
WALW * SE17	119	D2
Queens Ter PLSTW E13	82	B5
STJWD NW8	73	D5
WCHPL * E1	90	C3
Queensthorpe Ms SYD * SE26	157	D4
Queensthorpe Rd SYD SE26	157	D4
Queenstown Rd VX/NE SW8	116	B5
Queen St MANHO EC4N	23	F5
MYFR/PICC W1J	30	C3
Queen Street Pl CANST EC4R	35	F2
Queensville Rd CLAP SW4	135	D5
Queens Wk CDALE/KGS NW9	50	C5
Queensway BAY/PAD W2	15	D4
Queenswood Gdns WAN E11	64	A3
Queenswood Rd BFN/LL DA15	145	E3
FSTH SE23	157	E3
Queen's Wood Rd HGT N6	56	B1
Queen's Yd FITZ W1T	19	F1
Queen Victoria St BLKFR EC4V	34	C1
MANHO EC4N	23	F5
Queen Victoria Ter WAP * E1W	102	B1
Quemerford Rd HOLWY N7	75	F2
Quentin Pl LEW SE13	141	E1
Quentin Rd BKHTH/KID SE3	141	E1
Quernmore Rd FSBYPK N4	58	A1
Querrin St FUL/PGN SW6	114	C5
Quex Ms KIL/WHAMP NW6	72	A5
Quex Rd KIL/WHAMP NW6	72	A5
Quick Rd CHSWK W4	111	E1
Quick St IS N1	11	D2
Quickswood HAMP NW3	73	E4
Quill St FSBYPK N4	58	A5
Quilp St STHWK SE1	35	E5
Quilter St BETH E2	90	A2
WOOL/PLUM SE18	127	F1
Quinton St WAND/EARL SW18	150	C2
Quixley St POP/IOD E14	105	D1
Quorn Rd EDUL SE22	137	E2

R

Rabbit Rw KENS * W8	26	B3
Rabbits Rd MNPK E12	83	E1
Raby St POP/IOD * E14	91	E5
Racton Rd FUL/PGN SW6	114	A2
Radbourne Cl CLPT E5	79	D1
Radbourne Rd BAL SW12	134	C5
Radcliffe Av WLSDN NW10	88	A1
Radcliffe St STHWK SE1	49	D2
Radcot St LBTH SE11	118	A1
Raddington Rd NKENS W10	89	E4
Radfield Wy ELTH/MOT SE9	145	D5
Radford Est WLSDN * NW10	87	E2
Radford Rd LEW SE13	140	C4
Radford Wy BARK IG11	97	F2
Radipole Rd FUL/PGN SW6	113	F4

Radland Rd CAN/RD E16..........94 A5
Radlet Av FSTH SE23..........156 B3
Radlett CI FSTGT E7..........81 F3
Radlett PI STJWD NW8..........73 E5
Radley Av GDMY/SEVK IG3..........85 F1
Radley Ct BERM/RHTH SE16..........103 D3
Radley Ms KENS W8..........38 B3
Radley Sq CLPT * E5..........60 C4
Radley Ter CAN/RD * E16..........93 F4
Radlix Rd LEY E10..........62 A3
Radnor Ms BAY/PAD W2..........16 B5
Radnor PI BAY/PAD W2..........16 C5
Radnor Rd KIL/WHAMP NW6..........71 E5
  PECK SE15..........120 A3
Radnor St FSBYE EC1V..........11 F4
Radnor Ter WKENS W14..........101 F5
Radnor Wk CHEL SW3..........115 E1
Radnor Wy WLSDN NW10..........86 B3
Radstock St BTSEA * SW11..........115 E3
Raeburn CI EFNCH N2..........54 C1
Raeburn Rd BFN/LL DA15..........145 E4
Raeburn St BRXS/STRHM SW2..........135 E2
Raglan Rd WOOL/PLUM SE18..........126 C1
Raglan St KTTN NW5..........74 B3
Ragley CI ACT W3..........98 C3
Railey Ms KTTN NW5..........74 C2
Railton Rd HNHL SE24..........136 A3
Railway Ap STHWK SE1..........36 B3
Railway Ar BRXN/ST * SW9..........136 A2
Railway Av BERM/RHTH SE16..........102 C3
Railway Cottages SHB * W12..........100 C3
  SRTFD * E15..........93 E1
  WIM/MER * SW19..........150 B4
Railway Gv NWCR SE14..........121 F3
Railway Ri EDUL SE22..........137 E2
Railway Side BARN SW13..........129 E1
Railway Station Whf LEY * E10..........61 E3
Railway St IS N1..........9 D2
Railway Ter LEW SE13..........140 B3
Rainborough CI WBLY HA9..........68 C3
Rainbow Av POP/IOD E14..........122 B1
Rainbow St CMBW SE5..........119 E3
Raine St WAP E1W..........102 B2
Rainham CI BTSEA SW11..........133 E4
  ELTH/MOT SE9..........145 E4
Rainham Rd WLSDN NW10..........88 C2
Rainhill Wy BOW E3..........92 A2
Rainsborough Av DEPT SE8..........103 E5
Rainsford Rd WLSDN NW10..........86 B2
Rainsford St BAY/PAD W2..........16 C4
Rainton Rd CHARL SE7..........124 A1
Rainville Rd HMSMTH W6..........112 C2
Raleana Rd POP/IOD E14..........104 C2
Raleigh Ms IS N1..........76 B5
Raleigh St IS N1..........76 B5
Ralston CI CHEL SW3..........115 F1
Ramac Wy CHARL SE7..........106 B5
Rambler CI STRHM/NOR SW16..........152 C4
Rame CI TOOT SW17..........152 A5
Ramillies CI BRXS/STRHM SW2..........135 E4
Ramillies PI SOHO/CST W1F..........19 E5
Ramillies Rd CHSWK W4..........99 D4
Ramillies St SOHO/CST W1F..........90 B5
Rampart St WCHPL E1..........90 B5
Rampayne St PIM SW1V..........98 C4
Ramsay Rd ACT W3..........81 F1
  FSTGT E7..........81 F1
Ramsdale Rd TOOT SW17..........152 A5
Ramsden Ga BAL * SW12..........134 B5
Ramsden Rd BAL SW12..........134 A5
Ramsey CI CDALE/KGS NW9..........51 F1
Ramsey St BETH E2..........90 A3
Ramsey Wk IS * N1..........77 D3
Ramsgate St HACK * E8..........77 F3
Ram St WAND/EARL SW18..........132 B3
Rancliffe Gdns ELTH/MOT SE9..........143 E2
Rancliffe Rd EHAM E6..........95 E1
Randall Av CRICK NW2..........51 E4

Randall CI BTSEA SW11..........115 E4
Randall PI GNWCH SE10..........122 C3
Randall Rd LBTH SE11..........117 F1
Randall Rw LBTH SE11..........45 E5
Randall's Rd IS N1..........75 E5
Randisbourne Gdns CAT * SE6..........158 B3
Randlesdown Rd CAT SE6..........158 A4
Randolph Ap CAN/RD E16..........94 C5
Randolph Av KIL/WHAMP NW6..........2 C1
Randolph CI KUTN/CMB * KT2..........146 C5
Randolph Crs MV/WKIL W9..........15 E1
Randolph Gdns KIL/WHAMP NW6..........2 C1
Randolph Ms MV/WKIL W9..........15 F1
Randolph Rd MV/WKIL W9..........15 E1
Randolph St CAMTN NW1..........74 C4
Ranelagh Av BARN SW13..........112 A5
  FUL/PGN SW6..........131 F1
Ranelagh Gdns CHSWK W4..........110 C3
  FUL/PGN SW6..........131 E1
  IL IG1..........66 A3
Ranelagh Gv BGVA SW1W..........116 A1
Ranelagh Rd EHAM E6..........84 A5
  PIM SW1V..........116 C1
  WAN E11..........81 E1
  WLSDN NW10..........87 F1
Rangeworth PI BFN/LL DA15..........163 F5
Rangoon St TWRH * EC3N..........25 E5
Ranmere St BAL SW12..........152 B1
Rannoch Rd HMSMTH W6..........112 C2
Rannock Av CDALE/KGS NW9..........51 D2
Ransom Rd CHARL * SE7..........124 C1
Ranston St CAMTN NW1..........71 F1
Ranulf Rd CRICK NW2..........71 F1
Ranwell CI BOW * E3..........79 F5
Raphael St SKENS SW7..........41 E1
Rastell Av BAL SW12..........153 D2
Ratcliffe CI LEE/GVPK SE12..........142 A5
Ratcliffe Cross St WCHPL * E1..........91 D5
Ratcliffe La POP/IOD E14..........91 E5
Ratcliff Rd FSTGT E7..........82 C2
Rathbone Market CAN/RD * E16..........93 F4
Rathbone PI FITZ W1T..........20 A3
Rathbone St CAN/RD E16..........93 F3
  FITZ W1T..........19 F3
Rathfern Rd FSTH SE23..........157 F1
Rathgar Rd BRXN/ST SW9..........136 B1
Rathmell Dr CLAP SW4..........135 D4
Rathmore Rd CHARL SE7..........124 B1
Rattray Rd BRXS/STRHM SW2..........136 A2
Raul Rd PECK SE15..........120 A5
Raveley St KTTN NW5..........74 C1
Ravencroft Crs ELTH/MOT SE9..........161 F3
Ravenet St BTSEA SW11..........116 B4
Ravenfield Rd TOOT SW17..........151 F3
Ravenhill Rd PLSTW E13..........82 C5
Ravenna Rd PUT/ROE SW15..........131 D3
Raven Rw WCHPL E1..........90 B4
Ravensbourne Pk BROCKY SE4..........140 A5
Ravensbourne Park Crs CAT SE6..........139 F5
Ravensbourne PI DEPT SE8..........122 B5
Ravensbourne Rd FSTH SE23..........139 F5
Ravensbury Rd WAND/EARL SW18..........150 B2
Ravensbury Ter WAND/EARL SW18..........150 B2
Ravenscar Rd BMLY BR1..........159 E4
Ravenscourt Av HMSMTH W6..........100 A5
Ravenscourt Gdns HMSMTH W6..........99 F5
Ravenscourt Pk HMSMTH W6..........100 A5
Ravenscourt PI HMSMTH W6..........100 B5
Ravenscourt Rd HMSMTH W6..........100 B5
Ravenscourt Sq HMSMTH W6..........100 A4
Ravenscroft Av GLDGN NW11..........53 F2
Ravenscroft CI CAN/RD E16..........94 A4
Ravenscroft Rd CAN/RD E16..........94 A4
  CHSWK W4..........98 C5
Ravenscroft St BETH E2..........13 F2
Ravensdale Rd STNW/STAM N16..........59 F2
Ravensdon St LBTH SE11..........118 A1
Ravenshaw St KIL/WHAMP NW6..........71 F2

Ravenslea Rd *BAL* SW12 ....**133** F5
Ravensmede Wy *CHSWK* W4 ....**99** F5
Ravens Ms *BKHTH/KID* * SE3 ......**142** A3
Ravenstone Rd *CDALE/KGS* * NW9 ......**51** F1
Ravenstone St *BAL* SW12 ....**152** A1
Ravens Wy *LEE/GVPK* SE12 ......**142** A3
Ravenswood Rd *BAL* SW12 ....**134** B5
Ravensworth Rd *ELTH/MOT* SE9 ......**161** F4
   WLSDN NW10 ....**88** B2
Ravent Rd *LBTH* SE11 ....**45** F5
Ravey St *SDTCH* EC2A **12** C5
Ravine Gv *WOOL/PLUM* SE18 ......**127** E2
Rav Pinter Cl *STNW/STAM* N16 ......**59** E2
Rawlings St *CHEL* SW3 ....**41** E4
Rawreth Wk *IS* * N1 ....**76** C5
Rawson St *BTSEA* SW11 ....**116** A4
Rawsthorne Cl *CAN/RD* E16 ......**107** F2
Rawstone Pl *FSBYE* * EC1V **10** C3
Rawstorne St *FSBYE* EC1V **10** C3
Ray Bell Ct *BROCKY* * SE4 ......**121** F5
Raydon St *KTTN* NW5 ....**56** B4
Rayford Av *LEE/GVPK* SE12 ......**141** F5
Rayleas Cl *WOOL/PLUM* SE18 ......**126** B4
Rayleigh Rd *CAN/RD* E16 ......**106** B2
Raymere Gdns *WOOL/PLUM* SE18 ......**127** D3
Raymond Buildings *GINN* * WC1R **21** F2
Raymond Cl *SYD* SE26 ......**156** C5
Raymond Rd *GNTH/NBYPK* IG2 ......**67** D2
   PLSTW E13 ....**82** C4
Raymouth Rd *BERM/RHTH* SE16 ......**102** B5
Rayner's Rd *PUT/ROE* SW15 ......**131** E3
Raynes Av *WAN* E11 ....**64** C2
Raynham Rd *HMSMTH* W6 ......**100** B5
Raynor Pl *IS* N1 ....**76** C5
Ray St *CLKNW* EC1R **22** B1
Ray Street Br *CLKNW* * EC1R **22** B1
Reachview Cl *CAMTN* NW1 ......**74** C4
Reading La *HACK* E8 ....**78** B3
Reads Cl *IL* IG1 ....**66** B5
Reapers Cl *CAMTN* NW1 ......**75** D1
Reardon Pth *WAP* E1W **102** B2
Reardon St *WAP* E1W **102** B2
Reaston St *NWCR* SE14 ......**120** C3
Reckitt Rd *CHSWK* W4 ......**111** E1
Record St *PECK* SE15 ......**120** C2
Recovery St *TOOT* SW17 ......**151** E4
Recreation Rd *SYD* SE26 ......**157** D4
Rector St *IS* N1 ....**76** C5
Rectory Field Crs *CHARL* SE7 ......**124** C3
Rectory Gv *CLAP* SW4 ......**134** C1
Rectory La *TOOT* SW17 ......**152** A5
Rectory Orch *WIM/MER* SW19 ......**149** E4
Rectory Pl *WOOL/PLUM* SE18 ......**108** A5
Rectory Rd *BARN* SW13 ......**112** A5
   MNPK E12 ....**83** F2
   STNW/STAM N16 ....**59** F4
Rectory Sq *WCHPL* E1 ......**91** D4
Reculver Rd *BERM/RHTH* SE16 ......**120** C1
Red Anchor Cl *CHEL* * SW3 ......**115** D2
Redan Pl *BAY/PAD* W2 ......**14** C5
Redan St *WKENS* W14 ......**101** D4
Redan Ter *CMBW* SE5 ......**118** B5
Red Barracks Rd *WOOL/PLUM* SE18 ......**107** F5
Redberry Gv *SYD* SE26 ......**156** C3
Redbridge Gdns *CMBW* SE5 ......**119** E3
Redbridge La East *REDBR* IG4 ......**65** D1
Redbridge La West *WAN* E11 ......**64** B1
Redburn St *CHEL* SW3 ......**115** F2
Redcar St *CMBW* * SE5 ......**118** C3
Redcastle Cl *WCHPL* E1 ......**102** C1
Redchurch St *BETH* E2 ......**13** E5
Redcliffe Cl *ECT* SW5 ......**114** B1
Redcliffe Gdns *IL* IG1 ......**66** A3
   WBPTN SW10 ....
Redcliffe Ms *WBPTN* SW10 ......**114** A1
Redcliffe Pl *WBPTN* SW10 ......**114** B2
Redcliffe Rd *WBPTN* SW10 ......**114** C1
Redcliffe Sq *WBPTN* SW10 ......**114** B1

Redcliffe St *WBPTN* * SW10 ......**114** B2
Redclyffe Rd *EHAM* E6 ......**82** C5
Redcross Wy *STHWK* SE1 ......**35** F5
Reddins Rd *PECK* SE15 ......**120** A3
Rede Pl *BAY/PAD* W2 ......**14** B5
Redesdale St *CHEL* SW3 ......**115** F2
Redfern Rd *CAT* SE6 ......**140** C5
   WLSDN NW10 ....**69** E4
Redfield La *ECT* SW5 ......**38** C5
Redford Wk *IS* * N1 ......**76** B5
Redgate Ter *PUT/ROE* SW15 ......**131** D4
Redgrave Rd *PUT/ROE* SW15 ......**131** D2
Redgrave Ter *BETH* * E2 ......**90** A2
Redhall Ter *ACT* * W3 ......**98** A1
Red Hl *CHST* BR7 ......**162** A5
Redhill St *CAMTN* NW1 ......**7** D2
Redington Gdns *HAMP* NW3 ......**72** B1
Redington Rd *HAMP* NW3 ......**54** B5
Redlands Wy *BRXS/STRHM* SW2 ......**135** E5
Red Lion Cl *WALW* SE17 ......**119** D2
Red Lion Ct *FLST/FETLN* EC4A **22** B5
Red Lion La *WOOL/PLUM* * SE18 ......**126** A4
Red Lion Pl *WOOL/PLUM* * SE18 ......**126** A4
Red Lion Rw *WALW* SE17 ......**118** C2
Red Lion Sq *BMSBY* WC1N **21** E3
   WAND/EARL * SW18 ......**132** A3
Red Lion St *GINN* WC1R **21** E3
Red Lion Yd *MYFR/PKLN* * W1K **30** B3
Redman's Rd *WCHPL* E1 ......**90** C4
Redmead La *WAP* E1W **102** A2
Redmore Rd *HMSMTH* W6 ......**100** B5
Red Pl *MYFR/PKLN* W1K **30** A1
Red Post Hl *HNHL* SE24 ......**137** D3
Redriffe Rd *PLSTW* E13 ......**93** F1
Redriff Rd *BERM/RHTH* SE16 ......**103** E4
Redruth Rd *HOM* E9 ......**78** C5
Redstart Cl *EHAM* E6 ......**95** E4
   NWCR * SE14 ......**121** E3
Redvers St *IS* N1 ......**13** D3
Redwald Rd *CLPT* E5 ......**79** D1
Redwood Cl *BERM/RHTH* SE16 ......**103** E2
Reece Ms *SKENS* SW7 ......**40** A4
Reed Cl *CAN/RD* E16 ......**94** A4
   LEE/GVPK SE12 ......**142** A3
Reedham St *PECK* * SE15 ......**120** A5
Reedholm Vls *STNW/STAM* N16 ......**77** D1
Reed's Pl *CAMTN* NW1 ......**74** C4
Reedworth St *LBTH* SE11 ......**46** B5
Reesland Cl *MNPK* E12 ......**84** A3
Rees St *IS* N1 ......**76** C5
Reets Farm Cl *CDALE/KGS* NW9 ......**51** E1
Reeves Av *CDALE/KGS* NW9 ......**51** D2
Reeves Ms *MYFR/PKLN* W1K **30** A2
Reeves Rd *BOW* E3 ......**92** B3
   WOOL/PLUM SE18 ......**126** B2
Reform St *BTSEA* SW11 ......**115** F5
Regal Cl *WCHPL* E1 ......**90** A4
Regal La *CAMTN* NW1 ......**74** A5
Regan Wy *IS* N1 ......**12** C3
Regency Lawn *KTTN* * NW5 ......**56** B5
Regency Ms *WLSDN* NW10 ......**70** A3
Regency Pde *HAMP* * NW3 ......**73** D4
Regency Pl *WEST* * SW1P **44** A4
Regency St *WEST* SW1P **44** B5
Regency Ter *HGT* * N6 ......**55** F2
   SKENS * SW7 ......**115** D1
Regent Pde *STNW/STAM* * N16 ......**59** F2
Regent Pl *WIM/MER* SW19 ......**150** C5
Regent Rd *HNHL* SE24 ......**136** B4
Regents Bridge Gdns *VX/NE* SW8 ......**117** E2
Regents Ms *STJWD* NW8 ......**3** F1
Regents Pk *CAMTN* NW1 ......**6** B3
Regent's Park Rd *HAMP* NW3 ......**73** F5
Regent's Park Ter *CAMTN* NW1 ......**74** B5
Regents Plaza *KIL/WHAMP* * NW6 ......**2** C1
Regent Sq *BOW* E3 ......**92** B2
   STPAN WC1H **9** D4

Regent's Rw *HACK* E8 ....78 A5
Regent St *CHSWK* W4 ....110 A1
   CONDST W1S 19 E5
   STJS SW1Y 32 A2
   WLSDN NW10 ....89 D2
Regents Whf *IS* * N1 ....9 E1
Reginald Rd *DEPT* SE8. ....122 A3
   FSTGT E7 ....82 A4
Reginald Sq *DEPT* SE8. ....122 A3
Regina Rd *FSBYPK* N4 ....57 F3
Regis Rd *KTTN* NW5 ....74 B2
Regnart Buildings *CAMTN* NW1. ....7 F4
Reidhaven Rd *WOOL/PLUM* SE18 ...109 E5
Reigate Rd *BMLY* BR1 ....160 A3
   GDMY/SEVK IG3. ....67 F4
Reighton Rd *CLPT* E5 ....60 A5
Relay Rd *SHB* W12 ....100 C1
Relf Rd *PECK* SE15 ....138 A1
Reliance Ar *BRXN/ST* * SW9 ....136 A2
Relton Ms *SKENS* SW7 ....41 D2
Rembrandt Cl *BCVA* * SW1W 116 A1
   POP/IOD E14 ....105 D4
Rembrandt Rd *LEW* SE13 ....141 E2
Remington Rd *EHAM* E6. ....95 E5
   SEVS/STOTM N15 ....59 D1
Remington St *IS* N1 ....11 D2
Remnant St *HOL/ALD* WC2B. 21 E4
Remus Rd *BOW* E3 ....80 A4
Rendlesham Rd *CLPT* E5. ....78 A1
Renforth St *BERM/RHTH* SE16. ....102 C3
Renfrew Cl *EHAM* E6. ....108 A1
Renfrew Rd *LBTH* SE11 ....46 C4
Rennell St *LEW* SE13 ....140 C1
Rennets Cl *ELTH/MOT* SE9 ....145 D3
Rennets Wood Rd *ELTH/MOT* SE9 ..145 D3
Rennie Est *BERM/RHTH* SE16. ....102 B5
Rennie St *STHWK* SE1 ....34 C3
Renters Av *HDN* NW4 ....52 C1
Renton Cl *BRXS/STRHM* * SW2 .....135 F4
Rephidim St *STHWK* SE1 ....48 B3
Replingham Rd *WAND/EARL* SW18 ..149 F1
Reporton Rd *FUL/PGN* SW6 ....113 E4
Repository Rd *WOOL/PLUM* SE18 ...125 F2
Repton St *POP/IOD* E14 ....91 E5
Reservoir Rd *BROCKY* SE4 ....121 E5
Resolution Way *DEPT* SE8. ....122 A3
Restell Cl *BKHTH/KID* SE3 ....123 E2
Reston Pl *SKENS* SW7 ....39 E1
Restons Crs *ELTH/MOT* SE9 ....145 D4
Retford St *BETH* * E2. ....13 D2
The Retreat *BARN* SW13 ....129 E1
Retreat Pl *HOM* E9. ....78 C3
Reunion Sq *WAP* * E1W 102 B1
Reveley Sq *BERM/RHTH* SE16 ....103 F3
Revell Ri *WOOL/PLUM* SE18 ....127 F2
Revelon Rd *BROCKY* SE4 ....139 E2
Revelstoke Rd *WIM/MER* SW19 ......150 A3
Reventlow Rd *ELTH/MOT* SE9 ....162 C1
Reverdy Rd *STHWK* SE1 ....102 A5
Review Rd *CRICK* NW2 ....51 F4
Rewell St *FUL/PGN* * SW6 ....114 C3
Rex Pl *MYFR/PKLN* W1K 30 B3
Reydon Av *WAN* E11 ....64 C1
Reynard Pl *NWCR* * SE14 ....121 E2
Reynolds Av *MNPK* E12. ....84 A2
Reynolds Cl *GLDGN* NW11 ....54 B2
Reynolds Pl *BKHTH/KID* SE3. ....124 B3
Reynolds Rd *CHSWK* W4 ....98 C4
   PECK SE15 ....138 C3
Rheidol Ms *IS* N1 ....11 D1
Rheidol Ter *IS* N1 ....11 D1
Rhoda St *BETH* E2 ....13 F5
Rhodesia Rd *BRXN/ST* SW9 ....117 E5
   WAN E11. ....63 D4
Rhodes St *HOLWY* N7 ....75 F2
Rhodeswell Rd *BOW* E3 ....91 E4
Rhondda Gv *BOW* E3 ....91 E2
Rhyl St *KTTN* NW5 ....74 A3

Ribblesdale Rd *STRHM/NOR* SW16 ...152 B5
Ribbon Dance Ms *CMBW* SE5. ....119 D4
Ricardo St *POP/IOD* E14 ....92 B5
Ricards Rd *WIM/MER* SW19 ....149 F5
Richard Cl *WOOL/PLUM* SE18. ....107 E5
Richard House Dr *CAN/RD* E16 ....95 D5
Richardson Cl *HACK* * E8. ....77 F5
Richardson Rd *SRTFD* * E15 ....93 E1
Richardson's Ms *FITZ* W1T 19 E1
Richard's Pl *CHEL* SW3 ....41 D4
Richard St *WCHPL* E1 ....90 B5
Richbell Pl *BMSBY* WC1N 21 E2
Richborne Ter *VX/NE* SW8 ....117 F3
Richborough Rd *CRICK* NW2 ....71 D1
Riches Rd *IL* IG1 ....66 C4
Richford Ga *HMSMTH* * W6 ....100 C4
Richford Rd *SRTFD* E15. ....81 F5
Richford St *HMSMTH* W6 ....100 C3
Richmond Av *IS* N1 ....75 F5
   WLSDN NW10 ....70 B3
Richmond Buildings *SOHO/CST* W1F ...20 A5
Richmond Cl *WALTH* E17. ....61 F1
Richmond Crs *IS* N1 ....75 F5
Richmond Gv *IS* N1 ....76 B4
Richmond Ms *SOHO/CST* W1F 20 A5
Richmond Park Rd
   MORT/ESHN SW14 ....128 C3
Richmond Pl *WOOL/PLUM* SE18 .....108 C5
Richmond Rd *FSTGT* E7. ....82 B2
   HACK E8. ....77 F4
   IL IG1. ....66 C5
   SEVS/STOTM N15. ....59 E1
   WAN E11. ....63 D4
Richmond Ter *PLSTW* E13. ....94 A1
Richmond Ter *WHALL* SW1A 32 C5
Richmond Wy *SHB* W12 ....101 D3
   WAN E11. ....64 A4
Richmount Gdns *BKHTH/KID* SE3 ...142 A3
Rich St *POP/IOD* E14 ....103 F1
Rickard Cl *BRXS/STRHM* SW2 ....154 A1
Rickett St *FUL/PGN* SW6 ....114 A2
Rickman St *WCHPL* E1 ....90 C3
Rick Roberts Wy *SRTFD* E15. ....81 D5
Rickthorne Rd *ARCH* N19 ....57 E4
Riddons Rd *LEE/GVPK* SE12 ....160 C3
Rideout St *WOOL/PLUM* SE18 ....107 F5
Rider Cl *BFN/LL* DA15. ....145 E4
Ridgdale St *BOW* E3 ....92 A1
Ridgebrook Rd *ELTH/MOT* SE9 ....142 C2
Ridge Cl *THMD* SE28 ....109 D3
Ridge Hl *GLDGN* NW11. ....53 E5
Ridge Rd *CEND/HSY/T* N8. ....57 F1
   CRICK NW2. ....53 F5
   GLDGN NW11. ....53 F3
The Ridgeway *ACT* W3 ....98 A4
   GLDGN NW11. ....53 F3
Ridgeway Dr *BMLY* BR1 ....160 B4
Ridgeway East *BFN/LL* DA15. ....145 F3
Ridgeway West *BFN/LL* DA15. ....145 E3
Ridgewell Cl *IS* N1. ....157 F4
   SYD SE26. ....157 D1
Ridgmount Gdns *GWRST* WC1E. 20 A2
Ridgmount Rd *WAND/EARL* SW18 ...132 B3
Ridgmount St *GWRST* WC1E. 20 A2
Ridgway Rd *BRXN/ST* SW9 ....136 B3
Ridgwell Rd *CAN/RD* E16 ....94 C4
The Riding *GLDGN* NW11 ....53 F2
Riding House St *GTPST* W1W 19 E3
Ridley Rd *FSTGT* E7 ....82 C1
   HACK E8. ....77 F1
   WLSDN NW10 ....88 A1
Riefield Rd *ELTH/MOT* SE9 ....144 C1
Riffel Rd *CRICK* NW2 ....70 C2
Rifle Pl *NTGHL* W11 ....101 D2
Rifle St *POP/IOD* E14 ....92 B4
Rigault Rd *FUL/PGN* SW6 ....113 E5
Rigby Ms *IL* IG1 ....66 A4
Rigden St *POP/IOD* E14. ....92 B5
Rigeley Rd *WLSDN* NW10 ....88 A2

Rigg Ap LEY E10 .... **61** D3
Rigge Pl CLAP SW4 .... **135** D2
Riggindale Rd STRHM/NOR SW16 .... **153** D5
Riley Rd STHWK SE1 .... **49** E2
Riley St WBPTN SW10 .... **115** D3
Rinaldo Rd BAL SW12 .... **134** B5
Ringcroft St HOLWY N7 .... **76** A2
Ringford Rd WAND/EARL SW18 .... **131** F3
Ringlet Cl CAN/RD E16 .... **94** B4
Ringmer Av FUL/PGN SW6 .... **113** F4
Ringmore Ri FSTH SE23 .... **138** B5
Ringstead Rd CAT SE6 .... **140** B5
Ringwood Gdns PUT/ROE SW15 .... **148** A2
Ringwood Rd WALTH E17 .... **61** F1
Ripley Gdns MORT/ESHN SW14 .... **129** D1
Ripley Ms WAN * E11 .... **63** E1
Ripley Rd CAN/RD E16 .... **94** C5
  GDMY/SEVK IG3 .... **67** F4
Ripon Gdns IL IG1 .... **65** E1
Ripon Rd WOOL/PLUM SE18 .... **126** B2
Ripple Rd BARK IG11 .... **84** C4
Ripplevale Gv IS N1 .... **75** F3
Rippolson Rd WOOL/PLUM SE18 .... **127** F1
Risborough St STHWK SE1 .... **35** D2
Risdon St BERM/RHTH SE16 .... **102** C3
The Rise WLSDN NW10 .... **51** D5
Riseldine Rd FSTH SE23 .... **139** E4
Risinghill St IS N1 .... **10** A1
Rita Rd VX/NE SW8 .... **117** E3
Ritchie St IS N1 .... **10** B1
Ritherdon Rd TOOT SW17 .... **152** A2
Ritson Rd HACK E8 .... **78** F3
Ritter St WOOL/PLUM SE18 .... **126** A2
Rivaz Pl HOM E9 .... **78** C3
Riverbank Rd BMLY BR1 .... **160** A3
Riverdale Dr WAND/EARL SW18 .... **150** B1
Riverdale Rd WOOL/PLUM SE18 .... **127** F1
Riverdene Rd IL IG1 .... **66** A5
River Pl IS N1 .... **76** C4
River Rd BARK IG11 .... **97** E1
Riversdale Rd HBRY N5 .... **58** B5
Riverside CHARL SE7 .... **106** B4
  HDN NW4 .... **52** B2
  RCH/KEW * TW9 .... **110** A2
Riverside Cl CLPT E5 .... **60** C3
Riverside Dr CHSWK W4 .... **111** D3
  GLDGN * NW11 .... **53** E1
Riverside Gdns HMSMTH W6 .... **112** B1
Riverside Rd IL IG1 .... **66** B5
  SEVS/STOTM N15 .... **60** A1
  SRTFD E15 .... **92** C1
  TOOT SW17 .... **150** B4
River St CLKNW EC1R **10** A3
River Ter HMSMTH W6 .... **112** C1
Riverton Cl MV/WKIL * W9 .... **89** F2
Riverview Gdns BARN SW13 .... **112** B2
Riverview Pk CAT SE6 .... **158** A2
Riverview Rd CHSWK W4 .... **110** B3
River Wy GNWCH SE10 .... **105** F4
Rivington Pl SDTCH SE2A **13** D4
Rivington St SDTCH EC2A **13** D4
Rivington Wk HACK * E8 .... **78** A5
Rixon St HOLWY N7 .... **58** A5
Rixsen Rd MNPK E12 .... **83** E2
Roach Rd HOM E9 .... **80** A4
Roads Pl ARCH N19 .... **57** E4
Roan St GNWCH SE10 .... **122** C2
Robert Adam St MBLAR W1H **18** A4
Roberta St BETH E2 .... **90** A2
Robert Cl MV/WKIL W9 .... **15** F1
Robert Keen Cl PECK SE15 .... **120** A4
Robert Lowe Cl NWCR SE14 .... **121** D3
Robert St HOLWY N7 .... **58** A5
Roberts Cl ELTH/MOT SE9 .... **163** D1
Roberts Ct WLSDN NW10 .... **69** E3
Roberts House WOOL/PLUM SE18 .... **125** E4

Roberts Ms KTBR * SW1X **42** A3
Robertson Rd SRTFD E15 .... **80** C5
Robertson St VX/NE SW8 .... **134** B1
Robert's Pl CLKNW * EC1R **10** B5
Robert St CAMTN NW1 .... **7** D4
  CHCR WC2N **33** D2
  WOOL/PLUM SE18 .... **109** D5
Robeson St BOW E3 .... **91** F4
Robin Gv HGT N6 .... **56** A4
Robin Hood Gdns POP/IOD * E14 .... **104** C1
Robin Hood La POP/IOD E14 .... **104** C1
  PUT/ROE SW15 .... **147** E3
Robin Hood Rd PUT/ROE SW15 .... **147** E4
Robin Hood Wy PUT/ROE SW15 .... **147** E4
Robinia Crs LEY E10 .... **62** B4
Robinson Rd BETH E2 .... **90** C1
Robinson St CHEL SW3 .... **115** F2
Robinwood Pl RCHPK/HAM TW10 .... **147** D2
Robsart St BRXN/ST SW9 .... **117** F5
Robson Av WLSDN NW10 .... **70** A5
Robson Cl EHAM E6 .... **95** E5
Robson Rd WNWD SE27 .... **154** B3
Rochdale Wy DEPT SE8 .... **122** A3
Rochelle Cl BTSEA SW11 .... **133** D2
Rochelle St BETH E2 .... **13** E4
Rochemont Wk HACK * E8 .... **77** F5
Rochester Av BKHTH/KID SE3 .... **124** B4
Rochester Gdns IL IG1 .... **65** F2
Rochester Ms CAMTN NW1 .... **74** C4
Rochester Pl CAMTN NW1 .... **74** C3
Rochester Rd CAMTN NW1 .... **74** C3
Rochester Rw WEST SW1P **43** F4
Rochester Sq CAMTN NW1 .... **74** C4
Rochester St WEST SW1P **44** A3
Rochester Ter CAMTN NW1 .... **74** C3
Rochester Wk STHWK * SE1 .... **36** A3
Rochester Way Relief Rd
  ELTH/MOT SE9 .... **143** E3
Rochford Cl EHAM E6 .... **95** D1
Rochford Wk HACK * E8 .... **78** A4
Rock Av MORT/ESHN SW14 .... **129** D1
Rockbourne Rd FSTH SE23 .... **157** D1
Rockell's Pl EDUL SE22 .... **138** B4
Rock Grove Wy BERM/RHTH SE16 .... **102** A5
Rockhall Rd CRICK NW2 .... **71** D3
Rockhampton Rd STRHM/NOR SW16 ...... **154** A4
Rock Hl NRWD SE19 .... **155** F4
Rockingham Cl PUT/ROE SW15 .... **129** F2
Rockingham St STHWK SE1 .... **47** E3
Rockland Rd PUT/ROE SW15 .... **131** E2
Rockley Rd SHB W12 .... **101** D3
Rockmount Rd WOOL/PLUM SE18 .... **127** F1
Rocks La BARN SW13 .... **130** A1
Rock St FSBYPK N4 .... **58** A4
Rockwell Gdns NRWD SE19 .... **155** E4
Rocliffe St IS N1 .... **11** D2
Rocombe Crs FSTH * SE23 .... **138** C5
Rocque La BKHTH/KID SE3 .... **141** F1
Rodborough Rd GLDGN NW11 .... **54** A3
Rodenhurst Rd CLAP SW4 .... **134** C5
Rodney Pl STHWK SE1 .... **47** F4
Rodney Rd WALW SE17 .... **47** F5
Rodney St IS N1 .... **9** F1
Rodway Rd PUT/ROE SW15 .... **130** A5
Rodwell Rd EDUL SE22 .... **137** F4
Roedean Crs PUT/ROE SW15 .... **129** E4
Roehampton Cl PUT/ROE SW15 .... **130** A2
Roehampton Ga PUT/ROE SW15 .... **129** E4

Roehampton High St
PUT/ROE SW15 ....130 A5
Roehampton La PUT/ROE SW15 ....130 A3
Roehampton V PUT/ROE SW15 ....147 F3
Roffey St POP/IOD E14 ....104 C3
Rogers Rd CAN/RD E16 ....95 F5
TOOT SW17 ....151 D4
Roger St BMSBY WC1N 21 F1
Rojack Rd FSTH SE23 ....157 D1
Rokeby Rd BROCKY * SE4 ....121 F5
Rokeby St SRTFD E15 ....81 E5
Rokesby Cl WELL DA16 ....127 D5
Roland Gdns SKENS SW7 ....114 C1
Roland Ms WCHPL * E1 ....91 C4
Roland Wy WALW SE17 ....119 D1
WBPTN SW10 ....114 C1
Rollins St PECK SE15 ....120 C2
Rollit St HOLWY N7 ....76 A2
Rolls Buildings FLST/FETLN EC4A 22 A4
Rollscourt Av HNHL SE24 ....136 C3
Rolls Rd STHWK SE1 ....119 F1
Rolt St DEPT SE8 ....121 E2
Roman Cl ACT W3 ....98 B3
Romanfield Rd BRXS/STRHM SW2 ..135 F5
Roman Rd BETH E2 ....91 D1
CHSWK W4 ....99 E5
EHAM E6 ....95 E3
IL IG1 ....84 D3
Roman Wy HOLWY N7 ....75 F3
Romberg Rd TOOT SW17 ....152 A3
Romborough Gdns LEW SE13 ....140 C3
Romborough Wy LEW SE13 ....140 C3
Romero Sq BKHTH/MOT SE9 ....142 C2
Romeyn Rd STRHM/NOR SW16 ....153 F3
Romford Rd MNPK E12 ....66 A3
SRTFD E15 ....81 E4
Romford St WCHPL E1 ....90 A4
Romilly Rd FSBYPK N4 ....58 A3
Romilly St SOHO/SHAV W1D 32 B1
Rommany Rd WNWD SE27 ....155 D4
Romney Cl GLDGN NW11 ....54 B3
Romney Rd GNWCH SE10 ....122 C2
WOOL/PLUM SE18 ....108 B4
Romney Rw CRICK * NW2 ....53 D4
Romola Rd BRXS/STRHM SW2 ....154 B3
Ronald Av SRTFD E15 ....93 E2
Ronalds Rd HBRY N5 ....76 A2
Ronaldstone Rd BFN/LL DA15 ....145 E4
Rona Rd HAMP NW3 ....74 A1
Rona Wk IS N1 ....77 D3
Rondu Rd CRICK NW2 ....71 E2
Ron Leighton Wy EHAM E6 ....83 E5
Ronver Rd LEE/GVPK SE12 ....160 A1
Rood La FENCHST EC3M 36 C1
Rook Cl WBLY HA9 ....50 B5
Rookery Cl CLAP SW4 ....134 C4
Rookstone Rd TOOT SW17 ....151 F5
Rookwood Rd STNW/STAM N16 ....59 F1
Rootes Dr NKENS W10 ....89 D3
Ropemaker Rd BERM/RTHH SE16 ...103 E3
Ropemaker's Flds POP/IOD * E14 ...103 F1
Ropemaker St BARB EC2Y 24 A2
Roper La STHWK SE1 ....49 D1
Roper St ELTH/MOT SE9 ....143 F3
Ropery St BOW E3 ....91 F3
Rope St BERM/RHTH SE16 ....103 E4
Ropewalk Gdns WCHPL E1 ....90 A5
Ropewalk Ms HACK * E8 ....77 F4
Rope Yard Rails WOOL/PLUM SE18 ..108 B4
Ropley St BETH E2 ....90 A1
Rosa Alba Ms HBRY N5 ....76 C1
Rosaline Rd FUL/PGN SW6 ....113 E3
Rosaline Ter FUL/PGN * SW6 ....113 E3
Rosamond St SYD SE26 ....156 B3
Rosamond Vls MORT/ESHN * SW14 ..129 D2
Rosary Gdns SKENS SW7 ....39 F5
Rosaville Rd FUL/PGN SW6 ....113 E3

Roscoe St STLK EC1Y 23 F1
Rose Aly STHWK SE1 ....35 F3
Rosebank Est BOW E3 ....91 F1
Rosebank Gdns ACT * W3 ....87 D5
BOW * E3 ....91 E1
Rosebank Rd LEY E10 ....62 A3
Rosebank Wk CAMTN * NW1 ....75 D4
Rosebank Wy ACT W3 ....87 D5
Roseberry Gdns FSBYPK N4 ....58 B1
Roseberry Pl HACK E8 ....77 F3
Rosebery Av BFN/LL DA15 ....145 E5
CLKNW EC1R 10 A5
MNPK E12 ....83 B5
Rosebery Ct CLKNW EC1R 10 A5
Rosebery Rd CLAP SW4 ....135 E4
Rosebury Rd FUL/PGN SW6 ....114 B5
Rose Ct WCHPL E1 ....25 E3
Rosecroft Av HAMP NW3 ....55 E4
Rose Croft Gdns CRICK NW2 ....52 A5
Rose & Crown Yd STJS * SW1Y 31 F4
Rosedale Rd FSTGT E7 ....82 C2
Rosedene STRHM/NOR SW16 ....153 F3
Rosedene Ter LEY E10 ....62 B4
Rosedew Rd HMSMTH W6 ....113 D2
Rosefield POP/IOD E14 ....104 A1
Rosefield Gdns POP/IOD E14 ....104 A1
Rosehart Ms NTGHL * W11 ....14 A5
Rosehill Rd WAND/EARL SW18 ....132 C4
Roseleigh Av HBRY N5 ....76 B1
Rosemary Dr POP/IOD E14 ....93 D5
Rosemary La MORT/ESHN SW14 .....128 C1
Rosemary Rd PECK SE15 ....119 F3
TOOT SW17 ....150 B3
WELL DA16 ....127 F4
Rosemary St IS N1 ....77 D5
Rosemead CDALE/KGS NW9 ....51 F2
Rosemont Rd ACT W3 ....98 B3
HAMP NW3 ....72 C3
Rosemoor St CHEL SW3 ....41 E5
Rosenau Crs BTSEA SW11 ....115 F4
Rosenau Rd BTSEA SW11 ....115 E4
Rosendale Rd DUL SE21 ....154 C1
HNHL SE24 ....136 C5
Roseneath Rd BTSEA SW11 ....134 A4
Rosenthal Rd CAT SE6 ....140 B4
Rosenthorpe Rd PECK SE15 ....139 D3
Roserton St POP/IOD E14 ....104 C3
Rosery Ga BTSEA SW11 ....116 B3
Rose Sq CHEL * SW3 ....115 D1
Rose St COVGDN WC2E 32 C1
Rosethorn Cl BAL SW12 ....134 C5
Rosetta Cl VX/NE SW8 ....117 E3
Roseveare Rd LEE/GVPK SE12 ....160 C4
Roseway DUL SE21 ....137 D4
Rose Wy LEE/GVPK SE12 ....142 A3
Rosher Cl SRTFD E15 ....81 D4
Rosina St HOM E9 ....79 D2
Roskell Rd PUT/ROE SW15 ....131 D1
Roslin Rd ACT W3 ....98 B4
Roslin Wy BMLY BR1 ....160 A5
Rosmead Rd NTGHL W11 ....101 E1
Rosoman Pl CLKNW EC1R 10 B5
Rosoman St CLKNW EC1R 10 B4
Rossdale Dr CDALE/KGS NW9 ....50 C3
Rossdale Rd PUT/ROE SW15 ....130 C2
Rosse Ms BKHTH/KID SE3 ....124 B4
Rossendale St CLPT E5 ....60 B4
Rossendale Wy CAMTN NW1 ....74 C5
Rossetti Rd BERM/RHTH SE16 ....102 C5
Ross House WOOL/PLUM SE18 ....60 B4
Rossington St CLPT * E5 ....60 B4
Rossiter Rd BAL SW12 ....152 B1
Rosslyn Av BARN SW13 ....129 E1
Rosslyn Hl HAMP NW3 ....73 D1
Rosslyn Ms HAMP * NW3 ....73 D2
Rosslyn Park Ms HAMP NW3 ....73 D2
Rosslyn Rd BARK IG11 ....85 D4
Rossmore Cl CAMTN * NW1 ....17 D1

Rossmore Rd *CAMTN* NW1 ....5 D5
Ross Wy *ELTH/MOT* SE9 ....143 E1
Rostella Rd *TOOT* SW17 ....151 D4
Rostrevor Av *SEVS/STOTM* N15 ....59 F1
Rostrevor Rd *FUL/PGN* SW6 ....113 F4
  WIM/MER SW19 ....150 A5
Rotary St *STHWK* SE1 ....46 C2
Rothbury Rd *HOM* E9 ....79 F4
Rotherfield St *IS* N1 ....76 C4
Rotherham Wk *STHWK* * SE1 ....35 D4
Rotherhithe New Rd
  BERM/RHTH SE16 ....120 B1
Rotherhithe Old Rd
  BERM/RHTH SE16 ....103 D5
Rotherhithe St *BERM/RHTH* SE16 ......102 B3
Rotherhithe Tnl *BERM/RHTH* SE16 .....102 C3
Rotherwick Rd *GLDGN* NW11 ....54 A2
Rotherwood Rd *PUT/ROE* SW15 ....131 D1
Rothery St *IS* N1 ....76 B5
Rothery Ter *BRXN/ST* * SW9 ....118 B3
Rothesay Av *RCHPK/HAM* TW10 ....128 B2
Rothsay Rd *FSTGT* E7 ....82 C4
Rothsay St *STHWK* SE1 ....48 C2
Rothschild Rd *CHSWK* W4 ....98 C5
Rothschild St *WNWD* SE27 ....154 B4
Rothwell St *CAMTN* NW1 ....73 F5
Rotterdam Dr *POP/IOD* E14 ....104 C4
Rouel Rd *BERM/RHTH* SE16 ....102 A4
Roundel Cl *BROCKY* SE4 ....139 F2
Roundhay Cl *FSTH* SE23 ....157 D2
Round Hl *FSTH* SE23 ....156 B2
Roundtable Rd *BMLY* BR1 ....159 F3
Roundwood Pk *WLSDN* * NW10 ....70 A5
Roundwood Rd *WLSDN* NW10 ....69 E5
Rounton Rd *BOW* E3 ....92 A3
Roupell Rd *BRXS/STRHM* SW2 ....153 F1
Roupell St *STHWK* SE1 ....34 B4
Rousden St *CAMTN* NW1 ....74 C1
Rouse Gdns *DUL* SE21 ....155 E4
Routemaster Cl *PLSTW* E13 ....94 B2
Routh Rd *WAND/EARL* SW18 ....133 E5
Routh St *EHAM* E6 ....95 F4
Rowallan Rd *FUL/PGN* SW6 ....113 E3
Rowan Cl *IL* IG1 ....85 D2
Rowan Rd *HMSMTH* W6 ....101 D5
Rowan Wk *EFNCH* N2 ....54 C1
  NKENS * W10 ....89 E3
Rowberry Cl *FUL/PGN* SW6 ....113 D3
Rowcross St *STHWK* SE1 ....119 F1
Rowditch La *BTSEA* SW11 ....116 A5
Rowdon Av *WLSDN* NW10 ....70 B4
Rowe Gdns *BARK* IG11 ....97 F1
Rowe La *HOM* E9 ....78 C2
Rowena Crs *BTSEA* SW11 ....115 E5
Rowfant Rd *TOOT* SW17 ....152 A2
Rowhill Rd *CLPT* E5 ....78 B1
Rowington Cl *BAY/PAD* W2 ....14 C2
Rowland Gv *SYD* SE26 ....156 B3
Rowland Hill St *HAMP* NW3 ....73 E2
Rowlands Cl *HGT* * N6 ....56 A1
Rowley Cottages *WKENS* * W14 ....101 F5
Rowley Gdns *FSBYPK* N4 ....58 C2
Rowley Wy *STJWD* NW8 ....72 C5
Rowntree Cl *KIL/WHAMP* * NW6 ....72 A3
  PLSTW E13 ....94 B3
Rowse Cl *SRTFD* E15 ....80 C5
Rowstock Gdns *HOLWY* N7 ....75 D2
Rowton Rd *WOOL/PLUM* SE18 ....126 C3
Roxburgh Rd *WNWD* SE27 ....154 B5
Roxby Pl *FUL/PGN* SW6 ....114 A2
Roxley Rd *LEW* SE13 ....140 B4
Roxwell Rd *SHB* W12 ....100 A3
Royal Albert Rd *EHAM* E6 ....108 A1
Royal Albert Wy *CAN/RD* E16 ....107 D1
Royal Ar *CONDST* W1S 31 E2
Royal Arsenal West
  WOOL/PLUM SE18 ....126 A1
Royal Av *CHEL* SW3 ....115 F1

Royal Circ *WNWD* SE27 ....154 A3
Royal Cl *DEPT* SE8 ....121 F2
  STNW/STAM * N16 ....59 E3
Royal College St *CAMTN* NW1 ....74 C4
Royal Ct *BANK* EC3V 24 C5
  ELTH/MOT * SE9 ....161 F1
Royal Crs *NTGHL* W11 ....101 D3
Royal Crescent Ms *NTGHL* W11 ....101 D3
Royal Docks Rd *EHAM* E6 ....96 B4
Royal Herbert Pavilions
  WOOL/PLUM SE18 ....125 F4
Royal Hl *GNWCH* SE10 ....122 C3
Royal Hospital Rd *CHEL* SW3 ....115 F2
The Royal Ms *WHALL* SW1A 43 D2
Royal Ms *BAL* SW12 ....134 B5
Royal Mint Pl *WCHPL* E1 ....37 F1
Royal Mint St *TWRH* EC3N 37 F1
Royal Naval Rd *NWCR* SE14 ....121 F3
Royal Oak Pl *EDUL* SE22 ....138 B4
Royal Oak Rd *HACK* E8 ....78 B3
Royal Opera Ar *STJS* * SW1Y 32 A3
Royal Orchard Cl *WAND/EARL* SW18 ...131 E5
Royal Pde *BKHTH/KID* SE3 ....123 F5
  FUL/PGN * SW6 ....113 E3
Royal Pl *GNWCH* SE10 ....122 C3
Royal Rd *CAN/RD* E16 ....94 C3
  WALW SE17 ....118 B2
Royal St *STHWK* SE1 ....45 F1
Royal Victor Pl *BOW* E3 ....91 D1
Roycraft Av *BARK* IG11 ....97 F1
Roycroft Cl *BRXS/STRHM* * SW2 ....154 A1
Roydene Rd *WOOL/PLUM* SE18 ....127 E2
Royston Gdns *IL* IG1 ....65 D1
Royston St *BETH* E2 ....90 C1
Rozel Rd *CLAP* SW4 ....116 C5
Rubens St *CAT* SE6 ....157 F2
Ruby St *PECK* SE15 ....120 B2
Ruby Triangle *PECK* * SE15 ....120 B2
Ruckholt Cl *LEY* E10 ....62 B5
Ruckholt Rd *LEY* E10 ....62 C5
Rudall Crs *HAMP* NW3 ....73 D1
Ruddington Cl *CLPT* E5 ....79 E1
Ruddstreet Cl *WOOL/PLUM* SE18 ....108 B5
Rudgwick Ter *STJWD* * NW8 ....73 E5
Rudloe Rd *BAL* SW12 ....134 C5
Rudolf Pl *VX/NE* SW8 ....117 E2
Rudolph Rd *KIL/WHAMP* NW6 ....2 B2
  PLSTW E13 ....93 F1
Rufford St *IS* N1 ....75 E5
Rufus St *IS* N1 ....12 C4
Rugby Rd *CHSWK* W4 ....99 E3
Rugby St *BMSBY* WC1N 21 E1
Rugg St *POP/IOD* E14 ....104 A1
Ruislip St *TOOT* SW17 ....151 F4
Rumbold Rd *FUL/PGN* SW6 ....114 B3
Rum Cl *WAP* E1W 102 B1
Rumsey Rd *BRXN/ST* SW9 ....135 F1
Runbury Cir *CDALE/KGS* NW9 ....51 D4
Runcorn Pl *NTGHL* W11 ....101 E1
Rupack St *BERM/RHTH* * SE16 ....102 C3
Rupert Ct *SOHO/SHAV* W1D 32 A1
Rupert Gdns *BRXN/ST* SW9 ....118 B5
Rupert Rd *ARCH* N19 ....57 D5
  CHSWK W4 ....99 E4
  KIL/WHAMP NW6 ....89 F1
Rupert St *SOHO/SHAV* * W1D 32 A1
Rusbridge Cl *HACK* E8 ....78 A2
Ruscoe Rd *CAN/RD* E16 ....93 F5
Rusham Rd *BAL* SW12 ....133 F4
Rushbrook Rd *ELTH/MOT* SE9 ....162 C2
Rush Common Ms
  BRXS/STRHM SW2 ....135 F5
Rushcroft Rd *BRXS/STRHM* SW2 ....136 A3
Rushey Gn *CAT* SE6 ....140 B5
Rushey Md *BROCKY* SE4 ....140 A3
Rushford Rd *BROCKY* SE4 ....139 F4
Rushgrove St *WOOL/PLUM* SE18 ....107 F5

Rush Hill Ms *BTSEA* SW11 ....**134** A1
Rush Hill Rd *BTSEA* SW11 ....**134** A1
Rushmead *BETH* E2 ....**90** B2
Rushmere Pl *WIM/MER* SW19 ....**149** D5
Rushmore Rd *CLPT* E5 ....**78** C1
Rusholme Gv *NRWD* SE19 ....**155** E5
Rusholme Rd *PUT/ROE* SW15 ....**131** D4
Rushton St *IS* N1 ....**12** B1
Rushworth St *STHWK* SE1 ....**35** D5
Ruskin Av *MNPK* E12 ....**83** E3
RCH/KEW TW9 ....**110** A3
Ruskin Cl *GLDGN* NW11 ....**54** B1
Ruskin Wk *HNHL* SE24 ....**136** C5
Rusper Cl *CRICK* NW2 ....**52** C5
Russell Cl *CHARL* SE7 ....**124** C3
WLSDN NW10 ....**68** C4
Russell Ct *WHALL* SW1A **31** F4
Russell Gdns *GLDGN* NW11 ....**53** E1
WKENS * W14 ....**101** E4
Russell Gardens Ms *WKENS* W14 ....**101** E3
Russell Gv *BRXN/ST* SW9 ....**118** A4
Russell Kerr Cl *CHSWK* * W4 ....**110** C3
Russell Pde *GLDGN* * NW11 ....**53** E1
Russell Pl *HAMP* NW3 ....**73** D3
Russell Rd *CAN/RD* E16 ....**94** A3
CDALE/KGS NW9 ....**51** F1
CEND/HSY/T N8 ....**57** D1
LEY E10 ....**62** B3
WKENS W14 ....**101** E4
Russell Sq *GWRST* WC1E **20** B2
Russell St *HOL/ALD* WC2B **21** C5
Russet Crs *HOLWY* * N7 ....**75** F2
Russia Dock Rd *BERM/RHTH* * SE16 ....**103** E2
Russia La *BETH* E2 ....**90** D1
Russia Rw *CITYW* EC2V **23** F5
Rusthall Av *CHSWK* W4 ....**99** D4
Ruston Ms *NTGHL* * W11 ....**89** E5
Ruston Rd *WOOL/PLUM* SE18 ....**107** E4
Ruston St *BOW* E3 ....**79** F5
Rust Sq *CMBW* SE5 ....**119** D3
Rutford Rd *STRHM/NOR* SW16 ....**153** E5
Rutherford St *WEST* SW1P **44** A4
Rutherford Wy *WBLY* HA9 ....**50** A5
Ruthin Cl *CDALE/KGS* NW9 ....**51** E1
Ruthin Rd *BKHTH/KID* SE3 ....**124** A2
Ruthven St *HOM* E9 ....**79** D5
Rutland Cl *MORT/ESHN* SW14 ....**128** B1
Rutland Ct *SKENS* SW7 ....**41** D1
Rutland Gdns *FSBYPK* N4 ....**58** B1
SKENS SW7 ....**41** D1
Rutland Ga *SKENS* SW7 ....**40** C1
Rutland Gate Ms *SKENS* * SW7 ....**40** C1
Rutland Gv *HMSMTH* W6 ....**112** B1
Rutland Ms *STJWD* * NW8 ....**72** B5
Rutland Ms South *SKENS* * SW7 ....**40** C2
Rutland Pk *CAT* SE6 ....**157** F2
CRICK NW2 ....**70** C3
Rutland Pl *FARR* EC1M **23** D2
Rutland Pl *FSTGT* E7 ....**83** D4
HOM E9 ....**79** D5
IL IG1 ....**84** B1
WALTH E17 ....**62** A1
Rutland St *SKENS* SW7 ....**41** D2
Rutland Wk *CAT* SE6 ....**157** F2
Rutley Cl *LBTH* SE11 ....**118** B2
Rutt's Ter *NWCR* SE14 ....**121** D4
Ruvigny Gdns *PUT/ROE* SW15 ....**131** D1
Ryan Cl *ELTH/MOT* SE9 ....**142** C5
Ryculff Sq *BKHTH/KID* SE3 ....**123** F5
Rydal Gdns *PUT/ROE* SW15 ....**147** E5
Rydal Rd *STRHM/NOR* SW16 ....**153** D5
Ryder Dr *BERM/RHTH* SE16 ....**120** B1
Ryder St *STJS* SW1Y **31** E2
Ryde Vale Rd *BAL* SW12 ....**152** B2
Rydon St *IS* N1 ....**76** C5
Rydston Cl *HOLWY* N7 ....**75** F4
Ryecotes Md *DUL* SE21 ....**155** E1
Ryecroft Rd *LEW* SE13 ....**140** C3

Ryecroft St *FUL/PGN* SW6 ....**114** B4
Ryedale *EDUL* SE22 ....**138** B4
Rye Hill Pk *PECK* SE15 ....**138** C2
Ryelands Crs *LEE/GVPK* SE12 ....**142** C4
Rye La *PECK* SE15 ....**120** A4
Rye Rd *PECK* SE15 ....**139** D2
Rye Wk *PUT/ROE* SW15 ....**131** D3
Ryfold Rd *WIM/MER* SW19 ....**150** A3
Rylandes Rd *CRICK* NW2 ....**52** A5
Ryland Rd *KTTN* * NW5 ....**74** B3
Rylett Crs *SHB* W12 ....**99** F4
Rylett Rd *SHB* W12 ....**99** F3
Rymer St *HNHL* SE24 ....**136** B4
Rymill St *CAN/RD* E16 ....**108** A2
Rysbrack St *CHEL* SW3 ....**41** E2

S

Sabbarton St *CAN/RD* E16 ....**93** F5
Sabine Rd *BTSEA* SW11 ....**133** F1
Sach Rd *CLPT* E5 ....**60** B4
Sackville Est *STRHM/NOR* SW16 ....**153** E3
Sackville Gdns *IL* IG1 ....**65** F3
Sackville St *MYFR/PICC* W1J **31** F2
Saffron Av *POP/IOD* E14 ....**105** D1
Saffron Hl *HCIRC* EC1N **22** B2
Saffron St *FARR* EC1M **22** B2
Sage Cl *EHAM* E6 ....**95** F4
Sage St *WCHPL* E1 ....**102** C1
Sage Wy *FSBYW* WC1X **9** E4
Saigasso Cl *CAN/RD* E16 ....**95** D5
Sail St *LBTH* SE11 ....**45** F4
Sainfoin Rd *TOOT* SW17 ....**152** A2
Sainsbury Rd *NRWD* SE19 ....**155** E5
St Agnes Cl *HOM* * E9 ....**78** C5
St Agnes Pl *CMBW* SE5 ....**118** B2
St Agnes Well *STLK* EC1Y **12** B5
St Aidan's Rd *EDUL* SE22 ....**138** B4
St Albans Av *CHSWK* W4 ....**99** D4
EHAM E6 ....**95** F2
St Albans Gv *KENS* W8 ....**39** D2
KENS W8 ....**39** D2
St Albans La *GLDGN* NW11 ....**54** A3
St Alban's Ms *BAY/PAD* W2 ....**16** B2
St Alban's Pl *IS* N1 ....**76** B5
St Albans Rd *GDMY/SEVK* IG3 ....**67** F3
KTTN NW5 ....**56** A5
WLSDN NW10 ....**69** E5
St Alban's St *STJS* SW1Y **32** A2
St Albans Ter *HMSMTH* * W6 ....**113** E2
St Alfege Rd *CHARL* SE7 ....**125** D2
St Alphage Gdn *BARB* EC2Y **23** F3
St Alphage Gdns *BARB* * EC2Y **23** F3
St Alphage Highwalk *BARB* EC2Y **23** F3
St Alphonsus Rd *CLAP* SW4 ....**134** C2
St Amunds Cl *CAT* SE6 ....**158** A4
St Andrews Cl *BERM/RHTH* * SE16 ....**120** B1
CRICK * NW2 ....**52** B5
St Andrew's Ct *WAND/EARL* SW18 ....**150** C2
St Andrew's Gv *STNW/STAM* N16 ....**59** D3
St Andrew's Hl *BLKFR* EC4V **35** D1
St Andrews Ms *BAL* SW12 ....**153** D1
STNW/STAM * N16 ....**59** E2
St Andrew's Pl *CAMTN* NW1 ....**6** C5
St Andrew's Rd *ACT* W3 ....**87** F5
CDALE/KGS NW9 ....**51** D3
GLDGN NW11 ....**53** F1
IL IG1 ....**65** F2
PLSTW E13 ....**94** B2
WAN E11 ....**63** E1
WKENS * W14 ....**113** E2
WLSDN NW10 ....**70** B3
St Andrew's Sq *NTGHL* * W11 ....**89** E5
St Andrew St *HCIRC* EC1N **22** B3
St Andrews Wy *BOW* E3 ....**92** B3

St Anne's CI *HGT* N6............................56 A5
St Annes Ct *SOHO/CST* W1F...............20 A5
St Anne's Pas *POP/IOD* * E14.............91 F5
St Anne's Rd *WAN* E11.......................63 D4
St Anne's Rw *POP/IOD* E14.................91 F5
St Anne St *POP/IOD* E14.....................91 F5
St Ann's Bark IG11..............................84 C5
St Ann's Crs *WAND/EARL* SW18..........132 B4
St Ann's Gdns *HAMP* NW3...................74 A3
St Ann's HI *WAND/EARL* SW18.............132 B3
St Ann's Park Rd *WAND/EARL* SW18.....132 C4
St Ann's Rd *BARK* IG11......................84 C4
  BARN SW13...................................111 F5
  NTGHL W11...................................101 D1
  SEVS/STOTM N15..............................59 E1
St Ann's St *WEST* SW1P......................44 B2
St Ann's Ter *STJWD* NW8......................4 D1
St Ann's Vls *NTGHL* W11....................101 D1
St Anselm's PI *MYFR/PKLN* W1K..........30 C1
St Anthonys CI *TOOT* SW17.................151 E2
  WAP * E1W..................................102 A2
St Antony's Rd *FSTGT* E7....................82 B4
St Asaph Rd *PECK* SE15....................139 D1
St Aubyn's Av *WIM/MER* SW19............149 F5
St Augustine's Rd *CAMTN* NW1...........75 D4
St Austell Rd *LEW* SE13.....................122 C5
St Awdry's Rd *BARK* IG11...................85 D4
St Barnabas Rd *WALTH* E17.................62 A1
St Barnabas Ter *HOM* E9.....................79 D2
St Barnabas Vls *VX/NE* SW8...............117 E4
St Barnabus St *BGVA* SW1W...............116 A1
St Bartholomew's CI *SYD* SE26............156 C1
St Bartholomew's Rd *EHAM* E6.............83 E5
St Benets CI *TOOT* * SW17.................151 E2
St Bernards CI *WNWD* SE27................155 D4
St Bernard's Rd *EHAM* E6....................83 D5
St Botolph St *HDTCH* EC3A...................25 E4
St Bride St *FLST/FETLN* EC4A...............22 C4
St Catherines Ct *TOOT* * SW17.............151 E2
St Catherine's Dr *NWCR* SE14..............121 D5
St Catherines La *CHEL* SW3...................41 E4
St Chad's PI *FSBYW* WC1X......................9 D3
St Chad's St *STPAN* WC1H........................9 D3
St Charles PI *NKENS* W10.....................89 D4
St Charles Sq *NKENS* W10.....................89 D4
St Christopher's PI *MHST* W1U..............18 B5
St Clair Rd *PLSTW* E13..........................94 B1
St Clare St *TWRH* EC3N........................25 E1
St Clement's La *LINN* WC2A....................21 F5
St Clements Yd *EDUL* * SE22...............137 F3
St Cloud Rd *WNWD* SE27....................154 C4
St Crispins CI *HAMP* NW3......................73 E1
St Cross St *HCIRC* EC1N........................22 B2
St Cuthbert's Rd *CRICK* NW2.................71 F3
St Cyprian's St *TOOT* SW17.................151 F4
St Davids CI *BERM/RHTH* * SE16..........120 B1
  WBLY HA9......................................50 C5
St Davids Ms *BOW* * E3.......................91 E2
St David's PI *HDN* NW4..........................52 B2
St Davids Sq *POP/IOD* E14..................122 B1
St Denis Rd *FUL/PGN* SW6...................113 F5
St Dionis Rd *FUL/PGN* SW6..................113 F5
St Donatt's Rd *NWCR* SE14..................121 F4
St Dunstan's Av *ACT* W3.......................99 D1
St Dunstan's Gdns *ACT* W3....................99 D1
St Dunstan's HI *MON* * EC3R.................36 C2
St Dunstan's La *MON* * EC3R.................36 C2
St Dunstans Rd *FSTGT* E7.....................82 B3
  HMSMTH W6.................................113 D1
St Edmund's CI *STJWD* NW8...................73 F5
  TOOT SW17.................................151 E2
St Edmund's Rd *IL* IG1..........................65 F1
St Edmunds Sq *BARN* SW13................112 C2
St Edmund's Ter *STJWD* NW8..................5 D1
St Edward's CI *GLDGN* NW11..................54 A1
St Elmo Rd *ACT* W3..............................99 F3
St Elmos Rd *BERM/RHTH* SE16............103 E3

St Erkenwald Ms *BARK* IG11.................85 D5
St Erkenwald Rd *BARK* IG11.................85 D5
St Ervans Rd *NKENS* W10......................89 E4
St Faith's Rd *HNHL* SE24.....................154 B1
St Fillans Rd *CAT* SE6.........................158 C1
St Francis Rd *EDUL* SE22....................137 E2
St Francis Wy *IL* IG1............................85 D1
St Gabriel's CI *WAN* E11......................64 B3
St Gabriel's Rd *CRICK* NW2...................71 D2
St George's Av *FSTGT* E7......................82 B4
  HOLWY N7....................................76 C1
St George's Circ *STHWK* SE1.................46 C1
St George's CI *GLDGN* NW11.................53 F1
St George's Dr *PIM* SW1V....................116 B1
  PIM * SW1V................................116 B1
St Georges Flds *BAY/PAD* W2..............17 D5
St George's Gv *TOOT* SW17................151 D3
St George's La *MON* * EC3R..................36 B1
St George's Ms *CAMTN* NW1.................73 F4
  CHSWK * W4................................110 C2
  DEPT SE8...................................103 F5
St Georges Pde *CAT* * SE6..................157 F2
St Georges Rd *CHSWK* W4....................99 D3
  FSTGT E7....................................82 B4
  GLDGN NW11...............................53 F1
  IL IG1...65 F2
  LEY E10......................................62 C5
  STHWK SE1..................................46 C3
St George's Sq *FSTGT* E7......................82 B4
  PIM SW1V..................................117 D1
  PIM * SW1V................................117 D1
St George's Square Ms *PIM* SW1V........117 D1
St George's Ter *CAMTN* NW1.................73 F4
  PECK * SE15...............................120 A3
St George St *CONDST* W1S....................31 D1
St George's Wy *PECK* SE15...................119 E2
  PECK * SE15...............................119 E2
St Gerards CI *CLAP* SW4.....................134 C3
St German's PI *BKHTH/KID* SE3............124 A4
St German's Rd *FSTH* SE23..................157 E1
St Giles Churchyard *BARB* * EC2Y.........23 F3
St Giles High St *LSO/SEVD* WC2H...........20 B4
St Giles Rd *CMBW* SE5......................119 E4
St Gothard Rd *WNWD* SE27................155 D3
St Helena Rd *BERM/RHTH* SE16...........103 D5
St Helena St *FSBYW* WC1X....................10 A4
St Helen's Gdns *NKENS* W10..................89 D4
St Helen's PI *OBST* EC2N......................24 C4
St Helen's Rd *IL* IG1.............................65 F1
St Helier's Rd *LEY* E10..........................62 B1
St Hildas CI *KIL/WHAMP* * NW6..............71 D4
  TOOT SW17.................................151 E2
St Hilda's Rd *BARN* SW13...................112 B1
St Hughes CI *TOOT* * SW17.................151 E2
St James CI *STJWD* NW8........................5 E1
St James' Ct *WESTW* * SW1E.................43 F2
St James Ms *POP/IOD* * E14...............104 C4
St James' Rd *FSTGT* E7.........................81 F2
St James's *NWCR* SE14......................121 E4
St James's Av *BETH* E2..........................90 C1
St James's Chambers *STJS* * SW1Y.........31 F4
St James's Ct *TOOT* * SW17.................151 F2
  WOOL/PLUM SE18........................126 C4
St James's Ct *WESTW* SW1E.................43 F2
St James's Crs *BRXN/ST* SW9..............136 A1
St James's Dr *BAL* SW12.....................151 F1
St James's Gdns *CAMTN* NW1.................7 E4
  NTGHL W11................................101 E2
St James's Gv *BTSEA* * SW11................115 F5
St James's Market *STJS* * SW1Y.............32 A2
St James's PI *WHALL* SW1A....................31 E4
St James's Rd *BERM/RHTH* SE16..........102 A4
St James's Sq *STJS* SW1Y.....................32 A3
St James's St *WHALL* SW1A....................31 E3
St James's Terrace Ms *STJWD* NW8........73 F5
St James St *HMSMTH* W6....................112 C1
St James Ter *BAL* * SW12....................152 A1

St James Wk *CLKNW* EC1R **10** C5
St John Cl *FUL/PGN * SW6 ....**114** A3
St John's Av *PUT/ROE* SW15 ......**131** D3
  WLSDN NW10 ....**69** F5
St John's Church Rd *HACK * E8 ......**78** C2
St John's Cl *FUL/PGN * SW6 ....**114** A3
St John's Crs *BRXN/ST* SW9 ......**136** A1
St John's Dr *WAND/EARL* SW18 ..**150** B1
St John's Gdns *NTGHL* W11 ......**101** E5
St John's Gv *ARCH* N19 ....**56** C4
  *BARN * SW13 ....**111** F5
St John's Hl *BTSEA* SW11 ....**133** E2
St John's Hill Gv *BTSEA* SW11 ....**133** D2
St John's La *FARR* EC1M ....
St John's Pk *BKHTH/KID* SE3 ....**124** A3
St John's Pl *FARR* EC1M **22** C1
St John's Rd *BARK* IG11 ....**85** E5
  BTSEA SW11 ....**133** D2
  CAN/RD E16 ....**94** A5
  EHAM E6 ....**85** E5
  GLDGN NW11 ....**53** F1
  GNTH/NBYPK IG2 ....**67** G2
  SEVS/STOTM N15 ....**59** E1
St John's Sq *FARR* EC1M **22** C1
St John's Ter *FSTGT* E7 ....**82** B3
  NKENS W10 ....**89** D3
  WOOL/PLUM SE18 ....**126** C2
St John St *FSBYE* EC1V **10** B2
St John's V *BROCKY* SE4 ....**122** A5
St John's Vls *ARCH* N19 ....**57** D4
  KENS W8 ....**39** D3
  *KENS * W8 ....**39** D3
St John's Wy *ARCH* N19 ....**56** C4
St John's Wood High St *STJWD* NW8 ..**4** B5
St John's Wood Pk *STJWD* NW8 ....**73** D5
St John's Wood Rd *STJWD* NW8 ....**4** A5
St John's Wood Ter *STJWD* NW8 ....**4** C1
St Josephs Cl *NKENS* W10 ....**89** E4
St Joseph's St *VX/NE * SW8 ....**116** B4
St Joseph's V *BKHTH/KID* SE3 ..**123** D5
St Jude's Rd *BETH* E2 ....**90** B1
St Jude St *STNW/STAM* N16 ....**77** E2
St Julian's Cl *STRHM/NOR * SW16 ..**154** A4
St Julian's Farm Rd *WNWD* SE27 ..**154** A4
St Julian's Rd *KIL/WHAMP* NW6 ....**71** F4
St Katharine's Prec *CAMTN* NW1 ....**6** C1
St Katharine's Wy *TWRH* E1CN **37** F3
St Katherines Wk *NTGHL * W11 ....**101** D1
St Keverne Rd *ELTH/MOT* SE9 ....**161** E4
St Kilda's Rd *STNW/STAM* N16 ....**59** D3
St Kitts Ter *NRWD* SE19 ....**155** E5
St Laurence's Cl *KIL/WHAMP* NW6 ..**71** D1
St Lawrence Cottages
  *POP/IOD * E14 ....**104** C2
St Lawrence Ter *POP/IOD* E14 ....**104** C2
St Lawrence Ter *NKENS* W10 ....**89** E4
St Lawrence Wy *BRXN/ST * SW9 ..**118** A5
St Leonards Gdns *IL* IG1 ....**84** C2
St Leonards Rd *MORT/ESHN* SW14 ..**128** C1
  POP/IOD E14 ....**92** C4
  WLSDN NW10 ....**87** D3
St Leonards Sq *KTTN* NW5 ....**74** A3
St Leonard's St *BOW* E3 ....**92** B2
St Leonard's Ter *CHEL* SW3 ......**115** F1
  *CHEL * SW3 ....**115** F1
St Loo Av *CHEL* SW3 ....**115** E2
St Louis Rd *WNWD* SE27 ....**154** C4
St Lucia Dr *SRTFD* E15 ....**81** F5
St Luke's Av *CLAP* SW4 ....**135** D2
  IL IG1 ....**84** B2
St Luke's Est *FSBYE * EC1V **12** A4
St Luke's Ms *NTGHL* W11 ....**89** F5
St Luke's Rd *NTGHL* W11 ....**89** F4
St Lukes Cl *FSBYE* EC1V **11** F5
St Luke's Sq *CAN/RD* E16 ....**93** F5
St Luke's St *CHEL* SW3 ....**115** E1
St Lukes Yd *MV/WKIL * W9 ....**89** F1
St Margarets *BARK* IG11 ....**85** D4

RCHPK/HAM * TW10 ....**146** C5
St Margarets Av *BFN/LL* DA15 ......**163** D3
St Margarets Ct *PUT/ROE * SW15 ..**130** B2
St Margaret's Crs *PUT/ROE * SW15 ..**130** B3
St Margaret's Gv *WAN* E11 ....**63** F5
  WOOL/PLUM SE18 ....**126** C2
St Margarets La *KENS* W8 ....**38** C3
St Margarets Ms
  *RCHPK/HAM * TW10 ....**146** C5
St Margaret's Rd *BROCKY* SE4 ......**139** F2
  MNPK E12 ....**64** C4
  WLSDN NW10 ....**88** C2
St Margaret's Ter *WOOL/PLUM* SE18 ..**126** C1
St Margaret St *WEST* SW1P **44** C1
St Marks Cl *FUL/PGN* SW6 ....**114** A4
St Mark's Crs *CAMTN * NW1 ....**74** A5
St Marks Ga *HOM* E9 ....**79** E4
St Mark's Gv *WBPTN * SW10 ......**114** B3
St Mark's Pl *NTGHL* W11 ....**89** E5
St Mark's Ri *HACK* E8 ....**77** F2
St Mark's Rd *NKENS* W10 ....**89** D4
St Marks Sq *CAMTN* NW1 ....**74** A5
St Mark St *WCHPL* E1 ....**25** F5
St Marks Vls *HOLWY * N7 ....**57** F4
St Martin's Av *EHAM* E6 ....**95** D1
St Martin's Cl *CAMTN* NW1 ....**74** C5
St Martin's Ct *LSQ/SEVD * WC2H **32** C1
  LSQ/SEVD WC2H **32** C1
St Martin's La *CHCR* WC2N **32** C1
St Martin's Le Grand *STBT* EC1A ..**23** E4
St Martin's Pl *CHCR* WC2N **32** C2
St Martin's Rd *BRXN/ST* SW9 ......**117** F5
St Martin's St *LSQ/SEVD * WC2H **32** B2
St Martin's Wy *TOOT* SW17 ....**150** C4
St Mary Abbot's Pl *KENS * W8 ......**101** F4
  *KENS * W8 ....**101** F4
St Mary Abbots Ter *WKENS * W14 ..**101** F4
St Mary At Hl *MON* EC3R **36** C2
St Mary Axe *HDTCH* EC3A **24** C5
St Marychurch St *BERM/RHTH* SE16 ..**102** C3
St Mary Graces Ct *TWRH * EC3N **37** F2
St Mary Newington Cl *WALW * SE17 ..**119** E1
St Marys *BARK* IG11 ....**97** D1
St Mary's Ap *MNPK* E12 ....**83** F2
St Mary's Av *WAN* E11 ....**64** B1
St Marys Ct *SHB * W12 ....**99** F4
St Marys Est *BERM/RHTH * SE16 ....**102** C3
St Marys Gdns *LBTH * SE11 ....**46** B4
  LBTH SE11 ....**46** B4
St Mary's Ga *KENS* W8 ....**38** C3
  *KENS * W8 ....**38** C3
St Mary's Gv *BARN* SW13 ....**130** B1
  CHSWK W4 ....**110** B2
  IS N1 ....**76** B3
St Mary's Man *BAY/PAD* W2 ....**15** F2
St Mary's Ms *KIL/WHAMP* NW6 ....**72** B4
St Mary's Pth *IS * N1 ....**76** B5
St Marys Pl *KENS* W8 ....**38** C3
  *KENS * W8 ....**39** D3
St Mary's Rd *GLDGN* NW11 ....**53** E2
  IL IG1 ....**66** C4
  LEY E10 ....**62** C5
  PECK SE15 ....**120** C4
  PLSTW E13 ....**94** B3
  WIM/MER SW19 ....**149** E5
  WLSDN NW10 ....**69** E5
St Mary's Sq *BAY/PAD* W2 ....**16** A2
St Mary's Ter *BAY/PAD* W2 ....**16** A2
St Mary St *WOOL/PLUM* SE18 ....**107** F5
St Marys Wk *LBTH * SE11 ....**46** B4
  LBTH SE11 ....**46** B4
St Matthew's Rd *BRXS/STRHM* SW2 ..**135** F1
St Matthew's Rw *BETH* E2 ....**90** A2
St Matthew St *WEST* SW1P **44** A2
St Maur Rd *FUL/PGN* SW6 ....**113** F4
St Merryn Cl *WOOL/PLUM* SE18 ..**127** D3
St Michael's Aly *BANK* EC3V **24** B5
St Michael's Av *WBLY* HA9 ....**68** A3

St Michaels Cl CAN/RD E16 .... 95 D4
St Michaels Ct GLDGN * NW11 .... 53 F2
St Michael's Gdns NKENS W10 .... 89 D4
St Michael's Rd BRXN/ST SW9 .... 117 F5
  CRICK NW2 .... 70 C1
St Michael's St BAY/PAD W2 .... 16 B4
St Michaels Ter HGT * N6 .... 56 A3
St Mildred's Ct LOTH * EC2R 24 A5
St Mildreds Rd CAT SE6 .... 141 E5
St Nicholas Rd WOOL/PLUM SE18 ..... 127 F1
St Nicholas St DEPT SE8 .... 121 F4
St Norbert Rd BROCKY SE4 .... 139 E2
St Olaf's Rd FUL/PGN SW6 .... 113 E3
St Olave's Rd EHAM E6 .... 84 A5
St Oswald's Pl LBTH SE11 .... 117 F1
  LBTH * SE11 .... 117 F1
St Oswulf St WEST * SW1P 44 B5
St Pancras Gdns CAMTN * NW1 .... 8 A1
St Pancras Wy CAMTN NW1 .... 74 C4
St Paul's Av BERM/RHTH * SE16 .... 103 D2
  CRICK NW2 .... 70 B3
St Paul's Church Yd BLKFR * EC4V 23 D5
St Paul's Cl CHARL SE7 .... 125 D1
St Pauls Crs CAMTN NW1 .... 75 D4
  CAMTN NW1 .... 75 D4
St Paul's Dr SRTFD E15 .... 81 D2
St Pauls Ms CAMTN NW1 .... 75 D4
St Paul's Pl IS N1 .... 77 D3
St Pauls Rd BARK IG11 .... 84 C5
  IS N1 .... 76 B3
St Pauls Ter WALW * SE17 .... 118 B2
St Paul St IS N1 .... 76 C5
St Paul's Wy POP/IOD E14 .... 91 F4
St Peter's Av BETH * E2 .... 90 A1
St Petersburgh Ms BAY/PAD W2 .... 26 C1
St Petersburgh Pl BAY/PAD W2 .... 26 C1
St Peter's Cl BETH E2 .... 90 A1
  TOOT SW17 .... 151 E4
St Peters Ct LEE/GVPK * SE12 .... 141 F3
St Peter's Gdns WNWD SE27 .... 154 A3
St Peter's Gv HMSMTH W6 .... 100 A5
St Peters Pl MV/WKIL W9 .... 14 C1
St Peter's Rd HMSMTH * W6 .... 112 A1
  HMSMTH W6 .... 100 A5
St Peter's Sq BETH * E2 .... 90 A1
  HMSMTH W6 .... 100 A5
St Peter's St IS N1 .... 76 B5
St Peter's Ter FUL/PGN SW6 .... 113 E3
St Peter's Vls HMSMTH W6 .... 100 A5
St Peter's Wy IS * N1 .... 77 E4
St Philip Sq VX/NE * SW8 .... 116 B5
St Philip's Rd HACK E8 .... 78 A3
St Philip's St VX/NE SW8 .... 116 B5
St Philip's Wy IS N1 .... 76 C5
St Quentin Rd WELL DA16 .... 145 F1
St Quintin Av NKENS W10 .... 88 C4
St Quintin Rd PLSTW E13 .... 94 B2
St Raphael's Wy WLSDN NW10 .... 68 C2
St Rule St VX/NE SW8 .... 116 C5
St Saviour's Est STHWK SE1 .... 49 E2
St Saviour's Rd BRXS/STRHM SW2 ... 135 F1
Saints Cl WNWD SE27 .... 154 A4
Saints Dr FSTGT E7 .... 83 D2
St Silas Pl KTTN NW5 .... 74 A3
St Simon's Av PUT/ROE SW15 .... 130 C3
St Stephen's Av SHB W12 .... 100 B2
St Stephens Cl ST/JWD NW8 .... 73 E5
St Stephen's Crs BAY/PAD * W2 .... 14 B4
St Stephen's Gdns BAY/PAD W2 .... 14 A4
St Stephen's Gv LEW SE13 .... 140 C1
St Stephen's Ms BAY/PAD W2 .... 14 B3
St Stephens Pde WHALL SW1A 32 C5
St Stephen's Rd BOW E3 .... 79 E5
  EHAM E6 .... 82 C4
St Stephens Ter VX/NE * SW8 .... 117 E3
  VX/NE SW8 .... 117 F3
St Stephen's Wk SKENS SW7 .... 39 E4
St Swithin's La MANHO EC4N 36 A1
St Swithun's Rd LEW * SE13 .... 141 D3

St Thomas Gdns IL IG1 .... 84 C3
  CHSWK W4 .... 110 C3
St Thomas Rd CAN/RD E16 .... 94 A5
St Thomas's Gdns HAMP NW3 .... 74 A3
St Thomas's Pl HOM * E9 .... 78 C4
St Thomas's Rd FSBYPK N4 .... 58 A4
  WLSDN NW10 .... 69 E5
St Thomas's Sq HACK E8 .... 78 B4
St Thomas St STHWK SE1 .... 36 B4
St Thomas's Wy FUL/PGN SW6 .... 113 F3
St Vincent Cl WNWD SE27 .... 154 B5
St Vincent St MHST W1U 18 A3
St Winefride's Av MNPK E12 .... 83 F2
  WALTH E17 .... 61 F2
Salamanca Pl LBTH SE11 .... 45 E5
Salamanca St LBTH SE11 .... 45 E5
Salcombe Rd STNW/STAM N16 .... 77 F2
  WALTH E17 .... 61 F2
Salcott Rd BTSEA SW11 .... 133 E3
Salehurst Rd BROCKY SE4 .... 139 F4
Salem Rd BAY/PAD W2 .... 27 D1
Sale Pl BAY/PAD W2 .... 16 C4
Sale St BETH E2 .... 90 A3
Salford Rd BAL SW12 .... 153 D1
Salisbury Av BARK IG11 .... 85 D3
Salisbury Cl WALW SE17 .... 48 A4
Salisbury Ct EMB EC4Y 22 B5
Salisbury Pavement FUL/PGN * SW6 .. 114 A3
Salisbury Pl BRXN/ST SW9 .... 118 B3
  MBLAR W1H 17 E2
Salisbury Rd FSTGT E7 .... 82 A3
  GDMY/SEVK IG3 .... 67 E4
  LEY E10 .... 62 C4
Salisbury Sq EMB * EC4Y 22 B5
Salisbury St ACT W3 .... 98 C3
  ST/JWD NW8 .... 16 B1
Salisbury Ter PECK SE15 .... 138 C1
Sally Murray Cl MNPK E12 .... 84 A1
Salmen Rd PLSTW E13 .... 93 F1
Salmon La POP/IOD E14 .... 91 E5
Salmon Ms KIL/WHAMP * NW6 .... 72 A2
Salmon St POP/IOD * E14 .... 91 F5
  WBLY HA9 .... 50 C4
Salomons Rd PLSTW E13 .... 94 C4
Salop Rd WALTH E17 .... 61 D1
Saltcoats Rd CHSWK W4 .... 99 E3
Saltcroft Cl WBLY HA9 .... 50 B3
Salter Rd BERM/RHTH SE16 .... 103 D2
Salters' Hall Ct MANHO * EC4N 36 A1
Salters' Hi NRWD SE19 .... 155 D5
Salters Rd NKENS W10 .... 89 D3
Salters Rw IS * N1 .... 77 D3
Salter St POP/IOD E14 .... 104 A1
  WLSDN NW10 .... 88 A2
Salterton Rd HOLWY N7 .... 57 E5
Saltley Cl EHAM E6 .... 95 E5
Saltoun Rd BRXS/STRHM SW2 .... 136 A2
Saltram Crs MV/WKIL W9 .... 89 F2
Saltwell St POP/IOD E14 .... 104 A1
Saltwood Gv WALW * SE17 .... 119 D1
Salusbury Rd KIL/WHAMP NW6 .... 71 F3
Salvador TOOT SW17 .... 151 E5
Salvin Rd PUT/ROE SW15 .... 131 D1
Salway Pl SRTFD E15 .... 81 D3
Salway Rd SRTFD E15 .... 81 D3
Samantha Cl WALTH E17 .... 61 F2
Sam Bartram Cl CHARL SE7 .... 124 C1
Samels Cl HMSMTH W6 .... 112 A1
Samford St ST/JWD NW8 .... 16 C1
Sampson St WAP * E1W 102 A2
Samson St PLSTW E13 .... 94 C1
Samuel Cl HACK E8 .... 77 F5
  NWCR SE14 .... 121 D2
  WOOL/PLUM SE18 .... 107 F5
Samuel St PECK SE15 .... 119 F3
  WOOL/PLUM SE18 .... 107 F5
Sancroft Cl CRICK NW2 .... 52 B5
Sancroft Rd LBTH SE11 .... 118 A1
The Sanctuary WEST SW1P 44 B2

Sanctuary St *STHWK* SE1 ....47 F1
Sandall Rd *KTTN* NW5 ....74 C3
Sandal St *SRTFD* E15 ....81 E5
Sandalwood Cl *WCHPL* E1 ....91 E3
Sandbach Pl *WOOL/PLUM* SE18 ...126 C1
Sandbourne Rd *BROCKY* SE4 ......121 E5
Sandbrook Rd *STNW/STAM* N16 ....59 E5
Sandby Gn *ELTH/MOT* SE9 ....143 E1
Sandell St *STHWK* SE1 ....34 A5
Sanderson Cl *KTTN* * NW5 ....74 B1
Sanderstead Av *CRICK* NW2 ....53 E4
Sanderstead Cl *BAL* SW12 ....134 C5
Sanderstead Rd *LEY* E10 ....61 E3
Sandford Rd *EHAM* E6 ....95 F2
Sandford Rw *WALW* SE17 ....119 D1
Sandford St *FUL/PGN* SW6 ....114 B3
Sandgate La *WAND/EARL* SW18 ...151 E1
Sandgate St *PECK* SE15 ....120 B2
The Sandhills *WBPTN* * SW10 .....114 C2
Sandhurst Dr *GDMY/SEVK* IG3 .....85 F1
Sandhurst Market *CAT* * SE6 ......158 C1
Sandhurst Pde *CAT* * SE6 ....158 C1
Sandhurst Rd *BFN/LL* DA15 ....163 F3
   CAT SE6 ....159 D1
Sandifer Dr *CRICK* NW2 ....53 D5
Sandilands Rd *FUL/PGN* SW6 .....114 B4
Sandison St *PECK* SE15 ....137 F1
Sandland St *GINN* WC1R 21 F3
Sandling Ri *ELTH/MOT* SE9 ....162 A3
Sandlings Cl *PECK* SE15 ....120 B5
Sandmere Rd *CLAP* SW4 ....135 E2
Sandown Ct *SYD* * SE26 ....156 B3
Sandpiper Cl *BERM/RHTH* SE16 ...103 F3
Sandpit Pl *CHARL* SE7 ....159 E5
Sandpit Rd *BMLY* BR1 ....56 C4
Sandridge St *ARCH* N19 .... F2
Sandringham Cl *WIM/MER* * SW19 ..149 D1
Sandringham Dr *WELL* DA16 ....154 C1
Sandringham Gdns *CEND/HSY/T* N8 ...57 E1
Sandringham Rd *BARK* IG11 ....160 A5
   BMLY BR1 ....70 B2
   CRICK NW2 ....82 C2
   FSTGT E7 ....53 E2
   GLDGN NW11 ....77 F2
   HACK E8 ....77 F2
   LEY E10 ....63 D2
Sandrock Rd *LEW* SE13 ....140 A1
Sands End La *FUL/PGN* SW6 ......114 B4
Sandstone Rd *LEE/GVPK* SE12 ....160 B2
Sandtoft Rd *CHARL* SE7 ....124 B2
Sandwell Crs *KIL/WHAMP* NW6 .....72 A3
Sandwich St *STPAN* WC1H 8 C4
Sandycombe Rd *RCH/KEW* TW9 ...110 A5
Sandy Hill Av *WOOL/PLUM* SE18 ..126 B1
Sandy Hill La *WOOL/PLUM* SE18 ..108 B5
Sandyhill Rd *IL* IG1 ....84 B1
Sandy Hill Rd *WOOL/PLUM* SE18 ..126 B1
Sandy Rd *GLDGN* NW11 ....54 B4
Sandy's Rw *WCHPL* E1 ....25 D3
Sanford La *STNW/STAM* N16 ....59 F4
Sanford St *NWCR* SE14 ....121 E2
Sanford Ter *STNW/STAM* N16 ....59 F5
Sangley Rd *CAT* SE6 ....140 B5
Sangora Rd *BTSEA* SW11 ....133 D2
Sansom Rd *WAN* * E11 ....63 F4
Sansom St *CMBW* SE5 ....119 D3
Sans Wk *CLKNW* EC1R 10 C5
Santley St *BRXS/STRHM* SW2 ......135 E2
Santos Rd *PUT/ROE* SW15 ....132 A3
Saperton Wk *LBTH* SE11 ....45 F4
Sapphire Rd *DEPT* SE8 ....103 E5
Saracen St *POP/IOD* E14 ....92 A5
Sarah St *BETH* E2 ....13 D3
Saratoga Rd *CLPT* E5 ....78 C1
Sardinia St *HOL/ALD* WC2B 21 E5
Sarre Rd *CRICK* NW2 ....71 F2
Sarsfeld Rd *BAL* SW12 ....151 F1
Sartor Rd *PECK* SE15 ....139 D2

Sarum Ter *BOW* * E3 ....91 F3
Satanita Cl *CAN/RD* E16 ....95 D5
Satchwell Rd *BETH* E2 ....90 A2
Sattar Ms *STNW/STAM* * N16 ......59 D5
Sauls Gn *WAN* E11 ....63 E5
Saunders Cl *POP/IOD* * E14 ....103 F1
Saunders Ness Rd *POP/IOD* E14 ..105 D5
Saunders Rd *WOOL/PLUM* SE18 ..127 F1
Saunders St *LBTH* SE11 ....46 A4
Savage Gdns *EHAM* E6 ....95 F5
   TWRH EC3N 37 D1
Savernake Rd *HAMP* NW3 ....73 F1
Savile Rw *CONDST* W1S 31 E1
Saville Rd *CAN/RD* E16 ....107 E2
   CHSWK W4 ....99 D4
Savona St *VX/NE* SW8 ....116 C3
Savoy Cl *SRTFD* E15 ....81 E5
Savoy Ct *TPL/STR* * WC2R 33 D2
Savoy Hl *TPL/STR* WC2R 33 D2
Savoy Pl *CHCR* WC2N 33 D2
Savoy Rw *TPL/STR* WC2R 33 E1
Savoy Steps *TPL/STR* * WC2R 33 E2
Savoy St *TPL/STR* WC2R 33 E1
Savoy Wy *TPL/STR* WC2R 33 E2
Sawkins Cl *WIM/MER* SW19 ....149 D2
Sawley Rd *SHB* W12 ....100 A3
Sawyer St *STHWK* SE1 ....35 E5
Saxby Rd *BRXS/STRHM* SW2 ......135 E5
Saxham Rd *BARK* IG11 ....85 E5
Saxon Cl *WALTH* E17 ....62 A2
Saxon Dr *ACT* W3 ....86 B5
Saxonfield Cl *BRXS/STRHM* SW2 ..135 F5
Saxon Rd *BOW* E3 ....91 F1
   EHAM E6 ....95 F3
   IL IG1 ....84 B3
   WBLY HA9 ....50 C5
Saxton Cl *LEW* SE13 ....141 D1
Sayes Court St *DEPT* SE8 ....121 F1
Scala St *FITZ* W1T 19 F2
Scampston Ms *NKENS* W10 ....89 D5
Scandrett St *WAP* * E1W 102 B2
Scarba Wk *IS* N1 ....77 D3
Scarborough Rd *FSBYPK* N4 ....58 A2
   WAN E11 ....63 D3
Scarborough St *WCHPL* E1 ....25 F5
Scarlet Rd *CAT* SE6 ....159 E3
Scarsbrook Rd *BKHTH/KID* SE3 ...143 D1
Scarsdale Pl *KENS* * W8 ....38 C2
Scarsdale Vls *KENS* W8 ....38 B3
Scarth Rd *BARN* SW13 ....129 F1
Scawen Rd *DEPT* SE8 ....121 E1
Scawfell St *BETH* E2 ....13 F2
Sceptre Rd *BETH* E2 ....90 C2
Scholars Rd *BAL* SW12 ....152 C1
Scholefield Rd *ARCH* N19 ....57 D3
Schonfeld Sq *STNW/STAM* N16 ....59 D4
Schoolhouse La *WAP* * E1W 103 D1
School Rd *MNPK* E12 ....83 F1
   WLSDN NW10 ....87 D3
Schooner Cl *POP/IOD* E14 ....105 D4
Schubert Rd *PUT/ROE* SW15 ......131 F3
Sclater St *WCHPL* E1 ....13 E5
Scoles Crs *BRXS/STRHM* SW2 ....154 A1
Scoresby St *STHWK* SE1 ....34 C4
Scotia Rd *BRXS/STRHM* SW2 ......136 A5
Scotsdale Rd *LEE/GVPK* SE12 ....142 B3
Scotswood St *CLKNW* * EC1R 10 B5
Scott Ellis Gdns *STJWD* NW8 ....4 A4
Scott Lidgett Crs *BERM/RHTH* SE16 ...102 A3
Scotts Pas *WOOL/PLUM* * SE18 ..108 B5
Scott's Rd *LEY* E10 ....62 C3
   SHB W12 ....100 B3
Scott St *WCHPL* E1 ....90 B3
Scoulding Rd *CAN/RD* E16 ....93 F5
Scouler St *POP/IOD* E14 ....105 D1
Scout La *CLAP* SW4 ....134 C1
Scovell Crs *STHWK* * SE1 ....47 E1
Scovell Rd *STHWK* SE1 ....47 E1

Shakspeare Ms *STNW/STAM* N16 ....77 E1
Shakspeare Wk *STNW/STAM* N16 ....77 E1
Shalbourne Sq *HOM* E9 ....79 F3
Shalcomb St *WBPTN* SW10 ....114 C2
Shalfleet Dr *NKENS* W10 ....101 D1
Shalford Ct *IS* * N1 ....10 C1
Shalimar Gdns *ACT* W3 ....98 C1
Shalimar Rd *ACT* W3 ....98 C1
Shallons Rd *ELTH/MOT* SE9 ....162 B4
Shalstone Rd *MORT/ESHN* SW14 ....128 B1
Shamrock St *CLAP* SW4 ....135 D1
Shandon Rd *CLAP* SW4 ....134 C4
Shand St *STHWK* SE1 ....37 D5
Shandy St *WCHPL* E1 ....91 D4
Shannon Cl *CRICK* NW2 ....53 D5
Shannon Gv *BRXN/ST* SW9 ....135 F2
Shannon Pl *STJWD* NW8 ....5 D1
Shardcroft Av *HNHL* SE24 ....136 B3
Shardeloes Rd *BROCKY* SE4 ....121 F5
    BROCKY * SE4 ....139 F3
Shard's Sq *PECK* SE15 ....120 A2
Sharon Gdns *HOM* E9 ....78 C5
Sharon Rd *CHSWK* W4 ....111 D1
Sharples Hall St *CAMTN* NW1 ....73 F4
Sharratt St *PECK* SE15 ....120 C2
Sharsted St *WALW* SE17 ....118 B1
Shavers Pl *MYFR/PICC* W1J 32 A2
Shawbrooke Rd *ELTH/MOT* SE9 ....143 D2
Shawbury Rd *EDUL* SE22 ....137 F3
Shawfield St *CHEL* SW3 ....115 E1
Shaw Rd *BMLY* BR1 ....159 F3
    EDUL SE22 ....137 E2
Shaws Cottages *FSTH* * SE23 ....157 E3
Shearling Wy *HOLWY* N7 ....75 E3
Shearman Rd *BKHTH/KID* SE3 ....141 F2
Sheen Common Dr
    RCHPK/HAM TW10 ....128 A2
Sheen Court Rd *RCHPK/HAM* TW10 ....128 A2
Sheenewood *SYD* SE26 ....156 B5
Sheen Gate Gdns *MORT/ESHN* SW14 ....128 C2
Sheen Gv *IS* N1 ....76 A5
Sheen La *MORT/ESHN* SW14 ....128 A2
Sheen Wd *MORT/ESHN* SW14 ....128 A3
Sheepcote La *BTSEA* SW11 ....115 F5
Sheep La *HACK* E8 ....78 B5
Sheerwater Rd *CAN/RD* E16 ....95 D4
Sheffield Rd *LINN* * WC2A 21 E5
Sheffield Ter *KENS* W8 ....26 A5
Shelburne Rd *HOLWY* N7 ....75 F1
Shelbury Rd *EDUL* SE22 ....138 B3
Sheldon Av *HGT* N6 ....55 F2
Sheldon Cl *LEE/GVPK* SE12 ....142 B3
Sheldon Rd *CRICK* NW2 ....71 D1
Sheldrake Cl *CAN/RD* E16 ....107 F2
Sheldrake Pl *KENS* W8 ....101 F3
Shelduck Cl *FSTGT* E7 ....81 F2
Shelford Pl *STNW/STAM* N16 ....59 D5
Shelgate Rd *BTSEA* SW11 ....133 F3
Shelley Av *MNPK* E12 ....83 E3
Shelley Dr *WELL* DA16 ....127 E4
Shelley Rd *WLSDN* NW10 ....69 D5
Shellgrove Rd *STNW/STAM* * N16 ....77 E2
Shellness Rd *CLPT* E5 ....78 B2
Shell Rd *LEW* SE13 ....140 B1
Shellwood Rd *BTSEA* SW11 ....115 F5
Shelmerdine Cl *BOW* E3 ....92 A4
Shelton St *LSO/SEVD* * WC2H 20 C5
Shenfield St *IS* N1 ....13 D2
Shenley Rd *CMBW* SE5 ....119 E4
Shepherdess Pl *FSBYE* EC1V 11 F3
Shepherdess Wk *IS* N1 ....11 F1
Shepherd Market *MYFR/PICC* * W1J 30 C4
Shepherd's Bush Gn *SHB* W12 ....100 B4
Shepherd's Bush Market *SHB* W12 ....100 B3
Shepherd's Bush Pl *SHB* * W12 ....101 D3
Shepherd's Bush Rd *HMSMTH* W6 ....100 B4
Shepherd's Cl *HGT* N6 ....56 B1
Shepherd's Hl *HGT* N6 ....56 B1

Shepherd's La *HOM* * E9 ....79 D2
Shepherd's Leas *ELTH/MOT* * SE9 ....145 D2
Shepherds Pl *MYFR/PKLN* W1K 30 A1
Shepherd St *MYFR/PICC* W1J 30 C4
Shepherds Wk *CRICK* NW2 ....52 A4
    HAMP NW3 ....73 D3
Sheppard Dr *BERM/RHTH* SE16 ....120 B1
Sheppard Cl *CAN/RD* E16 ....93 F3
Shepperton Rd *IS* N1 ....77 D5
Sheppey Wk *IS* * N1 ....76 C4
Shepton Houses *BETH* * E2 ....90 C2
Sherard Rd *ELTH/MOT* SE9 ....143 E3
Sherborne La *MANHO* EC4N 36 A1
Sherborne St *IS* N1 ....77 D5
Sherboro Rd *SEVS/STOTM* N15 ....59 F1
Sherbrooke Rd *FUL/PGN* SW6 ....113 E3
Sherbrooke Ter *FUL/PGN* * SW6 ....113 E3
Sherfield Gdns *PUT/ROE* SW15 ....129 F4
Sheridan Rd *FSTGT* E7 ....63 F5
    MNPK E12 ....83 E2
Sheridan St *WCHPL* E1 ....90 B5
Sheridan Wk *GLDGN* NW11 ....54 A1
Sheringham Av *MNPK* E12 ....83 F1
Sheringham Dr *BARK* IG11 ....85 F2
Sheringham Rd *HOLWY* N7 ....76 A3
Sherington Rd *CHARL* SE7 ....124 B2
Sherlock Ms *MHST* W1U 18 A2
Sherrard Rd *FSTGT* E7 ....82 C3
Sherrick Green Rd *WLSDN* NW10 ....70 B2
Sheriff Rd *KIL/WHAMP* NW6 ....72 A3
Sherry Ms *BARK* IG11 ....85 D4
Sherwin Rd *NWCR* SE14 ....121 D4
Sherwood Cl *MBLAR* W1H 17 E3
Sherwood Gdns *BARK* IG11 ....85 D4
    POP/IOD E14 ....104 A5
    STHWK SE1 ....120 A1
Sherwood Rd *WELL* DA16 ....145 E1
Sherwood St *SOHO/SHAV* W1D 31 F1
Shetland Rd *BOW* E3 ....91 F1
Shifford Pth *FSTH* * SE23 ....157 D3
Shillibeer Pl *MBLAR* W1H 17 D3
Shillingford St *IS* N1 ....76 B5
Shinfield St *SHB* W12 ....88 D3
Shipka Rd *BAL* SW12 ....152 B1
Ship La *MORT/ESHN* SW14 ....128 C1
Shipman Rd *CAN/RD* E16 ....94 B5
    FSTH SE23 ....157 D2
Ship & Mermaid Rw *STHWK* * SE1 ....36 B5
Ship St *DEPT* SE8 ....122 A4
Ship Tavern Pas *BANK* EC3V 36 C1
Shipton St *BETH* E2 ....13 F3
Shipwright Rd *BERM/RHTH* SE16 ....103 E3
Shipwright Yd *STHWK* * SE1 ....36 C4
Shirburn Cl *FSTH* SE23 ....138 C5
Shirbutt St *POP/IOD* E14 ....104 A1
Shirebrook Rd *BKHTH/KID* SE3 ....125 D5
Shirehall Cl *HDN* NW4 ....53 D1
Shirehall Gdns *HDN* NW4 ....53 D1
Shirehall La *HDN* NW4 ....53 D1
Shirehall Pk *HDN* NW4 ....53 D1
Shirland Ms *MV/WKIL* W9 ....89 F2
Shirland Rd *MV/WKIL* W9 ....2 A5
Shirley Gdns *BARK* IG11 ....85 E3
Shirley Gv *BTSEA* SW11 ....134 A1
Shirley Rd *BFN/LL* DA15 ....163 E3
    CHSWK W4 ....99 D3
    SRTFD E15 ....81 E4
Shirley St *CAN/RD* E16 ....93 F5
Shirlock Rd *HAMP* NW3 ....73 F1
Shobroke Cl *CRICK* NW2 ....52 C5
Shoebury Rd *EHAM* E6 ....83 F4
Shoe La *FLST/FETLN* EC4A 22 B4
Shooters Hl *WOOL/PLUM* SE18 ....125 F4
Shooters Hill Rd *BKHTH/KID* SE3 ....123 E4
Shoot-Up Hl *CRICK* NW2 ....71 E3
Shoreditch High St *BETH* E2 ....13 D4
    WCHPL E1 ....25 D2
Shoreham Cl *WAND/EARL* SW18 ....132 B3

Shore Pl *HOM* E9 ....78 C4
Shore Rd *HOM* E9 ....78 C4
Shorncliffe Rd *STHWK* SE1 ....119 F1
Shorndean St *CAT* SE6 ....158 C1
Shorrolds Rd *FUL/PGN* SW6 ....114 A3
Shorter St *WCHPL* E1 ....37 E1
Shortlands *HMSMTH* W6 ....101 D5
Shortlands Rd *LEY* E10 ....62 B2
Short Rd *CHSWK* W4 ....111 E2
     WAN E11 ....63 E4
Shorts Gdns *LSQ/SEVD* * WC2H 20 C5
Short St *STHWK* SE1 ....34 B5
Shortway *ELTH/MOT* SE9 ....145 E1
Shottendane Rd *FUL/PGN* * SW6 ...114 A4
Shottery Cl *ELTH/MOT* SE9 ....161 D3
Shottfield Av *MORT/ESHN* SW14 ...129 E2
Shoulder of Mutton Aly
     POP/IOD E14 ....103 E1
Shouldham St *MBLAR* W1H 17 D3
Shrapnel Cl *WOOL/PLUM* SE18 ......125 D3
Shrapnel Rd *ELTH/MOT* SE9 ....143 F1
Shrewsbury Av *MORT/ESHN* SW14 ...128 C2
Shrewsbury Crs *WLSDN* NW10 ....69 D5
Shrewsbury La *WOOL/PLUM* SE18 ...126 B4
Shrewsbury Ms *BAY/PAD* W2 ....14 A4
Shrewsbury Rd *BAY/PAD* W2 ....14 A3
     MNPK E12 ....83 D3
Shrewsbury St *NKENS* W10 ....88 C3
Shroffold Rd *BMLY* BR1 ....159 E4
Shroton St *CAMTN* NW1 ....16 C2
Shrubbery Rd *STRHM/NOR* SW16 ...153 E4
Shrubland Cl *HACK* E8 ....78 A5
     LEY E10 ....62 A2
Shrublands Cl *SYD* SE26 ....156 C1
Shrubsall Cl *ELTH/MOT* SE9 ....161 E1
Shuna Wk *IS* * N1 ....77 D3
Shurland Gdns *PECK* * SE15 ....119 F3
Shuters Sq *WKENS* * W14 ....113 F1
Shuttle Cl *BFN/LL* DA15 ....145 F5
Shuttle St *WCHPL* E1 ....90 A3
Shuttleworth Rd *BTSEA* SW11 ....115 D5
Sibella Rd *CLAP* SW4 ....117 D5
Sibley Gv *MNPK* E12 ....83 E4
Sibthorpe Rd *LEE/GVPK* SE12 ....142 B5
Sicilian Av *NOXST/BSQ* * WC1A 21 D3
Sicilion Av *NOXST/BSQ* WC1A 21 D3
Sidbury St *FUL/PGN* SW6 ....113 E4
Sidcup By-Pass Rd *SCUP* DA14 ....163 E4
Sidcup Rd *ELTH/MOT* SE9 ....161 D1
     LEE/GVPK SE12 ....142 B3
Siddons La *CAMTN* NW1 ....17 F1
Siddons Rd *FSTH* SE23 ....157 E2
Sidewood Rd *ELTH/MOT* SE9 ....163 D1
Sidford Pl *STHWK* SE1 ....45 F3
The Sidings *WAN* E11 ....62 C3
Sidmouth Pde *CRICK* * NW2 ....70 C4
Sidmouth Rd *LEY* E10 ....62 C5
     WLSDN NW10 ....70 C4
Sidmouth St *STPAN* WC1H 9 D4
Sidney Elson Wy *EHAM* E6 ....96 A1
Sidney Gv *FSBYE* EC1V 10 C1
Sidney Rd *BRXN/ST* SW9 ....117 F5
     FSTGT E7 ....64 A5
Sidney Sq *WCHPL* * E1 ....90 C4
Sidney St *WCHPL* E1 ....90 B4
Sidworth St *HACK* E8 ....78 B4
Siebert Rd *BKHTH/KID* SE3 ....124 A2
Siemens Rd *WOOL/PLUM* SE18 ......107 D4
Sienna Ter *CRICK* * NW2 ....52 A4
Sigdon Rd *HACK* E8 ....78 A2
Signmakers Yd *CAMTN* * NW1 ....74 B5
Silbury St *IS* * N1 ....12 A3
Silchester Rd *NKENS* W10 ....89 D5
Silesia Buildings *HACK* E8 ....78 B4
Silex St *STHWK* SE1 ....47 D1
Silk Cl *LEE/GVPK* SE12 ....142 A3
Silk Mills Pth *LEW* SE13 ....140 C1

Silk St *BARB* EC2Y 23 F2
Silver Birch Cl *CAT* SE6 ....157 F3
Silverbirch Wk *HAMP* * NW3 ....73 F3
Silver Cl *NWCR* * SE14 ....121 E3
Silver Crs *CHSWK* W4 ....98 B5
Silverdale *CAMTN* NW1 ....7 E2
     SYD SE26 ....156 C4
Silverdale Dr *ELTH/MOT* SE9 ....161 E2
Silver Dene *PUT/ROE* * SW15 ....130 C3
Silvermere Rd *LEW* SE13 ....140 A4
Silver Rd *SHB* W12 ....101 D1
Silverthorne Rd *VX/NE* SW8 ....116 B5
Silverton Rd *HMSMTH* W6 ....113 D3
Silvertown Wy *CAN/RD* E16 ....93 F5
Silver Wk *BERM/RHTH* SE16 ....103 F2
Silvester Rd *EDUL* SE22 ....137 F3
Silvester St *STHWK* SE1 ....48 A1
Silwood St *BERM/RHTH* SE16 ....121 D1
Simmons Rd *WOOL/PLUM* SE18 ......126 B1
Simms Rd *STHWK* SE1 ....102 A5
Simnel Rd *LEE/GVPK* SE12 ....142 B5
Simon Cl *NTGHL* W11 ....101 F1
Simonds Rd *LEY* E10 ....62 A4
Simons Wk *SRTFD* E15 ....81 D2
Simpson Dr *ACT* W3 ....87 D5
Simpson's Rd *POP/IOD* E14 ....104 B1
Simpson St *BTSEA* SW11 ....115 E5
Sinclair Gdns *WKENS* W14 ....101 E1
Sinclair Gv *GLDGN* NW11 ....53 D1
Sinclair Rd *WKENS* W14 ....101 E1
Singer St *FSBYE* EC1V 12 B4
Sir Abraham Dawes Cottages
     PUT/ROE * SW15 ....131 E2
Sir Alexander Cl *ACT* W3 ....99 F1
Sirdar Rd *NTGHL* W11 ....101 D1
Sir John Kirk Cl *CMBW* SE5 ....118 C3
Sir Thomas Moore Est *CHEL* SW3 ...115 D2
Sise La *MANHO* * EC4N 24 A5
Sisley Rd *BARK* IG11 ....85 E5
Sispara Gdns *WAND/EARL* SW18 .....131 F4
Sissinghurst Cl *BMLY* BR1 ....159 E5
Sister Mabel's Wy *PECK* * SE15 ....120 A3
Sisters Av *BTSEA* SW11 ....133 F2
Sistova Rd *BAL* SW12 ....152 B1
Sisulu Pl *BRXN/ST* SW9 ....136 A1
Siward Rd *TOOT* SW17 ....150 C3
Sixth Av *MNPK* E12 ....83 F1
     NKENS W10 ....89 E3
Skardu Rd *CRICK* NW2 ....71 E2
Skeena Hl *WIM/MER* SW19 ....131 E5
Skeffington Rd *EHAM* E6 ....83 F5
Skelbrook St *WAND/EARL* SW18 .....150 B2
Skelgill Rd *PUT/ROE* SW15 ....131 F2
Skelley Rd *SRTFD* E15 ....81 F4
Skelton Cl *HACK* * E8 ....77 F3
Skelton Rd *FSTGT* E7 ....82 A3
Skelton's La *LEY* E10 ....62 B2
Skelwith Rd *HMSMTH* W6 ....112 C2
Sketchley Gdns *BERM/RHTH* SE16 ...121 D1
Skiers St *SRTFD* E15 ....81 E5
Skiffington Cl *BRXS/STRHM* SW2 ....154 A1
Skinner Pl *BGVA* * SW1W 42 A5
Skinners La *BLKFR* EC4V 35 F1
Skinner St *CLKNW* EC1R 10 B4
Skipsea Av *EHAM* E6 ....95 F2
Skipworth Rd *HOM* E9 ....78 C5
Skylines Village *POP/IOD* * E14 ....104 C3
The Slade *WOOL/PLUM* SE18 ....127 E2
Sladebrook Rd *BKHTH/KID* SE3 ......143 D1
Sladedale Rd *WOOL/PLUM* SE18 .....127 E1
Sladen Pl *CLPT* E5 ....78 B1
Slades Dr *CHST* BR7 ....162 C3
Slade Wk *WALW* SE17 ....118 B2
Slagrove Pl *BROCKY* SE4 ....140 A3
Slaidburn St *WBPTN* SW10 ....114 C2
Slaithwaite Rd *LEW* SE13 ....140 C2
Slaney Pl *HOLWY* N7 ....75 F3
Sleaford St *VX/NE* SW8 ....116 C3

Slievemore Cl CLAP SW4 ....135 D1
Slingsby Pl COVGDN WC2E 32 C1
Slippers Pl BERM/RHTH SE16 ....102 B4
Sloane Av CHEL SW3 ....41 D5
Sloane Ct East CHEL SW3 ....116 A1
Sloane Ct West CHEL SW3 ....116 A1
Sloane Gdns BGVA SW1W 42 A5
Sloane Sq BGVA SW1W 41 F5
Sloane St KTBR SW1X 41 F3
Sloane Ter SW1X 41 F4
Sly St WCHPL * E1 ....90 B5
Smallbrook Ms BAY/PAD W2 ....16 A5
Smalley Cl STNW/STAM N16 ....59 F5
Smallwood Rd TOOT SW17 ....151 D4
Smart's Pl HHOL WC1V 21 D4
Smart St BETH E2 ....91 D2
Smeaton Rd WAND/EARL SW18 ....132 A5
Smeaton St WAP E1W 102 B2
Smedley St VX/NE SW8 ....117 D5
Smeed Rd BOW E3 ....80 A4
Smiles Pl LEW SE13 ....122 C5
Smith Cl BERM/RHTH SE16 ....103 D2
Smith Sq WEST SW1P 48 A1
Smith Ter CHEL SW3 ....115 F1
Smithfield St STBT EC1A 22 C3
Smith's Ct SOHO/SHAV * W1D 32 A1
Smith St CHEL SW3 ....115 F1
Smith Ter CHEL SW3 ....115 F1
Smithwood Cl WIM/MER SW19 ....149 E1
Smithy St WCHPL E1 ....90 C4
Smugglers Wy WAND/EARL SW18 ....132 B2
WALW SE17 ....119 E1
Smyrks Rd WALW * SE17 ....119 E1
Smyrna Rd KIL/WHAMP NW6 ....72 A4
Smythe St POP/IOD E14 ....104 B1
Snarsgate St NKENS W10 ....88 C4
Sneath Av GLDGN NW11 ....53 F2
Sneyd Rd CRICK NW2 ....70 C2
Snowbury Rd FUL/PGN SW6 ....114 B5
Snowden Dr CDALE/KGS NW9 ....51 E1
Snow Hl STBT EC1A 22 C3
Snowsfields STHWK SE1 ....36 B5
Snowshill Rd MNPK E12 ....83 E2
Soames St PECK SE15 ....137 F1
Soho Sq SOHO/SHAV W1D 20 A4
Soho St SOHO/SHAV W1D 20 A4
Sojourner Truth Cl HACK * E8 ....78 B3
Solander Gdns WCHPL E1 ....102 B1
Solebay St WCHPL E1 ....91 E1
Solent Ri PLSTW E13 ....94 A2
Solent Rd KIL/WHAMP NW6 ....72 A4
Solna Av PUT/ROE SW15 ....130 C3
Solomon's Pas PECK SE15 ....138 B2
Solon New Rd CLAP SW4 ....135 E2
Solon Rd CLAP SW4 ....135 E2
Solway Cl HACK E8 ....77 F3
Solway Rd EDUL SE22 ....138 A2
Somali Rd CRICK NW2 ....71 F1
Somerby Rd BARK IG11 ....85 D4
Somerfield Rd FSBYPK N4 ....58 B4
Somerford Gv STNW/STAM N16 ....77 F1
Somerford Wy WCHPL E1 ....90 B3
Somerford Wy BERM/RHTH SE16 ....103 E3
Somerleyton Rd BRXN/ST SW9 ....136 A2
Somers Cl CAMTN * NW1 ....8 A1
Somers Crs BAY/PAD W2 ....16 C5
Somerset Av RWEL DA16 ....145 F3
Somerset Gdns HGT N6 ....56 A2
LEW SE13 ....122 B5
Somerset Rd CHSWK W4 ....99 D4
WIM/MER SW19 ....149 D3
Somerset Sq WKENS * W14 ....101 E1
Somerset St Little TWRH EC3N 25 E5
Somers Pl BRXS/STRHM SW2 ....135 F5
Somers Rd BRXS/STRHM SW2 ....135 F4
Somerton Av RCH/KEW TW9 ....128 B1
Somerton Rd CRICK NW2 ....53 D5
PECK SE15 ....138 B2
Somertrees Av LEE/GVPK SE12 ....160 B2
Somerville Av BARN SW13 ....112 C2

Sonderburg Rd HOLWY N7 ....57 F4
Sondes St WALW SE17 ....119 D2
Sonia Gdns CRICK NW2 ....69 F1
Soper Cl FSTH SE23 ....157 D3
Sophia Cl HOLWY N7 ....75 F3
Sophia Rd CAN/RD E16 ....94 B5
LEY E10 ....62 B3
Sophia Sq BERM/RHTH SE16 ....103 E1
Sopwith Wy VX/NE SW8 ....116 B3
Sorrel Gdns EHAM E6 ....95 E4
Sorrel La POP/IOD E14 ....93 D5
Sorrell Cl BRXN/ST * SW9 ....118 A5
NWCR SE14 ....121 E3
Sotheby Rd HBRY N5 ....76 C1
Sotheran Cl HACK E8 ....78 A5
Soudan Rd BTSEA SW11 ....115 F4
Souldern Rd WKENS * W14 ....101 D4
South Access Rd WALTH E17 ....61 E2
South Africa Rd SHB W12 ....100 B1
Southall Pl STHWK SE1 ....48 A1
Southampton Buildings LINN * WC2A 22 A3
Southampton Pl NOXST/BSQ WC1A 21 D3
Southampton Rd HAMP NW3 ....73 F2
Southampton Rw RSQ WC1B 21 D2
Southampton St COVGDN WC2E 33 D1
Southampton Wy CMBW SE5 ....119 D3
Southam St NKENS W10 ....89 D3
South Audley St MYFR/PKLN W1K 30 B2
South Av RCH/KEW * TW9 ....110 A5
South Bank STHWK SE1 ....34 B2
South Birkbeck Rd WAN E11 ....63 D5
South Black Lion La HMSMTH W6 ....112 A1
South Bolton Gdns WBPTN SW10 ....114 B1
Southborough Rd HOM E9 ....78 C5
Southbourne Gdns IL IG1 ....84 C2
LEE/GVPK SE12 ....142 B3
Southbrook Rd LEW SE13 ....141 E4
South Carriage Dr KTBR SW1X 29 E5
SKENS SW7 ....40 C1
Southchurch Rd EHAM E6 ....95 F1
South Cl HGT N6 ....56 B1
The South Colonnade POP/IOD E14 ....104 B2
South Colonnade POP/IOD E14 ....104 A2
Southcombe St WKENS W14 ....101 E5
Southcote Rd ARCH N19 ....74 C1
South Crs CAN/RD E16 ....93 D3
Southcroft Av WELL DA16 ....145 E1
South Croxted Rd DUL SE21 ....155 D3
Southdean Gdns WIM/MER SW19 ....149 F2
South Eaton Pl BGVA SW1W 42 B4
South Edwardes Sq KENS W8 ....101 E4
South End KENS W8 ....39 D2
Southend Cl ELTH/MOT SE9 ....144 B4
Southend Crs ELTH/MOT SE9 ....144 A4
Southend La CAT SE6 ....157 F4
South End Rd HAMP NW3 ....73 E1
South End Rw KENS W8 ....39 D2
Southerngate Wy NWCR SE14 ....121 E3
Southern Gv BOW E3 ....91 F2
Southern Rd PLSTW E13 ....94 B1
Southern Rw NKENS W10 ....89 D3
Southern St IS N1 ....9 E1
Southerton Rd HMSMTH * W6 ....100 C5
South Esk Rd FSTGT E7 ....82 C3
Southey Rd BRXN/ST SW9 ....118 A4
Southfield Rd CHSWK W4 ....99 D3
Southfields Ms WAND/EARL * SW18 ....132 A4
Southfields Rd WAND/EARL SW18 ....132 A4
South Gdns WBLY * HA9 ....50 A4
Southgate Gv IS N1 ....77 D4
Southgate Rd IS N1 ....77 D5
South Gv HGT N6 ....56 A3
South Hill Pk HAMP NW3 ....73 E1
South Hill Park Gdns HAMP NW3 ....73 E1
Southill St POP/IOD E14 ....92 B5
South Island Pl BRXN/ST SW9 ....117 F3
South Kensington Station Ar
    SKENS SW7 ....40 B4

South Lambeth Pl VX/NE SW8............117 E2
South Lambeth Rd VX/NE SW8............117 E2
Southland Rd WOOL/PLUM SE18............127 F3
Southlands Dr WIM/MER SW19............149 D2
Southmead Rd WIM/MER SW19............149 E1
South Molton La MYFR/PKLN W1K............30 B3
South Molton Rd CAN/RD E16............94 A5
South Molton St MYFR/PKLN W1K............18 C5
Southmoor Wy HOM E9............79 F3
South Oak Rd STRHM/NOR SW16............153 F4
Southold Ri ELTH/MOT SE9............161 F3
Southolm St VX/NE SW8............116 B4
Southover BMLY BR1............160 A5
South Pde CHEL SW3............199 D5
CHSWK W4............99 D5
South Park Crs CAT SE6............159 E1
IL IG1............67 D5
South Park Dr GDMY/SEVK IG3............85 E2
IL IG1............67 E5
South Park Ms FUL/PGN SW6............132 B1
South Park Rd IL IG1............67 D5
South Park Ter IL IG1............67 D5
South Pl LVPST EC2M............24 B3
South Place Ms LVPST EC2M............24 B3
Southport Rd WOOL/PLUM SE18............109 D5
South Ri BAY/PAD * W2............29 D1
South Rd FSTH SE23............157 D2
South Rw BKHTH/KID SE3............124 D1
South Sea St BERM/RHTH SE16............103 F4
South Side HMSMTH W6............99 F4
Southspring ELTH/MOT SE9............145 D5
South Sq GINN WC1R............22 A3
GLDGN NW11............54 A1
South St MYFR/PKLN W1K............30 B3
South Tenter St WCHPL E1............37 F1
South Ter SKENS SW7............40 C4
Southvale Rd BKHTH/KID SE3............123 E5
Southview Av WLSDN NW10............69 F2
Southview Cl TOOT SW17............152 A5
South View Crs GNTH/NBYPK IG2............66 B1
Southview Rd BMLY BR1............159 D4
South Vls CAMTN NW1............75 D3
Southville VX/NE SW8............117 D4
Southwark Br CANST EC4R............35 F2
Southwark Bridge Rd STHWK SE1............35 F3
Southwark Park Est
  BERM/RHTH * SE16............102 B5
Southwark Park Rd
  BERM/RHTH SE16............49 F4
Southwark St STHWK SE1............35 D3
Southway GLDGN NW11............54 B1
South Wy WBLY HA9............68 A2
Southwell Gdns SKENS SW7............39 E4
Southwell Grove Rd WAN E11............63 E4
Southwell Rd CMBW SE5............136 C1
Southwest Rd WAN E11............63 D3
South Wharf Rd BAY/PAD W2............16 A4
Southwick Ms BAY/PAD W2............16 B4
Southwick Pl BAY/PAD W2............16 C5
Southwick St BAY/PAD W2............16 C4
Southwick Yd BAY/PAD * W2............17 D5
Southwold Rd CLPT E5............60 B4
Southwood Av HGT N6............56 B2
Southwood La HGT N6............56 A2
Southwood Lawn Rd HGT N6............56 A2
Southwood Pk HGT * N6............56 B2
Southwood Rd ELTH/MOT SE9............162 B2
Southwood Smith St IS * N1............76 A5
South Worple Wy MORT/ESHN SW14............129 D1
Sovereign Cl WAP E1W............102 B1
Sovereign Crs BERM/RHTH SE16............103 E1
Sovereign Ms BETH * E2............13 E1
Sovereign Pk WLSDN NW10............86 B3
Sowerby Cl ELTH/MOT SE9............143 F3
Spafield St CLKNW * EC1R............10 A5
Spa Green Est CLKNW * EC1R............10 B3
Spalding Rd HDN NW4............52 C1
  TOOT SW17............152 B2

Spanby Rd BOW E3............92 A3
Spaniards Cl GLDGN NW11............54 C3
Spaniards End GLDGN NW11............54 C3
Spaniards Rd HAMP NW3............54 C4
Spanish Pl MHST * W1U............18 B4
Spanish Rd WAND/EARL SW18............132 C3
Sparke Ter CAN/RD * E16............93 F5
Sparks Cl ACT W3............87 D5
Spa Rd BERM/RHTH SE16............49 E5
Sparrows La ELTH/MOT SE9............144 C5
Sparsholt Rd ARCH N19............57 F3
  BARK IG11............85 E5
Sparta St LEW SE13............122 C4
Spearman St WOOL/PLUM * SE18............126 A2
Spear Ms ECT SW5............38 B5
Spears Rd ARCH N19............57 E3
Spedan Cl HAMP NW3............54 B5
Speedwell St DEPT SE8............122 A3
Spekehill ELTH/MOT SE9............161 F5
Speldhurst Rd CHSWK W4............99 D4
  HOM E9............79 D4
Spellbrook Wk IS * N1............76 C5
Spelman St WCHPL E1............90 A4
Spence Cl BERM/RHTH SE16............103 F3
Spencer Dr EFNCH N2............54 C1
Spencer Gdns MORT/ESHN SW14............128 C3
Spencer Ms HMSMTH W6............113 E2
Spencer Pk WAND/EARL SW18............133 D3
Spencer Pl IS N1............76 B4
  WEST SW1P............43 F3
Spencer Ri KTTN NW5............74 B1
Spencer Rd ACT W3............98 C2
  BTSEA SW11............133 D2
  CHSWK W4............110 C3
  EHAM E6............83 D5
  GDMY/SEVK IG3............67 F3
Spencer St FSBYE EC1V............10 C4
Spencer Wk PUT/ROE SW15............131 D2
Spenser Gv STNW/STAM N16............77 E3
Spenser Ms DUL SE21............155 D1
Spenser Rd HNHL SE24............136 B3
Spenser St WESTW SW1E............43 F2
Spensley Wk STNW/STAM N16............59 D5
Speranza St WOOL/PLUM SE18............127 F1
Spert St POP/IOD E14............103 E1
Spey St POP/IOD E14............92 C4
Spezia Rd WLSDN NW10............88 A1
Spicer Cl CMBW SE5............118 B5
Spindle Cl WOOL/PLUM SE18............107 E4
Spindrift Av POP/IOD E14............104 B5
Spinel Cl WOOL/PLUM SE18............127 F1
The Spinney BARN * SW13............112 B2
  STRHM/NOR SW16............152 C3
Spinney Gdns NRWD SE19............155 F5
Spirit Quay WAP E1W............102 A2
Spital Sq WCHPL E1............25 D2
Spital St WCHPL E1............90 A4
Spital Yd WCHPL * E1............25 D2
Spode Wk KIL/WHAMP * NW6............72 B2
Sportsbank St CAT SE6............140 C5
Spratt Hall Rd WAN E11............64 A1
Spray St WOOL/PLUM SE18............108 B5
Sprimont Pl CHEL SW3............115 F1
Springall St PECK SE15............120 B3
Springbank Rd LEW SE13............141 E4
Springbank Wk CAMTN NW1............75 D4
Springdale Rd STNW/STAM N16............77 D1
Springfield CLPT E5............60 B3
Springfield Gdns CLPT E5............60 B3
Springfield Gv CHARL SE7............124 C2
Springfield La KIL/WHAMP NW6............72 A5
Springfield Ri SYD SE26............156 B4
Springfield Rd EHAM E6............83 F4
  SRTFD * E15............93 E2
  STJWD NW8............72 C5
  SYD SE26............156 B5
  WALTH E17............61 F1
  WIM/MER SW19............149 F5

Springfield Wk KIL/WHAMP NW6 ....72 B5
Spring Gdns HBRY N5 ....76 C2
   WHALL SW1A 32 C3
Spring Gv CHSWK W4 ....110 A1
Spring Hl CLPT E5 ....60 A2
   SYD SE26 ....156 C4
Spring La CLPT E5 ....60 B3
Spring Ms MHST * W1U 17 F2
Springpark Dr FSBYPK N4 ....58 C3
Spring Pl KTTN NW5 ....74 A2
Springrice Rd LEW SE13 ....140 C4
Spring St BAY/PAD W2 ....16 A5
Spring Tide Cl PECK * SE15 ....120 A4
Springvale Ter WKENS W14 ....101 D4
Spring Wk WCHPL E1 ....90 A4
Springwater Cl WOOL/PLUM * SE18 ....126 A4
Springwell Av WLSDN NW10 ....69 F5
Springwell Rd STRHM/NOR SW16 ....154 A4
Sprowston Ms FSTGT E7 ....82 A3
Sprowston Rd FSTGT E7 ....82 A2
Sprules Rd BROCKY SE4 ....121 E5
Spurgeon St STHWK SE1 ....48 A3
Spurling Rd EDUL * SE22 ....137 F2
Spur Rd BARK IG11 ....96 C2
   STHWK SE1 ....46 A1
   WHALL SW1A 43 E1
Spurstowe Rd HACK E8 ....78 B3
Spurstowe Ter HACK E8 ....78 A2
The Square HMSMTH W6 ....112 C1
Squarey St TOOT SW17 ....150 C3
Squire Gdns STJWD NW8 ....4 A4
Squires Ct WIM/MER SW19 ....150 A4
Squire's Mt HAMP NW3 ....55 D5
The Squirrels LEW SE13 ....141 D1
Squirries St BETH E2 ....90 A2
Stable Ms WNWD SE27 ....154 C5
Stables Wy LBTH SE11 ....118 A1
Stable Wy NKENS W10 ....88 C5
Stable Yard Rd WHALL SW1A 31 F4
Stacey St HOLWY N7 ....58 A5
   LSO/SEVD WC2H 20 B5
Stackhouse St KTBR SW1X 41 E2
Stacy Pth CMBW * SE5 ....119 E3
Stadium Rd WOOL/PLUM SE18 ....125 F3
Stadium St WBPTN SW10 ....114 C3
Staffa Rd LEY E10 ....61 E3
Stafford Cl KIL/WHAMP NW6 ....2 A1
   WALTH E17 ....61 F1
Stafford Pl WESTW SW1E 43 E2
Stafford Rd BOW E3 ....91 F1
   FSTGT E7 ....82 C4
   KIL/WHAMP NW6 ....2 A3
   SCUP DA14 ....163 E4
Staffordshire St PECK SE15 ....120 A4
Stafford Ter KENS W8 ....38 A2
Stag Pl WESTW SW1E 43 E2
Stainer St STHWK SE1 ....36 B4
Staines Rd IL IG1 ....85 D1
Stainforth Rd GNTH/NBYPK IG2 ....67 D2
Staining La CITYW EC2V 23 F4
Stainsbury St BETH E2 ....90 C1
Stainsby Pl POP/IOD * E14 ....92 A5
Stainsby Rd POP/IOD E14 ....92 A5
Stainton Rd LEW SE13 ....141 D5
Stalbridge St CAMTN NW1 ....17 D2
Stalham St BERM/RHTH SE16 ....102 B4
Stamford Brook Av HMSMTH W6 ....99 F4
Stamford Brook Gdns HMSMTH W6 ....99 F4
Stamford Brook Rd HMSMTH W6 ....99 F4
Stamford Cottages FUL/PGN * SW6 ....114 B3
Stamford Gv East STNW/STAM N16 ....60 A3
Stamford Gv West STNW/STAM N16 ....60 A3
Stamford Hl STNW/STAM N16 ....59 F3
Stamford Rd EHAM E6 ....83 E5
   IS N1 ....77 D4
Stamford St STHWK SE1 ....34 A4
Stamp Pl BETH E2 ....13 E3

Stanborough HACK E8 ....77 F3
Stanbridge Rd PUT/ROE SW15 ....130 C1
Stanbury Ct HAMP NW3 ....73 F3
Stanbury Rd PECK SE15 ....120 B4
Standard Pl SDTCH EC2A 13 D4
Standard Rd WLSDN NW10 ....86 C3
Standen Rd WAND/EARL SW18 ....132 A5
Standish Rd HMSMTH W6 ....100 A5
Stane Wy WOOL/PLUM SE18 ....125 D3
Stanfield Rd BOW E3 ....91 E1
Stanford Pl STHWK SE1 ....48 C5
Stanford Rd KENS W8 ....39 D3
Stanford St WEST SW1P 44 A5
Stanhope Cl BERM/RHTH * SE16 ....103 D3
Stanhope Gdns FSBYPK N4 ....58 B1
   HGT N6 ....56 B1
   IL IG1 ....65 F3
   SKENS SW7 ....39 F4
Stanhope Ga BAY/PAD W2 ....29 E1
   MYFR/PKLN W1K 30 B4
Stanhope Ms East SKENS SW7 ....39 F4
Stanhope Ms South SKENS SW7 ....39 F5
Stanhope Ms West SKENS SW7 ....39 F4
Stanhope Pde CAMTN NW1 ....7 D3
Stanhope Pl BAY/PAD W2 ....17 E5
Stanhope Rd HGT N6 ....56 C1
Stanhope Rw MYFR/PICC * W1J 30 C4
Stanhope St CAMTN NW1 ....7 E3
Stanhope Ter BAY/PAD W2 ....28 B1
Stanier Cl ECT SW5 ....113 F1
Stanlake Rd SHB W12 ....100 C2
Stanlake Vls SHB W12 ....100 C2
Stanley Av BARK IG11 ....97 F2
Stanley Gdns ACT W3 ....99 E3
   CRICK NW2 ....70 C2
   NTGHL W11 ....101 F1
Stanley Gv VX/NE SW8 ....116 A5
Stanley Pas CAMTN NW1 ....8 C2
Stanley Rd ACT W3 ....98 B4
   IL IG1 ....67 D4
   LEY E10 ....62 B1
   MNPK E12 ....83 E2
   MORT/ESHN SW14 ....128 B2
   SRTFD E15 ....81 D5
Stanley St DEPT SE8 ....121 F3
Stanley Ter ARCH * N19 ....57 E4
Stanmer St BTSEA SW11 ....115 E4
Stanmore Rd WAN E11 ....63 F3
Stanmore St IS N1 ....75 F5
Stannard Ms HACK * E8 ....78 A3
Stannard Rd HACK E8 ....78 A3
Stannary St LBTH SE11 ....118 A2
Stansfeld Rd CAN/RD E16 ....95 D5
Stansfield Rd BRXN/ST SW9 ....135 F1
Stanstead Gv FSTH SE23 ....157 F1
Stanstead Rd FSTH SE23 ....157 D1
Stanswood Gdns CMBW SE5 ....119 E3
Stanthorpe Cl STRHM/NOR * SW16 ....153 E5
Stanthorpe Rd STRHM/NOR SW16 ....153 E5
Stanton Rd BARN SW13 ....111 F5
Stanton St PECK * SE15 ....120 A4
Stanton Wy SYD SE26 ....157 F4
Stanway Gdns ACT W3 ....98 A2
Stanway St IS N1 ....13 D1
Stanwick Rd WKENS W14 ....101 F5
Stanworth St STHWK SE1 ....49 E1
Staplefield Cl BRXS/STRHM * SW2 ....153 E1
Stapleford Cl WIM/MER SW19 ....131 E5
Staplehurst Rd LEW SE13 ....141 D3
Staple Inn HHOL WC1V 22 A3
Staples Cl BERM/RHTH SE16 ....103 E2
Staple St STHWK SE1 ....48 B1
Stapleton Hall Rd FSBYPK N4 ....57 F2
Stapleton Rd TOOT SW17 ....152 A3
Stapleton Vls STNW/STAM * N16 ....77 E1
Starboard Wy POP/IOD E14 ....104 A4
Starcross St CAMTN NW1 ....7 F4

Starfield Rd *SHB* W12 ....**100** A3
Star La *CAN/RD* E16 ....**93** E3
Star Rd *WKENS* W14 ....**113** F2
Star St *BAY/PAD* W2 ....**16** B4
Star Yd *LINN* WC2A **22** A4
Statham Gv *FUL/PGN* SW6 ....**131** D4
Station Ap *BKHTH/KID* SE3 ....**142** B1
  CAMTN * NW1 ....**18** A1
  CAT SE6.......................................**157** F5
  FSTGT * E7 ....**82** B1
  FUL/PGN * SW6 ....**131** E1
  GLDGN * NW11 ....**53** D2
  RCH/KEW TW9 ....**110** A4
  STRHM/NOR SW16 ....**153** D5
  WAN * E11 ....**81** E1
  WELL DA16 ....**127** F5
  WLSDN NW10 ....**87** E2
Station Approach Rd *CHSWK* W4 ...**110** C3
Station Ar *GTPST* * W1W **19** D1
Station Chambers *EA* * W5 ....**86** A3
Station Crs *BKHTH/KID* SE3 ....**124** A1
Stationers Hall Ct *STP* * EC4M **23** D5
Station Gdns *CHSWK* W4 ....**110** C3
Station Pde *ACT* * W3 ....**86** A5
  BAL * SW12....................................**152** A1
  BARK IG11 ....**84** C4
  CHSWK * W4 ....**98** C5
  CHSWK * W4 ....**110** C3
  CLPT * E5 ....**60** B5
  CRICK NW2.....................................**70** C3
  EHAM * E6 ....**82** C5
  EHAM * E6 ....**83** E4
  RCH/KEW TW9 ....**110** A4
Station Pas *PECK* SE15 ....**120** C4
Station Pl *FSBYPK* N4 ....**58** A4
Station Ri *WNWD* SE27 ....**154** B2
Station Rd *ARCH* N19 ....**56** C5
  BARN SW13 ....**111** F5
  HDN NW4 ....**52** A1
  IL IG1...**66** B5
  LEW SE13 ....**140** C1
  MNPK E12 ....**83** D1
  WALTH E17 ....**61** E1
  WLSDN NW10 ....**87** F1
Station St *SRTFD* E15 ....**81** D4
Station Ter *CMBW* SE5 ....**118** C4
  WLSDN NW10 ....**89** D1
Staunton St *DEPT* SE8 ....**121** F2
Staveley Gdns *HOLWY* * N7 ....**75** F3
  PECK SE15 ....**120** C4
Staveley Rd *CHSWK* W4 ....**110** C2
Staverton Rd *CRICK* NW2 ....**70** C4
Stave Yard Rd *BERM/RHTH* SE16 ..**103** E2
Stavordale Rd *HBRY* N5 ....**76** A1
Stayner's Rd *WCHPL* E1 ....**91** D3
Stead St *WALW* SE17 ....**48** A5
Stean St *HACK* E8 ....**77** F5
Stebondale St *POP/IOD* E14 ....**122** C1
Steedman St *WALW* SE17 ....**47** E5
Steele Rd *CHSWK* W4 ....**98** C4
  WAN E11 ....**81** E1
  WLSDN NW10 ....**86** C1
Steele's Ms North *HAMP* * NW3 ....**73** F3
Steele's Ms South *HAMP* NW3 ....**73** F3
Steele's Rd *HAMP* NW3 ....**73** F3
Steeles Studios *HAMP* * NW3 ....**73** F3
Steel's La *WCHPL* E1 ....**90** C5
Steelyard Pas *CANST* EC4R **36** A2
Steep Hl *STRHM/NOR* SW16 ....**153** D2
Steeple Cl *FUL/PGN* SW6 ....**131** E1
  WIM/MER SW19 ....**149** E4
Steeple Wk *IS* * N1 ....**76** C5
Steerforth St *WAND/EARL* SW18 ...**150** B2
Steers Wy *BERM/RHTH* SE16 ....**103** E3
Stellman Cl *CLPT* E5 ....**60** A5
Stephan Cl *HACK* E8 ....**78** A5
Stephendale Rd *FUL/PGN* SW6 .....**114** B5

Stephen Ms *FITZ* W1T **20** A3
Stephen Pl *CLAP* SW4 ....**134** C1
Stephenson St *CAN/RD* E16 ....**93** E4
  WLSDN NW10 ....**87** E2
Stephenson Wy *CAMTN* NW1 ....**7** F5
Stephen's Rd *SRTFD* E15 ....**81** E5
Stephen St *FITZ* W1T **20** A4
Stepney Cswy *WCHPL* E1 ....**91** D5
Stepney Gn *WCHPL* E1 ....**90** C4
Stepney High St *WCHPL* E1 ....**91** D4
Stepney Wy *WCHPL* E1 ....**90** B5
Sterling Cl *WLSDN* NW10 ....**70** A4
Sterling Gdns *NWCR* SE14 ....**121** E2
Sterling St *SKENS* SW7 ....**41** D1
Sterndale Rd *WKENS* * W14 ....**101** D4
Sterne St *SHB* W12 ....**101** D3
Sternhall La *PECK* SE15 ....**138** A1
Sternhold Av *BRXS/STRHM* SW2 ...**153** D2
Sterry Rd *BARK* IG11 ....**85** F5
Sterry St *STHWK* SE1 ....**48** A1
Steucers La *WAN* SE23 ....**157** E1
Steve Biko La *CAT* SE6 ....**158** A4
Steve Biko Rd *HOLWY* N7 ....**58** A5
Stevedore St *WAP* E1W **102** B2
Stevenage Rd *EHAM* E6 ....**84** A3
  FUL/PGN SW6 ....**113** D4
Stevens Av *HOM* E9 ....**78** C3
Stevenson Crs *BERM/RHTH* SE16 ..**120** A1
Stevens St *STHWK* SE1 ....**49** D2
Steventon Rd *SHB* W12 ....**99** F1
Steward St *WCHPL* E1 ....**25** D2
Stewart Cl *CDALE/KGS* * NW9 ....**50** C1
  CHST BR7 ....**162** B5
Stewart Rd *WAN* E11 ....**81** D1
Stewart's Gv *CHEL* SW3 ....**115** D1
  CHEL * SW3 ....**115** D1
Stewart's Rd *VX/NE* SW8 ....**116** B3
Stewarts Rd *VX/NE* SW8 ....**116** C3
  VX/NE SW8 ....**116** C3
Stewart St *POP/IOD* E14 ....**104** C3
Stew La *BLKFR* EC4V **35** E1
Steyne Rd *ACT* W3 ....**98** B2
Steyning Gv *ELTH/MOT* SE9 ....**161** F4
Stile Hall Gdns *CHSWK* W4 ....**110** A1
Stillingfleet Rd *BARN* SW13 ....**112** A3
Stillington St *WEST* SW1P **43** F4
Stillness Rd *FSTH* SE23 ....**139** E4
Stirling Rd *ACT* W3 ....**98** B4
  BRXN SW9 ....**117** E5
  PLSTW E13 ....**94** B1
St John's Est *IS* N1 ....**12** B2
  STHWK SE1 ....**37** E5
Stockfield Rd *STRHM/NOR* SW16 ..**153** F3
Stockholm Rd *BERM/RHTH* SE16 ...**120** C1
Stockholm Wy *WAP* * E1W **102** A2
Stockhurst Cl *PUT/ROE* SW15 ....**112** C5
Stock Orchard Crs *HOLWY* * N7 ......**75** F1
Stock Orchard St *HOLWY* N7 ....**75** F2
Stocks Pl *POP/IOD* E14 ....**103** F1
Stock St *PLSTW* E13 ....**94** A1
Stockwell Av *BRXN/ST* SW9 ....**135** F1
Stockwell Gdns *BRXN* SW9 ....**117** F4
Stockwell Gn *BRXN/ST* SW9 ....**117** F5
Stockwell La *BRXN/ST* SW9 ....**117** F5
Stockwell Park Crs *BRXN/ST* SW9 .**117** F4
Stockwell Park Rd *BRXN/ST* SW9 ..**117** F4
Stockwell Park Wk *BRXN/ST* SW9 .**135** F1
Stockwell Rd *BRXN/ST* SW9 ....**117** F5
Stockwell St *GNWCH* SE10 ....**122** C2
Stockwell Ter *BRXN/ST* SW9 ....**117** F4
Stoford Cl *WIM/MER* SW19 ....**149** E1
Stokenchurch St *FUL/PGN* SW6 ....**114** B4
Stoke Newington Church St
  STNW/STAM N16...........................**59** D5
Stoke Newington Common
  STNW/STAM N16...........................**59** F5
Stoke Newington High St
  STNW/STAM N16...........................**59** F5

Stoke Newington Rd
  STNW/STAM N16..............................77 F2
Stoke Pl WLSDN NW10 ....87 F2
Stokesley St SHB W12 ....87 F5
Stokes Rd EHAM E6................................95 E3
Stoll Cl CRICK NW2...............................52 C5
Stondon Pk FSTH SE23 ....139 E5
Stonebridge Pk WLSDN NW10 ....69 D4
Stonebridge Wy WBLY HA9..................68 B3
Stone Buildings LINN WC2A 21 F3
Stonechat Sq EHAM E6..........................95 E4
Stone Cl CLAP SW4 ....116 C5
Stonecutter St FLST/FETLN EC4A 22 C4
Stonefield St IS N1 ....76 A5
Stonefield Wy CHARL SE7 ....125 D3
Stonehall Av IL IG1 ....65 E1
Stone Hall Gdns KENS * W8 ....38 C3
Stone Hall Pl KENS * W8 ....38 C3
Stonehill Cl MORT/ESHN SW14..........129 D3
Stonehill Rd CHSWK W4 ....110 A1
  MORT/ESHN SW14 ....128 C3
Stonehills Ct DUL SE21 ....155 E3
Stone House Ct HDTCH EC3A 25 D4
Stoneleigh Pl NTGHL W11 ....101 D1
Stoneleigh St NTGHL W11 ....101 D1
Stonenest St FSBYPK N4........................57 F3
Stones End St STHWK SE1......................47 E1
Stonewall EHAM E6................................96 A4
Stoney Aly WOOL/PLUM SE18 ....126 A5
Stoneyard La POP/IOD E14..................104 B3
Stoneycroft Cl LEE/GVPK SE12 ....141 F5
Stoney La HDTCH EC3A 25 D4
Stoney St STHWK SE1 ....36 A3
Stonhouse St CLAP SW4 ....134 C1
Stonnell's Rd BTSEA SW11 ....133 F3
Stonor Rd WKENS W14 ....101 F5
Stopes St PECK SE15 ....119 F3
Stopford Rd PLSTW E13 ....82 A5
  WALW SE17 ....118 B1
Store Rd CAN/RD E16 ....108 A3
Storers Quay POP/IOD E14 ....105 D5
Store St GWRST WC1E 20 A3
  SRTFD E15..81 D2
Storey Rd HGT N6..................................55 F1
Storeys Ga STJSPK * SW1H 44 B3
  WEST SW1P 44 B1
Stories Ms CMBW * SE5 ....119 E5
Stories Rd CMBW SE5 ....137 E1
Stork Rd FSTGT E7 ....81 F3
Storks Rd BERM/RHTH * SE16 ....102 A4
Stormont Rd BTSEA SW11 ....134 A2
  HGT N6 ....55 F2
Story St IS N1 ....75 F4
Stothard St WCHPL E1 ....90 C3
Stott Cl WAND/EARL SW18 ....133 D4
Stoughton Cl PUT/ROE SW15..............148 A1
Stourcliffe St BAY/PAD W2 ....17 E5
Stourhead Cl WIM/MER SW19 ....131 D5
Stour Rd BOW E3 ....80 A4
The Stowage DEPT SE8........................122 A2
Stowe Rd SHB W12 ....100 B3
Stracey Rd WLSDN NW10 ....69 D5
Stradbroke Rd HBRY N5 ....76 C1
Stradella Rd HNHL SE24 ....136 C4
Strafford Rd ACT W3 ....98 C3
Strafford St POP/IOD E14....................104 A3
Strahan Rd BOW E3................................91 E2
Straightsmouth GNWCH SE10 ....122 C3
Strait Rd EHAM E6................................107 F1
Straker's Rd EDUL SE22 ....138 B2
Strand CHCR WC2N 32 C3
Strandfield Cl WOOL/PLUM SE18........127 E1
Strand-on-the-Green CHSWK W4 ....110 A2
Strangways Ter WKENS W14 ....101 F4
Stranraer Wy IS N1 ....75 E4
Strasburg Rd BTSEA SW11 ....116 A4
Stratford Gv PUT/ROE SW15 ....131 D2
Stratford Pl MHST W1U 18 B5

Stratford Rd KENS W8 ....38 B3
  PLSTW E13 ....82 A5
Stratford Vls CAMTN NW1 ....74 C4
Strathan Cl WAND/EARL SW18 ....131 E4
Strathaven Rd LEE/GVPK SE12 ....142 B4
Strathblaine Rd BTSEA SW11 ....133 D3
Strathdale STRHM/NOR SW16 ....153 F5
Strathdon Dr TOOT SW17 ....151 D3
Strathearn Pl BAY/PAD W2 ....28 C1
Strathearn Rd WIM/MER SW19 ....150 A5
Stratheden Rd BKHTH/KID SE3 ....124 A4
Strathfield Gdns BARK IG11 ....85 D3
Strathleven Rd BRXS/STRHM SW2 ....135 E3
Strathmore Rd WIM/MER SW19 ....150 A3
Strathnairn St STHWK SE1 ....102 A5
Strathray Gdns HAMP * NW3 ....73 E3
Strath Ter BTSEA SW11 ....133 E2
Strathville Rd WAND/EARL SW18........150 A2
Strattondale St POP/IOD E14 ....104 C4
Stratton Dr BARK IG11..........................85 E2
Stratton St MYFR/PICC W1J 31 D3
Strauss Rd CHSWK * W4 ....99 D3
Streakes Field Rd CRICK NW2 ....52 A4
Streamline Ms EDUL SE22 ....156 B1
Streatfeild Av EHAM E6 ....83 F5
Streatham Cl STRHM/NOR * SW16 ....153 E2
Streatham Common North
  STRHM/NOR SW16 ....153 F5
Streatham Ct STRHM/NOR SW16 ......153 E3
Streatham Gn STRHM/NOR * SW16....153 E4
Streatham High Rd
  STRHM/NOR SW16 ....153 E4
Streatham HI BRXS/STRHM SW2 ....153 E1
Streatham Pl BRXS/STRHM SW2 ....135 E5
Streatham St NOXST/BSQ WC1A 20 C4
Streathbourne Rd TOOT SW17 ....152 A2
Streatleigh Pde STRHM/NOR * SW16 ..153 E2
Streatley Pl HAMP NW3 ....73 D1
Streatley Rd KIL/WHAMP NW6 ....71 F4
Streetfield Ms BKHTH/KID SE3............124 A5
Streimer Rd SRTFD E15 ....92 C1
Strelley Wy ACT W3 ....99 E1
Strickland Rw WAND/EARL SW18 ......133 D5
Strickland St DEPT SE8 ....122 A5
Stride Rd PLSTW E13 ....93 F1
Strode Rd FSTGT E7 ....82 A1
  FUL/PGN SW6 ....113 D3
  WLSDN NW10 ....70 A3
Strone Rd FSTGT E7 ....82 C3
Strongbow Crs ELTH/MOT SE9 ....143 F3
Strongbow Rd ELTH/MOT SE9 ....143 F3
Stronsa Rd SHB W12 ....99 F3
Stroud Crs PUT/ROE SW15 ....147 F3
Stroud Green Rd FSBYPK N4 ....57 F3
Stroud Rd WIM/MER SW19 ....150 A3
Stroughton Cl LBTH SE11 ....45 F5
Strout's Pl BETH E2 ....13 E5
Strutton Gnd WEST SW1P 44 A2
Strype St WCHPL E1 ....25 E3
Stuart Av CDALE/KGS NW9 ....52 A2
Stuart Rd ACT W3 ....98 C2
  BARK IG11 ....85 F5
  KIL/WHAMP NW6 ....2 A4
  PECK SE15 ....138 C2
  WIM/MER SW19 ....150 A3
Stubbs Dr BERM/RHTH SE16 ....120 B1
Stucley Pl CAMTN NW1 ....74 B4
Studdridge St FUL/PGN SW6 ....114 A5
Studd St IS N1 ....76 B5
Studholme Ct KIL/WHAMP * NW6 ....72 A1
Studholme St PECK SE15 ....120 B3
Studio Pl KTBR * SW1X 41 F1
Studland Cl BFN/LL DA15 ....163 F3
Studland Rd SYD SE26 ....157 D5
Studland St HMSMTH W6 ....100 B5
Studley Cl CLPT E5 ....79 E2
Studley Dr REDBR IG4 ....65 D1
Studley Rd CLAP SW4 ....117 E4

FSTGT E7 ....82 B3
Stukeley Rd *FSTGT* E7 ....82 B4
Stukeley St *HOL/ALG* WC2B 21 D4
Sturdy Rd *PECK* SE15 ....120 B5
Sturgeon Rd *WALW* SE17 ....118 C1
Sturges Av *HDN* NW4 ....52 B3
Sturge St *STHWK* SE1 ....47 E1
Sturry Rd *POP/IOD* E14 ....92 B3
Sturt St *IS* N1 ....11 F2
Stutfield St *WCHPL* E1 ....90 A5
Styles Gdns *BRXN/ST* SW9 ....136 B1
Sudbourne Rd *BRXS/STRHM* SW2 ....135 E3
Sudbrooke Rd *BAL* SW12 ....133 E4
Sudbury *EHAM* E6 ....96 A5
Sudbury Crs *BMLY* BR1 ....160 A5
Sudbury Rd *BARK* IG11 ....85 F2
Sudeley St *IS* N1 ....11 D2
Sudlow Rd *WAND/EARL* SW18 ....132 A2
Sudrey St *STHWK* SE1 ....47 E1
Suffolk La *CANST* EC4R 36 A1
Suffolk Rd *BARK* IG11 ....85 E1
   BARN SW13 ....111 F3
   GDMY/SEVK IG3 ....67 E3
   PLSTW E13 ....93 F2
   SEVS/STOTM N15 ....59 D1
   WLSDN NW10 ....69 E4
Suffolk St *FSTGT* E7 ....82 A3
   STJS SW1Y 32 B3
Suffolk Vls *WAND/EARL* * SW18 ......132 A5
Sugar House La *SRTFD* E15 ....92 C1
Sugar Loaf Wk *BETH* * E2 ....90 C2
Sugden Rd *BTSEA* SW11 ....134 A1
Sugden Wy *BARK* IG11 ....97 F1
Sulgrave Gdns *SHB* W12 ....100 C3
Sulgrave Rd *HMSMTH* W6 ....100 C3
Sulina Rd *BRXS/STRHM* SW2 ....135 E5
Sulivan Ct *FUL/PGN* SW6 ....114 A5
Sulivan Rd *FUL/PGN* SW6 ....132 A1
Sullivan Av *CAN/RD* E16 ....95 D4
Sullivan Cl *BTSEA* SW11 ....133 E1
Sullivan Rd *LBTH* SE11 ....46 B4
Sultan St *CMBW* SE5 ....118 C3
Sumatra Rd *KIL/WHAMP* NW6 ....72 C3
Sumburgh Rd *BAL* SW12 ....134 A4
Summercourt Rd *WCHPL* E1 ....90 C5
Summerfield Av *KIL/WHAMP* NW6 ......89 E1
Summerfield St *LEE/GVPK* SE12 ......141 F5
Summerhouse Rd *STNW/STAM* N16 ....59 E4
Summerlands Av *ACT* W3 ....98 C1
Summerley St *WAND/EARL* SW18 ......150 B2
Summersby Rd *HGT* N6 ....56 B1
Summers Cl *WBLY* HA9 ....50 B3
Summers St *CLKNW* EC1R 22 A1
Summerstown *TOOT* SW17 ....150 C3
Summit Est *STNW/STAM* * N16 ....60 A2
Sumner Av *PECK* SE15 ....119 F4
Sumner Pl *SKENS* SW7 ....40 B5
Sumner Place Ms *SKENS* SW7 ....40 B5
Sumner Rd *PECK* SE15 ....119 F4
Sumner St *STHWK* SE1 ....35 E3
Sumpter Cl *HAMP* NW3 ....72 C3
Sunbeam Crs *NKENS* W10 ....88 C3
Sunbeam Rd *WLSDN* NW10 ....86 C3
Sunbury Av *MORT/ESHN* SW14 ....129 D2
Sunbury La *BTSEA* SW11 ....115 D4
Sunbury St *WOOL/PLUM* SE18 ....107 F4
Suncroft Pl *SYD* SE26 ....156 C3
Sunderland Mt *FSTH* * SE23 ....157 D2
Sunderland Rd *FSTH* SE23 ....157 D1
Sunderland Ter *BAY/PAD* W2 ....14 C4
Sunderland Wy *MNPK* E12 ....65 D4
Sundew Av *SHB* W12 ....100 A1
Sundorne Rd *CHARL* SE7 ....124 B1
Sundridge Av *WELL* DA16 ....127 D5
Sunfields Pl *BKHTH/KID* SE3 ....124 B3
Sun in Sands Rbt *BKHTH/KID* SE3 ....124 B3
Sun La *BKHTH/KID* SE3 ....124 B3

Sunlight Sq *BETH* E2 ....90 B2
   BARK IG11 ....85 D5
Sunningdale Av *ACT* W3 ....99 E1
   BARK IG11 ....85 D5
Sunningdale Cl *BERM/RTH* * SE16 ....120 B1
Sunningdale Gdns *KENS* W8 ....38 B3
Sunninghill Ct *ACT* * W3 ....98 C3
Sunninghill Rd *LEW* SE13 ....122 B5
Sunny Crs *WLSDN* NW10 ....68 C4
Sunnydale Rd *LEE/GVPK* SE12 ....142 B3
Sunnydene St *SYD* SE26 ....157 E4
Sunnyhill Cl *CLPT* E5 ....79 E1
Sunnyhill Rd *STRHM/NOR* SW16 ......153 E4
Sunnymead Rd *CDALE/KGS* NW9 ......51 D2
   PUT/ROE SW15 ....130 B3
Sunnyside *CRICK* NW2 ....53 F5
   FSTH * SE23 ....139 F5
Sunnyside Rd *ARCH* N19 ....57 D2
   IL IG1 ....66 C5
   LEY E10 ....62 A3
Sun Pas *BERM/RTH* SE16 ....102 A4
Sunray Av *CMBW* SE5 ....137 D2
Sun Rd *WKENS* W14 ....113 F1
Sunset Rd *CMBW* SE5 ....136 C2
   WIM/MER SW19 ....148 B5
Sun St *SDTCH* EC2A 24 B2
Surma Cl *WCHPL* E1 ....90 A3
Surrendale Pl *MV/WKIL* W9 ....14 B1
Surrey Canal Rd *BERM/RTH* SE16 ....120 C2
Surrey Crs *CHSWK* W4 ....110 A1
Surrey Gdns *FSBYPK* N4 ....58 C1
Surrey Gv *WALW* SE17 ....119 E1
Surrey La *BTSEA* SW11 ....115 E4
Surrey Ms *WNWD* SE27 ....155 E4
Surrey Quays Rd *BERM/RTH* SE16 ..102 C4
Surrey Rd *BARK* IG11 ....85 E4
   PECK SE15 ....139 D3
Surrey Rw *STHWK* SE1 ....34 C5
Surrey Sq *WALW* SE17 ....119 E1
Surrey St *PLSTW* E13 ....94 B2
   TPL/STR WC2R 33 F1
Surrey Ter *WALW* SE17 ....49 D5
Surrey Water Rd *BERM/RTH* SE16 ....103 D2
Surr St *HOLWY* N7 ....75 E2
Susannah St *POP/IOD* E14 ....92 B5
Susan Rd *BKHTH/KID* SE3 ....124 B5
Sussex Cl *ARCH* * N19 ....57 E4
   REDBR IG4 ....65 F1
Sussex Gdns *BAY/PAD* W2 ....16 B5
Sussex Ms East *BAY/PAD* * W2 ....28 B1
Sussex Ms West *BAY/PAD* W2 ....28 B1
Sussex Pl *BAY/PAD* W2 ....16 B5
   CAMTN NW1 ....5 E5
   HMSMTH W6 ....112 C1
Sussex Rd *EHAM* E6 ....96 C1
Sussex Sq *BAY/PAD* W2 ....28 B1
Sussex St *PIM* SW1V 116 B1
   PLSTW E13 ....94 B2
Sussex Wy *ARCH* N19 ....57 D2
Sutcliffe Rd *WOOL/PLUM* SE18 ......127 E2
Sutherland Av *MV/WKIL* W9 ....3 E4
   MV/WKIL W9 ....14 B1
   WELL DA16 ....145 D2
Sutherland Gdns *MORT/ESHN* SW14 ..129 E1
Sutherland Gv *WAND/EARL* SW18 ....131 F5
Sutherland Pl *BAY/PAD* W2 ....14 A4
Sutherland Rd *BOW* E3 ....91 F1
   CHSWK W4 ....111 D2
Sutherland Rw *PIM* * SW1V 116 B1
Sutherland Sq *WALW* SE17 ....118 C1
Sutherland St *PIM* SW1V 116 B1
Sutherland Wk *WALW* SE17 ....118 C1
Sutlej Rd *CHARL* SE7 ....124 C3
Sutterton St *HOLWY* N7 ....75 F3
Sutton Cl *CHSWK* * W4 ....110 C2
Sutton Ct *CHSWK* * W4 ....110 C2
Sutton Court Rd *CHSWK* W4 ....110 C2
   PLSTW E13 ....94 C2
The Sutton Est *IS* * N1 ....76 B4

Sutton Est CHEL * SW3 ....115 E1
  IS * N1 ....76 B4
Sutton La CHSWK W4 ....110 C1
Sutton La South CHSWK W4 ....110 C2
Sutton Pl HOM E9 ....78 C2
Sutton Rd BARK IG11 ....97 E1
  PLSTW E13 ....93 F3
Sutton Rw SOHO/SHAV W1D 20 A4
Sutton Sq HOM * E9 ....78 C2
Sutton St WCHPL E1 ....90 C5
Sutton Wy NKENS W10 ....88 C4
Swaby Rd WAND/EARL SW18 ....150 C2
Swaffield Rd WAND/EARL SW18 ....132 C5
Swain's La KTTN NW5 ....56 A5
Swainson Rd ACT W3 ....99 F3
Swain St STJWD NW8 ....16 B1
Swallands Rd CAT SE6 ....158 A3
Swallow Cl NWCR SE14 ....120 C4
Swallow Dr WLSDN NW10 ....69 D3
Swallowfield Rd CHARL SE7 ....124 B3
Swallow Gdns STRHM/NOR SW16 .....153 D5
Swallow Pl REGST W1B 19 D5
Swallow St CONDST W1S 31 F2
  EHAM E6 ....95 E4
Swanage Rd WAND/EARL SW18 ....132 C4
Swan Ap EHAM E6 ....95 E4
Swandon Wy WAND/EARL SW18 ....132 B3
Swanfield St BETH E2 ....13 E4
Swan La CANST EC4R 36 B2
Swan Md STHWK SE1 ....48 C3
Swan Ms BRXN/ST SW9 ....117 F5
Swan Pas WCHPL E1 ....37 F2
Swan Pl BARN SW13 ....111 F5
Swan Rd BERM/RHTH SE16 ....102 C3
Swanscombe Rd CHSWK W4 ....111 E1
  NTGHL W11 ....101 D2
Swan St STHWK SE1 ....47 F1
Swanton Gdns WIM/MER SW19 ....149 D1
Swan Wk CHEL SW3 ....115 F2
Swanwick Cl PUT/ROE SW15 ....129 F5
Swan Yd IS N1 ....76 B3
Swaton Rd BOW E3 ....92 A3
Sweden Ga BERM/RHTH SE16 ....103 E5
Sweeney Crs STHWK SE1 ....49 F1
Swete St PLSTW E13 ....94 A1
Sweyn Pl BKHTH/KID SE3 ....124 A5
Swift St FUL/PGN SW6 ....113 E4
Swinbrook Rd NKENS W10 ....89 D3
Swinburne Rd PUT/ROE SW15 ....130 A2
Swindon Cl GDMY/SEVK IG3 ....67 E4
Swindon St SHB * W12 ....100 B2
Swinford Gdns BRXN/ST SW9 ....136 B1
Swingate La WOOL/PLUM SE18 ....127 E3
Swinnerton St HOM E9 ....79 E2
Swinton Cl WBLY HA9 ....50 B3
Swinton Pl FSBYW WC1X 9 E1
Swinton St FSBYW WC1X 9 E1
Swithland Gdns ELTH/MOT SE9 ....161 F4
Sybil Phoenix Cl DEPT SE8 ....121 D1
Sybourn St WALTH E17 ....61 F2
Sycamore Av BFN/LL DA15 ....145 F4
  BOW E3 ....79 F5
Sycamore Cl ACT W3 ....99 E2
  CAN/RD E16 ....93 E3
Sycamore Gdns SHB W12 ....100 B3
Sycamore Gv CAT SE6 ....140 C4
  CDALE/KGS NW9 ....50 C2
Sycamore Ms CLAP SW4 ....134 C1
Sycamore St FSBYE EC1V 23 E1
Sycamore Wk NKENS W10 ....89 E3
Sydcote DUL * SE21 ....154 C2
Sydenham Av SYD SE26 ....156 B5
Sydenham Cottages
  LEE/GVPK * SE12 ....160 C2
Sydenham Hl SYD SE26 ....156 A3
Sydenham Pk SYD SE26 ....156 C3
Sydenham Park Rd SYD SE26 ....156 C3
Sydenham Ri FSTH SE23 ....156 B2

Sydenham Rd SYD SE26 ....157 D5
Sydenham Station Ap SYD SE26 ....156 C4
Sydmons Ct FSTH * SE23 ....138 C5
Sydner Rd STNW/STAM N16 ....77 F1
Sydney Cl SKENS SW7 ....40 B5
Sydney Ms SKENS SW7 ....40 B5
Sydney Pl SKENS SW7 ....40 B5
Sydney Rd SCUP DA14 ....163 E4
  WAN E11 ....64 B1
Sydney St CHEL SW3 ....115 E1
Sylvan Gv CRICK NW2 ....71 D1
  PECK SE15 ....120 B3
Sylvan Rd FSTGT E7 ....82 A3
  IL IG1 ....66 C4
Sylvan Ter PECK * SE15 ....120 B3
Sylvester Pth HACK * E8 ....78 B3
Sylvester Rd HACK * E8 ....78 B3
  WALTH * E17 ....61 F2
Sylvia Gdns WBLY HA9 ....68 B4
Symes Ms CAMTN NW1 ....7 E1
Symington Ms HOM * E9 ....79 D2
Symister Ms IS * N1 ....12 C4
Symons St CHEL SW3 ....41 F5
Symphony Ms NKENS * W10 ....89 E2

T

Tabard Garden Est STHWK SE1 ....36 A5
Tabard St STHWK SE1 ....48 A2
Tabernacle Av PLSTW E13 ....94 A3
Tabernacle St SDTCH EC2A 24 B1
Tableer Av CLAP SW4 ....134 C3
Tabley Rd HOLWY N7 ....75 E1
Tabor Rd HMSMTH W6 ....100 B4
Tachbrook St PIM SW1V 43 F5
Tack Ms BROCKY SE4 ....140 A1
Tadema Rd WBPTN SW10 ....114 C3
Tadmor St SHB W12 ....101 D2
Tadworth Rd CRICK NW2 ....52 A4
Taeping St POP/IOD E14 ....104 B5
Talacre Rd KTTN NW5 ....74 A3
Talbot Ct BANK EC3V 36 B1
Talbot Pl BKHTH/KID SE3 ....123 E5
Talbot Rd BAY/PAD W2 ....14 B4
  EDUL SE22 ....137 E2
  EHAM E6 ....95 F1
  FSTGT E7 ....82 A1
  HGT N6 ....56 A1
  NTGHL W11 ....89 F5
Talbot Sq BAY/PAD W2 ....16 A5
Talbot Wk NTGHL W11 ....89 E5
  WLSDN * NW10 ....69 E3
Talbot Yd STHWK SE1 ....36 A4
Talcott Pth BRXS/STRHM * SW2 ....154 A1
Talfourd Pl PECK SE15 ....119 F4
Talfourd Rd PECK SE15 ....119 F4
Talgarth Rd HMSMTH W6 ....113 D1
Talisman Sq SYD SE26 ....156 A4
Tallack Rd LEY E10 ....61 F3
Tallis Cl CAN/RD E16 ....94 B5
Tallis Gv CHARL SE7 ....124 B2
Tallis St EMB EC4Y 34 B1
Tallis Vw WLSDN NW10 ....69 D3
Talmage Cl FSTH SE23 ....138 C5
Talma Rd BRXS/STRHM SW2 ....136 A3
Talwin St BOW E3 ....92 B2
Tamar Cl BOW * E3 ....79 F5
Tamarind Yd WAP E1W 102 A2
Tamarisk Sq SHB W12 ....99 F1
Tamar St CHARL SE7 ....107 E5
Tamworth St FUL/PGN SW6 ....114 A2
Tancred Rd FSBYPK N4 ....58 B1
Tanfield Av CRICK NW2 ....69 F1
Tangier Rd RCHPK/HAM TW10 ....128 B3
Tangley Gv PUT/ROE SW15 ....129 F5
Tanhouse Fld KTTN * NW5 ....75 D2

Tankerton Houses *STPAN* * WC1H 9 D4
Tankerton St *STPAN* WC1H 9 D4
Tankridge Rd *CRICK* NW2 ....52 B4
The Tanneries *WCHPL* * E1 ....90 C3
Tanner's Hl *DEPT* SE8 ....122 A4
Tanner St *BARK* IG11 ....84 C3
   STHWK SE1 ....49 D1
Tannington Ter *FSBYPK* * N4 ....58 A5
Tannsfeld Rd *SYD* SE26 ....157 D5
Tansley Cl *HOLWY* * N7 ....75 D2
Tanswell St *STHWK* * SE1 ....46 A1
Tansy Cl *EHAM* E6 ....96 A5
Tantallon Rd *BAL* SW12 ....152 A1
Tant Av *CAN/RD* E16 ....93 F5
Tanza Rd *HAMP* NW3 ....73 F1
Taplow St *IS* N1 ....11 F2
Tappesfield Rd *PECK* SE15 ....138 C1
Tapp St *BETH* * E2 ....90 B3
Taransay Wk *IS* N1 ....77 D3
Tara Ter *BROCKY* * SE4 ....139 E1
Tarbert Rd *EDUL* SE22 ....137 E3
Tarbert Wk *WCHPL* E1 ....102 C1
Tarleton Gdns *FSTH* SE23 ....156 B1
Tarling Rd *CAN/RD* E16 ....93 F5
Tarling St *WCHPL* E1 ....90 B5
Tarn St *STHWK* SE1 ....47 E3
Tarnwood Pk *ELTH/MOT* SE9 ....161 F1
Tarragon Cl *NWCR* * SE14 ....121 E3
Tarrant Pl *MBLAR* W1H 17 E3
Tarriff Crs *DEPT* SE8 ....103 F5
Tarrington Cl *STRHM/NOR* * SW16 ....153 D4
Tarver Rd *WALW* SE17 ....118 B1
Tarves Wy *GNWCH* SE10 ....122 B3
Tasker Rd *HAMP* NW3 ....73 F2
Tasman Rd *BRXN/ST* SW9 ....135 E1
Tasso Rd *HMSMTH* W6 ....113 E2
Tate Rd *CAN/RD* E16 ....107 F2
Tatnell Rd *FSTH* SE23 ....139 E4
Tattersall Cl *ELTH/MOT* SE9 ....143 E3
Tatton Crs *CLPT* E5 ....59 F2
Tatum Rd *WLSDN* NW10 ....68 C4
Tatum St *WALW* SE17 ....48 B5
Tauheed Cl *FSBYPK* N4 ....58 C4
Taunton Ms *CAMTN* NW1 ....17 E1
Taunton Pl *CAMTN* NW1 ....5 E5
Taunton Rd *LEW* SE13 ....141 E5
Taverners Cl *NTGHL* * W11 ....101 E2
Taverner Sq *HBRY* * N5 ....76 C1
Tavistock Av *STNW/STAM* * N16 ....77 E2
Tavistock Ct *COVGDN* * WC2E 33 D1
Tavistock Crs *NTGHL* W11 ....89 F4
Tavistock Gdns *GDMY/SEVK* IG3 ....85 E1
Tavistock Ms *NTGHL* * W11 ....89 F5
Tavistock Pl *STPAN* WC1H 8 B5
Tavistock Rd *FSBYPK* N4 ....59 D1
   NTGHL W11 ....89 F4
   SRTFD E15 ....81 F3
   WLSDN NW10 ....87 F1
Tavistock Sq *STPAN* WC1H 8 B5
Tavistock St *COVGDN* WC2E 33 D1
Tavistock Ter *ARCH* N19 ....57 D5
Taviton St *STPAN* WC1H 8 A5
Tavy Cl *LBTH* SE11 ....118 A1
Tawny Wy *BERM/RHTH* SE16 ....103 D5
Taybridge Rd *BTSEA* SW11 ....134 A1
Tayburn Cl *POP/IOD* E14 ....92 C5
Taylor Av *RCH/KEW* TW9 ....110 B5
Taylor Cl *DEPT* SE8 ....121 F2
Taylor's Buildings *WOOL/PLUM* SE18 ....108 B5
Taylors Cl *SCUP* DA14 ....163 F4
Taylor's Gn *ACT* * W3 ....87 E5
Taylor's La *SYD* SE26 ....156 B4
   WLSDN NW10 ....69 E3
Taymount Ri *FSTH* SE23 ....156 C2
Tayport Cl *IS* N1 ....75 F4
Teak Cl *BERM/RHTH* SE16 ....103 E2
Teal Cl *CAN/RD* E16 ....95 D4
Teale St *BETH* E2 ....90 A1

Teasel Wy *SRTFD* E15 ....93 E2
Tedworth Gdns *CHEL* SW3 ....115 F1
Tedworth Sq *CHEL* * SW3 ....115 F1
The Tee *ACT* W3 ....87 E5
Teesdale Cl *BETH* E2 ....90 A1
Teesdale Rd *WAN* E11 ....63 F1
Teesdale St *BETH* E2 ....90 B1
Teesdale Yd *BETH* * E2 ....90 B1
Teignmouth Cl *CLAP* SW4 ....135 D2
Teignmouth Rd *CRICK* NW2 ....71 D2
Telegraph Hl *HAMP* NW3 ....54 B5
Telegraph Pl *POP/IOD* E14 ....104 B5
Telegraph Rd *PUT/ROE* SW15 ....130 B5
Telegraph St *LOTH* EC2R 24 A4
Telephone Pl *FUL/PGN* * SW6 ....113 F2
Telferscot Rd *BAL* SW12 ....153 D1
Telford Av *BAL* SW12 ....153 D1
Telford Cl *WALTH* E17 ....61 E2
Telford Rd *CDALE/KGS* NW9 ....51 F1
   CHST BR7 ....163 D2
   NKENS W10 ....89 E4
Telfords Yd *WAP* * E1W 102 A1
Telford Ter *PIM* * SW1V 116 C2
Telford Wy *ACT* W3 ....87 E4
Telham Rd *EHAM* E6 ....96 A1
Tell Gv *EDUL* SE22 ....137 F2
Tellson Av *WOOL/PLUM* SE18 ....125 E4
Temeraire St *BERM/RHTH* SE16 ....102 C3
Tempelhof Av *NW* 52 C2
Temperley Rd *BAL* SW12 ....134 A5
Templars Av *GLDGN* NW11 ....53 F1
Templar St *CMBW* SE5 ....118 B5
Temple Av *EMB* EC4Y 34 B1
Temple Cl *WAN* E11 ....63 E2
   WOOL/PLUM SE18 ....108 C4
Templecombe Rd *HOM* E9 ....78 C5
Temple Dwellings *BETH* * E2 ....90 B1
Temple Fortune La *GLDGN* NW11 ....53 F1
Temple Gdns *EMB* * EC4Y 34 A1
   GLDGN NW11 ....53 F1
Temple Gv *GLDGN* NW11 ....54 A1
Temple La *EMB* EC4Y 22 B5
Templemead Cl *ACT* W3 ....87 E5
Temple Mills La *LEY* E10 ....80 B1
Temple Pl *TPL/STR* WC2R 33 F1
Temple Rd *CHSWK* W4 ....98 C4
   CRICK NW2 ....70 C1
   EHAM E6 ....83 E5
Temple Sheen Rd *MORT/ESHN* SW14 ....128 C2
Temple St *BETH* E2 ....90 B1
Templeton Cl *STNW/STAM* * N16 ....77 E2
Templeton Pl *ECT* SW5 ....38 B5
Templeton Rd *SEVS/STOTM* N15 ....59 D1
Templewood Av *HAMP* NW3 ....54 B5
Templewood Gdns *HAMP* NW3 ....54 B5
Temple Yd *BETH* * E2 ....90 A2
Tenbury Cl *FSTGT* E7 ....83 D2
Tenbury Ct *BAL* SW12 ....153 D1
Tench St *WAP* * E1W 102 B2
Tenda Rd *BERM/RHTH* SE16 ....102 B5
Tenham Av *BRXS/STRHM* SW2 ....153 D2
Tenniel Cl *BAY/PAD* W2 ....15 E5
Tennis St *STHWK* SE1 ....36 A5
Tennyson Av *MNPK* E12 ....83 E4
   WAN E11 ....64 A2
Tennyson Cl *WELL* DA16 ....127 E4
Tennyson Rd *KIL/WHAMP* NW6 ....71 F5
   SRTFD E15 ....81 E4
   WALTH E17 ....61 F1
Tennyson St *VX/NE* SW8 ....116 B5
Tenterden Cl *ELTH/MOT* SE9 ....161 F4
Tenterden St *CONDST* W1S 19 D5
Tenter Gnd *WCHPL* * E1 ....25 E3
Tent St *WCHPL* E1 ....90 B3
Terling Cl *WAN* E11 ....63 F5
Terling Wk *IS* * N1 ....76 C5
Terminus Pl *PIM* SW1V 43 D3
The Terrace *BARN* SW13 ....111 E5

BETH * E2..90 C2
DEPT * SE8...103 F5
FSTH * SE23..139 E5
KIL/WHAMP NW6..72 A5
Terrace Gdns BARN SW13...........................111 F5
Terrace Rd HOM E9...................................79 D4
PLSTW E13...82 A5
Terrapin Rd TOOT SW17............................152 B3
Terretts Pl IS N1.......................................76 B4
Terrick St SHB W12...................................88 B5
Testerton Wk NTGHL * W11........................101 D1
Tetcott Rd WBPTN SW10............................114 C3
Teversham La VX/NE SW8..........................117 E4
Teviot St POP/IOD E14...............................92 C4
Tewkesbury Av FSTH SE23.........................156 B1
Tewkesbury Rd FSBYPK N4........................59 D2
Tewson Rd WOOL/PLUM SE18.....................127 E1
Thackeray Ms HACK * E8............................78 A3
Thackeray Rd EHAM E6..............................95 D3
VX/NE SW8..116 B5
Thackeray St KENS W8..............................39 D2
Thakeham Cl SYD SE26.............................156 B5
Thalia Cl GNWCH SE10..............................123 C3
Thame Rd BERM/RHTH SE16......................103 D3
Thames Av WBPTN SW10............................114 C4
Thames Bank MORT/ESHN SW14................110 C5
Thames Cir POP/IOD E14...........................104 A5
Thames Pth BERM/RHTH SE16....................103 F4
BOW E3...92 C1
CHSWK W4...111 F4
CLPT E5...61 D5
GNWCH SE10...106 A4
LBTH SE11...117 E1
WEST SW1P..45 D3
Thames Pl PUT/ROE SW15.........................131 D1
Thames Quay WBPTN * SW10....................114 C4
Thames Rd CAN/RD E16............................107 D2
CHSWK W4...110 B2
Thames St GNWCH SE10............................122 B2
Thames Village CHSWK W4........................110 C4
Thanet St STPAN WC1H................................8 C4
Thane Vls HOLWY N7..................................57 F5
Thant Cl LEY E10.......................................80 B1
Thaxted Rd ELTH/MOT SE9.......................162 C2
Thaxton Rd WKENS W14............................113 F2
Thayer St MHST W1U..................................18 B3
Theatre St BTSEA SW11.............................133 F1
Theberton St IS N1....................................76 A5
Theed St STHWK SE1.................................34 A4
Theobald Rd WALTH E17............................61 F2
Theobald's Rd FSBYW WC1X......................21 E2
Theobald St STHWK SE1.............................48 A3
Theodore Rd LEW SE13..............................141 D4
Therapia Rd EDUL SE22............................138 C4
Theresa Rd HMSMTH W6..........................100 A5
Thermopylae Ga POP/IOD E14...................104 B5
Theseus Wk IS N1.......................................11 D2
Thessaly Rd VX/NE SW8............................117 D4
Theydon Rd CLPT E5...................................60 C4
Theydon St WALTH E17...............................61 F2
Third Av ACT W3...99 E2
MNPK E12...83 E1
NKENS W10..89 E2
PLSTW E13...94 A2
Third Wy WBLY HA9....................................68 B1
Thirleby Rd WEST SW1P.............................43 F3
Thirlmere Rd STRHM/NOR SW16................153 D4
Thirsk Rd BTSEA SW11..............................134 A1
Thistle Gv WBPTN * SW10.........................114 C1
Thistlewaite Rd CLPT E5.............................60 B5
Thistlewood Cl HOLWY N7...........................57 F4
Thomas Baines Rd BTSEA SW11................133 D1
Thomas Cribb Ms EHAM E6.........................95 F5
Thomas Dean Rd SYD SE26.......................157 F4
Thomas Dinwiddy Rd
LEE/GVPK SE12.......................................160 B2
Thomas Doyle St STHWK SE1.....................46 C2

Thomas' La CAT SE6................................140 B5
Thomas More St WAP * E1W.....................102 A1
Thomas North Ter CAN/RD * E16................93 F4
Thomas Pl KENS W8..................................38 C3
Thomas Rd POP/IOD E14............................91 F5
Thomas St WOOL/PLUM SE18....................108 A5
Thompson Av RCH/KEW TW9.....................128 B1
Thompson Cl IL IG1....................................66 C4
Thompson Rd EDUL SE22..........................137 F4
Thompson's Av CMBW * SE5.....................118 C3
Thorburn Sq STHWK SE1...........................102 A5
Thoresby St IS N1..11 F3
Thornbury Cl STNW/STAM N16....................77 E2
Thornbury Rd CLAP SW4...........................135 E4
Thornby Rd CLPT E5...................................60 C5
Thorncliffe Rd CLAP SW4...........................135 D4
Thorncombe Rd EDUL SE22.......................137 E3
Thorncroft St VX/NE SW8..........................117 E3
Thorndean St WAND/EARL SW18................150 C2
Thorndike Cl WBPTN SW10........................114 C3
Thorndike St PIM * SW1V............................44 A5
Thorne Cl CAN/RD E16................................94 A5
WAN * E11..81 E1
Thorne Rd VX/NE SW8...............................117 E3
Thorne St BARN SW13...............................129 E1
Thorney Crs BTSEA * SW11........................115 D3
Thorney Hedge Rd CHSWK W4....................98 B5
Thorney St WEST SW1P..............................44 C4
Thornfield Rd SHB W12..............................100 B3
Thornford Rd LEW SE13............................140 C3
Thorngate Rd MV/WKIL W9...........................2 B5
Thorngrove Rd PLSTW E13..........................82 B5
Thornham Gv SRTFD E15............................81 D2
Thornham St GNWCH SE10........................122 B2
Thornhaugh St STPAN WC1H.......................20 B1
Thornhill Av WOOL/PLUM SE18..................127 E3
Thornhill Bridge Whf IS * N1........................75 D3
Thornhill Crs IS N1......................................75 F4
Thornhill Gdns BARK IG11...........................85 E4
LEY E10..62 B4
Thornhill Gv IS N1.......................................75 F4
Thornhill Rd IS N1.......................................76 A4
LEY E10..62 B4
Thornhill Sq IS N1..75 F5
Thornlaw Rd WNWD SE27..........................154 A4
Thornsbeach Rd CAT SE6..........................158 C4
Thornsett Rd WAND/EARL SW18.................150 B2
Thornton Av BAL SW12...............................153 D1
CHSWK W4...99 E5
Thornton Gdns BAL SW12..........................153 D1
Thornton Pl MBLAR W1H.............................17 E2
Thornton Rd BAL SW12..............................135 D5
BMLY BR1..160 A5
IL IG1...84 B1
MORT/ESHN SW14...................................129 D1
WAN E11...63 D4
Thornton St BRXN/ST SW9........................118 A5
Thorntree Rd CHARL SE7..........................125 D1
Thornville St DEPT SE8...............................122 A4
Thornwood Rd LEW SE13...........................141 E3
Thorogood Gdns SRTFD E15........................81 E2
Thorold Rd IL IG1.......................................66 B4
Thorparch Rd VX/NE SW8..........................117 D4
Thorpebank Rd SHB W12...........................100 A2
Thorpe Cl NKENS W10.................................89 E5
SYD * SE26...157 D4
Thorpedale Rd FSBYPK N4..........................57 E3
Thorpe Rd BARK IG11..................................85 D4
EHAM E6..83 F5
FSTGT E7...64 A5
SEVS/STOTM N15.......................................59 E1
Thorpewood Av FSTH SE23.......................156 B2
Thorsden Wy NRWD * SE19.......................155 E5
Thorverton Rd CRICK NW2...........................53 E5
Thoydon Rd BOW E3...................................91 E1
Thrale Rd STRHM/NOR SW16.....................152 C5
Thrale St STHWK SE1..................................35 F4
Thrasher Cl HACK * E8................................77 F5

Thrawl St *WCHPL* E1 ....25 F3
Threadneedle St *LOTH* EC2R 24 B5
Three Colts La *BETH* 90 B3
Three Colt St *POP/IOD* * E14 ......103 F1
Three Kings Yd *MYFR/PKLN* W1K 30 C1
Three Mill La *SRTFD* E15 ....92 C2
Three Oak La *STHWK* SE1 ....37 E5
Threshers Pl *NTGHL* W11 ....101 E1
Thriftwood *FSTH* SE23 ....156 C3
Throckmorten Rd *CAN/RD* E16 ....94 B5
Throgmorton Av *OBST* EC2N 24 B4
Throgmorton St *LOTH* EC2R 24 B5
Thrush St *WALW* SE17 ....118 C1
Thurbarn Rd *CAT* SE6 ....158 B5
Thurland Rd *BERM/RHTH* SE16 ....102 A4
Thurlby Rd *WNWD* SE27 ....154 A4
Thurleigh Av *BAL* SW12 ....134 A4
Thurleigh Rd *BAL* SW12 ....133 F4
Thurlestone Av *GDMY/SEVK* IG3 .....85 F1
Thurlestone Rd *WNWD* SE27 ....154 A3
Thurloe Cl *SKENS* SW7 ....40 C4
Thurloe Pl *SKENS* SW7 ....40 B4
Thurloe Place Ms *SKENS* * SW7 ....40 B4
Thurloe Sq *SKENS* SW7 ....40 B4
Thurloe St *SKENS* SW7 ....40 B4
Thurlow Hl *DUL* SE21 ....154 C1
Thurlow Park Rd *DUL* SE21 ....154 B2
Thurlow Rd *HAMP* NW3 ....73 D2
Thurlow St *WALW* SE17 ....119 E1
Thurlow Ter *KTTN* NW5 ....73 F2
Thurlow Wk *WALW* SE17 ....119 E1
Thursley Gdns *WIM/MER* SW19 ....149 D2
Thursley Rd *ELTH/MOT* SE9 ....161 F3
Thurso St *TOOT* SW17 ....151 D4
Thurston Rd *DEPT* SE8 ....122 B5
Thurtle Rd *BETH* E2 ....13 F1
Tibbat's Rd *BOW* E3 ....92 B3
Tibbenham Pl *CAT* SE6 ....158 A2
Tibberton Sq *IS* * N1 ....76 C4
Tibbets Cl *WIM/MER* SW19 ....149 D1
Tibbet's Ride *PUT/ROE* SW15 ....131 D5
Tiber Gdns *IS* N1 ....5 E5
Ticehurst Rd *FSTH* SE23 ....157 E2
Tidal Basin Rd *CAN/RD* E16 ....105 F1
Tideswell Rd *PUT/ROE* SW15 ....130 C2
Tideway Wk *VX/NE* * SW8 ....116 C2
Tidey St *BOW* E3 ....92 A4
Tidford Rd *WELL* DA16 ....127 F5
Tidworth Rd *BOW* E3 ....92 A3
Tierney Rd *BRXS/STRHM* SW2 ......153 E1
Tierney Ter *BRXS/STRHM* * SW2 ....153 E1
Tiger Wy *CLPT* E5 ....78 B1
Tilbrook Rd *BKHTH/KID* SE3 ....142 C1
Tilbury Cl *PECK* SE15 ....119 F3
Tilbury Rd *EHAM* E6 ....95 F1
   LEY E10 ....62 C2
Tildesley Rd *PUT/ROE* SW15 ....130 C4
Tilehurst Rd *WAND/EARL* SW18 ...151 D1
Tile Kiln La *HGT* N6 ....56 B3
Tileyard Rd *HOLWY* N7 ....75 E4
Tilford Gdns *WIM/MER* SW19 ....149 D3
Tilia Rd *CLPT* E5 ....78 B1
Tiller Rd *POP/IOD* E14 ....104 A4
Tillett Cl *WLSDN* NW10 ....68 C3
Tillet Wy *BETH* E2 ....90 B3
Tilling Rd *CRICK* NW2 ....52 B3
Tillman St *WCHPL* E1 ....90 B5
Tilloch St *IS* * N1 ....75 F4
Tillotson Rd *IL* IG1 ....66 A3
Tilney Gdns *IS* N1 ....77 D3
Tilney St *MYFR/PKLN* W1K 30 A1
Tilson Cl *CMBW* SE5 ....119 E3
Tilson Gdns *CLAP* SW4 ....135 E3
Tilston Cl *WAN* E11 ....63 F5
Tilton St *FUL/PGN* SW6 ....113 D3
The Tiltwood *ACT* W3 ....98 C1
Tilt Yard Ap *ELTH/MOT* SE9 ....143 F4
Timbercroft La *WOOL/PLUM* SE18 ..127 E2

Timberland Cl *PECK* * SE15 ....120 A3
Timberland Rd *WCHPL* * E1 ....90 B5
Timber Mill Wy *CLAP* SW4 ....135 D1
Timber Pond Rd *BERM/RHTH* SE16 ..103 D3
Timber St *FSBYE* * EC1V 11 E5
Timberwharf Rd *SEVS/STOTM* N15 ..60 A1
Time Sq *HACK* * E8 ....77 F2
Timothy Rd *POP/IOD* E14 ....91 F4
Tindal St *BRXN/ST* SW9 ....118 B4
Tinniswood Cl *HOLWY* * N7 ....76 A2
Tinsley Rd *WCHPL* E1 ....90 C4
Tintagel Crs *EDUL* SE22 ....137 F2
Tintern Cl *PUT/ROE* SW15 ....131 E3
Tintern St *CLAP* SW4 ....135 E2
Tinto Rd *CAN/RD* E16 ....94 A4
Tinworth St *LBTH* SE11 ....117 E1
Tipthorpe Rd *BTSEA* SW11 ....134 A1
Tisdall Pl *WALW* SE17 ....48 B5
Titchborne Rw *BAY/PAD* W2 ....17 D5
Titchfield Rd *STJWD* NW8 ....73 D5
Titchwell Rd *WAND/EARL* SW18 ...133 D5
Tite St *CHEL* SW3 ....115 F2
Titmuss St *SHB* * W12 ....100 B3
Tiverton Dr *ELTH/MOT* SE9 ....162 C1
Tiverton Rd *SEVS/STOTM* N15 ....59 D1
   WLSDN NW10 ....71 D5
Tiverton St *STHWK* SE1 ....47 E2
Tivoli Gdns *CHARL* SE7 ....107 E5
Tivoli Rd *WNWD* SE27 ....154 C5
Tobago St *POP/IOD* * E14 ....104 A3
Tobin Cl *HAMP* NW3 ....73 E4
Tokenhouse Yd *LOTH* EC2R 24 A4
Tokyngton Av *WBLY* HA9 ....68 A3
Toland Sq *PUT/ROE* SW15 ....130 A3
Tollbridge Cl *NKENS* W10 ....89 E3
Tollet St *WCHPL* E1 ....91 D3
Tollgate Dr *DUL* SE21 ....155 E2
Tollgate Gdns *KIL/WHAMP* NW6 ....2 C1
Tollgate Rd *EHAM* E6 ....95 E4
Tollhouse Wy *ARCH* N19 ....56 C4
Tollington Pk *HOLWY* N7 ....57 F4
Tollington Pl *FSBYPK* N4 ....57 F4
Tollington Rd *HOLWY* N7 ....75 F1
Tollington Wy *HOLWY* N7 ....57 E5
Tolmer's Sq *CAMTN* NW1 ....4 A5
Tolpuddle Av *PLSTW* E13 ....82 C5
Tolpuddle St *IS* N1 ....10 A1
Tolsford Rd *CLPT* E5 ....78 B2
Tom Cribb Rd *WOOL/PLUM* SE18 ..108 C4
Tom Jenkinson Rd *CAN/RD* E16 ....106 A2
Tomlin's Gv *BOW* E3 ....92 A2
Tomlinson Cl *BETH* E2 ....13 F4
   CHSWK W4 ....110 B1
Tomlins Orch *BARK* IG11 ....84 C5
Tomlin's Ter *POP/IOD* E14 ....91 E5
Tom Mann Cl *BARK* IG11 ....85 E5
Tom Nolan Cl *SRTFD* E15 ....93 E1
Tompion St *FSBYE* EC1V 10 C4
Tom Smith Cl *GNWCH* SE10 ....123 E2
Tonbridge St *STPAN* WC1H 8 C4
Tonsley Hl *WAND/EARL* SW18 ....132 B3
Tonsley Pl *WAND/EARL* SW18 ....132 B3
Tonsley Rd *WAND/EARL* SW18 ......132 B3
Tonsley St *WAND/EARL* SW18 ....132 B3
Took's Ct *FLST/FETLN* EC4A 22 A4
Tooley St *STHWK* SE1 ....36 B3
Tooting Bec Gdns *STRHM/NOR* SW16 ..153 D4
Tooting Bec Rd *TOOT* SW17 ....152 A3
Tooting Gv *TOOT* SW17 ....151 E5
Tooting High St *TOOT* SW17 ....151 E4
Tooting Market *TOOT* * SW17 ....151 F4
Topham St *CLKNW* * EC1R 10 A5
Topley St *ELTH/MOT* SE9 ....142 C2
Topmast Point *POP/IOD* * E14 ....104 A3
Topsham Rd *TOOT* SW17 ....151 F3
Torbay Rd *KIL/WHAMP* NW6 ....71 F4
Torbay St *CAMTN* * NW1 ....74 B4
Torcross Dr *FSTH* SE23 ....156 C2

Tor Gdns KENS W8 .... 26 A5
Tormount Rd WOOL/PLUM SE18 .... 127 E2
Toronto Av MNPK E12 .... 83 F1
Toronto Rd IL IG1 .... 66 B3
Torquay St BAY/PAD W2 .... 14 C3
Torrens Rd BRXS/STRHM SW2 .... 135 F3
Torrens Sq SRTFD E15 .... 81 F3
Torrens St FSBYE EC1V 10 C2
Torriano Av KTTN NW5 .... 75 D2
Torriano Ms KTTN NW5 .... 74 C2
Torridge Gdns PECK SE15 .... 138 C2
Torridon Rd CAT SE6 .... 159 D1
    LEW SE13 .... 141 D5
Torrington Pl FITZ W1T 19 F2
    WAP E1W 102 A2
Torrington Sq GWRST WC1E 20 B1
Torwood Rd PUT/ROE SW15 .... 130 A3
Tothill St STJSPK SW1H 44 B4
Tottan Ter WCHPL * E1 .... 91 D5
Tottenham Court Rd FITZ W1T 19 F1
Tottenham La CEND/HSY/T N8 .... 57 E1
Tottenham Ms FITZ * W1T 19 F2
Tottenham Rd IS N1 .... 77 E3
Tottenham St GTPST W1W 19 F2
Totterdown St TOOT SW17 .... 151 F4
Toulmin St STHWK SE1 .... 47 E1
Toulon St CMBW SE5 .... 118 C3
Tournay Rd FUL/PGN SW6 .... 113 F3
Toussaint Wk BERM/RHTH SE16 .... 102 A4
Towcester Rd BOW E3 .... 92 B3
Tower Br TWRH EC3N 37 E3
Tower Bridge Ap TWRH EC3N 37 E3
Tower Bridge Rd STHWK SE1 .... 48 C4
Tower Buildings WAP * E1W 102 A3
Tower Cl HAMP NW3 .... 73 D2
Tower Ct LSQ/SEVD * WC2H 20 C5
Tower Hamlets Rd FSTGT E7 .... 81 F2
Tower Hl TWRH EC3N 37 D2
Tower Hill Ter MON EC3R 37 D2
Tower Ms CLPT * E5 .... 79 E2
Tower Mill Rd PECK * SE15 .... 119 E3
Tower Pl MON EC3R 37 D2
Tower Rd WLSDN NW10 .... 70 A4
Tower Royal MANHO * EC4N 35 F1
Tower St LSQ/SEVD * WC2H 20 B5
Towncourt Pth FSBYPK N4 .... 58 C3
Townhall Av CHSWK W4 .... 111 D1
Town Hall Pde BRXS/STRHM * SW2 ...... 135 F2
Town Hall Rd BTSEA SW11 .... 133 F1
Townley Ct SRTFD E15 .... 81 F3
Townley Rd DUL SE21 .... 137 E3
Townley St WALW * SE17 .... 119 D1
Townmead Rd FUL/PGN SW6 .... 114 C5
    RCH/KEW TW9 .... 110 B5
Town Quay BARK IG11 .... 84 B5
Townsend La CDALE/KGS NW9 .... 51 D2
Townsend Rd WOOL/PLUM SE18 .... 108 B4
Townsend St WALW SE17 .... 48 C5
Townsend Yd HGT N6 .... 56 B3
Townshend Est STJWD NW8 .... 4 C1
Townshend Rd CHST BR7 .... 162 B5
    STJWD NW8 .... 73 E5
Towton Rd WNWD SE27 .... 154 C2
Toynbec Cl CHST BR7 .... 162 B4
Toynbee St WCHPL E1 .... 25 E3
Toyne Wy HGT N6 .... 55 F1
Tracey Av CRICK * NW2 .... 70 C2
Trader Rd EHAM E6 .... 96 B5
Tradescant Rd VX/NE SW8 .... 117 E4
Trading Estate Rd WLSDN * NW10 .... 86 C3
Trafalgar Av PECK SE15 .... 119 F4
Trafalgar Chambers CHEL * SW3 .... 115 D1
Trafalgar Gdns WCHPL E1 .... 91 D4
Trafalgar Gv GNWCH SE10 .... 123 D2
Trafalgar Rd GNWCH SE10 .... 123 E1
Trafalgar Sq CHCR WC2N 32 B3
Trafalgar St WALW SE17 .... 119 D1
Trafalgar Wy POP/IOD E14 .... 104 C2

Trafford Cl SRTFD E15 .... 80 B2
Tramway Av SRTFD E15 .... 81 D4
Tranley Ms HAMP * NW3 .... 73 E1
Tranmere Rd WAND/EARL SW18 .... 150 C1
Tranquil V BKHTH/KID SE3 .... 123 E5
Transept St CAMTN NW1 .... 17 D3
Transom Sq POP/IOD E14 .... 122 B1
Tranton Rd BERM/RHTH SE16 .... 102 B4
Travers Rd HOLWY N7 .... 58 A5
Treadgold St NTGHL W11 .... 101 D1
Treadway St BETH E2 .... 90 B1
Treaty St IS N1 .... 75 F5
Trebeck St MYFR/PICC W1J 30 C3
Trebovir Rd ECT SW5 .... 114 A1
Treby St BOW E3 .... 91 F3
Trecastle Wy HOLWY * N7 .... 75 D1
Tredegar Rd BOW E3 .... 91 F1
Tredegar Sq BOW E3 .... 91 F2
Trederwen Rd HACK E8 .... 78 A5
Tredown Rd SYD SE26 .... 156 C5
Tredwell Rd WNWD SE27 .... 154 B4
Treen Av BARN SW13 .... 129 E1
Tree Rd CAN/RD E16 .... 94 C5
Treewall Gdns BMLY BR1 .... 160 B4
Trefoil Rd WAND/EARL SW18 .... 132 C3
Tregaron Av CEND/HSY/T N8 .... 57 E2
Tregarvon Rd BTSEA SW11 .... 134 A2
Trego Rd HOM E9 .... 80 A4
Tregothnan Rd BRXN/ST SW9 .... 135 E1
Tregunter Rd WBPTN SW10 .... 114 C2
Treherne Ct BRXN/ST * SW9 .... 118 B4
Trehern Rd MORT/ESHN SW14 .... 129 D1
Trehurst St CLPT E5 .... 79 E2
Trelawney Est HOM * E9 .... 78 C3
Trelawn Rd BRXS/STRHM SW2 .... 136 A3
    LEY E10 .... 62 C5
Tremadoc Rd CLAP SW4 .... 135 D2
Tremlett Gv ARCH N19 .... 56 C5
Tremlett Ms ARCH * N19 .... 56 C5
Trenchard St GNWCH SE10 .... 123 D1
Trenchold St VX/NE * SW8 .... 117 E2
Trenmar Gdns WLSDN NW10 .... 88 B2
Trentham St WAND/EARL SW18 .... 150 A5
Trent Rd BRXS/STRHM SW2 .... 135 F3
Treport St WAND/EARL SW18 .... 132 B5
Tresco Gdns GDMY/SEVK IG3 .... 67 F4
Tresco Rd PECK SE15 .... 138 B2
Tresham Crs STJWD NW8 .... 4 C4
Tresham Rd BARK IG11 .... 85 F4
Tressell Cl IS * N1 .... 76 B4
Tressillian Crs BROCKY SE4 .... 140 A1
Tressillian Rd BROCKY SE4 .... 140 A1
Trevanion Rd WKENS * W14 .... 113 E1
Trevelyan Av MNPK E12 .... 83 F1
Trevelyan Gdns WLSDN * NW10 .... 70 C5
Trevelyan Rd FSTGT E7 .... 81 E1
Treveris St STHWK SE1 .... 35 D4
Treverton St NKENS W10 .... 89 D3
Treville St PUT/ROE SW15 .... 130 B5
Treviso Rd FSTH SE23 .... 157 D2
Trevithick St DEPT SE8 .... 122 A2
Trevor Pl SKENS SW7 .... 41 D1
Trevor Sq SKENS SW7 .... 41 D1
Trevor St SKENS SW7 .... 41 D1
Trewint St WAND/EARL SW18 .... 150 C2
Trewsbury Rd SYD SE26 .... 157 D5
Triangle Est LBTH * SE11 .... 117 F1
Triangle Pl CLAP SW4 .... 135 D2
Triangle Rd HACK E8 .... 78 B5
Trident Pl CHEL * SW3 .... 115 D2
Trident St BERM/RHTH SE16 .... 103 D5
Trig La BLKFR EC4V 35 E1
Trigon Rd VX/NE SW8 .... 117 F3
Trilby Rd FSTH SE23 .... 157 D2
Trim St NWCR SE14 .... 121 F2
Trinder Gdns ARCH N19 .... 57 E3
Tring Av WBLY HA9 .... 68 A3
Trinidad St POP/IOD E14 .... 103 F1

Trinity Buoy Whf *POP/IOD* * E14 ....93 D4
Trinity Church Rd *BARN* SW13 ....112 B2
Trinity Church Sq *STHWK* SE1 ....47 F2
Trinity Ct *CLAP* * SW4 ....134 C2
   HACK * E8 ....77 F3
   LEW SE13 ....141 D2
   WAN E11 ....63 E4
Trinity Ct *ELTH/MOT* SE9 ....144 B4
Trinity Crs *TOOT* SW17 ....151 E2
Trinity Gdns *BRXN/ST* SW9 ....135 F2
   CAN/RD E16 ....93 F4
Trinity Gn *WCHPL* * E1 ....90 C4
Trinity Gv *GNWCH* SE10 ....122 C4
Trinity Ri *HNHL* SE24 ....136 B5
Trinity Rd *TOOT* SW17 ....151 F2
   WAND/EARL SW18 ....133 D4
Trinity Sq *TWRH* EC3N 37 D2
Trinity St *CAN/RD* E16 ....93 F4
   STHWK SE1 ....47 F1
Trinity Wy *ACT* W3 ....99 F1
Trio Pl *STHWK* SE1 ....47 F1
Tristan Ct *BKHTH/KID* SE3 ....141 E1
Tristram Rd *BMLY* BR1 ....159 F4
Triton Sq *CAMTN* NW1 ....7 E5
Tritton Rd *WNWD* SE27 ....155 D3
Triumph Rd *EHAM* E6 ....95 F5
Troon Cl *BERM/RHTH* * SE16 ....120 B1
Troon St *WCHPL* E1 ....91 E5
Trossachs Rd *EDUL* SE22 ....137 E3
Trothy Rd *STHWK* SE1 ....102 A5
Trott St *BTSEA* SW11 ....115 D4
Troughton Rd *CHARL* SE7 ....124 B1
Troutbeck Rd *NWCR* SE14 ....121 E4
Trouville Rd *BAL* SW12 ....134 C4
Trowbridge Rd *HOM* E9 ....79 F3
Troy Ct *KENS* W8 ....38 A2
Troy Town *PECK* SE15 ....138 A1
Truman's Rd *STNW/STAM* N16 ....77 E4
Trumpington Rd *FSTGT* E7 ....81 F1
Trump St *CITYW* EC2V 23 F5
Trundle St *STHWK* SE1 ....35 E5
Trundleys Rd *DEPT* SE8 ....121 E2
   DEPT SE8 ....121 D1
Trundley's Ter *DEPT* SE8 ....103 D5
Truro Gdns *IL* IG1 ....65 E2
Truro St *KTTN* NW5 ....74 A3
Trusedale Rd *EHAM* E6 ....95 F5
Truslove Rd *WNWD* SE27 ....154 A5
Trussley Rd *HMSMTH* W6 ....100 C4
Tryon Crs *HOM* E9 ....78 C5
Tryon St *CHEL* SW3 ....115 F1
Tuam Rd *WOOL/PLUM* SE18 ....127 D2
Tubbs Rd *WLSDN* NW10 ....87 F1
Tudor Cl *BRXS/STRHM* * SW2 ....135 F4
   CDALE/KGS NW9 ....50 C4
   HAMP NW3 ....73 E2
   HGT N6 ....56 C2
Tudor Ct *ELTH/MOT* * SE9 ....143 E2
   WALTH E17 ....61 F2
Tudor Ct North *WBLY* HA9 ....68 A2
Tudor Ct South *WBLY* HA9 ....68 A2
Tudor Est *WLSDN* * NW10 ....86 B1
Tudor Gdns *ACT* W3 ....86 A5
   BARN SW13 ....129 E1
   CDALE/KGS NW9 ....50 C4
Tudor Gv *HOM* E9 ....78 C4
Tudor Pde *ELTH/MOT* * SE9 ....143 E2
Tudor Rd *BARK* IG11 ....85 F4
   EHAM E6 ....82 C5
   HACK E8 ....78 B5
Tudor St *EMB* EC4Y 34 B1
Tudor Wy *ACT* W3 ....98 A3
Tudway Rd *ELTH/MOT* SE9 ....142 C2
Tufnell Park Rd *HOLWY* N7 ....75 D1
Tufton St *WEST* SW1P 44 C3
Tugboat St *THMD* SE28 ....109 E3
Tugela St *CAT* SE6 ....157 F2
Tulip Cl *EHAM* E6 ....95 F4

Tulip Gdns *IL* IG1 ....84 B3
Tulse Hl *BRXS/STRHM* SW2 ....136 A5
Tulsemere Rd *WNWD* SE27 ....154 C2
Tunis Rd *SHB* W12 ....100 C2
Tunley Rd *BAL* SW12 ....152 A2
   WLSDN NW10 ....69 E5
Tunmarsh La *PLSTW* E13 ....94 C2
Tunnan Leys *EHAM* E6 ....96 A5
Tunnel Av *GNWCH* SE10 ....105 D3
Tunnel Rd *BERM/RHTH* SE16 ....102 C3
Tunstall Rd *BRXN/ST* SW9 ....135 F2
Tunworth Cl *CDALE/KGS* NW9 ....50 C1
Tunworth Crs *PUT/ROE* SW15 ....129 E4
Tupelo Rd *LEY* E10 ....62 B4
Turene Cl *BTSEA* SW11 ....132 C2
Turin St *BETH* E2 ....90 A2
Turks Rw *CHEL* SW3 ....115 F1
Turle Rd *FSBYPK* * N4 ....57 F4
Turlewray Cl *FSBYPK* N4 ....57 F3
Turley Cl *SRTFD* E15 ....81 E5
Turnagain La *STP* * EC4M 22 C4
Turnberry Cl *BERM/RHTH* * SE16 ....120 B1
Turner Cl *CDALE/KGS* NW9 ....50 C4
   GLDGN NW11 ....54 B1
Turner Ct *CMBW* * SE5 ....137 D2
Turner Dr *GLDGN* NW11 ....54 B1
Turner's Rd *POP/IOD* E14 ....91 F4
Turner St *CAN/RD* E16 ....93 F4
   WCHPL E1 ....90 B4
Turner's Wd *GLDGN* NW11 ....54 C3
Turneville Rd *WKENS* W14 ....113 F2
Turney Rd *DUL* SE21 ....136 C5
Turnham Green Ter *CHSWK* W4 ....99 E5
Turnham Rd *BROCKY* SE4 ....139 E3
Turnmill St *FARR* EC1M 22 B1
Turnpike Cl *DEPT* SE8 ....121 F3
Turnstone Cl *PLSTW* E13 ....94 A2
Turpentine La *PIM* SW1V 116 B1
Turpins Yd *CRICK* * NW2 ....52 B4
Turquand St *WALW* SE17 ....47 F5
Turret Gv *CLAP* SW4 ....134 C1
Turville St *BETH* * E2 ....13 E5
Tuscan Rd *WOOL/PLUM* SE18 ....127 D1
Tuskar St *GNWCH* SE10 ....123 E1
Tweedmouth Rd *PLSTW* E13 ....94 B1
Twelvetrees Crs *BOW* E3 ....92 C3
Twickenham Rd *WAN* E11 ....63 D4
Twig Folly Cl *BOW* E3 ....91 D1
Twig Folly Whf *BETH* * E2 ....91 D1
Twilley St *WAND/EARL* SW18 ....132 B5
Twine Ct *WCHPL* E1 ....102 C1
Twine Ter *BOW* * E3 ....91 F3
Twisden Rd *KTTN* NW5 ....74 B1
Twybridge Wy *WLSDN* NW10 ....68 C4
Twyford Av *ACT* W3 ....98 A1
Twyford Crs *ACT* W3 ....98 A2
Twyford Rd *IL* IG1 ....84 C2
Twyford St *IS* N1 ....75 F5
Tyas Rd *CAN/RD* E16 ....93 F3
Tyburn Wy *MBLAR* W1H 29 F1
Tyers Ga *STHWK* SE1 ....48 C1
Tyers St *LBTH* SE11 ....117 F1
Tyers Ter *LBTH* SE11 ....117 F1
Tylehurst Gdns *IL* IG1 ....84 C2
Tyler Cl *BETH* E2 ....13 E1
Tyler St *GNWCH* SE10 ....123 E1
Tylney Av *NRWD* SE19 ....155 F5
Tylney Rd *FSTGT* E7 ....82 C1
Tyndale La *IS* N1 ....76 B4
Tyndale Ter *IS* N1 ....76 B4
Tyndall Rd *LEY* E10 ....62 C4
   WELL DA16 ....145 F1
Tyneham Cl *BTSEA* * SW11 ....134 A1
Tyneham Rd *BTSEA* SW11 ....116 A5
Tynemouth Cl *EHAM* E6 ....96 B5
Tynemouth Rd *WOOL/PLUM* SE18 ....127 E1
Tynemouth St *FUL/PGN* SW6 ....114 C5
Tyne St *WCHPL* E1 ....25 F4

Tynsdale Rd WLSDN NW10 ....69 E3
Type St BETH E2 ....91 D1
Tyrawley Rd FUL/PGN SW6 ....114 B4
Tyrone Rd EHAM E6 ....95 F1
Tyron Wy SCUP DA14 ....163 E4
Tyrrell Rd EDUL SE22 ....138 A2
Tyrrel Wy CDALE/KGS NW9 ....51 F2
Tyrwhitt Rd BROCKY SE4 ....140 A1
Tysoe St CLKNW EC1R 10 A4
Tyson Gdns FSTH * SE23 ....138 C5
Tyson Rd FSTH SE23 ....138 C5
Tyssen Rd STNW/STAM * N16 ....59 F5
Tyssen St HACK E8 ....77 F3
Tytherton Rd ARCH N19 ....57 D5

U

Uamvar St POP/IOD E14 ....92 B4
Udall St WEST SW1P 43 F5
Uffington Rd WLSDN NW10 ....70 A5
    WNWD SE27 ....154 A4
Ufford St STHWK SE1 ....34 B5
Ufton Gv IS N1 ....77 E4
Uhura Sq STNW/STAM * N16 ....59 F5
Ullathorne Rd STRHM/NOR SW16 ....152 C4
Ullin St POP/IOD E14 ....92 C4
Ullswater Cl KUTN/CMB * KT2 ....147 D4
Ullswater Crs PUT/ROE SW15 ....147 D5
Ullswater Rd BARN SW13 ....112 A3
    WNWD SE27 ....154 B3
Ulster Pl CAMTN NW1 ....18 C1
Ulundi Rd BKHTH/KID SE3 ....123 E2
Ulva Rd PUT/ROE SW15 ....131 D2
Ulverscroft Rd EDUL SE22 ....138 A3
Ulysses Rd KIL/WHAMP NW6 ....71 F2
Umberston St WCHPL * E1 ....90 A4
Umbria St PUT/ROE SW15 ....130 A4
Umfreville Rd FSBYPK N4 ....58 B1
Undercliff Rd LEW SE13 ....140 A1
Underhill Rd EDUL SE22 ....138 A3
Underhill St CAMTN NW1 ....74 B5
Undershaft HDTCH EC3A 24 C5
Undershaw Rd BMLY BR1 ....159 E3
The Underwood ELTH/MOT SE9 ....161 F2
Underwood Rd WCHPL E1 ....90 A3
Underwood Rw IS N1 ....11 F3
Underwood St IS N1 ....11 F3
Undine Rd POP/IOD E14 ....104 B5
Undine St TOOT SW17 ....151 F5
Union Cl WAN E11 ....81 D1
Union Ct CLAP SW4 ....117 E5
Union Dr WCHPL * E1 ....91 E3
Union Gv VX/NE SW8 ....117 D5
Union Rd CLAP SW4 ....117 D5
Union Sq IS N1 ....76 C5
Union St SRTFD E15 ....81 D5
    STHWK SE1 ....35 D4
Union Wk BETH E2 ....13 E3
Unity Cl WLSDN NW10 ....70 A3
    WNWD SE27 ....154 C5
Unity Ms CAMTN NW1 ....8 A1
Unity Wy WOOL/PLUM SE18 ....107 D4
University Cl FITZ W1T 19 F1
University Wy EHAM E6 ....108 A1
Unwin Cl PECK SE15 ....120 A2
Unwin Rd SKENS SW7 ....40 B2
Upbrook Ms BAY/PAD W2 ....15 F5
Upcerne Rd WBPTN SW10 ....114 C3
Updale Rd SCUP DA14 ....163 F4
Uphall Rd IL IG1 ....84 B2
Upham Park Rd CHSWK W4 ....99 E5
Upland Rd EDUL SE22 ....138 A5
    PLSTW E13 ....94 A3
Uplands Cl MORT/ESHN SW14 ....128 B3
Upney La BARK IG11 ....85 F4
Upnor Wy WALW SE17 ....119 E1

Uppark Dr GNTH/NBYPK IG2 ....66 C1
Upper Addison Gdns WKENS W14 ....101 E3
Upper Bardsey Wk IS * N1 ....76 C3
Upper Belgrave St KTBR SW1X 42 B2
Upper Berenger Wk WBPTN * SW10 ......115 D3
Upper Berkeley St BAY/PAD W2 ....17 E5
Upper Blantyre Wk WBPTN * SW10 ....115 D3
Upper Brockley Rd BROCKY SE4 ....121 F5
Upper Brook St MYFR/PKLN W1K 30 A1
Upper Caldy Wk IS * N1 ....76 C3
Upper Camelford Wk NTGHL * W11 ....89 E5
Upper Cheyne Rw CHEL SW3 ....115 E2
Upper Clapton Rd CLPT E5 ....60 B4
Upper Clarendon Wk NTGHL * W11 ....89 E5
Upper Dartrey Wk WBPTN * SW10 ....114 C3
Upper Dengie Wk IS * N1 ....76 C5
Upper Grosvenor St MYFR/PKLN W1K 30 A2
Upper Gnd STHWK SE1 ....34 A3
Upper Gulland Wk IS * N1 ....76 C3
Upper Handa Wk IS * N1 ....77 D3
Upper Harley St CAMTN NW1 ....18 B1
Upper Hawkwell Wk IS * N1 ....76 C5
Upper John St REGST W1B 31 F1
Upper Ldg KENS * W8 ....27 D4
Upper Lismore Wk IS * N1 ....76 C5
Upper Marsh STHWK SE1 ....45 F2
Upper Montagu St MBLAR W1H 17 E2
Upper North St POP/IOD E14 ....92 A4
Upper Park Rd HAMP NW3 ....73 F3
Upper Phillimore Gdns KENS W8 ....38 A1
Upper Ramsey Wk IS N1 ....77 D5
Upper Rawreth Wk IS * N1 ....77 D3
Upper Richmond Rd PUT/ROE SW15 ......130 B2
Upper Richmond Rd West
    RCHPK/HAM TW10 ....128 A2
Upper Rd PLSTW E13 ....94 A2
Upper St Martin's La LSQ/SEVD WC2H 20 C5
Upper Sheppey Wk IS N1 ....76 C3
Upper St IS N1 ....10 B1
Upper Tachbrook St PIM SW1V 43 F4
Upper Talbot Wk NTGHL * W11 ....89 E5
Upper Ter HAMP NW3 ....54 C5
Upper Thames St BLKFR EC4V 35 E1
Upper Tollington Pk FSBYPK N4 ....58 A3
Upperton Rd SCUP DA14 ....163 F5
Upperton Rd East PLSTW E13 ....94 C2
Upperton Rd West PLSTW E13 ....94 C2
Upper Tooting Pk TOOT SW17 ....151 F2
Upper Tooting Rd TOOT SW17 ....151 F4
Upper Tulse HI BRXS/STRHM SW2 ....135 F5
Upper Whistler Wk WBPTN * SW10 ....114 C3
Upper Wimpole St CAVSO/HST W1G 18 B2
Upper Woburn Pl CAMTN NW1 ....8 B4
Upstall St CMBW SE5 ....118 B4
Upton Av FSTGT E7 ....82 A4
Upton La FSTGT E7 ....82 B3
Upton Park Rd FSTGT E7 ....82 B4
Upton Rd WOOL/PLUM SE18 ....126 C2
Upwood Rd LEE/GVPK SE12 ....142 A4
Urlwin St CMBW SE5 ....118 C2
Urlwin Wk BRXN/ST SW9 ....118 A4
Urmston Dr WIM/MER SW19 ....149 E1
Ursula Ms FSBYPK N4 ....58 B3
Ursula St BTSEA SW11 ....115 E4
Urswick Rd CLPT E5 ....78 C2
Usborne Ms VX/NE SW8 ....117 F3
Usher Rd BOW E3 ....79 F5
Usk Rd BTSEA SW11 ....132 C2
Usk St BETH E2 ....91 D2
Uverdale Rd WBPTN SW10 ....114 C3
Uxbridge Rd SHB W12 ....100 A2
Uxbridge St KENS W8 ....26 A3

V

The Vale *ACT* W3.....................................**99** D2
  CHEL SW3...**115** D2
  CRICK NW2...**53** D5
Vale Cl *MV/WKIL* W9..................................**3** E4
Vale Cottages *PUT/ROE* * SW15.......**147** E3
Vale Ct *ACT* * W3.......................................**99** F2
Vale Crs *PUT/ROE* SW15..........................**147** E4
Vale End *EDUL* SE22...............................**137** F2
Vale Gv *ACT* W3..**99** D2
  FSBYPK N4..**58** C2
Vale La *ACT* W3...**86** A4
Valentia Pl *BRXN/ST* SW9....................**136** A4
Valentine Pl *STHWK* SE1...........................**34** C5
Valentine Rd *HOM* * E9.............................**79** D3
Valentines Rd *IL* IG1...................................**66** B3
Vale of Health *HAMP* NW3........................**54** C5
Valerian Wy *SRTFD* E15............................**93** D2
Vale Ri *GLDGN* NW11.................................**53** F3
Vale Rd *FSBYPK* N4.....................................**58** C2
  FSTGT E7...**82** B3
Vale Royal *HOLWY* N7................................**75** D4
Valeswood Rd *BMLY* BR1........................**159** F5
Vale Ter *FSBYPK* N4....................................**58** C1
Valetta Gv *PLSTW* E13..............................**94** A1
Valetta Rd *ACT* W3.....................................**99** E3
Valette St *HACK* * E8...................................**78** B3
Valiant Wy *EHAM* E6...................................**95** F4
Vallance Rd *WCHPL* E1...............................**90** A3
Valleyfield Rd *STRHM/NOR* SW16.....**153** F5
Valley Gv *CHARL* SE7..............................**124** C1
Valley Rd *STRHM/NOR* SW16.............**153** F4
Valliere Rd *WLSDN* NW10...........................**88** A2
Valliers Wood Rd *BFN/LL* DA15..........**163** D5
Valmar Rd *CMBW* SE5.............................**118** C4
Valnay St *TOOT* SW17..............................**151** F5
Valonia Gdns *WAND/EARL* SW18......**131** F4
Vambery Rd *WOOL/PLUM* SE18...........**126** C2
Vanbrugh Flds *BKHTH/KID* SE3...........**123** F2
Vanbrugh Hl *GNWCH* SE10....................**123** E1
Vanbrugh Pk *BKHTH/KID* SE3..............**123** F2
Vanbrugh Park Rd *BKHTH/KID* SE3....**123** F3
Vanbrugh Park Rd West
  BKHTH/KID SE3....................................**123** F3
Vanbrugh Rd *CHSWK* W4............................**99** D4
Vanbrugh Ter *BKHTH/KID* SE3.............**123** F4
Vanburgh Cl *CAN/RD* E16............................**95** D4
Vancouver Rd *FSTH* SE23.......................**157** E2
Vanderbilt Rd *WAND/EARL* SW18........**150** B1
Vanderbilt Vls *SHB* * W12......................**101** D3
Vandome Cl *CAN/RD* E16.............................**94** B5
Vandon Pl *STJSPK* SW1H............................**43** E3
Vandyke Cl *PUT/ROE* SW15....................**131** D4
Vandyke Cross *ELTH/MOT* SE9.............**143** E3
Vandy St *SDTCH* EC2A................................**24** C1
Vane Cl *HAMP* NW3.....................................**73** D2
Vanguard Cl *CAN/RD* E16............................**94** A4
Vanguard St *DEPT* SE8...........................**122** A4
Vanneck Sq *PUT/ROE* * SW15................**130** A3
Vanoc Gdns *BMLY* BR1............................**160** A4
Vansittart Rd *FSTGT* E7...............................**82** A1
Vansittart St *NWCR* SE14.......................**121** E3
Vanston Pl *FUL/PGN* SW6........................**114** A3
Vant Rd *TOOT* SW17.................................**151** F5
Varcoe Rd *BERM/RHTH* SE16................**120** B3
Vardens Rd *BTSEA* SW11........................**133** D2
Varden St *WCHPL* E1....................................**90** B5
Varley Rd *CAN/RD* E16.................................**94** B5
Varna Rd *FUL/PGN* SW6..........................**113** E3
Varndell St *CAMTN* NW1..............................**7** E3
Varsity Rw *MORT/ESHN* SW14..............**110** C5
Vartry Rd *SEVS/STOTM* N15.....................**59** E1
Vassall Rd *BRXN/ST* SW9.......................**118** A3
Vauban Est *BERM/RHTH* SE16................**49** F3
Vauban St *BERM/RHTH* SE16...................**49** F3
Vaughan Av *HMSMTH* W6............................**99** F5

Vaughan Est *BETH* * E2...............................**13** E3
Vaughan Gdns *IL* IG1...................................**65** F2
Vaughan Rd *CMBW* SE5..........................**118** C5
  SRTFD E15..**81** F3
  WELL DA16...**127** F5
Vaughan St *BERM/RHTH* SE16.............**105** F3
Vaughan Wy *WAP* E1W..............................**102** A1
Vaughan Williams Cl *DEPT* SE8...........**122** A3
Vauxhall Br *VX/NE* SW8.............................**117** E1
Vauxhall Bridge Rd *PIM* SW1V.................**43** E3
Vauxhall Gv *VX/NE* SW8............................**117** F2
Vauxhall St *LBTH* SE11..............................**117** F1
Vauxhall Wk *LBTH* SE11............................**117** F1
Vawdrey Cl *WCHPL* E1.................................**90** C3
Veda Rd *LEW* SE13....................................**140** A2
Venables St *STJWD* NW8.............................**16** B1
Vencourt Pl *HMSMTH* W6.........................**112** A1
Venetian Rd *CMBW* SE5..........................**118** C5
Venetia Rd *FSBYPK* N4.................................**58** B1
Venn St *CLAP* SW4.....................................**134** C2
Ventnor Gdns *BARK* IG11.............................**85** E3
Ventnor Rd *NWCR* SE14............................**121** D3
Venue St *POP/IOD* E14.................................**92** B4
Venus Rd *WOOL/PLUM* SE18...................**107** F4
Vera Lynn Cl *FSTGT* E7................................**82** A1
Vera Rd *FUL/PGN* SW6.............................**113** E4
Verbena Cl *CAN/RD* E16...............................**93** E3
Verbena Gdns *HMSMTH* W6....................**112** A1
Verdant La *CAT* SE6...................................**159** E1
Verdun Rd *BARN* SW13............................**112** A3
Vereker Rd *WKENS* * W14.........................**113** E1
Vere St *MHST* W1U.......................................**18** C5
Vermont Rd *WAND/EARL* SW18............**132** B4
Verney Rd *BERM/RHTH* SE16.................**120** B3
Verney St *WLSDN* NW10...............................**51** D5
Verney Wy *BERM/RHTH* SE16.................**120** B3
Vernham Rd *WOOL/PLUM* SE18............**126** C2
Vernon Av *MNPK* E12....................................**83** F1
Vernon Pl *BMSBY* WC1N..............................**21** D5
Vernon Ri *FSBYW* WC1X................................**9** F3
Vernon Rd *BOW* E3..**91** F1
  GDMY/SEVK IG3..**67** F3
  MORT/ESHN SW14.................................**129** D1
  SRTFD E15..**81** E4
  WAN E11..**63** E3
Vernon Sq *FSBYW* * WC1X..........................**9** F3
Vernon St *WKENS* SE14...........................**101** E5
Vernon Yd *NTGHL* W11.............................**101** F1
Veronica Rd *TOOT* SW17..........................**152** B3
Verran Rd *BAL* * SW12..............................**134** B5
Verulam Av *WALTH* E17................................**61** F2
Verulam Ct *CDALE/KGS* * NW9.................**52** A2
Verulam St *FSBYW* WC1X...........................**22** A2
Vespan Rd *SHB* W12.................................**100** A3
Vesta Rd *BROCKY* SE4...............................**121** E5
Vestris Rd *FSTH* SE23...............................**157** D2
Vestry Rd *CMBW* SE5...............................**119** E4
Vestry St *IS* N1...**12** A3
Vevey St *FSTH* SE23..................................**157** F2
Viaduct Pl *BETH* E2......................................**90** B2
Viaduct St *BETH* E2......................................**90** B2
Vian St *LEW* SE13......................................**140** B1
Vibart Gdns *BRXS/STRHM* SW2.............**135** F5
Vibart Wk *IS* * N1...**75** E5
Vicarage Crs *BTSEA* SW11.......................**115** D4
Vicarage Dr *BARK* IG11...............................**84** C4
  MORT/ESHN SW14.................................**129** D1
Vicarage Gdns *KENS* * W8...........................**26** B5
Vicarage Ga *KENS* W8.................................**26** C4
Vicarage Gv *CMBW* SE5............................**119** D4
Vicarage La *EHAM* E6...................................**95** F2
  IL IG1...**67** D3
  SRTFD E15..**81** E3
Vicarage Ms *CHSWK* * W4.........................**111** E2
Vicarage Pk *WOOL/PLUM* SE18.............**126** C1
Vicarage Rd *HDN* NW4.................................**52** A1
  LEY E10..**62** B2
  MORT/ESHN SW14.................................**128** C3

SRTFD E15 ....81 F4
WOOL/PLUM SE18 ....126 C1
Vicarage Wk *BTSEA* * SW11 ....115 D4
Vicarage Wy *WLSDN* NW10 ....51 D5
Vicar's CI *HACK* E8 ....78 C5
SRTFD E15 ....82 A5
Vicars HI *LEW* SE13 ....140 B2
Vicar's Rd *KTTN* NW5 ....74 A2
Viceroy Rd *VX/NE* SW8 ....117 E4
Victoria Ar *PIM* SW1V 43 D3
Victoria Av *EHAM* E6 ....83 D5
WBLY HA9 ....68 B3
Victoria Cottages *WCHPL* * E1 ....90 A4
Victoria Ct *WBLY* HA9 ....68 A3
Victoria Dock Rd *CAN/RD* E16 ....93 F5
Victoria Dr *WIM/MER* SW19 ....131 D5
Victoria Emb *TPL/STR* WC2R 33 E2
WHALL SW1A 45 D1

Victoria Embankment Gdns
CHCR * WC2N...33 D2
Victoria Ga *BAY/PAD* W2 ....28 B1
Victoria Gv *KENS* W8 ....39 E2
Victoria Grove Ms *NTGHL* * W11 ....26 C2
Victoria Ms *KIL/WHAMP* NW6 ....72 A5
WAND/EARL SW18 ....150 C1
Victorian Gv *STNW/STAM* N16 ....59 E5
Victorian Rd *STNW/STAM* N16 ....59 E5
Victoria Pde *RCH/KEW* * TW9 ....110 A4
Victoria Park Rd *HOM* E9 ....79 D5
Victoria Park Sq *BETH* E2 ....90 C2
Victoria Park Studios *HOM* * E9 ....78 C3
Victoria Ri *CLAP* SW4 ....134 B3
Victoria Rd *ACT* W3 ....84 B3
BARK IG11 ....87 D4
BFN/LL DA15 ....163 F3
CHST BR7 ....162 A5
FSBYPK N4 ....57 F2
KENS W8 ....39 E3
KIL/WHAMP NW6 ....89 F1
MORT/ESHN SW14 ....129 D1
PLSTW E13 ....94 A1
WAN E11 ....81 D1
Victoria Sq *BGVA* SW1W 43 D3
Victoria St *PIM* SW1V 43 D3
SRTFD E15 ....81 E4
Victoria Ter *FSBYPK* N4 ....58 A3
Victoria Wy *CHARL* SE7 ....124 B1
Victoria Yd *WCHPL* * E1 ....90 A5
Victor Rd *WLSDN* NW10 ....88 B2
Victory PI *WALW* SE17 ....47 F4
Victory Wy *BERM/RHTH* SE16 ....103 E3
View CI *HGT* N6 ....55 F2
Viewfield Rd *WAND/EARL* SW18 ....131 F4
Viewland Rd *WOOL/PLUM* SE18 ....127 F1
View Rd *HGT* N6 ....55 F2
Vigilant CI *SYD* SE26 ....156 A4
Vigo St *MYFR/PICC* W1J 31 E2
Viking CI *BOW* E3 ....91 E1
Viking PI *LEY* E10 ....61 F3
The Village *CHARL* SE7 ....124 C2
GLDGN * NW11 ....54 C4
Village CI *HAMP* * NW3 ....73 D2
Village Ms *CDALE/KGS* * NW9 ....51 E3
Village Mt *HAMP* * NW3 ....72 C1
Village Wy *HNHL* SE24 ....137 D2
WLSDN NW10 ....69 D1
Villa Rd *BRXN/ST* SW9 ....136 A1
Villas Rd *WOOL/PLUM* SE18 ....108 C5
Villa St *WALW* SE17 ....119 D1
Villiers Rd *CRICK* NW2 ....70 A3
Villiers St *CHCR* WC2N 33 D3
Vincennes Est *WNWD* * SE27 ....155 D4
Vincent CI *BFN/LL* DA15 ....163 E1
Vincent Gdns *CRICK* NW2 ....51 F5
Vincent Pde *ARCH* * N19 ....57 E3
Vincent Rd *ACT* W3 ....98 C4
WOOL/PLUM * SE18 ....108 B5
Vincents CI *BERM/RHTH* SE16 ....103 E3

Vincent Sq *WEST* SW1P 43 F4
Vincent St *CAN/RD* E16 ....94 A4
WEST SW1P 44 A4
Vincent Ter *IS* N1 ....10 C1
Vince St *FSBYE* EC1V 12 B4
Vine Cottages *WCHPL* * E1 ....90 A4
Vine Ct *WCHPL* E1 ....84 C2
Vine Gdns *IL* IG1 ....84 C2
Vinegar St *WAP* E1W 102 B2
Vinegar Yd *STHWK* SE1 ....36 C5
Vine HI *CLKNW* EC1R 22 A1
Vine La *STHWK* SE1 ....37 D4
The Vineries *CAT* * SE6 ....158 A1
Vine Rd *BARN* SW13 ....129 F1
SRTFD E15 ....81 F4
Vine Sq *WKENS* * W14 ....113 F1
Vine St *CONDST* W1S 31 F2
TWRH EC3N 25 E5
Vine Street Br *FARR* EC1M 22 B1
Vine Street Crs *TWRH* * EC3N 37 E1
Vine Yd *STHWK* SE1 ....35 F5
Vineyard CI *CAT* SE6 ....158 A1
Vineyard Hill Rd *WIM/MER* SW19 ....150 A4
Vineyard Ms *CLKNW* * EC1R 10 A5
Vineyard Pth *MORT/ESHN* SW14 ....129 D1
Vineyard Wk *CLKNW* EC1R 10 A5
Viney Rd *LEW* SE13 ....140 B1
Vining St *BRXN/ST* SW9 ....136 A2
Viola Sq *SHB* W12 ....99 F1
Violet CI *CAN/RD* E16 ....93 E3
DEPT SE8 ....121 F2
Violet HI *STJWD* NW8 ....3 E2
Violet Rd *BOW* E3 ....92 B3
LEY E10 ....62 A1
Violet St *BETH* E2 ....90 B3
Virgil St *STHWK* SE1 ....45 F2
Virginia Rd *BETH* E2 ....13 E4
Virginia St *WAP* * E1W 102 A1
Viscount Dr *EHAM* E6 ....95 F4
Viscount St *STLK* EC1Y 23 E1
The Vista *ELTH/MOT* SE9 ....143 D4
Vivian Av *WBLY* HA9 ....68 A3
Vivian Gdns *WBLY* HA9 ....68 A3
Vivian Rd *BOW* E3 ....91 E1
Vivian Sq *PECK* SE15 ....138 C1
Vixen Ms *HACK* * E8 ....77 F5
Voce Rd *WOOL/PLUM* SE18 ....127 D3
Voltaire Rd *CLAP* SW4 ....135 D1
Volt Av *WLSDN* NW10 ....87 D2
Voluntary PI *WAN* E11 ....64 A1
Vorley Rd *ARCH* N19 ....56 C4
Voss St *BETH* E2 ....90 A2
Vulcan CI *EHAM* E6 ....96 A5
Vulcan Rd *BROCKY* SE4 ....121 F5
Vulcan Ter *BROCKY* SE4 ....121 F5
Vulcan Wy *HOLWY* N7 ....75 F3
Vyner Rd *ACT* W3 ....99 D1
Vyner St *BETH* E2 ....90 B1

W

Wadding St *WALW* SE17 ....48 A5
Waddington Rd *SRTFD* E15 ....81 D2
Waddington St *SRTFD* E15 ....81 D3
Wade House *STHWK* * SE1 ....102 A3
Wade Rd *CAN/RD* E16 ....94 C5
Wadeson St *BETH* E2 ....90 B1
Wade's PI *POP/IOD* E14 ....104 B1
Wadham Gdns *HAMP* NW3 ....73 E4
Wadham Rd *PUT/ROE* SW15 ....131 E2
Wadhurst Rd *CHSWK* W4 ....99 D4
Wadley Rd *WAN* E11 ....63 E2
Wager St *BOW* E3 ....91 F3
Waghorn Rd *PLSTW* E13 ....82 C5
Waghorn St *PECK* SE15 ....138 A1
Wagner St *PECK* SE15 ....120 C3

Wainford Cl *WIM/MER* SW19 ....149 D1
Waite Davies Rd *LEE/GVPK* SE12 ....141 F5
Waite St *PECK* SE15 ....119 F2
Wakefield Gdns *IL* IG1 ....65 E1
Wakefield Ms *STPAN* WC1H 9 D4
Wakefield St *BMSBY* WC1N 9 D5
   EHAM E6 ....83 E5
Wakeham St *IS* N1 ....77 D3
Wakehurst Rd *BTSEA* SW11 ....133 E3
Wakeling St *WCHPL* * E1 ....91 E5
Wakelin Rd *SRTFD* E15 ....93 E1
Wakeman Rd *WLSDN* NW10 ....88 C2
Wakering Gdns *IL* G11 ....84 C4
Wakerly Cl *EHAM* E6 ....95 F5
Wakley St *FSBYE* EC1V 10 C3
Walberswick St *VX/NE* SW8 ....117 E3
Walbrook *MANHO* EC4N 36 A1
Walburgh St *WCHPL* E1 ....90 B5
Walcorde Av *WALW* SE17 ....47 F5
Walcot Sq *LBTH* SE11 ....46 B4
Walcott St *WEST* * SW1P 43 F4
Waldeck Gv *WNWD* SE27 ....154 B3
Waldeck Rd *CHSWK* W4 ....110 A2
   MORT/ESHN SW14 ....128 C1
Waldemar Av *FUL/PGN* SW6 ....113 E4
Waldemar Rd *WIM/MER* SW19 ....150 A3
Walden Av *CHST* BR7 ....161 F4
Waldenshaw Rd *FSTH* SE23 ....156 C1
Walden St *WCHPL* * E1 ....90 B5
Waldo Cl *CLAP* SW4 ....134 C3
Waldo Rd *WLSDN* NW10 ....88 A2
Waldram Crs *FSTH* SE23 ....156 C1
Waldram Park Rd *FSTH* SE23 ....157 D1
Waldron Ms *CHEL* SW3 ....115 D2
Waldron Rd *WAND/EARL* SW18 ....150 C3
Walerand Rd *LEW* SE13 ....122 C5
Wales Cl *PECK* SE15 ....120 B3
Wales Farm Rd *ACT* W3 ....87 D4
Waley St *WCHPL* * E1 ....91 D4
Walford Rd *STNW/STAM* N16 ....77 E1
Walham Green Ct *FUL/PGN* * SW6 ....114 B3
Walham Gv *FUL/PGN* SW6 ....114 A3
Walham Yd *FUL/PGN* SW6 ....114 A3
Walkden Rd *CHST* BR7 ....162 A4
Walker Cl *WOOL/PLUM* SE18 ....108 C5
Walker's Ct *SOHO/CST* W1F 32 A1
Walkerscroft Md *DUL* SE21 ....154 C1
Walker's Pl *PUT/ROE* * SW15 ....131 E2
Wallace Rd *IS* N1 ....76 C3
Wallbutton Rd *BROCKY* SE4 ....121 E5
Wallcote Av *CRICK* NW2 ....53 D3
Wall End Rd *EHAM* E6 ....84 A4
Waller Rd *NWCR* SE14 ....121 D4
Wallflower St *SHB* W12 ....99 F1
Wallgrave Rd *ECT* SW5 ....38 C4
Wallingford Av *NKENS* W10 ....89 D4
Wallington Rd *GDMY/SEVK* IG3 ....67 F2
Wallis Cl *BTSEA* SW11 ....133 D1
Wallis Rd *HOM* E9 ....79 F3
Wallorton Gdns *MORT/ESHN* SW14 ......129 D2
Wallside *BARB* * EC2Y 23 F3
Wall St *IS* N1 ....77 D3
Wallwood Rd *WAN* E11 ....63 D2
Wallwood St *POP/IOD* E14 ....91 F4
Walmer Rd *NTGHL* W11 ....101 E1
Walmer Ter *WOOL/PLUM* SE18 ....108 C5
Walm La *CRICK* NW2 ....71 D2
Walney Wk *IS* * N1 ....76 C3
Walnut Cl *DEPT* SE8 ....121 F2
Walnut Gdns *SRTFD* E15 ....81 E2
Walnut Rd *LEY* E10 ....62 A4
Walnut Tree Cl *BARN* SW13 ....111 F4
Walnut Tree Rd *GNWCH* * SE10 ....123 E1
Walnut Tree Wk *LBTH* SE11 ....46 A4
Walpole Gdns *CHSWK* W4 ....110 A1
Walpole Ms *STJWD* NW8 ....73 D3
Walpole Rd *EHAM* E6 ....82 C4
Walpole St *CHEL* SW3 ....115 F1

Walsham Cl *STNW/STAM* N16 ....60 A3
Walsham Rd *NWCR* SE14 ....121 D5
Walsingham Rd *BTSEA* SW11 ....134 A4
   CLPT E5 ....60 A5
Walter St *BETH* E2 ....91 D2
Walters Wy *FSTH* SE23 ....139 D4
Walter Ter *WCHPL* E1 ....91 D5
Walterton Rd *MV/WKIL* W9 ....89 F3
Waltham Av *CDALE/KGS* NW9 ....50 A1
Walton Cl *CRICK* NW2 ....52 B4
   VX/NE SW8 ....117 E3
Walton Dr *WLSDN* NW10 ....69 D3
Walton Gdns *ACT* W3 ....86 B4
Walton Pl *CHEL* SW3 ....41 E2
Walton Rd *MNPK* E12 ....84 A1
   PLSTW E13 ....94 C1
Walton St *CHEL* SW3 ....41 D4
Walton Vls *IS* * N1 ....77 E4
Walton Wy *ACT* W3 ....86 B4
Walt Whitman Cl *HNHL* * SE24 ....136 B2
Walworth Pl *WALW* SE17 ....118 C1
Walworth Rd *WALW* SE17 ....47 E4
Wanborough Dr *PUT/ROE* SW15 ....148 B1
Wandle Rd *TOOT* SW17 ....151 E2
Wandle Wy *WAND/EARL* SW18 ....150 B1
Wandon Rd *FUL/PGN* SW6 ....114 B3
Wandsworth Br *WAND/EARL* SW18 ......132 C1
Wandsworth Bridge Rd
   FUL/PGN SW6 ....114 B4
Wandsworth Common West Side
   WAND/EARL SW18 ....132 C3
Wandsworth High St
   WAND/EARL SW18 ....132 A3
Wandsworth Rd *CLAP* SW4 ....134 B1
   VX/NE SW8 ....117 E3
Wanless Rd *HNHL* SE24 ....136 C1
Wanley Rd *CMBW* SE5 ....137 D2
Wanlip Rd *PLSTW* E13 ....94 B3
Wansbeck Rd *HOM* E9 ....79 F4
Wansdown Pl *FUL/PGN* SW6 ....114 B3
Wansey St *WALW* SE17 ....47 F5
Wanstead La *IL* IG1 ....65 E1
Wanstead Park Av *MNPK* E12 ....65 D4
Wanstead Park Rd *IL* IG1 ....65 E3
Wanstead Pl *WAN* E11 ....64 A1
Wantage Rd *LEE/GVPK* SE12 ....141 F3
Wapping Dock St *WAP* * E1W 102 B2
Wapping High St *WAP* E1W 102 A2
Wapping La *WAP* E1W 102 B1
Wapping Wall *WAP* E1W 102 C2
Warbeck Rd *SHB* W12 ....100 B2
Warburton Cl *IS* N1 ....77 E3
Warburton Rd *HACK* E8 ....78 B5
Warburton St *HACK* E8 ....78 B5
Wardalls Gv *NWCR* * SE14 ....120 C3
Warden Rd *KTTN* NW5 ....74 A3
Wardens Gv *STHWK* SE1 ....35 E4
Wardle St *HOM* E9 ....79 D2
Wardley St *WAND/EARL* SW18 ....132 B5
Wardo Av *FUL/PGN* SW6 ....113 E4
Wardour Ms *SOHO/CST* W1F 19 F5
Wardour St *SOHO/CST* W1F 19 F5
Ward Rd *ARCH* N19 ....74 C1
   SRTFD * E15 ....81 D5
Wardrobe Pl *BLKFR* * EC4V 23 D5
Wards Rd *GNTH/NBYPK* IG2 ....67 D2
Warepoint Dr *THMD* SE28 ....109 D3
Warfield Rd *WLSDN* NW10 ....89 D2
Warfield Yd *WLSDN* * NW10 ....89 D2
Wargrave Av *SEVS/STOTM* N15 ....59 F1
Warham Rd *CMBW* SE5 ....118 C3
Waring St *WNWD* SE27 ....154 C4
Warland Rd *WOOL/PLUM* SE18 ....127 D3
Warley St *BETH* E2 ....91 D2
Warlock Rd *MV/WKIL* W9 ....89 F3
Warlters Cl *HOLWY* * N7 ....75 E1
Warlters Rd *HOLWY* N7 ....75 E1
Warltersville Rd *ARCH* N19 ....57 E2

Warming Cl *CLPT* * E5 ....61 D5
Warmington Rd *HNHL* SE24 ....136 C4
Warmington St *BERM/RHTH* SE16 .....102 C5
Warndon St *BERM/RHTH* SE16 ..102 C5
Warneford St *HOM* E9 ....78 B5
Warner Cl *CDALE/KGS* NW9 ....51 F2
  SRTFD E15 ....81 E2
Warner Pl *BETH* E2 ....90 A1
Warner Rd *CMBW* SE5 ....118 C4
Warner St *CLKNW* EC1R 22 A1
Warner Ter *POP/IOD* * E14 ....92 A4
Warner Yd *CLKNW* EC1R 22 A1
Warple Ms *ACT* * W3 ....99 E3
Warple Wy *ACT* W3 ....99 E3
The Warren *MNPK* E12 ....83 E1
  WAN * E11 ....63 D5
The Warren Dr *WAN* E11 ....64 C2
Warrender Rd *ARCH* N19 ....56 C5
Warren La *WOOL/PLUM* SE18 .....108 B4
Warren Ms *GTPST* W1W 19 E1
Warren Rd *CRICK* NW2 ....51 F4
  LEY E10 ....62 C5
  WAN E11 ....64 C1
Warren St *FITZ* W1T 19 E1
Warriner Gdns *BTSEA* SW11 ....115 F4
Warrington Crs *MV/WKIL* W9 ....15 E1
Warrington Gdns *MV/WKIL* W9 ......15 E1
Warrington Pl *POP/IOD* * E14 .....104 C2
Warrior Sq *MNPK* E12 ....84 A1
Warspite Rd *WOOL/PLUM* SE18 ...107 E4
Warton Rd *SRTFD* E15 ....80 C5
Warwall *EHAM* E6 ....96 B5
Warwick Av *MV/WKIL* W9 ....15 D1
Warwick Ct *HHOL* WC1V 21 F3
Warwick Crs *BAY/PAD* W2 ....15 E2
Warwick Dr *BARN* SW13 ....130 B1
Warwick Gdns *IL* IG1 ....66 B3
  WKENS W14 ....101 F4
Warwick Gv *CLPT* E5 ....60 B3
Warwick House St *STJS* SW1Y 32 B3
Warwick La *STP* EC4M 23 D4
Warwick Pl *MV/WKIL* W9 ....15 E2
Warwick Pl North *PIM* * SW1V 43 E5
Warwick Rd *FSTGT* E7 ....81 F3
  MNPK E12 ....82 E2
  WKENS W14 ....101 F5
Warwick Rw *WESTW* SW1E 43 E2
Warwick Sq *PIM* SW1V 116 C1
  STP * EC4M 23 D4
Warwick Square Ms *PIM* SW1V 44 A5
Warwick St *REGST* W1B 31 F1
Warwick Ter *WOOL/PLUM* SE18 ..127 D2
Warwick Wy *PIM* SW1V 43 D5
Warwick Yd *STLK* * EC1Y 23 E1
Washington Av *MNPK* E12 ....83 E1
Washington Cl *BOW* E3 ....92 B2
Washington Rd *BARN* SW13 ....112 A3
  EHAM E6 ....82 C4
Wastdale Rd *FSTH* SE23 ....157 D1
Watchfield Ct *CHSWK* * W4 ....110 C1
Waterbank Rd *CAT* SE6 ....158 B3
Watercress Pl *IS* N1 ....77 F4
Waterden Rd *SRTFD* E15 ....80 A2
Waterfield Cottages
  MORT/ESHN * SW14 ....128 B2
Waterford Rd *FUL/PGN* SW6 ....114 B3
The Water Gdns *BAY/PAD* W2 ....16 C4
Watergate *DEPT* SE8 ....122 A2
Waterhouse Cl *HAMP* NW3 ....73 D2
Water La *CAMTN* NW1 ....74 B3
  CDMY/SEVK IG3 ....67 F5
  PECK SE15 ....120 C3
  SRTFD E15 ....81 E5
Waterloo Br *STHWK* SE1 ....33 F2
Waterloo Gdns *BETH* E2 ....90 C1
Waterloo Pl *RCH/KEW* TW9 ....110 A2
  STJS SW1Y 32 A3

Waterloo Rd *CRICK* NW2 ....52 A4
  EHAM E6 ....82 C4
  FSTGT E7 ....81 F2
  LEY E10 ....62 A2
  STHWK SE1 ....33 F3
Waterloo Ter *IS* N1 ....76 B4
Waterlow Rd *ARCH* N19 ....56 C3
Waterman St *PUT/ROE* SW15 ......131 D1
Waterman Wy *WAP* E1W 102 B2
Watermeadow La *FUL/PGN* SW6 ..114 C5
Watermead Rd *CAT* SE6 ....158 C4
Water Ms *PECK* SE15 ....138 C2
Watermint Quay *CLPT* E5 ....60 A2
Water's Edge *FUL/PGN* * SW6 .....113 D4
Waterside *WALTH* E17 ....60 C1
Waterside Cl *BERM/RHTH* SE16 ..102 A3
  HOM E9 ....79 F5
Waterside Ct *LEW* * SE13 ....141 D2
Waterside Wy *TOOT* SW17 ....150 C4
Waterson St *BETH* E2 ....13 D3
Waters Rd *CAT* SE6 ....159 E3
Waterworks La *CLPT* E5 ....61 D4
Waterworks Rd *BRXS/STRHM* SW2 ..135 E4
Watford Cl *BTSEA* SW11 ....115 E4
Watford Rd *CAN/RD* E16 ....94 A4
Watkin Rd *WBLY* HA9 ....50 B5
Watkinson Rd *HOLWY* N7 ....75 F3
Watling Ct *STP* EC4M 23 F5
Watling St *STP* EC4M 23 E5
Watlington Gv *SYD* SE26 ....157 E5
Watney Market *WCHPL* E1 ....90 B5
Watney Rd *MORT/ESHN* SW14 ....128 C1
Watney St *WCHPL* E1 ....90 B5
Watson Av *EHAM* E6 ....84 A4
Watson Cl *STNW/STAM* N16 ....77 D2
Watson's Ms *CAMTN* NW1 ....17 D3
Watson's St *DEPT* SE8 ....122 A3
Wattisfield Rd *CLPT* E5 ....60 C5
Watts Gv *BOW* E3 ....92 A4
Watts St *WAP* E1W 102 B2
Wat Tyler Rd *BKHTH/KID* SE3 .....122 C5
Wavell Dr *BFN/LL* DA15 ....145 E4
Wavel Ms *KIL/WHAMP* NW6 ....72 B4
Wavel Pl *NRWD* SE19 ....155 F4
Wavendon Av *CHSWK* W4 ....111 D1
Waveney Av *PECK* SE15 ....138 D2
Waveney Cl *WAP* E1W 102 A2
Waverley Crs *WOOL/PLUM* SE18 ..127 D2
Waverley Gdns *BARK* IG11 ....97 E1
  EHAM E6 ....95 E4
Waverley Pl *FSBYPK* * N4 ....58 B3
  STJWD NW8 ....4 A1
Waverley Rd *CEND/HSY/T* N8 ....57 D1
  WOOL/PLUM SE18 ....126 C1
Waverton Rd *WAND/EARL* SW18 ..132 C5
Waverton St *MYFR/PICC* W1J 30 B3
Wavertree Rd *BRXS/STRHM* SW2 ..153 F1
Waxlow Rd *WLSDN* NW10 ....86 C1
Wayford St *BTSEA* SW11 ....115 E5
Wayland Av *HACK* E8 ....78 A2
Waylett Pl *WNWD* SE27 ....154 B3
Waynflete Sq *NKENS* W10 ....101 E1
Waynflete St *WAND/EARL* SW18 ..150 C2
Wayside *CRICK* NW2 ....53 E3
  MORT/ESHN SW14 ....128 C2
Wayside Gv *CHST* BR7 ....161 F4
Wayside Ms *GNTH/NBYPK* IG2 ......66 A1
Weald Cl *BERM/RHTH* SE16 ....120 B1
Weald Sq *CLPT* * E5 ....60 B4
Weardale Rd *LEW* SE13 ....141 D3
Wear Pl *BETH* E2 ....90 B2
Wearside Rd *LEW* SE13 ....140 B2
Weaver Cl *EHAM* E6 ....108 B1
Weaver's La *STHWK* SE1 ....37 D4
Weavers Ter *FUL/PGN* * SW6 ....114 A2
Weaver St *WCHPL* E1 ....90 A3
Weavers Wy *CAMTN* NW1 ....75 D5

Weaver Wk *WNWD* SE27 ....154 B4
Webb Cl *NKENS* W10 ....88 C3
Webber Rw *STHWK* SE1 ....46 B1
Webber St *STHWK* SE1 ....34 B5
Webb Est *CLPT* * E5 ....60 A2
Webb Pl *WLSDN* NW10 ....87 F2
Webb Rd *BKHTH/KID* SE3 ....123 F2
Webb's Rd *BTSEA* SW11 ....133 F3
Webb St *STHWK* SE1 ....48 C3
Webster Rd *BERM/RHTH* SE16........102 A4
  LEY E10 ....62 C5
Wedderburn Rd *BARK* IG11 ....85 D5
  HAMP NW3 ....73 D2
Wedgwood Wk *KIL/WHAMP* * NW6 ...72 B2
Wedlake St *NKENS* W10 ....89 E3
Wedmore Gdns *ARCH* N19 ....57 E4
Wedmore St *ARCH* N19 ....57 D5
Weech Rd *KIL/WHAMP* NW6 ....72 A1
Weedington Rd *KTTN* NW5 ....74 A2
Weekley Sq *BTSEA* * SW11 ....133 D1
Weigall Rd *LEE/GVPK* SE12 ....142 A2
Weighhouse St *MYFR/PKLN* W1K 30 B1
Weimar St *PUT/ROE* SW15 ....131 E1
Weir Rd *BAL* SW12 ....152 C1
  WIM/MER SW19 ....150 B3
Weirs Pas *CAMTN* NW1 ....8 B3
Weiss Rd *PUT/ROE* SW15 ....131 D1
Welbeck Av *BMLY* BR1 ....160 A4
Welbeck Rd *EHAM* E6 ....95 D2
Welbeck St *MHST* W1U 18 C4
Welbeck Wy *MHST* W1U 18 C3
Welby St *CMBW* SE5 ....118 B4
Welfare Rd *SRTFD* E15 ....81 E4
Welford Cl *CLPT* E5 ....61 E4
Welford Pl *WIM/MER* SW19 ....61 D5
Welham Rd *TOOT* SW17 ....149 E4
Welland Ms *WAP* E1W 152 A5
Welland St *GNWCH* SE10 ....122 C2
Well Cl *STRHM/NOR* SW16 ....153 F4
Wellclose Sq *WAP* E1W 102 A1
Wellclose St *WAP* E1W 102 A1
Well Cottage Cl *WAN* E11 ....64 C2
Well Ct *MANHO* EC4N 23 F5
Wellers Ct *CAMTN* NW1 ....9 D3
Weller St *STHWK* SE1 ....35 E5
Wellesley Av *HMSMTH* W6 ....100 B4
Wellesley Cl *CHARL* * SE7 ....124 C1
Wellesley Ct *MV/WKIL* W9 ....3 E3
Wellesley Pl *CAMTN* * NW1 ....8 A4
  KTTN NW5 ....74 A2
Wellesley Rd *CHSWK* W4 ....110 A1
  IL IG1 ....66 B4
  KTTN NW5 ....74 A2
  WALTH E17 ....62 A1
Wellesley Ter *IS* N1 ....11 F3
Wellfield Rd *STRHM/NOR* SW16 .....153 E4
Wellfit St *HNHL* SE24 ....136 B1
Wellgarth Rd *GLDGN* NW11 ....54 B3
Well Hall Pde *ELTH/MOT* SE9 ....143 F2
Well Hall Rd *ELTH/MOT* SE9 ....143 F1
Wellington Av *SEVS/STOTM* N15 ......60 A1
  WOOL/PLUM SE18 ....108 C4
Wellington Cl *NTGHL* W11 ....14 A5
  NWCR SE14 ....121 D2
Wellington Gdns *CHARL* SE7 ....124 C1
Wellington Gv *GNWCH* SE10 ....123 D3
Wellington Ms *HOLWY* N7 ....75 F3
Wellington Park Est *CRICK* * NW2 .....52 A4
Wellington Pl *STJWD* NW8 ....4 B3
Wellington Rd *FSTGT* E7 ....82 A2
  LEY E10 ....61 E3
  STJWD NW8 ....4 B2
  WIM/MER SW19 ....150 A2
  WLSDN * NW10 ....89 D2
Wellington Rw *BETH* E2 ....13 F3
Wellington Sq *CHEL* SW3 ....115 F1
Wellington St *COVGDN* WC2E 33 D1

WOOL/PLUM SE18 ....108 A5
Wellington Ter *NTGHL* W11 ....26 B2
  WAP * E1W 102 B2
Wellington Wy *BOW* E3 ....92 A2
Welling Wy *ELTH/MOT* SE9 ....145 D1
Well La *MORT/ESHN* SW14 ....128 C3
Wellmeadow Rd *LEW* SE13 ....141 E4
Well Rd *HAMP* NW3 ....55 D5
Wells Dr *CDALE/KGS* NW9 ....51 D3
Wells Gdns *IL* IG1 ....65 E2
Wells House Rd *WLSDN* NW10 ....87 E4
Wellside Gdns *MORT/ESHN* SW14 ..128 C2
Wells Ms *FITZ* * W1T 19 F3
Wells Park Rd *SYD* SE26 ....156 A3
Wells Pl *CMBW* SE5 ....119 E3
  WAND/EARL SW18 ....132 C5
Wells Ri *STJWD* NW8 ....73 F5
Wells Rd *HMSMTH* W6 ....100 C3
Wells Sq *FSBYW* WC1X 9 E4
Wells St *GTPST* W1W 19 E3
Wellstead Rd *EHAM* E6 ....96 A1
Wells Ter *FSBYPK* N4 ....58 A4
Well St *HOM* E9 ....78 C4
  SRTFD E15 ....81 E3
Wells Wy *CMBW* SE5 ....119 D2
  SKENS SW7 ....40 A2
Well Wk *HAMP* NW3 ....55 D5
Welsford St *STHWK* SE1 ....120 A1
Welsh Cl *PLSTW* E13 ....94 A2
Welshpool St *HACK* * E8 ....78 A5
Welstead Wy *CHSWK* W4 ....99 F4
Weltje Rd *HMSMTH* W6 ....112 A1
Welton Rd *WOOL/PLUM* SE18 ....127 E3
Welwyn St *BETH* E2 ....90 C2
Wembley Wy *WBLY* HA9 ....68 B3
Wembury Rd *HGT* N6 ....56 B2
Wemyss Rd *BKHTH/KID* SE3 ....123 F5
Wendell Rd *SHB* W12 ....99 F3
Wendon St *BOW* E3 ....79 F5
Wendover Rd *ELTH/MOT* SE9 ....143 D1
  WLSDN NW10 ....87 F1
Wenlock Rd *IS* N1 ....11 E2
Wenlock St *IS* N1 ....11 F2
Wennington Rd *BOW* E3 ....91 D1
Wensley Cl *ELTH/MOT* SE9 ....143 F4
Wentland Cl *CAT* SE6 ....159 D2
Wentland Rd *CAT* SE6 ....159 D2
Wentworth Crs *PECK* SE15 ....120 A3
Wentworth Ms *BOW* E3 ....91 E3
Wentworth Rd *GLDGN* NW11 ....53 F1
  MNPK E12 ....83 D1
Wentworth St *WCHPL* E1 ....25 E4
Wernbrook St *WOOL/PLUM* SE18 ...126 C2
Werrington St *CAMTN* NW1 ....7 F2
Werter Rd *PUT/ROE* SW15 ....131 E2
Wesleyan Pl *KTTN* NW5 ....74 B1
Wesley Av *CAN/RD* E16 ....106 A2
  WLSDN NW10 ....87 D2
Wesley Cl *HOLWY* N7 ....57 F4
  WALW SE17 ....47 D5
Wesley Rd *LEY* E10 ....62 C2
  WLSDN NW10 ....68 C5
Wesley Sq *NTGHL* W11 ....89 D5
Wesley St *CAVSQ/HST* W1G 18 B3
Wessex Cl *GDMY/SEVK* IG3 ....67 F3
Wessex Gdns *CRICK* NW2 ....53 E3
Wessex St *BETH* E2 ....90 C2
Wessex Wy *GLDGN* NW11 ....53 E2
Wesson Md *CMBW* * SE5 ....118 C3
West Arbour St *WCHPL* E1 ....91 D5
West Bank *BARK* IG11 ....84 B5
  STNW/STAM N16 ....59 E2
Westbere Rd *CRICK* NW2 ....71 E1
Westbourne Av *ACT* W3 ....87 D5
Westbourne Crs *BAY/PAD* W2 ....28 A1
Westbourne Crescent Ms
  BAY/PAD W2 ....28 A1
Westbourne Dr *FSTH* SE23 ....157 D1

Westbourne Gdns *BAY/PAD* W2	14 C4
Westbourne Ga *BAY/PAD* W2	28 B2
Westbourne Gv *BAY/PAD* W2	14 B5
NTGHL W11	101 F1
Westbourne Grove Ms *NTGHL* W11	14 A4
Westbourne Grove Ter *BAY/PAD* W2	14 C4
Westbourne Park Rd *BAY/PAD* W2	14 A4
NTGHL W11	89 F5
Westbourne Park Vls *BAY/PAD* W2	14 B3
Westbourne St *BAY/PAD* W2	28 A1
Westbourne Ter *BAY/PAD* W2	15 E3
Westbourne Terrace Ms *BAY/PAD* W2	15 E4
Westbourne Terrace Rd *BAY/PAD* W2	15 E3
Westbridge Cl *SHB* W12	100 A2
Westbridge Rd *BTSEA* SW11	115 D4
Westbrooke Rd *BFN/LL* DA15	163 D2
Westbrook Rd *BKHTH/KID* SE3	124 A4
Westbury Dr *BARK* IG11	85 D5
FSTGT E7	82 B3
IL IG1	65 F3
Westbury Ter *FSTGT* E7	82 B3
West Carriage Dr *BAY/PAD* W2	28 A2
West Central St *NOXST/BSQ* WC1A	20 C4
Westcombe Hl *BKHTH/KID* SE3	124 A2
Westcombe Park Rd *BKHTH/KID* SE3	124 A3
Westcote Rd *STRHM/NOR* SW16	152 C5
Westcott Cl *SEVS/STOTM* N15	59 F1
Westcott House *POP/IOD* * E14	104 A1
Westcott Rd *WALW* SE17	118 B2
Westcroft Cl *CRICK* NW2	71 E1
Westcroft Ms *HMSMTH* * W6	100 A5
Westcroft Sq *HMSMTH* W6	100 A5
Westcroft Wy *CRICK* NW2	71 E1
West Cross Route *NTGHL* W11	101 D1
Westdale Rd *WOOL/PLUM* SE18	126 B2
Westdean Av *LEE/GVPK* SE12	160 B1
Westdean Cl *WAND/EARL* SW18	132 A4
Westdown Rd *CAT* SE6	140 A5
SRTFD E15	80 C1
West Dr *TOOT* SW17	152 B4
West Eaton Pl *KTBR* SW1X	42 A4
West Eaton Place Ms *KTBR* SW1X	42 A4
West Ella Rd *WLSDN* NW10	69 E4
West End Cl *WLSDN* NW10	68 C4
West End La *KIL/WHAMP* NW6	72 A1
Westerdale Rd *GNWCH* SE10	124 A1
Westerham Rd *LEY* E10	62 B1
Westerley Crs *SYD* * SE26	157 F5
Western Av *ACT* W3	86 B3
GLDGN NW11	53 D1
Western Gdns *ACT* W3	98 A1
Western Gtwy *CAN/RD* E16	106 B3
Western La *BAL* SW12	134 A5
Western Ms *MV/WKIL* W9	89 F3
Western Rd *BRXN/ST* SW9	136 A1
PLSTW E13	82 B5
WLSDN NW10	86 C3
Western Ter *HMSMTH* * W6	112 A1
Westernville Gdns *GNTH/NBYPK* IG2	66 C2
Western Wy *THMD* SE28	109 E3
Westferry Circ *POP/IOD* E14	104 A2
Westferry Rd *POP/IOD* E14	103 F1
Westfield Cl *FUL/PGN* * SW6	114 C3
Westfields *BARN* SW13	129 F1
Westfields Av *BARN* SW13	129 E1
Westfields Rd *ACT* W3	86 B4
Westfield St *WOOL/PLUM* SE18	107 D4
Westfield Wy *WCHPL* E1	91 E2
West Gdns *WAP* E1W	102 B1
Westgate St *HACK* E8	78 B5
Westgate Ter *WBPTN* SW10	114 B1
West Gv *GNWCH* SE10	122 C4
Westgrove La *GNWCH* SE10	122 C4
West Halkin St *KTBR* SW1X	42 A2
West Hallowes *ELTH/MOT* SE9	161 D1
West Hall Rd *RCH/KEW* TW9	110 B4
West Ham La *SRTFD* E15	81 D4

West Hampstead Ms	
KIL/WHAMP NW6	72 B3
West Harding St *FLST/FETLN* * EC4A	22 B4
Westhay Gdns *MORT/ESHN* SW14	128 B3
West Heath Av *GLDGN* NW11	54 A5
West Heath Cl *HAMP* NW3	54 A5
West Heath Dr *GLDGN* NW11	54 A5
West Heath Gdns *HAMP* NW3	54 A4
West Heath Rd *HAMP* NW3	54 A4
West Hl *HGT* N6	56 A3
PUT/ROE SW15	131 D5
Westhill Pk *HGT* N6	55 F4
West Hill Rd *WAND/EARL* SW18	131 F4
Westhorne Av *ELTH/MOT* SE9	142 C4
Westhorpe Rd *PUT/ROE* SW15	130 C1
West House Cl *WIM/MER* SW19	149 E1
Westhurst Dr *CHST* BR7	162 B5
West India Av *POP/IOD* E14	104 A2
West India Dock Rd *POP/IOD* E14	91 F5
Westland Pl *FSBYE* EC1V	12 A4
Westlands Ter *BAL* SW12	134 C4
West La *BERM/RHTH* SE16	102 B3
Westleigh Av *PUT/ROE* SW15	130 C3
West Lodge Av *ACT* W3	98 A3
West Lodge Ct *ACT* * W3	98 A3
Westmead *PUT/ROE* SW15	130 B5
West Ms *PIM* SW1V	43 D5
Westminster Br *WEST* SW1P	45 D1
Westminster Bridge Rd *STHWK* SE1	45 E1
Westminster Gdns *BARK* IG11	97 E1
Westmoor St *CHARL* SE7	107 D5
Westmoreland Av *WELL* DA16	145 E1
Westmoreland Pl *PIM* * SW1V	116 B1
Westmoreland Rd *BARN* SW13	111 F4
WALW SE17	119 D2
Westmoreland St *CAVSQ/HST* W1G	18 B3
Westmoreland Ter *PIM* SW1V	116 B1
Westmorland Cl *MNPK* E12	65 D4
Westmorland Rd *LEY* E10	62 A1
Westmount Rd *ELTH/MOT* SE9	125 F5
Weston Rd *CEND/HSY/T* N8	57 F1
Weston Ri *FSBYW* WC1X	9 F3
Weston Rd *CHSWK* W4	98 C4
Weston St *STHWK* SE1	48 B1
Weston Wk *HACK* E8	78 B4
Westover Hl *HAMP* NW3	54 A4
Westover Rd *WAND/EARL* SW18	132 C4
West Pk *ELTH/MOT* SE9	161 E2
West Park Av *RCH/KEW* TW9	110 A4
West Park Rd *RCH/KEW* TW9	110 A4
West Parkside *GNWCH* SE10	105 E3
West Pl *WIM/MER* SW19	148 C5
Westport Rd *PLSTW* E13	94 B3
Westport St *WCHPL* E1	91 D5
West Poultry Av *FARR* EC1M	22 C3
West Quarters *SHB* SW12	88 A5
West Ri *BAY/PAD* * W2	29 D1
West Rd *CHEL* SW3	115 F1
CLAP SW4	135 D3
SRTFD E15	81 F5
West Rw *NKENS* W10	89 E3
Westrow Dr *BARK* IG11	85 F3
Westrow Gdns *GDMY/SEVK* IG3	67 F4
West Side Common *WIM/MER* SW19	148 C5
West Smithfield *STBT* EC1A	22 C3
West Sq *LBTH* SE11	46 C3
West St *BETH* E2	90 B1
LSQ/SEVD * WC2H	20 B5
WAN E11	63 E5
West Temple Sheen	
MORT/ESHN SW14	128 B3
West Tenter St *WCHPL* E1	25 F5
West Ter *BFN/LL* * DA15	163 E1
Westview Cl *NKENS* W10	88 C5
WLSDN NW10	69 F2
Westville Rd *SHB* W12	100 A3
West Warwick Pl *PIM* * SW1V	43 E5
Westway *NTGHL* W11	89 F4

SHB W12 ....99 F1
West Wy *WLSDN* NW10 ....69 D1
Westwick Gdns *HMSMTH* W6 ....101 D3
Westwood Gdns *BARN* SW13 ....129 F1
Westwood HI *SYD* SE26 ....156 A5
Westwood Pk *FSTH* SE23 ....138 B5
Westwood PI *SYD* SE26 ....156 A5
Westwood Rd *BARN* SW13 ....129 F1
CAN/RD E16 ....106 B2
GDMY/SEVK IG3 ....67 F3
Wetherby Gdns *ECT* SW5 ....39 E5
Wetherby Ms *ECT* SW5 ....114 B1
Wetherby PI *ECT* SW5 ....39 E5
Wetherden St *WALTH* E17 ....61 F2
Wetherell Rd *HOM* E9 ....79 D5
Wexford Rd *BAL* SW12 ....133 F5
Weybourne St *WAND/EARL* SW18 ......150 C2
Weybridge Ct *STHWK* * SE1 ....120 B1
Weydown CI *WIM/MER* SW19 ....149 E1
Weyhill Rd *WCHPL* * E1 ....90 A5
Weyman Rd *BKHTH/KID* SE3 ....124 C4
Weymouth CI *EHAM* E6 ....96 B5
Weymouth Ms *CAVSQ/HST* W1G 18 C2
Weymouth St *CAVSQ/HST* W1G 18 B2
Weymouth Ter *BETH* E2 ....13 F1
Weymouth Vls *HOLWY* * N7 ....57 F4
Whadcoat St *FSBYPK* N4 ....58 A4
Whales Yd *SRTFD* * E15 ....81 E4
Wharfdale Rd *IS* N1 ....9 D1
Wharfedale St *WBPTN* SW10 ....114 B4
Wharf PI *BETH* E2 ....78 A5
Wharf Rd *IS* N1 ....11 E2
SRTFD E15 ....81 D5
Wharfside Rd *CAN/RD* E16 ....93 E4
Wharf St *CAN/RD* E16 ....93 E4
Wharton Cottages *FSBYW* * WC1X 9 F4
Wharton St *FSBYW* WC1X 9 F4
Whateley Rd *EDUL* SE22 ....137 F3
Whatman Rd *FSTH* SE23 ....139 D5
Wheastone Rd *NKENS* * W10 ....89 E4
Wheatlands Rd *TOOT* SW17 ....152 A3
Wheatley St *CAVSQ/HST* W1G 18 B3
Wheat Sheaf CI *POP/IOD* E14 ....104 A5
Wheatsheaf La *FUL/PGN* SW6 ....112 C3
VX/NE SW8 ....117 E3
Wheatsheaf Ter *FUL/PGN* * SW6 ....113 F3
Wheatstone Rd *NKENS* W10 ....89 E4
Wheeler Gdns *IS* N1 ....5 E5
Wheeler La *WCHPL* E1 ....25 E2
Wheelers Cross *BARK* IG11 ....97 D1
Wheelwright St *HOLWY* N7 ....75 F4
Wheler St *WCHPL* E1 ....25 E1
Whellock Rd *CHSWK* W4 ....99 E4
Whetstone Pk *LINN* WC2A 21 E4
Whetstone Rd *BKHTH/KID* SE3 ....124 C5
Whewell Rd *ARCH* N19 ....57 E4
Whichcote St *STHWK* * SE1 ....34 A4
Whidborne CI *DEPT* SE8 ....122 A5
Whidborne St *STPAN* WC1H 9 D4
Whinchat Rd *THMD* SE28 ....109 D4
Whinfell CI *STRHM/NOR* SW16 ....153 D5
Whinyates Rd *ELTH/MOT* SE9 ....143 E1
Whiskin St *CLKNW* EC1R 10 C4
Whistlers Av *BTSEA* * SW11 ....115 D3
Whistler St *HBRY* N5 ....76 B1
Whistler Wk *WBPTN* * SW10 ....114 C3
Whiston Rd *BETH* E2 ....13 E1
Whitbread Rd *BROCKY* SE4 ....139 E2
Whitburn Rd *LEW* SE13 ....140 B3
Whitby Av *WLSDN* NW10 ....86 B3
Whitby Rd *WOOL/PLUM* SE18 ....107 F5
Whitby St *WCHPL* E1 ....13 E5
Whitcher CI *NWCR* SE14 ....121 E2
Whitcher PI *CAMTN* NW1 ....74 C3
Whitchurch Rd *NKENS* W10 ....101 D1
Whitcomb St *SOHO/SHAV* W1D 32 A1
Whitcome Ms *RCH/KEW* TW9 ....110 B4

Whitear Wk *SRTFD* E15 ....81 D3
Whitebeam CI *BRXN/ST* * SW9 ....117 F3
White Bear PI *HAMP* * NW3 ....73 D1
White Bear Yd *CLKNW* * EC1R 22 A1
Whitechapel High St *WCHPL* E1 ....25 F4
Whitechapel Rd *WCHPL* E1 ....90 A5
White Church La *WCHPL* E1 ....90 A5
White City CI *SHB* W12 ....100 C1
White City Rd *SHB* W12 ....100 B1
White Conduit St *IS* N1 ....10 B1
Whitecross St *STLK* EC1Y 11 F5
Whitefield Av *CRICK* NW2 ....52 C2
Whitefield CI *WAND/EARL* SW18 ....131 E4
Whitefoot La *CAT* SE6 ....159 A4
Whitefoot Ter *BMLY* BR1 ....159 F3
Whitefriars St *EMB* EC4Y 22 B5
Whitehall *WHALL* SW1A 32 C4
Whitehall Ct *WHALL* SW1A 32 C4
Whitehall Gdns *ACT* W3 ....98 A2
CHSWK W4 ....110 B2
WHALL SW1A 32 C4
Whitehall Pk *ARCH* N19 ....56 C3
Whitehall Park Rd *CHSWK* W4 ....110 B2
Whitehall PI *WHALL* SW1A 32 C4
White Hart La *BARN* SW13 ....111 E5
White Hart Rd *WOOL/PLUM* SE18 ....109 E5
White Hart St *LBTH* SE11 ....118 A1
White Hart Yd *STHWK* SE1 ....36 A4
Whitehaven St *STJWD* NW8 ....16 C1
Whitehead CI *WAND/EARL* SW18 ....132 C5
Whiteheads Gv *CHEL* SW3 ....41 D5
CHEL SW3 ....115 E1
White Horse HI *CHST* BR7 ....162 A4
White Horse La *WCHPL* E1 ....91 D3
White Horse Rd *EHAM* E6 ....95 F2
Whitehorse Rd *WCHPL* E1 ....91 E4
White Horse St *MYFR/PICC* W1J 31 D4
White Kennett St *WCHPL* E1 ....25 D4
Whitelegg Rd *PLSTW* E13 ....93 F1
White Lion Ct *BANK* EC3V 24 C5
PECK * SE15 ....120 C2
White Lion HI *BLKFR* EC4V 35 D1
White Lion St *IS* N1 ....10 A2
White Lodge CI *EFNCH* N2 ....55 D1
White Lyon Ct *BARB* EC2Y 23 E2
White Oak Gdns *BFN/LL* DA15 ....145 F5
White Post La *HOM* E9 ....79 F4
White Post St *PECK* SE15 ....120 C3
White Rd *SRTFD* E15 ....81 E4
Whites Av *GNTH/NBYPK* IG2 ....67 E1
White's Grounds *STHWK* SE1 ....37 D5
Whites Grounds Est *STHWK* SE1 ....37 D5
White's Rw *WCHPL* E1 ....25 E3
White's Sq *CLAP* SW4 ....135 D2
Whitestone La *HAMP* NW3 ....54 C5
Whitestone Wk *HAMP* NW3 ....54 C5
Whitethorn St *BOW* E3 ....92 A3
Whitfield PI *FITZ* W1T 19 E1
Whitfield Rd *EHAM* E6 ....82 C4
GNWCH SE10 ....123 D4
Whitfield St *FITZ* W1T 19 F2
Whitgift St *LBTH* SE11 ....45 E4
Whitings Wy *EHAM* E6 ....96 A4
Whitlock Dr *WIM/MER* SW19 ....131 E5
Whitman Rd *BOW* E3 ....91 E3
Whitmore Est *IS* N1 ....77 E5
Whitmore Gdns *WLSDN* NW10 ....88 C1
Whitmore Rd *IS* N1 ....77 E5
Whitnell Wy *PUT/ROE* * SW15 ....130 C3
Whitney Rd *LEY* E10 ....62 A2
Whittaker Rd *EHAM* E6 ....82 C4
Whittaker St *BGVA* SW1W 42 A5
Whitta Rd *MNPK* E12 ....83 D1
Whittell Gdns *SYD* SE26 ....156 C3
Whittingstall Rd *FUL/PGN* SW6 ....113 F4
Whittington Av *BANK* EC3V 24 C5
Whittle CI *WALTH* E17 ....61 E1

Whittlesey St *STHWK* SE1 ....34 B4
Whitwell Rd *PLSTW* E13 ....94 A2
Whitworth Rd *WOOL/PLUM* SE18 ....126 A3
Whitworth St *GNWCH* SE10 ....123 E1
Whorlton Rd *PECK* SE15 ....138 A1
Whyteville Rd *FSTGT* E7 ....82 B3
Wickersley Rd *BTSEA* SW11 ....116 A5
Wickers Oake *NRWD* * SE19 ....155 F4
Wicker St *WCHPL* * E1 ....90 A5
Wickford St *WCHPL* E1 ....90 C3
Wickham Close *WCHPL* E1 ....90 C4
Wickham Gdns *BROCKY* SE4................139 F1
Wickham Rd *BROCKY* SE4....................139 F1
Wickham St *LBTH* SE11 ....117 F1
   WELL DA16.....................................127 E5
Wick La *BOW* E3 ....80 A5
Wickliffe Gdns *WBLY* HA9 ....50 A4
Wicklow St *FSBYW* WC1X 9 E3
Wick Rd *HOM* E9 ....79 D3
Wicks Cl *LEE/GVPK* SE12 ....161 D4
Wickwood St *CMBW* SE5 ....118 B5
Widdenham Rd *HOLWY* N7 ....75 F1
Widdin St *SRTFD* E15............................81 E4
Widecombe Rd *ELTH/MOT* SE9 ....161 E3
Widegate St *WCHPL* E1 ....25 D3
Widgeon Cl *CAN/RD* E16 ....94 B5
Widley Rd *MV/WKIL* W9 ....2 B4
Wigginton Av *WBLY* HA9 ....68 A3
Wigmore Pl *CAVSQ/HST* * W1G..........18 C4
Wigmore St *MBLAR* W1H 18 B4
Wigram Rd *WAN* E11 ....64 C1
Wigston Rd *PLSTW* E13.........................94 B3
Wigton Pl *LBTH* SE11...........................118 A1
Wilberforce Rd *FSBYPK* N4 ....58 B4
Wilbraham Pl *KTBR* SW1X 41 F4
Wilby Ms *NTCHL* W11 ....101 F1
Wilcox Cl *VX/NE* SW8 ....117 E3
Wilcox Rd *VX/NE* SW8 ....117 E3
Wild Ct *HOL/ALD* WC2B 21 E4
Wildcroft Rd *PUT/ROE* SW15 ....130 C5
Wilde Cl *HACK* E8 ....78 A5
Wilderton Rd *STNW/STAM* N16 ....59 E2
Wildfell Rd *CAT* SE6 ....140 B5
Wild Goose Dr *PECK* SE15 ....120 C4
Wild Hatch *GLDGN* NW11 ....54 A1
Wild's Rents *STHWK* SE1 ....48 C2
Wild St *HOL/ALD* WC2B 21 D5
Wildwood Cl *LEE/GVPK* SE12 ....141 F5
Wildwood Gv *GLDGN* NW11 ....54 C3
Wildwood Ri *GLDGN* NW11 ....54 C3
Wildwood Rd *GLDGN* NW11 ....54 C2
Wilfred St *WESTW* SW1E 43 E2
Wilfrid Gdns *ACT* W3 ....86 C4
Wilkes St *WCHPL* E1 ....25 F2
Wilkinson Rd *CAN/RD* E16 ....94 C5
Wilkinson St *VX/NE* SW8 ....117 F3
Wilkinson Wy *CHSWK* W4 ....99 D3
Wilkin St *KTTN* NW5 ....74 A3
Wilkin Street Ms *KTTN* * NW5...............74 B3
Wilks Pl *IS* N1 ....13 D2
Willan Wall *CAN/RD* E16 ....105 F1
Willard St *VX/NE* SW8 ....134 B1
Willcott Rd *ACT* W3 ....98 B2
Will Crooks Gdns *ELTH/MOT* SE9 ....143 D2
Willenhall Rd *WOOL/PLUM* SE18 ....126 B1
Willerfield Rd *WLSDN* NW10 ....86 C2
Willersley Av *BFN/LL* DA15 ....163 F1
Willersley Cl *BFN/LL* DA15 ....163 F1
Willesden La *KIL/WHAMP* NW6 ....71 D4
Willes Rd *KTTN* NW5 ....74 B3
William Barefoot Dr *ELTH/MOT* SE9 ...162 A4
William Cl *LEW* SE13 ....140 C1
William Ellis Wy *BERM/RHTH* * SE16 ...102 A4
William Gdns *PUT/ROE* SW15 ....130 B3
William Guy Gdns *BOW* E3 ....92 B2
William IV St *CHCR* WC2N 32 C2
William Margrie Cl *PECK* * SE15..........120 A5
William Ms *KTBR* SW1X 41 F1

William Morley Cl *EHAM* E6 ....83 D5
William Morris Wy *FUL/PGN* SW6........132 C1
William Rd *CAMTN* NW1 ....7 E4
William's Buildings *BETH* * E2 ....90 C3
Williams Cl *CEND/HSY/T* * N8...............57 D1
   FUL/PGN SW6 ....113 E3
Williams La *MORT/ESHN* SW14............128 C1
Williamson Cl *GNWCH* SE10 ....123 F1
Williamson Rd *FSBYPK* N4 ....58 B1
Williamson St *HOLWY* * N7 ....75 E1
William Sq *BERM/RHTH* SE16 ....103 E2
William St *BARK* IG11 ....84 C4
   KTBR SW1X 41 F1
   LEY E10 ....62 B1
Willingham Cl *KTTN* NW5 ....74 C2
Willingham Ter *KTTN* * NW5 ....74 C2
Willington Rd *BRXN/ST* SW9 ....135 E1
Willis Rd *SRTFD* E15 ....93 F1
Willis St *POP/IOD* E14 ....92 B5
Willoughby Rd *HAMP* NW3 ....73 D1
Willoughby Wy *CHARL* SE7 ....106 B5
Willow Av *BARN* SW13 ....111 F5
Willow Bridge Rd *IS* * N1 ....76 C3
Willowbrook Est *PECK* * SE15 ....119 F3
Willowbrook Rd *PECK* SE15 ....119 F2
Willowdene *HGT* * N6 ....55 F2
Willowfields Cl *WOOL/PLUM* SE18......127 E1
Willow La *WOOL/PLUM* SE18 ....107 F5
Willow Pl *WEST* SW1P 43 F4
Willow Rd *HAMP* NW3 ....73 D1
Willows Ter *WLSDN* * NW10 ....87 F1
Willow St *SDTCH* EC2A 12 C5
Willow Tree Cl *HOM* E9 ....79 E5
   WAND/EARL SW18...........................150 B1
Willow V *SHB* W12 ....100 A2
Willow Wk *STHWK* SE1 ....49 D4
Willow Wy *NTGHL* W11 ....101 D1
   SYD SE26...156 B3
Willshaw St *NWCR* SE14 ....122 A4
Wilman Gv *HACK* E8 ....78 A4
Wilmer Gdns *IS* N1 ....77 E5
Wilmer Lea Cl *SRTFD* E15 ....80 C4
Wilmer Pl *STNW/STAM* N16 ....59 F4
Wilmington Av *CHSWK* W4 ....111 D3
Wilmington Gdns *BARK* IG11 ....85 D4
Wilmington Sq *FSBYW* WC1X 10 A4
Wilmington St *FSBYW* WC1X 10 A4
Wilmot Cl *PECK* * SE15........................120 A3
Wilmot Pl *CAMTN* NW1 ....74 C4
Wilmot Rd *LEY* E10 ....62 B4
Wilmot St *BETH* E2 ....90 B3
Wilmount St *WOOL/PLUM* SE18..........108 B5
Wilna Rd *WAND/EARL* SW18 ....132 C5
Wilsham St *NTCHL* W11 ....101 D2
Wilson Gv *BERM/RHTH* SE16 ....102 B3
Wilson Rd *CMBW* SE5 ....119 D4
   IL IG1 ....65 F2
   PLSTW E13 ....95 D2
Wilson's Pl *POP/IOD* E14.......................91 F5
Wilson's Rd *HMSMTH* W6 ....113 D1
Wilson St *SDTCH* EC2A 24 B3
Wilson Wk *HMSMTH* * W6 ....99 F5
Wilton Av *CHSWK* W4 ....111 E1
Wilton Crs *KTBR* SW1X 42 A1
Wilton Est *HACK* * E8 ....78 A3
Wilton Ms *HACK* * E8 ....78 B3
   KTBR SW1X 42 B2
Wilton Pl *KTBR* SW1X 30 A5
Wilton Rd *PIM* SW1V 43 E3
Wilton Row *KTBR* SW1X 42 A1
Wilton Sq *IS* N1 ....77 D5
Wilton St *KTBR* SW1X 42 C2
Wilton Ter *KTBR* SW1X 42 A2
Wilton Vis *IS* N1 ....77 D5
Wilton Wy *HACK* E8 ....78 A3
Wiltshire Cl *CHEL* SW3 ....41 D5
Wiltshire Gdns *FSBYPK* N4 ....58 C1
Wiltshire Rd *BRXN/ST* SW9 ....136 A1

Wiltshire Rw *IS* N1 ....77 D5
Wimbart Rd *BRXS/STRHM* * SW2...135 F5
Wimbledon Park Rd *WIM/MER* SW19...149 E3
Wimbledon Park Side
  WIM/MER SW19 ....149 D5
Wimbledon Rd *TOOT* SW17 ....150 C4
Wimbolt St *BETH* E2 ....90 A2
Wimborne Cl *LEE/GVPK* SE12 ....141 F3
Wimbourne St *IS* N1 ....12 A1
Wimpole Ms *CAVSQ/HST* W1G 18 C2
Wimpole St *CAVSQ/HST* W1G 18 C3
Winans Wk *BRXN/ST* SW9...............118 A5
Wincanton Rd *WAND/EARL* SW18...131 F5
Winchcomb Gdns *ELTH/MOT* SE9 ...143 D1
Winchelsea Cl *PUT/ROE* SW15 ....131 D3
Winchelsea Rd *FSTGT* E7 ....82 A1
  WLSDN NW10 ....69 D5
Winchendon Rd *FUL/PGN* SW6 ....113 F3
Winchester Av *KIL/WHAMP* NW6.......71 E5
Winchester Cl *LBTH* * SE11 ....47 D5
Winchester Pl *HACK* E8 ....77 F2
  HGT N6 ....56 B3
Winchester Rd *HAMP* NW3 ....73 D4
  HGT N6 ....56 B3
  IL IG1 ....67 D5
Winchester Sq *STHWK* SE1 ....36 A3
Winchester St *ACT* W3 ....98 C2
  PIM SW1V 116 B1
Winchester Wk *STHWK* SE1 ....36 A3
Winchfield Rd *SYD* SE26 ....157 E5
Wincott St *LBTH* SE11 ....46 B4
Wincrofts Dr *ELTH/MOT* SE9 ....145 D2
Windermere Av *KIL/WHAMP* NW6.......71 E5
Windermere Rd *ARCH* * N19 ....56 C4
  PUT/ROE SW15 ....147 E4
Winders Rd *BTSEA* SW11 ....115 E3
Windfield Cl *SYD* SE26 ....157 D4
Windlass Pl *DEPT* SE8 ....103 E5
Windlesham Gv *WIM/MER* SW19...149 D1
Windley Cl *FSTH* SE23 ....156 F1
Windmill Cl *BERM/RHTH* * SE16 ......102 A5
  LEW * SE13 ....122 C5
Windmill Dr *CLAP* SW4......................134 B3
Windmill Hl *HAMP* NW3 ....54 C3
Windmill La *SRTFD* E15 ....81 D3
Windmill Pas *CHSWK* * W4 ....99 D5
Windmill Rd *CHSWK* W4 ....99 E5
  WAND/EARL SW18..............................133 D4
  WIM/MER SW19 ....148 B5
Windmill Rw *LBTH* * SE11 ....118 A1
Windmill St *FITZ* W1T 20 A3
Windmill Wk *STHWK* * SE1 ....34 B4
Windrose Cl *BERM/RHTH* SE16 ....103 D3
Windrush Cl *BTSEA* * SW11 ....133 D2
  CHSWK * W4 ....110 C3
Windrush La *FSTH* SE23 ....157 D3
Windrush Rd *STNW/STAM* NW10 ......69 D5
Windsor Cl *CHST* BR7 ....162 B5
  WNWD SE27 ....154 C4
Windsorne Cl *CHST* BR7 ....162 B5
Windsor Crs *WBLY* HA9 ....50 A5
Windsor Gdns *WV/WKIL* * W9 ....14 A1
Windsor Gv *WNWD* SE27 ....154 C4
Windsor Ms *CAT* SE6 ....158 C1
Windsor Rd *CRICK* NW2 ....70 B3
  FSTGT E7 ....82 B2
  HOLWY N7 ....57 F3
  IL IG1 ....84 C1
  LEY E10 ....62 B4
  WAN E11 ....64 A3
Windsor St *IS* N1 ....76 B5
Windsor Ter *IS* N1 ....11 F3
Windsor Wk *CMBW* SE5 ....119 D5
Windsor Wy *HMSMTH* W6 ....101 D5
Windspoint Dr *PECK* * SE15 ....120 A2
Windus Rd *STNW/STAM* N16 ....59 F3
Windy Ridge Cl *WIM/MER* SW19 ...149 D5
Wine Cl *WAP* E1W 102 C1
Winforton St *GNWCH* SE10..............122 C4

Winfrith Rd *WAND/EARL* SW18 ......132 C5
Wingate Rd *HMSMTH* W6 ....100 B4
  IL IG1 ....84 B2
Wingfield Ms *PECK* * SE15 ....138 A1
Wingfield Rd *SRTFD* E15.....................81 E2
Wingfield St *PECK* SE15 ....138 A1
Wingford Rd *CLAP* SW4.....................135 E4
Wingmore Rd *HNHL* SE24.................136 C1
Wingrave Rd *HMSMTH* W6 ....112 C2
Wingrove Rd *CAT* SE6 ....159 E2
Winifred St *CAN/RD* E16 ....107 F2
Winkley St *BETH* E2 ....90 B1
Winkworth Cottages *WCHPL* * E1 .....90 C3
Winlaton Rd *BMLY* BR1 ....159 D4
Winn Common Rd
  WOOL/PLUM SE18 ....127 E2
Winnett St *SOHO/SHAV* W1D 32 A1
Winnington Cl *EFNCH* N2 ....55 D1
Winnington Rd *EFNCH* N2 ....55 D1
Winn Rd *LEE/GVPK* SE12 ....160 A1
Winscombe St *KTTN* NW5 ....56 B5
Winsford Rd *CAT* SE6 ....157 F3
Winsham Gv *BTSEA* SW11 ....134 A3
Winslade Rd *BRXS/STRHM* SW2 .....135 E3
Winsland Ms *BAY/PAD* W2 ....16 A4
Winsland St *BAY/PAD* W2 ....16 A4
Winsley St *GTPST* W1W 19 E4
Winslow Cl *WLSDN* NW10 ....51 E5
Winslow Rd *HMSMTH* W6 ....112 C2
Winsor Ter *EHAM* E6 ....96 A4
Winstanley Rd *BTSEA* SW11 ....133 D1
Winston Av *CDALE/KGS* NW9 ....51 E2
Winston Rd *STNW/STAM* N16 ....77 D1
Winston Wy *IL* IG1 ....66 B5
Winter Av *EHAM* E6 ....83 E5
Winterbourne Rd *FSTH* SE23 ....157 F1
Winterbrook Rd *HNHL* SE24..............136 C4
Winterfold Cl *WIM/MER* SW19 ....149 E2
Winterstoke Rd *FSTH* SE23................157 F1
Winterton Pl *WBPTN* SW10 ....114 C2
Winterwell Rd *BRXS/STRHM* SW2 ...135 E3
Winthorpe Rd *PUT/ROE* SW15 ....131 E3
Winthorpe St *WCHPL* E1.....................90 B4
Winthrop St *WCHPL* * E1 ....90 B4
Winton Wy *STRHM/NOR* SW16 ....154 A5
Wiseman Rd *LEY* E10 ....62 A4
Wise Rd *SRTFD* E15 ....80 C5
Wiseton Rd *TOOT* SW17 ....151 E1
Wishart Rd *BKHTH/KID* SE3 ....125 D4
Wisley Rd *BTSEA* SW11 ....133 F3
Wisteria Cl *IL* IG1 ....84 B2
Wisteria Rd *LEW* SE13 ....141 D2
Witan St *BETH* E2 ....90 B2
Witherington Rd *HBRY* * N5 ....76 A2
Witherston Wy *ELTH/MOT* SE9 ....162 A2
Witley Rd *ARCH* N19 ....56 C4
Witney Pth *FSTH* * SE23 ....157 D3
Wittersham Rd *BMLY* BR1 ....159 F5
Wivenhoe Cl *PECK* SE15 ....138 A1
Wix's La *BTSEA* SW11 ....134 B2
Woburn Pl *STPAN* WC1H 8 B3
Woburn Sq *STPAN* WC1H 20 B1
Woburn Wk *STPAN* WC1H 8 B4
Wodehouse Av *PECK* SE15 ....119 F4
Woking Cl *PUT/ROE* SW15 ....129 F2
Wolfe Crs *CHARL* SE7 ....125 D1
Wolferton Rd *MNPK* E12 ....83 F1
Wolffington Rd *WNWD* SE27 ....154 B1
Wolfram Cl *LEW* SE13 ....141 E3
Wolftencroft Cl *BTSEA* SW11 ....133 E1
Wollaston Cl *WALW* SE17.....................47 D5
Wolseley Av *WAND/EARL* SW18 ......150 A2
Wolseley Gdns *CHSWK* W4 ....110 B2
Wolseley Rd *CEND/HSY/T* N8............57 D1
  CHSWK W4 ....98 C3
  FSTGT E7 ....82 B4
Wolseley St *STHWK* SE1 ....49 F1
Wolsey Av *EHAM* E6 ....96 A2

Wolsey Ct *ELTH/MOT* * SE9	**143**	F4
Wolsey Ms *KTTN* NW5	**74**	C3
Wolsey Rd *IS* N1	**77**	D2
Wolsey St *WCHPL* E1	**90**	C4
Wolverley St * E2	**90**	B2
Wolverton Gdns *HMSMTH* W6	**101**	D5
Womersley Rd *CEND/HSY/T* N8	**55**	F1
Wontner Cl *IS* * N1	**76**	C4
Wontner Rd *BAL* SW12	**151**	F2
Woodbank Rd *BMLY* BR1	**159**	F3
Woodberry Down *FSBYPK* N4	**58**	C3
Woodberry Gv *FSBYPK* N4	**58**	C2
Woodbine Pl *WAN* E11	**64**	A1
Woodbine Ter *HOM* E9	**78**	C3
Woodborough Rd *PUT/ROE* SW15	**130**	B2
Woodbourne Av *STRHM/NOR* SW16	**153**	D3
Woodbridge Cl *HOLWY* N7	**57**	F4
Woodbridge Rd *BARK* IG11	**85**	F2
Woodbridge St *CLKNW* EC1R	**10**	C5
Woodbury St *TOOT* SW17	**151**	E5
Woodchester Sq *BAY/PAD* W2	**14**	C2
Woodchurch Cl *BFN/LL* DA15	**163**	D3
Woodchurch Rd *KIL/WHAMP* NW6	**72**	A4
Wood Cl *BETH* E2	**90**	A3
CDALE/KGS NW9	**51**	D2
Woodcocks *CAN/RD* E16	**94**	C4
Woodcombe Crs *FSTH* SE23	**156**	C1
Woodcote Pl *WNWD* * SE27	**154**	B5
Woodcote Rd *WAN* E11	**64**	A2
Woodcroft *ELTH/MOT* SE9	**161**	F3
Woodcroft Ms *DEPT* SE8	**103**	E5
Wood Dene * SE15	**120**	B4
Wooden Bridge Ter *WNWD* * SE27	**154**	B3
Wooder Gdns *FSTGT* E7	**81**	F1
Woodfall Rd *FSBYPK* N4	**58**	A3
Woodfall St *CHEL* SW3	**115**	F1
Woodfarrs *CMBW* SE5	**137**	D2
Wood Fld *HAMP* * NW3	**73**	F2
Woodfield Av *STRHM/NOR* SW16	**153**	D3
Woodfield Gv *STRHM/NOR* SW16	**153**	D3
Woodfield Pl *MV/WKIL* W9	**89**	F3
Woodfield Rd *MV/WKIL* W9	**89**	F4
Woodford Rd *FSTGT* E7	**82**	B1
Woodger Rd *SHB* W12	**100**	C3
Woodget Cl *EHAM* E6	**95**	E5
Woodgrave Rd *FSTGT* E7	**82**	A2
Woodhall Av *DUL* SE21	**155**	F3
Woodhall Dr *DUL* SE21	**155**	F3
Woodham Rd *CAT* SE6	**158**	C3
Woodhatch Cl *EHAM* E6	**95**	E4
Woodheyes Rd *WLSDN* NW10	**69**	E2
Woodhill *CHARL* SE7	**107**	E5
Woodhouse Gv *MNPK* E12	**83**	E3
Woodhouse Rd *WAN* E11	**63**	F5
Woodhurst Rd *ACT* W3	**98**	C2
Woodington Cl *ELTH/MOT* SE9	**144**	B4
Woodison St *BOW* E3	**91**	E3
Woodland Cl *CDALE/KGS* NW9	**50**	C1
Woodland Crs *GNWCH* SE10	**123**	E1
Woodland Rd *NRWD* SE19	**155**	E5
The Woodlands *CMBW* * SE5	**118**	B3
LEW SE13	**141**	D5
Woodlands Av *ACT* W3	**98**	B2
BFN/LL DA15	**163**	E1
WAN E11	**64**	B3
Woodlands Gv *GNWCH* SE10	**123**	E1
Woodlands Park Rd *BKHTH/KID* SE3	**123**	D4
Woodlands Rd *BARN* SW13	**129**	F1
IL IG1	**66**	C3
WAN * E11	**64**	B3
Woodlands St *LEW* SE13	**141**	D5
Woodland St *HACK* * E8	**77**	F3
Woodlands Wy *PUT/ROE* SW15	**131**	F3
Woodland Ter *CHARL* SE7	**107**	E5
Woodland Wk *HAMP* NW3	**73**	E2
Wood La *CDALE/KGS* NW9	**51**	D2
HGT N6	**56**	B1

SHB W12	**88**	C5
Woodlawn Cl *PUT/ROE* SW15	**131**	F3
Woodlawn Rd *FUL/PGN* SW6	**113**	D3
Woodlea Rd *STNW/STAM* N16	**59**	E5
Woodleigh Gdns *STRHM/NOR* SW16	**153**	E3
Woodmans Gv *WLSDN* NW10	**69**	F2
Woodman St *CAN/RD* E16	**108**	A2
Woodmere *ELTH/MOT* SE9	**143**	F5
Woodmere Cl *BTSEA* SW11	**134**	A1
Woodnook Rd *STRHM/NOR* SW16	**152**	B5
Woodpecker Ms *LEW* SE13	**141**	D2
Woodquest Av *HNHL* SE24	**136**	B3
Woodriffe Rd *WAN* E11	**63**	D2
Woodrow *WOOL/PLUM* SE18	**107**	E5
Woodrush Cl *NWCR* SE14	**121**	E3
Woodseer St *WCHPL* E1	**25**	F2
Woodsford Sq *WKENS* W14	**101**	E3
Woodside *WIM/MER* SW19	**149**	E5
Woodside Av *CHST* BR7	**162**	C5
Woodside Crs *BFN/LL* DA15	**163**	E1
Woodside Pde *BFN/LL* * DA15	**163**	E3
Woodside Rd *BFN/LL* DA15	**163**	E3
PLSTW E13	**94**	C3
Wood's Ms *MYFR/PKLN* W1K	**29**	F1
Woodsome Rd *KTTN* NW5	**56**	A5
Wood's Pl *STHWK* SE1	**49**	D3
Woodspring Rd *WIM/MER* SW19	**149**	E2
Wood's Rd *PECK* SE15	**120**	B4
Woodstock Av *GLDGN* NW11	**53**	E2
SHB W12	**101**	D3
Woodstock Ms *CAVSQ/HST* W1G	**18**	D3
Woodstock Rd *CHSWK* W4	**99**	E5
FSBYPK N4	**58**	A3
FSTGT E7	**82**	C4
GLDGN NW11	**53**	F2
Woodstock St *CAN/RD* E16	**93**	F5
MYFR/PKLN W1K	**18**	C5
Woodstock Ter *POP/IOD* E14	**104**	B1
Wood St *BARB* EC2Y	**23**	F3
CAN/RD E16	**106**	B1
CHSWK W4	**111**	E1
Woodsyre *NRWD* SE19	**155**	F4
Wood Ter *CRICK* * NW2	**51**	F4
Woodthorpe Rd *PUT/ROE* SW15	**130**	B2
Wood V *EDUL* SE22	**156**	B1
Woodvale Wy *CRICK* NW2	**53**	D5
Woodview Cl *KUTN/CMB* KT2	**147**	D4
Woodville Cl *LEE/GVPK* SE12	**142**	A3
Woodville Rd *GLDGN* NW11	**53**	E2
KIL/WHAMP * NW6	**89**	F1
STNW/STAM N16	**77**	E2
WAN E11	**63**	F3
Woodville St *CHARL* SE7	**107**	E5
Woodwarde Rd *EDUL* SE22	**137**	E4
Woodwell St *WAND/EARL* SW18	**132**	C3
Wood Whf *GNWCH* SE10	**122**	B2
Woodyard Cl *KTTN* NW5	**74**	A2
Woodyard La *DUL* SE21	**137**	E5
Woodyates Rd *LEE/GVPK* SE12	**142**	A4
Woolacombe Rd *BKHTH/KID* SE3	**124**	C5
Woolands Rd *WAN* E11	**63**	E4
Wooler St *WALW* SE17	**119**	D1
Woolf Ms *STPAN* WC1H	**8**	C5
Woollaston Rd *FSBYPK* N4	**58**	B1
Woolmead Av *CDALE/KGS* NW9	**52**	A2
Woolmore St *POP/IOD* E14	**104**	C1
Woolneigh St *FUL/PGN* SW6	**132**	B1
Woolridge Wy *HOM* * E9	**78**	C4
Woolstaplers Wy *BERM/RHTH* SE16	**102**	A4
Woolstone Rd *FSTH* SE23	**157**	E2
Woolwich Church St *CHARL* SE7	**107**	D5
Woolwich Common		
WOOL/PLUM SE18	**126**	A2
Woolwich High St *WOOL/PLUM* SE18	**108**	A4
Woolwich Manorway *CAN/RD* E16	**108**	B3
Woolwich Manor Wy *CAN/RD* E16	**108**	B2
EHAM E6	**95**	F3

Woolwich New Rd
WOOL/PLUM SE18 ....126 A1
Woolwich Rd *CHARL* SE7 ....106 C5
CHARL SE7 ....124 B1
Wooster Gdns *POP/IOD* E14 ....93 D5
Wootton St *STHWK* SE1 ....34 E5
Worcester Cl *CRICK* NW2 ....52 A5
Worcester Dr *CHSWK* W4 ....99 E4
Worcester Gdns *IL* IG1.........................65 E2
Worcester Ms *KIL/WHAMP* NW6 ....72 B3
Worcester Rd *MNPK* E12 ....65 F5
WIM/MER SW19 ....149 F5
Wordsworth Av *MNPK* E12 ....83 E4
Wordsworth Pl *HAMP* NW3 ....73 F2
Wordsworth Rd *STHWK* SE1 ....49 E5
STNW/STAM N16.............................77 E1
WELL DA16 ....127 E4
Worfield St *BTSEA* SW11 ....115 E3
Worgan St *BERM/RHTH* SE16 ....103 D4
LBTH SE11 ....117 F1
Worland Rd *SRTFD* E15 ....81 E4
Worlds End Est *WBPTN* * SW10 ....115 D3
Worlds End Pas *WBPTN* * SW10 ....115 D3
Worlidge St *HMSMTH* W6 ....112 C1
Worlingham Rd *EDUL* SE22 ....137 F2
Wormholt Rd *SHB* W12 ....100 A2
Wormholt Ter *SHB* * W12 ....100 A2
Wormwood St *LVPST* EC2M 24 C4
Wornington Rd *NKENS* W10 ....89 E4
Woronzow Rd *STJWD* NW8 ....73 D5
Worple St *MORT/ESHN* SW14 ....129 D1
Worship St *SDTCH* EC2A 24 A1
Worslade Rd *TOOT* SW17 ....151 D4
Worsley Bridge Rd *CAT* SE6 ....157 F5
Worsley Gv *CLPT* E5...........................78 A1
Worsley Rd *WAN* E11 ....81 E1
Worsopp Dr *CLAP* SW4 ....134 C3
Worth Gv *WALW* * SE17 ....119 D1
Worthing Cl *SRTFD* E15.......................81 E5
Wortley Rd *EHAM* E6............................83 D4
Wotton Rd *CRICK* NW2 ....70 C1
Wouldham Rd *CAN/RD* E16 ....93 F5
Wragby Rd *WAN* * E11 ....63 E5
Wray Crs *FSBYPK* N4 ....57 E4
Wrekin Rd *WOOL/PLUM* SE18 ....126 C3
Wren Av *CRICK* NW2 ....70 C1
Wren Cl *CAN/RD* E16 ....93 F5
Wren Ms *LEW* * SE13 ....141 E2
Wren Rd *CMBW* SE5 ....119 D4
Wren St *FSBYW* WC1X 9 F5
Wrentham Av *WLSDN* NW10 ....89 D1
Wrenthorpe Rd *BMLY* BR1 ....159 E4
Wrexham Rd *BOW* E3 ....92 A1
Wricklemarsh Rd *BKHTH/KID* SE3 ....124 B5
Wrigglesworth St *NWCR* SE14 ....121 D3
Wright Cl *LEW* SE13 ....141 D2
Wrights La *KENS* * W8 ....38 B2
KENS W8 ....38 C2
Wrights Pl *WLSDN* * NW10 ....68 C3
Wright's Rd *BOW* E3 ....91 F1
Wrotham Rd *CAMTN* * NW1 ....74 C4
Wrottesley Rd *WLSDN* NW10 ....88 A2
WOOL/PLUM SE18 ....126 C2
Wroughton Rd *BTSEA* SW11 ....133 F4
Wroxton Rd *PECK* SE15 ....120 B5
Wulfstan St *SHB* W12 ....87 F5
Wyatt Dr *BARN* SW13 ....112 B2
Wyatt Park Rd *BRXS/STRHM* SW2 .....155 F2
Wyatt Rd *FSBYPK* N4............................58 C5
FSTGT E7 ....82 A3
Wybert St *CAMTN* NW1 ....7 D5
Wyborne Wy *WLSDN* NW10 ....68 C4
Wychcombe Studios *HAMP* * NW3 ......73 F3
Wycherley Cl *BKHTH/KID* SE3...........123 F3
Wychwood End *HGT* N6.........................56 C2
Wycliffe Cl *WELL* DA16 ....127 F4
Wycliffe Rd *BTSEA* SW11 ....116 A3
Wyclif St *FSBYE* EC1V 10 C4

Wycombe Gdns *CRICK* NW2 ....53 F4
Wycombe Pl *WAND/EARL* SW18 ....132 C4
Wycombe Rd *ALP/SUD* HA0 ....68 A5
Wydeville Manor Rd *LEE/GVPK* SE12 ...160 B4
Wye St *BTSEA* SW11 ....133 D1
Wyfold Rd *FUL/PGN* SW6 ....113 E4
Wyke Rd *BOW* E3 ....80 A4
Wyldes Cl *GLDGN* NW11 ....54 C3
Wyld Wy *WBLY* HA9 ....68 B3
Wyleu St *FSTH* SE23 ....139 E5
Wyllen Cl *WCHPL* E1 ....90 C3
Wymering Rd *MV/WKIL* W9 ....2 B1
Wymond St *PUT/ROE* SW15 ....130 C1
Wynan Rd *POP/IOD* E14 ....122 B1
Wyncham Av *BFN/LL* DA15 ....163 E1
Wyndale Av *CDALE/KGS* NW9 ....50 A1
Wyndcliff Rd *CHARL* SE7 ....124 B2
Wyndham Crs *KTTN* NW5 ....56 C5
Wyndham Est *CMBW* SE5 ....118 C3
Wyndham Ms *MBLAR* W1H 17 E3
Wyndham Pl *MBLAR* W1H 17 E3
Wyndham Rd *CMBW* SE5 ....118 C3
EHAM E6 ....83 D4
Wyndham St *MBLAR* W1H 17 E3
Wyneham Rd *HNHL* SE24 ....137 D3
Wynell Rd *FSTH* SE23 ....157 D3
Wynford Rd *IS* N1 ....9 E1
Wynford Wy *ELTH/MOT* SE9 ....161 F3
Wynne Rd *BRXN/ST* SW9 ....118 A5
Wynnstay Gdns *KENS* W8 ....38 B2
Wynter St *BTSEA* SW11 ....132 C2
Wynton Pl *ACT* W3 ....86 B5
Wynyard Ter *LBTH* * SE11 ....117 F1
Wynyatt St *FSBYE* EC1V 10 C1
Wythburn Pl *MBLAR* W1H 17 E5
Wythes Rd *CAN/RD* E16 ....107 E2
Wythfield Rd *ELTH/MOT* SE9 ....143 F4
Wyvil Rd *VX/NE* SW8 ....117 E3
Wyvis St *POP/IOD* E14.........................92 B4

Y

Yabsley St *POP/IOD* E14 ....104 C2
Yalding Rd *BERM/RHTH* SE16 ....102 A4
Yardley St *FSBYW* WC1X 10 A4
Yarmouth Pl *MYFR/PICC* W1J 30 C4
Yarrow Crs *EHAM* E6 ....95 E4
Yateley St *WOOL/PLUM* SE18 ....107 D3
Yeate St *IS* N1 ....77 D4
Yeatman Rd *HGT* N6 ....55 F1
Yeats Cl *BKHTH/KID* * SE3 ....123 D5
WLSDN NW10 ....69 E3
Yeldham Rd *HMSMTH* W6 ....113 D1
Yeldham Vls *HMSMTH* * W6 ....113 D1
Yelverton Rd *BTSEA* SW11 ....115 D5
Yeoman Cl *EHAM* E6 ....108 B1
Yeoman's Rw *CHEL* SW3 ....41 D3
Yeoman St *BERM/RHTH* SE16 ....103 E5
Yeo St *BOW* E3 ....92 B4
Yerbury Rd *ARCH* N19 ....57 D5
Yewfield Rd *WLSDN* NW10 ....69 F4
Yew Gv *CRICK* NW2 ....71 D1
Yew Tree Rd *SHB* W12 ....99 F1
Yoakley Rd *STNW/STAM* N16 ....59 E4
Yoke Cl *HOLWY* N7 ....75 E3
Yolande Gdns *ELTH/MOT* SE9 ....143 E3
Yonge Pk *HOLWY* N7 ....58 A5
York Av *BFN/LL* DA15 ....163 E2
MORT/ESHN SW14 ....128 C3
York Br *CAMTN* NW1 ....6 A5
York Buildings *CHCR* WC2N 33 D2
York Cl *CMBW* * SE5 ....118 C5
EHAM E6 ....95 F5
York Ga *CAMTN* NW1 ....18 B1
York Gv *PECK* SE15 ....120 C4
York Hl *STRHM/NOR* SW16 ....154 B3

York House Pl KENS W8 ....26 C5
Yorkland Av WELL DA16 ....145 F2
York Ms IL IG1 ....66 A4
KTTN NW5 ....74 B2
York Pde CDALE/KGS * NW9 ....52 A1
York Pl BTSEA SW11 ....132 C2
IL IG1 ....66 A5
York Ri KTTN NW5 ....56 B5
York Rd ACT W3 ....86 C5
BTSEA SW11 ....132 C2
FSTGT E7 ....82 A3
IL IG1 ....66 A5
LEY E10 ....63 C5
STHWK SE1 ....35 F5
Yorkshire Cl STNW/STAM N16 ....59 E5
Yorkshire Grey Yd HHOL * WC1V 21 E3
Yorkshire Rd POP/IOD E14 ....91 E5
York Sq POP/IOD * E14 ....91 E5
York St BARK IG11 ....84 B5
MBLAR W1H 17 E3
York St Chambers MHST * W1U 17 F2
York Ter East CAMTN NW1 ....18 B1
York Ter West CAMTN NW1 ....18 A1
Yorkton St BETH E2 ....90 A1

York Wy IS N1 ....9 D1
York Way Ct IS N1 ....75 E5
York Way Est HOLWY N7 ....75 E5
Young Rd CAN/RD E16 ....94 C5
Young St KENS W8 ....38 C1
Yoxley Ap GNTH/NBYPK IG2 ....66 C5
Yoxley Dr GNTH/NBYPK IG2 ....66 C1
Yukon Rd BAL SW12 ....134 B5
Yuletide Cl WLSDN NW10 ....69 E3

Z

Zampa Rd BERM/RHTH SE16 ....120 C1
Zander Ct BETH E2 ....90 A2
Zangwill Rd BKHTH/KID SE3 ....125 D4
Zealand Rd BOW E3 ....91 E1
Zennor Rd BAL SW12 ....152 C1
Zenoria St EDUL SE22 ....137 F2
Zetland St POP/IOD E14 ....92 C4
Zoar St STHWK SE1 ....35 E3
Zoffany St ARCH N19 ....57 D4

Index - featured places

6th Form Centre FSTGT E7 ....82 B3
Abbey Business Centre VX/NE SW8 ....116 C4
Abbey Medical Centre STJWD NW8 ......72 B5
Abbey Park Industrial Estate BARK IG11 ...96 B1
Abbey Road Health Centre SRTFD E15 ...81 E5
Abbey School for the English Language
STJWD NW8 ....3 F2
ABC Cinema CAT SE6 ....158 B1
HAMP NW3 ....73 C2
PUT/ROE SW15 ....151 E1
STRHM/NOR SW16 ....153 E2
Abercorn Place School STJWD NW8 ......3 F2
Aberdeen Wharf WAP E1W 102 B2
Abney Park Cemetery STNW/STAM N16 ...59 E4
Acacia Business Centre WAN E11 ....63 E5
Acland Burghley School KTTN NW5 .....74 B1
Acton Business Centre WLSDN NW10 ...87 D5
Acton Central Industrial Estate ACT W3 ...98 B1
Acton Health Centre ACT W3 ....98 A3
Acton High School ACT W3 ....98 A3
Acton Hospital ACT W3 ....98 A4
Acton Lane Medical Centre CHSWK W4 ...99 D5
Acton Park Industrial Estate ACT W3 ...99 F2
CHSWK W4 ....99 D3
Acton Superbowl ACT W3 ....86 A3
Acton Swimming Baths ACT W3 ....98 C2
Admiral Hyson Industrial Estate
BERM/RHTH SE16 ....102 C5
Admiralty Arch STJS SW1Y 32 B3
ADT Technology College PUT/ROE SW15 ...131 F3
The Adult College of Barking & Dagenham
BARK IG11 ....85 E3
Adult Education Centre POP/IOD E14 ...104 C4
Africa Centre COVGDN WC2E 33 D1
Agora Shopping Centre PECK SE15 ....120 A5
Airedale Physiotherapy Clinic CHSWK W4 ...111 F1
AIU London MHST W1U 18 B3
Aksaray Sports Club STNW/STAM N16 ...77 D1
Albany Centre & Theatre DEPT SE8 ...121 F3
Albemarle Independent College
BAY/PAD W2 ....27 D1
Albemarle Primary School
WIM/MER SW19 ....149 E2
Albert Memorial SKENS SW7 ....28 A5
Albery Theatre CHCR WC2N 32 C1
Albion Health Centre WCHPL E1 ....90 B4
Albion J & I School BERM/RHTH SE16 ...102 C3

Albion Street Health Centre
BERM/RHTH SE16 ....102 C3
The Alchemy Gallery CLKNW EC1R 10 A5
Aldersbrook Primary School BAL SW12 ...134 B5
Aldersbrook County Secondary School
MNPK E12 ....64 C3
Aldersbrook Primary School WAN E11 ...64 C3
Alderwood Primary School
ELTH/MOT SE9 ....145 D4
Aldgate Bus Station HDTCH EC3A 25 E4
Aldwych Theatre HOL/ALD WC2B 21 E5
Alfred Salter Primary School
BERM/RHTH SE16 ....103 D3
Allegory Clinic CAVSQ/HST W1G 18 C4
Allen Edwards Primary School CLAP SW4 ...117 E4
The All England Lawn Tennis
& Croquet Club
WIM/MER SW19 ....149 D3
Alleyns School EDUL SE22 ....137 E3
Allfarthing JMI School WAND/EARL SW18 ...132 C4
All Saints CE Primary School
BKHTH/KID SE3 ....123 E5
CRICK NW2 ....53 F5
FUL/PGN SW6 ....113 E5
PUT/ROE SW15 ....130 C1
All Souls CE Primary School GTPST W1W ...19 E3
Allum Medical Centre WAN E11 ....63 D2
Alma Primary School BERM/RHTH SE16 ...102 A5
Almeida Theatre IS N1 ....76 B4
Al Muntada Islamic School FUL/PGN SW6 ...113 F4
Alpine Business Centre EHAM E6 ....96 A4
Aiscot Road Industrial Estate STHWK SE1 ...49 F4
Altmore Infant School EHAM E6 ....83 F4
The Alton POP/ROE SW15 ....129 F5
Ambler Primary School FSBYPK N4 .....58 B5
AMC Business Centre WLSDN NW10 ...86 B2
American Intercontinental University
MHST W1U 18 B3
AMF Bowling LEW SE13 ....140 C1
Amherst Primary School HACK E8 ....78 A2
Ampthill Square Medical Centre
CAMTN NW1 ....7 E2
Anchorage Point Industrial Estate
CHARL SE7 ....106 C4
Anchor Retail Park WCHPL E1 ....90 C3
Andover Medical Centre HOLWY N7 .....57 F5
Andrew Skelton Theatre WCHPL E1 .....90 A4
Angerstein Business Park GNWCH SE10 ...106 A5
Anglian Industrial Estate BARK IG11 ...97 F3
Annandale Primary School GNWCH SE10 ...105 F3
GNWCH SE10 ....123 F1
The Anna Scher Theatre IS N1 ....76 A5
Annemount School EFNCH NW2 ....54 C1
Anson Primary School CRICK NW2 ....71 D2
Apex Industrial Estate WLSDN NW10 ...87 F3
Apollo Theatre SOHO/SHAV W1D 32 A1
Apollo Victoria Theatre PIM SW1V 43 E3

Apostolic Nuncio *WIM/MER* SW19 .... **148** C3
Apsley House, The Wellington Museum
BAY/PAD W2 .... **30** A3
Aquarius Business Park *CRICK* NW2 ...... **52** A3
Aquarius Golf Club *EDUL* SE22 .... **138** C3
Archbishop Michael Ramsey
Technology College *CMBW* SE5 .... **118** B3
Archbishop Sumners CE Primary School
LBTH SE11 .... **46** B5
Archbishop Tenison's School *VX/NE* SW8 .... **117** F2
Arches Leisure Centre *GNWCH* SE10 ...... **123** D2
Archway Business Centre *ARCH* N19 ...... **57** D5
Archway Leisure Centre *ARCH* N19 .... **56** C4
Arena Estate *FSBYPK* N4 .... **58** B1
Argyle Primary School *STPAN* WC1H **8** C3
Arklow Trading Estate *NWCR* SE14 .... **121** E2
Armourers & Braziers' Hall *LOTH* EC2R **24** A5
Arndale Health Centre *WAND/EARL* SW18 ... **132** A4
Arnhem Wharf Primary School
POP/IOD E14 .... **103** F4
Arnold House School *STJWD* NW8 .... **4** A1
Arnot Abbey *FARR* EC1M **22** C2
Arsenal FC (Highbury) *HBRY* N5 .... **58** A5
Arts Centre *HAMP* NW3 .... **72** B2
Arts Theatre *LSQ/SEVD* WC2H **32** B1
PUT/ROE SW15 .... **131** D2
Ashbourne Independent Sixth Form College
KENS W8 .... **27** D5
Ashburnham Primary School *WBPTN* SW10 ... **117** D5
Ashby Mill School *CLAP* SW4 .... **135** E5
Ashleigh Commercial Estate *CHARL* SE7 ... **106** C5
Ashmead Primary School *BROCKY* SE4 .... **122** A5
Ashmole Primary School *VX/NE* SW8 .... **117** F2
Ashmount Primary School *ARCH* N19 ...... **56** C2
Aspen House Secondary & Primary School
BRXS/STRHM SW2 .... **135** E3
Associated Newspapers
BERM/RHTH SE16 .... **103** D5
The Association of British
Language Schools *WCHPL* E1 .... **90** B4
Athelney Primary School *CAT* SE6 .... **158** A3
Athena Medical Centre *CLPT* E5 .... **78** C1
Atherton Leisure Centre *FSTGT* E7 .... **81** F3
Athlone House Hospital *HGT* N6 .... **55** F3
Atlas Business Centre *CRICK* NW2 .... **52** B4
Atlas Transport Estate *BTSEA* SW11 .... **114** C5
Australia House *HOL/ALD* WC2B **21** F5
Avenue Primary School *KIL/WHAMP* NW6 ... **71** E4
MNPK E12 .... **83** E1
Avigdor Primary School *STNW/STAM* N16 ... **59** D4
Avondale Park Primary School
NTGHL W11 .... **101** D1
Avon Trading Estate *WKENS* W14 .... **101** F5
Axis Business Centre *SRTFD* E15 .... **80** B5
The Aylesham Centre *PECK* SE15 .... **120** A4
Aylwin Girls School *BERM/RHTH* SE16 ... **49** F4
Bacons City Technology College
BERM/RHTH SE16 .... **103** D3
Bacon's College *BERM/RHTH* SE16 .... **103** E2
Baden Powell House *SKENS* SW7 .... **39** F5
Baden Powell Primary School *CLPT* E5 .... **60** B5
Bakers Hall *MON* EC3R **37** D2
Balaam Leisure Centre *PLSTW* E13 .... **94** A3
Bales College *NKENS* W10 .... **89** D2
Balham Health Centre *BAL* SW12 .... **152** B2
Balham Leisure Centre *TOOT* SW17 .... **152** A2
Balham Preparatory School *TOOT* SW17 ... **151** F4
Balmoral Trading Estate *BARK* IG11 .... **97** F4
Baltic Exchange *HDTCH* EC3A **25** D4
Bangabandhu Primary School *BETH* E2 ... **90** C2
Bank of England (& Museum) *LOTH* EC2R ... **24** A5
Bank of England Extension *STP* EC4M **23** E5
Bankside Gallery *STHWK* SE1 .... **35** D2
Bankside Jetty *STHWK* SE1 .... **35** E2
Bannockburn Primary School
WOOL/PLUM SE18 .... **109** F5
Banqueting House *WHALL* SW1A **32** C4
Barber Surgeons' Hall *BARB* EC2Y **23** F3
Barbican Cinema *BARB* EC2Y **23** E2
The Barbican *BARB* EC2Y **23** E2
Barbican Theatre *BARB* EC2Y **23** F2
Barclay J & I School *LEY* E10 .... **63** D1
Baring Primary School *LEE/CVPK* SE12 ... **142** A5
Baring Road Medical Centre
LEE/CVPK SE12 .... **160** A2
Barkantine Clinic *POP/IOD* E14 .... **104** A3
Barking Abbey Comprehensive School
BARK IG11 .... **85** F3
BARK IG11 .... **85** D2
Barking Abbey Industrial Estate
BARK IG11 .... **84** B5
Barking Hospital *BARK* IG11 .... **85** F4
Barking Industrial Park *BARK* IG11 .... **85** F5
Barlby Primary School *NKENS* W10 .... **89** D3
Barn Croft Primary School *WALTH* E17 .... **61** E1

Barn Elms Athletics Track *BARN* SW13 .... **112** B5
Barn Elms Water Sports Centre
BARN SW13 .... **112** C5
Barnes Hospital *MORT/ESHN* SW14 .... **129** E1
Barnes Sports Club *BARN* SW13 .... **111** F4
Barnsbury School for Girls *IS* N1 .... **76** A3
Barons Court Theatre *WKENS* W14 .... **113** E1
Barratt Industrial Park *BOW* E3 .... **92** C3
Barrow Hill Junior School *STJWD* NW8 .... **4** C2
Barton House Health Centre
STNW/STAM N16 .... **59** D5
Bassett House School *NKENS* W10 .... **89** D5
Bath Factory Estate *HNHL* SE24 .... **136** C4
Battersea Business Centre *BTSEA* SW11 ... **134** A1
Battersea Dogs' Home *VX/NE* SW8 .... **116** B3
Battersea Power Station (disused)
VX/NE SW8 .... **116** B2
Battersea Sports Centre *BTSEA* SW11 .... **133** D1
Battersea Technology College
BTSEA SW11 .... **115** F4
Battersea Tutorial College *TOOT* SW17 ... **152** A2
BBC Studios *MV/WKIL* W9 .... **2** C5
BBC Television Centre *SHB* W12 .... **100** C5
Beatrix Potter Primary School
WAND/EARL SW18 .... **150** C1
Beaumont Primary School *LEY* E10 .... **62** B3
Beckford Primary School
KIL/WHAMP NW6 .... **71** F2
Beckton Ski Centre *EHAM* E6 .... **96** A3
Beckton Special School *CAN/RD* E16 ...... **95** D4
Beckton Triangle Retail Park *EHAM* E6 ... **96** B2
Bective House Clinic *PUT/ROE* SW15 ...... **131** F2
Beechwood School *STRHM/NOR* SW16 ... **153** E2
Belmont Park School *LEY* E10 .... **62** C1
Belmont Primary School *CHSWK* W4 .... **99** D5
Belvedere Day Hospital *WLSDN* NW10 .... **70** A5
Benedict Primary School
BFN/LL DA15 .... **163** F4
Ben Jonson Primary School *WCHPL* E1 ... **91** E3
Benthal Primary School *STNW/STAM* N16 ... **60** A5
Bentworth Primary School *SHB* W12 .... **88** B5
Beormund School *STHWK* SE1 .... **48** A1
Berger Primary School *HOM* E9 .... **79** D3
Berlitz Schools of Languages *LINN* WC2A ... **21** F3
Bermondsey Town Hall *STHWK* SE1 .... **49** F3
Bermondsey Trading Estate
BERM/RHTH SE16 .... **102** C5
Berrymede Infant School *ACT* W3 .... **98** B3
Berrymede Junior School *ACT* W3 .... **98** B3
Bertram House School *TOOT* SW17 .... **152** A2
Bessemer Grange J & I School *CMBW* SE5 ... **137** E2
Bessemer Park Industrial Estate
HNHL SE24 .... **136** D2
Bethnal Green Museum of Childhood
BETH E2 .... **90** B2
Bethnal Green Technology College
BETH E2 .... **13** F4
Bevington Primary School *NKENS* W10 ... **89** E4
BFI London IMAX Cinema *STHWK* SE1 ... **33** F4
Big Ben *WEST* SW1A **45** D1
Bigland Green Primary School *WCHPL* E1 ... **90** D5
Billingsgate Fish Market *POP/IOD* E14 ... **104** B2
Birkbeck College *STPAN* WC1H **8** A5
Bishop Challoner RC School *WCHPL* E1 ... **102** C1
Bishop Challoner RC Secondary School
WCHPL E1 .... **90** C5
Bishop Gilpin Primary School
WIM/MER SW19 .... **149** F5
Bishopsgate Institute *WCHPL* E1 .... **25** D3
Bishop Thomas Grant School
STRHM/NOR SW16 .... **153** F5
Blackfriars Millennium Pier *EMB* EC4Y ... **34** B1
Blackfriars Pier *BLKFR* EC4V **35** D1
Blackheath Bluecoat CE School
BKHTH SE3 .... **124** B3
Blackheath Business Centre *GNWCH* SE10 ... **124** E4
The Blackheath Clinic *BKHTH/KID* SE3 ... **142** A4
Blackheath High School
BKHTH SE3 .... **123** F5
Blackheath High Senior School
BKHTH SE3 .... **124** A3
Blackheath Hospital *BKHTH/KID* SE3 ..... **141** F1
Blackwall Trading Estate *POP/IOD* E14 ... **93** D4

Blake College *GTPST* W1W 19 E2
Blessed John Roche Catholic School
  POP/IOD E14 .... 92 A5
Blessed Sacrament RC Primary School
  IS N1 .... 75 D5
Bloomfield Clinic (Guys Hospital)
  STHWK SE1 .... 36 B5
Bloomsbury College *FUL/PGN* SW6 .... 114 A3
Bloomsbury Theatre *STPAN* WC1H 8 A5
Blossoms Inn Medical Centre *BLKFR* EC4V ... 35 F1
Blue Gate Fields Primary School
  WCHPL E1 .... 102 C1
BMI Medical Centre *CAVSQ/HST* W1G 19 E2
Bnois Jerusalem School *STNW/STAM* N16 ... 59 D2
The Bob Hope Theatre *ELTH/MOT* SE9 .... 143 F4
Bodywise Natural Health Centre *BETH* E2 .... 90 C2
Boleyn Cinema *EHAM* E6 .... 95 D1
Bolingbroke Hospital *BTSEA* SW11 .... 133 E3
Bolingbroke Primary School *BTSEA* SW11 ... 115 D4
Bonner Primary School *BETH* E2 .... 91 D1
Bonneville Primary School *CLAP* SW4 .... 134 C4
Bonus Pastor School *BMLY* BR1 .... 159 E4
Borough Market *STHWK* SE1 .... 36 A3
Bousfield CE Primary School *ECT* SW5 .... 114 B1
Boutcher CE Primary School *STHWK* SE1 .... 49 E3
Bowater House *SKENS* SW7 .... 41 E1
Bow County Court *SRTFD* E15 .... 95 D1
Bow Cross Secondary School *BOW* E3 .... 92 A2
Bow Industrial Park *SRTFD* E15 .... 80 A4
Bow Street Magistrates Court
  HOL/ALD WC2B 21 D5
Bow Triangle Business Centre *BOW* E3 .... 92 A3
Brackenbury Health Centre
  HMSMTH W6 .... 100 B4
Brackenbury Primary School
  HMSMTH W6 .... 100 B4
Brady Recreation Centre *WCHPL* E1 .... 90 A4
Braincroft Primary School *CRICK* NW2 .... 51 F5
Braman's Tea & Coffee Museum
  STHWK SE1 .... 35 F4
Brampton Manor School *PLSTW* E13 .... 95 D3
Brampton Primary School *EHAM* E6 .... 95 E2
Brandlehow Primary School
  PUT/ROE SW15 .... 131 F2
Branollys Health Centre *PLSTW* E13 .... 94 A3
Brecknock Primary School *HOLWY* N7 .... 75 D3
Bredinghurst School *PECK* SE15 .... 138 C2
Brent Adult College *WLSDN* NW10 .... 69 D5
Brent Arts Council *CRICK* NW2 .... 52 A5
Brent Child & Family Clinic *WLSDN* NW10 ... 69 F2
Brent Cross Shopping Centre *HDN* NW4 .... 52 C2
Brentfield Medical Centre *WLSDN* NW10 ...... 69 D3
Brentfield Primary School *WLSDN* NW10 ...... 69 D3
Brentford Fountain Leisure Centre
  CHSWK W4 .... 110 A1
Brent Knoll School *SYD* SE26 .... 157 D3
Brent Magistrates Court House
  WLSDN NW10 .... 69 E5
Brent Sparks Montessori School
  WKENS W14 .... 101 D3
Brent Trading Estate *WLSDN* NW10 .... 69 E2
Brewers Hall *CITYW* EC2V 23 F3
Brewery Industrial Estate *IS* N1 .... 11 E2
Brick Lane Music Hall *SDTCH* EC2A 13 D4
Brick Lane Music House *WCHPL* E1 .... 25 F1
Bricklayer Arms Industrial Estate
  STHWK SE1 .... 49 E5
The Bridewell Theatre *EMB* EC4Y 22 C5
Bridge Lane Theatre *BTSEA* SW11 .... 115 E4
The Bridge Leisure Centre *SYD* SE26 .... 157 F4
Bridge Park Business & Leisure Centre
  WLSDN NW10 .... 68 B2
Bright Sparks Montessori School
  WKENS W14 .... 101 D3
Bright Sparks School *STRHM/NOR* SW16 ... 155 E4
Brindishe Primary School *LEE/GVPK* SE12 ... 141 F3
Britannia Business Centre *CRICK* NW2 .... 71 D1
Britannia Leisure Centre *IS* N1 .... 77 D5
Britannia Village Primary School
  CAN/RD E16 .... 106 B2
British Airways London Eye *WHALL* SW1A ... 33 D5
British Dental Association
  CAVSQ/HST W1G 18 C3
British Friends of Diaspora Museum
  KTTN NW5 .... 74 A3
British Library *CAMTN* NW1 .... 8 B3
British Medical Association *STPAN* WC1H 8 B5
British Museum *RSQ* WC1B 20 C3
British Telecom Tower *GTPST* W1W 19 E2

Broadway Shopping Centre
  HMSMTH W6 .... 112 C1
Broadway Squash & Fitness Centre
  HMSMTH W6 .... 101 D5
Brocklebank Health Centre
  WAND/EARL SW18 .... 132 B5
Brocklebank Industrial Estate
  GNWCH SE10 .... 106 A5
Brockley Cross Business Centre
  BROCKY SE4 .... 139 F1
Brockley Primary School *BROCKY* SE4 .... 139 F3
Brockwell Lido *HNHL* SE24 .... 136 A5
Brockwell Primary School
  BRXS/STRHM SW2 .... 136 A4
Bromley Road Retail Park *CAT* SE6 .... 158 B2
Brompton Cemetery *WBPTN* SW10 .... 114 B2
Brompton Medical Centre *WBPTN* SW10 ..... 114 B1
Brompton Oratory *SKENS* SW7 .... 40 C3
Bromyard Leisure Centre *ACT* W3 .... 99 E2
Brondesbury College for Boys
  KIL/WHAMP NW6 .... 71 D4
Brookfield Primary School *ARCH* N19 .... 56 B3
Brooklands Primary School
  BKHTH/KID SE3 .... 142 A1
Brookmarsh Industrial Estate *DEPT* SE8 ..... 122 B3
Broomsleigh Business Park *CAT* SE6 .... 157 F5
Broomwood Hall School *BAL* SW12 .... 134 A5
Brunel Engine House *BERM/RHTH* SE16 ...... 102 C3
Brunswick Housing & Shopping Centre
  BMSBY WC1N 21 D1
Brunswick Medical Centre *BMSBY* WC1N 8 C5
Brunswick Park Primary School
  CMBW SE5 .... 119 D3
BT Centre *STBT* EC1A 23 E4
Buckingham Palace *WHALL* SW1A 43 D1
Buckingham Road Cemetery *IL* IG1 .... 67 D3
Buckingham Centre *GWRST* WC1E 20 A3
Burbage School *IS* N1 .... 12 C1
Burdett Coutts CE Primary School
  WEST SW1P 44 A4
Burgess Industrial Park *CMBW* SE5 .... 119 D3
Burlington Danes School *SHB* W12 .... 88 B5
Burnley Road Clinic *WLSDN* NW10 .... 70 A2
Burnt Ash Infant School *BMLY* BR1 .... 160 A5
Burnt Ash School *BMLY* BR1 .... 159 F5
Burntwood School *TOOT* SW17 .... 151 D2
Burrells Wharf *POP/IOD* E14 .... 122 B1
Burwell Industrial Estate *LEY* E10 .... 61 E3
Bush House (BBC) *HOL/ALD* WC2B 21 E5
Bush Industrial Estate *ARCH* N19 .... 56 C5
  WLSDN NW10 .... 87 D2
The Business Centre *IL* IG1 .... 66 B4
The Business Design Centre *IS* N1 .... 76 A5
Bute House Preparatory School for Girls
  HMSMTH W6 .... 100 C5
Butler's Wharf *STHWK* SE1 .... 37 F4
Butler's Wharf Business Centre
  STHWK SE1 .... 37 F5
Butler's Wharf Pier *STHWK* SE1 .... 37 F5
Butterfly Sports Club *ELTH/MOT* SE9 .... 144 B4
Buzzard Creek Industrial Estate
  BARK IG11 .... 97 F2
Byam Shaw School of Art *ARCH* N19 .... 56 C4
Bygrove JMI School *POP/IOD* E14 .... 92 B5
Cabinet War Rooms *WHALL* SW1A 32 B5
Calder House School *BTSEA* SW11 .... 115 F4
Caledonian Market *STHWK* SE1 .... 49 D2
Cally Pool *IS* N1 .... 75 F5
Calverton Primary School *CAN/RD* E16 .... 95 D5
Camberwell Business Centre *CMBW* SE5 ..... 119 D3
Camberwell College of Arts *CMBW* SE5 ...... 119 E4
Camberwell New Cemetery *FSTH* SE23 .... 139 D4
Camberwell Trading Estate *CMBW* SE5 .... 118 B5
Cambridge School *HMSMTH* W6 .... 100 B5
Cambridge Theatre *LSQ/SEVD* WC2H 20 C5
Camden Community Trust Day Hospital
  CAMTN NW1 .... 74 C3
Camden House Clinic *BKHTH/KID* SE3 .... 123 F4
Camden Market *CAMTN* NW1 .... 74 A4
Camden Peoples Theatre *CAMTN* NW1 .... 7 F4
Camden Road for Girls *CAMTN* NW1 .... 74 C3
Camden Theatre *CAMTN* NW1 .... 7 E1
Camden Town Hall & St Pancras Library
  CAMTN NW1 .... 8 C3
Camelot Primary School *PECK* SE15 .... 120 B3
Cameron House School *CHEL* SW3 .... 115 D2
Camperdown House *WCHPL* E1 .... 25 F5
Canada House *STJS* SW1Y 32 B3
Canada Square *POP/IOD* E14 .... 104 A2
Canada Water Retail Park
  BERM/RHTH SE16 .... 103 D4
Canada Wharf Museum
  BERM/RHTH SE16 .... 103 F2
Canal Cafe Theatre *BAY/PAD* W2 .... 15 D2
Canary Riverside *BERM/RHTH* SE16 .... 103 F2

Canary Wharf Pier *BERM/RHTH* SE16........... 103 F2
Canary Wharf Tower *POP/IOD* E14............. 104 B2
Canberra Primary School *SHB* W12............. 100 B1
Cann Hall Primary School *WAN* E11............. 65 F5
The Canning School *KENS* W8..................... 38 A2
Cannon Sports Club *CANST* EC4R............... 35 F1
Cannon Trading Estate *WBLY* HA9............. 68 B1
Cannon Wharf Business Centre
  DEPT SE8... 103 E5
Cannon Workshops *POP/IOD* E14............. 104 A1
Canon Barnett Primary School
  WCHPL E1.. 25 F4
Canonbury Business Centre *IS* N1............. 76 C5
Canonbury Primary School *IS* N1............... 76 B5
Canon Palmer RC High School *IL* IG1......... 67 E3
Canterbury Industrial Estate *PECK* SE15..... 121 D2
Cantium Retail Park *STHWK* SE1............... 120 A2
Capital Radio *LSO/SEVD* WC2H................. 32 B2
Capital Wharf *WAP* E1W........................... 102 A2
Cardinal Hinsley High School
  WLSDN NW10....................................... 70 A5
Cardinal Pole RC School *HOM* E9............... 79 E3
Cardinal Pole RC Secondary Lower School
  HOM E9.. 79 D4
Cardinal Vaughan Memorial School
  WKENS W14... 101 E3
Cardwell Primary School
  WOOL/PLUM SE18................................ 107 F5
Carlton Gate Development *MV/WKIL* W9..... 14 B2
Carlton House *STJS* SW1Y....................... 32 A4
Carlton Primary School *KTTN* NW5............. 74 A2
Carlton Vale Infant School *MV/WKIL* W9..... 89 F2
Carlyle's House *CHEL* SW3....................... 115 E2
Carnwath Road Industrial Estate
  FUL/PGN SW6...................................... 132 B1
Carpenters Business Park *HOM* E9............. 80 A3
Carpenters' Hall *LVPST* EC2M.................. 24 B3
Carpenters Primary School *SRTFD* E15....... 80 C5
Cassidy Medical Centre *FUL/PGN* SW6...... 114 A3
Castlecombe Primary School
  ELTH/MOT SE9.................................... 161 E5
Castle Industrial Estate *WALW* SE17......... 47 E4
Catford Cricket & Sports Club *CAT* SE6..... 158 B1
Catford Cyphers Cricket Club *CAT* SE6...... 157 F2
Catford Girls School *CAT* SE6................. 159 D3
Catford Trading Estate *CAT* SE6............. 158 B2
Catford Wanderers Sports Club *CAT* SE6... 158 C4
Cathall Leisure Centre *WAN* E11............. 65 D5
Cathedral School of St Saviour &
  St Mary Overie *STHWK* SE1.................. 35 F5
Cavendish College *FITZ* W1T................... 20 A3
Cavendish Primary School *CHSWK* W4....... 111 E3
The Cavendish School *CAMTN* NW1........... 74 B5
Caxton Hall *STJSPK* SW1H...................... 44 A2
Cayley Primary School *POP/IOD* E14......... 91 E4
The Cedar School *FSTGT* E7................... 82 C5
Cedar Way Industrial Estate *CAMTN* NW1... 75 D4
Cenotaph *WHALL* SW1A......................... 32 C5
Central Business Centre *WLSDN* NW10....... 69 E2
Central Criminal Court *STP* EC4M............. 22 C4
Central Foundation Boys School
  SDTCH EC2A....................................... 12 B5
Central Foundation Girls School *BOW* E3... 91 E2
Central Hall *STJSPK* SW1H...................... 44 B1
Central London County Court
  CAVSO/HST W1G.................................. 18 C1
Central London Golf Club *TOOT* SW17....... 151 D2
Central London Markets *FARR* EC1M......... 22 C3
Central Middlesex Hospital *WLSDN* NW10... 86 C2
Central Park Primary School *EHAM* E6....... 95 D1
Central St Martins College of Art & Design
  RSQ WC1B... 21 D3
Central School of Ballet *CLKNW* EC1R....... 22 B1
Central School of Fashion *CTPST* W1W..... 19 E3
Central School of Speech & Drama
  HAMP NW3... 73 D4
Central Speech & Drama
  CAMTN NW1....................................... 75 D3
Centre Point *LSO/SEVD* WC2H................. 20 B4
Chalcot School *CAMTN* NW1.................... 74 B3
Chalkhill Primary School *WBLY* HA9......... 50 B5
Chambers Wharf *BERM/RHTH* SE16........... 102 A3
Chancellors Wharf
  Development *HMSMTH* W6..................... 112 C1
Channelsea Business Centre *SRTFD* E15... 93 D1
Channing School *HGT* N6........................ 56 B3
Chapman Park Industrial Estate
  WLSDN NW10..................................... 69 F3
Charing Cross Hospital *HMSMTH* W6......... 113 D2
Charing Cross & Westminster
  Medical School *HMSMTH* W6................ 113 D1
The Charles Dickens Museum
  BMSBY WC1N..................................... 21 E1
Charles Dickens Primary School
  STHWK SE1....................................... 47 E1
Charles Edward Brook Lower School
  CMBW SE5.. 118 B4
Charles Edward Brook Upper School
  CMBW SE5.. 118 B4
Charles Lamb Primary School *IS* N1......... 76 C5
Charlotte Sharman Primary School
  LBTH SE11.. 46 C3
Charlton Athletic FC (The Valley)
  CHARL SE7....................................... 124 C1
Charlton Health & Fitness Centre
  CHARL SE7....................................... 124 C1
Charlton House *CHARL* SE7.................... 125 D2
Charlton Manor Primary School
  CHARL SE7....................................... 125 D3
Charlton RFC *ELTH/MOT* SE9................. 144 B5
Charlton School *CHARL* SE7.................. 125 E2
Charter Clinic *CHEL* SW3...................... 115 F1
Charterhouse *FARR* EC1M..................... 23 D2
Charteris Road Sports Centre
  KIL/WHAMP NW6............................... 71 F5
The Charter School *HNHL* SE24.............. 137 D5
Chartfield School *PUT/ROE* SW15........... 130 B3
Chase Road Trading Estate *WLSDN* NW10... 87 D3
Chelsea Barracks *BGVA* SW1W............... 116 A1
Chelsea Bridge Business Centre
  VX/NE SW8....................................... 116 B3
Chelsea Centre & Theatre *WBPTN* SW10... 115 D3
Chelsea Cinema *CHEL* SW3.................... 115 E1
Chelsea College of Art & Design
  CHEL SW3.. 115 D1
  FUL/PGN SW6................................... 114 C5
Chelsea FC (Stamford Bridge)
  FUL/PGN SW6................................... 114 B3
Chelsea Leisure Centre *CHEL* SW3.......... 115 E1
Chelsea Old Town Hall *CHEL* SW3........... 115 E1
Chelsea Physic Garden *CHEL* SW3........... 115 F2
Chelsea & Westminster Hospital
  WBPTN SW10.................................... 114 C2
Chelsea Wharf *WBPTN* SW10................. 115 D3
Chiltonian Industrial Estate
  LEE/GVPK SE12................................ 141 F4
Chinnocks Wharf *POP/IOD* E14............. 103 E1
Chisenhale Primary School *BOW* E3......... 91 E1
Chislehurst Cemetery *CHST* BR7........... 163 E5
Chiswick & Bedford Park
  Preparatory School *CHSWK* W4............ 99 E5
Chiswick Business Park *CHSWK* W4......... 98 B5
Chiswick Community School *CHSWK* W4... 111 D3
Chiswick House *CHSWK* W4.................. 111 D2
Chrisp Street Health Centre *POP/IOD* E14... 92 B5
Christ Church Bentinck CE Primary School
  CAMTN NW1..................................... 16 C2
Christ Church Brondesbury CE J & I School
  KIL/WHAMP NW6.............................. 71 F5
Christ Church CE Primary School
  BRXN/ST SW9.................................. 118 A4
  BRXS/STRHM SW2........................... 153 F1
  CHEL SW3....................................... 115 E1
  FSTH SE23...................................... 157 D2
Christchurch CE Primary School
  HAMP NW3...................................... 55 D5
  WCHPL E1....................................... 25 F3
Christ Church CE Primary School
  WOOL/PLUM SE18............................ 126 A4
Christchurch Industrial Centre *STHWK* SE1... 34 C3
Christchurch Primary School
  BTSEA SW11................................... 133 E1
Christchurch Primary School *IL* IG1........ 66 C5
Christ Church CE Primary School *CAMTN* NW1... 7 D3
Christine King 6th Form College
  LEW SE13....................................... 141 D1
Christopher Hutton Primary School
  FSBYW WC1X................................... 22 A1
Christ's College *BKHTH/KID* SE3........... 124 A4
Christ the King RC Primary School
  FSBYPK N4....................................... 57 F4
Chrysalis Theatre *BAL* SW12................. 152 A1
Chrysanthemum Clinic *CHSWK* W4......... 110 C3
Chrysostra Primary School *STHWK* SE1... 48 B2
Church Down Adult School
  LEE/GVPK SE12............................... 160 A2
Church End Medical Centre *WLSDN* NW10... 69 E3
Churchfield School *WOOL/PLUM* SE18..... 109 F5
Church House *WEST* SW1P.................... 44 B2
Churchill Clinic *STHWK* SE1.................. 46 B1

Churchill College *TOOT* SW17 .... **151** F2
Churchill Gardens Primary School
   PIM SW1V ....
Church Mead Infant School *LEY* E10 ...... **62** A3
Church Mead Junior School *LEY* E10 ...... **62** A3
Church Stairs *BERM/RHTH* SE16 .... **102** B3
City Banking College *STHWK* SE1 .... **36** B5
City Business Centre *BERM/RHTH* SE16 .... **102** C3
City Business College *FSBYE* EC1V **11** D4
City Central Estate *FSBYE* EC1V **11** E2
City College of Higher Education *IS* N1 .. **12** B3
City & Guilds of London Art School
   LBTH SE11 .... **118** B3
City Health Centre *FSBYE* **12** A1
City & Islington College *FSBYE* EC1V **11** F4
   FSBYPK N4 .... **58** B4
   HOLWY N7 .... **75** E1
   IS N1 .... **76** C5
   STLK EC1Y **24** A1
City & Islington College Sixth Form Centre
   HOLWY N7 .... **75** F1
City of London Cemetery *MNPK* E12 ...... **65** E4
City of London Crematorium
   MNPK E12 .... **65** D5
City of London College *OBST* EC2M **24** C4
City of London College *WCHPL* E1 .... **90** C4
City of London Magistrates Court
   MANHO EC4N **24** A5
City of London Polytechnic Sports Ground
   ELTH/MOT SE9 .... **160** C2
City of London School *BLKFR* EC4V **35** D1
City of London School for Girls
   BARB EC2Y **23** E2
City of Westminster College *BAY/PAD* W2 . **16** A1
   MV/WKIL W9 .... **2** A4
City of Westminster Vehicle Pound
   BAY/PAD W2 ....
City University *FSBYE* EC1V **29** F2
   FSBYE EC1V **10** C3
City University Business School
   BARB EC2Y **23** C4
Civil Service Recreation Centre
   WEST SW1P **44** B3
Civil Service Sport Ground
   ELTH/MOT SE9 .... **142** C4
Clapham Common Clinic *CLAP* SW4 .... **135** D2
Clapham Manor Primary School
   CLAP SW4 .... **134** C1
Clapham Manor Street Public Baths
   CLAP SW4 .... **135** D1
Clapham North Business Centre
   CLAP SW4 .... **135** D1
Clapham Park School *CLAP* SW4 .... **135** D3
Clapham Park Picture House *CLAP* SW4 ... **134** C2
Clapton City Technology College
   CLPT E5 .... **78** C1
Clapton Jewish Boys School
   STNW N16 .... **59** E4
Clara Grant Primary School *BOW* E3 ...... **92** A3
Claremont Clinic *FSTGT* E7 .... **82** B2
Claremont Way Industrial Estate
   CRICK NW2 .... **52** C3
Clarence House *WHALL* SW1A **31** F5
Claridges Hotel *MYFR/PKLN* W1K **30** C1
Cleopatra's Needle *CHCR* WC2N **33** E3
Clerkenwell Country Court *IS* N1 .... **10** C1
Clerkenwell Heritage Centre *FARR* EC1M . **22** C1
Clerkenwell Parochial CE Primary School
   CLKNW EC1R **10** A4
Cleveland Primary School *IL* IG1 .... **84** B1
Cleves Primary School *EHAM* E6 .... **83** D5
Clink Exhibition *STHWK* SE1 .... **36** A3
Clissold Leisure Centre *STNW/STAM* N16 . **59** D5
Clissold Park Natural Health Centre
   STNW/STAM N16 .... **59** E4
Clitterhouse Primary School *CRICK* NW2 . **53** D4
Clock Museum *CITYW* EC2V ....
Cloisters Business Centre *VX/NE* SW8 ... **116** B3
Clore Gallery *WEST* SW1P **44** C5
Clothworkers' Hall *FENCHST* EC3M **37** D1
Clouster's Green *WAP* E1W **102** A2
Cobbold Estate *WLSDN* NW10 .... **69** F5
Cobourg Primary School *CMBW* SE5 ...... **119** F1
Cochrane Theatre *GINN* WC1R **21** E5
The Cockpit Theatre *STJWD* NW8 .... **16** C1
Coldharbour Industrial Estate
   CMBW SE5 .... **118** C5
Coldharbour Leisure Centre
   ELTH/MOT SE9 .... **161** F2
Coldharbour Sports Ground
   ELTH/MOT SE9 .... **162** A2
Colebrooke Primary School *IS* N1 .... **10** C1
Colegrave Primary School *SRTFD* E15 .... **81** D2
Coleridge Primary School *HGT* N6 .... **57** D2
Colfes Preparatory School *LEE/GVPK* SE12 **142** B4

Coliseum Theatre *CHCR* WC2N **32** C2
College of Arms *BLKFR* EC4V **23** E5
College of Central London *SDTCH* EC2A .. **12** C5
College of Fuel Technology *HGT* N6 ..... **56** A1
The College of Law *FLST/FETLN* EC4A **22** A2
College of North West London
   KIL/WHAMP NW6 .... **72** A5
   WBLY HA9 .... **50** A5
   WLSDN NW10 .... **69** F2
College of Organists *FLST/FETLN* EC4A ... **22** B4
College Park School *BAY/PAD* W2 .... **14** B5
Collingwood Business Centre *ARCH* N19 .. **57** E5
Collins Method School *CRICK* NW2 ...... **70** C3
The Colonnades Shopping Centre
   BGVA SW1W **42** C4
Columbia Primary School *BETH* E2 ...... **13** F3
Colvestone Primary School *HACK* E8 .... **77** F2
Colville Primary School *NTGHL* W11 .... **89** F5
Comber Grove Primary School
   CMBW SE5 .... **118** C3
Comedy Theatre *STJS* SW1Y **32** A2
Comelle House Trading Estate
   DEPT SE8 .... **121** E1
Commonwealth Institute *KENS* W8 .... **101** F4
Community Arts Centre *GNWCH* SE10 ..... **122** B3
Community Centre (Island History Trust)
   POP/IOD E14 .... **104** C5
Community College & School
   GNWCH SE10 .... **122** C3
Complementary Health Centre *LEW* SE13 . **141** E4
Concord Business Centre *ACT* W3 .... **86** B4
Connaught Girls School *WAN* E11 .... **63** E3
Connaught School *BAY/PAD* W2 .... **17** E5
Consort Clinic *PECK* SE15 .... **138** E1
Consulate General of Monaco *SKENS* SW7 . **40** A4
Consulate General of the
   Republic of Guinea Bissau *KENS* W8 ... **39** E2
Consulate of Burkina Faso *BTSEA* SW11 .. **132** C1
Consulate of Chile *CAVSQ/HST* W1G **18** C1
Consulate of Colombia *GTPST* W1W **19** E4
Consulate of Eritrea *IS* N1 .... **10** B1
Consulate of Guinea *MYFR/PKLN* W1K **30** A2
Consulate of Panama *MYFR/PICC* W1J **30** C4
Convent of Jesus & Mary Infant School
   CRICK NW2 .... **70** C3
Convent of Jesus & Mary Language College
   WLSDN NW10 .... **69** F5
Conway Hall *FSBYW* WC1X **21** E2
Conway Medical Centre
   WOOL/PLUM SE18 .... **127** D1
Conway Primary School
   WOOL/PLUM SE18 .... **109** E5
Coopers' Hall *LVPST* EC2M **25** D3
Coopers Lane Primary School
   LEE/GVPK SE12 .... **160** A4
Cordwainers School *HOM* E9 .... **78** C4
Cornhill Sports Club *BECK* BR5 .... **158** A5
Coronet Cinema *NTGHL* W11 .... **26** A3
Corpus Christi RC Primary School
   BRXS/STRHM SW2 .... **135** F3
Cosmopolitan College *IS* N1 .... **9** E2
Courtauld Institute Galleries
   HOL/ALD WC2B **33** E1
Counterpoint Theatre *STPAN* WC1H **9** D3
Courtfield Medical Centre *ECT* SW5 .... **39** D5
Covent Garden Flower Market
   VX/NE SW8 .... **117** E2
Covent Garden Medical Centre
   LSQ/SEVD WC2H **20** C5
CPFC Soccer & Sports Centre
   BRXN/ST SW9 .... **135** F1
Crafts Council *IS* N1 .... **10** B2
Crampton Primary School *WALW* SE17 .... **47** F5
Cranbrook College *IL* IG1 .... **66** A4
The Craven Clinic *HMSMTH* W6 .... **100** B5
Craven Park Health Centre *WLSDN* NW10 . **69** D5
Craven Park Medical Centre *WLSDN* NW10 . **69** D5
Craven Park Primary School
   SEVS/STOTM N15 .... **60** A1
Crawford Primary School *CMBW* SE5 ..... **118** C4
Crawford Upper School *MBLAR* W1H **17** E3
Creekmouth Industrial Estate *BARK* IG11 **97** F5
Creek Road Health Centre *DEPT* SE8 .... **122** A2
Creek Road Industrial Estate *DEPT* SE8 . **122** B2
Cremer Business Centre *BETH* E2 .... **13** E2
Crewe House *MYFR/PICC* W1J **30** C3
Cricket Pavilion *WEST* SW1P **44** A4
Cricklefield Stadium *IL* IG1 .... **67** E4
Cricklewood Trading Estate *CRICK* NW2 . **53** E5
Criterion Theatre *MYFR/PICC* W1J **31** F2
Crofton Leisure Centre *BROCKY* SE4 .... **140** A4
Crofton School *BROCKY* SE4 .... **140** A4
Cromwell Business Centre *BARK* IG11 ... **97** E3
Cromwell Hospital *KENS* W8 .... **38** C4

Cromwell Industrial Estate LEY E10 ....61 E3
Crouch Hill Recreation Centre ARCH N19 .....57 E2
Crown Close Business Centre BOW E3 ....80 A5
Crown Court at the Borough STHWK SE1 ......35 D5
Crowndale Health Centre CAMTN NW1 ....7 F1
Crown Lane Primary School WNWD SE27 .....154 B5
Crown Woods School ELTH/MOT SE9 ....144 C3
Crusader Industrial Estate FSBYPK N4 ....58 C1
Crusoe House School IS N1 ....12 A3
Cubitt Town Primary School
POP/IOD E14 ....104 C4
Culloden Primary School POP/IOD E14 ....93 D5
Cumberland Business Park WLSDN NW10 .....86 B2
Cumberland Comprehensive School
CAN/RD E16 ....93 F4
Cumberland Park Industrial Estate
WLSDN NW10 ....88 A2
The Cuming Museum WALW SE17 ....47 E5
Curwen Primary School PLSTW E13 ....94 A1
Curzon Mayfair Cinema MYFR/PICC W1J 32 C4
Curzon Soho Cinema SOHO/SHAV W1D 32 B1
Cutlers' Hall STP EC4M 23 D4
Cutty Sark GNWCH SE10 ....122 C2
Cygnet Clinic Beckton EHAM E6 ....96 B5
Cygnus Business Centre WLSDN NW10 ......69 C2
Cyprus College of Art WNWD SE27 ....154 B4
Cyril Jackson Primary School
POP/IOD E14 ....103 F1
Daily Mirror Industrial Estate FLST/FETLN EC4A ..22 B3
Daily Telegraph POP/IOD E14 ....104 A4
Dali Universal Exhibition STHWK SE1 ....35 D5
Dallington School FSBYE EC1V 11 D5
Dalmain Primary School FSTH SE23 ....157 E1
Damilola Taylor Centre PECK SE15 ....119 F3
Darell Primary School RCH/KEW TW9 ......128 A1
Datapoint Business Centre CAN/RD E16 .....93 D3
Daubeney Primary School CLPT E5 ....79 F1
David Game College KENS W8 ....26 A5
David Game Tutorial College SKENS SW7 ....40 A5
David Lloyd Leisure Centre SKENS SW7 .....39 E4
Davies Lane Primary School WAN E11 ......63 F4
Davies's College STHWK SE1 ....35 J4
Dawlish Primary School LEY E10 ....62 C4
Days Lane Primary School BFN/LL DA15 ....145 F4
De Beauvoir Primary School IS N1 ....77 E3
Department for Environment,
Food & Rural Affairs WHALL SW1A 32 C3
Department of Health WHALL SW1A 32 C5
Department of Trade & Industry
STJSPK SW1H 44 B2
Deptford Business Centre DEPT SE8 ....121 F1
Deptford Green School NWCR SE14 ....121 F3
Deptford Park Business Centre
DEPT SE8 ....121 E1
Deptford Park Primary School DEPT SE8 ....121 E1
Deptford Trading Estate DEPT SE8 ....121 E1
Dersingham Infant School MNPK E12 ....83 F2
Derwentwater Primary School ACT W3 .....98 A2
Discovery Business Park
BERM/RHTH SE16 ....102 A4
Design Museum STHWK SE1 ....37 F4
Devonshire Hospital MHST W1U 18 B2
Devonshire Road Preparatory School
HAMP NW3 ....72 C2
Devonshire House School HAMP NW3 ....72 C2
Diamond College SOHO/SHAV W1D 20 B4
The Dickens House Museum
BMSBY WC1N 21 E1
Docklands Medical Centre POP/IOD E14 ....104 A5
Docklands Sailing Centre POP/IOD E14 .....104 A5
Docklands Sailing & Watersports Centre
POP/IOD E14 ....103 F4
Dockmaster's House POP/IOD E14 ....104 A1
Dockyard Industrial Estate
WOOL/PLUM SE18 ....107 E4
Dog Kennel Hill Primary School
CMBW SE5 ....137 E1
Dolphin School BTSEA SW11 ....133 F3
Dome GNWCH SE10 ....105 E2
Dominion Business Centre NOXST/BSQ WC1A ...20 B4
Donmar Warehouse Theatre
LSQ/SEVD WC2H 20 C5
Donnington Primary School WLSDN NW10 ...70 B4
Dorma Trading Park LEY E10 ....61 D3
Dorset Road Infant School
ELTH/MOT SE9 ....161 E2
Douglas Bader Foundation
PUT/ROE SW15 ....130 A4
Downderry Primary School BMLY BR1 ....159 E4
Downham Health Centre BMLY BR1 ....159 F4
Downhall Primary School
CNTH/NBYPK IG2 ....67 E2
Downsview School CLPT E5 ....78 B1
Drapers Hall LOTH EC2R 24 B4
Drapers Sports Ground SRTFD E15 ....80 C1

Drayton Park Primary School HBRY N5 ......76 A2
DRCA Business Centre BTSEA SW11 ....116 A4
Drew Primary School CAN/RD E16 ....107 E2
Dr Johnson's House FLST/FETLN EC4A 22 B5
Drury Way Industrial Estate WLSDN NW10 ...69 D1
Duchess Theatre COVGDN WC2E 33 E1
Duff Miller College SKENS SW7 ....39 F4
Duke of York Column STJS SW1Y 32 A4
Duke of York's HQ CHEL SW3 ....41 F5
Duke of York Theatre CHCR WC2N 32 C2
Dulverton Primary School BFN/LL DA15 ....163 D2
Dulwich College DUL SE21 ....155 E1
Dulwich College Preparatory School
DUL SE21 ....155 E3
Dulwich College Track DUL SE21 ....155 E3
Dulwich Hamlet FC CMBW SE5 ....137 E2
Dulwich Hamlet Junior School
HNHL SE24 ....137 D4
Dulwich Hospital DUL SE22 ....137 E2
Dulwich Leisure Centre EDUL SE22 ....138 A2
Dulwich Medical Centre EDUL SE22 ....138 A3
Dulwich Picture Gallery DUL SE21 ....137 D5
Dulwich & Sydenham Hill Golf Club
DUL SE21 ....156 A2
Dulwich Village CE Infant School
DUL SE21 ....137 E4
Dunbar Wharf POP/IOD E14 ....103 F1
Duncombe Primary School ARCH N19 ....57 E3
Dundee Wharf POP/IOD E14 ....103 F1
Dunraven School (Lower School)
STRHM/NOR SW16 ....153 F3
Dunraven School (Upper School)
STRHM/NOR SW16 ....153 F3
Durand Primary School BRXN/ST SW9 .....117 F4
Eaglesfield School WOOL/PLUM SE18 ......126 A4
Ealdham Primary School ELTH/MOT SE9 ...143 C2
Earlham Primary School FSTGT E7 ....81 F2
Earl's Court Exhibition Centre ECT SW5 ...114 A1
Earlsfield Primary School
WAND/EARL SW18 ....150 C2
Earth Gallery (Geological Museum)
SKENS SW7 ....40 A3
East Acton Primary School ACT W3 ....99 E1
East Beckton District Centre EHAM E6 ......95 F5
Eastbury Comprehensive School
BARK IG11 ....85 D4
Eastbury Comprehensive School
BARK IG11 ....85 F5
Eastbury Infant School BARK IG11 ....85 E4
Eastcote Primary School ELTH/MOT SE9 ...145 D1
East Greenwich Christ Church CE
Primary School GNWCH SE10 ....105 E5
East Ham Industrial Estate EHAM E6 ....95 D5
East Ham Jewish Cemetery EHAM E6 ....95 E2
East Ham Leisure Centre EHAM E6 ....83 F5
East Ham Memorial Hospital FSTGT E7 .....83 D4
East Ham Nature Reserve EHAM E6 ....95 F2
Eastlea Community School CAN/RD E16 .....93 E3
East London Business College WAN E11 ....63 E3
East London Cemetery PLSTW E13 ....93 F2
East London Crematorium PLSTW E13 ......93 F2
East London RFC EHAM E6 ....93 F1
East London RUFC PLSTW E13 ....93 F1
Eastman Dental Hospital FSBYW WC1X 9 E5
East Sheen Cemetery RCHPK/HAM TW10 ...128 C3
East Sheen Primary School
MORT/ESHN SW14 ....129 C2
East Wickham Primary School
WELL DA16 ....127 F4
Eaton House School KTBR SW1X 42 A4
Eaton Square Preparatory School
BGVA SW1W 42 C4
Eaton Square School PIM SW1V 43 E5
Ecclesbourne Primary School IS N1 ....77 D4
Eckerd College GWRST WC1E 20 A2
Ecole De Mime Corporel Theatre
De Lange Foux ARCH N19 ....57 E2
Eden College STHWK SE1 ....47 D2
Eden Medical Centre WKENS W14 ....101 F5
Edgebury Primary School CHST BR7 ....162 C4
Edge Business Centre CRICK NW2 ....52 B4
Edgware College HAMP NW3 ....72 C3
Edith Neville Primary School CAMTN NW1 ....8 A2
Edmund Waller Primary School
NWCR SE14 ....121 D5
Education Centre WOOL/PLUM SE18 ......104 A5
Edward Wilson Primary School
BAY/PAD W2 ....14 C2
Effra Primary School BRXS/STRHM SW2 ...136 A3
Effra Road Retail Park BRXS/STRHM SW2 ..136 A3
Eglinton Infant School WOOL/PLUM SE18 ..126 A2
Eglinton Junior School WOOL/PLUM SE18 ...126 A2
Eleanor Palmer Primary School
KTTN NW5 ....74 C1
Eleanor Smith Special School &
Primary Support Service PLSTW E13 ....94 A1

Electric Cinema *NTGHL* W11 .... 89 F5
Elephant & Castle Leisure Centre
LBTH SE11 .... 47 D4
Elephant & Castle Shopping Centre
STHWK SE1 .... 47 D3
Elfrida Primary School *CAT* SE6 .... 158 B4
Eliot Bank Primary School *FSTH* SE23 .... 156 B2
Elizabeth Garrett Anderson Hospital
CAMTN NW1 .... 8 B4
Elizabeth Garrett Anderson School *IS* N1 .... 9 F1
Elizabeth Selby Infant School *BETH* E2 .... 90 A2
Elizabeth Trading Estate *NWCR* SE14 .... 121 D2
Ellen Wilkinson Primary School *EHAM* E6 .... 95 D4
Ellerslie Square Industrial Estate
CLAP SW4 .... 135 C2
Elliott Foundation School
PUT/ROE SW15 .... 130 C4
Elm Court School *WNWD* SE27 .... 154 B2
Elmhurst Primary School *FSTGT* E7 .... 82 B4
Elm Wood Primary School *WNWD* SE27 .... 155 D5
Elsdale Street Health Centre *HOM* E9 .... 78 C4
Elsley Primary School *BTSEA* SW11 .... 134 A1
Eltham Bus Station *ELTH/MOT* SE9 .... 143 F5
Eltham Cemetery *ELTH/MOT* SE9 .... 144 C2
Eltham CE Primary School
ELTH/MOT SE9 .... 143 F3
Eltham College *ELTH/MOT* SE9 .... 161 D2
Eltham College Junior School
ELTH/MOT SE9 .... 161 D1
Eltham Crematorium *ELTH/MOT* SE9 .... 145 D2
Eltham Green School *ELTH/MOT* SE9 .... 143 D4
Eltham Health Clinic *ELTH/MOT* SE9 .... 143 E3
Eltham Health & Fitness Centre
ELTH/MOT SE9 .... 144 A4
Eltham Hill Technology College
ELTH/MOT SE9 .... 143 E4
Eltham Palace (Remains) *ELTH/MOT* SE9 .... 143 F5
Eltham Pools *ELTH/MOT* SE9 .... 143 E3
Eltham Warren Golf Club *ELTH/MOT* SE9 .... 144 B3
Emanuel School *WAND/EARL* SW18 .... 133 D3
Embankment Pier *CHCR* WC2N 33 E5
Embassy of Thailand *SKENS* SW7 .... 39 F3
Embassy of Afghanistan *SKENS* SW7 .... 40 A1
Embassy of Albania *BCVA* SW1W 43 D3
Embassy of Algeria *NTGHL* W11 .... 101 D2
Embassy of Angola *MYFR/PKLN* W1K 30 A2
Embassy of Argentina *MYFR/PKLN* W1K 30 C1
Embassy of Armenia *KENS* W8 .... 38 C2
Embassy of Austria *KTBR* SW1X 42 A2
Embassy of Bahrain *SKENS* SW7 .... 39 E3
Embassy of Belarus *KENS* W8 .... 39 D1
Embassy of Belgium *KTBR* SW1X 42 B3
Embassy of Bolivia *KTBR* SW1X 42 B3
Embassy of Bosnia-Herzegovina
CAVSO/HST W1G 19 D4
Embassy of Brazil *MYFR/PKLN* W1K 30 A1
Embassy of Bulgaria *SKENS* SW7 .... 39 F2
Embassy of Cameroon *WKENS* W14 .... 101 D2
Embassy of China *CAVSO/HST* W1G 18 C2
Embassy of Costa Rica *BAY/PAD* W2 .... 27 F1
Embassy of Cote d'Ivoire *KTBR* SW1X 42 B2
Embassy of Croatia *GTPST* W1W 19 D1
Embassy of Cuba *HHOL* WC1V 20 C4
Embassy of the Democratic Republic
of the Congo *KTBR* SW1X 41 F3
Embassy of Denmark *KTBR* SW1X 41 E2
Embassy of The Dominican Republic
BAY/PAD W2 .... 15 D3
Embassy of Ecuador *KTBR* SW1X 41 E2
Embassy of Egypt *MYFR/PICC* W1J 30 C3
Embassy of Estonia *SKENS* SW7 .... 39 F1
Embassy of Ethiopia *SKENS* SW7 .... 40 B1
Embassy of France *KTBR* SW1X 29 F5
Embassy of Gabon *SKENS* SW7 .... 39 F3
Embassy of Georgia *KENS* W8 .... 38 C1
Embassy of Germany *KTBR* SW1X 42 A2
Embassy of Ghana *HGT* N6 .... 56 B3
Embassy of Greece *KENS* W8 .... 101 F2
Embassy of Guatemala *WBPTN* SW10 .... 114 A3
Embassy of Honduras *MBLAR* W1H 17 F2
Embassy of Hungary *KTBR* SW1X 42 A4
Embassy of Iceland *KTBR* SW1X 42 A4
Embassy of Indonesia *MYFR/PKLN* W1K 30 B2
Embassy of Iran *SKENS* SW7 .... 40 B1
Embassy of Iraq *SKENS* SW7 .... 39 F2
Embassy of Ireland *KTBR* SW1X 42 C1
Embassy of Israel *KENS* W8 .... 27 D5
Embassy of Italy *MYFR/PICC* W1K 30 B1
Embassy of Japan *MYFR/PICC* W1J 31 D4
Embassy of Jordan *SKENS* SW7 .... 38 C3
Embassy of Korea *WESTW* SW1E 43 F2
Embassy of Kryrgyzstan *MBLAR* W1H 17 F2
Embassy of Kuwait *KTBR* SW1X 29 F5
Embassy of Latvia *CAMTN* NW1 .... 18 C1

Embassy of Lebanon *KENS* W8 .... 26 C3
Embassy of Liberia *BAY/PAD* W2 .... 26 B1
Embassy of Lithuania *MBLAR* W1H 17 E3
Embassy of Luxembourg *KTBR* SW1X 42 A1
Embassy of Mexico *MYFR/PICC* W1J 30 C4
Embassy of Mongolia *KENS* W8 .... 39 D1
Embassy of Morocco *SKENS* SW7 .... 39 E4
Embassy of Mozambique *FITZ* W1T 19 E1
Embassy of Myanmar *MYFR/PICC* W1J 30 C3
Embassy of Nepal *KENS* W8 .... 26 C3
Embassy of The Netherlands *SKENS* SW7 .... 39 F1
Embassy of Norway *KTBR* SW1X 42 B2
Embassy of Paraguay *SKENS* SW7 .... 39 D3
Embassy of Peru *KTBR* SW1X 41 F2
Embassy of The Philippines *KENS* W8 .... 26 C4
Embassy of Poland *CAVSO/HST* W1G 18 C2
Embassy of Portugal *KTBR* SW1X 42 A1
Embassy of Qatar *MYFR/PKLN* W1K 30 B3
Embassy of The Republic of Senegal
CRICK NW2 .... 70 C4
Embassy of Romania *KENS* W8 .... 26 C5
Embassy of Russian Federation *KENS* W8 .... 26 C3
Embassy of Saudi Arabia *MYFR/PICC* W1J 30 C3
Embassy of Slovak Republic *KENS* W8 .... 26 C5
Embassy of Slovenia *CAVSO/HST* W1G 18 C4
Embassy of South Vietnam *KENS* W8 .... 39 D2
Embassy of Spain *KTBR* SW1X 42 B2
Embassy of Sudan *WHALL* SW1A 31 E4
Embassy of Sweden *MBLAR* W1H 17 E3
Embassy of Switzerland *MBLAR* W1H 17 F3
Embassy of Syria *KTBR* SW1X 42 A1
Embassy of Tunisia *SKENS* SW7 .... 40 B1
Embassy of Turkey *KTBR* SW1X 42 B1
Embassy of Turkmenistan *GTPST* W1W 19 E1
Embassy of Ukraine *NTGHL* W11 .... 101 F2
Embassy of the United Arab Emirates
SKENS SW7 .... 28 B5
Embassy of Uruguay *SKENS* SW7 .... 41 D2
Embassy of USA *MYFR/PKLN* W1K 30 A1
Embassy of Uzbekistan *NTGHL* W11 .... 101 F2
Embassy of Venezuela *KENS* W8 .... 40 B3
Embassy of Yemen *SKENS* SW7 .... 40 A4
Emery Theatre *POP/IOD* E14 .... 92 B5
Emmanuel CE Primary School
KIL/WHAMP NW6 .... 72 A2
Empire Cinema *LSO/SEVD* WC2H 32 B5
English Martyrs RC Primary School
WALW SE17 .... 48 A5
WCHPL E1 .... 25 F1
Ennersdale Primary School *LEW* SE13 .... 141 D3
Ensham Secondary School *TOOT* SW17 .... 151 E4
Enterprise Business Park *POP/IOD* E14 .... 104 B3
Enterprise Industrial Estate
BERM/RHTH SE16 .... 120 C1
Eric Liddell Sports Centre *ELTH/MOT* SE9 .... 161 D2
Ernest Bevin School *TOOT* SW17 .... 151 E4
Eros *MYFR/PICC* W1J 32 A2
Essendine Primary School
MV/WKIL W9 .... 2 B4
Essex Primary School *MNPK* E12 .... 83 E3
Ethelburga GM School *BTSEA* SW11 .... 115 E4
Euro Business Centre *SRTFD* E15 .... 81 F5
Eurolink Business Centre
BRXS/STRHM SW2 .... 136 A2
European School of Economics
KTBR SW1X 42 C1
European Vocational College
HDTCH EC3A 25 D5
Euro Way School London *FSBYPK* N4 .... 58 C2
Euston Centre *CAMTN* NW1 .... 7 F5
Euston Tower *CAMTN* NW1 .... 7 F5
Eveline Lowe Primary School *STHWK* SE1 .... 120 A1
Everyman Cinema *HAMP* NW3 .... 72 C1
EW Fact/Emile Woolf Colleges *HOLWY* N7 .... 75 E5
ExCeL Exhibition Centre *CAN/RD* E16 .... 106 C1
Exchange Square *SDTCH* EC2A 24 C2
The Exchange *IL* IG1 .... 66 B4
Exhibition Halls *STLK* EC1Y 23 F2
Eye Clinic *LSO/SEVD* WC2H 20 B4
Eye Hospital *HHOL* WC1V 20 C4
Faircharm Trading Estate *DEPT* SE8 .... 122 B5
Fairfax *EHAM* E6 .... 11 E1
The Faircross Complementary
Medical Centre *BARK* IG11 .... 85 E3
Fairlawn Primary School *FSTH* SE23 .... 138 C5
Fairley House School *WEST* SW1P 44 A3
Fairways Business Park *LEY* E10 .... 61 E4
Falconbrook JMI School *BTSEA* SW11 .... 115 D5
Falcon Business Centre *BTSEA* SW11 .... 133 E2
Falcon Park Industrial Estate
WLSDN NW10 .... 69 E2
Falkner House School *SKENS* SW7 .... 114 C1
Fanmakers' Hall *LVPST* EC2M 24 C4

Fan Museum *GNWCH* SE10 .... 122 C3
Faraday Building *BLKFR* EC4V 23 D5
Farm Lane Trading Estate *FUL/PGN* SW6 ... 114 A2
Fashion & Textile Design Museum
   STHWK SE1 .... 49 D1
Fenstanton J & I School
   BRXS/STRHM SW2 .... 154 A1
Fenton House *HAMP* NW3 .... 54 C5
Ferrier Industrial Estate
   WAND/EARL SW18 .... 132 B2
Festival Pier *STHWK* SE1 .... 33 F3
Financial Times *POP/IOD* E14 .... 92 C5
   STHWK SE1 .... 35 F3
Fine Arts College *HAMP* NW3 .... 73 G3
Finsbury Circus Medical Centre
   LVPST EC2M 24 B3
Finsbury Health Centre *CLKNW* EC1R 10 A5
Finsbury Leisure Centre *FSBYE* EC1V 11 F4
Finsbury Park Track *FSBYPK* N4 .... 58 B2
Firehouse School *TOOT* SW17 .... 151 F2
Fircroft Primary School *TOOT* SW17 ...... 151 F2
Fire Brigade HQ *STHWK* SE1 .... 45 E4
Fire Brigade Museum *STHWK* SE1 .... 35 E5
Firepower (Museum of Artillery)
   WOOL/PLUM SE18 .... 108 B4
Fisher Athletic FC *BERM/RHTH* SE16 ..... 103 D2
Fishmonger's Hall *CANST* EC4R 36 A2
Fitness Unlimited Leisure Centre *BOW* E3 ... 92 A1
Fitzjohns Primary School *HAMP* NW3 ...... 73 D2
Fitzrovia Medical Clinic *GTPST* W1W 19 E1
Fitzroy Nuffield Hospital *MBLAR* W1H 17 F4
Five Bridges School *LBTH* SE11 .... 117 F1
Flamsteed House Museum *GNWCH* SE10 ... 123 D3
Flaxman Sports Centre *CMBW* SE5 .... 118 C5
Fleet Primary School *HAMP* NW3 .... 73 F2
Fleming Lab Museum *BAY/PAD* W2 .... 16 B3
Flora Gardens Primary School
   HMSMTH W6 .... 100 B5
Florence Nightingale Museum *STHWK* SE1 ... 45 E4
Florida State University *RSQ* WC1B 20 B5
Flutters Leisure Centre *FUL/PGN* SW6 .... 114 A3
FOB School *CLPT* E5 .... 60 A2
The Foot Clinic *WIM/MER* SW19 .... 149 E5
The Ford College *CONDST* W1S 31 D1
Foreign & Commonwealth Office
   WHALL SW1A 32 B5
Foreland Medical Centre *NTGHL* W11 .... 101 E1
Forest Business Park *WALTH* E17 .... 61 D2
Forest Gate Community School *FSTGT* E7 ... 82 A2
Forest Hill Business Centre *FSTH* SE23 ... 156 C2
Forest Hill Industrial Estate *FSTH* SE23 .. 156 C2
Forest Hill School *FSTH* SE26 .... 157 D3
Forest Hills Pools *FSTH* SE23 .... 156 C2
Forest House Business Centre *WAN* E11 .. 63 F2
The Former Health Centre *CHARL* SE7 .... 107 D5
Forster Park Primary School *CAT* SE6 .... 159 E3
Fortune Theatre *HOL/ALD* WC2B 21 D5
Fossdene Primary School *CHARL* SE7 .... 124 B1
The Foundling Museum *BMSBY* WC1N 9 D5
Fountayne Road Health Centre *CLPT* E5 .. 60 A4
Foxfield Primary School
   WOOL/PLUM SE18 .... 126 C1
Fox Primary School *KENS* W8 .... 26 A4
Freuchen Medical Centre *WLSDN* NW10 ... 87 F1
Freud Museum *HAMP* NW3 .... 73 D3
Friars Primary Foundation School
   STHWK SE1 .... 34 C5
Friends House *CAMTN* NW1 .... 8 A4
Friends of Bar Ilan University
   GLDGN NW11 .... 54 A3
Friends of the Hebrew University
   CAMTN NW1 .... 74 B5
Froebel College *PUT/ROE* SW15 .... 130 A4
Frogmore Industrial Estate *HBRY* N5 ...... 76 C1
   WLSDN NW10 .... 86 C2
Fryent Country Park *WBLY* HA9 .... 50 A2
Fryent Medical Centre *CDALE/KGS* NW9 .. 50 C2
Fryent Primary School *CDALE/KGS* NW9 .. 50 C2
Fulham Clinic *FUL/PGN* SW6 .... 113 F2
Fulham Cross School *FUL/PGN* SW6 ..... 113 D3
Fulham FC (Craven Cottage) *BARN* SW13 ... 112 C4
Fulham Medical Centre *FUL/PGN* SW6 .... 114 B3
Fulham Palace *FUL/PGN* SW6 .... 113 E5
Fulham Preparatory School *FUL/PGN* SW6 . 113 E5
Fulham Primary School *FUL/PGN* SW6 .... 114 A2
Fulham & South Kensington Institute
   WBPTN SW10 .... 114 C1

Fulham Warner Village Cinema
   FUL/PGN SW6 .... 114 A3
Fuller Smith & Turner Sports Club
   CHSWK W4 .... 111 E4
Future Business College *CONDST* W1S 19 D5
Gainsborough Primary School *HOM* E9 ..... 79 F5
   SRTFD E15 .... 93 E2
Galleywall Primary School
   BERM/RHTH SE16 .... 102 B5
Gallions Mount Primary School
   WOOL/PLUM SE18 .... 127 F1
Gallions Primary School *EHAM* E6 .... 96 B5
Gants Hill Medical Centre
   CNTH/NBYPK IG2 .... 66 A1
Gardener Industrial Estate *BECK* BR3 .... 157 E5
Garden House School *BCVA* SW1W 116 A1
Garratt Park Secondary Special Sch
   WAND/EARL SW18 .... 150 B3
Garrick Theatre *LSQ/SEVD* WC2H 32 C2
Gascoigne Primary School *BARK* IG11 .... 84 C5
Gate Cinema *NTGHL* W11 .... 26 A3
Gatehouse School *BETH* E2 .... 91 D1
The Gatehouse Theatre *HGT* N6 .... 56 A2
The Gate Theatre *NTGHL* W11 .... 26 A3
Gateway Industrial Estate *WLSDN* NW10 .. 87 F2
Gateway Primary School *STJWD* NW8 .... 2 B3
Gayhurst Primary School *HACK* E8 .... 78 A4
Geffrye Museum *BETH* E2 .... 13 D2
Gemini Business Estate *NWCR* SE14 .... 121 D3
General Medical Clinics *WCHPL* E1 .... 25 E2
Genesis Cinema *WCHPL* E1 .... 90 C3
Geoffrey Chaucer School *STHWK* SE1 .... 48 B3
The Geoffrey Lloyd Foulkes Clinic *IL* IG1 .. 66 A4
George Eliot J & I School *STJWD* NW8 .... 72 C5
George Green Mixed School *POP/IOD* E14 .. 122 C1
George Lowe Court *BAY/PAD* W2 .... 14 C2
George Mitchell School *LEY* E10 .... 62 B3
George Mitchell School Annexe *LEY* E10 .. 62 B3
George Tomlinson Primary School
   WAN E11 .... 63 E3
Germal College *FSBYPK* N4 .... 58 B3
Gibbs Green Special School *WKENS* W14 .. 113 F1
The Gielgud Theatre *SOHO/SHAV* W1D ... 32 A1
Giffin Business Centre *DEPT* SE8 .... 122 C4
Gilbert Collection *TPL/STR* WC2E 33 E1
   WAP E1W 102 B1
Gillespie Primary School *FSBYPK* N4 ...... 58 B5
Gilwell Hall *CITYW* EC2V 23 F3
Gladstone Court Business Centre
   VX/NE SW8 .... 116 C4
Gladstone Medical Centre *CRICK* NW2 .... 69 C4
Gladstone Park Primary School
   WLSDN NW10 .... 70 B2
Glaziers/Scientific Instrument Makers Hall
   STHWK SE1 .... 36 A3
Gleen Lecky Health Centre
   PUT/ROE SW15 .... 131 D2
Glenbrook Primary School *CLAP* SW4 .... 135 D4
Glendower Preparatory School
   SKENS SW7 .... 39 F4
Glenham College *IL* IG1 .... 66 B4
Globe Primary School *BETH* E2 .... 90 C2
Globe Wharf *BERM/RHTH* SE16 .... 103 D1
Gloucester Primary School *PECK* SE15 .. 119 E3
Godolphin & Latymer School
   HMSMTH W6 .... 100 B5
Godwin Junior School *FSTGT* E7 .... 82 B1
Golborne Medical Centre *NKENS* W10 .... 89 F3
Golden Hinde Educational Museum
   STHWK SE1 .... 36 A2
Golders Green Crematorium *GLDGN* NW11 ... 54 A2
Golders Green Health Centre
   GLDGN NW11 .... 54 B3
Golders Hill Health Centre *EFNCH* N2 .... 54 C1
Golders Hill School *GLDGN* NW11 .... 54 A2
Goldhawk Industrial Estate *SHB* W12 .... 100 B4
Goldsmiths College *BROCKY* SE4 .... 122 A4
   DEPT SE8 .... 122 A2
   LEW SE13 .... 141 E2
   NWCR SE14 .... 121 E4
Goldsmiths Hall *STBT* EC1A 23 E4
Goodinge Health Centre *HOLWY* N7 ...... 75 E5
Goodrich J & I School *EDUL* SE22 .... 138 A4
Good Shepherd RC Primary School
   BMLY BR1 .... 159 F4
The Good Shepherd RC Primary School
   SHB W12 .... 99 F3
Goose Green Trading Estate *EDUL* SE22 .. 138 A2
Gordonbrock Primary School
   BROCKY SE4 .... 140 A3
Gordon Hospital *WEST* SW1P 44 A5
Gordon Infant School *IL* IG1 .... 67 D5
Gordon Primary School *ELTH/MOT* SE9 .. 143 F2
Gospel Oak Primary School *HAMP* NW3 .. 74 A1
Gower House School *CDALE/KGS* NW9 ... 50 C4

Grace Theatre at the Latchmere
  BTSEA SW11 .... 115 F5
Grafton Primary School *HOLWY* N7 ...... 57 E5
Granard Primary School *PUT/ROE* SW15 .. 130 B4
Granby Sports Club *ELTH/MOT* SE9 ...... 161 G5
Grande Vitesse Industrial Centre
  STHWK SE1 .... 35 D4
Grand Union Industrial Estate
  WLSDN NW10 .... 86 B1
Grange Infant School *CAN/RD* E16 .... 93 F2
The Grange Museum *CRICK* NW2 .... 69 F1
Grange Primary School *STHWK* SE1 ...... 48 C3
Grangewood Independent School
  FSTGT E7 .... 83 D4
Granville Road Industrial Estate
  CRICK NW2 .... 53 F4
Grasmere Primary School
  STNW/STAM N16 .... 77 D1
Grazebrook Primary School
  STNW/STAM N16 .... 59 E3
Great Chapel Street Medical Centre
  SOHO/SHAV W1D 20 A4
Greater London Authority Headquarters
  (City Hall) *STHWK* SE1 .... 37 D4
Great Jubilee Wharf *WAP* E1W 102 C2
Greenacres Primary School
  ELTH/MOT SE9 .... 162 A2
Greenfield Medical Centre *CRICK* NW2 ... 53 E5
Greenfields Junior School *SHB* W12 ...... 99 F1
Greengate Medical Centre *PLSTW* E13 .... 94 B2
Greenhalth Business Centre *BETH* E2 ..... 90 B2
Greenhill Park Medical Centre
  WLSDN NW10 .... 69 G5
Greenland Pier *BERM/RHTH* SE16 .... 103 F4
Green Lane Business Park *ELTH/MOT* SE9 . 162 A2
Greenmead Primary School
  PUT/ROE SW15 .... 130 B3
Greenshields Industrial Estate
  CAN/RD E16 .... 106 A2
Greenside Primary School *SHB* W12 ...... 100 A3
Greenside Primary School
  WOOL/PLUM SE18 .... 127 D1
Greenvale School *FSTH* SE23 .... 157 E3
Greenwich Centre Business Park
  DEPT SE8 .... 122 B3
Greenwich Cinema *GNWCH* SE10 .... 122 C3
Greenwich College *GNWCH* SE10 .... 122 C3
Greenwich Community College
  WOOL/PLUM SE18 .... 108 B5
  WOOL/PLUM SE18 .... 127 D2
Greenwich Hospital *GNWCH* SE10 .... 123 F1
Greenwich Industrial Estate *CHARL* SE7 .. 106 B5
  GNWCH SE10 .... 122 B3
Greenwich Natural Health Centre
  GNWCH SE10 .... 122 C3
Greenwich Theatre & Art Gallery
  GNWCH SE10 .... 123 D3
Greenwich University Library
  GNWCH SE10 .... 122 C2
Greenwood School *WOOL/PLUM* SE18 ... 127 G4
Greenwood Theatre *STHWK* SE1 .... 36 B5
Gresham College *FLST/FETLN* EC4A 22 A3
Gresham Way Industrial Estate
  WIM/MER SW19 .... 150 B3
The Greycoat Hospital *WEST* SW1P 44 A5
Grey Coat Hospital Upper School
  WEST SW1P 44 A3
Griffen Manor School *WOOL/PLUM* SE18 . 127 G4
Grinling Gibbons Primary School
  DEPT SE8 .... 121 F2
Grocers' Hall *CITYW* EC2V 24 C5
Grove Hall School *WB* 26 B3
Grove Park School *CHSWK* W4 .... 110 C2
Grove Health Centre *HMSMTH* W6 ...... 100 B5
Grove House School *WWWD* SE27 .... 154 B2
Grove Medical Centre *DEPT* SE8 .... 103 E5
The Grove Medical Centre *ARCH* N19 .... 56 C4
Grove Park Primary School *CHSWK* W4 ... 110 C2
Guardian Angels RC Primary School
  BOW E3 .... 91 E3
Guardian Newspapers *POP/IOD* E14 ..... 104 B3
Guards' Chapel & Museum *WHALL* SW1A . 44 A1
Guildhall Art Gallery *LOTH* EC2R 24 A4
Guildhall *BARB* EC2Y 23 F2
Guildhall School of Music & Drama
  STLK EC1Y 23 F1
Guildhall University *WCHPL* E1 .... 90 A5
Gunnersbury Park Museum *ACT* W3 ...... 98 A4
Guys Hospital *STHWK* SE1 .... 36 B4
Guys Kings & St Thomas School of Medicine
  CMBW SE5 .... 118 C5
Gwyn Jones Primary School *WAN* E11 .... 63 D2
GX Superbowl *EHAM* E6 .... 96 A4
Gypsy Moth IV *GNWCH* SE10 .... 122 C2

Haberdashers Askes Hatcham College
  NWCR SE14 .... 121 E4
  NWCR SE14 .... 121 E5
Haberdashers' Hall *CITYW* EC2V 23 F4
Hackney Business Centre *HACK* E8 ...... 78 B3
Hackney Community College *CLPT* E5 .... 60 B5
  IS N1 .... 12 C2
Hackney Empire Variety Theatre
  HACK E8 .... 78 B3
Hackney Free & Parochial CE School
  HOM E9 .... 78 C3
Hackney Hospital *HOM* E9 .... 79 E2
The Hackney Museum *HOM* E9 .... 78 C5
Hackney Sports Centre *HOM* E9 .... 80 A1
Hadlow College *LEE/GVPK* SE12 .... 160 C1
The Haelan Clinic *CEND/HSY/T* N8 ...... 57 D1
Haggerston School *BETH* E2 .... 13 F1
Haggerston Swimming Pool *BETH* E2 .... 77 F5
Hague Primary School *BETH* E2 .... 90 B3
Haimo Primary School *ELTH/MOT* SE9 ... 143 G3
The Hale Clinic *REGST* W1B 19 D1
Half Moon Theatre *WCHPL* E1 .... 91 D3
Halley Primary School *POP/IOD* E14 .... 91 E4
Hallfield Clinic *BAY/PAD* W2 .... 15 E5
Hallfield J & I School *BAY/PAD* W2 ...... 15 D5
The Hall Junior School *HAMP* NW3 ..... 73 D5
Hallmark Trading Estate *WBLY* HA9 ..... 68 C1
Hall School Wimbledon *PUT/ROE* SW15 .. 148 A3
The Hall Senior School *HAMP* NW3 ...... 73 D3
Hallsville Primary School *CAN/RD* E16 ... 94 A5
Halstow Primary School *GNWCH* SE10 ... 123 F1
Hamer Indoor Market *BOW* E3 .... 91 F1
Hamilton Road Industrial Estate
  WNWD SE27 .... 155 D4
Hammersmith Apollo *HMSMTH* W6 ..... 112 C1
Hammersmith Cemetery *HMSMTH* W6 .. 113 D1
The Hammersmith Hospitals *SHB* W12 .. 88 A5
Hammersmith Industrial Estate
  HMSMTH W6 .... 112 C2
Hammersmith New Cemetery
  RCH/KEW TW9 .... 110 B5
Hammersmith Palais *HMSMTH* W6 ..... 100 C5
Hammersmith Physio & Sports Injury Clinic
  HMSMTH W6 .... 100 C5
Hammersmith & West London College
  WKENS W14 .... 101 D5
Hampden Gurney School *MBLAR* W1H 17 D3
The Hampshire School (Knightsbridge)
  SKENS SW7 .... 40 C1
The Hampshire School *BAY/PAD* W2 .... 27 D1
Hampstead Cricket Club *KIL/WHAMP* NW6 72 B2
Hampstead Golf Club *EFNCH* N2 .... 54 C2
Hampstead Hill School *HAMP* NW3 ...... 73 F1
Hampstead Medical Centre *HAMP* NW3 .. 72 C1
Hampstead Parochial CE School
  HAMP NW3 .... 72 C1
Hampstead School *CRICK* NW2 .... 71 E1
Hampstead School of English
  KIL/WHAMP NW6 .... 72 A1
Hampstead Theatre *HAMP* NW3 .... 73 D4
Hanover Primary School *IS* N1 .... 11 D1
Hanover Trading Estate *HOLWY* N7 ..... 75 E2
Hanover West Industrial Estate
  WLSDN NW10 .... 86 C2
Harbinger Primary School *POP/IOD* E14 .. 104 A5
Harborough School *ARCH* N19 .... 57 D4
Hargrave Park Primary School *ARCH* N19 . 56 C4
Haringey Magistrates Court *HGT* N6 .... 56 A1
Harlesden Primary School *WLSDN* NW10 . 87 E1
Harley Medical Centre *CAVSQ/HST* W1G .. 18 C4
The Harley Medical Centre *CANST* EC4R .. 35 F1
Harley Street Clinic *CAVSQ/HST* W1G 18 C2
  CAVSQ/HST W1G 18 C3
Harp Business Centre *CRICK* NW2 ...... 52 A4
Harpley School *WCHPL* E1 .... 90 C3
Harrington Hill Primary School *CLPT* E5 . 60 B3
Harrodian School *BARN* SW13 .... 111 F5
Harrods Store *CHEL* SW3 .... 41 E2
Harrow Road Health Centre *BAY/PAD* W2 . 14 B2
Harry Gosling Primary School *WCHPL* E1 . 90 A5
Hartley Primary School *EHAM* E6 ...... 83 E5
Haselrigge School *CLAP* SW4 .... 135 D2
Haseltine Primary School *CAT* SE6 ...... 157 F4
Haslemere Industrial Estate
  WAND/EARL SW18 .... 150 B2
Hastings Clinic *BRXS/STRHM* SW2 ...... 135 F3
Hatcham Mews Business Centre
  NWCR SE14 .... 121 D3
Haverstock School *CAMTN* NW1 .... 74 A3
Hawkins Clinic *PUT/ROE* SW15 .... 131 D2
Hawley Infant School *CAMTN* NW1 ..... 74 B4
Haymerle School *PECK* SE15 .... 120 A2
Hays Galleria *STHWK* SE1 .... 36 C3
Hayward Gallery *STHWK* SE1 .... 33 F4
Hazeldene Medical Centre *WBLY* HA9 ... 68 B5

Healy Medical Centre *CLPT* E5 .... 60 B3
The Heart Hospital *CAVSQ/HST* W1G 18 B3
Heathbrook Primary School *VX/NE* SW8 .... 116 C5
Heath House Preparatory School
  BKHTH/KID SE3 .... 123 E5
Heathmere Primary School
  PUT/ROE SW15 .... 148 A1
Heatside Preparatory School
  HAMP NW3 .... 72 C1
Heber Primary School *EDUL* SE22 .... 137 F4
Heckford Street Business Centre
  WAP E1W 103 D1
Hedges & Butler Estate *SRTFD* E15 .... 92 C1
Helena Road Clinic *WLSDN* NW10 .... 70 B1
Heliport Industrial Estate *BTSEA* SW11 ... 115 D5
Hellenic College of London *KTBR* SW1X ... 41 E3
Helston Court Business Centre
  WIM/MER SW19 .... 148 B5
Hendon FC *CRICK* NW2 .... 53 D4
Hendon Youth Sports Centre *CRICK* NW2 ... 53 D2
Henry Cavendish Primary School
  BAL SW12 .... 152 C1
Henry Compton School *FUL/PGN* SW6 ..... 113 D4
Henry Fawcett Primary School
  LBTH SE11 .... 118 A2
Henwick Primary School *ELTH/MOT* SE9 ... 143 D1
Herbert Morrison Primary School
  VX/NE SW8 .... 117 E3
Hereward House School *HAMP* NW3 .... 73 E3
Her Majestys Theatre *STJS* SW1Y 32 B5
Hermitage Primary School *WAP* E1W 102 A2
Herne Hill School *HNHL* SE24 .... 136 C3
Herne Hill Stadium (Cycle Centre)
  HNHL SE24 .... 137 D4
Heron Industrial Estate *SRTFD* E15 .... 92 B1
Heronsgate Primary School *THMD* SE28 ... 109 D4
Heron Trading Estate *ACT* W3 .... 86 B4
Heythrop College *KENS* W8 .... 38 C2
Higgs Industrial Estate *BRXN/ST* SW9 ..... 136 B1
Highbury Corner Magistrates Court
  HOLWY N7 .... 76 A3
Highbury Fields School *HBRY* N5 .... 76 B2
Highbury Grove School *HBRY* N5 .... 76 C2
Highbury Park Clinic *HBRY* N5 .... 58 B5
Highbury Pool *HBRY* N5 .... 76 B3
Highbury Quadrant Primary School
  HBRY N5 .... 76 C1
High Commission of Angola
  MYFR/PKLN W1K 30 B1
High Commission of Antigua & Barbuda
  MHST W1U 18 A4
High Commission of Bahamas
  MYFR/PICC W1J 30 B3
High Commission of Bangladesh
  SKENS SW7 .... 39 F2
High Commission of Barbados *FITZ* W1T ... 20 A4
High Commission of Belize
  CAVSQ/HST W1G 18 C4
High Commission of Botswana
  OXSTW W1C 18 C5
High Commission of Brunei *BAY/PAD* W2 ... 16 B3
  KTBR SW1X 42 A2
High Commission of Cyprus *CONDST* W1S ... 19 D5
High Commission of Dominica *ECT* SW5 ... 30 A4
High Commission of Fiji *SKENS* SW7 .... 39 E1
High Commission of the Gambia *KENS* W8 ... 39 D1
High Commission of Grenada *ECT* SW5 ..... 114 B1
High Commission of Guyana *NTGHL* W11 ... 26 C2
High Commission of Jamaica *SKENS* SW7 ... 40 A1
High Commission of Kenya
  CAVSQ/HST W1G 18 C2
High Commission of Lesotho *KTBR* SW1X ... 42 A2
High Commission of Malawi
  MYFR/PKLN W1K 30 C1
High Commission of Malaysia *KTBR* SW1X ... 42 B1
  MBLAR W1H 17 E4
High Commission of the Maldives
  MHST W1U 18 A2
High Commission of Malta
  MYFR/PICC W1J 31 F2
High Commission of Mauritius *SKENS* SW7 ... 39 F3
High Commission of Namibia
  CAVSQ/HST W1G 19 D3
High Commission of New Zealand
  STJS SW1Y 32 A3
High Commission of Nigeria
  CHCR WC2N 32 C3
  EMB EC4Y 22 B5
High Commission of Pakistan *KTBR* SW1X ... 41 F2
High Commission of Papua New Guinea
  STJS SW1Y 32 A3
High Commission of St Vincent &
  The Grenadines *KENS* W8 .... 39 D1

High Commission of Seychelles
  MBLAR W1H 17 F2
High Commission of Sierra Leone
  OXSTW W1C 19 E4
High Commission of Singapore
  KTBR SW1X 41 F1
  STJS SW1Y 32 A3
  WEST SW1P 43 F4
High Commission of South Africa
  CHCR WC2N 32 B3
High Commission of Sri Lanka
  BAY/PAD W2 .... 28 B1
High Commission of Swaziland
  WESTW SW1E 43 E2
High Commission of Tonga *MBLAR* W1H ... 17 D3
High Commission of Trinidad & Tobago
  KTBR SW1X 42 A2
High Commission of Uganda *STJS* SW1Y ... 32 B3
High Commission of Zambia *SKENS* SW7 ... 39 E1
High Commission of Zimbabwe
  CHCR WC2N 32 C2
Highfield School *WAND/EARL* SW18 .... 133 E5
Highgate Cemetery *HGT* N6 .... 56 A3
Highgate Golf Club *HGT* N6 .... 55 E1
Highgate Junior School *HGT* N6 .... 55 F2
Highgate Pre-Preparatory School *HGT* N6 ... 55 F1
Highgate Primary School *HGT* N6 .... 55 F1
Highgate Private Hospital *HGT* N6 .... 55 F1
Highgate School *HGT* N6 .... 55 F1
Highlands J & I School *IL* IG1 .... 65 F3
Highlands Primary School *IL* IG1 .... 65 F3
Highshore School *PECK* SE15 .... 119 F4
High View Primary School *BTSEA* SW11 ... 133 D2
The Highway Trading Centre *WAP* E1W ... 103 D1
Hillbrook Primary School *TOOT* SW17 ..... 151 F4
Hill House International School
  KTBR SW1X 41 E3
Hill House School *CHEL* SW3 .... 115 E2
Hill Mead Infant School *HNHL* SE24 .... 136 B2
Hillmead Primary School *BRXN/ST* SW9 ... 136 B2
Hilly Fields Medical Centre *BROCKY* SE4 ... 140 A3
Hinley Clinic *LBTH* SE11 .... 46 C5
Hispaniola *WHALL* SW1A 33 D4
Hitherfield Primary School
  STRHM/NOR SW16 .... 154 A2
Hither Green Cemetery *CAT* SE6 .... 159 F2
Hither Green Primary School *LEW* SE13 ... 141 D4
HM Prison *CLAP* SW4 .... 135 E4
  HOLWY N7 .... 75 F5
  HOLWY N7 .... 75 E1
  SHB W12 .... 88 A5
  WAND/EARL SW18 .... 133 D4
HMS Belfast *STHWK* SE1 .... 32 C2
HMS President *EMB* EC4Y 34 B1
Hogarth Business Park *CHSWK* W4 .... 111 E2
Hogarth Industrial Estate *WLSDN* NW10 ... 88 A3
Hogarth Primary School *CHSWK* W4 .... 111 E1
Hogarth's House *CHSWK* W4 .... 111 D2
Holbeach Primary School *CAT* SE6 .... 140 A5
Holborn College *WKENS* W14 .... 113 E2
Holborn Medical Centre *BMSBY* WC1N ... 21 E1
Holborn Town Hall *HHOL* WC1V 21 D4
Holland Park School *KENS* W8 .... 101 F3
Holland Park Theatre *KENS* W8 .... 101 F3
Holland Street Clinic *KENS* W8 .... 38 B1
Holloway School *HOLWY* N7 .... 75 D2
Hollydale Primary School *PECK* SE15 ..... 120 C5
The Holme *CAMTN* NW1 .... 5 F4
Holmleigh Primary School
  STNW/STAM N16 .... 59 F3
Holy Cross Primary School *FUL/PGN* SW6 ... 114 A4
Holy Cross RC Primary School *CAT* SE6 ... 158 C1
Holy Family RC Primary School
  ELTH/MOT SE9 .... 142 B2
  POP/IOD E14 .... 104 A1
Holy Ghost RC Primary School *BAL* SW12 ... 133 F5
Holy Trinity CE Primary School
  BGVA SW1W 42 A1
  BRXS/STRHM SW2 .... 135 F5
  FSTH SE23 .... 156 C2
  KIL/WHAMP NW6 .... 72 C3
  RCHPK/HAM TW10 .... 128 A3
Holy Trinity Haverstock Hill CE
  Primary School *CAMTN* NW1 .... 74 B4
Holy Trinity Primary School *HACK* E8 ..... 77 E3
Holy Trinity School *CHEL* SW3 .... 41 F4
Homerton Hospital *CLPT* E5 .... 79 D2
Homerton House School *HOM* E9 .... 78 C2
Homoeopathic Health Centre *PLSTW* E13 ... 94 A3
Honeywell Primary School *BTSEA* SW11 ... 133 F4
Honor Oak Crematorium *FSTH* SE23 .... 139 D3
Honor Oak Gallery *FSTH* SE23 .... 139 D4
Honor Oak Health Centre *BROCKY* SE4 ... 139 E2
Honourable Artillery Company HQ
  STLK EC1Y 24 A1

Horizon Industrial Estate *PECK* SE15 ...... 120 A2
Horizon School *STNW/STAM* N16 .... 77 E1
The Horniman Museum & Gardens
    FSTH SE23 .... 156 B1
Horniman Primary School *FSTH* SE23 ...... 156 B1
Horn Park Primary School
    LEE/GVPK SE12 .... 142 B5
Hornsby House School *BAL* SW12 .... 152 A1
Hornsey Rise Health Centre *ARCH* N19 ..... 57 D2
Horseferry Road Magistrates Court
    WEST SW1P 44 B3
Horse Guards Parade *WHALL* SW1A 32 B4
Hospital & Counselling Centre
    CAMTN NW1 .... 17 C2
Hospital of St John & St Elizabeth
    STJWD NW8 .... 4 A2
Hotham Primary School *PUT/ROE* SW15 ... 131 D2
House of Detention *CLKNW* EC1R 10 B5
House of St Barnabas *SOHO/SHAV* W1D 20 A5
Houses of Parliament *WEST* SW1P 45 D1
Howland Quay *BERM/RHTH* SE16 .... 103 D4
Hoxton Hall Community Theatre *IS* N1 .... 12 C1
HQS Wellington (Master Mariners)
    TPL/STR WC2R 34 C1
Hughesfields Primary School *DEPT* SE8 ... 122 A2
Hugh Myddelton Primary School
    CLKNW EC1R 10 B4
The Humana Wellington Hospital
    STJWD NW8 .... 4 B3
Humber Trading Estate *CRICK* NW2 .... 52 B4
Hungerford Primary School *HOLWY* N7 ...... 75 D3
Hunter Street Health Centre *STPAN* WC1H .. 8 C5
Huntsman Sports Club *BKHTH/KID* SE3 ... 142 A5
Hurlingham Business Park *FUL/PGN* SW6 ... 132 A1
Hurlingham & Chelsea School
    FUL/PGN SW6 .... 132 A1
Hurlingham House *FUL/PGN* SW6 .... 131 F1
Hurlingham Private School
    PUT/ROE SW15 .... 131 F2
Huron College *SKENS* SW7 .... 39 F4
Huron University *SKENS* SW7 .... 40 B2
Hyelford School *IL* IG1 .... 85 E2
Hythe Road Industrial Estate
    WLSDN NW10 .... 88 A3
Ian Mikardo High School *BOW* E3 .... 92 B2
Ibstock Place School *PUT/ROE* SW15 .... 129 E4
ICA Cinema *STJS* SW1Y 32 B4
Ichthus Primary School *CMBW* SE5 .... 119 D3
Ickburgh School *CLPT* E5 .... 60 B5
Ihlara Sport FC *HBRY* N5 .... 76 C1
Ikra Primary School *STNW/STAM* N16 .... 59 F2
Ilderton Primary School
    BERM/RHTH SE16 .... 120 C2
Ilford County Court *IL* IG1 .... 67 D4
Ilford Golf Club *IL* IG1 .... 65 E5
Ilford Medical Centre *IL* IG1 .... 66 B5
Ilford Preparatory School *GDMY/SEVK* IC3 ... 67 F3
Ilford Retail Park *IL* IG1 .... 66 C4
Ilford Swimming Pool *IL* IG1 .... 67 D4
Imperial College *PUT/ROE* SW15 .... 113 D5
    SKENS SW7 .... 40 A2
Imperial College of Science
    FUL/PGN SW6 .... 114 A2
Imperial College of Science & Technology
    SKENS SW7 .... 40 B1
Imperial College of Science &
    Medicine *SKENS* SW7 .... 39 F2
Imperial College School of Medicine
    PIM SW1V 44 A5
Imperial War Museum *STHWK* SE1 .... 46 B3
Imperial War Museum Annexe *STHWK* SE1 .. 46 B3
India House *HOL/ALD* WC2B 33 E1
Indoor Market *DEPT* SE8 .... 122 A4
    WOOL/PLUM SE18 .... 108 B5
Infant College *IL* IG1 .... 66 A4
Inner London Sessions House
    (Crown Court) *STHWK* SE1 .... 47 E2
Inner Temple *EMB* EC4Y 34 B1
Innholders Hall *CANST* EC4R 35 F1
Inns of Court & Chancery *TPL/STR* WC2R ... 22 A5
Inns of Court School of Law *GINN* WC1R ... 21 F2
Institut Francais *SKENS* SW7 .... 40 A4
International Community School
    CAMTN NW1 .... 18 A1
International Financial Centre *OBST* EC2N ... 24 C4
International Medical Centre *ECT* SW5 ...... 38 B5
International School of London *ACT* W3 ..... 98 A5
Invicta Industrial Estate *SRTFD* E15 .... 81 F2
Invicta Primary School *BKHTH/KID* SE3 ... 124 A2
IQRA Independent Primary School *BRXN/ST* SW9 .. 136 A1
Ironmonger Row Baths *FSBYE* EC1V 11 E4
Ironmongers Hall *STBT* EC1A 23 E3
Islamia Girls School *KIL/WHAMP* NW6 .... 71 E5
Islamic College for Advanced Studies
    WLSDN NW10 .... 70 B4

The Islamic Grammar School
    WAND/EARL SW18 .... 131 F5
Island Clinic *POP/IOD* E14 .... 104 C3
Islington Arts & Media School *FSBYPK* N4 .. 57 F5
Islington Business Centre *IS* N1 .... 76 C3
Islington Green Medical Centre *IS* N1 .... 76 B5
Islington Green School *IS* N1 .... 76 B5
Islington Tennis Centre *HOLWY* N7 .... 75 E3
Islington Town Hall *IS* N1 .... 76 B4
Ismaili Centre *SKENS* SW7 .... 40 B4
Italia Conti Academy of Theatre Arts
    BRXN/ST SW9 .... 135 E1
Italian Hospital *WEST* SW1P 43 E4
Ivydale Primary School *PECK* SE15 .... 139 D2
Jack Taylor School *KIL/WHAMP* NW6 .... 72 C5
Jack Tizzard School *FUL/PGN* SW6 .... 113 D4
Jacques Prevert School *HMSMTH* W6 .... 101 D5
Jamahiriya School *CHEL* SW3 .... 115 E2
James Allens Preparatory Girls School
    HNHL SE24 .... 137 D3
Jamestown Mental Health Centre
    HAMP NW3 .... 73 F4
James Wolfe Primary School
    GNWCH SE10 .... 122 B3
Janet Adegoke Leisure Centre *SHB* W12 ... 100 A1
The Japanese School *ACT* W3 .... 98 A1
Japan Green Medical Centre *ACT* W3 .... 98 B2
Jenner Health Centre *FSTH* SE23 .... 157 E1
Jenny Hammond Primary School
    WAN E11 .... 81 E1
Jermyn Street Theatre *STJS* SW1Y 31 F2
Jessop Primary School *HNHL* SE24 .... 137 E5
Jewel Tower *WEST* SW1P 44 C2
Jewin Cemetery *GLDGN* NW11 .... 54 A1
Jewish Community Theatre *CMBW* SE5 ...... 137 D1
Jewish Free School *KTTN* NW5 .... 75 D3
The Jewish Museum *CAMTN* NW1 .... 74 B5
Johanna Primary School *STHWK* SE1 .... 46 A1
John Ball Primary School *BKHTH/KID* SE3 .. 123 F5
John Betts Primary School *HMSMTH* W6 ... 100 A4
John Burns Primary School *BTSEA* SW11 ... 116 A5
John Dixon Clinic *BERM/RHTH* SE16 .... 102 B4
John Donne Primary School *PECK* SE15 ... 120 B4
John F Kennedy Special School
    SRTFD E15 .... 81 D5
John Keble CE Primary School
    WLSDN NW10 .... 69 F5
John Kelly Boys & Girls Technology College
    CRICK NW2 .... 51 F5
John Milton Primary School *VX/NE* SW8 ... 116 C3
John Orwell Sports Centre *WAP* E1W 102 A2
John Paul II RC School *WIM/MER* SW19 ... 131 D5
John Perryn Primary School *ACT* W3 .... 87 E4
John Roan Lower School *BKHTH/KID* SE3 ... 123 F2
John Roan School *BKHTH/KID* SE3 .... 123 E3
John Ruskin Primary School *WALW* SE17 ... 118 C2
John Scott Health Centre *FSBYPK* N4 .... 58 C3
John Scurr JMI School *WCHPL* E1 .... 90 C3
John Smith House *WALW* SE17 .... 47 E5
John Stainer Primary School
    BROCKY SE4 .... 139 E1
Joseph Lancaster Primary School *STHWK* SE1 .. 47 F3
Joseph Tritton Primary School
    BTSEA SW11 .... 132 C2
Jubilee JMI School *STNW/STAM* N16 .... 60 A3
Jubilee Market *COVGDN* WC2E 33 D1
Julians Primary School
    STRHM/NOR SW16 .... 154 A4
Juno Way Industrial Estate *NWCR* SE14 ... 121 D2
JVC Business Park *CRICK* NW2 .... 52 A3
Kangley Business Centre *SYD* SE26 .... 157 F5
Katella Trading Estate *BARK* IG11 .... 97 E2
Katherine Road Medical Centre *FSTGT* E7 .. 82 C3
Keats House Museum *HAMP* NW3 .... 73 D1
Keen Students Supplementary School
    WCHPL E1 .... 90 A4
Keir Hardie Primary School *CAN/RD* E16 ... 94 A4
Kelmscott Leisure Centre *WALTH* E17 .... 61 F1
Kelmscott School *WALTH* E17 .... 61 F1
Kelvin Grove Primary School *SYD* SE26 ... 156 B3
Ken Barrington Centre *LBTH* SE11 .... 117 F2
Kender Primary School *NWCR* SE14 .... 121 D2
Kenmont Primary School *WLSDN* NW10 ... 88 A2
Kenmore Park Infants School
    KENS W8 .... 90 A4
Kensal Rise Primary School *WLSDN* NW10 .. 89 D1
Kensington & Chelsea Town Hall *KENS* W8 .. 38 B1
Kensington Business Centre *SKENS* SW7 ... 40 D2
Kensington & Chelsea College *NKENS* W10 .. 89 E4
    WBPTN SW10 .... 114 C3
The Kensington Clinic *KENS* W8 .... 38 C5
Kensington Market *KENS* W8 .... 38 C1
Kensington Palace State Apartments &
    Royal Ceremonial Dress Collection
    KENS W8 .... 27 D4
Kensington Park School *REGST* W1B 19 D3

Kensington Preparatory School
FUL/PGN SW6 ...... 113 F4
Kensington Primary School *MNPK* E12 ...... 83 F3
Kensington School of Business
HCIRC EC1N 22 B2
Kensington Wharf *WBPTN* SW10 ...... 115 D5
Kentish Town Church CE Primary School
KTTN NW5 ...... 74 C2
Kentish Town Health Centre *KTTN* NW5 ...... 74 C3
Kentish Town Industrial Estate *KTTN* NW5 ...... 74 B2
Kentish Town Sports Centre *KTTN* NW5 ...... 74 A3
Kent Park Industrial Estate *PECK* SE15 ...... 120 D2
Kenwood House *HGT* N6 ...... 73 F1
Kew College *RCH/KEW* TW9 ...... 110 A3
Kew Retail Park *RCH/KEW* TW9 ...... 110 B4
Keyplan & Roxburghe College *FITZ* W1T 19 F1
Keyworth Primary School *WALW* SE17 ...... 118 B1
Kidbrooke Park Primary School
BKHTH/KID SE3 ...... 124 C5
Kidbrooke School *BKHTH/KID* SE3 ...... 125 D5
Kilburn Park Junior School
KIL/WHAMP NW6 ...... 2 A2
Killick Street Medical Centre *IS* N1 ...... 9 E1
Kilmorie Primary School *FSTH* SE23 ...... 157 E1
King Alfred School *GLDGN* NW11 ...... 54 B3
King Edward VII Hospital for Officers
MHST W1U 18 B2
King Fahad Academy
(Boys School & Girls Lower School)
ACT W3 ...... 99 E1
The Kingfisher Medical Centre *DEPT* SE8 ...... 121 F2
Kingford Community Primary School *PLSTW* E13 ...... 94 C3
Kingham Industrial Estate *WLSDN* NW10 ...... 87 D2
King Henry's Reach Development
BARN SW13 ...... 112 C2
King & Queen Wharf *BERM/RHTH* SE16 ...... 103 D1
Kings Acre Primary School *CLAP* SW4 ...... 135 E3
Kingsbury Trading Estate
CDALE/KGS NW9 ...... 50 C3
Kings College Hospital *CMBW* SE5 ...... 136 C1
Kings College London *CMBW* SE5 ...... 119 D5
HAMP NW5 ...... 72 A1
STHWK SE1 ...... 35 F3
TPL/STR WC2R 35 F1
WBPTN SW10 ...... 114 C3
WEST SW1P 43 F4
Kings College School of
Medicine & Dentistry *HNHL* SE24 ...... 137 D4
Kingsdale School *DUL* SE21 ...... 155 E3
Kingsgate Primary School
KIL/WHAMP NW6 ...... 72 A4
Kings Head Leisure Centre *CLPT* E5 ...... 78 C2
Kings Head Theatre *IS* N1 ...... 76 A5
Kingsland Health Centre *HACK* E8 ...... 77 F4
Kingsland School *HACK* E8 ...... 77 F2
Kingsland Shopping Centre *HACK* E8 ...... 77 F3
Kings Mall Shopping Centre
HMSMTH W6 ...... 100 C5
Kingsmead Primary School *CLPT* E5 ...... 79 E1
Kings Private Clinic *GDMY/SEVK* IG3 ...... 67 F3
MHST W1U 18 A2
Kings Stairs *BERM/RHTH* SE16 ...... 102 B3
Kingston University *KUTN/CMB* KT2 ...... 147 D5
King Street College *HMSMTH* W6 ...... 100 C5
Kingsway College *CLKNW* EC1R 10 B5
KTTN NW5 ...... 74 A3
STPAN WC1H 9 D4
Kingswood Primary School *WNWD* SE27 ...... 155 D1
Kisharon School *GLDGN* NW11 ...... 53 F1
KLC School of Design *WBPTN* SW10 ...... 114 C4
Knightsbridge Barracks *SKENS* SW7 ...... 41 D1
Knightsbridge Medical Centre *KTBR* SW1X 41 F2
Knightsbridge School *KENS* W8 ...... 40 A5
Knowledge Point School *HOLWY* N7 ...... 75 F3
Kobi Nazrul Primary School *WCHPL* E1 ...... 90 A5
Kubrick Business Estate *FSTGT* E7 ...... 82 B1
Laburnum Primary School *HACK* E8 ...... 122 B5
Lady Edens School *KENS* W8 ...... 39 E2
Lady Margaret School *FUL/PGN* SW6 ...... 114 A4
Ladywell arena *LEW* SE13 ...... 140 B4
Ladywell Cemetery *BROCKY* SE4 ...... 139 F3
Ladywell Leisure Centre *LEW* SE13 ...... 140 C3
Laker Industrial Estate *BECK* BR3 ...... 157 E5
Lambeth College *CLAP* SW4 ...... 134 C3
STHWK SE1 ...... 37 D4
Lambeth Crematorium *TOOT* SW17 ...... 150 C4
Lambeth Hospital *BRXN/ST* SW9 ...... 136 A1
Lambeth Palace *STHWK* SE1 ...... 45 E3
Lambs Court *POP/IOD* E14 ...... 105 E1
The Lanark Medical Centre *MV/WKIL* W9 ...... 3 D3
Lancaster House *WHALL* SW1A 31 F3
Langbourne Primary School *DUL* SE21 ...... 155 E3
Langdon Park Secondary School
POP/IOD E14 ...... 92 B5
Langdon School *EHAM* E6 ...... 96 B3

Langford Primary School *FUL/PGN* SW6 ...... 114 B5
Langthorne Health Centre *WAN* E11 ...... 63 D5
Langthorne Hospital *WAN* E11 ...... 81 D1
Lansbury Lawrence Primary School
POP/IOD E14 ...... 92 B5
Lansdowne College *BAY/PAD* W2 ...... 26 C2
Lansdowne School *BRXN/ST* SW9 ...... 135 F1
La Retraite RC Girls School *BAL* SW12 ...... 134 C5
Lark Hall Junior School *CLAP* SW4 ...... 117 D5
Lark Hall Primary School *CLAP* SW4 ...... 117 D5
Larmenier Infant School *HMSMTH* W6 ...... 101 D5
La Sainte Union Convent School
KTTN NW5 ...... 56 A5
Latchmere Leisure Centre *BTSEA* SW11 ...... 115 F5
Lathom Junior School *EHAM* E6 ...... 83 E4
Latimer Industrial Estate *SHB* W12 ...... 88 C5
Latymer Upper School *HMSMTH* W6 ...... 100 A5
Lauderdale Primary School *BMLY* BR1 ...... 160 A4
Lauriston Primary School *HOM* E9 ...... 79 D5
Lawdale Junior School *BETH* E2 ...... 90 A2
Lawrence Trading Estate *GNWCH* SE10 ...... 105 E5
Lawrence University *SKENS* SW7 ...... 39 F5
Lawrence Wharf *BERM/RHTH* SE16 ...... 103 F2
Laycock Primary School *IS* N1 ...... 76 A3
Lea Bridge Industrial Estate *LEY* E10 ...... 61 E3
Lea Bridge Road Industrial Estate *LEY* E10 ...... 61 E3
Leadenhall Market *BANK* EC3V 24 C5
Lea Park Trading Estate *LEY* E10 ...... 61 F2
Leathermarket Gardens *STHWK* SE1 ...... 48 C1
Leathersellers Sports Ground
ELTH/MOT SE9 ...... 142 C5
Leathers Hall *HDTCH* EC3A 24 C4
L'écoles des Petits *FUL/PGN* SW6 ...... 114 B5
Lee Manor Primary School *LEW* SE13 ...... 141 E4
Leeside Court *BERM/RHTH* SE16 ...... 103 D2
Lee Valley Ice Centre *LEY* E10 ...... 61 D4
Leighton House Museum & Art Gallery
WKENS W14 ...... 101 F4
Lena Gardens Primary School
HMSMTH W6 ...... 100 C4
Leopold Primary School *WLSDN* NW10 ...... 69 H4
Leopold Street Clinic *BOW* E3 ...... 91 F4
Lewisham Bridge Primary School
LEW SE13 ...... 140 B1
Lewisham Business Centre *NWCR* SE14 ...... 121 D2
Lewisham Centre *LEW* SE13 ...... 140 C1
Lewisham College *DEPT* SE8 ...... 122 A4
Lewisham Crematorium *CAT* SE6 ...... 159 F2
Leyton Business Centre *LEY* E10 ...... 61 F4
Leyton FC *LEY* E10 ...... 61 F3
Leyton Industrial Village *LEY* E10 ...... 61 D2
Leyton Leisure Centre *LEY* E10 ...... 62 B2
Leyton Orient FC (Matchroom Stadium)
LEY E10 ...... 62 B5
Leytonstone School *WAN* E11 ...... 63 E1
Leyton VI Form College *LEY* E10 ...... 61 D1
Leyton Youth Sports Ground *LEY* E10 ...... 62 B3
The Liberty City Clinic *SDTCH* EC2A 12 C5
Library & Community Centre
BTSEA SW11 ...... 133 D1
Lilian Baylis School *LBTH* SE11 ...... 45 F5
VX/NE SW8 ...... 117 E2
Lilian Baylis Theatre *FSBYE* EC1V 10 C1
Lilian Bishop School of English
SKENS SW7 ...... 40 A4
Lillie Road Fitness Centre *FUL/PGN* SW6 ...... 113 G5
Limehouse Town Hall *POP/IOD* E14 ...... 91 F5
Lincoln's Inn *LINN* WC2A 21 F4
Linden Lodge School *WIM/MER* SW19 ...... 149 E1
Linford Christie Stadium *SHB* W12 ...... 88 A4
Linley Sambourne House *KENS* W8 ...... 38 A1
Linnet House Clinic *STJWD* NW8 ...... 4 C2
Lion House School *PUT/ROE* SW15 ...... 131 D2
Lisson Grove Health Centre *STJWD* NW8 ...... 4 C5
Lister Community School *PLSTW* E13 ...... 94 B2
The Lister Hospital *BGVA* SW1W 116 B1
Lister House Clinic *CAVSQ/HST* W1G 18 C4
Little Angel Theatre *IS* N1 ...... 76 B5
Little Ilford School *MNPK* E12 ...... 83 F2
Little Wandsworth School *TOOT* SW17 ...... 152 A2
Livesey Museum for Children *PECK* SE15 ...... 120 B2
Lloyds Register Cricket Club *DUL* SE21 ...... 155 F5
Locks View Court *POP/IOD* E14 ...... 103 E1
Lombard Business Centre *BTSEA* SW11 ...... 115 D5
Lombard Business Park
WAND/EARL SW18 ...... 133 D4
Lombard Trading Estate *CHARL* SE7 ...... 106 B5
London Academy of Music & Dramatic Art
HMSMTH W6 ...... 113 D1
London Aquarium *STHWK* SE1 ...... 33 E5
London Arena *POP/IOD* E14 ...... 104 B4
London Balloon *STHWK* SE1 ...... 117 F1
London Bridge City Pier *STHWK* SE1 ...... 36 C3
London Bridge Hospital *STHWK* SE1 ...... 36 B2
London Bridge Sports Centre *CANST* EC4R 36 A2
London Business School *CAMTN* NW1 ...... 5 E5

The London Canal Museum *IS* N1 .... 9 D1
London Capital College *CAMTN* NW1 .... 74 B5
London City Airport *CAN/RD* E16 .... 107 F2
London City College *STHWK* SE1 .... 34 A4
London City Mission *STHWK* SE1 .... 37 D5
The London Clinic *MHST* W1U 18 B1
London College of Business & Computing
  BETH E2 .... 90 B1
London College of Fashion
  CAVSO/HST W1G 19 D4
  MHST W1U 18 B5
  SDTCH EC2A 13 D5
London College of Further Education
  LBTH SE11 .... 46 C5
London College of Higher Education
  CLAP SW4 .... 134 B1
London College of International
  Business Studies *HHOL* WC1V 21 D3
London College of Printing *LBTH* SE11 ...... 47 D5
The London Dungeon *KENS* W8 .... 26 A3
London Commodity Exchange *WAP* E1W 37 F2
London Dungeon *STHWK* SE1 .... 36 B3
London Electronics College *ECT* SW5 .... 114 A1
London Executive College *TOOT* SW17 ..... 152 A5
London Eye Clinic *CAVSO/HST* W1G 18 C3
London Fields Primary School *HACK* E8 ...... 78 B5
London Foot Hospital *FITZ* W1T 19 E1
London Gender Clinic *HDN* NW4 .... 52 B2
London Group Business Park *CRICK* NW2 .... 51 F5
London Guildhall University *LVPST* EC2M 24 B3
  TWRH EC3N 25 E5
London Guildhall University Sports Ground
  LEE/GVPK SE12 .... 160 C2
London Heart Clinic *CAVSO/HST* W1G 18 C3
London Hospital Medical College *WCHPL* E1... 90 B4
The London Industrial Estate *EHAM* E6 .... 96 A4
London Industrial Park *EHAM* E6 .... 96 B4
The London Irish Youth Theatre *HCT* N6 ..... 56 B3
London Islamic School/Madrasah
  WCHPL E1 .... 90 B5
London Ladies & Girls FC *CAT* SE6 .... 158 B5
London Lighthouse *NTGHL* W11 .... 89 E5
London Living Theatre *SYD* SE26 .... 157 D4
London Nautical School *STHWK* SE1 .... 34 B5
London Open College *FSBYE* EC1V 11 D3
London Oratory School *FUL/PGN* SW6 ...... 114 A3
London Pavilion *REGST* W1B 32 A2
London School of Economics *HHOL* WC1V ... 20 C4
  LINN WC2A 21 F5
  STHWK SE1 .... 35 E3
London School of Hygiene &
  Tropical Medicine *GWRST* WC1E 20 B2
London Scottish Golf Club
  WIM/MER SW19 .... 148 B3
London Silver Vaults *LINN* WC2A 22 A3
The London Television Centre (LWT)
  STHWK SE1 .... 34 A3
London Tourist Board & Convention Centre
  BAY/PAD W2 .... 42 C2
London Toy & Model Museum
  BAY/PAD W2 .... 27 F1
London Transport Museum
  COVGDN WC2E 33 D1
London Underwriting Centre *MON* EC3R 37 D1
London Weather Centre *CLKNW* EC1R 22 A2
London Welsh School *CRICK* NW2 .... 70 C5
London Wetland Centre *BARN* SW13 .... 112 B4
London Zoo *CAMTN* NW1 .... 9 D4
Longlands Primary School *BFN/LL* DA15 ... 163 E3
Long Lane AFC *BKHTH/KID* SE3 .... 124 C5
Lord Lister Health Centre *FSTGT* E7 .... 82 A1
Lord's Tour & MCC Museum *STJWD* NW8 ...... 4 A4
Loughborough Primary School
  BRXN/ST SW9 .... 118 B5
Lower Clapton Health Centre *CLPT* E5 .... 78 C2
Lower Place Business Centre
  WLSDN NW10 .... 86 C1
Lower Sydenham Industrial Estate
  CAT SE6 .... 157 F5
Low Hall Sports Ground *WALTH* E17 .... 61 D1
Lowther Primary School *BARN* SW13 .... 112 A2
Loxford School of Science & Technology
  IL IG1 .... 85 D2
LT Lost Property Office *CAMTN* NW1 .... 17 F1
LTR Depot *SHB* W12 .... 101 D2
Lubavitch House School *STNW/STAM* N16 ... 59 F2
Lucas Vale Primary School *DEPT* SE8 .... 122 A4
Lucie Clayton Secretarial/Fashion
  Design College *SKENS* SW7 .... 39 E3
Lutomer House Business Centre
  POP/IOD E14 .... 104 B2
Lux Cinema *IS* N1 .... 11 C4
Lycee Francais *SKENS* SW7 .... 40 A4
The Lyceum Theatre *TPL/STR* WC2R 11 E5

Lyndhurst House Preparatory School
  HAMP NW3 .... 73 D2
Lyndhurst Primary School *CMBW* SE5 ...... 119 D5
Lyon Business Park *BARK* IG11 .... 97 E1
Lyric Theatre *HMSMTH* W6 .... 100 C5
  SOHO/SHAV W1D 32 A1
Macaulay CE Primary School *CLAP* SW4 .. 134 B2
Madame Tussaud's *CAMTN* NW1 .... 18 A1
Madni Girls School *WCHPL* E1 .... 90 B5
Mahatma Gandhi Industrial Estate
  BRXN/ST SW9 .... 136 B1
Maida Vale Medical Centre *MV/WKIL* W9 ...... 3 F5
Maida Vale Medical Centre *MV/WKIL* W9 ...... 2 C4
Malham Road Industrial Estate
  FSTH SE23 .... 157 D1
Mall Galleries *STJS* SW1Y 32 B3
Malmesbury Primary School *BOW* E3 .... 91 F2
Malories J & I School *KIL/WHAMP* NW6 ...... 71 D4
Malory Primary School *BMLY* BR1 .... 160 A4
Mandeville Primary School *CLPT* E5 .... 61 E5
Manford Primary School *POP/IOD* E14 ...... 92 B4
Manor House Hospital *GLDGN* NW11 .... 54 B3
Manor Infant School *BARK* IG11 .... 85 F3
Manor Park Cemetery *FSTGT* E7 .... 83 D1
Manor Park Crematorium *FSTGT* E7 .... 82 C1
Manor Park Methodist School *MNPK* E12 ... 83 F1
Manor Primary School *SRTFD* E15 .... 93 E1
Manor Special School *WLSDN* NW10 .... 87 E3
Mansion House *MANHO* EC4N 24 A5
Mapledown School *CRICK* NW2 .... 53 D2
Maples Business Centre *IS* N1 .... 76 A4
Marble Arch *BAY/PAD* W2 .... 29 F1
Maria Fidelis Convent Lower School
  CAMTN NW1 .... 7 F4
Maria Fidelis Convent Upper School
  CAMTN NW1 .... 8 A3
Maritime Industrial Estate *CHARL* SE7 ..... 106 B5
Maritime Museum *GNWCH* SE10 .... 105 E5
Marlborough Cricket Club *DUL* SE21 .... 156 A1
Marlborough Day Hospital *STJWD* NW8 .... 3 E1
Marlborough House *STJS* SW1Y 31 F4
Marlborough Primary School *CHEL* SW3 ..... 41 D5
Marlborough Trading Estate
  RCH/KEW TW9 .... 110 B4
Marlowe Business Centre *NWCR* SE14 ...... 121 E3
Marner Primary School *BOW* E3 .... 92 B3
Marshall Street Leisure Centre
  SOHO/CST W1F 19 E5
Marsh Gate Business Centre *SRTFD* E15 ... 92 C1
Marshgate Trading Estate *SRTFD* E15 .... 80 B4
Martan College *HOL/ALD* WC2B 21 D4
Marvels Lane Primary School
  LEE/GVPK SE12 .... 160 C4
Mary Boone School *WKENS* W14 .... 101 E5
Maryland Industrial Estate *SRTFD* E15 ..... 81 E2
Maryland Primary School *SRTFD* E15 .... 81 E2
Marylebone Health Centre *MHST* W1U 18 B1
Marylebone Magistrates Court
  CAMTN NW1 .... 17 D2
The Maudsley Hospital *CMBW* SE5 .... 119 D5
Mawbrey Brough Health Centre
  VX/NE SW8 .... 117 E3
Mayfair Medical Centre *MYFR/PKLN* W1K ... 18 B5
Mayflower Primary School *POP/IOD* E14 ... 92 A5
Maytime School *IL* IG1 .... 66 A5
Mayville Infant School *WAN* E11 .... 63 E4
Mayville Junior School *WAN* E11 .... 63 E4
Maze Hill School *GNWCH* SE10 .... 123 E2
Mazenod RC Primary School
  KIL/WHAMP NW6 .... 2 A4
McKay Trading Estate *NKENS* W10 .... 89 E3
MDO Majidiah (Uk) *WCHPL* E1 .... 102 B1
Meadowgate School *PECK* SE15 .... 139 D1
Meadowside Leisure Centre
  ELTH/MOT SE9 .... 146 B5
Medical Express Clinic *CAVSO/HST* W1G 18 C2
Mednurs Clinic *SEVS/STOTM* N15 .... 59 D1
Megabowl *BRXS/STRHM* SW2 .... 153 E2
Melcombe Primary School *HMSMTH* W6 ... 113 D2
Mellish Industrial Estate
  WOOL/PLUM SE18 .... 107 D2
Memorial Hospital *WOOL/PLUM* SE18 ...... 126 A5
Menorah Grammar School *GLDGN* NW11 .... 53 D1
Menorah Primary School *GLDGN* NW11 .... 53 E4
Mercers' Hall *CITYW* EC2V 23 F5
The Merchant Taylors Hall *BANK* EC3V 24 B5
Mercury Theatre *LSQ/SEVD* WC2H 33 D1
Meridian Clinic *BRXN/ST* SW9 .... 136 A1
Meridian Locality Mental Health Centre
  CHARL SE7 .... 124 C2
Meridian Primary School *GNWCH* SE10 ... 123 D1
Meridian Sports Club *CHARL* SE7 .... 125 E2
Meridian Trading Estate *CHARL* SE7 .... 106 A5

Merlin Primary School *BMLY* BR1 .... 160 A3
Merlin School *PUT/ROE* SW15 .... 131 D3
Mermaid Theatre *BLKFR* EC4V 35 D1
Merton Road Industrial Estate
  WAND/EARL SW18 .... 132 A5
Metropolitan Business Centre *HACK* E8 .... 77 E4
Metropolitan Hospital *STHWK* SE1 .... 46 B2
Metropolitan Tabernacle *LBTH* SE11 .... 47 D4
Metro Trading Centre *WBLY* HA9 .... 68 B1
Michael Faraday Primary School
  WALW SE17 .... 119 D1
Michael Manley Industrial Estate
  VX/NE SW8 .... 116 C5
Michael Sobell Sinai School
  KTN/HRWW/W HA3 .... 50 A1
The Michael Tippett School *LBTH* SE11 .... 48 B5
Middle Park Primary School
  ELTH/MOT SE9 .... 143 D5
Middle Row Primary School *NKENS* W10 .... 89 E3
Middlesex CCC (Lord's Cricket Ground)
  STJWD NW8 .... 4 B3
Middlesex Guildhall *WEST* SW1P 44 B1
Middlesex Hospital *GTPST* W1W 19 E3
Middlesex Hospital Medical School
  FITZ W1T 19 F2
Middlesex Hospital Nurses Home
  FITZ W1T 19 E2
Middlesex Hospital School of Physiotherapy
  FITZ W1T 19 F2
Middlesex Hospital Sports Ground
  CHST BR7 .... 163 F5
Middlesex University *CLDGN* NW11 .... 54 B3
Middle Temple Hall *TPL/STR* WC2R 34 A1
Midway Mission Hospital *BETH* E2 .... 7 J5
Mile End & Bow Business Centre
  WCHPL E1 .... 90 B4
Mile End Hospital *WCHPL* E1 .... 91 D2
Mile End Stadium *BOW* E3 .... 91 F4
Miles Coverdale Primary School
  SHB W12 .... 100 C3
Millbank Primary School *WEST* SW1P 44 B5
Millbank Millennium Pier *WEST* SW1P 44 C5
Millbank Tower *WEST* SW1P 44 B5
Millennium Arena *BTSEA* SW11 .... 116 A3
Millennium Balloon *STHWK* SE1 .... 37 D4
Millennium Harbour Development
  POP/IOD E14 .... 105 F3
Millennium Quay *DEPT* SE8 .... 122 B2
Millennium Wharf Development
  POP/IOD E14 .... 105 D4
Millfields J & I School *CLPT* E5 .... 78 C1
Mill Lane Medical Centre *KIL/WHAMP* NW6 .... 72 A2
Mill Street Clinic *STHWK* SE1 .... 37 F5
Mill Trading Estate *WLSDN* NW10 .... 86 B1
Millwall FC (The New Den)
  BERM/RHTH SE16 .... 120 C1
Milton Natural Health Centre *HCT* N6 .... 56 C2
Ministry of Defence *WHALL* SW1A 32 C4
Mini Town Hall *WOOL/PLUM* SE18 .... 127 E5
Mint Business Park *CAN/RD* E16 .... 94 A4
Mitchell Brook Primary School
  WLSDN NW10 .... 69 D3
Mitre Bridge Industrial Park *WLSDN* NW10 .... 88 B3
Moatbridge School *ELTH/MOT* SE9 .... 143 D4
Moberly Sports & Education Centre
  WLSDN NW10 .... 89 D2
Monega Primary School *MNPK* E12 .... 83 D2
Monson Primary School *NWCR* SE14 .... 121 D3
Montbelle Primary School
  ELTH/MOT SE9 .... 162 B3
The Monument *MON* EC3R 36 B2
Moorfields Eye Hospital *FSBYE* EC1V 12 A4
Moorfields Primary School *STLK* EC1Y 12 A5
Mora Primary School *CRICK* NW2 .... 70 C1
Morden College Homes *BKHTH/KID* SE3 .... 124 A5
Morden Mount Primary School
  LEW SE13 .... 122 B5
More House School *KTBR* SW1X 41 F3
Moreland Primary School *FSBYE* EC1V 11 D4
Morningside Primary School *HOM* E9 .... 78 C3
Morpeth School *BETH* E2 .... 90 C2
Mortimer Road Clinic *WLSDN* NW10 .... 88 C2
Mortimer School *STHM/NOR* SW16 .... 153 D2
Mortlake Cemetery *MORT/ESHN* SW14 .... 129 E1
Mortlake Crematorium *RCH/KEW* TW9 .... 110 B5
Mosiah Foundation Supplementary School
  STNW/STAM N16 .... 59 E3
The Mother & Baby Clinic *HOM* E9 .... 79 D3
Mottingham Community Health Clinic
  ELTH/MOT SE9 .... 161 E4
Mottingham Primary School
  ELTH/MOT SE9 .... 161 F3
Mount Carmel School *ARCH* N19 .... 57 D5
Mowlem Primary School *BETH* E2 .... 90 C1
MSP Business Centre *WBLY* HA9 .... 68 B1

Mudchute City Farm *POP/IOD* E14 .... 104 C5
Mulberry Business Centre
  BERM/RHTH SE16 .... 103 D3
Mulberry House School *CRICK* NW2 .... 71 D2
Mulberry School for Girls *WCHPL* E1 .... 90 B5
Mulgrave Primary School
  WOOL/PLUM SE18 .... 108 B4
Museum in Docklands *POP/IOD* E14 .... 104 A1
Museum of Fulham Palace *FUL/PGN* SW6 .... 113 D5
Museum of Garden History *STHWK* SE1 .... 45 D3
Museum of London
  (Archaeological Research Centre) *IS* N1 .. 11 F1
Museum of the Order of St John
  FARR EC1M 23 D1
Museum of the Royal College of Surgeons
  LINN WC2A 21 F4
Myatt Garden Primary School
  BROCKY SE4 .... 121 F5
Myatts Field Clinic *BRXN/ST* SW9 .... 118 B4
Nags Head Shopping Centre *HOLWY* N7 .... 75 F1
Naima Jewish Preparatory School
  KIL/WHAMP NW6 .... 2 C1
National Army Museum *CHEL* SW3 .... 115 F1
National Film Theatre *STHWK* SE1 .... 33 F3
National Gallery *LSQ/SEVD* WC2N 32 B2
National Hospital for Neurology &
  Neurosurgery *BMSBY* WC1N 20 C1
National Hospital for Sick Children
  (Great Ormond Street) *BMSBY* WC1N 21 D1
National Maritime Museum *GNWCH* SE10 .... 123 D2
National Portrait Gallery *LSQ/SEVD* WC2H 32 B2
National Temperance Hospital
  CAMTN NW1 .... 7 F4
National Youth Theatre of GB *HOLWY* N7 .... 57 E5
Natural History Museum *SKENS* SW7 .... 40 A3
Natural Therapy Clinic *TOOT* SW17 .... 152 B5
Nature Reserve *WALTH* E17 .... 60 C2
Navigation College *MANHO* EC4N 35 F1
Negus 6th Form Centre
  WOOL/PLUM SE18 .... 127 D3
Nelson Dock Museum *BERM/RHTH* SE16 .... 103 F2
Nelson Primary School *EHAM* E6 .... 96 A1
Nelson's Column *CHCR* WC2N 32 C3
Neo Clinic *PIM* SW1V 43 E5
Netley Primary School *CAMTN* NW1 .... 7 E4
The New Ambassadors Theatre
  LSQ/SEVD WC2H 20 C5
New Atlas Wharf Development
  POP/IOD E14 .... 103 F4
Newbury Park Health Centre
  GNTH/NBYPK IG2 .... 67 D1
Newbury Park Primary School
  GNTH/NBYPK IG2 .... 67 D1
The New Business Centre *WLSDN* NW10 .... 87 F2
New Caledonian Wharf
  BERM/RHTH SE16 .... 103 F4
New Chiswick Pool *CHSWK* W4 .... 111 E5
New City Primary School *PLSTW* E13 .... 94 C2
New Connaught Rooms *HOL/ALD* WC2B 21 D4
New Covent Garden Market *VX/NE* SW8 .... 117 D2
New Crane Wharf *WAP* E1W 102 C2
New Cross Sports Arena *NWCR* SE14 .... 121 E3
New End Primary School *HAMP* NW3 .... 72 C1
New End Theatre *HAMP* NW3 .... 54 C5
New England Industrial Estate *BARK* IG11 .... 96 C1
Newfield Primary School *WLSDN* NW10 .... 69 F4
The New Furness Primary School
  WLSDN NW10 .... 88 B2
Newham College of Further Education
  EHAM E6 .... 95 F1
  SRTFD E15 .... 76 C5
Newham Community College *CAN/RD* E16... .... 93 E5
Newham General Hospital *PLSTW* E13 .... 94 C3
Newham Leisure Centre *PLSTW* E13 .... 94 C4
Newham Medical Centre *PLSTW* E13 .... 94 C1
Newham Sixth Form College *PLSTW* E13 .... 94 B3
Newington Court Business Centre
  STHWK SE1 .... 47 E3
Newington Green Primary School
  STNW/STAM N16 .... 77 E2
Newington Industrial Estate *WALW* SE17 .... 47 D5
New Kings Primary School *FUL/PGN* SW6 .... 113 F5
New London Theatre *LSQ/SEVD* WC2H 21 D4
Newport J & I School *WAN* E11 .... 62 C4
New Rush Hall School *IL* IG1 .... 66 C4
New School *FUL/PGN* SW6 .... 113 F4
New Scotland Yard *STJSPK* SW1H 44 A2
New Spitalfields Market *LEY* E10 .... 62 A5
News International *WAP* E1W 102 B1
Newton Medical Centre *BAY/PAD* W2 .... 14 B4
Newton Preparatory School *VX/NE* SW8 .... 116 B3
The Woodlands School *BMLY* BR1 .... 159 E4
New York University London School
  RSQ WC1B 20 B3

Nightingale Clinic *PLSTW* E13 .... 94 C1
Nightingale Primary School *CLPT* E5 .... 78 A1
　WOOL/PLUM SE18 .... 126 B1
Nightingale School *STHWK* SE1 .... 45 E1
　TOOT SW17 .... 151 E2
Nineacres School *WOOL/PLUM* SE18 .... 127 D1
Norland Place Primary School *NTGHL* W11 .... 101 E2
Norlington School *LEY* E10 .... 63 D3
Normand Park Primary School
　FUL/PGN SW6 .... 113 F2
Norman Shaw Building (MP's Offices)
　WHALL SW1A 32 C5
North Acton Business Park *ACT* W3 .... 87 D5
North Beckton Primary School *EHAM* E6 ...... 95 F4
North Bridge House *HAMP* NW3 .... 72 C3
North Bridge House School *CAMTN* NW1 ...... 74 A3
　HAMP NW3 .... 73 D5
Northbrook CE School *LEW* SE13 .... 141 E3
Northbury Primary School *BARK* IG11 .... 84 B3
Northcote Lodge School *BTSEA* SW11 .... 133 E4
Northfields Industrial Estate
　ALP/SUD HA0 .... 68 A5
Northfields Prospect Business Centre
　WAND/EARL SW18 .... 131 F2
Northgate Clinic *CDALE/KGS* NW9 .... 51 E1
North London Centre of Physiotherapy
　ARCH N19 .... 56 C3
North London Tutorial College *HDN* NW4 ..... 52 C1
The North Street Health Centre
　CLAP SW4 .... 134 C1
Northview Primary School *WLSDN* NW10 ...... 69 E1
North West London Jewish J & I School
　CRICK NW2 .... 71 E4
North West London Medical Centre
　MV/WKIL W9 .... 3 E2
North Westminster Community School
　BAY/PAD W2 .... 16 A3
　STJWD NW8 .... 16 C2
North Westminster Community
Secondary School *MV/WKIL* W9 .... 2 B5
Northwood Primary School *CLPT* E5 .... 60 A4
Norwegian/British Monument
　BAY/PAD W2 .... 29 D4
Norwood Park Primary School
　WNWD SE27 .... 154 C4
Norwood School *WNWD* SE27 .... 154 C4
Notre Dame RC Girls School *STHWK* SE1 .... 46 C2
Notre Dame RC Primary School
　WOOL/PLUM SE18 .... 126 B2
N1 Shopping Centre *IS* N1 .... 10 B1
NTGB Sports Ground *EHAM* E6 .... 84 A3
Nutrition Clinic *MHST* W1U 18 A2
Oakfield Preparatory School *DUL* SE21 .... 155 D2
Oakington Manor School *WBLY* HA9 .... 68 B2
Oaklands Secondary School *BETH* E2 .... 90 A2
Oak Lodge School *BAL* SW12 .... 133 F5
Oak Tree Medical Centre *CDMY/SEVK* IG3 ... 66 B1
Oakwood Business Park *WLSDN* NW10 .... 87 D2
Oasis Sports Centre *LSQ/SEVD* WC2H 20 C4
Obstetrics Hospital *CWRST* WC1E 19 F1
Odeon Cinema *CAMTN* NW1 .... 74 B5
　ELTH/MOT SE9 .... 143 E2
　FITZ W1T 20 A3
　GNTH/NBYPK IG2 .... 66 A1
　HOLWY N7 .... 57 E5
　KENS W8 .... 38 A2
　LSQ/SEVD WC2H 74 D4
　MBLAR W1H 17 F5
　STJS SW1Y 32 A2
　STRHM/NOR SW16 .... 153 E3
Odeon Covent Gardens Cinema
　LSQ/SEVD WC2H 20 B5
Odeon Wardour Street Cinema
　SOHO/SHAV W1D 32 A1
Odessa Infant School *FSTGT* E7 .... 82 A2
Old Admiralty *WHALL* SW1A 32 B4
Old Barnes Cemetery *BARN* SW13 .... 112 B5
Old Bellgate Wharf Development
　POP/IOD E14 .... 103 F4
Old Brocklebians Sports Ground
　ELTH/MOT SE9 .... 142 C4
Old Cemetery *EDUL* SE22 .... 138 B4
Old Colfeian Sports Club *LEE/GVPK* SE12 ... 142 A3
Old Curiosity Shop *LINN* WC2A 21 E4
Old Ford Primary School *BOW* E3 .... 91 F1
Oldhill Medical Centre *STNW/STAM* N16 .... 59 F3
Old Jamaica Business Estate
　BERM/RHTH SE16 .... 49 F2
Old Oak Primary School *SHB* W12 .... 87 F5
Old Operating Theatre Museum
　STHWK SE1 .... 36 A4
Old Palace Primary School *BOW* E3 .... 92 B2
Old Royal Naval College *GNWCH* SE10 .... 123 D2

Old Royal Observatory Greenwich
　GNWCH SE10 .... 123 D3
Old Station Museum *CAN/RD* E16 .... 108 A3
Old Sun Wharf *POP/IOD* E14 .... 103 E1
Old Treasury *WHALL* SW1A 32 C5
Old Vic Theatre *STHWK* SE1 .... 34 B5
Old War Office *WHALL* SW1A 32 C4
Olga Primary School *BOW* E3 .... 91 E1
Oliver Business Park *WLSDN* NW10 .... 86 C1
Oliver Goldsmith Primary School
　CMBW SE5 .... 119 E4
Olympia *WKENS* W14 .... 101 E4
Olympic Industrial Estate *WBLY* HA9 .... 68 B3
Olympic Retail Park *WBLY* HA9 .... 68 A1
Olympic Trading Estate *WBLY* HA9 .... 68 B3
On Sai Clinic *ECT* SW5 .... 38 C5
On the Road Tours CC *WAND/EARL* SW18 ... 132 C4
Open Air Theatre *CAMTN* NW1 .... 9 E3
The Open University *FSBYW* WC1X 9 E3
　KIL/WHAMP NW6 .... 72 A1
Ophaboom Theatre *WLSDN* NW10 .... 88 B2
Optimax Laser Eye Clinic *HAMP* NW3 .... 72 C3
Orchard Business Centre *SYD* SE26 .... 157 F5
The Orchard Health Centre *BARK* IG11 .... 96 C1
Orchard House School *CHSWK* W4 .... 99 D5
Orchard Primary School *HOM* E9 .... 78 C4
Orient Industrial Park *LEY* E10 .... 62 A4
Orion Business Centre *BERM/RHTH* SE16 .. 121 D1
Osmani Primary School *WCHPL* E1 .... 90 A4
Our Lady of Dolours RC Primary School
　BAY/PAD W2 .... 14 C2
Our Lady of Grace RC Junior School
　CRICK NW2 .... 52 B5
Our Lady of Lourdes RC Primary School
　LEW SE13 .... 141 D1
　WAN E11 .... 63 F1
　WLSDN NW10 .... 68 C5
Our Lady of the Rosary RC Primary School
　BFN/LL DA15 .... 145 E4
Our Lady of the Sacred Heart School
　HOLWY N7 .... 75 F2
Our Lady of Victories RC Primary School
　PUT/ROE SW15 .... 131 D2
　SKENS SW7 .... 40 A5
Our Lady Queen of Heaven RC
　Primary School *WIM/MER* SW19 .... 131 D5
Our Lady & St Bonaventure School
　POP/IOD E14 .... 91 F5
Our Lady & St Joseph Primary School
　IS N1 .... 77 E2
Our Lady & St Philip Neri RC Primary School
　FSTH SE23 .... 157 D3
Our Ladys Convent High School
　STNW/STAM N16 .... 59 E2
Our Ladys RC Primary School
　CAMTN NW1 .... 74 C5
Outdoor Market *WOOL/PLUM* SE18 .... 108 A5
Oval Business Centre *LBTH* SE11 .... 117 F1
Oval House Theatre *LBTH* SE11 .... 118 A2
Oxford Gardens Primary School
　NKENS W10 .... 89 D5
Oxford House College *SOHO/SHAV* W1D 20 A4
Oxo Tower Wharf *STHWK* SE1 .... 34 B2
Paddington Bowling & Sports Club
　MV/WKIL W9 .... 2 C5
Paddington Community Hospital
　MV/WKIL W9 .... 14 A2
Paddington Green Primary School
　BAY/PAD W2 .... 16 A1
Paddington Recreation Ground
　Athletics Track *KIL/WHAMP* NW6 .... 2 B3
Paddock School *PUT/ROE* SW15 .... 129 F2
Pain Relief Clinic *HDN* NW4 .... 52 B1
Pakeman Primary School *HOLWY* N7 .... 57 F5
Palladium Theatre *REGST* W1B 19 E5
Panorama Pier *STHWK* SE1 .... 35 D2
Parayhouse School *WBPTN* SW10 .... 114 C3
Parent Infant Clinic *HAMP* NW3 .... 72 C2
Park Business Centre *KIL/WHAMP* NW6 .... 2 A4
Parkfield Industrial Estate *BTSEA* SW11 ...... 116 A5
Parkfield JMI School *HDN* NW4 .... 52 B2
Parkgate House School *CLAP* SW4 .... 134 A2
Park Hall Trading Estate *WNWD* SE27 .... 154 C3
Park House Medical Centre
　KIL/WHAMP NW6 .... 89 E1
Parkhouse Middle School
　WIM/MER SW19 .... 149 F4
Park Medical Centre *BERM/RHTH* SE16 ..... 103 D5
Park Mews Small Business Centre
　HNHL SE24 .... 136 C4
Park Primary School *SRTFD* E15 .... 81 F4
Park Royal Business Centre *WLSDN* NW10 ... 86 B3
Park School for Girls *IL* IG1 .... 66 B3
Parkside Business Estate *DEPT* SE8 .... 121 F2
Parkside Clinic *NTGHL* W11 .... 89 E5
Parkside Health *NTGHL* W11 .... 89 E5

Parkside Hospital *WIM/MER* SW19 .... 149 D3
Park Walk Primary School *WBPTN* SW10 ...... 115 D2
Parkwood Primary School *FSBYPK* N4 .... 58 B4
Parliament Hill Fields Athletics Track
   KTTN NW5 .... 73 F1
Parliament Hill School *KTTN* NW5 .... 74 A1
Parmiter Industrial Centre *BETH* E2 .... 90 B1
Parsons Green Health Clinic
   FUL/PGN SW6 .... 114 A4
Patent Office *HHOL* WC1V 22 A3
Peace Pagoda *BTSEA* SW11 .... 115 F3
The Peacock Theatre *HOL/ALD* WC2B 21 E5
Peckham Park Primary School
   PECK SE15 .... 120 A3
Peckham Pulse Healthy Living Centre
   PECK SE15 .... 120 A4
Peckham Rye Primary School *PECK* SE15 ... 138 B1
Pembridge Hall *BAY/PAD* W2 .... 26 B2
Pendragon Secondary School *BMLY* BR1 ... 160 A3
Penton Primary School *IS* N1 .... 10 D1
Percival David Foundation of Chinese Art
   STPAN WC1H 8 C5
Perrymount Primary School *FSTH* SE23 ..... 157 D2
Peterborough Primary School
   FUL/PGN SW6 .... 114 A5
Peter Hills School *BERM/RHTH* SE16 .... 103 A5
Peterley Business Centre *BETH* E2 .... 90 B1
Peter Pan Statue *BAY/PAD* W2 .... 28 A3
Pewterers' Hall *CITYW* EC2V 23 F5
Phoenix Business Centre *POP/IOD* E14 ...... 92 A4
Phoenix College *TOOT* SW17 .... 151 E4
Phoenix Court *POP/IOD* E14 .... 104 A5
Phoenix High School *SHB* W12 .... 100 A1
Phoenix Leisure Centre *CAT* SE6 .... 140 B5
Phoenix School *BOW* E3 .... 91 F2
   HAMP NW3 .... 73 D5
Phoenix Theatre *LSO/SEVD* WC2H 20 B5
Physical Energy Statue *BAY/PAD* W2 .... 28 A4
Piccadilly Theatre *SOHO/SHAV* W1D 32 A1
Picture House Cinema *SRTFD* E15 .... 93 D3
Pilgrims Way J & I School *PECK* SE15 .... 120 C2
Pilot Industrial Centre *WLSDN* NW10 .... 87 E3
Pimlico School *PIM* SW1V 116 C1
Plaisterers Hall *CITYW* EC2Y 23 E3
Plaistow Hospital *PLSTW* E13 .... 94 B1
Planetarium *CAMTN* NW1 .... 18 A1
Plantation House Medical Centre
   LOTH EC2R 24 B4
Plashet Jewish Cemetery *MNPK* E12 .... 83 D5
Plashet Road Medical Centre *FSTGT* E7 ..... 82 A5
Plashet School *EHAM* E6 .... 83 E4
Players Theatre *CHCR* WC2N 32 C5
The Playhouse *HOLWY* N7 .... 75 E3
Pleasance Theatre *HOLWY* N7
Plumcroft Primary School
   WOOL/PLUM SE18 .... 126 C2
Plumstead Leisure Centre
   WOOL/PLUM SE18 .... 127 F1
Plumstead Manor School
   WOOL/PLUM SE18 .... 127 D1
The Pointer School *BKHTH/KID* SE3 .... 124 A4
Police Cadet School *WAN* E11 .... 64 A3
The Polish Institute & Sikorski Museum
   SKENS SW7 .... 40 B1
Pollock's Toy Museum *FITZ* W1T 19 F2
Poole's Park Primary School *HOLWY* N7 ... 57 F4
Pope John Primary School *SHB* W12 .... 100 B1
Pop In Business Centre *WBLY* HA9 .... 68 B2
Poplar Business Park *POP/IOD* E14 .... 104 C1
Pop Up Theatre *FSBYE* EC1V 10 C2
Porchester Leisure Centre *BAY/PAD* W2 .... 14 C4
Portcullis House *WHALL* SW1A 45 E1
The Portland Hospital *REGST* W1B 19 D1
Portland Place School *REGST* W1B 19 D2
The Portman Clinic *HAMP* NW3 .... 73 D5
The Portman Gallery *HAMP* NW3
Portobello Market *NKENS* W10 .... 89 E4
Portobello Medical Centre *NTGHL* W11 ...... 89 E5
Portway Primary School *SRTFD* E15 .... 93 E3
Pound Park Nursery School *CHARL* SE7 .... 125 D1
Powergate Business Park *WLSDN* NW10 .... 87 D2
Premier Cinema *PECK* SE15 .... 120 A5
Prendergast School *BROCKY* SE4 .... 140 A2
PRG for Schools *SYD* SE26
Primrose Hill School *CAMTN* NW1 .... 74 A5
Primrose Montessori School *HBRY* N5 .... 58 C5
Prince Charles Cinema *SOHO/SHAV* W1D .. 32 B1
Prince Edward Theatre *SOHO/SHAV* W1D .. 20 A5
Prince of Wales Theatre *STJS* SW1Y 32 A2
Princes College *NOXST/BSQ* WC1A 20 C4
Princes Court Business Centre *WAP* E1W .. 102 B1
Princess Frederica CE J & I School
   WLSDN NW10 .... 88 B1
Princess Grace Hospital *MHST* W1U 18 A1
Princess Louise Hospital *NKENS* W10 .... 88 B1

Princess May Primary School
   STNW/STAM N16 .... 77 E2
Prior Western Primary School *STLK* EC1Y .. 23 F1
Priory CE Middle School *WIM/MER* SW19 .. 150 B5
Priory House School *CAT* SE6 .... 158 B1
Priory Council *STJS* SW1Y 32 A4
Privy Council Office *WHALL* SW1A 32 C4
Prospect House School *PUT/ROE* SW15 .... 131 D5
Prospect of Whitby *WAP* E1W 102 C2
Proud Gallery *CHCR* WC2N 32 C2
Psychiatric Home *BRXN/ST* SW9 .... 135 E1
Public Record Office *LINN* WC2A 22 A4
Public Record Office Museum
   RCH/KEW TW9 .... 110 B3
Pump House *BERM/RHTH* SE16 .... 103 E2
Purdy Hicks Gallery *STHWK* SE1 .... 34 C3
Pursuit Centre *WAP* E1W 102 A1
Putney Animal Hospital *PUT/ROE* SW15 ... 131 D2
Putney Exchange Shopping Centre
   PUT/ROE SW15 .... 131 D2
Putney High School *PUT/ROE* SW15 .... 131 D3
Putney Hospital *PUT/ROE* SW15 .... 130 C1
Putney Leisure Centre *PUT/ROE* SW15 ..... 130 C2
Putney Lower Common Cemetery
   PUT/ROE SW15 .... 112 B5
Putneymead Medical Centre
   PUT/ROE SW15 .... 130 C2
Putney Park School *PUT/ROE* SW15 .... 130 B2
Putney School of Art *PUT/ROE* SW15 .... 131 E2
Putney Vale Cemetery *PUT/ROE* SW15 ...... 148 A2
Putney Vale Crematorium
   PUT/ROE SW15 .... 148 A2
Pylon Trading Estate *CAN/RD* E16 .... 93 D3
Quadrant Business Park *KIL/WHAMP* NW6 . 71 E5
Queen Charlottes & Chelsea Hospital
   HMSMTH W6 .... 100 A4
Queen Elizabeth College *KENS* W8 .... 26 A5
Queen Elizabeth Conference Centre
   WEST SW1P 44 B1
Queen Elizabeth Hall *STHWK* SE1 .... 33 E3
Queen Elizabeth Hospital *CHARL* SE7 .... 125 F2
Queen Elizabeth II School *MV/WKIL* W9 .... 89 F3
Queenhithe Stairs *BLKFR* EC4V 35 E3
Queen Mary's Hospital *HAMP* NW3 .... 54 C5
Queen Mary's University Hospital
   PUT/ROE SW15 .... 130 A2
Queen Mary & Westfield College
   WCHPL E1 .... 91 D3
Queen Mother Sports Centre *PIM* SW1V 43 E4
Queensbridge Infant School *HACK* E8 .... 77 F4
Queensbridge Sports Centre *HACK* E8 .... 77 F4
Queen's Club *WKENS* W14 .... 113 E1
Queens College *CAVSQ/HST* W1G 18 C3
Queen's Gallery *WHALL* SW1A 43 D1
The Queens House *GNWCH* SE10 .... 123 D2
Queens Ice Skating Club *BAY/PAD* W2 ...... 27 D2
Queens Manor Primary School
   FUL/PGN SW6 .... 112 C3
Queensmill School *FUL/PGN* SW6 .... 114 A5
Queens Park Community School Gm
   WLSDN NW10 .... 70 C5
Queens Park Health Centre *NKENS* W10 .... 89 E2
Queens Park Primary School *NKENS* W10 .. 89 E2
Queens Park Rangers FC
   (Loftus Road Stadium) *SHB* W12 .... 100 B1
Queens Road Practice *NWCR* SE14 .... 121 D4
Queens Theatre *SOHO/SHAV* W1D 32 A1
Queen Victoria Memorial *WHALL* SW1A 44 A1
Quicksilver Theatre *IS* N1 .... 77 E4
Quintin Kynaston School *STJWD* NW8 .... 73 D5
Radcliffe College *HNHL* SE24 .... 136 B3
Railton Road Clinic *HNHL* SE24 .... 136 B3
Rainbow Quay *BERM/RHTH* SE16 .... 103 E4
Raines Foundation School *BETH* E2 .... 90 B2
Ramac Industrial Estate *CHARL* SE7 .... 124 C1
Ram Brewery & Visitor Centre
   WAND/EARL SW18 .... 132 B3
RAM College *WEST* SW1P 117 E1
Randal Cremer Primary School *BETH* E2 ... 13 E1
Ranelagh Gardens
   (Site of Chelsea Flower Show)
   CHEL SW3 .... 116 A2
Ranelagh Primary School *SRTFD* E15 .... 93 E1
Rangefield Primary School *BMLY* BR1 .... 159 E5
Rangers House (The Wernher Collection)
   GNWCH SE10 .... 123 D4
Ransomes Dock Business Centre
   BTSEA SW11 .... 115 E3
Rathfern Primary School *FSTH* SE23 .... 157 F1
Ravensbourne College of Design &
   Communication *CHST* BR7 .... 161 F5
Ravenscourt Park Preparatory School
   HMSMTH W6 .... 100 A5
Ravenscroft Medical Centre *GLDGN* NW11 . 53 F2
Ravenscroft Primary School *PLSTW* E13 .... 94 B3

Ravenstone Primary School *BAL* SW12 ...... 152 A1
RCA *SKENS* SW7 .... 39 F3
RCA Sculpture School *BTSEA* SW11 ...... 115 E3
Reay Primary School *BRXN/ST* SW9 ...... 117 F3
Records Office *CLKNW* EC1R 10 B5
Redbridge Museum IL IG1 .... 66 D5
Redcliffe School *WBPTN* SW10 .... 114 C2
Redhill Junior School *CHST* BR7 .... 162 B5
Redlands Primary School *WCHPL* E1 .... 90 C4
Redriff Community Primary School
 BERM/RHTH SE16 .... 103 E2
Regent Clinic *CAVSQ/HST* W1G 18 C3
Regent's College *CAMTN* NW1 .... 6 A3
Regent's Park Barracks *CAMTN* NW1 .... 6 C1
Regents Park Clinic *CAMTN* NW1 .... 5 F5
Regents Park Medical Centre *CAMTN* NW1 .... 7 D3
Regent's Park Track *CAMTN* NW1 .... 5 E1
Renoir Cinema *BMSBY* WC1N 9 D5
Reynolds Sports Centre *ACT* W3 .... 98 A3
Rhyl Primary School *KTTN* NW5 .... 74 A3
Riba Drawings Collection & Heinz Gallery
 MBLAR W1H 17 F4
Ricards Lodge High School
 WIM/MER SW19 .... 149 F5
Richard Atkins Primary School
 BRXS/STRHM SW2 .... 135 E5
Richard Cloudesley School *STLK* EC1Y 23 E1
Richard Cobden Primary School
 CAMTN NW1 .... 74 C3
Rich Industrial Estate *PECK* SE15 .... 120 B2
 STHWK SE1 .... 49 D3
Richmond College *KENS* W8 .... 58 C2
Richmond Park Golf Club *PUT/ROE* SW15 .... 128 E5
Rio Cinema *HACK* E8 .... 77 F2
Ripple J & I School *BARK* IG11 .... 85 D5
Ritzy Cinema *BRXN/ST* SW9 .... 136 A2
River Place Health Centre *IS* N1 .... 76 C4
River Road Business Park *BARK* IG11 .... 97 E2
Riverdale Primary School
 WAND/EARL SW18 .... 150 A1
Riverside Business Centre
 WAND/EARL SW18 .... 150 B1
Riverside Community Health Care
 WKENS W14 .... 101 D4
Riverside Primary School
 BERM/RHTH SE16 .... 102 A3
Riverside Studios Cinema *BARN* SW13 .... 112 C1
Riverston School *LEE/GVPK* SE12 .... 142 A3
RNLI Lifeboat Station *TWRH* EC3N 37 D3
Robert Blair Primary School *HOLWY* N7 .... 75 D3
Robert Browning Primary School
 WALW SE17 .... 119 D1
Robin Hood Primary School
 KUTN/CMB KT2 .... 147 D5
Robinsfield Infant School *STJWD* NW8 .... 4 B1
The Roche School *WAND/EARL* SW18 .... 132 A3
Rockcliffe Manor Primary School
 WOOL/PLUM SE18 .... 127 E5
Roehampton Church School
 PUT/ROE SW15 .... 130 B5
Roehampton Golf Club *PUT/ROE* SW15 .... 129 F2
Roehampton Institute *PUT/ROE* SW15 .... 129 F3
 WAND/EARL SW18 .... 131 E4
The Roehampton Priory Hospital
 PUT/ROE SW15 .... 129 F2
Roehampton Recreation Centre
 PUT/ROE SW15 .... 130 A5
Rokeby School *SRTFD* E15 .... 81 D3
Roman Bath *TPL/STR* WC2R 33 F1
Roman Road Primary School *EHAM* E6 .... 95 D3
Roman Wall Remains *BARB* EC2Y 23 E3
Ronald Rose Primary School
 WIM/MER SW19 .... 131 D5
Rood Lane Medical Centre *FENCHST* EC3M 36 C1
Roosevelt Memorial *MYFR/PKLN* W1K 30 B1
Ropery Business Park *CHARL* SE7 .... 106 C5
The Rosary RC Primary School *HAMP* NW3.... 73 F2
Rosemary (Primary) School *IS* N1 .... 76 C5
Rosemary Secondary School *CLKNW* EC1R 10 E5
Rose McAndrew Clinic *BRXN/ST* SW9 .... 117 F5
Rosemead Preparatory School *DUL* SE21 .... 154 C2
Rosendale Primary School *DUL* SE21 .... 136 C5
Rose Theatre Exhibition *STHWK* SE1 .... 35 E3
Rosetta Primary School *POP/IOD* E16 .... 94 B4
Rosslyn Park RFC *PUT/ROE* SW15 .... 129 F2
Rotherfield Primary School *IS* N1 .... 76 C3
Rotherhithe Civic Centre
 BERM/RHTH SE16 .... 102 C3
Rotherhithe Primary School
 BERM/RHTH SE16 .... 102 C5
The Roundhouse Theatre *CAMTN* NW1 .... 74 A4
Roundwood Park Medical Centre
 WLSDN NW10 .... 70 A4
Rowan High School *CLAP* SW4 .... 135 D4
Rowley Industrial Park *ACT* W3 .... 98 B4

Roxwell Trading Park *LEY* E10 .... 61 E2
Royal Academy of Arts *MYFR/PICC* W1J 31 E2
Royal Academy of Dramatic Art
 GWRST WC1E 20 B1
Royal Academy of Music *CAMTN* NW1 ...... 18 B2
Royal Albert Hall *SKENS* SW7 .... 40 A1
Royal Arsenal *WOOL/PLUM* SE18 .... 108 B4
Royal Ballet School *LSQ/SEVD* WC2H 21 D5
The Royal Ballet School
 RCHPK/HAM TW10 .... 147 D1
Royal Blackheath Golf Club
 ELTH/MOT SE9 .... 143 F5
Royal Brompton & National Heart Hospitals
 CHEL SW3 .... 115 D1
Royal College of Anaesthetists *RSQ* WC1B 20 C2
Royal College of Art *SKENS* SW7 .... 39 F1
Royal College of Music *SHB* W12 .... 100 A4
 SKENS SW7 .... 40 A2
Royal College of Nursing *CAMTN* NW1 .... 7 F5
 IS N1 .... 76 B5
Royal College of Obstetricians &
 Gynaecologists *CAMTN* NW1 .... 5 E5
Royal College of Ophthalmologists
 CAMTN NW1 .... 18 A1
Royal College of Paediatrics & Child Health
 GTPST W1W 19 D2
The Royal College of Pathology
 STJS SW1Y 32 A4
Royal College of Physicians *CAMTN* NW1 .... 6 C5
Royal College of Surgeons *LINN* WC2A 21 F4
Royal Courts of Justice *LINN* WC2A 21 F5
Royal Court Theatre *BGVA* SW1W 42 A5
Royal Court Young Peoples Theatre
 NKENS W10 .... 89 E4
The Royal Dock Community School
 CAN/RD E16 .... 94 C5
Royal Docks Medical Centre *EHAM* E6 .... 96 A5
Royal Exchange *LOTH* EC2R 24 B5
Royal Festival Hall *STHWK* SE1 .... 33 E4
Royal Foundation of Grey Coat Hospital
 WESTW SW1E 43 D2
Royal Free Hospital *HAMP* NW3 .... 73 E2
Royal Free Hospital School of Medicine
 HAMP NW3 .... 73 E2
Royal Geographical Society *SKENS* SW7 .... 40 A1
Royal Horticultural Society New Hall
 WEST SW1P 44 A3
Royal Horticultural Society Old Hall
 WEST SW1P 44 A4
Royal Hospital Chelsea *CHEL* SW3 .... 115 F1
Royal Hospital for Neuro-Disability
 PUT/ROE SW15 .... 131 E4
Royal Hospital & Home *PUT/ROE* SW15 .... 130 B5
Royal Institute of British Architects
 REGST W1B 19 D2
Royal Institution's Faraday Museum
 MYFR/PICC W1J 31 D2
Royal London Homeopathic Hospital
 BMSBY WC1N 21 D2
Royal London Hospital *BETH* E2 .... 90 C1
The Royal London Hospital
 (Whitechapel) A & E *WCHPL* E1 .... 90 B4
Royal Marsden Hospital *CHEL* SW3 .... 115 D1
The Royal Mews *WHALL* SW1A 43 D2
Royal Mint Court *TWRH* EC3N 37 F2
Royal National Orthopaedic Hospital
 GTPST W1W 19 D1
Royal National Theatre *BRXN/ST* SW9 .... 118 A3
 STHWK SE1 .... 34 A3
Royal National Throat Nose & Ear Hospital
 FSBYW WC1X 9 E3
Royal Observatory Greenwich
 GNWCH SE10 .... 123 D2
Royal Opera House *COVGDN* WC2E 21 D5
The Royal School *HAMP* NW3 .... 73 D1
Royal Society of Arts *TPL/STR* WC2R 33 D2
Royal Society of Medicine
 CAVSQ/HST W1G 18 C4
Royal Veterinary College *CAMTN* NW1 .... 75 D5
Royal Victoria Docks Watersports Centre
 CAN/RD E16 .... 106 A1
Royal Wimbledon Golf Club
 WIM/MER SW19 .... 148 B5
RSPCA Animal Hospital *HOLWY* N7 .... 57 F4
Rudolph Steiner Hall *CAMTN* NW1 .... 5 E5
Rufus Business Centre *WAND/EARL* SW18 .... 150 B2
Rushey Green Primary School *CAT* SE6 .... 158 B1
Rushmore Junior School *CLPT* E5 .... 78 C1
Ruskin House School *HNHL* SE24 .... 136 C3
Ruxley Manor School *ELTH/MOT* SE9 .... 162 A4
Saatchi Gallery *STHWK* SE1 .... 33 E5
Sacred Heart High School *HMSMTH* W6 .... 100 C5
Sacred Heart Junior School *HMSMTH* W6 .... 101 D5
Sacred Heart RC Infant School
 BTSEA SW11 .... 115 E5

Sacred Heart RC Junior & Middle School
BTSEA SW11... 133 E1
Sacred Heart RC Primary School
PUT/ROE SW15 .... 130 A3
Sacred Heart RC School *CMBW* SE5 .... 118 C4
Sacred Heart RC School *HOLWY* N7 .... 75 D2
Saddlers Hall *CITYW* EC2V 23 E5
Sadler's Wells Theatre *CLKNW* EC1R........... 10 B3
SAE Technology College *HOLWY* N7 .... 75 E2
Sai Medical Centre *POP/IOD* E14 .... 104 C2
St Agnes RC Primary School *BOW* E3.......... 92 A2
CRICK NW2 .... 53 E5
St Aidans Primary School *FSBYPK* N4 .... 58 A2
St Aidans RC Primary School *IL* IG1 .... 67 D3
St Albans CE Primary School *FSBYW* WC1X... 22 A2
St Albans Health Clinic *KTTN* NW5 .... 56 A5
St Alfege with St Peter CE Primary School
GNWCH SE10 .... 122 C2
St Aloysius College *ARCH* N19 .... 56 C3
St Aloysius RC Infant School *CAMTN* NW1... 8 A3
St Aloysius RC Junior School *CAMTN* NW1... 7 A3
St Andrew & St Francis CE JMI School
CRICK NW2 .... 70 A3
St Andrews Greek School *CAMTN* NW1 .... 74 B3
St Andrews Hospital *BOW* E3........................ 92 B3
St Andrews Primary School
BRXN/ST SW9 .... 117 F5
PLSTW E13 .... 75 F5
St Andrews School *WLSDN* NW10 .... 70 B4
St Angelas School *FSTGT* E7 .... 82 B3
St Annes CE Primary School
WAND/EARL SW18 .... 132 B3
St Annes RC Primary School *LBTH* SE11..... 117 F1
St Anne's Trading Estate *POP/IOD* E14 ...... 91 F5
St Ansleims RC Primary School
TOOT SW17 .... 152 A3
St Anthony's Preparatory School
HAMP NW3 .... 73 D1
St Anthonys RC Primary School
EDUL SE22 .... 137 F4
FSTGT E7 .... 82 A4
St Anthony's School *HAMP* NW3 .... 72 C2
St Augustines CE School *KIL/WHAMP* NW6 ... 2 B1
St Augustines Primary School
KIL/WHAMP NW6 .... 2 B1
St Augustines RC Primary School
CAT SE6 .... 158 B5
FUL/PGN SW6 .... 113 E4
St Barnabas & Philip CE Primary School *KENS* W8 ... 38 A3
St Barnabas & St Philips CE Primary School
KENS W8 .... 38 A3
St Bartholomews CE Primary School
SYD SE26 .... 156 C4
St Bartholomews Hospital *STBT* EC1A 23 D3
St Bartholomews Medical School
FARR EC1M 23 D1
St Bartholomews & Royal London
School of Medicine *FARR* EC1M.............. 23 E2
St Bartholomew's the Great *STBT* EC1A 23 D3
St Bedes RC Infant School *BAL* SW12 .... 153 D1
St Bonaventure's School *FSTGT* E7............. 82 A4
St Boniface RC Primary School
TOOT SW17 .... 151 F5
St Bride's Church *EMB* EC4Y 22 C5
St Charles Hospital *NKENS* W10 .... 89 D4
St Charles RC Primary School *NKENS* W10 ... 89 D4
St Christmas Prep School *STJWD* NW8 .... 5 D1
St Christopher House *STHWK* SE1............... 35 E5
St Christophers School *HAMP* NW3 .... 73 D2
St Clement Danes CE Primary School
HOL/ALD WC2B 21 E5
St Clement & James CE Primary School
NTGHL W11 .... 101 F2
St Clements Hospital *BOW* E3...................... 91 F2
St Cuthbert with St Matthias CE
Primary School *ECT* SW5 .... 114 B1
St Dominics RC J & I School *HOM* E9 .... 79 D3
St Dominics RC Primary School
HAMP NW3 .... 73 F2
St Dunstans College *CAT* SE6 .... 157 F1
St Edmunds RC Primary School
POP/IOD E14 .... 104 A3
St Edwards RC JMI School *STJWD* NW8 ...... 16 C1
St Faiths CE School *WAND/EARL* SW18 ..... 132 B3
St Francesca Cabrini Primary School
FSTH SE23 .... 138 C4
St Francis of Assisi Primary School
NTGHL W11 .... 101 D1
St Francis RC Primary School *PECK* SE15... 120 A2
SRTFD E15 .... 81 E2
St Francis Xavier College *BAL* SW12 .... 134 B4
St Gabriels CE Primary School *PIM* SW1V ... 116 C1
St George's Cathedral *STHWK* SE1.............. 46 B2
St George's Cathedral RC Primary
STHWK SE1.. 46 C1

St Georges CE Primary School *PECK* SE15... 119 E3
VX/NE SW8 .... 116 C3
St Georges College *HOLWY* N7.................... 58 A5
St Georges Elizabethan Theatre *HOLWY* N7 ... 75 D1
St Georges Hanover Square CE
Primary School *MYFR/PKLN* W1K 30 B2
St Georges Hospital *TOOT* SW17 .... 151 E5
St Georges Pool *WCHPL* E1 .... 102 A1
St George the Martyr CE Primary School
BMSBY WC1N 21 E1
St George Wharf *VX/NE* SW8 .... 117 E1
St Gildas RC Junior School *CEND/HSY/T* N8... 57 E2
St Giles College London Central *RSO* WC1B ... 20 C2
St Helens RC Primary School
BRXN/ST SW9 .... 136 A1
PLSTW E13 .... 93 F3
St Ignatius RC Primary School
SEVS/STOTM N15 .... 59 E4
St James & St Michaels CE Primary School
BAY/PAD W2 .... 27 F1
St James CE J & I School *BERM/RHTH* SE16... 102 A4
St James CE Junior School *FSTGT* E7 .... 81 F2
St James Hatcham CE Primary School
NWCR SE14 .... 121 E4
St James's Palace *WHALL* SW1A 31 F4
St James the Great Catholic School
PECK SE15 .... 119 F4
St Joachims RC Primary School
CAN/RD E16... 94 C5
St Joan of Arc RC Primary School
HBRY N5 .... 76 B1
St John of Jerusalem CE Primary School
HOM E9 .... 78 C4
St John & St James CE Primary School
HACK E8 .... 78 C2
St Johns Angell Town CE Primary School
BRXN/ST SW9 .... 118 A5
St Johns CE Primary School *BETH* E2.......... 90 C1
WALW SE17 .... 47 F5
St John's CE Walham Green
FUL/PGN SW6 .... 113 E4
St Johns Concert Hall *WEST* SW1P 44 C3
St Johns Highbury Vale CE Primary School
HBRY N5 .... 58 B5
St John's Hospital *SOHO/SHAV* W1D 32 A1
St John's Hospital Day Centre
BTSEA SW11 .... 133 D2
St Johns RC Primary School
BERM/RHTH SE16 .... 103 E3
St Johns Upper Holloway
Primary School *ARCH* N19 .... 57 D3
St Johns Way Medical Centre *ARCH* N19..... 57 D3
St Johns Wood Prep School *STJWD* NW8 ..... 4 C3
St John the Baptist CE Primary School
CAT SE6 .... 158 C4
IS N1 .... 12 C2
St John the Divine CE Primary School
CMBW SE5 .... 118 B3
St John the Evangelist RC Primary School
IS N1 .... 10 C1
St Josephs Academic RC School
BKHTH/KID SE3....................................... 141 E1
St Josephs Catholic Infant School *LEY* E10... 61 F3
St Josephs Convent School *WAN* E11......... 64 C5
St Josephs Primary School
PUT/ROE SW15 .... 132 A3
St Josephs RC Junior School *CMBW* SE5 ... 118 C3
LEY E10 .... 61 F3
St Josephs RC Primary School *ARCH* N19 ... 56 B3
BARK IG11 .... 84 C5
BERM/RHTH SE16 .... 102 C4
CHEL SW3 .... 41 E5
DEPT SE8 .... 122 A3
GNWCH SE10 .... 123 E1
HOL/ALD WC2B 21 D4
MV/WKIL W9 .... 3 E4
STHWK SE1... 35 F5
STHWK SE1.. 102 A5
WLSDN NW10 .... 69 E4
St Judes CE Primary School *STHWK* SE1 ..... 46 C3
St Jude's CE Prim Sch *HNHL* SE24 .... 136 B4
St Judes & St Pauls CE Primary School
IS N1 .... 77 E3
St Katharine Pier *WAP* E1W 37 F3
St Lawrence University *FSBYW* WC1X 21 F1
St Leonards CE Primary School
STRHM/NOR SW16 .... 153 D5
St Leonards Hospital *IS* N1........................... 13 D1
St Lukes CE Primary School *CAN/RD* E16 ..... 93 F5
FSBYE EC1V 11 F4
MV/WKIL W9 .... 89 F1
POP/IOD E14 .... 105 D5
WNWD SE27 .... 154 C5
St Luke's Health Centre *CAN/RD* E16 .... 93 F5

St Lukes Hospital for the Clergy *FITZ* W1T 19 E1
St Margaret Lee CE Primary School
LEW SE13 .... 141 E2
St Margaret Lothbury *LOTH* EC2R 24 A4
St Margarets CE Primary School
WOOL/PLUM SE18 .... 126 C2
St Margarets Clitherow RC Primary School
WLSDN NW10 .... 51 D5
St Margarets Primary School *BARK* IG11 ...... 84 B5
St Margarets School *HAMP* NW3 .... 72 B1
St Marks CE Primary School *ARCH* N19 .... 57 E4
LBTH SE11 .... 117 F2
St Marks Industrial Estate *CAN/RD* E16 ..... 107 D2
St Martin-in-the-Fields High School
BRXS/STRHM SW2 .... 154 B1
St Martins Theatre *LSQ/SEVD* WC2H 32 B1
St Martins School *MYFR/PKLN* W1K 30 A1
St Martins School of Art *SOHO/SHAV* W1D 20 B5
St Mary Abbots CE Primary School
KENS W8 .... 38 C1
St Mary Abbots Church Hall *KENS* W8 .... 26 C5
St Mary Abchurch *MANHO* EC4N 36 A1
St Mary & St Josephs GM School
SCUP DA14 .... 163 F5
St Mary CE Primary School
PUT/ROE SW15 .... 131 D1
St Marylebone CE Secondary School
MHST W1U 18 B2
St Mary le Bow *MANHO* EC4N 23 F3
St Mary Magdalene CE Primary School
MV/WKIL W9 .... 14 C2
WOOL/PLUM SE18 .... 107 F5
PECK SE15 .... 120 B5
St Mary Magdalene Primary School
HOLWY N7 .... 76 A3
St Mary Magdalen RC Junior School
CRICK NW2 .... 70 B3
St Mary Magdalens RC Primary School
MORT/ESHN SW14 .... 129 D1
St Mary of the Angels RC Primary School
BAY/PAD W2 .... 14 A4
St Mary & St Pancras CE Primary School
CAMTN NW1 .... 8 A2
St Marys Bryanston Square CE
Primary School *MBLAR* W1H 17 E3
St Mary's Cemetery *BTSEA* SW11 .... 133 E3
St Marys CE Primary School *IS* N1 .... 76 B4
LEW SE13 .... 140 B3
WLSDN NW10 .... 69 E3
St Marys Hospital *BAY/PAD* W2 .... 16 B4
St Marys Hospital Medical School
BAY/PAD W2 .... 16 B4
St Mary's Kilburn Primary School
KIL/WHAMP NW6 .... 72 A5
St Marys Magdalens RC Primary School
BROCKY SE4 .... 139 E2
St Mary's Primary School *WKENS* W14 ...... 101 D4
St Marys RC Primary School *CHSWK* W4 .... 111 D1
CLAP SW4 .... 134 C3
ELTH/MOT SE9 .... 144 A3
KIL/WHAMP NW6 .... 2 A1
NKENS W10 .... 89 E3
VX/NE SW8 .... 116 B4
St Marys School *HAMP* NW3 .... 72 C2
St Marys Stoke Newington CE
Primary School *STNW/STAM* N16 .... 59 E4
St Matthews CE Primary School
WEST SW1P 44 B3
St Matthias CE Primary School *BETH* E2 .... 13 F5
STNW/STAM N16 .... 77 E2
St Michaels CE Primary School *HCT* N6 ...... 56 A2
WAND/EARL SW18 .... 131 F5
St Michaels CE Primary School *EHAM* E6 .... 95 F1
St Michaels RC Secondary School
BERM/RHTH SE16 .... 102 A3
St Michaels Sydenham CE Primary *SYD* SE26 157 E4
St Monicas RC Primary School *IS* N1 .... 12 C3
St Nicholas Preparatory School
CDALE/KGS NW9 .... 50 C4
St Olaves Preparatory School
ELTH/MOT SE9 .... 162 B2
St Osmunds RC Primary School
BARN SW13 .... 111 F4
St Pancras Hospital *CAMTN* NW1 .... 75 D5
St Patricks Church School *STHWK* SE1 .... 34 A4
St Patricks Infants School *WAP* E1W 102 B2
St Patricks International School
SOHO/CST W1F 19 F4
St Patricks Primary School *KTTN* NW5 .... 74 B3
St Patrick RC Primary School *WAP* E1W ... 102 B2
WOOL/PLUM SE18 .... 109 D5
St Paul's Cathedral *STP* EC4M 23 D5
St Paul's Cathedral School *STP* EC4M 23 E5
St Pauls CE Primary School *HAMP* NW3 ..... 73 E4
WALW SE17 .... 118 B1

WAP E1W 102 A1
St Pauls Girls School *HMSMTH* W6 .... 101 D5
St Pauls Preparatory School *BARN* SW13 ... 112 A1
St Pauls Primary School *HMSMTH* W6 .... 112 C1
St Pauls Road Medical Centre *IS* N1 .... 76 B3
St Pauls Way School *BOW* E3 .... 92 A3
St Pauls with St Lukes CE Primary School
BOW E3 .... 91 F4
St Paul's with St Michael's CE
Primary School *HACK* E8 .... 78 A5
St Paul with St Luke CE Primary School
POP/IOD E14 .... 91 F4
St Peter & Pauls RC Primary School *IL* IG1 ... 67 D5
St Peter & St Pauls Primary School
FSBYE EC1V 11 D5
St Peters CE Primary School *HMSMTH* W6 ... 112 A1
MV/WKIL W9 .... 14 A1
WALW SE17 .... 119 D1
St Peters Eaton Square CE Primary School
BCVA SW1W 42 C3
St Peter's Hospital *COVGDN* WC2E 33 D1
St Peters Primary School *WAP* E1W 102 C2
St Peters RC Primary School
WOOL/PLUM SE18 .... 126 B1
St Philips School *SKENS* SW7 .... 39 F5
St Phillips Infant School *SYD* SE26 .... 156 B4
St Quintins Health Centre *NKENS* W10 ...... 88 C4
St Raphaels Way Medical Centre
WBLY HA9 .... 68 C2
St Robert Southwell RC Primary School
CDALE/KGS NW9 .... 50 C1
St Saviour & St Olaves School *STHWK* SE1 ... 48 B3
St Saviours CE Primary School
HNHL SE24 .... 136 C1
MV/WKIL W9 .... 15 D1
POP/IOD E14 .... 92 B4
WALTH E17 .... 61 F2
St Saviours RC Primary School *LEW* SE13 ... 140 C2
St Scholastica's RC Primary School
STNW/STAM N16 .... 60 A5
St Stephens CE Primary School
BAY/PAD W2 .... 14 B3
DEPT SE8 .... 122 A5
SHB W12 .... 100 C2
St Stephens CE School *VX/NE* SW8 .... 117 E3
St Stephens Primary School *EHAM* E6 .... 82 C4
St Stephen Walbrook *MANHO* EC4N 36 A1
St Thomas CE Primary School *NKENS* W10 ... 89 E3
STNW/STAM N16 .... 59 F3
St Thomas' Hospital *STHWK* SE1 .... 45 E2
St Thomas' Hospital Operation Theatre
STHWK SE1 .... 36 B4
St Thomas More RC Primary School
ELTH/MOT SE9 .... 143 E1
St Thomas More RC School *CHEL* SW3 .... 41 E5
ELTH/MOT SE9 .... 144 A4
St Thomas of Canterbury RC
Primary School *FUL/PGN* SW6 .... 113 F3
St Thomas the Apostle College
PECK SE15 .... 120 C4
St Ursulas Convent School *GNWCH* SE10 ... 123 D3
St Vincent de Paul RC Primary School
WEST SW1P 43 E3
St Vincents Catholic Primary School
ELTH/MOT SE9 .... 161 E4
St Vincents RC Primary School *ACT* W3 ..... 98 B1
MHST W1U 18 A3
St Walter & St John Sports Ground
TOOT SW17 .... 151 E1
St William of York Primary School
TOOT SW17 .... 151 F1
St Winefrides Catholic Primary School
FSTH SE23 .... 157 E5
St Winefrides Catholic Primary School
MNPK E12 .... 83 F2
St Winifreds Junior School
LEE/GVPK SE12 .... 141 F4
St Winifreds RC Infant School *LEW* SE13 ... 141 E5
Salesian College *BTSEA* SW11 .... 115 E4
Salisbury Primary School *MNPK* E12 .... 82 D2
Salters' Hall *BARB* EC2Y 23 F3
Salusbury Primary School
KIL/WHAMP NW6 .... 71 E5
Salvation Army Heritage Centre
BLKFR EC4V 35 E1
Samaritan & Western Ophthalmic Hospital
MBLAR W1H 17 E2
Samuel Jones Industrial Estate
PECK SE15 .... 119 E3
Samuel Rhodes School *IS* N1 .... 76 A5
Sandgate Trading Estate
BERM/RHTH SE16 .... 120 B1
Sandhurst Primary School *CAT* SE6 .... 141 E5
Sandringham Primary School *FSTGT* E7 ..... 82 C3
Sapcote Trading Centre *WLSDN* NW10 .... 69 F2
Sarah Bonnell School *SRTFD* E15 .... 81 E3
Sarum Hall School *HAMP* NW3 .... 73 E4

Satmer Trust School *STNW/STAM* N16.......... **60** A4
Savoy Pier *TPL/STR* WC2R.......... **33** E2
Savoy Theatre *TPL/STR* WC2R.......... **33** E2
Sayer Clinics *MBLAR* W1H.......... **17** F5
Scarsdale Place Medical Centre *KENS* W8.......... **38** C2
Schiller International School *STHWK* SE1.......... **34** A4
Schomberg House *STJS* SW1Y.......... **31** F4
School of English *GLDGN* NW11.......... **54** A3
School of Oriental & African Studies
 STPAN WC1H.......... **20** B1
The School of Pharmacy *BMSBY* WC1N.......... **9** D5
Science Museum *SKENS* SW7.......... **40** B3
Science Museum Imax Cinema *SKENS* SW7.......... **40** A3
The Science Museum Library *SKENS* SW7.......... **40** A2
Scott Wilkie Primary School *CAN/RD* E16.......... **94** C5
Screen on Baker Street Cinema
 MHST W1U.......... **17** F2
Screen on the Green Cinema *IS* N1.......... **76** A5
Screen on the Hill Cinema *HAMP* NW3.......... **73** E2
Sebright Primary School *BETH* E2.......... **90** B1
Sedgehill School *CAT* SE6.......... **158** B5
Sedgewick Centre *WCHPL* E1.......... **25** F4
Selwyn Primary School *PLSTW* E13.......... **82** A5
Sergeant Industrial Estate
 WAND/EARL SW18.......... **132** B4
Serpentine Gallery *BAY/PAD* W2.......... **28** B4
Servite RC Primary School *WBPTN* SW10.......... **114** C2
Seven Islands Leisure Centre
 BERM/RHTH SE16.......... **102** C4
Seven Kings High School *GNTH/NBYPK* IG2.......... **67** E3
Seven Mills Primary School *POP/IOD* E14.......... **104** A3
Seymour Gardens Medical Centre *IL* IG1.......... **65** F3
Seymour Leisure Centre *MBLAR* W1H.......... **17** F3
Shaare Zedek Medical Centre
 GLDGN NW11.......... **53** F1
Shacklewell Primary School
 STNW N16.......... **77** F1
Shaftesbury Hospital *LSQ/SEVD* WC2H.......... **20** B5
Shaftesbury Park Primary School
 BTSEA SW11.......... **134** A1
Shaftesbury Primary School *FSTGT* E7.......... **82** C4
Shaftesbury Theatre *LSQ/SEVD* WC2H.......... **20** C4
Shahjalal Medical Centre *WCHPL* E1.......... **90** A5
Shakespeare Business Centre
 BRXN/ST SW9.......... **136** B1
Shakespeare's Globe Theatre *STHWK* SE1.......... **35** D2
The Shamrock Sports Club *ACT* W3.......... **86** C5
Shapla J & I School *WCHPL* E1.......... **102** A1
Sheen Lane Health Centre
 MORT/ESHN SW14.......... **128** C1
Sheen Mount Primary School
 RCHPK/HAM TW10.......... **128** B3
Sheen Sports Centre *MORT/ESHN* SW14.......... **129** E2
Sheen Sports Centre *MORT/ESHN* SW14.......... **129** E2
Shell Centre *STHWK* SE1.......... **33** F4
Shelley School *CLAP* SW4.......... **134** C1
Shepherd's Bush Cricket Club *ACT* W3.......... **99** E1
Shepherd's Bush Empire *SHB* W12.......... **100** C3
Shepherds Community School *YWAM*
 BROCKY SE4.......... **140** A1
Sheringdale Primary School
 WAND/EARL SW18.......... **149** F1
Sheringham Junior School *MNPK* E12.......... **83** F1
Sherington Primary School *CHARL* SE7.......... **124** B2
Sherlock Holmes Museum *CAMTN* NW1.......... **17** F1
Shooters Hill Golf Club *WOOL/PLUM* SE18.......... **126** C4
The Shopping Hall *EHAM* E6.......... **83** E5
Shore Business Centre *HOM* E9.......... **78** C4
Shoreditch Comprehensive School *IS* N1.......... **13** D2
Shoreditch County Court *STLK* EC1V.......... **12** B5
Showcase Newham Cinema Bowl *EHAM* IG11.......... **96** C2
Shrewsbury Road Health Centre *FSTGT* E7.......... **83** D4
Sidcup Sports Club *SCUP* DA14.......... **163** F4
Simon Marks Jewish Primary School
 STNW/STAM N16.......... **59** F3
Sinclair House School *FUL/PGN* SW6.......... **113** E4
Sion College *EMB* EC4Y.......... **34** B1
Sion Manning RC Girls School *NKENS* W10.......... **89** D4
Sir Francis Drake Primary School
 DEPT SE8.......... **121** E1
Sir James Barrie School *VX/NE* SW8.......... **117** E1
Sir John Cass Foundation/Redcoat School
 WCHPL E1.......... **91** D4
Sir John Cass Foundation School
 TWRH EC3N.......... **25** E5
Sir John Lilian Primary School *HMSMTH* W6.......... **113** F2
Sir John Soane's Museum *LINN* WC2A.......... **21** F4
Sir Thomas Abney Primary School
 STNW/STAM N16.......... **59** D2
Sir William Burrough School
 POP/IOD E14.......... **91** E5
Six Bridges Trading Estate *STHWK* SE1.......... **120** A1
Skillion Business Park *BARK* IG11.......... **97** D3

Skinners Company Lower
 Girls School *CLPT* E5.......... **60** B3
Skinners Companys School For Girls
 STNW/STAM N16.......... **59** F3
Slade School of Fine Art *STPAN* WC1H.......... **8** B4
Sleaford Industrial Estate *VX/NE* SW8.......... **116** C3
Smallwood Primary School *TOOT* SW17.......... **151** D4
SMA Medical Centre *LEY* E10.......... **62** B2
Smithy Street School *WCHPL* E1.......... **90** C4
Snowsfields Primary School *STHWK* SE1.......... **36** C5
Sobell Leisure Centre *HOLWY* N7.......... **57** F5
Sobell Medical Centre *HOLWY* N7.......... **76** A1
Soho Parish CE Primary School
 SOHO/CST W1F.......... **32** A1
Solent Road Health Centre
 KIL/WHAMP NW6.......... **72** A3
Somerset House *COVGDN* WC2E.......... **33** E1
Somers Town Community Sports Centre
 CAMTN NW1.......... **7** F2
Sorsby Health Centre *CLPT* E5.......... **79** D1
South Bank Business Centre *BTSEA* SW11.......... **116** A4
 VX/NE SW8.......... **117** D2
Southbank International School
 HAMP NW3.......... **72** C3
 NTCHL W11.......... **26** A2
Southbank University *STHWK* SE1.......... **46** C1
 STHWK SE1.......... **47** E2
 VX/NE SW8.......... **117** D4
South Camden Community School
 CAMTN NW1.......... **7** F1
South Chelsea College *BRXN/ST* SW9.......... **135** E2
South Eastern University *HOLWY* N7.......... **57** F5
Southern Road Primary School
 PLSTW E13.......... **94** B1
Southfield First & Middle School
 CHSWK W4.......... **99** E3
Southfield Medical Centre *CHSWK* W4.......... **99** D3
The Southfield Clinic *WAND/EARL* SW18.......... **132** A4
Southfields Community School
 WAND/EARL SW18.......... **150** A1
Southgate Road Medical Centre *IS* N1.......... **77** D4
South Grove Primary School *WALTH* E17.......... **61** E1
South Hampstead Cricket Club
 CRCK NW2.......... **70** C4
South Hampstead High School (Senior)
 HAMP NW3.......... **73** D3
Southlands College *PUT/ROE* SW15.......... **129** F2
South Lewisham Health Centre *CAT* SE6.......... **158** C4
South London Gallery *CMBW* SE5.......... **119** E4
South London Montessori School
 BTSEA SW11.......... **115** E4
The South London Natural Health Centre
 CLAP SW4.......... **154** C2
South London Theatre *WNWD* SE27.......... **154** E3
Southmead Primary School
 WIM/MER SW19.......... **149** E1
South Park Business Centre *IL* IG1.......... **67** E4
South Park Clinic *IL* IG1.......... **85** E1
South Park Primary School
 GDMY/SEVK IG3.......... **67** E5
South Quay Plaza *POP/IOD* E14.......... **104** B3
South Rise Primary School
 WOOL/PLUM SE18.......... **127** D1
Southside Industrial Estate *VX/NE* SW8.......... **116** C3
South Thames College *PUT/ROE* SW15.......... **131** D3
South Thames College/Roehampton
 Adult College *PUT/ROE* SW15.......... **129** F4
Southwark Bridge Business Centre
 STHWK SE1.......... **35** F4
Southwark Bridge Stairs *BLKFR* EC4V.......... **35** E2
Southwark Cathedral *STHWK* SE1.......... **36** A3
Southwark College *BERM/RHTH* SE16.......... **102** B4
 CMBW SE5.......... **119** E3
 STHWK SE1.......... **34** C5
 STHWK SE1.......... **49** D2
Southwark Crown Court *STHWK* SE1.......... **36** C3
Southwark Park Primary School
 BERM/RHTH SE16.......... **102** B4
Southwark Park Sports Centre
 BERM/RHTH SE16.......... **102** C5
Southwark Sports Ground *DUL* SE21.......... **155** F1
Southwark Hospital *HGT* N6.......... **56** A2
The Space Arts Centre Cinema
 POP/IOD E14.......... **105** F5
Speakers Corner *BAY/PAD* W2.......... **29** F1
Speke's Monument *BAY/PAD* W2.......... **27** F5
Spencer House *WHALL* SW1A.......... **31** E4
Spiritualist University *WLSDN* NW10.......... **70** A4
Spitalfields Health Centre *WCHPL* E1.......... **25** F3
Spitalfields Market Hall *WCHPL* E1.......... **25** E2
Springfield Christian School *PECK* SE15.......... **119** F3
Springfield Hospital *TOOT* SW17.......... **151** E3
Springfield Primary School *VX/NE* SW8.......... **117** D5

The Stables Gallery & Art Centre
  CRICK NW2 .... 70 A1
Stadium Business Centre WBLY HA9 .... 50 D5
Stadium Industrial Estate WBLY HA9 .... 68 B2
Stadium Retail Park WBLY HA9 .... 50 A5
Stamford Clinic HMSMTH W6 .... 100 A5
Stamford Hill Primary School
  SEVS/STOTM N15 .... 59 D1
Standard Industrial Estate CAN/RD E16 ..... 107 D3
Stanton Square Industrial Estate
  CAT SE6 .... 157 F4
Staple Inn Buildings HHOL WC1V 22 A3
Staples Corner Business Park CRICK NW2 ..... 52 B4
Star Primary School CAN/RD E16 .... 93 E3
Stationers Hall STP EC4M 23 D5
Stationery Office HOL/ALD WC2B 21 E4
Stephen Hawking Primary School
  POP/IOD E14 .... 91 E5
Stepney Day Hospital WCHPL E1 .... 90 C5
Stepney Greencoat CE Primary School
  POP/IOD E14 .... 91 F5
Stepney Green School WCHPL E1 .... 91 F4
Stewart Headlam Primary School
  WCHPL E1 .... 90 B5
Stillness Primary School BROCKY SE4 .... 139 E4
Stock Exchange OBST EC2N 24 B4
Stockwell Park School BRXN/ST SW9 .... 117 F4
Stockwell Primary School BRXN/ST SW9 ..... 135 F1
Stoke Newington School STNW/STAM N16 ..... 59 D5
The Stonebridge Primary School
  WLSDN NW10 .... 68 C5
Stonebridge Shopping Centre
  WLSDN NW10 .... 69 D5
Stone Lake Retail Park CHARL SE7 .... 106 C5
Storey Primary School CAN/RD E16 .... 108 A2
Stormont House School CLPT E5 .... 78 B1
Strand on the Green J & I School
  CHSWK W4 .... 110 A2
Strand Theatre HOL/ALD WC2B 33 E1
Stratford Magistrates Court SRTFD E15 ..... 81 D1
Stratford School FSTGT E7 .... 82 A4
Stratford Shopping Centre SRTFD E15 .... 81 D1
Stratford Station BAY/PAD W2 .... 14 B5
Streatham & Clapham High School
  STRHM/NOR SW16 .... 152 C3
Streatham & Clapham High School
  Preparatory School BRXS/STRHM SW2 ..... 153 F1
Streatham Cemetery TOOT SW17 .... 151 E3
Streatham Ice Rink STRHM/NOR SW16 .... 153 E3
Streatham Swimming Pool
  STRHM/NOR SW16 .... 153 E3
Streatham Wells Primary School
  BRXS/STRHM SW2 .... 153 F2
Stroud Green Primary School FSBYPK N4 ..... 58 A3
The Study Preparatory School
  WIM/MER SW19 .... 149 D5
Sudbourne Primary School
  BRXS/STRHM SW2 .... 135 F3
Sulivan Primary School FUL/PGN SW6 .... 114 A5
Sunnyhill Primary School
  STRHM/NOR SW16 .... 153 F4
Surrey Docks Farm BERM/RHTH SE16 .... 103 F3
Surrey Docks Health Centre
  BERM/RHTH SE16 .... 103 E4
Surrey Docks Watersports Centre
  BERM/RHTH SE16 .... 103 E4
Surrey Quays Leisure Park
  BERM/RHTH SE16 .... 103 D4
Surrey Quays Shopping Centre
  BERM/RHTH SE16 .... 103 D4
Surrey Square J & I School WALW SE17 ..... 119 D1
Surrey CCC (The Oval) LBTH SE11 .... 117 F2
Sussex House Preparatory School
  KTBR SW1X 41 E4
Sutcliffe Park Athletics Track
  ELTH/MOT SE9 .... 142 B3
Sutton House HOM E9 .... 78 C2
Swaffield Primary School
  WAND/EARL SW18 .... 132 C4
Swaminarayan School WLSDN NW10 .... 69 D3
Swan Business Centre CHSWK W4 .... 99 D5
Swan Lane Pier CANST EC4R 36 A2
Swanlea School WCHPL E1 .... 90 B3
Swedish School BARN SW13 .... 112 A2
Swiss Cottage School HAMP NW3 .... 73 D5
Swiss Re-Insurance Tower LVPST EC2M 24 C4
Sybourn Infant School LEY E10 .... 61 E3
Sybourn Junior School WALTH E17 .... 61 F2
Sydenham Girls School SYD SE26 .... 156 B3
Sydenham High School SYD SE26 .... 156 B5
Sydenham (Junior) High School
  SYD SE26 .... 156 B4
Syracuse University London Centre
  NTCHL W11 .... 101 F1
Tabard Theatre CHSWK W4 .... 99 D3

Talmud Torah School STNW/STAM N16 .... 59 D2
Tate Britain WEST SW1P 44 C5
Tate Modern STHWK SE1 .... 35 D3
Tavistock Clinic HAMP NW3 .... 73 D3
Telegraph Hill School BROCKY SE4 .... 121 E5
Telferscot Primary School BAL SW12 ...... 152 C1
Temple of Bacchus CMBW SE5 .... 118 C5
Temple of Mithras MANHO EC4N 24 A5
Terence McMillan Stadium PLSTW E13 ...... 94 C3
Thames Barrier CAN/RD E16 .... 107 D3
Thames Barrier Visitor Centre
  WOOL/PLUM SE18 .... 107 D4
Thames Christian College BTSEA SW11 ..... 133 D1
Thames House WEST SW1H 44 C4
Thameside Industrial Estate CAN/RD E16 .. 107 D5
Thames Magistrates Court BOW E3 .... 92 A2
Thames View Clinic BARK IG11 .... 97 F1
Thames Water Tower NTCHL W11 .... 101 D3
Thames Wharf Studios HMSMTH W6 .... 100 B2
Theatre for Mankind FSBYPK N4 .... 57 F3
Theatre Museum Library & Archive
  COVGDN WC2E 33 D1
Theatre of the Dispossessed
  WIM/MER SW19 .... 149 D1
Theatre Royal SRTFD E15 .... 81 D4
Theatre Royal, Drury Lane HOL/ALD WC2B .. 21 D5
Theatre Royal Haymarket STJS SW1Y 32 B2
Theodore McLeary Primary School
  BRXS/STRHM SW2 .... 135 F2
Thomas Buxton Primary School
  WCHPL E1 .... 90 A3
Thomas Fairchild Primary School IS N1 ... 12 A1
Thomas Gamuel Primary School
  WALTH E17 .... 62 A1
Thomas Jones Primary School
  NTCHL W11 .... 89 E5
Thomas London Independent Day School
  KENS W8 .... 39 D2
Thomas Road Industrial Estate
  POP/IOD E14 .... 92 A4
Thomas's Preparatory School
  BTSEA SW11 .... 115 D4
Thomas Tallis School BKHTH/KID SE3 ..... 142 B1
Thornhill Primary School IS N1 .... 76 A4
Thorntree Primary School CHARL SE7 ..... 125 D1
Three Mills Heritage Centre SRTFD E15 ... 92 C2
Thurlow Park School WNWD SE27 .... 154 B2
Thurston Industrial Estate LEW SE13 .... 140 B1
Tidemill Primary School DEPT SE8 .... 122 A3
Tideway Industrial Estate VX/NE SW8 .... 116 C2
Tiller Centre (Swimming Baths)
  POP/IOD E14 .... 104 A4
Tiller Leisure Centre POP/IOD E14 ...... 104 A4
Timbercroft Primary School
  WOOL/PLUM SE18 .... 127 E3
Tiverton Primary School SEVS/STOTM N15 .. 59 D1
Tobacco Dock WAP E1W 102 B1
Tokyngton Community Centre WBLY HA9 .... 68 B2
Toldos School STNW/STAM N16 .... 59 D3
Tollgate Primary School PLSTW E13 ...... 94 C3
Tom Hood School WAN E11 .... 63 F5
Toynbee Hall & Curtain Theatre WCHPL E1 . 25 E4
Tooting Bec Athletics Track TOOT SW17 ... 152 B4
Tooting Leisure Centre TOOT SW17 .... 151 D4
Torriano J & I School KTTN NW5 .... 74 C2
Torridon Primary School CAT SE6 .... 159 D2
Total Health Clinic SHB W12 .... 100 B5
Tower Bridge Experience STHWK SE1 ...... 37 E4
Tower Bridge Primary School STHWK SE1 .. 37 E5
Tower Bridge Wharf WAP E1W 102 A2
Tower Hamlets College POP/IOD E14 ...... 104 B1
  WCHPL E1 .... 90 C4
Tower House School MORT/ESHN SW14 ..... 130 C2
Tower Medical Centre WCHPL E1 .... 90 A5
Tower Millennium Pier MON EC3R 37 D3
Tower of London TWRH EC3N 37 E2
Towers Business Park WBLY HA9 .... 68 B1
Tower Stairs MON EC3R 36 C2
Tower Theatre IS N1 .... 76 B4
Townmead Business Centre
  FUL/PGN SW6 .... 132 C1
Townsend Industrial Estate WLSDN NW10 .. 68 C5
Townsend Primary School STHWK SE1 ...... 48 C4
Trabzon Spor FC STNW/STAM N16 .... 59 E3
Trade Union Congress NOXST/BSQ WC1A 20 B4
Trafalgar Business Centre BARK IG11 .... 97 F3
Tramshed Theatre WOOL/PLUM SE18 .... 108 B5
Trans Atlantic College BETH E2 .... 13 E1
Transport House WEST SW1P 44 C4
Treasury WHALL SW1A 32 C4
The Treehouse School BMSBY WC1N 9 E5
Trevor Roberts School HAMP NW3 .... 73 D4
Tricycle Cinema KIL/WHAMP NW6 .... 71 F4
Trident Business Centre TOOT SW17 ...... 151 F5

Trinity Business Centre
BERM/RHTH SE16 .... **103** F3

Trinity College *PECK* SE15 .... **119** E3

Trinity College Centre *PECK* SE15 .... **119** E3

Trinity College of Music *GNWCH* SE10 ... **122** C2

MHST W1U **18** B3

Trinity Hospital *GNWCH* SE10 ..... **123** D1

Trinity House *TWRH* EC3N **37** D1

Trinity St Marys Primary School
BAL SW12 .... **152** A1

Trocadero Centre *MYFR/PICC* W1J **32** A2

Trojan Business Centre *WLSDN* NW10 .. **69** F3

True Buddha School *IS* N1 .... **75** F5

Tudor Lodge Health Centre
WIM/MER SW19 .... **131** D5

Tufnell Park Primary School *HOLWY* N7 .. **75** D1

Tuke School *PECK* SE15 .... **120** B4

Tulloch Clinic *SHB* W12 .... **101** D2

Tunnel Avenue Trading Estate
GNWCH SE10 .... **105** D3

Turney School *DUL* SE21 .... **136** C5

Turnham Primary School *BROCKY* SE4 .. **139** E2

Twyford CE High School *ACT* W3 ... **98** B2

Twyford Sports Centre *ACT* W3 .... **98** B2

Tyburn Infant School *STJWD* NW8 ... **4** B5

The Type Museum *BRXN/ST* SW9 .... **117** F4

Tyssen Primary School *STNW/STAM* N16 .. **60** A3

UCI Cinema *BAY/PAD* W2 .... **15** D5

BERM/RHTH SE16 .... **103** D4

UCI Empire Cinema *LSQ/SEVD* WC2H ... **32** B2

UCI Filmworks Cinema *GNWCH* SE10 .. **105** F5

UCL Hospitals *FITZ* W1T **19** F1

UGC Cinema *CHEL* SW3 .... **115** D2

CRICK NW2 .... **52** B3

HMSMTH W6 .... **100** B5

SOHO/SHAV W1D **32** A1

United Medical & Dental Schools
STHWK SE1 .... **45** E2

United Services Sports Ground
CHSWK W4 .... **111** E4

Unity College *KTTN* NW5 .... **74** B1

University Church of Christ the King
STPAN WC1H **20** A1

University College Hospital *GWRST* WC1E .. **19** F1

HAMP NW3 .... **73** D3

University College Junior School
HAMP NW3 .... **72** C1

STPAN WC1H **8** A5

University College London *FITZ* W1T ... **19** F2

University College London, Astor College
FITZ W1T **19** F2

**University College London, Department of
Clinical Haematology** *GWRST* WC1E ... **20** A1

University College London
Medical School *FITZ* W1T **19** E2

University College School *HAMP* NW3 .. **72** C2

University Hospital Lewisham *LEW* SE13 .. **140** B3

University of California *WHALL* SW1A ... **31** E4

University of East London *PLSTW* E13 ... **94** B2

University of East London Campus
EHAM E6 .... **108** A1

University of Greenwich *GNWCH* SE10 .. **123** D1

WOOL/PLUM SE18 .... **108** A4

University of Greenwich (Mansion Site)
ELTH/MOT SE9 .... **144** C4

University of Greenwich (Southwood Site)
ELTH/MOT SE9 .... **144** C4

University of Greenwich Sports Ground
ELTH/MOT SE9 .... **143** E2

ELTH/MOT SE9 .... **144** C5

University of London *BAY/PAD* W2 ... **16** A5

BMSBY WC1N **21** D1

FITZ W1T **20** A4

NWCR SE14 .... **121** E4

STPAN WC1H **8** B5

University of North London *HOLWY* N7 .. **75** F1

University of Notre Dame *LSQ/SEVD* WC2H .. **32** B1

University of Westminster *CAMTN* NW1 .. **7** E5

CHSWK W4 .... **110** C4

GTPST W1W **19** E2

HGT N6 .... **56** B3

MHST W1U **18** A2

Uphall Primary School *IL* IG1 ...... **84** B2

Upper Montagu Street Clinic *MBLAR* W1H .. **17** E2

Upper Tooting Independent High School
TOOT SW17 .... **151** E2

Upton Cross Primary School *PLSTW* E13 .. **82** B5

Upton Lane Medical Centre *STGT* E7 ... **82** B2

Ursuline High School *IL* IG1 .... **66** B4

The Vale Medical Centre *FSTH* SE23 ... **157** E2

Valentine High School *IL* IG1 ...... **66** A1

Vale Park Industrial *ACT* W3 .... **99** E3

The Vale School *SKENS* SW7 .... **39** E3

Valmar Trading Estate *CMBW* SE5 .. **119** E3

Vanbrugh Theatre *GWRST* WC1E **20** A1

Vanguard Trading Estate *SRTFD* E15 ... **80** C5

Vaudeville Theatre *COVGDN* WC2E ... **33** D1

Vauxhall Primary School *LBTH* SE11 ... **117** F1

Vernon House Special School
WLSDN NW10 .... **68** C2

Vicarage Fields Health Clinic *BARK* IG11 .. **84** C4

The Vicarage Field Shopping Centre
BARK IG11 .... **84** C4

Victoria & Albert Museum *SKENS* SW7 .. **40** B3

Victoria Chiropractic Clinic *CHEL* SW3 .. **41** E1

Victoria Coach Station *BGVA* SW1W ... **42** C5

Victoria Industrial Estate *ACT* W3 ... **87** D4

Victoria Medical Centre *PIM* SW1V ... **43** E5

Victoria Palace Theatre *WESTW* SW1E .. **43** D5

Victoria Park Industrial Centre *HOM* E9 .. **79** F4

Victoria Place Shopping Centre *PIM* SW1V .. **43** D4

Victoria Rail/Air Terminal *PIM* SW1V ... **43** D4

Victoria Wharf *POP/IOD* E14 .... **103** E1

Victoria Wharf Industrial Estate
DEPT SE8 .... **121** F1

Victory Primary School *WALW* SE17 ... **47** F4

The Village School *HAMP* NW3 ...... **73** F3

The Vines School *BTSEA* SW11 ...... **134** A2

Vinopolis, City of Wine *STHWK* SE1 .. **35** F5

Vinters' Hall *BLKFR* EC4V **35** F1

VIP Trading Estate *CHARL* SE7 ...... **106** C5

Virginia Primary School *BETH* E2 .... **13** E4

Visitor Centre *STJS* SW1Y **32** A3

Voyager Business Estate
BERM/RHTH SE16 .... **102** A4

Waldorf School of SW London
STRHM/NOR SW16 .... **152** C2

Waldorf Steiner School of SW London
STRHM/NOR SW16 .... **153** D4

Wallace Collection *MHST* W1U **18** A4

Walmer Road Clinic *NTGHL* W11 ..... **101** E1

Walnut Tree Walk Primary School
LBTH SE11 .... **46** A4

Walworth Lower School *WALW* SE17 .. **119** D1

Walworth Town Hall *WALW* SE17 .... **47** E5

Walworth Upper School *WALW* SE17 .. **119** E1

Wandle Primary School
WAND/EARL SW18 .... **150** B1

Wandle Recreation Centre
WAND/EARL SW18 .... **132** B4

The Wandsworth Arndale Centre
WAND/EARL SW18 .... **132** B4

Wandsworth Cemetery
WAND/EARL SW18 .... **150** C1

Wandsworth Community Health Trust
TOOT SW17 .... **152** A5

Wandsworth County Court
PUT/ROE SW15 .... **131** E3

Wandsworth Trading Estate
WAND/EARL SW18 .... **132** B5

Wanstead Cricket Club *WAN* E11 .... **64** B2

Wanstead Golf Club *WAN* E11 ...... **64** C2

Wanstead High School *WAN* E11 .... **64** C1

Wanstead Leisure Centre *WAN* E11 .. **64** C1

Wapping Sports Centre *WAP* E1W ... **102** C2

Warner Village Cinema *ACT* W3 ..... **86** A3

HAMP NW3 .... **72** B3

SHB W12 .... **101** D3

SOHO/SHAV W1D **32** B1

Warwick Estate *BAY/PAD* W2 .... **15** D5

Warwick Leadlay Gallery *GNWCH* SE10 .. **122** C2

Warwick Park School *PECK* SE15 .... **119** F4

Waterfront Leisure Centre
WOOL/PLUM SE18 .... **108** A4

Watergate School *LEW* SE13 .... **140** B2

Waterloo Health Centre *STHWK* SE1 .. **46** A1

The Watermans Hall *MON* EC3R **36** C2

Water Rats Theatre *STPAN* WC1H **9** D3

Watersports Centre *FSBYPK* N4 ..... **58** C3

Wavelengths Leisure Pool & Library
DEPT SE8 .... **122** A3

Waverley Lower Secondary School
EDUL SE22 .... **138** B3

Waverley School *EDUL* SE22 .... **138** C3

Waxchandlers' Hall *CITYW* EC2V **23** F4

Welbeck Clinic *CRICK* NW2 .... **54** A5

Welfare Clinic *CMBW* SE5 .... **118** C4

GNWCH SE10 .... **122** C3

HGT N6 .... **56** A1

Wellcome Institute *CAMTN* NW1 ..... **8** A5

Wellington Medical Centre *WELL* DA16 .. **145** F2

Wellington Arch *MYFR/PICC* W1J **31** E3

Wellington Primary School *BOW* E3 .. **92** A2

Wembley Arena *WBLY* HA9 .... **68** A1

Wembley Park Business Centre
WBLY HA9 .... **50** B5

Wembley Stadium Industrial Estate
  WBLY HA9 .... 50 C5
  WBLY HA9 .... 68 A1
Wembley Stadium (under development)
  WBLY HA9 .... 68 A1
Wendell Park Primary School *SHB* W12 ...... 99 F3
Wentworth Tutorial College *GLDGN* NW11 .... 53 D1
Wesley's Chapel, House & Museum
  STLK EC1Y 12 A5
Wessex Gardens Primary School
  CRICK NW2 .... 53 E3
West Acton Primary School *ACT* W3 .... 86 B5
West Becton Health Centre *CAN/RD* E16 ..... 95 D5
Westbourne Green Sports Complex
  BAY/PAD W2 .... 14 B3
Westbridge College *BTSEA* SW11 .... 115 E4
Western Avenue Business Park *ACT* W3 ...... 86 B3
Western Trading Estate *WLSDN* NW10 .... 86 C3
Westfields Primary School *BARN* SW13 ...... 111 F5
Westgate Business Centre *NKENS* W10 .... 89 E3
West Ham Church Primary School
  SRTFD E15 .... 81 F5
West Ham Lane Clinic *SRTFD* E15 .... 81 E5
West Hampstead Clinic *KIL/WHAMP* NW6 ...... 72 A4
West Ham United FC (Upton Park) *EHAM* E6 .. 95 F1
West Hendon Clinic *CDALE/KGS* NW9 .... 51 F1
West Hill Primary School
  WAND/EARL SW18 .... 132 A3
West India Pier *POP/IOD* E14 .... 103 F3
West India Shopping Centre
  POP/IOD E14 .... 104 A2
Westland Heliport *BTSEA* SW11 .... 133 D1
West Lodge Preparatory School
  BFN/LL DA15 .... 163 F3
West London County Court *WKENS* W14 ...... 101 E5
West London Magistrates Court
  HMSMTH W6 .... 113 D1
West London Tamil School *WLSDN* NW10 ...... 87 F1
Westminster Abbey *WEST* SW1P 44 C2
Westminster Abbey Choir School
  WEST SW1P 44 B2
Westminster Business Square *LBTH* SE11 .... 117 F1
Westminster Cathedral *WEST* SW1P 43 E5
Westminster Cathedral Choir School
  WEST SW1P 43 F4
Westminster Cathedral RC Primary School
  PIM SW1V 117 D1
Westminster City Hall *WESTW* SW1E 43 F2
Westminster City School *WESTW* SW1E 43 F2
Westminster College *BTSEA* SW11 .... 116 A4
  SOHO/SHAV W1D 31 F1
Westminster Gallery *STJSPK* SW1H 44 B1
Westminster Industrial Estate
  WOOL/PLUM SE18 .... 107 D4
Westminster Natural Health Centre
  PIM SW1V 43 E5
Westminster Pier *WHALL* SW1A 45 D1
Westminster School *WEST* SW1P 44 C2
Westminster Technical College
  WEST SW1P 43 F4
Westminster Theatre *WESTW* SW1E 43 E2
Westminster Under School *WEST* SW1P 44 A5
Westmoor Community Clinic
  PUT/ROE SW15 .... 130 A3
West Norwood Clinic *WNWD* SE27 .... 154 C2
West Norwood Crematorium
  WNWD SE27 .... 154 C3
West One Shopping Centre
  MYFR/PKLN W1K 18 B5
Westpoint Trading Estate *ACT* W3 .... 86 B4
West 12 Shopping & Leisure Centre
  WKENS W14 .... 101 D3
West Twyford Primary School
  WLSDN NW10 .... 86 A1
Westway Business Centre *BAY/PAD* W2 .... 14 C3
Westway Sports Centre *NKENS* W10 .... 89 D5
Westwood Business Park *WELL* DA16 .... 145 E2
Westwood Technology College
  WELL DA16 .... 145 D2
Whaddon House Clinic *CMBW* SE5 .... 137 E1
Whipps Cross Hospital *WAN* E11 .... 63 D1
Whitechapel Art Gallery *WCHPL* E1 .... 90 A3
Whitechapel Sports Centre *WCHPL* E1 .... 90 A3
Whitefield School *CRICK* NW2 .... 53 D2
Whitehall Theatre *WHALL* SW1A 32 B3
Whiteleys Shopping Centre *BAY/PAD* W2 .... 14 C5
Whitmore Primary School *IS* N1 .... 77 D5
Whittington Hospital *ARCH* N19 .... 56 B4
Wigmore Hall *MHST* W1U 18 C4
Wilberforce Primary School *NKENS* W10 ..... 89 E2
Willesden Community Hospital
  WLSDN NW10 .... 70 A4
Willesden County Court *WLSDN* NW10 .... 87 E1
Willesden High School *WLSDN* NW10 .... 70 B5
Willesden Medical Centre *CRICK* NW2 .... 70 B5
Willesden Sports Centre *WLSDN* NW10 .... 70 B5
Willesden Sports Stadium *WLSDN* NW10 ..... 70 B5
William Davies Primary School *FSTGT* E7 ... 83 D3
William Ellis School *KTTN* NW5 .... 56 A5
William Morris Academy *HMSMTH* W6 .... 113 E1
William Patten Primary School
  STNW/STAM N16 .... 59 F4
William Tyndale Primary School *IS* N1 ..... 76 B4
Willoughby Hall School *HAMP* NW3 .... 73 D1
Willow Business Park *SYD* SE26 .... 156 C5
Willowfield School *HNHL* SE24 .... 136 C2
Wimbledon Common Golf Club
  WIM/MER SW19 .... 148 B5
Wimbledon (Gap Road) Cemetery
  WIM/MER SW19 .... 150 B4
Wimbledon Park Athletics Track
  WIM/MER SW19 .... 149 F2
Wimbledon Park Golf Club
  WIM/MER SW19 .... 149 F3
Wimbledon Park Primary School
  WIM/MER SW19 .... 150 A2
Wimbledon Stadium *TOOT* SW17 .... 150 B4
Wimbledon Stadium Business Centre
  WIM/MER SW19 .... 150 B3
Winchcombe Business Centre
  PECK SE15 .... 119 E2
Windmill School *BRXS/STRHM* SW2 .... 135 E3
Winfield House *CAMTN* NW1 .... 5 D3
Wingfield Primary School
  BKHTH/KID SE3 .... 142 A1
Winsor Primary School *EHAM* E6 .... 95 F5
Winston Churchill's Britain at
  War Experience *STHWK* SE1 .... 36 B4
Winton Primary School *IS* N1 .... 9 E2
Witnitz School *STNW/STAM* N16 .... 59 F3
Wix Primary School *BTSEA* SW11 .... 134 B1
Women's Theatre Workshop *REGST* W1B 31 F2
Woodbury Down Primary School
  FSBYPK N4 .... 58 C2
Woodentops School *BAL* SW12 .... 153 D1
Woodfield School *CDALE/KGS* NW9 .... 51 E3
Woodgrange Infant School *FSTGT* E7 .... 82 B1
Woodgrange Park Cemetery *FSTGT* E7 ...... 83 D2
Woodhill Primary School *CHARL* SE7 .... 107 E5
Woodlands J & I School *IL* IG1 .... 85 D2
Wood Lane School *FUL/PGN* SW6 .... 114 C4
Wood Wharf *POP/IOD* E14 .... 104 B2
Wood Wharf Business Park *POP/IOD* E14 .... 104 C1
Woolmore Primary School *POP/IOD* E14 ..... 104 C1
Woolwich Cemetery *WOOL/PLUM* SE18 .... 127 F3
Woolwich College *WOOL/PLUM* SE18 .... 107 D5
  WOOL/PLUM SE18 .... 108 C5
Woolwich County Court
  WOOL/PLUM SE18 .... 108 A4
Woolwich Crown Court *THMD* SE28 .... 109 E3
Working Mens College *CAMTN* NW1 .... 7 F1
World End Place *WBPTN* SW10 .... 114 C3
World Trade Centre *TWRH* EC3N 37 F3
World University Service *STLK* EC1Y 24 A1
Wormholt Park Primary School *SHB* W12 .... 100 A1
Wyborne Primary School *ELTH/MOT* SE9 .... 162 B1
Wykeham Primary School *WLSDN* NW10 ...... 51 D5
Wyndhams Theatre *LSQ/SEVD* WC2H 32 B1
Wyvil Primary School *VX/NE* SW8 .... 117 E3
Yale University Press *HAMP* NW3 .... 73 E1
Yerbury Primary School *ARCH* N19 .... 57 D5
Yeshivo Horomo Talmudical College
  STNW/STAM N16 .... 59 D3
Yesodey Hatorah Jewish School
  STNW/STAM N16 .... 59 F2
Yetev Lev Day School for Boys
  STNW/STAM N16 .... 60 A3
York Clinic *STHWK* SE1 .... 36 A4
York Hall *BETH* E2 .... 90 B1
York Water Gate *CHCR* WC2N 33 D3
Young England RFC *VX/NE* SW8 .... 117 E2
Young Victoria Theatre *STHWK* SE1 .... 34 B5
Zennor Road Industrial Estate *BAL* SW12 .. 152 C1
Ziam Trading Estate *WALTH* E17 .... 60 C3

336 Acknowledgements

The Post Office is a registered trademark of Post Office Ltd. in the UK and other countries.

Schools address data provided by Education Direct.

Petrol station information supplied by Johnsons

One-way street data provided by © Tele Atlas N.V. Tele Atlas

The boundary of the London congestion charging zone supplied by ⊖ Transport for London

Notes

Notes

AA **Street by Street** QUESTIONNAIRE

Dear Atlas User
**Your comments, opinions and recommendations are very
important to us. So please help us to improve our street atlases
by taking a few minutes to complete this simple questionnaire.**

You do NOT need a stamp (unless posted outside the UK). If you do not want to
remove this page from your street atlas, then photocopy it or write your answers
on a plain sheet of paper.

**Send to: The Editor, AA Street by Street, FREEPOST SCE 4598,
Basingstoke RG21 4GY**

ABOUT THE ATLAS...

Which city/town/county did you buy?
_____

**Are there any features of the atlas or mapping that you find particularly
useful?**
_____
_____
_____

Is there anything we could have done better?
_____
_____
_____

Why did you choose an AA Street by Street atlas?
_____
_____
_____

Did it meet your expectations?

Exceeded ☐ **Met all** ☐ **Met most** ☐ **Fell below** ☐

Please give your reasons
_____
_____
_____
_____

MN037y

continued overleaf

Where did you buy it?

For what purpose? (please tick all applicable)

To use in your own local area ☐ **To use on business or at work** ☐

Visiting a strange place ☐ **In the car** ☐ **On foot** ☐

Other (please state)

LOCAL KNOWLEDGE...

Local knowledge is invaluable. Whilst every attempt has been made to make the information contained in this atlas as accurate as possible, should you notice any inaccuracies, please detail them below (if necessary, use a blank piece of paper) or e-mail us at *streetbystreet@theAA.com*

ABOUT YOU...

Name (Mr/Mrs/Ms)

Address

Postcode

Daytime tel no

E-mail address

Which age group are you in?

Under 25 ☐ **25-34** ☐ **35-44** ☐ **45-54** ☐ **55-64** ☐ **65+** ☐

Are you an AA member? **YES** ☐ **NO** ☐

Do you have Internet access? **YES** ☐ **NO** ☐

Thank you for taking the time to complete this questionnaire. Please send it to us as soon as possible, and remember, you do not need a stamp (unless posted outside the UK).